THE FONDAS

Henry, Jane, & Peter

TRIPLE EXPOSURE

Volume Two (1961-1982) of a Two-Part Biography

This is Part Two of a Two-Part biography about Henry Fonda and his spawning of two of the most talked-about actors of the 20th Century.

Henry Fonda was an American Original, the sixth most renowned actor in the history of Hollywood, as determined by the American Film Institute.

His rebellious, emotionally tormented children, **Jane and Peter**, evolved into major-league celebrities too.

This is the story of how they handled their careers and their fame, and how they wove themselves into the fabric of the American Experience

WHAT IS BLOOD MOON PRODUCTIONS?

"Blood Moon, in case you don't know, is a small publishing house on Staten Island that cranks out Hollywood gossip books, about two or three a year, usually of five-, six-, or 700-page length, chocked with stories and pictures about people who used to consume the imaginations of the American public, back when we actually had a public imagination. That is, when people were really interested in each other, rather than in Apple 'devices.' In other words, back when we had vices, not devices."

—The Huffington Post

THE FONDAS

Henry, Jane, & Peter

TRIPLE EXPOSURE

Volume Two (1961-1982)
of a Two-Part Biography by
Darwin Porter & Danforth Prince

THE FONDAS
HENRY, JANE, & PETER
TRIPLE EXPOSURE

VOLUME TWO (1961-1982)
OF A TWO-PART BIOGRAPHY

Darwin Porter and Danforth Prince

Unless otherwise stated, all texts are copyright
© 2023 Blood Moon Productions, Ltd.
with all rights reserved.

www.BloodMoonProductions.com

ISBN 978-936003-86-0

Manufactured in the USA
Covers and Book Design by Danforth Prince

Thanks to Mike Sevick, Assistant Professor of Art at the University of Michigan, Flint,
for permission to use a replica of his celebrated painting,
The Dust Storm, as a background for this book's front cover

This book is distributed worldwide through
Ingram, Amazon.com, and internet vendors everywhere.

BLOOD MOON PRODUCTIONS

Proudly defines this book as

VOLUME TWO

of its two-part biography of Henry, Jane, and Peter Fonda, and as

VOLUME EIGHT

of its

Magnolia House Series

CONTENTS

HENRY

PROLOGUE
    AN ABBREVIATED RUNDOWN OF HENRY FONDA'S LIFE   PAGE 1

CHAPTER ONE   PAGE 5
    AS ONE OF THE FEW SURVIVING SUPERSTARS OF PRE-WAR CLASSIC HOLLYWOOD, HENRY WORKS. *The Longest Day, The Best Man, Fail Safe, Sex and the Single Girl, In Harm's Way, The Rounders, Battle of the Bulge, Welcome to Hard Times.*

CHAPTER TWO   PAGE 25
    HORRIFIED BY NEWFANGLED SOCIAL TRENDS, HENRY FONDA CHANGES WITH CHANGING TIMES: *Firecreek; Yours, Mine, & Ours; Madigan; The Boston Strangler; Once Upon a Time in the West; Our Town*

CHAPTER THREE   PAGE 39
    THE MOVIES CHANGE—AND TO SOME DEGREE, SO DOES HENRY: *The Cheyenne Social Club; Too Late the Hero; There Was a Crooked Man; Sometimes a Great Notion; The Smith Family; Night Flight from Moscow; Ash Wednesday; My Name is Nobody; Clarence Darrow.*

CHAPTER FOUR PAGE 59
    IGNORING HEALTH CONCERNS, HENRY WORKS UNTIL HE CAN'T.
    THE DECLINE AND COLLAPSE OF HENRY FONDA. *Midway, Tentacles, The Great Smokey Roadblock; Killer Bees: The Swarm; Fedora, Roots, The Next Generation; Meteor; City on Fire*; *The Oldest Living Graduate; Gideon's Trumpet; Summer Solstice.*

JANE

CHAPTER FIVE PAGE 75
    LADY OF CONTRADICTIONS, MISTRESS OF THE UNEXPECTED
    The Chapman Report; Period of Adjustment; Marilyn Monroe; In the Cool of the Day; Sunday in New York; Cat Ballou.

CHAPTER SIX PAGE 91
    JANE AND HER FRENCH INVASION
    America's Answer to Brigitte Bardot moves to France and inaugurates an affair with the French actor voted, prior to their meeting, as "The Handsomest Man in the World." (Alain Delon). Roger Vadim, the avant-garde director, enters Jane's life. BARDOT (Vadim, not God, created her.) DENEUVE ("the most beautiful woman in the world.") How the producers of *La Ronde* display an effigy of Jane, nude, above Times Square. Back in California, *The Chase* teams Jane with Marlon Brando and Robert Redford.

CHAPTER SEVEN PAGE 117
    JANE GETS MORPHED INTO THE SEX KITTEN OF THE 22ND CENTURY
    Barbarella. Jane and Roger Vadim host the "celebrity shindig of the year" at Malibu. *Any Wednesday.* Jane gets married! *The Game Is Over; Hurry Sundown; Barefoot in the Park, Myra Breckinridge.*

CHAPTER EIGHT PAGE 137
    THE ENCHANTED COUPLE AND THE VAGARIES OF VADIM.
    JANE MEETS THE CREAM OF AVANT GARDE EUROPE: Jean Marais; Jean-Paul Belmondo; Louis Jourdan; Luchino Visconti; Gunter Sachs, Marcello Mastroianni, Jean-Louis Trintignant, and Roman Polanski.

CHAPTER NINE PAGE 159
    JANE BECOMES THE PREFERRED ACTRESS OF BOTH THE COMMERCIAL AND AVANT-GARDE FILM INDUSTRIES: Existential anguish during the Great Depression (*They Shoot Horses, Don't They?).* Rock Hudson: Vadim directs him in an celebration of nymphet allure, *Pretty Maids All in a Row; Klute (*Jane plays a whore); *Steelyard Blues* (Jane plays another whore*);* the most respected director in France (Jean-Luc Godard) directs Jane in a socialist comedy, *Tout Va Bien;* Jane does Ibsen in *A Doll House;* Even Jane can't rescue the USSR's sloppy, confusing remake of *The Blue Bird; Fun with Dick and Jane;* Jane teams with Vanessa Redgrave in Lillian Hellman's fantasy version of an anti-Nazi activist in *Julia.*

CHAPTER TEN   PAGE 197
    JANE GETS AGGRESSIVE: BARBARELLA MORPHS INTO HANOI JANE;
    HER MARRIAGE TO TOM HAYDEN. HENRY FONDA (PÈRE) IS NOT AMUSED—NEITHER IS THE
    AMERICAN PUBLIC.

CHAPTER ELEVEN   PAGE 211
    JANE AGES GRACEFULLY:
    Coming Home; Comes a Horseman; California Suite; The China Syndrome; The Electric Horseman; 9 to 5.

PETER

CHAPTER TWELVE   PAGE 239
    PETER: AN ENTITLED CHILD OF HOLLYWOOD, HE'S "RESENTFULLY ROYAL" FROM BIRTH. *Tammy and the Doctor.* (WHAT? Peter Fonda in a Tammy rip-off?) , *PT 109* (Peter doesn't get to play JFK); *The Victors* (Before the final reel, Peter doesn't become one of them); his scandals with the draft board; Peter's rival (Warren Beatty) dates Peter's ex-stepmother, Afdera Franchetti; Peter hangs out with (and gets high with) the deeply depressed sons of other famous movie stars; Peter gets batty with Adam West (aka TV's campy *Batman);* Peter's competitive maneuverings with Tom Jones, George Hamilton, and *the Rifleman*, Chuck Connors.

CHAPTER THIRTEEN   PAGE 271
    SEX AND DRUGS AND ROCK AND ROLL:
    PETER VS. HOLLYWOOD'S OTHER "HEARTTHROBS OF THE MOMENT," NICK ADAMS, TOMMY KIRK, BRANDON DEWILDE; AND MICHAEL POLLARD. THEN-DARING FEATURE FILMS ABOUT TEENAGED PREGNANCIES (*The Young Lovers);* PETER'S CULTIVATION OF THE KING OF B-LIST FILMMAKING, ROGER CORMAN; MOTORCYCLE MANIA AND *The Wild Angels;* ROMANTIC DRAMAS, PLAYED OUT PUBLICLY, WITH NANCY SINATRA. PETER DROPS ACID, PUBLICLY AND WILFULLY, IN *THE TRIP.*

CHAPTER FOURTEEN   PAGE 293
    PETER BITES HARD (AND SWALLOWS) THE COMMERCIAL POTENTIAL OF THE COUNTER-CULTURE. *Certain Honorable Men;* Anachronistic Sex with Celebrities from the Past (Billy the Kid! Jean Harlow!) in a stage play, *The Beard* (Peter doesn't get the movie role); a politically provocative film (*The Queen*) that Peter covets the lead for never gets made; The Quirks and Private Anguish of Dennis Hopper (*Easy Rider* makes Peter rich): Marital abandonment and reconciliation in *The Hired Hand;* Peter embarasses himself in *The Last Movie,* reviewed by some as "the worst movie ever made."

CHAPTER FIFTEEN   PAGE 293
    WINDING DOWN ("THE SLOW GOODBYE) WITH PETER FONDA. THE EMBARASSING BUT INEVITABLE COLLAPSE OF HIS SCREEN CAREER, HIS SEPARATION AND DIVORCE FROM SUSAN BREWER, AND *Idaho Transfer; Two People; Dirty Mary, Crazy Larry; Open Season; Race with the Devil,* and *92 in the Shade.* How he emoted with Andy Warhol's self-enchanted porn star, Sylvia Miles, in Key West; and his love affair and marriage with Portia Rebecca Crockett.

CHAPTER SIXTEEN   PAGE 333
    PETER TUNES OUT, DROPS OUT, AND FADES AWAY.
    Killer Force; Navigating his way, aboard his private yacht, through the South Pacific, h Portia Crockett, *Fighting (Ho-Hum) Mad; Future World; Outlaw Blues;* and *Wanda Nevada.*

EPILOGUE   PAGE 349

    TWILIGHT TIME ON GOLDEN POND. HENRY FONDA, PÈRE, JOINS HIS DAUGHTER, JANE, IN A *TOUR DE FORCE* OF ACTING TALENT, AND MANAGE TO SALVAGE MEANING FROM THEIR DYSFUNCTIONAL, HIGHLY CONTENTIOUS PERSONAL PASTS. KATHARINE HEPBURN STANDS BY AS THEIR PRICKLY ON-SCREEN MATRIARCH.

AUTHORS' BIOS   PAGE 355

PREVIOUS WORKS BY DARWIN PORTER
PRODUCED IN COLLABORATION WITH BLOOD MOON

BIOGRAPHIES FROM BLOOD MOON'S MAGNOLIA HOUSE SERIES

Henry Fonda, He Did It His Way,
(Volume One —1905-1960—of a Two-Part Biography)

Lucille Ball & Desi Arnaz: They Weren't Lucy & Ricky Ricardo
(Volume One—1911-1960—of a Two-Part Biography)

The Sad & Tragic Ending of Lucille Ball
(Volume Two-1961-1989) of a Two-Part Biography

Marilyn: Don't Even Dream About Tomorrow
(a 2021 revised version of the best-selling
Marilyn at Rainbow's End: Sex, Lies, Murder, &
the Great Cover-Up (2012)

The Seductive Sapphic Exploits of Mercedes de Acosta
Hollywood's Greatest Lover

Jacqueline Kennedy Onassis, Her Tumultuous Life & Her Love Affairs

Judy Garland & Liza Minnelli, Too Many Damn Rainbows

Historic Magnolia House: Celebrity & The Ironies of Fame

Glamour, Glitz, & Gossip at Historic Magnolia House

***

BIOGRAPHIES FROM BLOOD MOON NOT ASSOCIATED WITH ITS MAGNOLIA HOUSE SERIES

Burt Reynolds, Put the Pedal to the Metal

Kirk Douglas, More Is Never Enough

Playboy's Hugh Hefner, Empire of Skin

Carrie Fisher & Debbie Reynolds,
Princess Leia & Unsinkable Tammy in Hell

Rock Hudson Erotic Fire

Lana Turner, *Hearts & Diamonds Take All*

Donald Trump, *The Man Who Would Be King*

James Dean, Tomorrow Never Comes

Bill and Hillary, *So This Is That Thing Called Love*

Peter O'Toole, *Hellraiser, Sexual Outlaw, Irish Rebel*

Love Triangle, *Ronald Reagan, Jane Wyman, & Nancy Davis*

Pink Triangle, *The Feuds and Private Lives of Tennessee Williams, Gore Vidal, Truman Capote, and Famous Members of their Entourages.*

Those Glamorous Gabors, *Bombshells from Budapest*

Inside Linda Lovelace's Deep Throat,
Degradation, Porno Chic, and the Rise of Feminism

Elizabeth Taylor, *There is Nothing Like a Dame*

J. Edgar Hoover and Clyde Tolson
Investigating the Sexual Secrets of America's Most Famous Men and Women

Frank Sinatra, *The Boudoir Singer. All the Gossip Unfit to Print*

The Kennedys*, All the Gossip Unfit to Print*

The Secret Life of Humphrey Bogart *(2003), and*
Humphrey Bogart, The Making of a Legend *(2010)*

Howard Hughes, *Hell's Angel*

Steve McQueen, *King of Cool, Tales of a Lurid Life*

Paul Newman, *The Man Behind the Baby Blues*

Merv Griffin, *A Life in the Closet*

Brando Unzipped

Katharine the Great, Hepburn, Secrets of a Lifetime Revealed

Jacko, His Rise and Fall, The Social and Sexual History of Michael Jackson

Damn You, Scarlett O'Hara,
The Private Lives of Vivien Leigh and Laurence Olivier

FILM CRITICISM
Blood Moon's 2005 Guide to the Glitter Awards
Blood Moon's 2006 Guide to Film
Blood Moon's 2007 Guide to Film, and
50 Years of Queer Cinema, 500 of the Best GLBTQ Films Ever Made

NON-FICTION
Hollywood Babylon, It's Back! and *Hollywood Babylon Strikes Again!*

NOVELS

Blood Moon,
Hollywood's Silent Closet,
Rhinestone Country,
Razzle Dazzle
Midnight in Savannah

OTHER PUBLICATIONS BY DARWIN PORTER NOT DIRECTLY ASSOCIATED WITH BLOOD MOON

NOVELS

The Delinquent Heart
The Taste of Steak Tartare
Butterflies in Heat
Marika (a roman à clef based on the life of Marlene Dietrich)
Venus (a roman à clef based on the life of Anaïs Nin)
Sister Rose

TRAVEL GUIDES

Many Editions and Many Variations of The Frommer Guides, The American Express Guides, and/or TWA Guides, et alia to:

Andalusia, Andorra, Anguilla, Aruba, Atlanta, Austria, the Azores, The Bahamas, Barbados, the Bavarian Alps, Berlin, Bermuda, Bonaire and Curaçao, Boston, the British Virgin Islands, Budapest, Bulgaria, California, the Canary Islands, the Caribbean and its "Ports of Call," the Cayman Islands, Ceuta, the Channel Islands (UK), Charleston (SC), Corsica, Costa del Sol (Spain), Denmark, Dominica, the Dominican Republic, Edinburgh, England, Estonia, Europe, "Europe by Rail," the Faroe Islands, Finland, Florence, France, Frankfurt, the French Riviera, Geneva, Georgia (USA), Germany, Gibraltar, Glasgow, Granada (Spain), Great Britain, Greenland, Grenada (West Indies), Haiti, Hungary, Iceland, Ireland, Isle of Man, Italy, Jamaica, Key West & the Florida Keys, Las Vegas, Liechtenstein, Lisbon, London, Los Angeles, Madrid, Maine, Malta, Martinique & Guadeloupe, Massachusetts, Melilla, Morocco, Munich, New England, New Orleans, North Carolina, Norway, Paris, Poland, Portugal, Provence, Puerto Rico, Romania, Rome, Salzburg, San Diego, San Francisco, San Marino, Sardinia, Savannah, Scandinavia, Scotland, Seville, the Shetland Islands, Sicily, St. Martin & Sint Maarten, St. Vincent & the Grenadines, South Carolina, Spain, St. Kitts & Nevis, Sweden, Switzerland, the Turks & Caicos, the U.S.A., the U.S. Virgin Islands, Venice, Vienna and the Danube, Wales, and Zurich.

BIOGRAPHIES

From Diaghilev to Balanchine, The Saga of Ballerina Tamara Geva

Greta Keller, Germany's Other Lili Marlene

Sophie Tucker, The Last of the Red Hot Mamas

Anne Bancroft, Where Have You Gone, Mrs. Robinson?
(co-authored with Stanley Mills Haggart)

Veronica Lake, The Peek-a-Boo Girl

Running Wild in Babylon, Confessions of a Hollywood Press Agent

HISTORIES

Thurlow Weed, Whig Kingpin

Chester A. Arthur, Gilded Age Coxcomb in the White House

Discover Old America, What's Left of It

**Each of the two volumes of this biography is gratefully dedicated
to the unsung heroes of the American Century,
the unlucky, hardworking men and women, some of them pawns of fate, as
Henry Fonda portrayed so poignantly in so many of his films.**

Biographies
from Blood Moon Productions

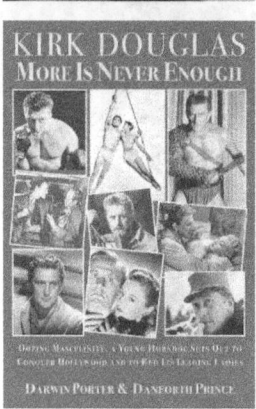

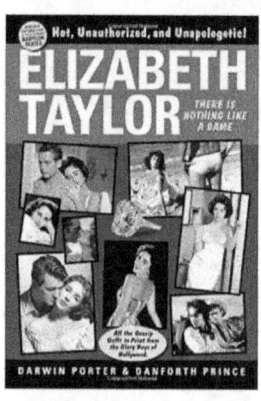

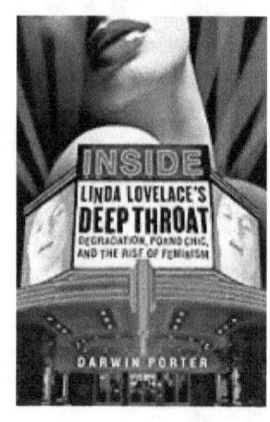

More Biographies
from Blood Moon Productions

WHAT WAS FIRST IN THIS TWO-VOLUME BIOGRAPHY?

It was this overview of "Mostly Henry" (as depicted below),
Volume One: Henry Fonda, (1905-1960) He Did It His Way

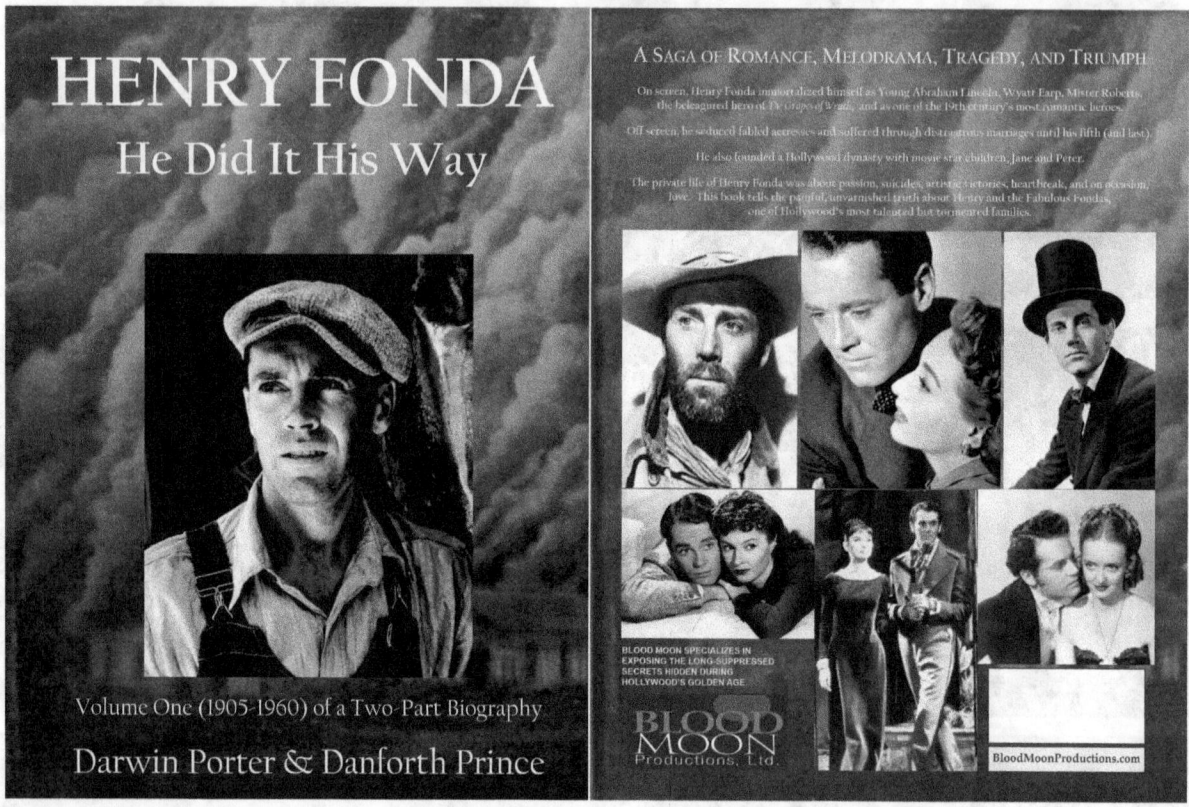

Throughout his forty-five year career, Henry Fonda—a stable, reassuring archetype of the American male—never gave a bad performance, immortalizing himself in such films as Young Mr. Lincoln, The Grapes of Wrath, and Mister Roberts. The torments of his introverted private life vied with his on-screen dilemmas.

Personal dramas included five wives (two of whom committed suicide) and involvements in many of the seminal events (including active service in the Navy during World War II) of the 20th Century. His affairs starred such mega-divas as Lucille Ball, Joan Crawford, and Bette Davis. With his second wife, Frances Seymour, he founded a Hollywood dynasty with movie star children, Jane and Peter.

This, Volume One (1905-1960) covers Henry's origins in Depression-era Nebraska, his rise to fame, his complicated dynamics with other celebrities, and his middle-aged years navigating his passion for acting with the business realities of Hollywood.

Unlike any other books published, these two volumes reflect the private agonies of a father, daughter, and son engulfed by the divisions of their respective generations and the ironies of the American Experience.

HENRY FONDA, HE DID IT HIS WAY
Volume One (1905-1960) of a Two-Part Biography , ISBN 978-1-936003-84-6   Available everywhere now

Hot, Show-Bizzy, Unauthorized, Unapologetic, and Newsworthy from Blood Moon Productions: **A new and Expanded Edition of the Scandalous Anthology** that made us famous when its (smaller, thinner) predecessor first appeared in 2008. This Time, We're Calling It:

HOLLYWOOD BABYLON
With Detours to Gomorrah

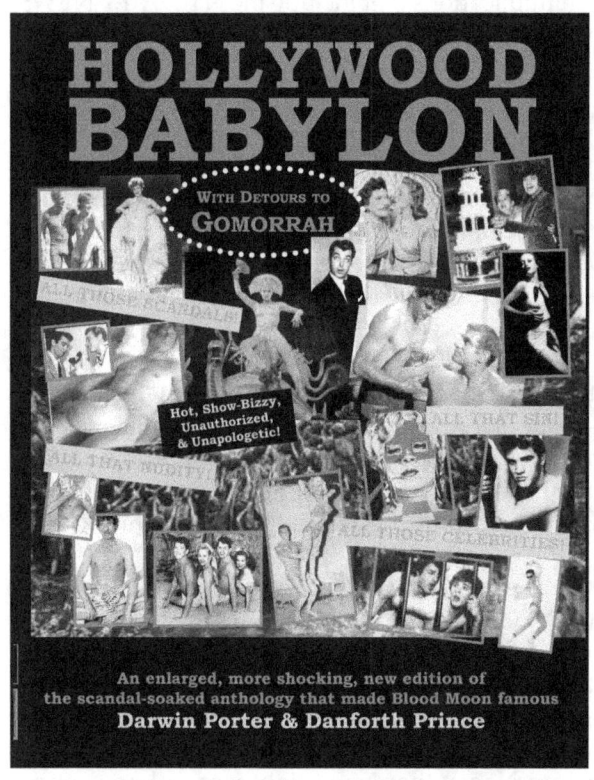

Dishing with abandon, the authors spare no one--especially not the dead. Marilyn Monroe had an affair with Ronald Reagan. Marilyn also had a tryst with Joan Crawford but refused to make it an ongoing affair. James Dean showed a disconcerting interest in a 12-year old boy in the early 1950s. Lucille Ball launched herself into show business as a hooker, and her husband Desi Arnaz had a fling with Cesar Romero. Cary Grant had an incestuous relationship with his stepson, Lance Reventlow. And this, by the way, is only the tip of the iceberg."

Rush & Molloy, *The NY Daily News*

MAKING AMERICA GREAT AGAIN
For Immediate Release, from Blood Moon Productions
Hollywood Babylon, with Detours to Gomorrah

In the tradition of GREAT AMERICAN GOSSIP, Blood Moon offers this COMPELLING ANTHOLOGY OF GOSSIP to anyone who ever had any nagging questions about Show-biz indiscretion, mendacity, and excess.

WHAT IS IT? According to Blood Moon's President, Danforth Prince, "It's the best feature-length compendium of Hollywood gossip ever compiled, lavishly illustrated, and loaded with examples of the PR hurricanes generated by the false gods of fame, physical beauty, lust, greed, narcissism, and exhibitionism. This book might not be everybody's fantasy about what they really wanna crawl into bed with, but as a publishing phenomenon, it's the very best of its genre."

HOW HAS IT BEEN REVIEWED SINCE ITS FIRST EDITION?
ANSWER: With spectacular praise and enthusiasm from publications that include the NY DAILY NEWS, London's EXPRESS, a passel of entertainment-industry publications "Down Under," and show-biz blogsites around the world.

HOW BIG IS IT AND HOW MUCH DOES IT COST?
ANSWER: This anthology was conceived and designed as a softcover **COLLECTOR'S ITEM** for placement on COFFEE TABLES in living rooms that need a little nudge. It has a BIG footprint—something akin to an 8 1/2 x 11" news magazine—and the central image of its front cover is Fritz Lang's 1920s 'perhaps demented' image of THE WHORE OF BABYLON. Debauched and persuasive, she hovers over a passel of spectacularly famous, partially undressed celebrities culled from a century of show-biz mania. In this case, you can acquire her "favors" for $60.

Danforth Prince continued: "We're marketing this as the most lewdly sophisticated 'coffee table book' of the holiday season. It's a one-of-a-kind 'conversation stopper' or (depending on your point of view) 'conversation starter.' This is a 'hipster to hipster' gift you'd give to an embittered survivor who's already deeply familiar with the casting couch. It's the best accumulation of tabloid trauma ever published....a drunken sorority party's first prize; a 'I'm ready for another martini' cocktail *klatsch's* most embarassing panty raid."

"We've doubled its content from its previous edition," Prince continued, "by adding the 'concentrated cream' from rip-snorting OTHER biographies within Blood Moon's (very extensive) backlist. This anthology is what happens when Classic Hollywood gets down and low with the literary *avant-garde* of the Fabulous 50s, the Free Love Sixties; the Sexy Seventies, and the big-haired teledrama-driven Eighties."

"WHO'S NEW? There's More about Ronald Reagan and Nancy than you might wanna know, and a cross-section of ONCE AGAIN IN THE NEWS stars you might, if not for this book, have forgotten."

IT'S BACK.! IT'S BABYLON! And it's available everywhere, now, through **Amazon.com, Barnes & Noble.com** and other online booksellers worldwide.

HOLLYWOOD BABYLON with DETOURS TO GOMORRAH
By Darwin Porter and Danforth Prince   www.BloodMoonProductions.com
488 pages, 8 1/2" x 11" softcover. ISBN 978-1-936003-88-4

A ONE-OF-A-KIND COLLECTOR'S ITEM AND COFFEE TABLE SHOWPIECE.

Challenging the Status Quo's Beliefs about Classic Hollywood

PROLOGUE TO VOLUME TWO

AN ABBREVIATED RUNDOWN OF HENRY FONDA'S LIFE

from his birth in 1905 until 1960, as laid out in Volume One (published in 2022), of this Two-part Biography

Welcome, readers, to the beginning of VOLUME TWO of our two-part saga of Henry, Peter, and Jane Fonda.

***

"**The Grapes of Wrath** *helped forge Henry Fonda's image as a quintessential American figure—the uncommon common man, who seemed to symbolize the decency and integrity in which Americans, ideally, saw themselves.*"
—Tony Thomas

"*All in all, I guess I'm still somewhat the gawky, naïve decent-to-the-core hayseed who sputtered, stuttered, and stumbled my way into movie stardom.*"
—Henry Fonda

Volume One (*Henry Fonda: He Did It His Way*, published in the summer of 2022) explored the life, career, five marriages, and lovers of the Fonda clan's patriarch, Henry, one of the leading movie stars of Hollywood's Golden Age. The American Film Institute ranks him as the sixth greatest move star of all time.

How did it all begin?

The Fonda ancestors can be traced to Genoa in the 15th century. Later, because of political and perhaps religious reasons, they fled north to the Netherlands.

By 1642, a branch of the family moved to the Dutch colony that later became the City of New York.

From there, a coven of Fondas headed 200 miles north into New York State, where they founded the settlement of Fonda, which still exists today.

***

Henry Fonda was born on May 16, 1905, to an advertising and printing jobber, William Brace Fonda and Elma Herberta (*née* Jaynes).

Throughout his long life, son Henry was an agnostic, despite having been born into a Christian Scientist family. That meant that whenever the boy got sick, his mother prayed for him instead of sending him to a doctor.

"My whole damn family was so nice," Henry recalled. "Mom, Dad, and my two sisters were a closely knit unit."

He grew up an awkward, bashful, shy boy who avoided girls, except for his sisters. He worked part time in his father's print shop. One of his earliest memories was watching an angry mob of white men lynch a black man. It made a lasting impression on Henry, and in time, he became a liberal, rejecting the early prejudices he encountered in his native Nebraska.

He grew to six feet, two inches, with smoky blue eyes and hollow cheeks. He walked with a loping cornhusker gait, speaking in a voice that had a certain tonelessness. All in all, he seemed enveloped in a Midwestern melancholy. In years to come, that mournful, weather-lashed look of his would be defined as "The Face of America."

He grew up when Omaha was still the Wild West, with numerous bordellos. They reached their peak when neighboring cowpokes descended onto the town's honky-tonk district every Saturday night.

He lost his virginity in an Omaha whorehouse to an overweight 45-year-old prostitute. "I was repulsed by it, a sort of *wham-bam*. The whole act was revolting, and she stank, having seduced five cowboys earlier without even taking a 'whore's bath.'"

Intending to become a journalist, he attended the University of Minnesota, but did not graduate.

At the age of 20, he was still in Omaha, where he caught the eye of the actress and arts activist, Dodie Brando, the mother of Marlon. She enticed Henry to appear on stage at the Omaha Community Theater. The neglected wife of brutal alcoholic, she "took a fancy to young Henry," and an affair began. "She taught me the pleasurable side of sex, not the whorehouse variety," he recalled.

At first, he was terrified walking out onto a stage, but he found he could "lose myself" during his portrayal of a character—in fact, "I became hooked, from that first night on stage, I dropped my goal of being a journalist and set out on the long road to becoming an actor."

After getting the lead in a play called *Merton of the Movies,* and receiving praise for his performance, "I realized the beauty of acting as a profession. My tongue-tied personality could speak the words of a character, keeping my own secrets to myself."

In 1928, he headed East to seek fame and fortune. To his deepest regret, that was in 1928, just a year before the Great Depression swept across America. "My timing was way off," he said.

That summer, he migrated to Cape Cod, where he found work at the Cape Playhouse in Dennis, Massachusetts. He later became a member of the University Players, a deeply respected intercollegiate summer stock company.

There, he worked with Margaret Sullavan, a tart-tongued, blonde-haired actress from Virginia. After he married her in 1931, she became the first of his five wives. Their union lasted for two tumultuous months. "She castrates a guy and makes him feel he's worth two cents and has two inches."

[Ironically, by 1936, Sullavan and Henry had each moved to Hollywood, overlooking their marital anguish and co-starring together in a film named The Moon's Our Home.*]*

On the Cape, Henry met and bonded with another rising young actor, James Stewart. They became best friends, a closely knit bonding that would last until their respective deaths. In Hollywood, they became known as "Hank and Jim."

After the summer season on Cape Cod, they each gravitated to Manhattan and became longtime roommates. During the day, they pounded the pavements around Broadway theaters, each of them looking for work as an actor.

Money was very scarce. At times, all they could afford was a bag of rice, without any salt to season it.

Henry found odd jobs and brief roles in theatrical productions from the late 1920s to 1934.

At long last, Henry got his first big break on Broadway when he starred in *The Farmer Takes a Wife*, which opened on Broadway in February of 1934.

The well-known director, Victor Fleming, asked him to repeat the role in the play's 1935 film adaptation. In it, he co-starred with Oscar-winning Janet Gaynor.

In time, he'd pull in $3,000 a week, a lot of money in that Depression era. Soon, James Stewart joined him, and they rented a house together.

Their neighbor was Greta Garbo, who wanted one of them to become her boxing partner in the practice ring in her backyard. Both men, especially Stewart, became far more than her boxing opponent.

As the 1930s moved on, both Henry and Stewart became movie stars. By 1935, Henry was starring with opera diva Lily Pons in *I Dream Too Much. The New York Times* announced him as "the most likable of the new crop of romantic juveniles."

That same year, he starred with Sylvia Sidney in one of his best-known films, *The Trail of the Lonesome Pine,* the first Technicolor movie shot outdoors.

That year (1936), he also married socialite Frances Ford Seymour. It was not a happy union. Having a daughter and son was probably the only reason they stayed together, the marriage on life support. Jane was born in 1937, Peter in 1940.

His greatest success came in 1938, when he was cast as Bette Davis' co-star in *Jezebel*. He had known her back in the late 1920s. They had an affair.

As bachelors, Stewart and Henry had brief flings with some of the biggest female stars in Hollywood. Stewart also dated a number of starlets, claiming that before 1940, he seduced 263 of them. Despite Henry's status as an (unhappy) married man, he began an affair with Lucille Ball that continued for years to come. His eventually famous daughter, Jane, was once quoted as saying, "Lucy was the love of my father's life."

As a lover, Henry attracted the ire of many detractors, including George Sanders, who called him "A Don Juan homosexual who has to prove himself with one woman after another."

Hollywood's biggest blockbuster year was 1939, which saw the release of *Gone With the Wind* and a number of other classics. Henry later defined it as "my good year, the best I've ever had."

He starred in *Jesse James* with Tyrone Power as the outlaw and with Henry as his brother, Frank. The film, directed by Henry King, was a hit for Fox. Another memorable film starring Fonda was *The Story of Alexander Graham Bell,* with Don Ameche cast as the inventor of the telephone.

Also in 1939, Henry starred in a role to which he'd be forever associated, *Young Mr. Lincoln* at Fox. It was directed by John Ford, who became his mentor. Ford followed that by casting Henry in *Drums Along the Mohawk,* also in 1939, co-starring Claudette Colbert.

His subtle, naturalistic acting style preceded by many years the soon-to-be-widespread style known as Method Acting.

In 1940 came the most memorable role of Henry's career, that of Tom Joad in *The Grapes of Wrath,* a film based on John Steinbeck's best-known, best-selling novel. Once again, John Ford was Henry's director

It told the story of a poverty-stricken family uprooted from their subsistence-level farm in Oklahoma in the aftermath of the Dust Storms. The Joads make their way to California, where they aren't made to feel welcome. Henry almost didn't get the role because Darryl F. Zanuck first considered Tyrone Power or Don Ameche.

Henry's portrayal of an "Oakie" was the most memorable of his career. For it, he was nominated for a Best Actor Oscar, losing to his best friend, James Stewart, for his performance in *The Philadelphia Story,* co-starring opposite Katharine Hepburn and Cary Grant.

His character's tender farewell speech to his mother, portrayed by Jane Darwell, is one of the most oft-quoted scenes in American film literature.

To get the role of Tom Joan in *The Grapes of Wrath,* Henry had to sign a seven-year contract with Darryl F. Zanuck at Fox. He called it "a slave contract."

Before he joined the U.S. Navy in World War II, Henry made a number of movies at Fox, none of which he admired or liked. *[Actually, some were quite notable and entertaining. One of them was* The Lady Eve *(1942) with Barbara Stanwyck. During the course of filming, they sparked an affair.]*

Henry served in the Pacific theater of World War II for three years, initially as a lowly quartermaster 3rd Class aboard a destroyer, the *USS Satterlee*. He was later commissioned as a Lt. Junior Grade in Air Combat Intelligence, eventually winning the Navy's Presidential citation and a Bronze Star.

After the war, despite his initial optimism, Henry returned to Hollywood to discover that many of the other stars of the 1930s had been virtually forgotten and replaced.

Fortunately, his mentor, John Ford, still wanted him, casting him in such pictures as *My Darling Clementine* (1946); a re-telling of the story of the *Gunfight at the OK Corral*; and in *Fort Apache* (1948) with John Wayne and Shirley Temple.

Otto Preminger cast him in *Daisy Kenyon* (1947), in which he was seduced by Joan Crawford both on and off the screen.

Exasperated with increasingly silly film offers in Hollywood, Henry returned to his first love, the Broadway stage, to star in the title role of *Mister Roberts,* a comedy-drama about the Navy. As a junior officer, he wages a private war against his ship's captain. In 1948, he won a Tony Award for his performance.

After an eight-year absence from Hollywood, he returned to star in the film version of *Mister Roberts* (1955), co-starring opposite James Cagney and Jack Lemmon. However, he and director John Ford came to blows. Each of them vowed, separately, never to work with the other ever again.

Opposite Audrey Hepburn in 1958, Henry starred in *War and Peace,* a film adaptation of a literary masterpiece by Leo Tolstoy. He was cast as Pierre Bezukhov, a moon-faced, soul-tortured introvert.

That same year, Alfred Hitchcock cast him in *The Wrong Man,* which became a sort of classic. He won even more acclaim when he played Juror #8 in *12 Angry Men,* smoothly guided by Sidney Lumet. For the role, Henry received another Oscar nomination.

Movie roles came and went, as many other aging actors were forced into retirement. As for Henry, he would continue as a major-league star until the final months before his death in 1982.

On the marriage front, Henry moved through four wives before he finally got it right. After his second wife's suicide in 1950, he married Susan Blanchard, the stepdaughter of Oscar Hammerstein II, but they divorced three years later.

In 1957, he married the brisk and brittle Italian countess, Afdera Franchetti. Their tumultuous union lasted until 1961.

At long last, Shirlee Mae Adams entered his life. They married in 1965. She was at his bedside when he died in 1982.

Volume Two, a **TRIPLE EXPOSURE** of Henry and his children's extraordinary lives, we're proud to announce, begins **HERE and NOW.**

CHAPTER ONE

IN THE EARLY 60S, AS ONE OF THE FEW SURVIVING SUPERSTARS OF PRE-WAR CLASSIC HOLLYWOOD,

HENRY WORKS

The Longest Day (1962)
Henry Fonda and John Wayne Join an All-Star Cast to Liberate France from the Nazi Yoke

The Best Man (1964)
Henry Fails in a Race for the Presidential Nomination

Fail Safe (1964)
As the U.S. President, Henry Orders the Atomic Bombardment of New York City, Where His First Lady is Shopping

Sex and the Single Girl (1964)
Cast as a Panty Hose Mogul, Henry is Wed to "Bogie's Baby," Lauren Bacall. Off Screen, Friends Urge Him to Marry Her.

In Harm's Way (1965)
As Admiral Nimitz, Henry Teams with Duke Wayne "To Defeat the Japs Once Again."

The Rounders (1965)
Aging Icons Glenn Ford & Henry Fonda Portray Gambling, Hard-Drinking, Bronco Busters in a Modern Western

Battle of the Bulge (1965)
Henry and the Cast Are Accused of Distorting the Facts About World War II's Nazi Breakthrough of the Allies' Western Lines.

Welcome to Hard Times (1967)
In This Gritty, Grimy Western, Henry Plays a Weak and Mangy Sheriff

By the early 1960s, many of the matinee idols of the 1930s had died, were retired, or reduced to secondary roles. Matinee idols like Humphrey Bogart had died in 1957, with Tyrone Power going in 1958. Errol Flynn joined them in 1959, with Gary Cooper following them in 1961. Even the former "King of Hollywood," Clark Gable, had died in 1960 after filming *The Misfits* with the forever-tardy Marilyn Monroe.

John Wayne was still around. So was Henry's best friend, James Stewart. But William Powell and James Cagney, box office champs of the 1930s, would fade after playing "second fiddle" to Henry in *Mister Roberts* (1955).

Cary Grant was flirting with the business world, and Bing Crosby was sometimes appearing on television.

In 1967, Wanda Hale in the *New York Daily News* wrote that "Henry Fonda remains one of the most sought-after actors in Hollywood. Not only that, but his daughter, Jane, is No. 4 among female stars."

Of course, Wayne, Henry, and Stewart were well aware of the coven of younger actors "rehearsing what wardrobe to wear at our funerals," in the words of Stewart.

Marlon Brando had been a box office champ since the 1950s, and the Welsh actor, Richard Burton, was on the rise even before he even met Elizabeth Taylor.

Rock Hudson had ended the 1950s as a box office champ, and Dustin Hoffman, Clint Eastwood, Warren Beatty, and Jack Nicholson were moving up fast. Paul Newman and Steve McQueen had also become established stars, as had Robert Redford.

***

Advise and Consent (1962)

A call from director Otto Preminger ended Henry Fonda's three-year hiatus from Hollywood. For its 1962 release of *Advise and Consent*, Columbia had purchased the screen rights to the Pulitzer Prize-winning novel about insiderish Washington politics by Allen Drew. The novel was so rich, it could have been the core of a 12-part TV series, but it had to be reduced to 140 minutes.

Henry was given star billing as Robert Leffingwell, a nominee for U.S. Secretary of State. He faced a formidable cast of scene-stealers. None was more notorious than Charles Laughton, who had been cast as Senator

Henry Fonda had been off the screen for three years when Otto Preminger lured him back to make *Advise and Consent*, based on Allen Drury's best-selling novel.

Henry tackled the then-controversial role of Robert Leffingwell, clearly based on Adlai Stevenson, who had run against Eisenhower twice in the 1950s.

Upper photo: **Henry Fonda** (left) confronts a bitter political foe, Senator Brigham Anderson (**Don Murray**). The senator's homosexual past emerges.

Lower photo: The President, **Franchot Tone** (left) has a tense meeting in the the Oval Office. Leffingwell (**Fonda**) admits to the President that he had once been a member of the Communist Party.

"Seab" Cooley of South Carolina, the curmudgeonly *pro tempore* of the U.S. Senate. A critic labeled Laughton in the role as "a ham's ham, a jowly, jiggling, panorama of obesity."

A key performance was delivered by Don Murray, who had been a sensation as the dumb cowboy opposite Marilyn Monroe in *Bus Stop* (1956), a role coveted by Elvis Presley.

Three actors had already rejected the part of Senator "Brig" Anderson of Utah, a character whose homosexual past is exposed as part of the movie's plot. Murray had no objection to shouldering such a role.

Frank Sinatra wanted to play Van Ackerman of Wyoming, but Preminger rejected him, assigning the role to George Grizzard instead.

Anderson (Murray), as committee chairman, demands that Leffington's denial of his communist past should have derailed his nomination as Secretary of State, but the President refuses to withdraw Henry as his choice to fill the position.

Anderson finds himself in trouble, too. An ambitious young senator, Fred van Ackerman (George Grizzard), threatens to blackmail him with the exposure of a long-ago homosexual encounter. The character of Anderson is unable to face the charge in public and commits suicide.

Franchot Tone was cast as the dying President, a Rooseveltian Democrat who nominated Leffington, although privately knowing he had once been a member of a Communist cell.

During the Senate confirmation hearing, Henry is confronted with someone from his past, Burgess Meredith as Herbert Gelman, "a trembling Judas."

Noting Henry's counter-attack, one reviewer claimed, "Like a bird of prey, Fonda circles and swoops down on the mouselike Meredith, dissolving him in confusion and pathos."

Later, Henry's character loses the nomination because Tone, portraying a U.S. President akin to that of "a beached flounder," dies in office. The "replacement" President, Harley Hudson, cast with Lew Ayres, wants to name his own Secretary of State.

As a Washington hostess, Gene Tierney, cast as Dolly Harrison, was making her comeback after years in a mental hospital.

The brother-in-law of President Kennedy, Peter Lawford, was cast as Senator Lafe Smith of Rhode Island. Preminger assigned him the role because he knew that Lawford could obtain permission from JFK to allow him to shoot scenes within the White House.

Other cast members included Walter Pidgeon, Eddie Hodges, Paul Ford, and Inge Swenson. Preminger offered the role of a black senator to Martin Luther King Jr., and he accepted, but, at the last moment, bowed out.

Henry recalled, "I used Adlai Stevenson as my inspiration for the role. Reviews were mixed, with one critic referring to my 'grieving cocker spaniel eyes,' but I must have done something right, because I would be returned to 'political office' in future movies."

***

The Longest Day (1962).

In the next two blockbuster films he accepted, Henry accepted only cameo roles, beginning with Darryl F. Zanuck's *The Longest Day*.

Based on Cornelius Ryan's epic chronicle, the movie followed the D-Day landings on June 6, 1944 as the Allied Armies—by sea and by air—invaded the Norman coast of Nazi-occupied France.

One of the most amazing and talented group of actors ever assembled for one picture included not only Henry Fonda and John Wayne, but Richard Todd, Robert Mitchum, Richard Burton, Sean Connery, Steve Forrest, Red Buttons, Tom Tryon, Rod Steiger, Leo Genn, Peter

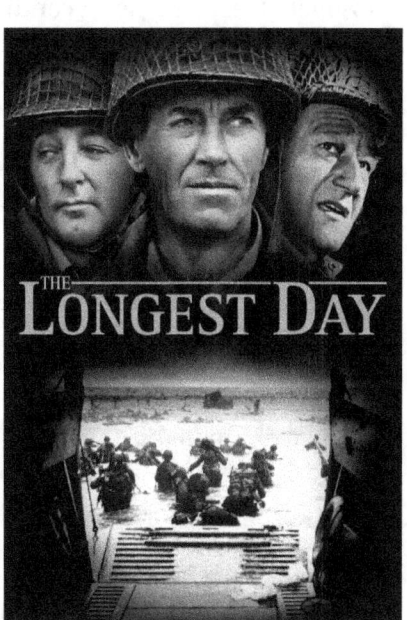

Robert Mitchum (left), Henry Fonda (middle) and **John Wayne** stopped—at least during filming—their animosities in favor of "the bigger (and very tragic) "America at War" focal point

Ambitious and focused on an accurate replication of the invasion of Normandy, **The Longest Day** poured millions of dollars and gallons of sweat into scenes like this—the blood-soaked Allied attack on Sword Beach—as the background for the dramas and strategies articulated by at least twenty, mostly male, big-name movie stars.

Lawford, Kenneth More, Eddie Albert, Stuart Whitman, Jeffrey Hunter, Curt Jurgens, George Segal, Robert Wagner, and singer Paul Anka.

Former President Dwight Eisenhower was considered for the role of himself, and he indicated that he was willing to star in the part. However, makeup artists were not able to make him look young enough. Subsequently, the role went to Henry Gracie, a set decorator who was a dead ringer for the young Ike. He had had no previous experience as an actor.

[Henry Fonda and John Wayne would team up again three years later to make In Harm's Way, a movie about the U.S. Navy in the aftermath of Pearl Harbor.]

In *The Longest Day*, Henry was cast as Theodore Roosevelt Jr., the eldest son of President Theodore Roosevelt. Despite a heart condition and arthritis that forced him to use a cane, General Roosevelt led the assault on Utah Beach. Regrettably, one month after the landing, he died of a heart attack in France. He was 56 years old.

***

How the West Was Won (1962)

Henry's next cameo was in *How the West Was Won*, a Western released by MGM in Cinerama. Narrated by Spencer Tracy, it, too, featured an all-star cast helmed by three directors: John Ford, George Marshall, and Henry Hathaway. On a budget of $15 million, the Western grossed $50 million and won the Best Picture of the Year Oscar.

Cast as Jethro Stuart, Henry played the white man's emissary to the Indians. He appears with a handlebar mustache as a buffalo hunter supplying meat to the railroaders. He wore what he later called "a hippie" wig with long hair.

His best friends, James Stewart and George Peppard, were also in the film.

The stunning cast also featured Carroll Baker, Gregory

Peck, Carolyn Jones, Karl Malden, Richard Widmark, Debbie Reynolds, Robert Preston, and Eli Wallach. Harry Morgan played Ulysses S. Grant, Raymond Massey portrayed Abraham Lincoln.

Hathaway hated the shoot, denouncing that "damned Cinerama. A waist-shot is as close as you can get with that thing. The film was nothing but god damn trouble. The producer, Sol Siegel, was drunk most of the time. Henry Fonda did it just for the dough."

On a nostalgic note, Henry took a long last walk around the Fox Studio grounds. The old sets were being torn down for a real estate development. During his tour, he stopped at one point and stared for a long time, remembering. It was at the shack, used in his first movie, *The Farmer Takes a Wife* (1935).

Henry, looking and playing it folksy, replete with buckskins and a handlebar mustache, **Winning the West** along with "24 (other) Great Stars."

***

Spencer's Mountain (1963)

To make up for not transmitting to Henry the script of Edward Albee's *Who's Afraid of Virginia Wolff?* Henry's new agents landed him the lead in *Spencer's Mountain* (1963).

Adapted from a novel by Earl Hammer Jr., it was set in the Blue Ridge Mountains of Virginia, but the producer and director, Delmer Daves, wanted it shot in the Grand Teton Mountains of Wyoming. The movie became a forerunner of the hit TV series, *The Waltons*.

Spencer's Mountain marked the second of three films Henry made with the flame-haired Irish beauty, Maureen O'Hara. [*During World War II, they had previously co-starred together in The Immortal Sergeant. Donald Crisp was cast as Grandpa Spencer, who is accidentally killed as part of the plot. Playing the local preacher was Wally Cox.*]

As a hayseed quarry worker, Henry, as Clay Spencer, is supposed to be dirt poor, but he seems to have enough money to buy whiskey and play poker. He is fiercely independent, navigating issues associated with religion and education, and hoping for a better future for his nine children.

One of his most controversial scenes is when he "whips the butt" of his wife, O'Hara, outdoors. One viewer outrageously claimed that watching that "was better than anal rape."

James MacArthur, the son of Helen Hayes, played Henry's oldest son, "Clayboy." After the release of the film, the studio was flooded with fan letters from homosexuals, who found his shirtless scenes alluring. When asked about this, he told reporters, "Better gay fans than no fans at all."

Although it's not really on exhibit in this movie, the real beefcake of the picture belonged to Mike Henry, cast as Clay's brother. The former football player for the Los Angeles Rams would become one in the series of movie Tarzans. Producer Sy Weintraub went looking for a "Burt Lancaster type" and

By today's standards, this politically incorrect shot of Henry Fonda whalloping the *derrière* of **Maureen** *("Kiss me, I'm Irish")* **O'Hara** in *Spencer's Mountain* was considered so cinematically "winning" that an important monthly film review placed it on the cover of its August, 1963 edition.

MORE MAUREEN: Here, **Maureen O'Hara** reacts to something that's only moderately shocking, with **Henry Fonda**, playing it *"gee, whiz!"* in this publicity banner for *Spencer's Mountain*.

found him in Mike Henry.

Henry later appeared in such movies as the 1968 *Tarzan and the Jungle Boy*. Wardrobe said he had to wear a heavy-duty jockstrap before the loincloth was attached.

Spencer's Mountain made money. Bosley Crowther in *The New York Times* wrote, "This papa, played by Henry Fonda, is a standard 'dang tootin'' type, acceptable as a poor dirt farmer and quarry laborer if you'll make certain allowances."

Judith Crist of the *New York Herald Tribune* felt that "Wyoming should sue."

Henry delivered his own review: "*Spencer's Mountain* will set the motion picture industry back twenty-five years."

Spencer's Mountain: Not until **Henry Fonda** starred with Lucille Ball in *Yours, Mine, and Ours* (1968) did any role he played place such an emphasis on home, hearth, and the (dubious) joys of too many children.

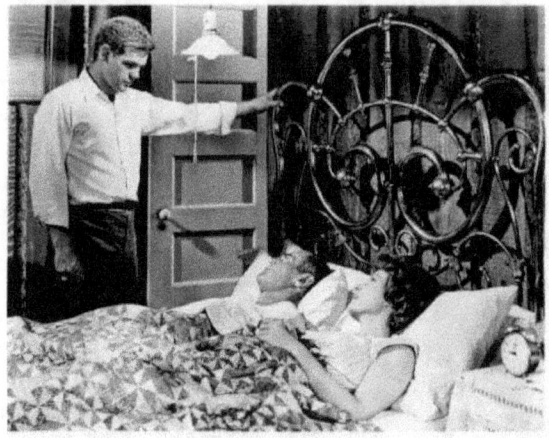

Cast as their eldest son, Clayboy (**James MacArthur**) wishes a good night to his screen parents, **Henry Fonda** and **Maureen O'Hara**.

Henry hated the picture, calling it "old-fashioned corn that will set films back 25 years."

TIME OUT FOR BEEFCAKE

Left photo, **James MacArthur,** the handsome adopted son of Helen Hayes, played Henry's stalwart oldest son (Clayboy) in *Spencer's Mountain*

Right photo, **Mike Henry,** Clayboy's younger brother, as he appeared not in *Spencer's Mountain*, but in one of his (later) *Tarzan* movies.

***

Tissue of Hate (1963)

Henry's previous major venture into TV drama had been in 1955, when he co-starred with Humphrey Bogart and Lauren Bacall in *The Petrified Forest*. Now, after a long absence from "the little box," he returned in May of 1963 as the star of an hour-long television drama, *Tissue of Hate*. It was hosted by Dean Martin as part of *The Dick Powell*

From an era when men wore jackets and neckties, no matter how dull it made them look, here's **Henry Fonda** with **John Larkin** in the made-for-TV drama about plastic surgeons and their clients.

Theater.

In it, he plays a rich plastic surgeon, Dr. Victor Fallon, who has a clientele of society ladies and (mostly female) movie stars hoping to retain their youth.

Dr. Burt Jacobson, played by Eduard Franz, lures him into a new venture. He begins to perform corrective surgery on deformed faces in a woman's prison, in the hopes that a more acceptable face will incite more acceptable behavior after their respective releases.

Henry's co-stars included Polly Bergen and heiress Gloria Vanderbilt, who at the time was pursuing an acting career.

That same year she worked with Henry, Bergen had appeared in *The Caretakers* with Joan Crawford and Robert Stack. For Bergen's performance, she was nominated for a Golden Globe as Best Supporting Actress in a Motion Picture Drama.

Vanderbilt was in the process of divorcing director Sidney Lumet, who would soon be helming Henry in the feature film, *Fail Safe*. Previously, she'd been married to the brilliant orchestra conductor, Leopold Stowkowski, 42 years her senior.

On the set, Vanderbilt flirted openly with Henry, as she had a record of seducing movie stars—namely, Errol Flynn, Frank Sinatra, and Orson Welles.

It is not known if Henry seduced the heiress. Marc Daniels, the director, noted that on two occasions, he spent more than an hour and a half alone with her in her dressing room.

Gloria Vanderbilt, shown here in a photo from 1959, had a temporary dream of a screen career, but that didn't work out. Today, she's better known as the mother of CNN's news anchor, Anderson Cooper.

***

The Best Man (1964)

"I wrote my Broadway play and screenplay, The Best Man, *back in the days when America was terrified of two evils—commies and queers."*

—Gore Vidal

The gay novelist and playwright, Gore Vidal, wrote both the Broadway play and the movie adaptation of *The Best Man*. United Artists released the film version in 1964 starring Henry Fonda and Cliff Robertson.

The plot has two candidates—each of them flawed—seeking the Democratic party's presidential nomination in Los Angeles at their national convention.

Henry portrays William Russell, a former Secretary of State clearly based on Adlai Stevenson.

As his rival, Robertson is Joe Cantwell, a sitting U.S. senator. Vidal later admitted that for this ruthless opportunist, willing to go to any length to get the nomination, he based the character on three men: Senator Joseph McCarthy, Bobby Kennedy, and Richard Nixon.

Margaret Leighton as Alice, Russell's wife, is willing to postpone their divorce until after the election. Edie Adams, cast as the wife of Cantwell, is glamourous and willing to do anything to see that her husband is nominated and eventually elected.

Ann Sothern as Sue Ellen Gamadge, the party's vice chair, had a colorful role. The character she plays is the

DOES 'THE BEST MAN' ALWAYS GET TO THE WHITE HOUSE?

America loved **Henry** in his roles of powerful, no-nonsense, American men. His portrayals of some of them got woven into the national fabric.

only known link between the KKK and the John Birch Society.

Lee Tracy, in his last film role, is Art Hockstader, the ailing, near-death former President of the United States. It takes no imagination to know that this is an impersonation of Harry S Truman.

Getting the worst reviews for his sleazy role was Shelley Berman as Sheldon Bascomb, a former Army comrade of Cantwell. He arrives at the convention to destroy Cantwell's bid for the nomination, by releasing details of his homosexuality that manifested itself during the months he was stationed in Alaska during World War II.

The Best Man marked one of the first times that a movie studio would actually dare to use the word "homosexual" on the screen. Up until then, the Production Code did not allow even a mention of the word.

As might be anticipated the two rivals cancel each other out, paving the way for the nomination as the Democratic Presidential candidate of the dull, blandly conventional Governor John Merwin, portrayed by William R. Ebersol.

In spite of its fine acting and heavy drama, *The Best Man* generated no lines at the box office. Critic John Simon labeled it as "impure hokum" *Time* magazine cited the film as being "remarkable not for its scorn or misanthropy, but for the even-handedness of its vision."

Preparing for a showdown in *The Best Man* are (*left to right*) **Cliff Robertson, Kevin McCarthy,** and **Henry Fonda.**

Once again, Fonda was inspired by Adlai Stevenson, with Robertson drawing upon both Bobby Kennedy and Richard Nixon. Standing between the two political enemies is Dick Jensen (Kevin McCarthy).

***

Fail Safe (1964)

Henry Fonda failed to win the presidency in his previous picture, *The Best Man,* but he was elevated to the office in his next film, *Fail Safe* (1964). Surely he regrets having won the office, since he has to make the most difficult decision a President has ever made—that is, dropping a hydrogen bomb on New York City, killing millions of his fellow citizens, including the First Lady, who was in the city at the time.

Sidney Lumet, its director, approved the advertising slogan devised during pre-production: "*Fail Safe* will have you sitting on the brink of eternity."

A Cold War thriller, the film was based on the 1962 novel of the same name by Harvey Wheeler and Eugene Burdick.

In the plot, a wing of SAC bombers pass the "fail safe" point of no return and head for the destruction of Moscow. Because of a breakdown in communications, the SAC crews cannot be recalled. The President, Fonda, is forced to give the order to shoot down their own pilots. One SAC bomber gets through and navigates his way toward the skies above Moscow with the intention of destroying it.

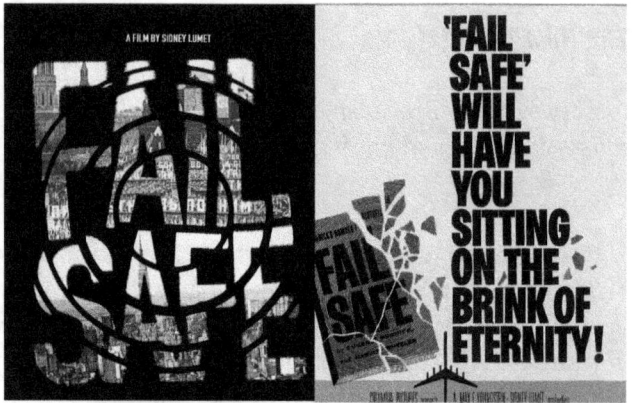

Henry Fonda, in his portrait of a U.S. President making impossible choices, orders the nuclear bombing of New York City in *Fail Safe.* It was a premise that many audiences found convincingly neurotic, but absurd and even worse, irritating.

BEFORE WE WERE PINK

The Best Man originated as a novel by the "Out and proud" American writer and politician, **Gore Vidal**, one of the most acerbic and scathing literary and political commentarians of the 20th Century.

In 2014, **Blood Moon Productions** published the world's first overview of the decades-long literary, romantic, and show-biz feuds that flourished (and festered) among the three most sought-after gay writers of the 20th century—an ongoing competition for stylish friends, better boyfriends, and more prominent roles in the pecking order of the *glitterati* of Broadway, *haute* society, and Hollywood.

PINK TRIANGLE, the widely reviewed overview of mid-Century America's most fascinating slugfest, by the authors of this two-part biography of the Fondas. Paperback, 708 pages, ISBN 978-1-936003-37-2, and available everywhere now.

In frantic calls, the President and the Soviet Premier reach history's harshest agreement. As "retribution" for destroying Moscow, the President will also destroy New York. He then orders the bombing of the great city, killing millions and hoping that the premier will not retaliate on an even larger scale.

The action in the movie takes place in three main locales, including SAC headquarters in Omaha, Henry's hometown. The War Room of the Pentagon is visited. The President is pictured for the most part in the bunker under the White House, where he communicates with the Russians through an emergency hot line. In the room with him is a Russian translator.

That role was played by Larry Hagman, the son of Mary Martin. He would soon become a household name. During the making of *Fail Safe,* he signed on to help craft a fantasy/comedy TV sitcom, *I Dream of Jeanie* (1965-1970). He'd go on to an even bigger TV series, playing the ruthless J.R. Ewing in the 1978-1991 soap opera, *Dallas.*

Even before the release of *Fail Safe,* a serious problem arose: Columbia had also signed to release *Dr. Strangelove,* a black comedy that satirized Cold War fears of a nuclear conflict between the Soviet Union and the U.S. Director Stanley Kubrick cast Peter Sellers, George C. Scott, and Sterling Hayden into its key roles.

***

In the "release wars" that quickly unfolded, Kubrick was victorious in getting *Dr. Strangelove* into movie theaters before *Fail Safe.*

After seeing Kubrick's eccentric satire, the public seemed to be in no mood to sit through a serious, mainstream version of a roughly equivalent Cold War disaster.

Lumet, who had helmed Henry in *12 Angry Men,* assured him that "We've created a masterpiece, even if nobody came to see it. You were Kennedy-esque throughout the film. How many roles will you ever have again when you hold the fate of mankind in your hands as the world faces Armageddon?"

Newsweek proclaimed, "Without question, the best thing in *Fail Safe* is Henry Fonda. Everyone else is hopeless and helpless."

***

Sex and the Single Girl (1964)

The mid-1960s found Henry starring in one film after another, mainly for a paycheck. He'd go from a comic Western to a sex romp, from a Cold War drama to a family frolic, even a couple of World War II battle spectacles.

"My kids weren't doing much better," he said. "Jane was compared to every star from Sandra Dee to the late Marilyn Monroe. Peter was in some flops, even playing a suicidal mental patient in *Lilith*."

"I hate to admit it, but in *Sex and the Single Girl*, I played a panty hose mogul wed to Lauren Bacall with her buzzsaw voice."

Helen Gurley Brown had written an international bestseller, *Sex and the Single Girl*, that sold two million copies in the first three weeks of its release. Soon-after, it was also published and released in 35 other countries, often in translation, during the same era when *Playboy's* Hugh Hefner was profitably promoting more liberated attitudes toward sexuality in publications of his own. Brown referred to *Sex and the Single Girl* as a "pippy-poo little book." In it, she encouraged women to become financially independent and to experience sexual relationships in and out of marriage.

Richard Quinn was designated as director of the book's film adaptation by Warner Brothers, who launched it in 1964 as a Technicolor comedy.

Left photo: Young **Larry Hagman**, pre-*Jeannie*, pre-*Dallas*, appears with his then very famous mother, stage diva **Mary Martin.** They did not always see eye to eye.

Above: **Hagman** as he appears as the world is about to explode in *Fail Safe*.

Both **Tony Curtis** (*left*) and **Henry Fonda** were lured into this silly picture because it was written by Joseph Heller—the author of *Catch-22*, one of their favorite books—and based on Helen Gurley Brown's hit novel. Neither actor was pleased with the final product.

NAUGHTY AND NICE, BUT STUPID

Tony Curtis, with **Natalie Wood**, puzzle over their (simulated) first glance at a thinly disguised clone of Helen Gurley Brown's "book that shook the world"—or at least its dating scene.

Henry Fonda was cast as a salesman who specializes in the wholesale distribution of nylon stockings, Here, he gets up close and personal with his product.

When seeing the film, he gave a snort of disgust.

Critic Judith Crist of the *New York Herald Tribune* claimed that the movie "was enough to put you off sex, single girls, and movies for the season."

His selection of players wasn't very astute. The picture focused on Tony Curtis, publisher of *Spot*, hailed as the filthiest rag in America. Curtis didn't want the role but needed the money to settle the terms of a recent divorce.

He's in love with Natalie Wood, cast as the psychologist/author of *Sex and the Single Girl*. "I hated the script, but I owed Warners one move movie, having signed a three-picture deal," Wood said. "I think Tony and I had made love on some night long ago, but who can keep track with all the men—everyone from Elvis Presley to Frank Sinatra. Tony himself has seduced stars from Marilyn Monroe to Rock Hudson."

Mel Ferrer admitted, "I stooped very low to take the thankless role of a psychiatrist."

In spite of the attacks it received, *Sex and the Single Girl* became one of the twenty highest-grossing films of 1964.

Lauren Bacall *(left)* and **Henry Fonda** did not become famous for their screen comedies. Here, she is cast as Sylvia, his sharp-tongued wife. Frank and Sylvia are noted for their epic battles.

***

The Rounders (1965)

For Henry's next film, he returned to the familiar Western genre when Burt Kennedy, the screenwriter and director, cast him with Glenn Ford in MGM's *The Rounders*.

During the first day of the shoot, Ford and Henry decided to play a practical joke on Kennedy. They showed up in jeans to meet him. Then, instead of shaking his hand, they unbuckled their jeans and mooned him. Henry quipped, "I hope you saw the saddle sores Glenn and I have earned in Westerns."

Kennedy shot back, "All I saw was two aging asses that looked like they've been plugged by half the studs of Hollywood."

The Rounders, set in the modern day, was a most unusual Western: No bank robberies, no duels on Main Street, no lynchings, no fistfights, no cattle rustling.

Glenn Ford had the lead role of Ben Jones, with Henry cast as "Howdy" Lewis. Together, they portrayed a duo of laidback, not-to-bright wranglers who make a meager living breaking in wild horses. In winter, they spend their time rounding up stray cows for slaughter.

Their employer, Jim

FOLKSY OL' COWPOKES & ROUNDERS

This photo evokes the camaradie that **Henry Fonda** managed to project with **Glenn Ford**, onscreen, in *The Rounders*.

Loaded with coy and sexually suggestive references *(wink wink, nudge nudge)*, **The Rounders** was marketed with taglines that included, "NOWADAYS, it's the GALS who make the West Wild."

Fonda and Ford strutted and joked their way through the movie, which, perhaps because of its unfunny toolbox of cornpone jokes and gaffes, more or less failed at the box office. **Sue Ann Langdon** and **Hope Holiday**, depicted in the illustration above, played the (sometimes bare-assed) bimbos.

Ed Lowe (Chill Wills), is a shrewd but larcenous businessman, always taking advantage of them and paying them meager wages.

One season, instead of being paid in cash, the cowpokes agree to accept a wild roan that no one has been able to ride for more than ten seconds. The cowboys decide to enter the beast in a rodeo, accepting bets that no one can stay on for more than ten seconds. As the plot moves on, complications are just beginning.

For relief, the cowboys come across two dim-witted strippers (portrayed by Hope Holiday and Sue Ann Langdon) stranded in a broken-down car. To jazz up the picture, Kennedy suggested that all four of them go skinny dipping. Consequently, Glenn Ford and the girls strip down, but Henry modestly opts to retain a jockstrap. In the film's final cut, the frontal nude scenes were cut.

During its filming, Henry was waging a relentless guerilla war with his son, Peter, over his heavy drug use. The young actor showed up in Arizona not for a reunion with his father, but to see his friend, the son of Glenn Ford, also named Peter.

[Ford's first marriage (1943-1959) had been to actress/dancer Eleanor Powell, with whom he had his only child, Peter Ford (born 1945). Glenn Ford and Eleanor Powell appeared to-

THAT'S SHOW BIZ
(All in the Family)

Left photo: **Glenn Ford** (right) with his son, **Peter Ford**, on the set of *The Long Ride Home* (aka, *A Time for Killing*; 1967), a potboiler that was advertised, somewhat shrilly, with the tagline, "Two Violent Men...and a Violated Woman."

Another Peter (Peter Fonda) also visited the set of *The Rounders*, culminating in an embarrassing outcome associated with hurt feelings about a surprise party organized for his father.

In the right photo appears **Eleanor Powell** in the 1930s, an era when she reigned at MGM as "The Queen of Tap Dancing." Powell was the first wife of Glenn Ford and the mother of their son, Peter

The most *risqué* scene in the movie occurred when **Henry Fonda** (left) and **Glenn Ford** (far right) stripped jaybird naked for a dip in the river.

Whereas the girls coyly cover their breasts, Fonda and Ford were completely naked, but their treasured assets weren't shown on the screen.

The Rounders: **GAFFES GALORE!**

In this view of **Henry Fonda** being thrown from a horse, its amazing that he wasn't seriously injured.

gether on screen only once, in a short film crafted as a fund-raiser for charity. It was ironically entitled Have Faith in Our Children *(1955).]*

When he learned that a surprise party was being staged for his father, young Peter threw a fit, in part because he had not been invited.

Kennedy tried to calm him down, pointing out that since the gathering had been conceived as a surprise party, his father could not have invited him. Nonetheless, Peter left the set in a rage.

Even though it was getting some good advance reviews, MGM didn't know what to do with this offbeat Western. They decided not to promote it, instead releasing it as the second feature on a double bill. *[The more heavily promoted film it was linked with was a piece of "claptrap teen bait," entitled* Get Yourself a College Girl, *starring Nancy Sinatra and Mary Ellen Mobley.]*

In reference to *The Rounders*, film critic Manny Farber wrote: "Henry Fonda fields Glenn Ford's act by doing a Stan Laurel, suggesting a catfish bag of bones in a hick foxtrot."

Running 85 minutes, *The Rounders* took in $1.5 million at the box office.

***

In Harm's Way (1965)

Henry signed to appear in two upcoming movies (*In Harm's Way* and *Battle of the Bulge*), each of which used World War II as their backdrop. Each was released in 1965.

As he headed out the door on his first assignment, he kissed his fifth (and final) wife Shirlee goodbye. "I'm back in the U.S. Navy," he said. "Not been there since I went AWOL from *Mr. Roberts*."

Producer and director Otto Preminger sent out a call to Henry, whom he referred to as "that darling man," to appear in a cameo in his latest film, *In Harm's Way*, based on the 1962 novel by James Bassett.

Henry's character was clearly inspired by Admiral Chester W. Nimitz, the commander of the U.S. Naval fleet in the Pacific Theater until his retirement in 1957.

As Admiral Chester W. Nimitz, **Henry Fonda** is in command of the Pacific Allied fleet moving ever forward toward the homeland of Japan. Though small, his role as the Navy boss was hailed as the most memorable in this gargantuan war epic.

Preminger rounded up an all-star cast headed by John Wayne as Captain Rock Torrey. He is removed from his command of a heavily armed cruiser for boldly pursuing the enemy, and then for mishandling the situation after it was attacked by a Japanese submarine in the immediate aftermath of Japan's December 7, 1941, assault on Pearl Harbor.

Henry was shocked to see the declining health of his former co-star, The Duke, when he arrived on the set. In the middle of a scene, he would sometimes erupt into an extended coughing fit. Henry urged him to see a doctor, but Wayne assured him, "I'm as fit as a fiddle."

In key roles, Preminger cast Kirk Douglas as the doomed commander Paul Eddington and Patricia Neal portrayed Lt. Maggie Haines of the nurse corps. Henry's longtime friend, Burgess Meredith, starred as Commander Powell based on Rear Admiral Gene Markey. Franchot Tone had the thankless role of Admiral Husband E. Kimmel, who was in charge of the base at Pearl Harbor at the time of its bombing.

The war drama took a realistic look behind the scenes, beginning on the night of December 6, 1941. It was a balmy night filled with dancing, drinking, and "making out." Within hours, Pearl Harbor would be in flames..

Near the end of filming, Henry learned that Wayne had lung cancer, leading to the removal of his entire left lung and two ribs.

Bosley Crowther of *The New York Times* reviewed the movie as "slick and shallow, a *cliché*-crowded melodrama. The only character who finally emerges with firmness is the admiral in command of the Pacific Fleet, as portrayed by Henry Fonda."

Despite the critical attacks, audiences flocked to see it, the film taking in $4.5 million at the box office.

[When news reached Henry that John Wayne was dying, he went to the hospital, where his son, Patrick, let him enter Wayne's hospital room. Alone with him, Henry found him in a deep slumber, a skeleton of his former self. Henry stood at the foot of his bed for five minutes, remembering their times together when they were young. When he left the room, a nurse reported seeing tears running down his cheeks.

Here are two A-list movie stars as they appeared in *In Harm's Way*, an "on the verge of death" **John Wayne** (left) alongside an equivalently battered **Kirk Douglas**.

On Monday, June 11, 1979, regular radio and TV programs were interrupted to announce the news: John Wayne was dead at the age of 72.

Listening to the news with great sadness, Henry turned to Shirlee, saying, "I'm next."]

***

Battle of the Bulge (1965)

In the next World War II drama film Henry made—a three-hour wide-screen Cinerama epic named *The Battle of the Bulge*—he was configured as the star. It was a highly fictionalized saga of one of the war's most poignant and notorious battles.

In a last-ditch effort to hold back the Allied advance, Nazi soldiers broke through the weakly defended outposts in the Ardennes Forests of eastern Belgium in attempts to recapture Antwerp. Ultimately, they would not succeed. The Allies won after great sacrifices of men and materiel.

Henry was cast as a military intelligence officer, Lt. Col. Daniel Kiley. He discovers that the Germans are planning an offensive and alerts his superiors. He is instantly dismissed as a "crackpot."

Henry with his wife, Shirlee, flew to Spain to shoot the movie, promising her a second honeymoon touring Europe after the end of the filming.

On his first day there, he met the British director Ken Annakin, later complaining, sarcastically that "He spoke no English and worked us from sunup to sundown."

Annakin had rounded up a strong supporting cast: Robert Shaw, Telly Savalas, Robert Ryan, Dana Andrews, and Charles Bronson.

Immediately after its release, *Battle of the Bulge* came under heavy fire from historians who cited numerous inaccuracies. Even so, it did reasonably well at the box office, taking in $4.5 million.

Variety found Henry "excellent in his warm, restrained underplaying."

Bosley Crowther, however, of *The New York Times* thought that Henry played Kiley "as though he was a pal of Bill Maudlin's

At this point in his career, **Henry Fonda** (left) had become a stalwart, reliable, and very familiar figurehead in cinematic replications of the American war machine. Here he poses, radiating genuine concern, with **Robert Ryan**, equivalently stressed and attired.

The demanding and authoritarian **Otto Preminger**—one of the most hated, but most respected, creative forces in Hollywood.

cartooned Willie."

Around the same time, Columbia was also in pre-production of yet another film about the Battle of the Bulge. Unimpressed with its forecast for potential earnings, the studio shut it down. It was to have starred Van Heflin as Eisenhower, John Wayne as General Patton, David Niven as General Montgomery, and Laurence Olivier as Hitler.

After the European honeymoon Henry had promised Shirlee, they lived out the remainder of the dying summer in a villa on the beach at Malibu. About a mile away, also along the beach at Malibu, Henry's daughter, Jane, went to bed every night with Roger Vadim—"that frog director" (Henry's words of contempt).

This is a filmmaker's replication of the midwinter battle for the Ardennes Forest, aka **The Battle of the Bulge**.

Many of the film's sometimes emotional viewers had been real-life participants in the actual fighting of a battle (and a war) which had ended only twenty years before the release of this film.

***

The Dirty Game (1965)

The producers of *The Dirty Game* were hoping to hop a ride aboard the "cash cow" enjoyed by *The Spy Who Came in From the Cold* (also released in 1965 and starring Richard Burton) to box offices around the world. In that, they failed, but not before valiantly trying.

After *Battle of the Bulge* Henry journeyed to Berlin to film this three-part anthology-style spy thriller.

All three episodes were narrated by Robert Ryan, cast as the fictional General Bruce, an archetype of a Head of CIA Intelligence in Europe

During the course of the film, Bruce recalls three spy cases in which he was involved.

Most critics agreed that Henry was miscast in his role of Lt. Col. Dmitri Koulov, an American undercover agent who has just escaped from East Berlin to the West. The Russians had imprisoned him there for seventeen years.

Hoping for freedom, he finds himself betrayed by a treacherous CIA agent based in Berlin. He awaits his fate in a lonely hotel room, where he will be murdered.

Henry's episode was noted for its grim and gritty drama, although the first two sequences were labeled as "James Bondism."

Terrence Young, who had helmed 007 films, was Henry's director.

The Dirty Game had a limited release, with most of its showings configured as part of a double-bill at drive-in theaters in the Midwest. It ended up configured as part of a package deal sold to television networks.

Critic Michael Kerbel wrote, "Fonda skillfully imparts all the world weariness of *The Spy Who Came in from the Cold.*"

The *New York World Journal Tribune* found that "*The Dirty Game* is a dirty shame."

Postwar **Henry Fonda** (the quintessential American) cast as an undercover agent stealing secrets from the Soviets.

He's world-weary, broken, and eventually, murdered, at least as the plot unfolds in *The Dirty Game*.

***

Generation (1965)

In October of 1965, Henry returned to his first love, the Broadway stage, to star in a play entitled *Generation,* produced in part by Frederick Brisson, the Danish-born husband of Rosalind Russell. Written by William Goodhart, the play was directed by Gene Saks and opened at Manhattan's Morosco Theatre. It would run for 300 performances and be marketed as "a generation gap comedy."

In the role of a conservative father, Jim Bolton, Henry plays a befuddled parent shocked at the advanced pregnancy of his daughter right before she marries.

Actress Holly Turner played Doris Owen. Her unconventional wedding is with Richard Jordan, cast as Walter Owen.

As the girl's father, Henry is shocked to learn that his new son-in-law plans to deliver the baby himself. Finally, however, Henry, portraying the father of the pregnant woman, fumblingly tries to fall into step with the "new generation" and agrees to assist in the delivery of the baby too.

John Chapman of *The Daily News* wrote that "Fonda is diverting as the father-in-law in his disbelieving agitated reactions. He does his best to keep Goodhart's thin little brew bubbling."

Richard Watts Jr. of the *New York Post* weighed in, too: "In spite of Fonda's winning skill, he can't cancel the unfortunate fact that Goodhart's *Generation* is a curiously irritating comedy."

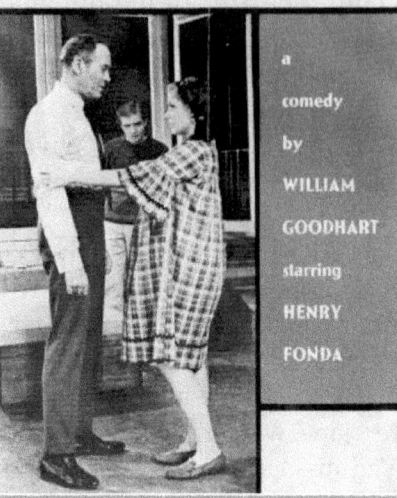

Henry Fonda, perhaps drawing on the sometimes traumatic example of his own family, became more and more convincing as a "back from the wars' befuddled but well-intentioned patriarch confused and baffled by changing times.

Here, he appears on the cover of the playbill for the Broadway show, *Generation.*

***

A Big Hand for the Little Lady (1966)

Marking Henry's involvement in what was his 60th motion picture, he returned to the Western genre with *A Big Hand for the Little Lady* (1966). This time, the script was permeated with what critics defined as "an O. Henry twist in the plot."

Churned out by Eden Productions, and released by Warners, it had been adapted from a screenplay by Sidney Carroll from a TV play, *Big Deal at Laredo,* which had aired on *The Dupont Show of the Week* in 1962.

A topnotch cast of often grizzled character actors were cast alongside Joanne Woodward, the actress wife of Paul Newman.

In key roles were Jason Robards Jr., portraying a rich cattleman; Kevin McCarthy as a lawyer; Charles Bickford as an undertaker; Burgess Meredith as the town "Doc;" and Paul Ford as a crooked banker.

On the set, Henry bonded with Robards, who had accepted this minor role, a genuine comedown for him. He was better known as an interpreter of the works of playwright Eugene O'Neill. He was a triple winner—two Oscars, a Tony, and an Emmy, for his previous stage or screen interpretations.

Lauren Bacall had divorced him in 1961. "Before you made off with Bogie's Baby, friends were urging me to marry Bacall," Henry said. "I turned her down because I like to wear the pants in the family."

Henry's character was named "Meredith" with Woodward as his "wife" Mary. On television, Meredith had been portrayed by Walter Matthau, who was rejected for the movie version.

Meredith is a "shamblin' gamblin' man," trying to reform from his addiction to gambling.

According to the plot, five of the richest men in the territory gather for their annual high-stakes poker game. They allow homesteader Meredith to join. He stakes all the money he has, hoping to build a farm for his family.

In the middle of the game, he collapses, and when it becomes apparent that he can't continue, Mary bravely replaces him at the poker table, using collateral borrowed from the bank.

POKER-FACED PRIDE

Clad in gingham and wearing a bonnet, **Joanne Woodward** (*right*) appears with **Robert Middleton** (*left*) and **Henry Fonda** as they plot their strategies at the gaming tables.

She has a winning hand, eventually making off with $16,000.

As it turns out, Meredith and Mary are not what they seem to be. Each is a die-hard card shark, always cheating and always crooked. And actually, she is not his wife, but his mistress, Ruby.

Richard Schnickel wrote: "Fonda transcends his customary image without sacrificing that graceful ease that is his hallmark."

The New York Times cited him as the "best of the bunch" of seasoned performers. "The actors are a skilled bunch of real film professionals, having at each other. Fonda is the most memorable of the lot."

Critic Michael Kerbel found that "Fonda gives a genuine performance, convincing us that he is a simpleton and a sucker."

Although critics tended to like the movie, the public stayed away.

***

Welcome to Hard Times (1967)

"Back in the saddle and gun-totin'" again, Henry Fonda starred in *Welcome to Hard Times*, a controversial Western. Although it had a small coterie of admirers, it came under heavy critical fire.

Burt Kennedy had both written and directed it, and he and Henry were glad to work with each other again, after doing so successfully in *The Rounders*.

The plot for *Hard Times* was based on a novel by E.L. Doctorow in which the character of "Will Blue," as portrayed by Henry, would appear.

In this grimy little Western, he played a reluctant lawman. In Kennedy's words, "I want you to be an anti-hero, coming as close as one is likely to see with a gun in Western garb.

An array of big-name actors was rounded up for supporting roles. Key parts went to Aldo Ray, Janice Rule, and Janis Paige. As the psychotic villain, Ray had launched himself into the movies by positioning himself on the casting couch of George Cukor during the filming of *Pat and Mike* (1952), co-starring

Spencer Tracy and Katharine Hepburn.

Janice Rule as Molly started out on Broadway as a dancer until she broke her ankle. Warner's later cast her as support for Joan Crawford in *Goodbye, My Fancy* (1951). Rule went on to an on-again, off-again career in TV dramas. In 1973, she began formal studies as a psychotherapist, eventually receiving a PhD and specializing in treating and/or counseling other actors.

Janis Paige, a noted singer, had played brassy showgirls in some of her previous movies. In *Hard Times*, she was a Wild West floozie named "Adah."

The supporting cast was loaded with big names of yesterday, many by this time nearly forgotten—Keenan Wynn, Warren Oates, Edgar Buchanan, Lon Chaney Jr., and Elisha Cook Jr.

Actress Ann McCrea had the most thankless role. The character played by Ray grabs her and hauls her to an upstairs bedroom, where he rapes and kills her.

The settlement of Hard Times is a small Western outpost invaded by the "Man from Bodie" (Ray). He terrorizes the locals, killing the residents and burning their ramshackle buildings.

Will Blue (Fonda) does nothing to stop him.

Janice Rule's character wants Will to stand up to the marauders, even to kill them. For her intervention, she is fatally shot.

After more drama and soul-searching, Will finally summons enough courage to face the killer.

As critic Craig Butler noted, "Kennedy directed Fonda in this revisionist Western, typical of the 1960s, disassembling the classic genre and reassembling it in ways that did not follow the traditions of the classic western."

Another critic likened Henry's movements "to those of an older, slower Wyatt Earp, but without his skill or cunning. He feels his way through a timid man's desperate efforts to remain among the living."

Bosley Crowther of *The New York Times* claimed, "It's listless, haphazard, and there isn't a single person in it with whom we can identify. Not even Mr. Fonda, who walks through drearily."

Charming and beautiful **Janice Rule** (who later quit acting to become a psychotherapist, specializing in counseling other actors) appears here with a cowardly sheriff portrayed by **Henry Fonda** in *Hard Times*.

Janis Page with **Keenan Wynn** in *Hard Times*. Even such talents as they were, cast as Adah and Zar, couldn't save this stinker.

Wynn arrives in town with a wagonload of party girls to entertain miners and relieve them of their gold.

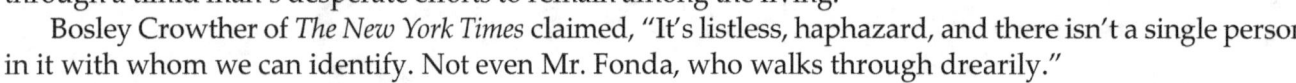

"People ask me from time to time what it was like growing up with Henry Fonda as my dad. I ask them, 'Have you seen Fort Apache? That Western he made with John Wayne? He was like that role he played of Colonel Owen Thursday.'"

—Peter Fonda

Henry was growing a beard for his next film role when he was called upon to testify on behalf of his son Peter at the Municipal Court in downtown Los Angeles. He had been arrested and charged with illegal drug possession.

After signing autographs, Henry entered the courtroom and sat through his son's testimony.

"Peter made the worst defendant," he later said. "Every time the prosecutor asked a question, he answered with a wisecrack. He

Peter Fonda from around the time his father testified on his behalf in court after he was hauled in for drug possession.

Witnesses to the trial later credited Henry for "saving his ass from jail."

seemed to be working the room for laughs instead of trying for an acquittal."

During lunch, Henry lectured Peter, criticizing his "hippie outfit."

"You look like you're on drugs, and cut out the fucking wisecracks, or you'll end up jailed for two or three years. Make yourself sound like a decent young man—not some junkie."

Henry later claimed that Peter followed his advice.

After Henry himself took the stand, the prosecutor claimed, "Fonda gave an Oscar-winning performance as Peter's father. He saved him from jail. The Fonda boy was found not guilty, though he was clearly guilty."

Peter later disputed Henry's account: "I wore a custom-tailored, double-breasted suit, a Battisoni shirt, an Hermès tie, and fine black leather shoes. That afternoon, I did not change my attitude to the prosecutor, judge, or jury, unlike what my father wrote in his so-called 'autobiography.'"

Before freeing Peter, the judge lectured him. "Make the most of your life by leading a productive and useful existence for your wife, your children, and your illustrious father. Don't ever make them ashamed and humiliated by your actions."

Many newspapers in Hollywood predicted the end of Peter's film career. *Easy Rider*, however, lay in his near future.

***

Stranger on the Run (1967)

"Never have I looked like such an alcoholic bum than I did in *Stranger on the Run*."

Henry was referring to the Western drama that NBC had recently telecast as Movie of the Week.

However, when the producers saw the film's final cut, they wanted to open it in neighborhood theaters nationwide. NBC objected, standing firm with their intention of broadcasting its exclusive first exposure. In contrast, however, theaters abroad ran it as a regular Hollywood release.

Henry had accepted the role of Ben Chamberlain largely because it had been written by Reginald Rose, the author of the Fonda movie classic, *12 Angry Men* (1957).

A native of Chicago, the son of a mandolin player, Don Siegel was hired to direct *Stranger on the Run*. *The New York Times* called him a director of "tough, cynical and forthright adventure films whose plots are centered on individualistic losers."

In 1956, Siegel had helmed the cult favorite, *Invasion of the Body Snatchers*. In time, he would direct five movies starring Clint Eastwood, such films as *Dirty Harry* (1971). From 1945 to 1963, he'd been married to the sultry Sweden-born screen actress, Viveca Lindfors.

Siegel assembled the cast, assigning Anne Baxter, the granddaughter of Frank Lloyd Wright, as its female lead. Baxter had won a Best Supporting Actress Oscar for *The Razor's Edge* (1946) starring Tyrone Power.

She had also been nominated for a Best Actress Oscar for her classic performance as the scheming Eve Harrington in *All About Eve* (1950), co-starring Bette Davis.

During World War II, she had appeared

Left photo: *Stranger on the Run*, as marketed for a TV audience, shows **Anne Baxter,** a then-ingenue in *All About Eve* (1950) in a low-tech cover shot with an attractively "graying at the temples" **Henry Fonda.**

Right photo: Shows how commercial artists "morphed" the made for TV project into a jazzier photo montage with the intention of "selling" it to movie audiences.

in a number of dramas, such as *Sunday Dinner for a Soldier* (1945), co-starring with John Hodiak. She later married him.

During lunch with Henry, she told him that during the war, "I received almost as much fan mail as the pinup girl, Betty Grable." The soldiers admired her legs, but I was the idealized girl they wanted to come home to."

Michael Parks was cast as the stoic, resilient, walrus-mustached Sheriff, Vinnie McKay.

Anne Baxter with **Henry Fonda** in *Stranger on the Run*

Dan Duryea played O.E. Hotchkiss. Known mainly for villain roles, he was noted for having co-starred with Bette Davis in *The Little Foxes* (1940).

He specialized in playing "sniveling, taunting, antagonists" in *film noir*. He would co-star with James Stewart and Gary Cooper in a trio of movies assigned to each actor. He told Henry, "I've made a career of slapping women around on the screen, where evil and death lurk in each nightmare alley."

Sal Mineo, the son of coffin makers in the Bronx, was cast as George Blaylock. He'd shot to fame as Plato in *Rebel Without a Cause* (1955), starring James Dean. Both Henry and Mineo had had cameos in Zanuck's *The Longest Day* (1962).

Sal Mineo in a photo unrelated to *Stranger on the Run*

"I felt sorry for Sal having to deny who he was every day," Henry said. "He'd go on the Johnny Carson show, bragging about all his female conquests, then retire to his home to sodomize some young man later that night."

In 1976, following a rehearsal for James Kirkwood's *P.S. Your Cat is Dead*, Mineo headed home to his apartment in West Hollywood. Directly in front of his house, he was fatally stabbed in the heart by a mugger.

In the plot for *Stranger on the Run*, drifter Ben Chamberlain (Fonda), a former prison inmate and alcoholic, arrives as a stranger in a small town. There, he's wrongly accused by a hostile sheriff (Michael Parks) of murdering a woman.

Ben is given a horse, some supplies, and a one-hour start into the desert before a thuggish posse will chase him down and kill him.

The plot thickens at this point, especially with the entry of Valverde Johnson, cast with Anne Baxter. She plays a lonely, widowed homesteader, whose troubles include an unstable son who wants to be a gunman. She and Ben start to develop a relationship, but this is interrupted when the posse arrives.

We won't give away the ending.

After the film was released, director Siegel delivered his opinion of it: "I think for a 'one-twenty' (i.e., a two-hour television film) that it's very good. I liked having Fonda. I like very much the fact that a man of his age is thrown off a freight car at the start of the picture. He's a bum and doesn't lick anybody. There isn't anybody in town he can lick. And then you go through a change at the end of the picture. Not that he could whip anybody, but he's a man. He faces up to responsibility. I thought the picture was surprisingly un-Hollywood—and I'm not using that term to be as contemptuous as it sounds."

Judith Crist reviewed *Stranger on the Run* for TV Guide like this: "An excellent movie cast, beautifully paced melodrama, replete with social and psychological significance and outstanding performances by Henry Fonda, Dan Duryea, and Michael Parks…The performances made *Stranger on the Run* of particular interest beyond its being one of the few tailored-for-TV films that provide character, along with skillfully paced melodramatics. Henry Fonda and Dan Duryea are their usual perfection; Michael Parks gives his best performance to date, and Anne Baxter is so good you don't even mind her chic or her flashy teeth, hardly the hallmark of the working frontierswoman."

CHAPTER TWO

The 1960s

ALTHOUGH HORRIFIED BY NEWFANGLED SOCIAL TRENDS

HENRY

AS A WORKING ACTOR, FATHER, CELEBRITY, AND CITIZEN,
CHANGES WITH CHANGING TIMES

FIRECREEK (1968)
After 20 Years, James Stewart and Henry Fonda co-star in a film, a grim Western where Henry plays a ruthless, enigmatic killer, a Loner like "Flint on Steel."

YOURS, MINE, AND OURS (1968)
Lucille Ball and Henry, at least on the screen, resume their on- and off affair that began one moonlit night in the late 1930s. In this comedy, a widow, 56, and a widower, 62, get married. Between them, they have 18 kids

MADIGAN (1968)
Richard Widmark and Henry Fonda are police officers in this cops-and-crime saga. "Widmark robbed the picture from me," Henry said. "We starred with Sheree North, sometimes described as 'Marilyn Monroe's replacement.'"

THE BOSTON STRANGLER (1969)
Henry's assignment involves grilling a murderous pervert, played by Tony Curtis, whose character confesses to ejaculating with a woman only when he's strangling her.

ONCE UPON A TIME IN THE WEST (1969)
Critically praised for a performance that evokes the killer instincts of a Cobra, Henry stars in his first "Spaghetti Western." Claudia Cardinale agrees with the film's director, Sergio Leone, in defining Henry as "an erotic rapist."

OUR TOWN (1969)
Henry returns to the stage in this romanticized version of life in a sleepy New England village. Its author, Thornton Wilder, defines Henry as "the theater's consummate actor."

As the "swinging 1960s" came to their "liberated," blood-soaked and controversial end, Henry Fonda worked steadily as an actor.

Everywhere, there were protests (some led by his daughter Jane) over the Vietnam war, major-league political assassinations (including both Martin Luther King Jr. and Robert Kennedy). Spearheaded or at least encouraged by feminists and pornographers alike, America experienced a highly confrontational sexual revolution where recreational drugs and gender preference didn't seem particularly important.

Henry seemed immune from all that. So was his friend, James Stewart, who talked about what was happening when they co-starred once again in a picture, a Western called *Firecreek*. "This," Henry said, "will be our version of *High Noon*, with Jim in the Gary Cooper role."

Before filming it, each of the veteran actors agreed not to discuss politics. Stewart was a Nixon supporter and an ardent Republican, and Henry was a liberal Democrat but "Far to the right of my daughter."

In December of 1968, Henry was saddened to learn of the death of his favorite author, John Steinbeck, who had written the best-selling novel, *The Grapes of Wrath*. He flew to New York for the author's burial, reading three poems. Later, Steinbeck's wife gave him the pair of pearl studs worn on his shirt during his acceptance of the Nobel Prize for Literature in 1962.

Ironically offers began pouring in for Henry to star in Westerns. He had to tell his potential directors, "Unlike my daughter, Jane, I hate horses. They have it in for me. Whenever I've been on one, it tries to kill me."

While Henry was away on one film set or another, making movies, his wife Shirlee was driving the roads of Southern California looking for a new home for them. Eventually she found one that she liked on Chalon Drive in Bel Air, a hacienda-inspired residence made of stone and brick. That night, Henry was taken there. After they toured it, he told her, "Let's live here for the rest of our lives."

Nedda Logan, the wife of director Joshua Logan, a longtime frenemy of Henry's, came to visit. "Hank's new wife," she said, "has caused him to open like a rose, emerging from a tiny bud. She gives him confidence. My god, Silent Slim has even become loquacious."

When Jane visited, she said, "Shirlee takes a lot of abuse from Dad. I least I think so, because she knows that underneath, he loves her very much. She even gets him to fly to do things she wants to do, including winging to Las Vegas at the invitation of Barbra Streisand or Frank Sinatra to attend one of their

10744 Chalon Road in Bel Air, California: 7 bedrooms, 7 baths, 9,385 square feet: Henry and Shirlee Fonda's home

On December 3, 1965, Henry married this former flight attendant. As he told James Stewart, "A last I've found the right girl, the one I should have married in the first place—not those other four disasters."

shows. But Henry cautions 'Don't expect me to gamble. Why? Because I hate to lose.'"

***

Firecreek (1968)

In many ways, *Firecreek,* Henry's next movie, evoked Gary Cooper's *High Noon* (1952), the Western classic made with a too young Grace Kelly.

Best friends James Stewart and Henry Fonda hadn't appeared in a film together since *On Our Merry Way* in 1948.

In *Firecreek,* Stewart would take top billing over Henry. Stewart was cast as Johnny Cobb, a farmer and part-time sheriff. In contrast, Henry would play "Larkin," a scruffy, unmitigated villain.

Before shooting began, Henry told Stewart, "You and I are a bit old for our roles, but what the hell!"

Still best friends after all these years, the former roommates, Stewart and Fonda, try to kill each other at the end of *Firecreek.*

For their leading lady, the Swedish-born actress Inger Stevens was cast as Evelyn.

In the plot, she takes Larkin into her modest home, where he is recovering from a bullet wound he'd received during a recent robbery.

The director, Vincent McEveenty, would become better known for helming such Emmy Award-winning television series as *The Untouchables, Gunsmoke,* and *Star Trek.* For *Firecreek,* he assembled a superb supporting cast, rounding up some of Hollywood's best character actors. For an added treat for the ladies and gay men, he threw in two handsome young men, James Best and Gary Lockwood.

Henry Fonda and James Stewart. Lifelong friends in private, the duo was pitted against each other in this cold-hearted, somber Western.

Stewart got top billing in the film's press and publicity campaigns.

Lockwood was married to actress Stefanie Powers at the time. He would become far better known when he played the astronaut in *2001: A Space Odyssey,* released the same year as *Firecreek.*

Two years older than Henry, Dean Jagger had won a Best Supporting Oscar for his performance in *Twelve O'Clock High* (1949), starring Gregory Peck.

A high note in Jagger's career was when he was cast as the Morman leader in *Brigham Young* (1940), starring Tyrone Power. Long before he played a father in *Firecreek,* he was the dad of Elvis Presley in *King Creole* (1958) and the father of Audrey Hepburn in *The Nun's Story* (1959).

One of Jagger's biggest successes was in the TV series *Mr. Novak (1963-1965)* with James Franciscus. Encountering Jagger one afternoon, Henry told him, "Your former co-star, James Franciscus, was the man who made a woman out of my daughter, Jane."

As Preacher Broyles, Ed Begley Sr. had won a Best Supporting Actor Oscar when cast as a political boss in Tennessee

Inger Stevens with Henry Fonda in *Firecreek.* Their love scene did not generate much fire on screen, contributing to a very mild box office response from the public.

Williams' *Sweet Bird of Youth* (1962). He'd also starred with Henry in *12 Angry Men* and was featured as Debbie Reynold's father in *The Unsinkable Molly Brown* (1964).

Jay C. Flippen was cast as Mr. Pittman, the father of Evelyn (Inger Stevens). He'd gotten his start in vaudeville, where he was known for appearing in blackface. He called himself "The Ham That Am."

In movies of the 1940s and '50s, he played weary crooks or police officers. On occasion, he supported Stewart in his film roles, and he was often seen in movies starring John Wayne. When he worked with Henry in *Firecreek,* he had already filmed *Cat Ballou* (1965) with Jane Fonda.

Cast as wild boy Drew, one of Larkin's gang, James Best was at home in feature films, in TV, or on the stage. During a 60-year career, he was also a writer, director, acting coach, artist, college professor, and musician. Best is most widely known for his role of Sheriff Rosco P. Coltrane in CBS's TV sitcom, *The Dukes of Hazzard* (1979-1985).

Jack Elam, a former cotton picker from Miami, Arizona, was known for having the meanest face of any actor in Hollywood Westerns. Part of his ghastly look came from a misaligned eye, the result of a schoolboy incident when a male student jabbed a sharpened pencil into his eyeball. Elam was a fixture in such movies as *High Noon* (1952) and *Once Upon a Time in the West* (1968).

Stewart's character was that of a mild-mannered Peace Officer, a kind a sheriff, who earns two dollars a month. He is only forced into action when his conscience will not permit evil to continue.

The action heats up when five "no good gun-totin' drifters" arrive at the frontier town. Their gang leader, Larkin (Henry) needs to recover from a gunshot wound. He finds refuge in the home of Evelyn (Inger Stevens) and her wheelchair-bound father, Mr. Pittman (Flippen).

In the meantime, the Larkin gang tear up the once-peaceful town.

Gang members Earl (Lockwood); Norman (Elam); and Drew (Best) run roughshod over the locals, even interrupting their church service.

Cobb has to leave town to tend to his pregnant wife who is about to deliver their baby.

Left behind is a dim-witted stable boy (J. Robert Porter). When a gang member abducts an Indian girl to rape her, Porter rushes to rescue her, killing her would-be rapist. Later, while Cobb is still out of town, the stable boy is hanged.

When Cobb returns to Firecreek, Larkin and Cobb, with guns loaded, meet for a showdown on the main street. However, it is Evelyn who enters the fray, fatally shooting Larkin from a second-floor window.

Howard Thompson of *The New York Times* wrote, "*Firecreek* is a good, sturdy, and occasionally powerful little Western. James Stewart is plain wonderful, and Henry Fonda almost matches him. The unpretentious little color movie, which looks as if it cost a dime, is almost exactly right every step of the way. Fonda, as a ruthless, enigmatic loner, plays it like flint on steel."

Critic Judith Crist, on the *NBC Today Show,* delivered her opinion: "Sometimes, there's a sleeper, a small Western that comes along, that really has more to offer than just grist for the Western mill. For the first time in twenty years, Henry Fonda and James Stewart are on screen together and it's a joy to watch these two old pros. Fonda, mind you, is the bad guy, leader of a gang that terrorizes the town and Stewart is the aging farmer and part-time sheriff who just gets rip-roaring mad. *Firecreek* has some explosive stuff, but it is, thanks to its stars and direction, a satisfyingly low-key and absorbing Western."

In spite of some good reviews, *Firecreek* was dumped into neighborhood theaters where it came and went quickly, eventually ending up on television.

Henry reviewed his own role: "Any man who kills James Stewart on screen is a marked man who is just plain rotten."

***

Yours, Mine, and Ours (1968)

Before selling Desilu, Lucille Ball had concluded a deal with United Artists to distribute her latest feature film, *Yours, Mine, and Ours,* set for a 1968 release.

As director, she had chosen Melville Shavelson, who was also a screenwriter and producer. He'd gotten his start in the entertainment industry as a writer for Bob Hope's radio shows. Lucille had met and been impressed with him when he'd directed Hope and her in *Sorrowful Jones* (1949).

Ultimately, *Yours, Mine, and Ours* became her all-time favorite feature film. John Wayne had been her first choice as leading man, although Art Carney and Jackie Gleason were temporary candidates too. None of those three was available, but Henry Fonda was. So once again, and for the final time, Lucille was re-teamed with her former co-star and off-screen lover. She desperately wanted this movie to be a hit, since she felt she'd bombed in her last picture, *Critic's Choice*, with Bob Hope.

The plot of *Yours, Mine, and Ours* was based on a true-to-life story. In a nutshell, it described a widowed mother of eight who marries a Naval officer—father of ten—who was also widowed.

The real Helen Beardsley wrote an autobiography entitled *Who Gets the Drumstick?*. It described her life as the story of a man and a wife coping with (and living with) an overcrowded schoolyard of their own kids.

Lucille insisted on personally casting each of the kiddie roles herself, and for a brief period, she considered casting Lucie Arnaz and Desi Jr. among the horde of children who eventually appeared in the film. At the last minute, however, she changed her mind.

As pre-production got underway, Fonda, also at the last minute, wanted to drop out of *Yours, Mine, and Ours*, and accept another role instead. Lucille turned to Fred MacMurray as a replacement, but then Fonda changed his mind and came aboard, although MacMurray might have been better-suited as the father, as he'd had such a hit with the TV sitcom *My Three Sons* (1960-1972).

Although her long-ago affair with Fonda was a distant memory, Lucille had long maintained a friendship with him. He'd once told her, "If you had married me, *Desilu* could have been named *Fondalu*."

Before the beginning of filming, she told *Variety*, "I'm getting tired of mini-skirted beauties ruling Hollywood. Our movie will mark a return to family values."

In his biography of Henry Fonda, Devin McKinney wrote: "*Yours, Mine, and Ours* is less honest than the youth-oriented exploitation movies it means to counteract. We wonder why Lucy, opposing the miniskirt oligarchy, goes through the film wearing thickly painted lips and false lashes that curl over

Van Johnson (left) is **Henry Fonda**'s best man at his wedding to **Lucille Ball.**

Decades before that, Fonda and Ball had been, in their private personal lives, secret lovers.

In the film, when, as a widow and widower, they tied the knot, they brought together two unruly households. All combined, that meant eighteen children who, at first, divided into warring camps.

Henry Fonda and Lucille Ball's ultimate "family friendly" joint venture included way too many children.

Here's a still from what many fans remember as one of their favorite scenes. Fonda's children have deliberately spiked the drinks of their about-to-become new stepmother with the intention of embarrassing her.

As with many "cutesie" movies of the late 60s, marital bliss, with the bizarre collusion of their collective eighteen children—wins out in the end.

her eyes like fried spiders. We ask how traditional morals are advanced by a screenplay sprinkled with, in Renata Adler's words, 'all sorts of sleazy, dirty lines, and cozy bedroom scenes and smiley, hesitant conversations about puberty.'"

Although Van Johnson, Lucille's longtime friend and former co-star, was no longer the box office attraction he'd been in the 1940s. she hired him as the third lead, Darrel Harrison, who convinces the pair that "you guys are made for each other."

Tom Bosley had a minor role as the family doctor.

Yours, Mine, and Ours became United Artists' #1 hit of the year and one of the top-grossing comedies of its era.

Made for $1.2 million, it took in more than $25 million at the box office.

To Lucille's regret, in this era of comparatively high income tax, most of her take-home pay ($2 million dollars) went to the IRS.

Time magazine asserted that the movie "relies for its levity on two unassailable assets, Fonda and Ball. At 62, Fonda can still leave a line wry and dry. At 56, Ball commands a solid slapstick style." The *Philadelphia Inquirer* noted that the two stars "curb their instincts for the extravagance the story suggests."

Variety found the film's overall impact to be wholesome— in the best sense of the word. *[The word wholesome is rarely used these days without derogation.]*

As the new owner of Desilu, Paramount pocketed $2 million of the revenue from the box office bonanza the film generated, thereby retrieving a chunk of the money they had paid to purchase Desilu. "That money could have gone to me," Lucille lamented.

Her accountants had not anticipated that *Yours, Mine, and Ours* would generate such a windfall, so they had not prepared a workable "tax shelter" for her in advance.

***

Madigan (1968)

For the release of the neo-*noir* film *Madigan*, Henry was reunited with director Don Siegel and Inger Stevens, with whom he had recently worked. Richard Widmark in the role of Detective Daniel Madigan took star billing over Henry.

He's married to Julia (Inger Stevens), who is socially and sexually frustrated at her husband's time-consuming job. One reason he doesn't spend a lot of time in bed with her is that he has a girl on the side. Cast as "Jonesy," Sheree North plays a nightclub singer. At the time, Fox was billing North as the

Ironically, the real-life **Henry Fonda** was notorious for not really liking children. Here, in this cutesie family-friendly stance against birth control, he's drowning in them.

No one played a "normal-looking" American of his era better than **Henry Fonda**. Here, in *Madigan*, dressed in the "business uniform" of hundreds of thousands of postwar American men, he's portrays a dedicated police officer intent on enforcing justice.

replacement for Marilyn Monroe.

He had long admired Widmark ever since he'd been nominated for an Oscar for his debut film as the villainous Tommy Udo in *Kiss of Death* (1947).

Widmark would spend most of his later career cast in gun-toting roles as cowboys, police officers, gangsters, and soldiers.

The screenplay was by two writers blacklisted in the 1950s by the McCarthy Witch Hunt during its obsession with ferreting out so-called "commies in the film industry." Their names were Abraham Polonski and Howard Rodman, writing under the shared pseudonym of Henry Simoun. What had intrigued Henry to star in the picture came after he read the 1962 novel, *The Commissioner,* by Richard Dougherty. But in the final draft of the screenplay, Henry was "pissed" at how his role of Police Commissioner Anthony X. Russell had been severely shortened.

Both Henry and Siegel feuded constantly with producer Frank P. Rosenberg, who seemed to want to direct the picture himself. Right from the beginning, during the filming of Henry's first scene, Rosenberg interfered.

In one scene, Commissioner Russell walks into a bedroom where his mistress Tricia Bentley (Susan Clark) is waking up. He says to her, "You can open the other eye now. I made coffee."

Rosenberg demanded the scene be reshot with Henry saying "the coffee" instead of simply "coffee." Siegel refused, but the producer later had Henry record the single word "the," which he then instructed his film editors to splice into the final cut.

At the time she worked with Henry, Clark, a Canadian actress, also shot *Coogan's Bluff* with Clint Eastwood and *Tell Them Willie Boy is Here* with Robert Redford.

Originally, the title of *Madigan* was *Friday, Saturday, and Sunday,* focusing on a police precinct in Harlem. Later, the setting had to be changed to Los Angeles because Harlem was viewed as too dangerous for a "full throttle" film crew. Some of the crew members were mugged and two cars were set on fire, one of them a very expensive model owned by Siegel himself.

In the plot, Madigan and his fellow detective, Rocco Bonaro (Harry Guardino), break into a sleazy apartment in Spanish Harlem and attempt to arrest Barney Benesch (played by Steve Ihnat), but he manages to elude them. For having botched the assignment, the detectives are lectured by Fonda in his role as the police commissioner.

A tangled plot follows until Madigan is fatally shot.

On screen, it is Widmark's character who seduces Sheree North, but off-screen, it was a different matter, as Henry was rumored to have had had a "quickie" with her.

Sheree was known for seducing her leading men such as Dean Martin, Gordon MacCrae, Bob Hope, and (in *The Trouble with Girls,* 1969) Elvis Presley.

Critic David Shipman said, "*Madigan* is a first-class thriller with Richard Widmark, somewhat flawed by the dull sequences involving police chief Fonda, who doesn't help by letting his integrity tipple over into sanctimoniousness."

Marilynesque bombshell of the Space Age: **Sheree North** on the cover of the March 21, 1955 edition of *Life* magazine.

Noted for his portrayals of tough, cynical gunmen and cops, **Richard Widmark** is remembered by the co-author of this book (Darwin Porter) as a short-term "man friend" in the convoluted history of his mother.

Their brief fling did not survive after *Slattery's Hurricane* (1949) with Linda Darnell and Veronica Lake blew out of town.

Andrew Sarris of *The Village Voice* found *Madigan* to be the "best American movie I have seen so far in 1968." But he had reservations. "Henry Fonda's police commissioner walks around as if he had something else on his mind—and he does."

Time magazine claimed "Henry Fonda is at his uptight best as the up-from-the-ranks police commissioner. As a cop, he was so righteous that he even sent back a turkey a local butcher had given him for Thanksgiving."

***

Shortly after the release of *Madigan*, Inger Stevens was found dead on April 30, 1970. She'd been dumped after an affair with Bing Crosby.

At the time, she was dating both Burt Reynolds and Ike Jones, the first black person to graduate from UCLA's School of Theater, Film, and Television.

After her death, Jones claimed that he had married Stevens in 1962. But, fearing for her career, she kept the union a secret.

Both Reynolds and Jones visited her very close to the moment of her death. Her body was found on the floor of the kitchen in her Hollywood Hills home.

Thomas Noguchi, the Los Angeles coroner, later ruled her death a suicide by "acute barbiturate poisoning."

However, rumors still persist to this day that either Reynolds or Jones murdered her. The full story with additional details is revealed in Blood Moon's biography, *Burt Reynolds, Put the Pedal to the Metal*.

In 1970, during affairs she was sustaining with both **Burt Reynolds** and Ike Jones, the suspicious death of **Inger Stevens** was defined (with enormous controversy) as a suicide by the same L.A. coroner who had prevailed at the botched murder investigation of Marilyn Monroe in 1962.

Burt Reynolds was one of the suspects.

Reynolds with Stevens are depicted in both of the photos above. The one on the left derived from their shared scene in the made-for-TV movie, *Run Simon, Run* (1970).

The ins and outs of her murky death was covered in excruciating detail in **Blood Moon's definitive 2019 biography of Burt Reynolds**.

Reynolds was the most financially successful and frequently employed actor of the 1970s.

***

The Boston Strangler (1968)

Jack the Ripper once inspired terror on the dark streets of London.

America, too, had its own Jack the Ripper, a malignant psychopath known as "the Boston Strangler." In the screen adaptation, he was portrayed by Tony Curtis.

In real life, he was Albert DeSalvo, a rapist and serial killer who "focused on" 13 women between 1962 and 1964. DeSalvo was imprisoned for life for committing a series of rapes. However, his murder confession has been disputed, and the debate continues as to which crimes he actually committed.

On November 25, 1973, he was found stabbed to death in a prison infirmary.

A noted author, Gerold Frank, went to Boston and delved deeply into the life and personal history of DeSalvo. He later wrote the best-seller, *The Boston Strangler,* on which the movie was based.

He also wrote several celebrity memoirs, inhad cluding, in 1975, one on Judy Garland. His *I'll Cry Tomorrow* (1954) was the "ghosted" autobiography of Lillian Roth, which became an international bestseller, as seven million copies moved off the shelves.

Film rights to *The Boston Strangler* were purchased by 20th Century Fox for $250,000 (the 2022 equivalent of $1.9 million).

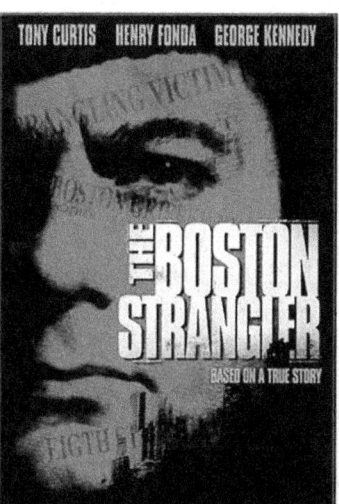

Producers James Cresson and Robert Fryer went into pre-production to turn it into a 1968 biographical film. Originally, Terence Rattigan was hired to write the screenplay, but the producers did not like his final draft. Edward Anhalt was given the difficult task of condensing this fact-and-sequence-loaded bio into 116 minutes of screen time.

A skilled director was needed, and the producers found one in Richard Fleischer, a helmer who in four decades released movies in many genres and styles, often rigorously budgeted ones such as the war epic *Tora! Tora! Tora!*. [It detailed the December 7, 1941 attack by the Japanese Empire on Pearl Harbor.]

The film was already in pre-production when he took the reins of *The Boston Strangler* project.

His choice of a leading man as the Strangler initially displeased the producers, since Tony Curtis was best known for his comedic, flippant style. That was demonstrated when he'd starred with Henry Fonda in *Sex and the Single Girl.*

Two implacable foes: The one played by **Henry Fonda** was notably dogged, dull, and unflashy. **Tony Curtis**, on the right, at least the way he played it, embodied evil.

Fleischer filmed a private screen test with Curtis as the Strangler, and both producers were amazed at the strength of his acting. Eventually, he was assigned the film's title role and male lead.

Fleischer next set out to cast John S. Bottomly, the real-life chief detective who rose to fame in part because of the exhausting hours he spent eliciting a confession from DeSalvo.

This role seemed ideal for Henry, who heads a "Strangler Bureau" to coordinate the probe from within Boston's Police Department.

Fleischer had already seen Henry play a dignified New York police commissioner in *Madigan,* and he thought he'd be perfect.

At first, Henry didn't want to play the dull, professor-like criminologist, but was eventually talked into it.

Before Henry's character gets to grill DeSalvo

Tony Curtis (left) being grilled by **Henry Fonda**.

Is he *The Boston Strangler?* In this film, Curtis played against his usualy flip image. The young actor tried to convince director Richard Fleischer to make the movie far more lurid than it had been perceived during its pre-production.

and break through his protective shell, he has to confront many of the deviants and perverts of Boston.

Fleischer worked smoothly with both Fonda and Curtis, as he would later in his career with Orson Welles, Robert Mitchum, or Charlton Heston.

Right from the start, Henry knew the picture belonged to Curtis, who would later win a Golden Globe for his performance. Fleischer carefully picked the character actors for the support Curtis and Fonda needed.

Cast in the role of Phil DiNatale, actor George Kennedy would in time star in a hundred films or TV drams. Before filming *The Boston Strangler*, he had starred in *Cool Hand Luke* (1967), which had earned him a Best Supporting Actor Oscar.

Murray Hamilton, as Frank McAfeem, was known to Henry since, years previously, he had performed with him on Broadway in *Mister Roberts*, having replaced David Wayne. In 1960, he'd also appeared on stage with Henry in *Critic's Choice* portraying an obnoxious director.

Sally Kellerman was cast as Dianne Cluny, one of the Strangler's victims. In one of the most dramatic scenes in the movie, Curtis attacks her, tying her to her bed with rags ripped from her dress. He tries to subdue her, but she bites him hard and he flees.

Later, Kellerman earned great fame as Major Margaret ("Hot Lips") Houlihan in Robert Altman's film *M*A*S*H* (1970).

Hurt Hatfield, cast as Terence Huntley, was known for playing winsome, narcissistic young men, notably in Oscar Wilde's *The Portrait of Dorian Gray* (1946). Wilde's ageless antihero made Hatfield a star, but he always regretted having taken the role

Over lunch one afternoon with Henry, the actor told him, "*Dorian Gray* was too *avant-garde,* with its hints of homosexuality. I became a leper in Hollywood. Some people would not even speak to me."

Hatfield claimed that one day, he was going to write a tell-all autobiography as an act of revenge. "I'll name names. Some top-ranking male stars seduced me. They ranged from Spencer Tracy to "Tarzan" Lex Barker during our filming together of *Tarzan and the Slave Girl* (1950).

Most critics did not applaud Henry's performance but heaped praise instead on Curtis. The acerbic Rex Reed wrote, "Fonda plays Bottomly more boring than the paper it's written on."

Renata Adler of *The New York*

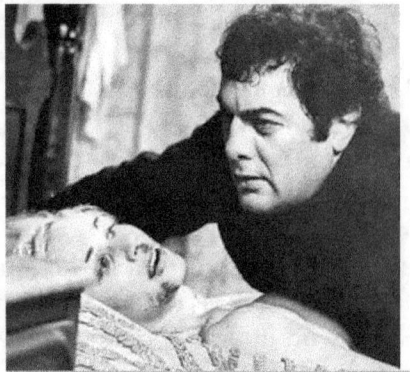

Above left, **Sally Kellerman**, horizontal and in danger of being strangled by a grim-looking **Tony Curtis** as the serial killer who terrorized Boston.

When filming was finished, Kellerman was famously quoted saying, "I was also the romantic lead in *The Boston Strangler*. I was the only one that lived to tell the story, so I called myself the romantic lead."

Above, right: Kellerman went on to portray a competent but lascivious medic in M*A*S*H.

Two views of **Hurt Hatfield,** left with **Donna Reed**, in *The Portrait of Dorian Gray*. right, as the youthful subject of that movie's namesake portrait.

34

Times wrote: "*The Boston Strangler* represents an incredible collapse of taste, judgment, decency, prose, insight, journalism, and movie technique, and yet—through certain prurient options that it does not take—it is not quite the popular exploitation film that one might think. It is as though someone had gone out to do a serious piece of reporting and come up with 4,000 clippings from a sensationalist tabloid. It has no depth, no timing, no facts of any interest, and yet, without any hesitation, it uses the name and pretends to report the story of a living man who was neither convicted nor indicted for the crimes it ascribes to him. Tony Curtis 'stars' as what the movie takes to be the Boston Strangler."

Another critic, Roger Ebert, awarded *The Boston Strangler* three out of four stars, but criticized the movie's content: "*The Boston Strangler* requires a judgment not only on the quality of the film (very good), but also on its moral and ethical implications. The events described in Gerold Frank's book have been altered considerably in the film. This is essentially a work of fiction 'based' on the real events. And based on them in such a way to entertain us, which it does, but for the wrong reasons, I believe. This film, which was made so well, should not have been made at all."

In spite of the bricks thrown at it, *The Boston Strangler* took in about $18 million at the box office. It had been shot on a budget of $4 million.

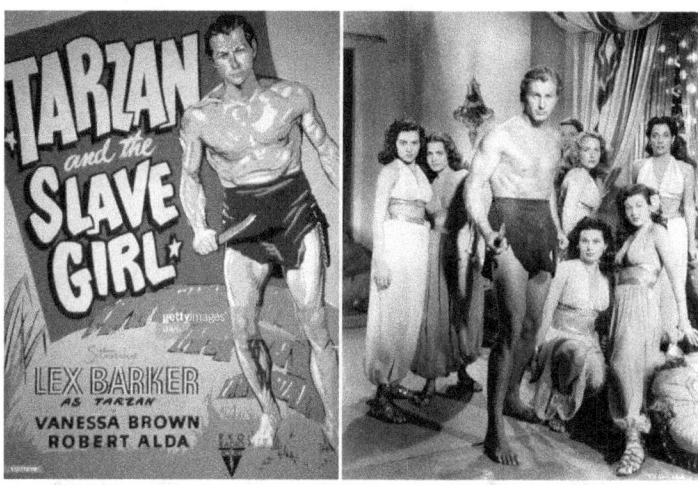

The film you might have seen with a date you were heavy petting with at a drive-in movie theater in the 50s.

Lex Barker, as Tarzan, is campily surrounded by slaves, each supposedly set to follow his instructions.

***

Once Upon a Time in the West (1969)

The greatest film within the genre known as "the Spaghetti Western" (the name derives from the fact that they were shot abroad) was *Once Upon a Time in the West*. In it, Henry was cast as "Frank," the merciless villain.

When he was first offered the role by Sergio Leone, the Italian director, he rejected it. *[It was not the first time he'd rejected and then re-considered his decision. He'd done the same thing in The Good, the Bad, and the Ugly (1966). For that film, Clint Eastwood had stepped up to bat, scoring one of his most memorable hits.]*

This time, Leone did not go away so easily. He flew

As a boy growing up in Italy, film director **Sergio Leone** developed a passion for Western movies. He hit "pay dirt" in his Clint Eastwood "Dollars" trilogy.

In *Once Upon a Time in the West*, he set out to make "the ultimate Western," drawing inspiration from Gary Cooper's *High Noon;* Alan Ladd's *Shane;* and any John Ford Western.

According to Leone, "Only Henry Fonda, not Eastwood, should star in my epic."

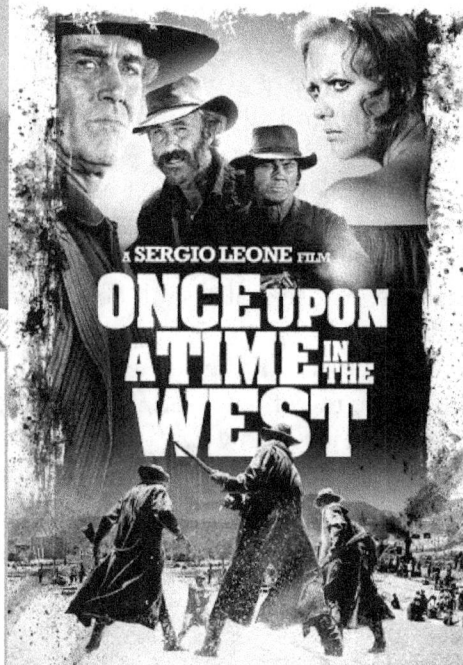

from Rome to Los Angeles, where he finally convinced Henry to accept the role of a bloody killer.

In his latest incarnation, Henry was no longer Tom Joad in *The Grapes of Wrath*. Instead, he played a veteran gunman who evolves into a ruthless murderer.

On his first day of filming, Henry showed up with a mustache and brown contact lenses. Leone immediately objected, ordering him to "lose" both the mustache and those contact lenses: "I want the audience to see your blue eyes, the cold blue eyes of a killer. Just picture it. The camera will shoot you below the belt as you pull your gun from its holster. The camera will them move up your body until the face of a heartless gunman is revealed. The audience will gasp because...it's Henry Fonda!"

Leone was right. An opening scene of Henry (as Frank) shooting homesteaders became one of the most horrifying, most memorable of his career.

The setting is 1870 Arizona, where railroad tracks are being laid and change is in the air. Homesteaders are forced to sell their land at ridiculously low prices. A holdout is Brett McBain, played by Frank Wolff. His land is where a railway station will stand, as it also contains the only water source in the area.

A corrupt official for the railroad company hires Frank to murder the McBain family.

Backed up by his henchmen, Frank arrives at the McBain homestead. McBain's wife, the audience learns, died six years ago, and he has remarried, with the understanding that his bride will arrive soon from New Orleans.

McBain's family includes a late teenaged daughter and her two younger brothers. Frank mows McBain and two of his children down, leaving a small eight-year-old boy who is still inside the house.

When the angelic, red-haired kid emerges from inside, he confronts the body of his slain family and looks hopelessly into the cold, "Arctic blue" eyes of a man he seems to know is about to kill him, too. He realizes that any attempt to escape is hopeless. He does not scream or shout. Instead, his eyes tear up as he awaits his fate. Frank fires a bullet into his head.

Claudia Cardinale took the female lead of Jill McBain, a former prostitute from New Orleans who had married Brett McBain. When she arrives, as planned, she learns of the McBain family's massacre.

Born in French-controlled Tunisia, she was voted "The Most Beautiful Italian Girl in Tunisia," which led to a film contract in Rome, where she would star in many Italian and European movies in the 1960 and 1970s. Her key roles were in Fellini's *8½* (1963) and in *The Pink Panther* (1964) with David Niven.

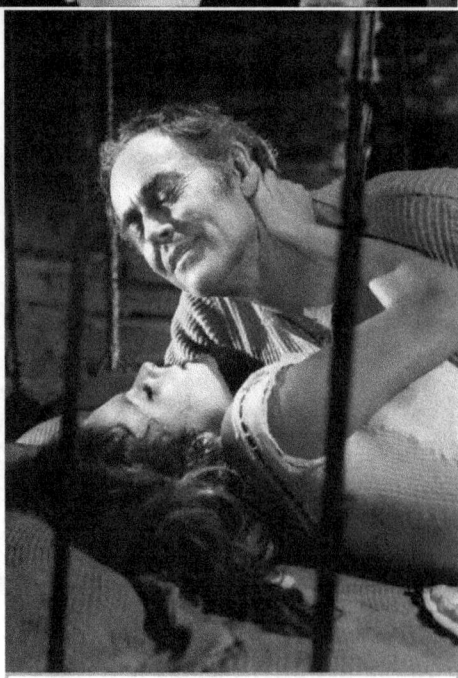

As Jill, she finds herself holding the most valuable property in the territory, in part because of its water source. At one point, she allows Frank to seduce her, seemingly as part of her attempt to save her life. Her sexual assault occurs on a bed suspended by ropes in a cave.

At the end of the scene, Leone lavishly praised Henry: "What an erotic rapist—wicked, cruel, but enticing. You've done this in real life, I just know it..."

Jason Robards Jr., in the role of "Cheyenne," worked with Henry again. They had recently co-starred in *A Big Hand for the Little Lady* (1966).

In the early 1970s, Charles Bronson would go on to become the number one box office attraction in the world. Before working with

> "I had just met Fonda, and our first scene together was a 'twisted love scene' with him," said **Claudia Cardinale**.
>
> "His wife was looking on. I was nervous and tense, and all these people were voyeurs. What could I do? I blotted them out and imagined that I was actually getting screwed by Mr. Fonda for real."
>
> His line to her was, "I'm beginning to think I might fell a little sorry killing you. You like being alive."

Henry, he had scored a big hit in *The Dirty Dozen* (1967).

With his ugly mug, Bronson took the role of "Harmonica," nicknamed for the musical instrument he always carries with him and plays at various intervals throughout the day. He was offered the role after Clint Eastwood rejected it.

Near the opening, Harmonica kills three men Frank sent to murder him. At the end, Frank learns why Harmonica wants revenge. As a young boy, as revealed in a flashback, he witnessed Frank kill his father and older brother.

At the end of the film, Harmonica draws first and fatally shoots Frank, stuffing his harmonica into the mouth of the dying gunslinger as partial payback for the murders of his family.

Once Upon a Time in the West opened in Europe, to great fanfare, in December of 1968. Across Europe, it became the seventh most popular movie of that year. In Paris, it played for two years at the same theater.

Its release in America did not come until May of 1969. By then, it had been "butchered" down to 145 minutes, and it flopped at the box office.

Sam Lesner of the *Chicago Daily News* compared Fonda's character to a cobra, citing it as "a performance of chilling malevolence."

John Russell Taylor in the *Times of London* wrote, "Who would think that Henry Fonda is 64? He is a little more weathered, a little thinner on the top, but as slim as he was in *The Farmer Takes a Wife* 34 years ago. He probably has many surprises in store for us."

Michael Kerbel posted his review: "*Warlock* and *Firecreek* prepared us for Fonda as a killer, and there was something calculating and potentially violent in his earlier characters. But never was he so thoroughly the embodiment of evil as he was in *Once Upon a Time in the West.*"

Leonard Maltin called Henry's performance "one of the weirdest villains in film history."

Over the years, *Once Upon a Time in the West* morphed into a cult film for a cult following. Directors George Lukas and Martin Scorsese each cited it as a great inspiration for them.

***

Our Town (1969)

Except for rare breaks here and there, Henry was kept busy in the 1960s starring in films. However, when a break occurred in 1968, he returned to his first love, the stage. Actress Martha Scott asked him to join the board of a newly formed theater group, the Plumstead Playhouse at Mineola, Long Island.

Her vision involved the establishment of a theater where veteran actors would appear in revivals of plays from the archives of America's most distinguished dramatic literature.

Henry willingly came aboard and almost immediately bonded with film actor Robert Ryan, who signed on, too.

He was not surprised when Scott wanted to launch their season with Thornton Wilder's *Our Town*. Scott's ultimate goal extended far beyond Long Island as she wanted to create an American National Theater. For *Our Town*, Henry was assigned the lead role of the "stage manager."

On Broadway in 1938, Scott had originated the character of *Our Town's* Emily Webb, who tragically dies in childbirth. She was assigned the same role in the play's 1940 film adaptation, for which she was nominated for a Best Actress Oscar.

Scott's greatest exposure came in film. On two different occasions, she was cast as the mother of Charlton Heston in Cecil

B. De Mille's epic, *The Ten Commandments* (1956). She was Heston's mother again in the William Wyler blockbuster, *Ben-Hur* (1959). Not only that, but on Broadway, she played the wife of Heston in *Design for a Stained Glass Window* and then again in *The Tumbler in the Window* presented in London.

Robert Ryan took the role of Mr. Webb. He was mostly known for his work in film, where he often portrayed hardened cops or ruthless villains. He was nominated for a Best Supporting Actor Oscar for his performance in the *film noir* drama *Crossfire* (1947) that focused on anti-Semitism.

As Mrs. Webb, Estelle Parsons won an Oscar for her interpretation of Blanche Barrow in *Bonnie and Clyde* (1967). She was also nominated for her involvement in *Rachel, Rachel* (1968).

Jo Van Fleet, portraying Mrs. Gibbs, had won an Oscar for Best Supporting Actress in *East of Eden* (1955), starring James Dean.

On November 27, 1969, *Our Town* opened on Broadway and ran for 36 performances.

John Simon in *Uneasy Stages* wrote, "Henry Fonda's Stage Manager was as comfortable as an old felt slipper, except in the area of the New England accent, where it pinched a little."

Richard Watts Jr. of the *New York Post* defined Henry as "an actor of rare grace and seemingly effortless skill.

Clive Barnes of *The New York Times* wrote, "I was hoping that *Our Town* stood the test of time. It hasn't. Apart from any literary comparison, it is deplorable that *Peyton Place* seems more relevant than Wilder's cozily romanticized New Hampshire town of Grover's Corners."

As a footnote, Henry agreed, in October of 1968, to play the minor role of a reporter in a revival of *The Front Page*. Written by Ben Hecht and Charles MacArthur, it was first produced on Broadway in 1928, which led to several film versions.

Clive Barnes in *The New York Times* claimed, "There is a kind of pleasure seeing Henry Fonda in the tiny cameo role of a reporter. My respect for him grew to watch as he so unobtrusively, yet still decisively, went about his business."

Henry Fonda in *Our Town* with **Mark Bramhill**, and (lower photo) with **Katherine Winn** and, again, with **Mark Bramhill**.

The widely disliked Broadway producer-director, Jed Harris, who had been "the other man" in Fonda's ill-fated marriage to Margaret Sullavan, hoped to revive his own sagging career. To that end, he lobbied to direct Henry Fonda in *Our Town*.

When Fonda heard about his request, he said, "Only when hell freezes over."

CHAPTER THREE

THE MOVIES CHANGE
(AND TO SOME DEGREE, SO DOES HENRY)

The Cheyenne Social Club
James Stewart Inherits a Seamy Bordello in the Old West. With His Grizzled Cowpoke Buddy (Henry Fonda), He Arrives to Appraise His Investment and to Sample the Merchandise.

Too Late the Hero
Producer/Director Robert Aldrick had previously hit the jackpot with *The Dirty Dozen* (1967). Now, three years later, this time with Henry Fonda, Cliff Robertson, and Michael Caine, he returns to World War II, this time battling not in Europe, but in the Pacific Theater.

There Was a Crooked Man
Joseph Mankiewicz casts Kirk Douglas and Henry Fonda in a picture that evokes both a Western and a Prison Drama. It's the character played by Henry, however, who rides off with gold that was hidden, years previously, in a rattlesnake nest

Sometimes a Great Notion
At last Henry is cast as a Geriatric, the crotchety head of a lumberjack clan. Paul Newman, who's been designated as the film's director, also stars as his son.

The Smith Family
ABC-TV hires Henry to Play an Embittered Veteran of the LAPD who—up close and personal— confronts "The Generation Gap" as Portrayed by his Onscreen Son, Ron Howard

Night Flight From Moscow
Henry Fonda and Yul Brynner Cash In on the James Bond Craze.

Ash Wednesday
Elizabeth Taylor Plays Henry's Neurotically Adulterous Wife
Facing "the Beauty Butchers"

My Name Is Nobody
In this Spaghetti Western, Henry sings his Swan Song to the Genre,
Having Already Appeared in 15 Westerns Since *Jesse James*.
He Faces Off Against a Wild Bunch of "Bad Guys,"
Dynamiting Them as He Closes the Final Curtain on the Old West.

Clarence Darrow
Henry Essays his Favorite Stage Role as the Fabled Attorney,
"The Champion of Dissenters and Underdogs"

As the turbulent 1960s came to an end, both James Stewart and Henry Fonda became aware that the public's taste in movies was undergoing a major change. Neither was sure where movies were going, wondering if they'd be offered a role—or roles—to play. Although each had reigned as a movie prince during the Golden Age, they feared that in the 1970s, many the big roles would go to Burt Reynolds.

In the years to come, Henry would face mounting criticism from reviewers who charged him with lending his prestigious presence to threadbare scripts not worthy of his talents. But he kept working and bringing in the money. "Even if a picture flops," he told Shirlee, "I'll still get paid."

Although he worked mostly in films at this advanced stage of his life (he had turned 65 in 1970), he also ventured into television drama, with an occasional appearance on the stage.

He launched the decade by starring in three films, including one with James Stewart in The Cheyenne Social Club, an innocuous name" for a seamy bordello in the Old West.

Henry followed that with There Was a Crooked Man, a prison drama in which he played second fiddle to Kirk Douglas.

A bit later, he also made Too Late the Hero with Cliff Robertson and Michael Caine.

He starred in an ABC television series, The Smith Family (1971-1972), and even played a part in a TV movie, John Steinbeck's The Red Pony (1973).

In a somewhat old-fashioned Hollywood melodrama, he played the alienated husband of Elizabeth Taylor, who was coping with plastic surgery as a means of holding on to her fading beauty.

In the mid-1970s, Henry starred in a "Spaghetti Western," My Name is Nobody. Terence Hill played "Nobody."

Henry attempted to cash in on the James Bond genre in Night Flight from Moscow.

In 1974, he returned to Broadway in the biographical drama based on the famous attorney, Clarence Darrow, for which he was nominated for a Tony.

Ironically, despite Henry's membership in the **Academy of Motion Picture Arts and Sciences (AMPAS)**, the organization that assesses and awards the Oscars, Henry opted never to vote in any of the Oscar nominations or awards, telling reporters, "I do not believe in Oscars. How can you compare the films of Laurence Olivier with those of Woody Allen?"

Around the same time that Henry's career was slowing down in ironic contrast, his children, Jane and Peter, were reveling in their greatest successes. In 1974, Jane won an Oscar for her performance as a prostitute in Klute.

A few years before that, Peter Fonda had enjoyed the biggest hit of his film career when Easy Rider was released during the closing months of 1969. It was still raking in profits in 1970.

One critic called it "The little movie that killed the big picture."

Peter was the producer, the leading man, and one of the trio of screenwriters. The film grossed more than $60 million, and 22% of that went into Peter's pockets.

"I'm in awe of my boy," Henry told the press.

***

The Cheyenne Social Club (1970)

One night in Henry's backyard, he and his longtime buddy, James Stewart, spent a moonlit night just sitting, talking, drinking, and speculating. Both of them, at their age, wondered if any director would cast either of them in an A-list feature film. The next day, their speculation ended.

An unlikely producer-director, Gene Kelly *[yes, that one, the singing and dancing co-star with Debbie Reynolds of* Singin' in the Rain *(1952)]* phoned and offered them co-starring roles in a comedy-western, *The Cheyenne Social Club*. It was scheduled for a 1970 release by a studio called National General Film.

Cheyenne would mark their third time in a film together. In this new and "modern" Western, they were cast as two grizzled, horny old cowpokes—Stewart as John O'Hara and Henry as the talkative Harley Sullivan.

At the opening of the film, John learns that his brother had died and left him "a social club" in the town of Cheyenne, Wyoming.

They journey on horseback from Texas, arriving in Cheyenne to learn that the social club is actually the local whorehouse. Conveniently located near the train station, it's run by "Jenny," (Shirley Jones), who employs a staff of six pretty girls, all of them in frilly dresses. They are particularly busy on Saturday nights.

John finds the idea of running a bordello distasteful and ponders converting it, perhaps into a saloon. Harley, however, who is now a partner, stays busy "sampling the wares," visiting one working girl after another in the upstairs bedrooms.

Following a barroom brawl, John is arrested and thrown into jail. When he gets out, he learns that Jenny has been ravished by an outlaw named Corey Bannister (Robert J. Wilke). He goes after him and guns him down. To seek revenge, Barrister's kin descend on the whorehouse for a shootout.

Although John and Harley survive, John doesn't want any more warfare. He turns the bordello over to Jenny before, with Harlan, he heads off into the sunset on the long trail back to Texas.

Most of the scenes were shot in New Mexico. During filming, Henry comforted Stewart—who had fallen into a deep depression based on the death of his stepson, Ronald, in Vietnam— as much as he could.

Shirley Jones—the previous co-star of wholesome musicals that included *Oklahoma* (1953) and *Carousel* (1956), both with Gordon MacRae, might have been an unusual choice as a whorehouse madam. Kelly, however, had seen her portray a vengeful prostitute in *Elmer Gantry* (1960) opposite Burt Lancaster. For that she had won an Oscar as Best Supporting Actress.

Variety wrote, "Stewart seems genuinely nervous in his role, while Fonda projects a genuine delight in his."

Critic Rex Reed expressed a different view: "Picture, if you have the heart, Jimmy Stewart and Henry Fonda lying in bed with their *toupées* slipping down on their foreheads. Stewart can't go to sleep because Fonda is keeping him awake cracking walnuts with his bare hands. It's a sad embarrassment when old pros like these two have to sink to this kind of corny old-fashioned material."

Jenny (played by **Shirley Jones**) welcomes **James Stewart** *(center)* and **Henry Fonda** to the local whorehouse.

Stewart plays John O'Hanlan, whose brother has died and left him a bordello. The madam just assumes these two grizzled old cowboys will want to sample her staff—a half-dozen pretty gals.

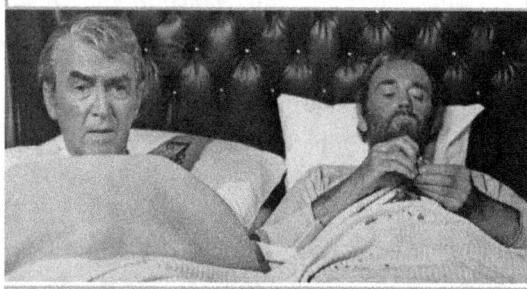

In bed together, **James Stewart** (left) and **Henry Fonda** duplicate a scene from their real-life early days when, as struggling actors, they shared a small apartment in Manhattan. Each night, they retired to a three-quarter bed, hoping to find an acting job the next day.

These roommates became lifelong friends. There were, of course, the inevitable rumors of homosexuality.

***

Too Late the Hero (1970)

At the end of 1970, Henry released *Too Late the Hero*. Robert Aldrich, its producer, director and screenwriter, had scored a big hit with *The Dirty Dozen* (1967), set in the European theater of World War II.

In contrast, this time he was to shoot a movie in the Pacific theater of that same war. The action would take place in what was known at the time as the New Hebrides Islands. *[Today, they're collectively known as the Republic of Vanuatu, an island nation in the South Pacific Ocean, northeast of New Caledonia, west of Fiji, and east of Australia. As a historic fact, these islands were never occupied by the Japanese. The Americans took them over in May of 1942.]*

In the plot, Sam Lawson (Cliff Robertson), a Japanese-to-English interpreter, has so far avoided combat. That is about to change when his commanding officer, John G. Nolan (Fonda) sends him to join a British infantry unit on a suicide mission to destroy a Japanese communications outpost.

Aldrich had originally intended to cast Laurence Olivier and Trevor Howard in those roles, but neither of them was available. Aldrich instructed ABC Films "to send me any actor, but not Cliff Robertson."

In almost defiant opposition to his preferences, almost as a means of deliberately defying him, they sent Robertson anyway. In the end, it was Robertson who portrayed Sam Lawson.

[Later, Henry wondered about Aldrich's problem with Robertson. Two years earlier, Robertson had won the Best Actor Oscar for his performance in the title role of Charley (1968), about an intellectually disabled adult who is selected by two doctors to undergo a surgical procedure that triples his IQ.]

The actual star of *Too Late the Hero* was Michael Caine, who had used his Cockney accent to full advantage in his depiction of Private Tosh Heame, the squad's cynical medic. He told Henry, "I keep my Cockney accent as a means of letting other working-class blokes know that if I made it, they can do it, too."

Fonda was less diplomatic and congenial: "If someone spent an extra minute or two in the latrine, shaking off the last drops, he would have missed my performance."

As a novelty, his sequence appeared before the opening credits. "If someone missed that in the first few minutes, they would never know when my name was connected to the movie. I was paid $50,000 for two days of work."

When ABC Films got around to tallying its profits, *Too Late the Hero* emerged as its all-time financial disaster, losing $6,750,000.

In *Too Late the Hero*, **Henry Fonda** plays Naval Captain Noland, a mere cameo that comes before the credit titles of this war drama.

Prominently featuring Michael Caine, the movie consists mostly of British players except for Cliff Robertson.

***

There Was a Crooked Man (1970)

Kirk Douglas had been in contact with director Joseph L. Mankiewicz since the late 1940s when he had helmed him in *A Letter to Three Wives*.

Since then, Mankiewicz had famously directed such classics as *All About Eve* (1950), and had been the guiding force behind the success of some of Kirk's favorite movies, including *The Barefoot Contessa* (1954), starring Humphrey Bogart and Ava Gardner; and *Suddenly, Last Summer* (1959) with Montgomery Clift, Eliza-

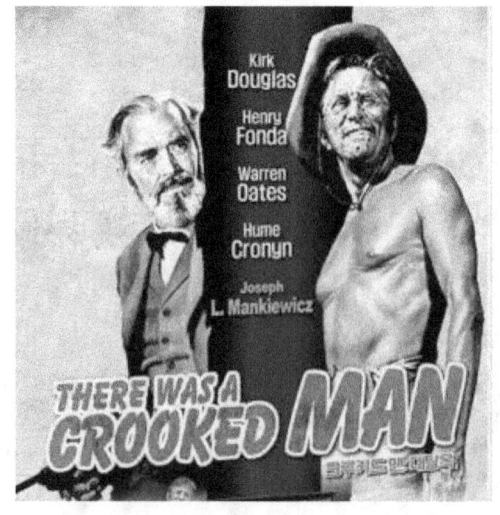

beth Taylor, and Katharine Hepburn.

At first, Kirk thought Mankiewicz was calling to cast him in a first-rate melodrama, perhaps within a Hollywood setting. "But after five minutes, I believed I had John Ford on the wire. Joe wanted me to star with Henry Fonda in a very gritty, very cynical Western set in the dying days of the Old West in the 1880s. Its title was *There Was a Crooked Man*."

"When I read the script two days later, I accepted," Kirk continued. "It was the first film script written by David Newman and Robert Benton since their success with *Bonnie and Clyde* (1967)."

In preparation for filming, Kirk repeatedly read and re-read the lines of the character he'd portray: Paris Pitman Jr., a ruthless villain and bandit who wears steel-rimmed glasses and is a bundle of explosive energy, plotting and scheming.

Although the script never called for it, he dyed his hair red. As a post-Civil War scoundrel, he lines up a small group of masked marauders.

He played this roguish criminal with a deadly charm, and did so with a certain relish, as if actually enjoying being such a nefarious character, spinning an intricate cobweb of confidence trickery—and not afraid to murder his own men.

In his memoirs, Henry Fonda never mentioned Kirk or *Crooked Man*. Fonda had agreed to accept second billing for his portrayal of a former sheriff, Woodward W. Lopeman, who becomes the warden of a notorious hell hole prison isolated in the desert.

[Fonda had already appeared in the brief role of a World War II Admiral in Kirk's In Harm's Way.]

Kirk revealed in a memoir that back in the late 1940s, he had first resented Fonda when he'd escorted, as his date, a beautiful young starlet to his first Hollywood party. She later disappeared, without telling him, but not before he spotted her exiting through a rear entrance with Fonda and his best friend, James Stewart.

Of all the crooked men in all the crooked west one man was the crookedest.

But who might the scriptwriter have been referring to when he wrote the tagline displayed above?

Could it have been **(GASP!)** the character portrayed by **Henry Fonda**?

"It was obvious that the bitch was a star-fucker and had tossed me aside for these two big stars. Perhaps they were fading into the night for a three-way. Fonda and Stewart had lived together as aspiring actors in a small room in Manhattan, and Hollywood gossips have buzzed about what went on between them back in those Depression days."

"I should have long ago recovered from that insult and let it die," Kirk continued. "But I was still mad as hell, even though today I'm the big star stealing beautiful trophies from lesser mortals."

There Was a Crooked Man was shot in the high desert plateau of the Joshua Tree National Monument, some 45 miles northwest of Indio, California. To construct the remote and isolated 1880s-era "hell hole" of a prison, one of the leading art directors in Hollywood, Edward Carrere, was hired. *[He had already won an Oscar for his set decoration of* The Wild Bunch *(1969).]*

For *Crooked Man*, he was given his biggest assignment to date. It involved creating a desert prison with thick walls, and more than a dozen buildings. They would include a barracks, a mess hall, seven lookout towers, a mule shed, a blacksmith shop, and a gallows. He even had to bring in large rocks for the prisoners to split. One of those prisoners was a shirtless Kirk.

Kirk, as Pitman, leads his gang in pulling off a $500,000 robbery of a rich rancher, Mr. Lomax (Arthur O'Connell).

In fleeing from the scene of the crime, Kirk's men are shot, except for one, who Pitman shoots so that he can escape with all the loot. He placed the swag, wrapped in a pair of women's bloomers, in a rattlesnake pit in the desert and then heads into town to patronize the local brothel.

Kirk and two nude women are shown in a bordello bedroom, enjoying a night of lust.

There, he is spotted by the rancher he'd robbed, who turns him in to the sheriff.

O'Connell was very effective in the role of the rancher. He had already been nominated twice for a

Best Supporting Actor Oscar—first, for *Picnic* (1955) starring William Holden, and second, for *Anatomy of a Murder* (1959) with James Stewart.

Arrested and tried, Kirk is sent to the most notorious and isolated prison in the entire Southwest. There, he joins a coven of depraved convicts.

Kirk charms his way into a relationship with the warden, Francis LeGoff (Martin Gabel), who wants to make a deal with him. He will allow him to escape if he'll split the loot with him.

Kirk had never worked with Gabel before, although he was a familiar figure to him on television, appearing as a frequent guest panelist on the hit TV series, *What's My Line?* His glamourous, blonde-haired wife, Anne Francis, was also a regular panelist on the show.

Two smelly old cowpokes, **Kirk Douglas** (left) and **Henry Fonda** take much-needed baths in (separate) rain barrels.

Everybody's a crook in this film, which is both a Western and a prison drama. Even Fonda, the warden, turns crooked in the end.

The warden's plan goes awry when he's killed in a prison uprising. Replacing him is Woodward W. Lopeman (Fonda), who seems to be decent and uncorruptible. Kirk, as Pitman, ingratiates himself with the new warden, ostensibly to improve prison conditions while plotting his escape from a ten-year sentence.

The Fonda and Kirk characters become so friendly that in one scene they're depicted bathing in the nude in two large wooden barrels.

Kirk and the warden cooperate to inaugurate a new dining hall, to which the governor of the state is invited, along with many distinguished guests, some of whom are women. The prisoners, who haven't seen a woman in months, virtually slobber over Lee Grant, cast as Mrs. Billard.

Kirk had not seen Grant since she co-starred with him in *Detective Story* (1951), almost twenty years before. She told him about what had happened in the interim: She had been blacklisted by the House Un-American Activities Committee, and her career had suffered, accordingly.

Pitman (Kirk) certainly lives up to his reputation as a crooked man, as he manipulates everyone around him with his personal charisma.

Burgess Meredith has the most colorful role in the movie, playing "The Missouri Kid," a grimy old pot-smoking codger who takes a bath once a year and wears the dirtiest long johns in the history of Arizona.

Kirk Douglas in *There Was a Crooked Man.* He portrayed Paris Pittman, who steals half a million dollars and hides it in a rattlesnake hole.

"Burgess looked totally repulsive," Kirk said. "A great character role, I could hardly believe that he was once married to the screen goddess, Paulette Goddard after Charlie Chaplin dumped her." Burgess had recently worked with Kirk, Fonda, and John Wayne on the set of *In Harm's Way* (1965).

Mankiewicz had selected a talented array of supporting players, including Hume Cronyn, who had co-starred with Kirk in *The Arrangement* (1969). He was cast as a homosexual con man and religious fake, Dudly Whinner, always sticking close to his lover, Cyrus McNutt (John Randolph).

Alan Hale Jr. played "Tobaccy," a prison guard. He had last worked with Kirk on location in Oregon shooting *The Indian Fighter* (1955).

Kirk also found himself speaking again with Gene Evans, cast as Colonel Wolff. They had worked on location together in *The War Wagon* (1967).

Warren Oates played an oafish gunman, Floyd Moon, who shoots the sheriff in the leg. Kentucky born, he had appeared in several films directed by Sam Peckinpah, including *The Wild Bunch* (1969).

Making his film debut was Yang Chuan-kwang *[also known as C.K. Yang]*, an Olympic decathlete from Taiwan, known as "The Iron Man of Asia." As a murderous Chinaman, he was one tough inmate who did not speak.

Michael Blodgett, as Coy Cavendish, had a tragic role. His character learns of his fate, a walk to the gallows, where he is to be hanged for accidentally shooting his girlfriend's father, who stumbled upon them making love.

When Blodgett got back to Hollywood, with some excitement, he told gossip columnist Marilyn Beck about the nudity being filmed in Kirk's latest movie. "Kirk stripped buck-assed naked. He sure isn't ashamed to pull off every stitch. I don't know what the censors will allow on the screen."

What might have become the most controversial scene in *Crooked Man* ended up on the cutting room floor, even though Hugh Hefner of *Playboy* wanted stills from it.

Love-starved prisoners attack starlet Barbara Rhoades and strip off her clothing. She is seen fleeing with "jiggling jugs," a decorative hat, and one full-length glove.

Here is busty **Barbara Rhoades** in *There Was a Crooked Man*.

Her biggest scene involved being stripped by prisoners and sexually assaulted shortly after her arrival in their midst, and her subsequent escape.

Blue-nosed censors demanded that the scene be removed.

In the same year, Blodgett went on to greater but dubious fame when he played the gigolo, Lance Rocke, in Rus Meyer's cult classic, *Beyond the Valley of the Dolls* (1970).

The roles that Blodgett was offered got so bad that he finally abandoned acting altogether and became a novelist and screenwriter, turning out scripts for Tom Hanks and Burt Reynolds.

Near the end of *Crooked Man*, Kirk engineers his escape from prison and returns to Rattlesnake Mountain to retrieve the swag he wrapped in that pair of women's bloomers and buried. He shoots all the rattlers and jubilantly lifts up the money. However, one snake has hidden within it. It lunges toward his neck with fangs exposed, and bites. Pitman dies shortly thereafter, an ironic twist to a plot riddled with ironies, deception, striving, and pain.

His body is found by Fonda, who has trailed him. He hauls it back to the gates of the prison, where he dumps it and rides off into the sunset.

Then the till-now morally upright warden portrayed by Fonda turns crooked, riding off with the $500,000 to destinations south, beyond the Mexican border, no doubt spending the rest of his days in grand luxury. *[One estimate evaluates the equivalent of $500,000 in the dollars of that era to $25 million in today's currency.]*

There Was a Crooked Man opened on Christmas Day of 1970. "What a stupid time," Kirk said. "No

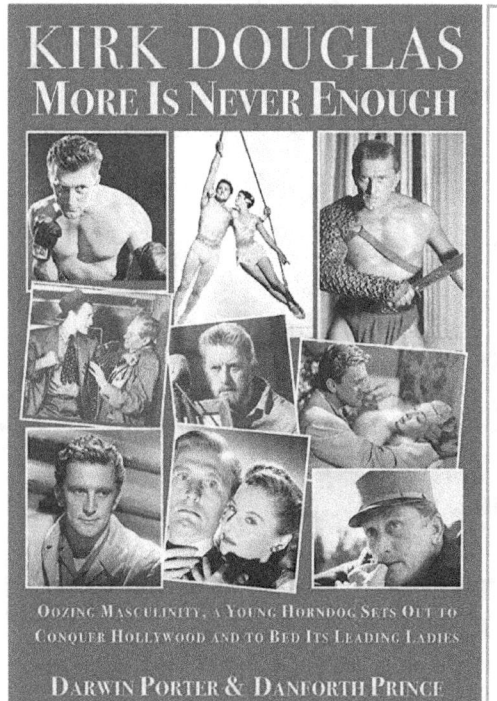

In 2019, the authors of this two-volume biography of the Fondas produced this, history's most complete overview of **Kirk Douglas**. Of the many male stars of Golden Age Hol-lywood, Kirk Douglas became the final survivor, the last icon of a fabled, optimistic era that the world will never see again.

Douglas was the son of Russian-Jewish immigrants, his father a collector and seller of rags. After service in the Navy during World War II, he moved to Hollywood, oozing masculinity and charm. Conquering Tinseltown and bedding its leading ladies, he became the personification of the American dream, moving from obscurity and (literally) rags to riches and major-league fame.

En route to his status as a myth and legend, his performances reflected both his personal pain and the brutalization of the characters he played, too. In *Champion* (1949), he was beaten to a fatal bloody pulp. As the sleazy, heartless reporter in *Ace in the Hole* (1951), he was stabbed with a knife in his gut. As Van Gogh in *Lust for Life* (1956), he writhed in emotional agony and unrequited love before slicing off his ear with a razor. His World War I movie, *Paths of Glory* (1957), grows more profound over the years. He lost an eye in *The Vikings* (1958), and, as the Thracian slave leading a revolt against Roman legions in *Spartacus* (1960), he was crucified.

All of this is brought out, with photos and stories you've probably never heard before, in this remarkable testimonial to the last hero of Hollywood's swashbuckling Golden Age, an inspiring testimonial to the values and core beliefs of an America that's Gone With the Wind, yet lovingly remembered as a time when it, in many ways, was truly great.
Kirk Douglas, More is Never Enough ISBN 978-1-936003-61-7.

wonder it did poorly at the box office and in the weeks to come. On Christmas, most Americans wanted to watch Jimmy Stewart, the 'plucker' of my girlfriend at that party back in the '40s, perform onscreen in *It's a Wonderful Life* (1946)."

Vincent Canby, of *The New York Times*, wrote, "*Crooked Man* is rather low-eyed and takes its own sweet time to reveal itself. It is a movie of the sort of tastes, intelligence, and somewhat bitter humor associated with Mankiewicz, who, in real life, is one of America's most sophisticated, least folksy raconteurs."

***

Fathers Against Sons Against Fathers (1970)

After he finished shooting some final TV commercials for the year, Henry signed to appear in a one-man play awkwardly entitled *Fathers Against Sons Against Fathers*.

The writer and director of the show, Sid Steibel, created a script based on the writings of Socrates, Shakespeare (especially *Hamlet* and *Macbeth*), Thoreau, Eugene O'Neill, and even Bob Dylan. Its premiere in April of 1970, focused entirely on the play's only character (Fonda) was at the Joslyn Art Museum in Omaha, Henry's hometown. It was clearly understood that after that, he'd go with it on a tour of regional theaters, often playing to college students.

For a change of pace, in November of 1971, Henry directed a revised stage version of *The Caine Mutiny Court-Martial* at the Ahmanson Theater in Los Angeles. It ran for 42 performances and starred John Forsythe as Lt. Barney Greenwald, the role Henry had originated on Broadway in 1954.

***

Sometimes a Great Notion (1971)

In the living room of the Fonda home, Henry, seated across from his wife Shirlee, had just finished reading the script of the latest film he'd been offered. It was *Sometimes a Great Notion*, based on the 1964 novel of the same name by Ken Kesey.

Paul Newman was to be both the director and star of this Universal motion picture.

"As you know, I've been playing characters meant for a younger actor on the screen," Fonda said to Shirlee. "At last, here's a role that matches my age. Get this: Paul Newman wants me to play his dad in his latest movie. I'm gonna do it, too."

Newman had wanted to star in Kesey's *One Flew Over the Cuckoo's Nest* (1962) but lost the role to Jack Nicholson.

After reading the script, Henry bought a copy of Kesey's novel and began to read it for a better understanding of the story. A counterculture icon, Kesey viewed himself as "the missing link" between the Beatniks of the 1950s and the hippies of the 1960s. When Fonda met him, he claimed, "I was too young to be a Beatnik and too old to be a hippie."

In the river scene above, **Paul Newman** rescues drowning victim **Richard Jaeckel**.

It took three hours of Newman giving the young actor mouth-to-mouth rescuscitation. George Kennedy originally had the role, but Newman ordered him fired:

"There's no way I'm going mouth to mouth for three hours *[the time allocated to shoot the scene]* with George," Newman said. "Richard is a cute guy, and I can do it with him."

The star of the picture is **Paul Newman** (right).

For the first time, **Henry Fonda** plays an old man, who is crude and earthy, declaring that "Life is about eating, drinking, and screwing."

A story about lumberjacks, *Sometimes a Great Notion* takes place in the fictional town of Wakonda, Oregon, whose economy is threatened when many of the town's lumberjacks go on strike against a large industrial conglomerate. Independent loggers, the Stamper family, hold out and continue working.

The angry strikers set about to sabotage the Stamper enterprise.

Although the patriarch of the family is Henry Stamper (played by Fonda), most of the plot centers on his son, Hank (Newman). He is unhappily married to Vic (Lee Remick).

To complicated matters, Leeland, Henry's mentally disturbed youngest son (Hank's half-brother), arrives on the scene. A heavy drinker, he admits to having attempted suicide after his mother did the same.

Complicating the plot is the unexpected arrival of Hank's cousin, Joe Ben Stamper.

Richard Jaeckel in *Sometimes a Great Notion*. For his role in the film, the young actor received an Academy Award nomination for Best Supporting Actor.

"I got Paul Newman to give me the longest kiss in film history, lasting three hours—and got paid for that. However, our screen kiss was cut down to a minute or two."

Michael Sarrazine with **Lee Remick**.

The actor played Henry's youngest son, who has rejected his family's long-sustained beliefs that male descendents should all become loggers.

Henry's wife, played by Remick, is the only person who understands the errant teenager.

Tragedy hits: A falling tree collapses unpredictably; Joe Ben is trapped in the river and almost drowns; and a huge log falls on Henry, who later dies in a hospital.

Newman, along with Fonda, and the rest of the crew headed north for location shooting near the towns of Lincoln City and Newport, Oregon, each opening onto views of the forested watersheds of the Siletz and Yaquina Rivers.

Newman had cast Lee Remick as his wife, despite his admission that there had been no chemistry between them when they co-starred in *The Long, Hot Summer* (1958).

She later recalled, "Newman, like Steve McQueen, was known for seducing his leading ladies. I can assure you that this is one leading lady who he will never sleep with. He turns me off."

Her big scene in *Sometimes a Great Notion* ended up on the cutting room floor. She and actor Michael Sarrazin, cast as the suicidal and alcoholic Leeland Stamper, were in bed together making love.

Another intimate scene, this one featuring George Kennedy and Paul Newman, was supposed to be filmed, but Newman replaced Kennedy with another actor before its filming began.

"There was no way I was going to get that intimate with Kennedy," Newman said. "I had no problem, however, going mouth-to-mouth with his replacement, Richard Jaeckel."

Fonda recalled that the script called for mouth-to-mouth rescuscitation delivered to a man who was drowning. "Newman and Jaeckel kissed each other on and off for three hours, the length of the shoot. They seemed to be enjoying it. Maybe they finished the scene in their motel room later that night."

For all that kissing, (and also for the genuinely emotive acting he delivered), Jaeckel won an Academy Award nomination for Best Supporting Actor.

Newman was bitterly disappointed, as he'd told Fonda that he expected to win for both Best Actor and Best Director.

"Best Director, my foot," Fonda said after hearing that. "Who does he think he is? Erich von Stroheim?"

Henry thought so little of *Sometimes a Great Notion* that he didn't even mention it in his memoirs.

"Paul Newman and my daughter, Jane, should make a movie together," Fonda said. "The director should strip them and film them in bed together. Those two on the screen would guarantee a big box office."

Sometimes a Great Notion did not evolve into a box office hit.

Vincent Canby, in *The New York Times*, wrote, "The film is an extremely interesting, if impure, example of a genre of action movies that flourished in the 1930s about tuna fishermen, bush pilots, and high-wire repairmen, and just about any physical pursuit you can think of."

Critic Michale Kerbel claimed, "Grizzled, foul-mouthed, and looking his age for a change, Fonda is extremely colorful."

***

The Trial of A. Lincoln (1971)

The playbill displayed above is from **The Trial of A. Lincoln** starring **Henry Fonda**. His two co-stars included Billy Dee Williams and Lee Philips. The play held its premiere at the Huntington Hartford Theatre in Los Angeles.

It was named for the A&P heir, a major-league patron of the Arts.

When Hartford bought the theater from CBS in 1953, he morphed it into a modern showcase for dramas and musicals, seating 970 people.

Hartford ran the theater for a decade, often showcasing big name stars. He opened it with *What Every Woman Knows*, starring Helen Hayes.

"These days, actors on stage or screen have to show their ass," Henry Fonda lamented to his agents. "I'll have none of that. I would be so nervous appearing nude in front of an audience, my dick would shrink to two inches."

That anxiety wasn't pertinent when he was presented with the script of a new play, *The Trial of A. Lincoln* by James Domico.

Henry had also told his agent that he did not want to be cast in any of those radical plays being presented at the time from coast to coast. But he changed his mind after reading the Domico play.

Early in his career, Henry had famously played the young, lanky, "Jackleg" future President in the film *Young Mr. Linoln* (1939).

This time, he would play Lincoln as a ghost-like spirit come back to earth to sue a group of attackers who had accused him of being a racist. The "spirit of Lincoln" filed a libel charge.

The courtroom drama is set in the basement of a municipal police station. Characters in the play include a mayor, members of a jury, a municipal judge, and lawyers.

In a secondary role, Billy Dee Williams played a black man of "low intelligence, speaking argot."

He had been accused of having disrespected Lincoln and inciting strife between blacks and whites within the police department. As the trial proceeds, rancor rises and the audience witnesses a kind of Civil War in microcosm.

As it turns out, the ghost trial is merely a "setup" staged by the police themselves, who hope to defuse racial tensions among the cops.

To make himself taller, Henry stood on four-inch lifts.

Its April 1971 premiere was presented in Tucson, Arizona. Because the play was so racially explosive, many members of the audience walked out in disdain, behavior that was repeated two nights later by an audience in Phoenix. "If this play reaches Detroit, there will be race riots," Henry lamented.

From Phoenix, the play moved to Los Angeles, where it drew mixed reviews. Finally, it arrived in Detroit. There were no race riots, as Henry had predicted.

But something happened to him. For reasons he never made clear, he dropped out of the play in Detroit and announced that would not reprise his performance on Broadway. No suitable replacement could be found, and *A. Lincoln* drew its final curtain and died.

***

The Smith Family (1971)

In the spring of a new decade (the 1970s), his last full decade on earth, Henry temporarily deserted feature films for a series of stage appearances and made-for-television movies.

Motivated mainly by its paychecks, he signed to appear in a TV series, *The Smith Family,* inaugurated by Don Fedderson Productions. Thirty-nine episodes would be aired on ABC in the 18-months between January of 1971 and June of 1972.

Its executive producer, Fedderson, might have been better suited for the 1950s. At least part of his reputation derived from signing faded older stars into harmless family dramas. *[One of his biggest hits had involved casting Fred MacMurray in* My Three Sons *(1960-1972), a sitcom that survived the age of Sputnik and beyond.]*

Henry was cast as Chad Smith, an LAPD police detective based in Los Angeles. As promised by Fedderson, the weekly stories "will touch on today's gap between generations and the problems of today's youth attempting to remodel the world."

The series focused on the sergeant's crime-fighting exploits and his relationships with his wife, Betty, and their three children, 18-year-old Cindy; 15-year-old Bob; and 7-year-old Brian.

The scripts were bad and Henry, who never really threw his heart into the lackluster saga, was dull.

One critic wrote that whenever Henry had to smile, "It appeared that he had indigestion, perhaps too much squid soup." Episodes had titles ranging from "The Greener Pastures" to "No Place to Hide."

Adding some luster to the series was Janet Blair, cast as Betty, Chad's wife. She had been a big band singer before evolving into a popular TV and film star. Her most memorable roles had been in *My Sister Eileen* (1942) with Rosalind Russell, and in *Tonight and Every Night* (1945) with Rita Hayworth.

Ron Howard was cast as Bob, Chad's older son. Within a few years of his birth in Okla-

The Smiths showcased America's not-always Silent Majority: .

The venue was within the California home of Potice Sergeant Chad Smith.

The cast, left to right, included son Bob (**Ron Howard**)' college-aged daughter Cindy (**Darleen Carr**); wife Betty (**Janet Blair**), Chad (**Henry Fonda**) and their 9-year-old son, Brian (**Michael-James Wood**).

Dad doesn't get the lingo of the younger generation, but then he shows genuine concern in his life-threatening work as a police detective. Call it a "dramedy"

Ads that focused on **Henry Fonda**'s endorsement of a then-newfangled slide-viewing device happened during the peak years of Madison Avenue's postwar advertising craze that later inspired the AMC series *Mad Men*.

On the left is one of Henry Fonda (embarrassing) endorsements of the fruits of American capitalism. This one met with profit-generating success.

homa in 1954, he evolved into a child star on TV, portraying Opie, the son of Sheriff Andy Taylor (Andy Griffith) on the TV sitcom, *The Andy Griffith Show,* from 1960 to 1968. He would go on to amazing success not only as an actor, but as a filmmaker. He was still going strong by the turn of the century, winning a Best Director Oscar for *A Beautiful Mind* (2001).

Around the same time, as part of an advertising gig, Henry signed to be the "pitchman" for the General Aniline and Film Corporation (GAF). To millions of viewers out there in TV land, he would be hyping View Master slide machines and vinyl flooring.

His contract called for him to appear in eleven commercials annually for a combined fee of $250,000.

Sales rose with his endorsements. Because he dared risk his reputation as a serious actor, other big names jumped into the advertising rat race, too. For example, around the same time, Kodak signed Laurence Olivier for endorsements too. He took time off from being "the greatest actor in the world" to sell cameras.

Henry claimed that working in GAF commercials was like hitting three bars on a slot machine. "The money just kept pouring out."

***

The Time of Your Life (1972)

Perhaps unnerved and exhausted from having filmed too many movies, Henry opted to link himself with the Plumstead Playhouse as the star of the lauded revival of William Saroyan's *The Time of Your Life* in the early 70s. Originally produced in 1939, it was the first play to win both a Pulitzer Prize and the New York Drama Critic's Circle Award. In 1948, James Cagney had starred in its film adaptation.

For its 1972 revival, Henry played the Cagney role of Joe, a loafer with money and a good heart.

The setting is a rundown dive in San Francisco. Joe uses his money to encourage his neighbors in their eccentricities. For example, Tom becomes his disciple, errand boy, and stooge, and Joe sets him up with a prostitute. Wesley is a black man who plays a mean and melancholy boogie-woogie piano.

Supporting players included Richard Dreyfuss, Ken Thompson, sultry Gloria Grahame, and Jane Alexander.

On January 12, 1972, *The Time of Your Life* held its premiere at the Eisenhower Theater at the Kennedy Center in Washington, D.C. In the spring and summer of that year, Henry went on a national tour with the play.

Clive Barnes of *The New York Times* wrote that, "This play is one of the best things I have ever seen with Henry Fonda. His performance is one of those stark patterns of opposites that so often the

The writer, **William Saroyan** (1908-1981) had long been a favorite of Henry Fonda. As such, he was eager to appear in the stage version of Saroyan's *The Time of Your Life.*

"When I took the role, it was viewed as an old chestnut. But I think it was perfectly valid of me to go back in time to the days that used to be. I took the role for appreciation of the writer—certainly not for the money."

Henry Fonda (left) starred with **Yul Brynner** in *Night Flight from Moscow.* "When we weren't due before the cameras, he told me of his many seductions of famous women," Henry said. "He provided clinical details, and I mean 'clinical,' almost like a doctor's report on a patient."

Brynner's list of conquests included Tallulah Bankhead, Marlene Dietrich, Anne Baxter, Ingrid Bergman, Yvonne De Carlo, Marilyn Monroe (why not?), Judy Garland, Gina Lollobrigida, and Maria Schell. According to Henry, "He claimed that Nancy Davis wanted to marry him, and that she later settled for Ronald Reagan."

greatest acting is all about. This is a lovely, overstated performance of a deliberately understated role."

A critic in Long Beach (California) claimed, "Seen now, in a new context, the play seems vapid, pointless, and pretentious. Since the play has not changed, apparently we have."

***

Night Flight from Moscow (aka *The Serpent*; 1973)

Henry worked steadily throughout the remainder of the 1970s (a period he called "the twilight of my career") in a series of films he had rather forget.

One of them was *Night Flight from Moscow (aka The Serpent)*. A Cold War thriller, it was financed by a conglomerate of companies based in Italy, France, and West Germany.

In *Night Flight from Moscow*, **Yul Brynner**, cast as KGB officer Colonel Alexei Viassov, flies into Paris, claiming that he is a defector with valuable information for The West's Allied Intelligence.

Is he for real, or is he a Russian implant?

It was produced, directed, and partially written by Henry Verneuil, who was called "the most American of French directors." He'd played key roles in the careers of Alain Delon, Jean Gabin, Omar Sharif, Yves Montand, Jean-Paul Belmondo, and Claudia Cardinale.

In top billing, Yul Brynner co-starred in it with Fonda.

The bald-headed Brynner was still an international sex symbol in spite of his lack of hair. He was best known for his portrayal of King Mongkut in the Rodgers and Hammerstein musical *The King and I*. On stage, he won a Tony for it; on film, an Oscar.

Other parts in *Night Flight from Moscow* went to Kirk Bogarde and Virni Lisi. Farley Granger and Robert Alda appeared in uncredited walk-ons.

The movie was inspired by several high-profile spy cases, including those of the British turncoats Kim Philby, Guy Burgess (cryptonym "Hicks"), and Donald MacLean (cryptonym "Hicks").

Aleksey Teodorovic Vlassov (Brynner) is a high-ranking KGB officer, who seemingly has defected to the West. He is grilled in long debriefings by Fonda, playing Allan Davies, the head of the CIA in Europe. He discovers there is something suspicious about Vlassov, as this complicated tale of intrigue commences.

In the third lead, Dirk Bogarde played Philip Boyle, No. 2 in the British Secret Service. He turns out to be working for the Soviets.

The British actor, **Dirk Bogarde**, plays a seasoned British intelligence officer, and he maintains that Viassov's intentions are sincere.

As a sign of good faith, the KGB officer reveals a list of double agents active in America, France, and West Germany. But before the CIA can move in to capture them, they're murdered by unknown assailants.

Several names cited as double agents commit suicide (or was it murder?). Bogarde turns out to be a Soviet "mole," and Vlassow, Henry discovers, is a Russian "plant." He is exchanged for a downed American pilot.

Perhaps as a means of offsetting all this male dominance, Virna Lisa was a glamourous addition to the cast. She played an Italian actress oddly named Annabel Lee. Throughout her career, her beauty seemed to override any talent she had. Her biggest regret, as she relayed to Fonda, was having rejected the role of the female lead in *From Russia With Love* (1963).

Hollywood studios tried to turn her into the "second coming of Marilyn Monroe."

Lisa was cast in the film alongside Jack Lemmon, Frank Sinatra, Tony Curtis, Rod Steiger, and Anthony Quinn. She later confessed to friends that she seduced all of them except Lemmon.

Two well-known actors, Robert Alda and Dirk Bogarde, were each cast into minor roles. Alda played an unnamed suspect questioned as a spy. *[On Broadway, he had originated the role of Sky Masterson in* Guys and Dolls *(1950), for which he'd won a Tony.]*

Bogarde, a gay British actor noted for his panache and style, had previously starred in a number of hits: *Death in Venice* (1971); *The Night Porter* (1974); and *A Bridge Too Far* (1977).

During the shoot, Henry dining several times with Bogarde and his long-time companion, Anthony Forwood, who had been wed to Glynis Johns in the 1940s.

Another gay actor, Farley Granger, had a minor role, too. Although he had worked steadily for years on stage and screen, his career had been to some degree "defined" by his starring role in Alfred Hitchcock's *Rope* (1948) and again in *Strangers on a Train* (1951).

In the *Cleveland Press*, Tony Mastroianni wrote: "The film demonstrates that in 1973, the computer has replaced the dagger in espionage. *The Serpent* has more good moments than bad."

"*The Serpent*" is a traditional spy fable," said *Time*. "The only thing that sets it apart is the totally consistent layer of impenetrable gloss with which Verneuil covers it."

TV Guide called it "a gritty, tightly directed look at international intrigue, and the performances are finely tuned."

***

Ash Wednesday (1973)

In September of 1972, the last of the co-starring films with Elizabeth Taylor and Richard Burton was shown on television on the NBC channel. Almost immediately, *Divorce His/Divorce Hers* was blasted by critics, one of them claiming, "The film holds all the joys of standing by at an autopsy."

"The Battling Burtons," as they'd been nicknamed, escaped together to Rome, where each of them would soonafter star in movies made in Italy.

Burton was to co-star with Marcello Mastroianni in *Massacre in Rome*, a World War II saga directed by Carlo Ponti, the husband of Sophia Loren.

For their first onscreen pairing, Elizabeth and Henry Fonda would co-star in *Ash Wednesday*. *[Actually, he had hoped to play opposite her in the then avant-garde and jarring* Who's Afraid of Virginia Woolf *(1966), but that role had gone to Burton.]*

The screenplay of *Ash Wednesday*, as conceived by Jean-

Virna Lisi in *Night Flight from Moscow*. To many of her fans, her role was far too small. As one of them said, "She should have at least done one nude scene. She's always being compared to Marilyn Monroe, but let's face the obvious: She's far more sensual than Monroe ever could be. Monroe was all pretend, but Virna is the real thing."

Film critic Tony Thomas wrote, "*Ash Wednesday* was sadly in line with most of the **Elizabeth Taylor** films made in the 1970s—of little success. It is something of a puzzle how an actress of such fame and perpetual exposure in the newspapers of the world could appear in films of such limited appeal."

Claude Tramont, focused on the effect of extensive cosmetic surgery on the hopes and dreams of a 55-year-old married woman whose looks have faded, the audience learns in the opening scenes. Elizabeth had been cast as Barbara Sawyer, a once-ravishing beauty of yesteryear. Henry was cast as her alienated husband, Mark Sawyer, a powerful attorney who has lost interest in her.

Elizabeth was to fly to Cortina d'Ampezzo in the Italian Alps to film *Ash Wednesday*. The film's producer, Dominick Dunne, had made a deal with her, agreeing to give her a hefty percentage of the profits and to pay all expenses during the shoot.

Its director would be Larry Peerce, whose reputation had been based on such films as *Goodbye Columbus* (1969) and *A Separate Peace* (1972).

From the beginning, Henry told Shirlee, "This is merely a soap opera, and the picture belongs totally to Elizabeth. But the dough is good for me."

Before flying to the Italian Alps for location shooting, Henry visited Taylor and Burton at their hotel in Rome, The Grand, where they had rented ten rooms.

As he was ushered into their very grand living room, Burton, clad only in his jockey shorts, was picking up dog shit. The Burtons had dogs *[her favorites, depending on the period, included Maltese terriers, Pekingese, and Lhasa Apsos]* with them, but they never seemed to take them for walks.

It was obvious that Burton had been drinking heavily. He did most of the talking. "Helmut Berger's gonna be in Eliza-

Our American Hero, **Henry Fonda**, on hiatus in Cortina d'Ampezzo re-courting his estranged, neurotically aging screen wife, *La Liz*.

Ash Wednesday was filmed during the peak years of the "Jetsetter Age."

Here is **Elizabeth Taylor**, starring with the then-29-year-old **Helmut Berger**, a spectacularly international then-famous beauty beloved of movie directors who (literally) included Luchino Visconti.

beth's movie, cast as a gigolo. Type casting, if you ask me. You know Helmut, don't you? Visconti's steady piece. But I know that Elizabeth will always come back to Daddy and his 11½ inches." Then he paused. "Perhaps I exaggerated an inch or two."

Because Elizabeth was still beautiful, Dunne brought in makeup artist Alberto Rossi "to age her face, which took two hours every morning before shooting the film's beginning scenes"

"I don't mind looking like an old hag in the first part of the film if I emerge gorgeous, youthful, and stunning in the end," she told Dunne.

During the shoot, Elizabeth, time and again, tested Henry's patience. Whereas he was always on time, she never was. Often, he had to wait three hours for her to show up, and on some days, she never appeared at all.

Henry arrived in the Alps weeks after the inauguration of filming because he only emerges in the final scenes of the film.

While waiting for her screen husband (Fonda) to fly to Italy, Barbara (i.e., Elizabeth) has an affair with

Erich, played by Helmut Berger.

All that plastic surgery doesn't do the trick for Mark (Fonda). In one of his first scenes, he compliments her on her beauty, then tells her that he has fallen in love with a younger woman and that he wants a divorce.

Burton had more or less predicted that that Helmut and Elizabeth would have a brief fling, and after a few days on the set with them, Henry began to more or less agree. A bisexual, Berger was a renowned seducer. An Austrian, "blonde and beautiful," as he was proclaimed, Berger was known for his portrayal of narcissistic, sexually ambiguous, high-testosterone men.

He was the long-time companion of the Italian director, Luchino Visconti, who cast him in a variety of films, notably as King Ludwig of Bavaria in the movie *Ludwig* (1972).

Berger was celebrated for his sexual conquests: Rudolf Nureyev, Nathalie *[wife of Alain Delon (1964-69)]* Delon, Ursula Andress, Tab Hunter, Linda Blair, Florinda Bolkan, Marisa Mell, Marilù Tolo, Britt Ekland, Anita Pallenberg, Jerry Hall, and both Mick and Bianca Jagger.

Ash Wednesday held its premiere in Manhattan on November 21, 1973. Privately, its producer, Dominick Dunne, gave this review: "It's a minor film. It's not *A Place in the Sun*. It's a nothing movie that I predict will mark the end of Taylor's screen career. There's nothing riveting about *Ash Wednesday*."

Don E. Stanke wrote, "Fonda seemed bored throughout."

Critic Rex Reed, who was usually an attack dog, actually seemed to write a love letter to Elizabeth. In the *New York Observer*, he wrote, "She's subtle, sensitive, glowing with freshness and beauty, fifty pounds lighter, her hair coiffed simply, her clothes ravishing, her make-up a symphony of perfection. For those who grew up in love with Elizabeth Taylor, the movie is pure magic. She is once again the kind of superstar that *marquées* light up for."

Reed added a bitchy footnote to his review: "This is the first time in recent years when Elizabeth didn't sound like a parody of Bette Davis in *Beyond the Forest*."

Vincent Canby of *The New York Times* was sarcastic: "The film was directed by Larry Peerce and written by Jean-Claude Tramont with all the fearlessness and perception demanded in the boiling of an egg."

Roger Ebert of the *Chicago Sun Times* wrote: "The movie's story is not really that interesting, but we're intrigued because the star is Taylor. She's 40 or 41 now, and yet she looks great. There's a kind of voyeuristic sensuality in watching her look at herself in the mirror. Maybe the fundamental problem with the movie is that we can't quite believe any man would leave Elizabeth Taylor. It's a good thing that we never see Henry Fonda's bimbo, because if we did, we wouldn't be convinced."

***

My Name Is Nobody (1973)

Henry had worked with the Italian director Sergio Leone successfully before during the filming of *Once Upon a Time in the West*. Leone came up with the idea, not the script, to star Henry in yet another Western, *My Name is Nobody* (1973), an Italian/French/German "spaghetti western."

This time around, the director would be Tonino Valerii, who specialized in spaghetti westerns. A native of Abruzzo in southern Italy, he started his film career as an assis-

tant director to Leone in *A Fistful of Dollars,* later moving on to direct films himself.

He personally called Henry to discuss his role in the film and to tell him that it would be shot on location in New Orleans, New Mexico, and Spain. It was set in 1899 as an old century was ending and a new one was on the verge of dawn.

Henry was informed that he would have second billing and that his leading man would be Terence Hill in the role of "Nobody."

"Do we have any nude love scenes together?" Henry jokingly asked Valerii. "It seems that every movie I go to see these days has actors taking off their clothes."

"No, it's not that kind of movie," Valerii said. "Of course, if you want love scenes with Terence, we'll write them in. You know I don't mean that."

Henry's knowledge of the Italian actor, Terence Hill, was very limited. A son of Venice, he was also a film director, screenwriter, and producer, having begun his career as a child actor.

At the time he worked with Henry, he was riding high in Italian popularity polls and was one of the highest-paid actors in the country. His film, *Lo chiamavano Trinità* (*They Call Me Trinity;* 1970), became the highest-grossing Italian film of all time.

In *My Name Is Nobody,* known in Italy as *Il mio nome è Nessuno,* he played "Nobody," a young man who craves excitement in the dying days of the Old West.

He attempts to get his idol, Jack Beauregard (Fonda), an aging gunslinger, to take on a wild gang of outlaws. He wants him to end his notorious career in a blaze of glory by singlehandedly taking on 150 members of "The Wild Bunch."

Despite daunting odds, Beauregard murders 100 of them in a single showdown. He had learned that several of them were carrying sacks of dynamite in their saddle bags. After blasting them with gunfire, an explosion rocks the cactus-studded plain.

Beauregard then sails for Eu-

Here's **Terence Hill.** Younger, more handsome, and much more of a star in Italy—site of this Spaghetti Western's greatest financial success—than Henry Fonda.

With ironic humor, its script, and Henry Fonda's acting talent, led to the conclusion that although he wasn't the stud Terence Hill was in *My Name is Nobody,* **Henry Fonda** was the more potent and skillful mass murderer.

Whereas the film was a commercial failure in the U.S. it prompted blockbuster sales in Italy

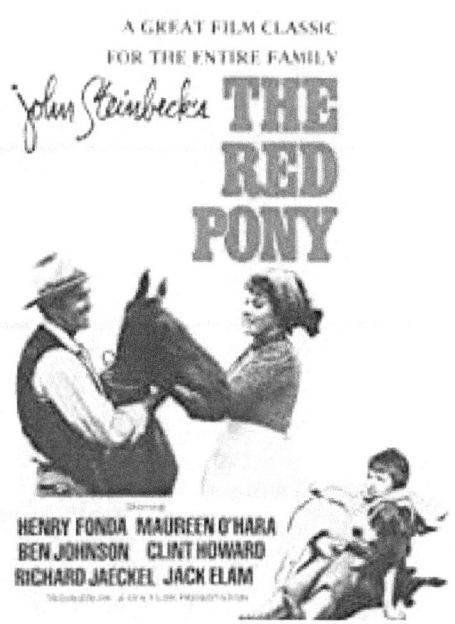

Adapting with muscle and grit to the TV age, **Henry Fonda** and **Maureen O'Hara**, two seasoned veterans of the big screen, continued their cinematic celebration of home, hearth, and family values in this made-for-TV adaptation of *The Red Pony,* a novel by John Steinbeck.

It wasn't the first time Henry had moved into the orbit of screen adaptations of literary works by Steinbeck—his breakthrough role as Tom Joad in *The Grapes of Wrath* (1940) had also been based on one of Steinbeck's then most-controversial novels.

rope to end his life in obscurity, with the audience realizing that his legacy will be kept alive in dozens of dime paperback novels of the Old West.

The movie marked Henry's swan song to Westerns. Since *Jesse James,* he had appeared in fifteen movies of this genre. In Italy, *Il mio nome è Nessuno* became the third-highest grossing film of the year. In the United States, it was drastically cut to 111 minutes and flopped at the box office.

Stanley Ralph Ross wrote, "Fonda plays the role with utmost believability, but nevertheless, he seems to be having a good time with his character.

Film studies expert Tony Thomas said, "As a picture about a man wrapping up his days in the Old West, it could hardly have had a better actor than the one who is doing exactly that."

Michael Kerbel wrote, "Fonda ideally embodies the slightly melancholy, stoic man of action at the end of his career, and the individual predestined by his own myth."

***

The Red Pony (1973)

Next, Henry enjoyed a reunion with the Irish beauty, Maureen O'Hara, co-starring with her in a made-for-television drama, *The Red Pony*. It was telecast on Sunday night, March 18, 1973. Its plot was based on a novel by John Steinbeck, who had remained Henry's favorite novelist, despite the passage of many years.

He and O'Hara had previously co-starred together in *The Immortal Sergeant* (1943). *The Red Pony* would mark her last picture before she retired.

The setting is a farm in California circa 1900, where a young boy named Jody (Clint Howard) forms an attachment to his pony, getting the love from the animal he does not get from his gruff father, Carl (Henry Fonda).

One critic wrote, "The chemistry and professionalism between Fonda and O'Hara is present and palpable and makes this a must-see for viewing two classic movie stars."

The supporting cast included familiar faces (familiar to Henry, at least): Richard Jaeckel, Ben Johnson, and Jack Elam.

***

The Alpha Caper (1973)

Henry followed *The Red Pony* with *The Alpha Caper*, a made-for-television crime thriller directed by Robert Michael Lewis. In some releases, it was entitled *The Inside Job.* It was first telecast on ABC on October 16, 1973.

Henry stars as Mark Forbes, an embittered parole officer who is forced into early retirement. He decides to take revenge and teams up with ex-cons Mitch (Leonard Nimoy), Scat (James McEachin), and Tudor (Larry Hagman) to pull a grand heist—$30 million in gold bullion—from a caravan of armored cars.

Henry had become friends with Hagman when they co-starred in *Fail Safe* (1964).

Nimoy originated the role of Spock (the half-Vulcan with the big ears) on *Star Trek* in 1964, appearing for the last time in the part in 2013.

***

As he aged and as major roles dried up, **Henry Fonda** insisted on working, even in relatively obscure made-for-television dramas such as *The Alpha Caper.*

He is billed as "a good guy who goes bad, especially when $30 million in gold is up for grabs" **Larry Hagman** and **Leonard Nimoy** were also in the cast.

The Last Days of Mussolini (1974)

After the filming of *My Name Is Nobody,* Henry remained in Rome for his small role in *The Last Days of Mussolini* (1974), directed by Carlo Lizzari. The historical drama depicts the days leading up to the execution of Benito Mussolini, the Italian dictator, during his attempt to flee from Milan in April of 1945 at the end of World War II. Rod Steiger was cast as Mussolini, supported by Franco Nero and Lisa Gastoni.

Henry appeared as Cardinal Alfredo Ildefonso Schuster, the Vatican's envoy who attempts to broker the dictator's surrender to Allied forces.

Despite its historic significance, Paramount, the film's U.S. distributor, encountered resistance among movie house managers.

Finally, the studio removed the reference to Mussolini in the title and renamed it *The Last 4 Days.*

[Steiger would go on to portray Mussolini once again in the 1981 Libyan-funded Lion of the Desert.*]*

Rod Steiger as Mussolini. Even the mention of the protagonist's name was so controversial that the distributor eventually removed the dictator's name from the title of the version released in the U.S., changing it to the blandly neutral *The Last 4 Days.*

In it, Henry Fonda played a diplomatically adroit and perhaps collusional Italian Cardinal.

***

Clarence Darrow (1974)

Of all his stage roles, Henry's favorite was the drama, *Clarence Darrow,* which opened on Broadway's Helen Hayes Theater on March 26, 1974.

It had to be temporarily shut down after only 29 performances because Henry collapsed in his dressing room.

The one-star play was based on the exploits of the fabled attorney as detailed in the book *Clarence Darrow for the Defense,* by Irving Stone. Stone was chiefly known for his biographical novels of noted artists, politicians, and intellectuals. His best-known work was *Lust for Life* (1934) about the tragic days of Vincent Van Gogh. *[In 1956, a film adaptation of* Lust for Life *would be made into a movie starring Kirk Douglas.]*

Stone also wrote *The Agony and the Ecstasy* (1961) about the turbulent life of the Renaissance artist, Michelangelo. *[In 1965, Charlton Heston was cast as Michelangelo in that novel's screen adaptation.]*

Stone's book on Darrow was not fictional, and highlighted events from his actual life. It featured his defense of those child killers, Richard Loeb and Nathan Leopold. It also dealt with Darrow's defense of teacher John T. Scopes in Tennessee in 1925. A biology teacher, Scopes went on trial for teaching evolution to his students.

On stage, Fonda reminisced about the life of Darrow with salty humor, courtroom gusto, and human relish. Darrow was an attorney not afraid of taking on popular causes, earning for himself the title of "The Champion of Dissenters and Underdogs."

Before accepting the role, Henry told his wife, Shirlee, "Here is one Old Lion who is going to play another Old Lion."

The first two weeks of rehearsal had gone badly, and Henry had several altercations with the director. Finally, he demanded that the producers fire him.

The distinguished John Houseman was brought in as a replacement. Henry had known Houseman, the Romanian-born British actor, for many years. He had originally become known for his highly publicized collaboration with Orson Welles. *[Welles had been the force behind the seminal film,* Citizen Kane *(1941), a few years after Welles' and Houseman's involvement with the Depression-era Federal Theatre. Meeting with Henry again, Houseman shared memories with him of directing his daughter Jane in the film* In the Cool of the Day *(1963).]*

Opening night was a brilliant critical success for Henry, although he suffered occasional attacks from reviewers.

Richard Watts, Jr., of the *New York Post* wrote: "If anyone ever had a doubt that the seemingly effortless Henry Fonda was one of the most brilliant actors living, it must have been demolished at the Helen Hayes Theatre last night."

In negative contrast, *Women's Wear Daily* interpreted Fonda as "a personality rather than an actor."

On April 23, 1974, patrons in the front rows of *Clarence Darrow* noticed that Henry was sweating profusely and seemed at times to forget his lines. Several times, he coughed rather violently.

As the curtain fell, he stumbled to his dressing room, where he collapsed. Shirlee was in the theater that night, and she was the first to discover him. He blamed it on exhaustion and spent the rest of the evening with her. Overnight, his condition worsened. He was admitted to a hospital the following morning.

At least three specialists examined him before the day's end, and he was forced to wear an oxygen mask. A specialist told him he had been fibrillating, and he was hooked up to a monitor to measure his irregular heartbeat. As a countermeasure, a doctor installed a temporary pacemaker.

Holders of tickets for upcoming performances of *Clarence Darrow* had their money refunded. Henry and Shirlee flew back to Bel Air, where he began a regime that included lots of rest and recuperation.

When doctors diagnosed continuing heart troubles, a decision was made for him to undergo an operation for the installation of a permanent pacemaker, a device pioneered by William O. Douglas, a cardiac surgeon.

Henry traveled to New York City for the operation. On May 7, 1974, he was released from the hospital, and he and Shirlee flew back to Bel Air.

After a month or so, he delivered some performances of *Clarence Darrow* again, this time at the Huntington Hartford Theatre in Los Angeles. Then it was back to Manhattan again for a taping of the television adaptation of *Clarence Darrow,* scheduled for a telecast on September 4 on NBC.

There arose such an outcry from frustrated former ticket holders who never got to see Henry perform in *Clarence Darrow* that he presented the show on Broadway on March 3, 1975 at the Minskoff Theatre. He fulfilled his commitment to appear in every performance of that production until the end of the play's run in mid-May.

Henry and Shirlee then flew to London, where he would open a production of *Clarence Darrow* at the Piccadilly Theatre. Some members of the London press hailed it as "the hottest ticket in the West End."

The *Daily Express* urged theater goers "to go see a noble man playing a noble man."

During his stint in the U.K., he spent as much time as possible with his longtime friend, James Stewart, who was in London at the time appearing in a revival of *Harvey.*

CHAPTER FOUR

THE DECLINE AND COLLAPSE OF HENRY FONDA

A Unique Array of Henry's Lesser-Known, Dying Efforts

Ignoring Health Concerns, Henry Works Until He Can't

MIDWAY
Bolstered by His Personal Wartime Experience in the U.S. Navy, Henry Fonda Portrays General Admiral Nimitz, Commander of U.S. Forces During the Bloody War Against the Japanese

A DISASTER HORROR FILM: TENTACLES
Henry Joins John Huston and Shelley Winters in the Italian Remake of *Jaws*. Instead of a Killer Shark, They Face a Devouring Giant Octopus with Deadly Tentacles

THE GREAT SMOKEY ROADBLOCK
Henry "Gets Off" as a Cross-Country Trucker Looking for Love He Stars Opposite Susan Sarandon playing a Prostitute and Eileen Brennan cast as a Bordello Madam

KILLER BEES: *THE SWARM*
Reviewed as the Worst Film Ever Made, Its Cast Included Five Oscar Winners. Despite the Best Efforts of Henry, Fred MacMurray, Olivia de Havilland, and Jose Ferrer, It Died an Embarrassing, Bee-Stung Death at the Box Office.

No, We're Not Talking about a Hat. She's a Clumsy Tribute to the Razzmatazz of Old Hollywood, and her name is

FEDORA

Hoping for another *Sunset Blvd.*, Director Billy Wilder casts William Holden once again As a male lead. But even Holden can't save this Gay Writer's Fantasy, a dull and convoluted tale of a former movie goddess like Marlene Dietrich or Greta Garbo living in mysterious exile. Henry Fonda appears as himself in a cameo.

ROOTS: THE NEXT GENERATIONS
Henry, Awkwardly Cast as a Confederate General with Olivia de Havilland as his Wife Lend Their Considerable Talents to this Sequel of the Best-Belling Mega-Hit, *Roots, The Saga of an American Family* (1976) by Alex Haley.

METEOR
Despite Henry's Vow to Never Appear in Another Disaster Movie, Sean Connery lured him back for a Cameo Appearance as President of the United States. Together, POTUS and 007 Face a Challenge:

A GIANT ASTEROID IS ON A COLLISION COURSE WITH EARTH. OFF SCREEN, TABLOIDS SCREAM AS NATALIE WOOD SHARES HER OVERUSED CHARMS WITH THIS FABLED ACTOR FROM SCOTLAND

CITY ON FIRE

RIDING ON THE COATTAILS OF *THE TOWERING INFERNO*, HENRY FONDA AND AVA GARDNER APPEAR IN CAMEOS IN YET ANOTHER DISASTER FILM. AUDIENCES YAWN, AND A CRITIC CLAIMS: "WITH FONDA AS OUR FIRE CHIEF, YOUR CITY IS LIKELY TO BURN TO THE GROUND."

THE OLDEST LIVING GRADUATE

HENRY LAUNCHED THE 1980S—THE LAST DECADE OF HIS LIFE—WITH AN NBC TELECAST FEATURING HIM AS A CRUSTY OLD CURMUDGEON WHO REFUSES TO RETIRE.

GIDEON'S TRUMPET

BASED ON A TRUE STORY, HENRY PLAYS CLARENCE EARL GIDEON, A SEMI-LITERATE FLORIDA DRIFTER CONVICTED OF PETTY LARCENY. DESPITE HIS ATTEMPTS TO DEFEND HIMSELF IN COURT, HE'S SENTENCED TO FIVE YEARS IN JAIL. IN PRISON, HE PETITIONS THE SUPREME COURT, CLAIMING HIS CIVIL RIGHTS WERE VIOLATED BECAUSE HE COULD NOT AFFORD A LAWYER. AFTER PUBLIC OUTCRY, THE BLACK-ROBED JUDGES REACH THE LANDMARK DECISION THAT ALL AMERICANS ARE ENTITLED TO HAVE A LAWYER DEFEND THEM.

SUMMER SOLSTICE

IN THIS MADE-FOR-TV MOVIE, TWO SCREEN LEGENDS—HENRY FONDA AND MYRNA LOY, EACH BORN IN 1905—BID *ADIEU* TO THE MOVIES. FROM THEIR LIVING ROOMS, AMERICANS EVALUATE THEM IN FLASHBACKS PORTRAYING THEIR HALF-CENTURY OF MARRIAGE. STEPHENS COLLINS AND LINDSAY CROUSE PORTRAY YOUNGER VERSIONS OF THE SAME CHARACTERS.

In February of 1976, X-rays at Cedars-Sinai Medical Center in Los Angeles revealed a tumor that had grown near Henry's lung. His doctor ordered surgery for him on March 17. The procedure lasted 7 ½ hours. Shirlee described it as "one of the most nerve-wracking of my life."

Although Henry's right lung was spared, the creeping growth had moved to the right side of his diaphragm. A part of it had to be cut away. A surgeon reported that the tumor was "the size of California's biggest grapefruit." Subsequently, gossip along the Hollywood grapevine surmised that Henry had inoperable cancer and had only months to live.

He was released in April and was sent home, where slowly, he began to recover under Shirlee's love and care.

To friends and the press, she put up a brave front, dismissing his operation "as only minor surgery."

Henry was forced to abandon the stage. On March 1, 1981, he made his last live appearance in a play called Showdown at the Adobe Hotel at the Hartman Theatre in Stamford, Connecticut.

With the belief that he was dying, official Hollywood began plotting some lifetime achievement awards. In 1979, he won a Tony for his cumulative work on the Broadway stage. During the course of 1981, he was presented with Lifetime awards from the American Film Institute, the Golden Globes, and the Kennedy Center.

Although by now his health had begun to plague him, he carried on.

That same year (1981) he starred in one of his greatest roles in On Golden Pond opposite both Katharine Hepburn and his daughter Jane. [For more details on the dramas associated with the making of that film, refer to the Epilogue of this book.]

For their performances in On Golden Pond, Hepburn and Henry won Best Actor and Best Actress Oscars, respectively. Because he was too weak to attend the Awards ceremony, Jane accepted the Oscar for him.

Henry said, "I'm not a religious person, but I thanked God every day that I could finish On Golden Pond. If you survive long enough, you can gather up enough awards on paper to cover the walls of a fair-sized room, and more than enough metal to build a stove. And I've been fortunate enough to harvest my share."

On August 8, 1982, he was once again rushed to a hospital.

Award-Winning Actor Henry Fonda Dies at 77
Began His Career With Amateur Production in Omaha; Received the Oscar for Final Picture

His days were dwindling down to a precious few. At the age of 77, on August 12, the Grim Reaper came for him in his sleep. His body was cremated, but his world-famous blue eyes were donated to the Manhattan Eye Institute.

In his final interview, he praised his wife Shirlee, calling her "an angel who stood by me every day of our marriage."

"I was never part of a family until I met Henry Fonda," she said.

***

Midway (1976)

Henry may have been miscast as a Vatican envoy in *The Last Days of Mussolini*, but he was perfectly cast as Admiral Chester W. Nimitz in the World War II drama, *Midway* (1976). Historians view the June 1942 battle wherein U.S. warships and planes defeated the Japanese fleet as "the most stunning and decisive blow in the history of naval warfare."

Nimitz was the admiral who directed the Allied offense in the Pacific Theater.

Universal distributed *Midway*, which had been directed by Jack Smight. He assembled an international cast of stars led by Charlton Heston, with support from James Coburn, Robert Wagner, Glenn Ford, Ed Nelson, Robert Mitchum, Cliff Robertson, and Toshiro Mifune.

Despite mixed reviews, *Midway* became the tenth most popular film released in the United States in 1976.

Variety wrote, "Perhaps because Henry Fonda is old enough to know about, and care about, the actual environment of the film, his performance as Nimitz towers over everything else."

Tony Thomas said, "Fonda's authoritative presence is as valuable to this movie as Admiral Nimitz's was in the actual battle."

Midway became one of the few films to use Sensurround, the brand name for a process used to enhance an audience's audio experience during screenings. The low-frequency sounds of throbbing engines and exploding torpedoes were more felt than heard, thereby providing a vivid complement to on-screen depictions of bomber formations and the like. Ultimately, however, the trend toward multiplex theaters presented challenges that made Sensurround impractical as a permanent feature of cinema.

During World War II, **Henry Fonda** witnessed first hand how Allied forces captured island by island in the Pacific on their way to conquer Tokyo. As Admiral Chester W. Nimitz in the film *Midway*, he was totally convincing as one of the great Naval heroes of American history.

***

Collision Course (1976)

As the years rolled on, Henry, his physicality weakening, continued to perform in feature films and television dramas.

In *Collision Course* (1976), which premiered on ABC-TV on January 1, 1976, he starred as General Douglas MacArthur.

Its script focused on the conflicts between President Harry S Truman (E. G. Marshall) and General MacArthur over how to fight the Korean War. The general wanted to expand it, perhaps even by attacking Red China. In loud and vivid contrast, the president preferred a cease fire. When the general flamboyantly disobeyed his Commander-in-Chief, Truman fired him.

Relieved of his command, MacArthur returned to America for public speaking tours of major cities. In Miami, much to the embarrassment of Truman, he was given a hero's welcome for his brilliant service as a warrior in the Pacific.

On the set, Henry had a reunion with Marshall, who had co-starred with him in *12 Angry Men* (1957) twenty years earlier. Lucille Benson played Bess Truman, and Lee Kessler was cast as their daughter, Margaret. Barry Sullivan starred as Dean Acheson, and John Larch was General Omar Bradley.

After his portrayal of Nimitz, **Henry Fonda** took on an even more challenging character when he was cast as General Douglas MacArthur.

The teledrama's plot unfolded during the Korean War, when then- President Harry Truman fired America's military hero, based in part on his policies of escalating conflicts with China.

***

Captains and the Kings (1976)

Henry starred as Senator Enfield Bassett in one episode of an eight-part miniseries, *Captains and the Kings*. It was telecast on NBC beginning on the night of September 30, 1976.

Part of the studio's *Best Sellers* anthology series, the stories were adapted from a novel by Taylor Caldwell. It was set against an Irish-American family who accumulates economic and political power during the 19th and 20th centuries.

Heading the cast was Richard Jordan as the ambitious Irish immigrant, Joseph Arnagh. Other regulars in the cast included Patty Duke, Robert Vaughan, Perry King, and Jane Seymour.

Henry was just one of a roster of stars who appeared in various episodes of the series. Others included John Houseman, Celeste Holm, Ray Bolger, Neville Brand, John Carradine, Burl Ives, William Prince, Ann Sothern, and Sally Kirkland.

***

Rollercoaster (1977)

Director James Goldstone hyped Henry's small role in an upcoming disaster suspense film called *Rollercoaster*. He described it like this: "It is not a disaster movie, but a Hitchcock-like suspense cat-and-mouse story."

Its male lead was assigned to George Segal as Harry Calder, a safety inspector of amusement parks. As Simon Davenport, Fonda was Segal's nasty boss.

In her first feature film, Helen Hunt played Segal's teenaged daughter. Steve Guttenberg, also in his first film role, had an uncredited part as a messenger boy.

Richard Widmark, who had previously co-starred with Henry in the police drama *Madigan* (1968), played FBI agent Hoyt.

At the start, Timothy Bottoms, credited only as "Young Man," sneaks into an amusement park and places a radio-controlled bomb on the tracks of a wooden rollercoaster. The bomb later explodes, killing or injuring riders. Bottoms told Henry, "This is my first time playing a villain."

Stanley Ralph Ross wrote, "Fonda has very little to do in this movie, and one wonders why he took the job."

Vincent Canby, in *The New York Times*, claimed, "Henry Fonda takes his role with the sort of gravity that never betrays the nature of the film."

Rollercoaster was made for $9 million but took in only $8.3 million at the box office. It was the third film to be presented in Sensurround.

"We almost made it pay off," Henry said, "but the opening of that same year of the first installment of the *Star Wars* franchise sucked our blood."

***

Tentacles (1977)

"What in hell are we doing in a piece of crap like this?" Henry asked his co-stars John Huston and Shelley Winters. He was referring to their having been cast in the Italian-American horror film, *Tentacles*, directed by the B-movie horror specialist Ovidio G. Assonitis.

It was obvious that low-budged *Tentacles* was an attempt to capitalize off the success of *Jaws* (1975), the Steven Spielberg man-eating shark epic that had ticket buyers lined up around the block.

In *Tentacles*, the menace derives from a giant octopus terrorizing a small seaside resort in California. Although it was often compared to *Jaws*, *Tentacles* actually evoked *It Came from Beneath the Sea* (1955), a sci-fi "giant monster" horror flick.

Huston was cast as Ned Turner, a crusading newspaper reporter with Winters as Tillie Turner. Years later, when asked about *Tentacles*, the actress said, "I hardly remember that stinker. Maybe I was Huston's wife, perhaps his daughter. In movies, I've been drowned by Monty Clift, run over by James Mason, crushed to death by Robert Mitchum. I've been strangled, raped, and otherwise done away with. I think I'm just about due for an incineration. In *Tentacles*, I didn't even get to wrestle in a fight with that monster octopus."

Henry was cast as Mr. Whitehead, the President of Trojan construction. His company's excavation of an underwater tunnel was credited with bringing the enraged killer octopus up from its watery depths.

If the picture belonged to anyone, it was to Bo Hopkins, who was cast as marine biologist Will Gleason. At film's end, the octopus is done in by a pair of killer whales trained by Gleason.

It cost only $750,000 to make, and it took in $3 million at the box office.

Reviews were universally negative. Lawrence Van Gelder in *The New York Times* attacked "the atrocious acting in minor roles."

In the *Los Angeles Times*, Linda Gross dismissed it as "a tedious movie, nightmarishly slow and intermittently out of synch."

Tom Milne in *The Monthly Film Bulletin* declared: "A devastatingly silly rehash of the *Jaws* formula, atrociously scripted, stiltedly acted, and reaching a low point in a grotesquely maudlin finale where the hero pours his heart out in a pep talk to the whales he has trained to graduate standards in communications."

***

The Great Smokey Roadblock (1977)

The early, working title of Henry's next film, a comedy road film, was *The Last of the Cowboys*. It would suffer through two or three more title changes before its release as *The Great Smokey Roadblock*. It marked the last time Henry received star billing. *[Even in* On Golden Pond, *he had second billing under Katharine Hepburn.]*

When director John Leone first presented the *Roadblock* film to him, Henry rejected it. "I'm not only the last of the cowboys, but I can no longer ride a horse."

"You don't have to ride a horse in this movie," Leone said. "You're a 60-year-old truck driver. Cross-country truckers sometimes call themselves 'cowboys.'"

The name of Henry's character was "Elegant John," although there wasn't much that was elegant about his character. Leone had written the script himself. Its producers were Allan F. Bodoh and Susan Sarandon, who cast herself in a minor role as a prostitute.

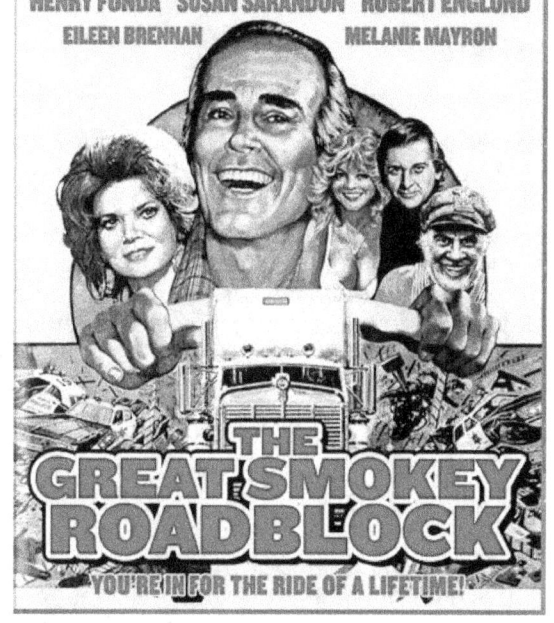

Cast as Penelope, Eileen Brennan played Henry's leading lady, the madam of a bordello with six beautiful girls for rent. This native of Los Angeles, born in 1932, had achieved recognition in Peter Bogdanovich's *The Last Picture Show* (1971). She went on to acclaim for her nomination as Best Supporting Actress for her performance as Goldie Hawn's nasty commanding officer in *Private Benjamin* (1980).

Other supporting roles in *Roadblock* were cast with John Bryner, Dub Taylor, and Daina House.

The film was shot for the most part in Oroville, California during a difficult time for Henry, who was plagued with a number of illnesses.

The movie opens with a view of an ailing Henry sprawled out on a hospital bed. His illness has caused him to miss many payments on his 18-wheel Kenworth rig.

Before the finance company can reclaim his vehicle, he makes an impulsive decision to make one last "and perfect" cross-country jaunt. He "steals" his impounded truck and heads out on what the audience learns is his character's last road adventure.

First, he heads for Wyoming, where his old flame Penelope (Brennan) runs a whorehouse. She, too, is in trouble. An undercover cop has exposed her operation, and she has 48 hours to get out of town.

Elegant John invites Penelope and her prostitutes to head out with him on the road. Along the way, the girls sell their favors to gas station attendants who gallantly fill up the truck's tank, without charge, with gasoline.

Soon after, state troopers are on their tail. A renegade cop arrests them and tosses all of them in jail. There, the girls strip naked and coyly lure the sheriff and his deputy into a cell, from which they then escape.
After Henry's eighteen-wheeler runs through a series of blockades, their daring exploits reach the news media The press amplifies and sensationalizes their story, nicknaming them "Elegant John and the Sweet Mystery Six."

At the end, with a smile on his face, John dies in the arms of Penelope.

Variety wrote, "This is an appealing film about a dying truck driver played with moral force by Henry Fonda."

Stanley Ralph Ross was quoted in *Motion Picture Guide* with "Fonda seems to be having the time of his life, giving a good performance despite the fact that he had a pacemaker installed and a hearing aid."

Years later, Eileen Brennan was interviewed about her performance as a whorehouse madam. She had little to say about her movie roles, but a lot to say about her ongoing (and horrifying) health issues: "In 1982, Goldie Hawn and I were leaving a restaurant in Venice when a speeding car hit me. I suffered massive injuries and was in recovery for three years, where I became addicted to painkillers."

"In 1989, I was appearing on stage in *Annie,* and I fell into the orchestra pit, breaking my leg. More recovery time. The following year, I was diagnosed with breast cancer. That was successfully treated. However, now I've been told that I have inoperable bladder cancer. What a career!"

Eileen Brennan, cast as a whorehouse madam, welcomes "Elegant John" (Fonda) to town. He is her old flame, but now is seriously ill—in fact, he dies in her arms.

***

Home to Stay (1978)

In 1978, a Canadian-American made-for-television drama, *Home to Stay,* starred Henry Fonda. It was telecast for the first time on May 1 on CBS.

Directed by Delbert Mann, it was based on *Grandpa and Frank* by Janet Majerus. Co-stars included Frances Hyland and Michael McGuire.

Henry played "Grandpa George," an elderly man who runs away from home with his young granddaughter after refusing to be moved into a retirement home. Together, they tour the Midwest. The film's producer, David Susskind, an almost legendary name back then, insisted that Henry play the lead. He told his associates, "Old Hank isn't gonna be around much longer. Get him now."

***

The Swarm (1978)

"I had the dishonor of having a small role in *The Swarm,* which some critics hailed as the worst film ever made," Henry claimed.

He was referring to the natural horror disaster film produced and directed by Irwin Allen and based on Arthur Herzog's 1974 novel.

At the time, Allen was called "The Master of the Disaster Movie." Henry was impressed with the cast he'd hired. It included five Oscar winners.

A rapidly aging **Henry Fonda** in *Home to Stay,* a press photo with his juvenile co-star, **Kristen Vigardi**.

Michael Caine had the lead role of Dr. Bradford Crane, an entomologist *[i.e., a zoologist specializing in insects].*

At that point in his life, Caine was being hailed as a British film icon, having appeared in such hits as *Alfie* (1966), for which he was nominated for a Best Actor Oscar. Near the end of his life, his movies would collectively gross some $8 billion at the box office.

Other stars in the cast included Katharine Ross, Richard Widmark, Richard Chamberlain, Olivia de Havilland, Ben Johnson, Cameron Mitchell, Lee Grant, Jose Ferrer, Patty Duke, Slim Pickins, Bradford Dillman, and Fred MacMurray in his last film role.

Henry had been assigned the cameo role of Dr. Walter Krim, another entomologist.

The Swarm is a tale about killer bees which invade, by the millions, the neighborhoods of Houston,

Texas. Authorities are charged with removing stingers from some 800,000 bees. One of them, with its stinger intact, slips through their barricades and attacks De Havilland, sending her to the hospital.

Released at the height of the disaster film craze, *The Swarm* cost $21 million to make, but generated only $7.7 million in ticket sales.

Reviews were heavily critical, sometimes morphing into attacks. Most of them moralized that Henry should be ashamed for appearing—even in a cameo—in this "disaster about a disaster."

Vincent Canby in *The New York Times* defined the film as "nothing less than the ultimate apotheosis of yesterday's B movie."

Richard Velt in the *Wilmington Morning Post* claimed that *The Swarm* "was as bad as any movie he'd ever seen." *Variety* labeled it as "a disappointing and tired non-thriller."

How does a scriptwriter kill off two vintage movie stars in the same horrible movie? Put them under contracts to appear in **The Swarm**, a "Disaster Film' hated by virtually everyone.

Upper photo shows an aging **Henry Fonda** in a death spasm. *Lower photo* shows **Olivia de Havilland** in equivalent straits, each the victim of killer bees and wounded pride.

***

Fedora (1978)

Director Billy Wilder, a year younger than Henry, came from a family of Polish Jews born in a town that then was a part of the Austro-Hungarian Empire. Or, as he put it, "a half hour from Vienna."

He lived in Berlin until the rise of the Nazi Party. By 1933, he was in Hollywood, where he became a film director, producer, and screenwriter..

He immortalized himself with *Sunset Blvd.* (1950), starring Gloria Swanson as the demented former silent screen vamp, opposite William Holden as the sullen, sexy, and doomed Joe Gillis, and Erich von Stroheim, who had come out of retirement.

When Wilder read Tom Tryon's novella, *Fedora,* he thought he had discovered a story to rival *Sunset Blvd.* [How wrong he was.] Perhaps borrowing from his previous triumph, he even opted to cast William Holden as its male lead.

The script's character of the exotically beautiful, foreign-born Fedora evoked memories of Greta Garbo and Marlene Dietrich. Fedora is an actress and movie star who's known for her "forever young" beauty that has survived intact for many decades.

She had retired and was living on a guarded private island near Corfu, to which she had withdrawn at the height of her fame.

Her legions of fans were shocked when she committed suicide by throwing herself in front of a train. The script evoked previous characters portrayed in various renditions of *Anna Karenina* by both Greta Garbo and Vivien Leigh.

One of the mourners at her funeral is the aging has-been producer named Dutch Detweiler, who was once Fedora's lover. He had arrived on Corfu in an attempt to persuade her to come out of retirement and to appear in a revised screen adaptation of *Anna Karenina.*

She confided to him that she'd been a prisoner of the elderly Polish "dragon," Countess Subryanski (played by Hildegard Kneff) and Dr. Vando (Jose Ferrer), a larcenous and lecherous cosmetic surgeon.

At the funeral, Detweiler accuses the countess and the doctor of murdering Fedora. The countess then shocks him by revealing that SHE is the actual Fedora. The woman who committed suicide was her daughter, Antonia, who had disguised herself as her mother after some botched cosmetic surgeries disfigured her, ruining her face.

In a brief cameo, Henry Fonda appears as himself in *Fedora*, a bittersweet saga evoking the old star system of Golden Age Hollywood. Director Billy Wilder failed to make another *Sunset Blvd.*

The deception went undetected until Antonia had fallen in love with actor Michael York (playing himself) during their filming of a movie together.

Although Antonia desperately wanted to admit the truth to York and others, the countess (aka "the real Fedora") has forced her into psychological torment and enforced. The loss of both her career and her lover morphs Antonia into a

GRAND ILLUSIONS: Shadow-soaked **Marthe Keller** emoting with with *(left photo)* **Henry Fonda** and *(right photo)* **William Holden** in separate scenes from *Fedora*.

As an independent film producer, the character played by Holden has traveled to a remote Greek island to lure Fedora back to the screen. Is he in for a surprise!

drug addict. After the loss of both her beauty and her sanity, she kills herself.

Detweiler makes a final decision not to expose the real Fedora's secret to the world. She dies within six weeks of telling him goodbye.

Henry had only a cameo role in the film, appearing as the President of the Academy who arrived on the island to present a lifetime achievement award to Fedora. With the belief that she is Fedora, he meets Antonia and is amazed at her youthful beauty.

Wilder told Henry that he had originally envisioned Marlene Dietrich as Fedora, with Faye Dunaway cast as her daughter. "But Dietrich told me she hated the movie script even more than she hated the Tryon novella.

Wilder had cast a Swiss-born actress, Marthe Keller, a former fashion model, in the dual role of Fedora/Antonia. She had recently completed her most famous role in *Marathon Man* (1976), for which she was nominated for a Golden Globe.

Before working with Henry, Keller had acted alongside Al Pacino in the romantic drama, *Bobby Deerfield* (1977) based on the Erich Maria Remarque novel, *Heaven Has No Favorites*.

Portraying the countess, Germany-born Hildegard Knef had led a dramatic life, as she candidly recounted in her autobiography, *The Gift Horse* in 1970.

In Germany during World War II, the Soviets had captured Knef and sent her to a prison camp, but she managed to escape.

Her reputation was hurt in America because she'd performed nude in scenes in the German film *Die Sünderin* (1950), and because she had fallen in love with a Nazi when she was 19.

Henry had worked with Jose Ferrer before, an actor from Puerto Rico who became the first Hispanic to win an Oscar for *Cyrano de Bergerac* in 1950. Ferrer had married (1953-1961) and divorced and remarried (1964-1967) the singer Rosemary Clooney.

Janet Maslin in *The New York Times* referred to *Fedora* as "old fashioned with a vengeance, a proud, passionate remembrance of the way movies used to be."

TV Guide found it a "campy melodrama. It's almost as if Wilder is bidding *adieu* to the Golden Age of Hollywood."

Variety found that Fonda "adds some flavor to this bittersweet bow to the old star system."

***

First Monday in October (1978)

Even as his years dwindled down to a precious few, Henry still appeared in stage roles. *First Monday in October* by Jerome Lawrence and Robert E. Lee premiered at Broadway's Majestic Theatre on October 3, 1978. Its title referred to the day the U.S. Supreme Court traditionally convenes following its summer recess.

Directed by Edwin Sherin, the drama was transferred that November to the ANTA Playhouse, where it ran for seventy-nine performances.

Fonda co-starred with Jane Alexander. He played Associate Justice Daniel Snow. The President appoints Ruth Loomis (Alexander) as the first woman to sit on the High Court. Snow is appalled at her conservative views, so different from his own liberal thinking. They even battle over the fictional pornographic film, *The Naked Nymphomaniac*.

The play originally opened in Cleveland in 1975, starring fading stars Jean Arthur and Melvyn Douglas. Reviews were poor, and it ran for only eleven performances. Suffering from a viral infection, Arthur entered a clinic and left the theater forever.

Henry teamed with Eva Marie Saint to bring the play to the Huntington Hartford Theatre in Los Angeles for a short run in March of 1979.

The usually acerbic John Simon claimed, "Henry Fonda is always the grand old ham, exploiting every bit of this high-minded hokum to the hilt."

Time Magazine gave its opinion. "Henry Fonda is one of the very few actors who could dive into this two-inch deep pool of a play and emerge from it with an Olympic gold medal."

The Christian Science Monitor weighed in too: "Mr. Fonda is in fine fettle as the cussing, curmudgeonly dissenter, a role apparently inspired in part by Justice William O. Douglas."

During the run of *First Monday in October*, there was a sad, frightening event that occurred in Henry's life. One critic maintained that during his performance, "audiences were eating him up like ice cream."

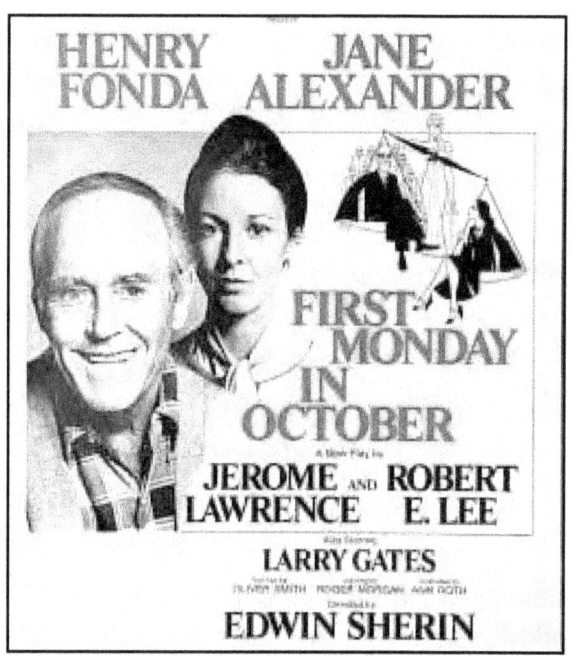

Dissatisfied with his recent film roles, **Henry Fonda** returned to his first love, the stage, to co-star with **Jane Alexander** in *First Monday in October*. His declining physicality allowed him only six weeks to perform.

One Sunday morning, he slept late. He had retired the previous night complaining of exhaustion. When he finally woke up around 11AM, he was alone in bed. Shirlee had slept with him but had retreated downstairs to cook.

He stretched his body, but as he did so, "something seemed to 'snap' in his left hip. He tried to get up and out of bed but could not. He collapsed back onto the bed and called for Shirlee.

During the previous two weeks, she had noticed that he was limping, and she had urged him to go to a doctor.

He finally agreed to go with her to see a Dr. Edward Newman. After an examination, he told Henry he might be suffering from arthritis or tendonitis.

After much resistance, he was finally put on a stretcher and hauled to a hospital in an ambulance, with its red dome light flashing and its siren wailing. He had arrived at the Michael Reese Hospital on Lake Michigan on Chicago's South Side.

There, he was extensively X-rayed, and Dr. Newman went over the pictures with him. Henry seemed a the time more concerned about missing a stage performance of *First Monday in October*.

Six specialists were also called in to go over the x-rays. One picture depicted a chalk-white growth, a nodule on the prostate gland that had propelled splinters into his hip bone.

At 1AM that morning, a call came in from Los Angeles. It was from Jane. She was joyous, having won the Oscar for *Coming Home*, her second. He had watched the awards hours before, and he was proud of her. He feared she'd deliver a political speech, but he saw her as a gracious lady who thanked the audience and left the stage.

[*In* Coming Home *(1978), the screenplay had been written by Waldo Salt, who had also written the screenplay for* Midnight Cowboy, *which had been voted Best Picture of the Year in 1969. Jon Voight had played the hustler.*

Along with Bruce Dern, he was also Jane's co-star in Coming Home, *a mature, gripping film that dealt with the Vietnam War, especially its effects on the people back home. While her husband (Dern) is overseas, Jane falls in love with Voight, who is a paraplegic.*]

During her phone call, Henry did not tell her he had cancer, but told her only that he had a leg injury. He and Shirlee would be flying out of Chicago in the morning, heading to Los Angeles, where he would be a patient at Cedars-Sinai.

Dr. Joseph Kaplan operated and removed the cancerous growth. The surgery was a success, but, as he said, "I had to learn to walk again—first on crutches, then with a cane."

Spring had come for Shirlee and Henry at their Bel Air home. He slowly strolled among his blossoming fruit trees with Shirlee at his side. He told her, "I'm alive, and you're with me. I'm going to go on. I'm not licked yet."

***

Battle Force (1978)

A 1978 film in which Henry had a key role is so obscure it is sometimes left off his anthology of movies. It had a limited release, and was sometimes billed as *Biggest Battle* or *Battle Force*. It got its greatest exposure in Italy, where it was known as *Il Grande Attacco* or *The Great Attack*.

Umberto Lenzi, the Italian director, also wrote most of the screenplay. He assembled an all-star cast that featured Helmut Berger, Giuliano Gemma, Stacy Keach, Ray Lovelock, Samantha Eggar, Evelyn Stewart, and the director, John Huston.

The movie was a production financed by three companies in West Germany, Italy, and Yugoslavia.

Its plot focuses on a group of Nazi and Allied nations during the early years of World War II. Henry's role was that of the American Brigadier General Harold Foster. Other roles featured

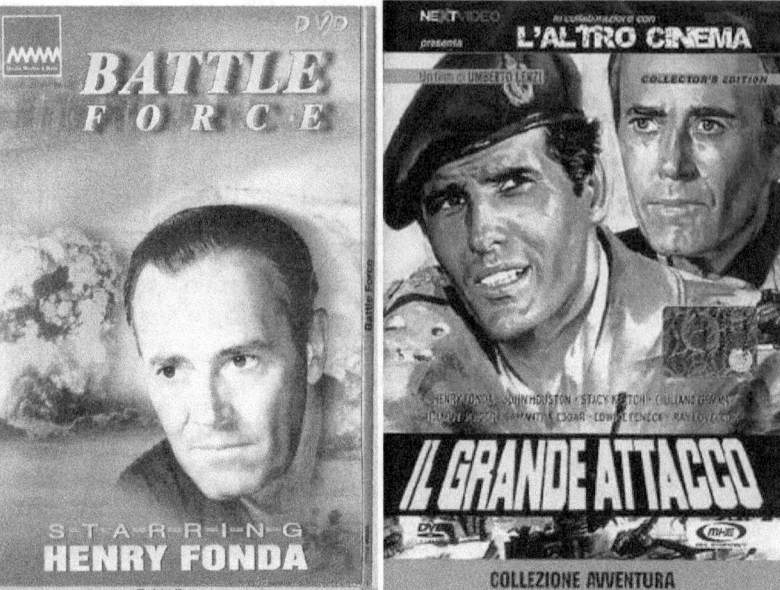

Although judged as a pretentious and muddled commercial failure in the US , its Italian campaign, when it was distributed as *Il Grande Attacco*, was somewhat more effective.

Still, it did absolutely nothing for **Henry Fonda's** then-ironclad reputation as a grand master from the Golden Age of filmmaking—despite more than a few recent stinkers.

John Huston as war correspondent Sean O'Hara. Eggar was cast as a German actress Annelise Hackerman. Lovelock played Fonda's son, John. Helmut Berger was cast as a Nazi lieutenant.

Battle Force reaches its climax in a re-creation of the Battle of the Mareth Line in Tunisia. The Allies scored a victory but at a great cost.

The film performed badly on the international market and had a limited release. Leonard Maltin defined it as an "Amateurish muddle about World War II *[that]* combines tired vignettes and newsreel footage narrated by Orson Welles. A waste of everybody's time."

Mick Martin claimed that the film "has lots of phony battle scenes, bad acting, and a poor script."

***

Roots: The Next Generations (1979)

Henry Fonda joined an impressive array of actors, many of them movie stars, to appear in an episode of *Roots: The Next Generations*. This new series was based on the last seven chapters of Alex Haley's best-selling novel, *Roots: The Saga of an American Family* (1976).

Aired on ABC-TV on February 18 to the 24th, *The Next Generations* was a sequel to the 1977 miniseries, *Roots: The Saga of an American Family*, which traced the lives of slaves forcibly imported to the U.S from Africa, and their descendants, many of them in Henning, Tennessee, from 1882 to 1967. The author of the original book which inspired Henry's TV series had been Alex Haley.

[Haley, incidentally, had been associated for years with Hugh Hefner's Playboy *magazine, which published his interview of Martin Luther King, Jr. in January of 1965. King's interview with Haley was the longest the reverend had ever granted to a journalist. Around the same time, in a kind of "reverse image" of the interview with Dr. King, Haley also interviewed George Lincoln Rockwell.*

Haley had also been the ghostwriter for The Autobiography of Malcolm X, *published in 1965. By 1977, the book had sold six million copies.]*

The first personality in the saga Haley composed was an 18th century 17-year-old named Kunta Kinte, who was captured in

Roots, The Next Generations: Left to right: **Richard Thomas, Olivia de Havilland, Henry Fonda**, and **Marc Singer**.

Gambia, sold into slavery, and shipped under horrible conditions to the United States.

At first, the producers, David L. Wolper and Stan Margulies, were reluctant to produce this controversial mini-series, but were talked into filming it. Ernest Kinoy was hired to write the screenplay, which was shot for a budget of $16.6 million, nearly three times as much as the cost of the 1977 original. The saga reached 120 million viewers in America and went international.

Henry was cast as Colonel Frederick Warner, a Confederate officer, with Olivia de Havilland, his former co-star, playing Mrs. Warner. It was somewhat daring for both of them to appear before millions of American viewers as champions of slavery.

De Havilland had known Henry since the 1930s. In those days, she was involved in a torrid romance with his best friend, James Stewart. At the time, they had considered getting married.

"My regret," she told Henry, "is that you and I didn't co-star together as Mr. and Mrs. Ashley Wilkes in *Gone With the Wind*."

"Mine too," was all he had to say in answer to that.

Also appearing in *Roots, The Next Generation* was an array of talented actors who included a few big names such as Andy Griffith, Diahann Carroll, Norman Fell, Ossie Davis, James Earl Jones, Robert Culp, and a most unlikely choice, the Post Toasties heiress, Dina Merrill, who had once owned Mar-a-Lago.

Marlon Brando, a champion of civil rights for African Americans, phoned the producers and asked to be cast as George Lincoln Rockwell. Brando won an Emmy for his performance.

[A former U.S. Naval commander, Rockwell had founded the American Nazi Party. Loudly and frequently, he'd been broadcasting some of the most controversial views in America, denying the Holocaust and accusing Martin Luther King, Jr., of "being a tool of Jewish Communists." In a speech, he praised Hitler as "the White Savoir of the 20th Century."]

Haley ran into trouble after *Roots* was published. Author Harold Courlander sued him for plagiarism, charging that he had infringed on his novel, *The African*, the saga of a boy captured by slave traders.

Haley finally admitted that some passages from *The African* made it into *Roots*. The case was settled out of court in 1978 for $650,000.

***

Meteor (1979)

"*The Swarm*" should have taught me to avoid future disaster films," Henry said. "But fool that I am, I signed for a cameo in a last-ditch attempt to pump more blood out of yet another one. It was called *The Meteor*."

What had tempted him to sign for his portrayal of the President of the United States was that the script had been penned by Edmund H. North and Stanley Mann, who had scored big in their movie, *The Day the Earth Stood Still* (1951), one of the best sci-fi films ever made.

Meteor's plot premise follows a group of scientists struggling

Left photo: The fiery, real-life American Nazi, **George Lincoln Rockwell**.

Right photo: **Marlon Brando** portraying him in *Roots, The Next Generations*.

Left: A poster for ***Roots, The Next Generations*** and (*right*), a mature, post-Post Toasties and post Mar-a-Lago **Dina Merrill**.

with Cold War politics after computers predict that an asteroid has been detected that's on a collision course with Earth. This five-mile wide, high-velocity fragment will lead to the extinction of most of the species on the planet. Smaller asteroid fragments preceding the arrival of the meteor are the first to wreak havoc.

Ronald Neame was the film's director, and he hired a post-007 Sean Connery as Dr. Paul Bradley, the film's leading man. The leading lady was Natalie Wood, with whom Henry had last starred in *Sex and the Single Girl* (1964), a very different picture.

Other stars were Karl Malden as Harry Sherwood; Brian Keith as Dr. Alexi Dubov; Martin Landau as General Adlon; Trevor Howard as Sir Michael Hughes, and Joseph Campanella as General Easton.

Shooting began on January 9, 1978, but the movie wasn't released until eighteen months later because the many special effects that needed to be processed and tweaked.

Although the film was allocated a budget of $16 million, it generated only $6.4 million at the box office.

Critics were vicious, one reviewer finding the "romance" between Wood and Connery less convincing than that of Ma Kettle with James Bond.

The stars of the disaster film, *Meteor*, were **Sean Connery** and **Natalie Wood**, pictured above. In a cameo, Henry Fonda once again was cast as the President of the U.S. From the Oval Office, he orders the launching of nuclear missiles to destroy a meteor heading to destroy the earth.

Connery had far more success as Secret Agent 007 James Bond. He ranked *Meteor* as the low point of his career. So did his critics.

Meteor evolved into one of the biggest flops of the decade. *New Statesman* wrote, "It's not so much a disaster movie as a disaster itself."

Then, just as everyone thought they'd seen enough of **Henry Fonda** emulating an American President *(Who does he think he is, Ronald Reagan?)* he appeared behind a much-enlarged replica of the Seal of the President of the United States (who could possibly miss it?), in this "*shake 'em and wake 'em*" suspense drama (*Meteor*) that everyone disliked.

Fonda's previous and most memorable performance as a U.S. President had been in *Fail-Safe* (1964). In it, a squadron of SAC bombers is called back from their pre-defined mission to destroy Moscow, but the message does not reach them.

In a desperate call to the Kremlin, Fonda agrees to order American bombers to eradicate New York City as a means of avoiding World War III.

Philip Lisa wrote, "Into every actor's life, a little rain must fall. In Connery's case, it was a shower of meteors."

Another critic claimed, "This is not just a film about a disaster, it IS the disaster."

Janet Maslin of *The New York Times* claimed, "Henry Fonda has played the President so much, he ought to be him."

Meeting Henry again, many months after the release of their film, Connery told him, "*Meteor* was the worst piece of shit I've ever been in, and that includes my 1956 movie, *Tarzan's Greatest Adventure*."

***

City on Fire (1979)

Two fabled stars of yesterday, Henry Fonda and Ava Gardner, were asked to appear in cameo roles in *City on Fire*. Yet another disaster movie (despite Henry's previous vows never to appear in one again), it revolved around a disgruntled ex-employee who sabotages an oil refinery, setting an entire city on fire. Although no city was specifically mentioned in the film, it was shot in Montréal.

As the city's fire chief Albert Risley, Henry fights a losing battle against the roaring flames. He sums it up: "All is takes is one man with a match to destroy a city."

Canadian director Alvin Rakoff had helmed some of the world's finest actors, including Laurence Olivier, Peter Sellers, Judi Dench, Rex Harrison, and Rod Steiger. He had given Sean Connery his first leading role when he was an unknown extra. He also had nurtured the talent of Michael Caine.

Rakoff was hoping that his film would ride to success on the coattails of that other "blazing" movie, *The Towering Inferno* (1974).

The actual star of the picture was Barry Newman as Dr. Frank Whitman, who treats thousands of burn victims. A Bostonian, Newman was an actor of stage, screen, and television, having been nominated for Golden Globe and Emmy awards. He was known for his portrayal of Kowalski in *Vanishing Point* (1971).

Susan Clark, who had worked with Henry in *Madigan* (1968) played Diana Brockhurst-Lautrec, a socialite involved in an affair with the city's corrupt mayor, William Dudley.

The mayor's role went to Leslie Nielsen, whose career would span 60 years, as he appeared in 100 films and 150 television programs, portraying more than 200 characters. He would go on to gain recognition for his deadpan comedy performances in such films as *Airplane* (1981). Critic Roger Ebert labeled him "the Laurence Olivier of Spoof."

Henry had long known Shelley Winters, whose career had dimmed to the point where she was accepting minor roles such as that of the nurse, Andrea Harper.

Another fading star, Ava Gardner, played an alcoholic reporter, Maggie Grayson.

James Franciscus, as "Jimbo," her assistant, lunched with Henry and talked of their long-ago escapades on the French Riviera when he was having an affair with his daughter, Jane.

Shot on a budget of $3 million, *City on Fire* garnered only $750,000 at the box office.

Vincent Canby of *The New York Times* wrote, "The Japanese do this sort of disaster movie much, much better."

Variety cited Fonda for "being an amazingly slow fire chief."

***

City on Fire: Even the faded charms of **Ava Gardner** and **Shelley Winters** (cast as a well-meaning but shrill and frumpy nurse) couldn't rescue it from its firebombing by critics. On the right, above, Shelley appears in glam, more seductive days.

The Oldest Living Graduate (1980)

The Oldest Living Graduate was telecast live on April 7, 1980. A presentation on NBC-TV, it was the third and final play of a series known as *A Texas Trilogy*. The drama by Preston Jones had first been presented in its entirety at the Dallas Theatre Center in 1975.

Broadcast live from the Southern Methodist University, the drama starred Henry Fonda, George Grizzard, Cloris Leachman, and Timothy Hutton. When Henry encountered Grizzard, the actor confessed, "The biggest disappointment in my career was that you and I didn't get to star as the male leads in *Who's Afraid of Virginia Wolff?* (1966).

In Henry's 1962 film, *Advise and Consent*, Grizzard, a native son of North Carolina, had starred as an unscrupulous senator.

Before working with Henry again, Grizzard had recently completed the Western, *Comes a Horseman* (1978), alongside Henry's daughter, Jane. In *Comes a Horseman*, the other co-stars had included Jason Robards and James Caan.

Much of the action in *The Oldest Living Graduate* takes place in the summer of 1962 in the den of the Kincaid family's ranch-style

house on the outskirts of Bradleyville, Texas.

Henry, as Col. J.C. Kincaid, played the oldest living graduate of a southern military academy who refuses to change his habits, lifestyle, and points of view. His son, Floyd (Grizzard), tries to talk him into retiring, but he stubbornly refuses When confronted with the *hoopla* being focused on his status as "the oldest living graduate" of the nearby military academy, he becomes even more sour, miserable, and truculent.

At the end of the telecast, Henry appears as himself to make an announcement. The author of the play, Preston James, had died earlier that day.

***

Gideon's Trumpet (1980)

Even as his health continued to decline, Henry's agents continued to send him scripts for stage, film, and TV roles. He declined most of them, preferring quiet days and nights at home with his beloved Shirlee.

One made-for-television script, *Gideon's Trumpet*, intrigued him because it was the work of author David W. Rintels, who had penned a memorable biography of Clarence Darrow. Henry had brilliantly portrayed Darrow on the stage.

Its premiere was telecast on April 30, 1980 on CBS's Hallmark Hall of Fame. Henry's friend and former co-star, John Houseman, was both the executive producer and one of the co-stars, portraying the Chief Justice of the U.S. Supreme Court.

The movie depicts the historical events before and during the 1963 Supreme Court case of the Gideon vs. Wainwright that established the right of a lawyer for criminal defendants who could not afford one. After the ruling in Gideon's favor, its precedents sparked nationwide (and global) consequences.

Clarence Earl Gideon was an actual person, a semi-literate Florida drifter who was falsely accused of breaking and entering an establishment when he was drunk. He did not have enough money to pay a lawyer in court, and he was found guilty and sentenced to five years in jail.

He spent a lot of time in the prison library reading up on the law. Finally, he wrote a letter to the U.S. Supreme Court about his case. Amazingly, the justices heard his plea, and he was granted a second trial in which he was found not guilty and released.

Henry was assigned the role of the down-and-out Gideon, later pronouncing it as "fascinating."

Jose Ferrer was cast as Abe Fortes. Other justices of the court were portrayed by Sam Jaffe, Dean Jagger, and William Prince, among others.

The prison scenes were shot at the Men's Correctional facility in Chino, California, using prison inmates as extras.

Making a rare appearance was the Canadian-born actress, Fay Wray, cast as Edna Curtis. In 1933, Wray had immortalized herself as the female lead (Ann Darrow) in the horror film, *King Kong*.

Her scene with the giant ape atop the Empire State Building became one of the most memorable in motion picture history. Later, in a career that spanned six decades, she was referred to as "the Beauty who Tamed the Beast," and "The Original Scream Queen."

As he aged, whenever someone offered him a role he thought he was right for, **Henry Fonda** was never shy about his declining physicality, frail health, and diminished good looks.

Here, he appears ill and almost "used up" in his end-of-life portrayal of the self-educated prisoner who changed the face of America's legal defense system.

Henry Fonda wasn't the only near-decrepit actor from the Golden Age to appear in *Gideon's Trumpet*:

Fay Wray, shown above as she appeared in *King Kong* (1933), made an appearance in it before she died.

Henry was intrigued by her and lunched with her. She revealed that Jean Harlow had been offered her role in *King Kong*, but that she had not been available. "I was paid $10,000 for my performance, and *King Kong* saved RKO from bankruptcy."

Wray died on August 8, 2004, and two nights later, the Empire State Building was dimmed for fifteen minutes in honor of her iconic role in *King Kong*.

Robert Kennedy—then the Attorney General of the United States—commented on the Gideon case: "The whole course of legal history was changed by Clarence Earl Gideon."

***

Showdown at the Adobe Hotel (1981)

Henry had first appeared on stage in 1925 in Omaha. His last performance on stage was on February 10, 1981, in Stamford, Connecticut at the Hartman Theater in a premiere of *Showdown at the Adobe Hotel*. It ran for 24 performances.

The play was written by Edwin Sherin, who had directed Henry in *First Monday in October* about the Supreme Court. Henry was cast with Cecilia Hart and Art Lund as his supporting players.

As described by Dan Hulbert, Henry played "a stooped, unsteady, temperamental old coyote who spends long hours in a cane chair beside a Texas Interstate, watching trucks whiz by and fearing he'll end up, like many of his friends, flat on his back in a nursing home or eating dog food in some run-down boarding house up north.

In an interview with Hubert, Henry recalled his days as a young man when he'd lived in Connecticut. He also discussed the differences of regional theater vs. Broadway.

"Regional theater, after all, is the most exciting place in the theater world today. It's the answer to a sick theater on Broadway. It's regrettable, it's obscene the money they get for the thing they produce. The musicals and so on. The really good plays don't get put on. It's discouraging to producers. Broadway is not the goal anymore."

***

Here's an up-close-and-personal, autographed by Henry playbill from the brief run, off Broadway at a theater in Hartford, of *Showdown at the Adobe Hotel*.

Upper photo shows a frail but valiant **Henry Fonda** emoting onstage with **Cecilia Hart**.

Summer Solstice (1981)

With Shirlee at this side, Henry flew to Boston, where they then drove to Cape Cod. It was here that he would shoot his last movie, a made-for-television romantic drama, *Summer Solstice*, to be telecast on ABC-TV on December 30, 1981.

As he told his wife, "I'm back on Cape Cod, right where I started from." He spoke of his struggling days as an actor. He'd already shot his last feature film, *On Golden Pond* (also 1981) with Katharine Hepburn and his daughter Jane.

[For more on the crafting and filming of On Golden Pond, *refer to an upcoming chapter of this book, where it's reported from the point of view of his daughter and co-star, Jane.]*

He was waiting for its release.

On the set, director Ralph Richardson greeted Henry and ushered him over to the dressing room of his co-star, Myrna Loy, who had arrived on the Cape the night before.

Both Henry and Loy had struggled to memorize their lines from the script by Bill Phillips. It was the saga of an aging couple, Josh and Margaret Turner. At least some of their scenes unfolded on the same beach where they had first met decades before.

"So," Loy said to Henry. "We've come to this little nostalgic drama. The great Henry Fonda and Miss Myrna Loy—a combination that would have guaranteed box office in the late 1930s and '40s. We've both

Left photo: Director **Ralph Rosenblum** on location in Wellfleet, Massachusetts, with **Henry Fonda** (center) and **Myrna Loy** during the filming of *Summer Soltice*, one of their last hurrahs. *Right photo:* **Loy** in her youthful, glamourous, A-list glory.

arrived. And now it's twilight time."

"Look at it this way," he answered. "You and I were born in the same year—1905. You in the dusty streets of Helena, Montana, me in Omaha, Nebraska, a town that was still living the days of the Old West, stubbornly refusing to join the 20th Century. Considering our origins, I think we've done damn well for ourselves."

The two fading stars worked in smooth harmony together. When they weren't needed on camera, they spoke of their pasts, sharing moments together. Amazingly, she had seen more of his movies than he had. He shared his secret: "I try to avoid seeing any of my previous films that would cause me embarrassments."

In contrast, he had seen all of her major films.

She told him stories of her early life he'd never heard before: "I was discovered by Natacha Rambova, Valentino's second wife. She was a lesbian and fell madly in love with me. She got me minor roles as a vamp. One of them called for me to play a woman of Asian descent. That all changed when I was cast as Nora Charles opposite William Powell in *The Thin Man* (1934)."

Each of them agreed on the films that immortalized them as icons, respectively. For him, it was *The Grapes of Wrath* (1940). For her, it was Samuel Goldwyn's *The Best Years of Our Lives* (1946), a drama about civilians returning home from the battlefields of World War II. Her co-star had been Fredric March.

At the end of filming for *Summer Solstice*, Henry hugged Loy and kissed her goodbye. "Oh, Hank, where do we go from here?" she said. "The time has come for me to retire from pictures. I've given it all. There's nothing left for me to give!"

"Me, too," he said. "I've booked a date for Forest Lawn, or perhaps I'll ask to be buried somewhere on the wild plains of Nebraska."

***

By the time he and Shirlee arrived back in Bel Air, Henry's physical condition had weakened.

Unaware of his frailties, a Broadway producer offered him a script that called for him to play Harry Hopkins, confidant of Franklin D. Roosevelt. Henry rejected it. He knew he'd never fly to the East Coast, or appear on a stage, ever again.

A final offer intrigued him. Another producer wanted to stage a one-man show with him talking about and reading from the works of Walt Whitman.

That never happened. The Grim Reaper was on His way, and He'd scheduled a "date" with Henry at L.A.'s Cedars-Sinai Hospital.

Part Two
JANE

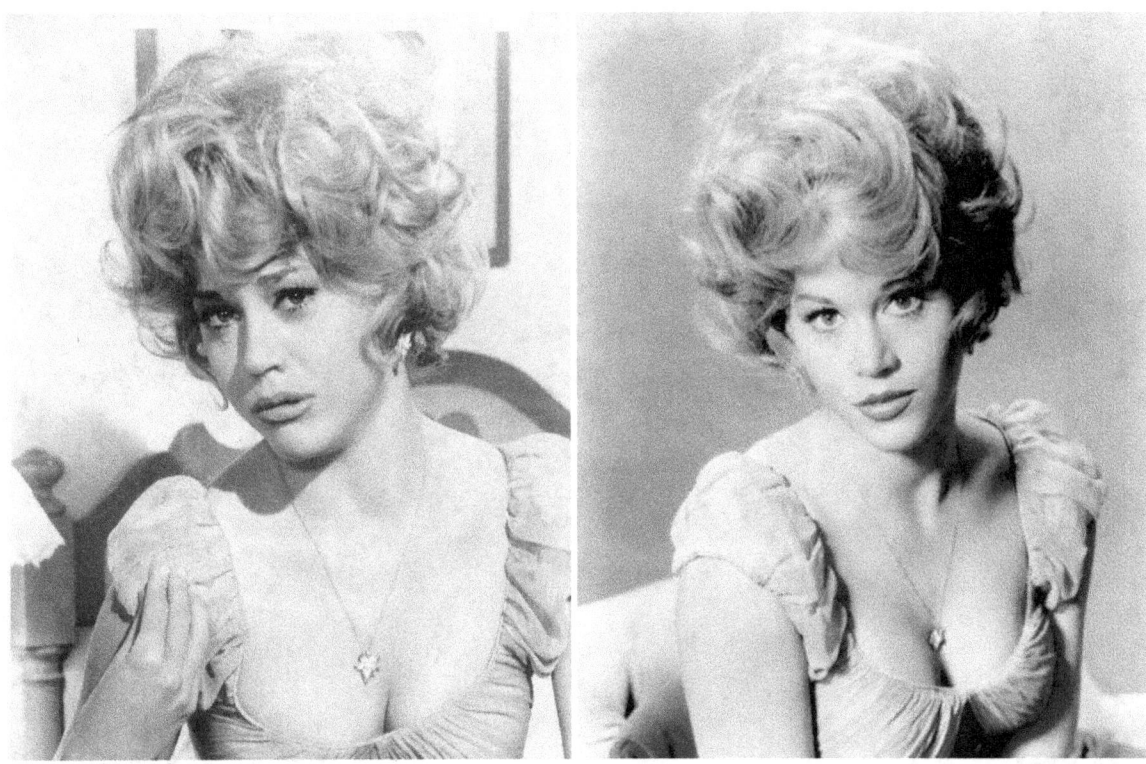

A battered, self-tormented, and drug-addicted soul, Tennessee Williams, sought help from a psychiatrist, who convinced him to write an unabashedly heterosexual play. The uneven result, written in 1960, was the soporific stage drama, *Period of Adjustment,* an effort forever after judged as one of his lesser efforts.

In 1962, the beautiful and fetching quasi-neophyte, **Jane Fonda** appeared in its film adaptation. In both photos above, she appears as the camera captured her in that almost-forgotten film which made only a modest profit but got Jane nominated for a Golden Globe award.

She had, at first, dreamed of a stage career, but during the making of this film, "I decided to become a movie star instead, even though the screen is far more ego-battering, and working in Hollywood gives one a certain expertise in the field of prostitution."

HERE'S JANE!

As she appeared in films, incidents, and episodes highlighted in VOLUME ONE (*Henry Fonda, He Did It His Way*) **of this two-part triple biography.**

Coronet
November, 1960
p. 64

A Jane To Be Fonda

CHAPTER FIVE

JANE FONDA

Lady of Contradictions & Mistress of the Unexpected

THE CHAPMAN REPORT
Jane stars with Shelley Winters in what one critic called
"The sexiest mainstream movie ever made."

PERIOD OF ADJUSTMENT
Jane plays a newlywed married to a young man nervous about taking off his jockey shorts.
Blame Tennessee Williams for this one

MARILYN MONROE
Jane dines with the doomed blonde goddess after Marilyn's weekend in Palm Springs with JFK

IN THE COOL OF THE DAY
As a dying, tubercular figure inspired by Camille,
Jane steals Peter Finch (playing a "piss-pot and hell-raiser")
from the sadistic Angela Lansbury

SUNDAY IN NEW YORK
"I played the only 22-year-old virgin left in Manhattan," Jane claims.
The dude editors at *The Harvard Lampoon* define her as "the year's worst actress"

CAT BALLOU
Jane shoots to bankable stardom in this Western spoof of a gun-totin'
siren who exudes sex appeal, even when robbing a train.

Henry Fonda's relationship with his children, Jane and Peter, was sometimes described as emotionally distant.

In an interview, he admitted, "I was not a good father. I figured it best if I stayed out of their way and let them pursue their own film careers as they chose. I wanted them to succeed because of their own hard work and not because they were coasting on my fame to achieve their goals."

In the 1960s, Henry paid scant attention to the movies starring his daughter Jane and his son, Peter,

Demure, sexy, and kittenish, **Jane** is very different from the *avant-garde* artist and activist she'd become.

Depicted immediately above and also to the left is **Jane Fonda** as she appeared in a harmless tale about academics, sports, and awakening sexuality alongside **Tony Perkins**, a college basketball star in *Tall Story* (1960).

Perkins, the not not-altogether heterosexual object of her perky adolescent affection, was engaged at the time in an affair with Tab Hunter.

In the trio of photos positioned vertically on the right, **Jane Fonda** appears in two of them with **Ephram Zimbalist, Jr.** in *Walk on the Wild Side* (1962).

Photographers and directors agreed that she was highly sexual and completely vulnerable—a winning formula that served her well in the years to come.

both of whom were blossoming into nationally recognized film stars. That was not surprising to those who knew Henry. He admitted that he didn't see most of his own pictures. "I can't stand to look at myself on the screen."

Jane's minor stage work at the Actors Studio and elsewhere served her well when she became a motion picture star in the "Swinging Sixties."

As previewed in **Volume One of this Fonda saga**, Jane made her screen debut in *Tall Story* (1960), starring Anthony Perkins. On and off the screen, she maintained a crush on this basketball star until she discovered he was gay. She later learned that he and Tab Hunter had been long-time lovers. Her future co-star, Robert Redford, appeared briefly in *Tall Story.*

The basketball story had focused on sweet, harmless love. In contrast, in Jane's next film, *Walk on the Wild Side,* she played a whore. Her co-star was the bisexual English actor, Laurence Harvey. The other leading star of the picture was Barbara Stanwyck, lusting after one of her in-house prostitutes, as portrayed by Capucine. Anne Baxter was cast in a role not worthy of her talents.

Paul V. Beckley of the *New York Herald Tribune* wrote, "Jane Fonda is a bouncy, wiggly, bratty little thief and prostitute, and she seems more like a Nelson Algren character than anyone else in the picture."

At around the time Henry was starring in such movies as *Advise and Consent* and *Fail Safe.* Jane went on to make *The Chapman Report.* (See below.)

Throughout the 1960s, as reviewed in this and upcoming chapters of this book, she averaged about two pictures a year, such movies as *Sunday in New York,* where she had Rod Taylor panting after her.

She and Jim Hutton appeared as newlyweds in Tennessee Williams' *Period of Adjustment.*

Newsweek declared that "Jane Fonda is the loveliest and most gifted of all our new young actresses."

But to spoil that accolade, the "bad-assed boys at the *Harvard Lampoon* named her as "the year's worst actress."

Half of the decade had already disappeared by the time she was cast in the title role of Cat Ballou in a Western spoof alongside Oscar-winning Lee Marvin. It was a hit and shot her up into the sky of bankable stars.

In that movie, she went from a schoolmarm to a gun-totin' wildcat anti-heroine. It received five Oscar nominations and became one of the top films released in 1965.

In the 1960s, a lot of Jane's life was spent in France, where she became emotionally involved with the *avant-garde* French director, Roger Vadim, later marrying him. Her days making movies abroad and her tortuous relationship with Vadim are previewed in a later chapter of this book.

Her most famous film with Vadim was the notorious *Barbarella* (1968), in which she was either scantily clad or nude.

As the 1960s came to an end, Jane starred in one of her greatest films, now hailed as a movie classic, *They Shoot Horses, Don't They?.* Her performance earned her a Best Actress Oscar nomination.

THE CHAPMAN REPORT: It was a scandalous, potboiling novel which was later adapted into a scandalous, potboiling movie.

Jane Fonda, the producers decided, was perfect as a sexually curious but deeply repressed participant in the early manifestations of the sexual and lifestyle revolutions then sweeping across the media landscapes of America.

Hugh Hefner, subject of a Porter and Prince. Blood Moon biography published in 2018, was the fast-rising magazine and lifestyle mogul everyone was watching at the time.

***

The Chapman Report (1962)

Jane's third film, *The Chapman Report,* gave her star billing alongside Shelley Winters. Its director was George Cukor, who had long been known for helming such legends as Greta Garbo and Katharine Hepburn. Privately, he was also known for his lavish gay lifestyle and the Sunday afternoon nude pool parties he regularly hosted.

Darryl F. Zanuck Productions shot it for a release through Warners. As featured supporting players, it included Claire Bloom, Efrem Zimbalist Jr., Glynis Johns, Ray Danton, Cloris Leachman, Chad Everett, and Jack Cassidy.

Jane heard that the key roles featured both a nymphomaniac and a woman who was frigid. "I dressed up like a whore and presented myself to Cukor only to learn that Bloom would play the nympho. He cast me instead as the frigid widow, Kathleen Brady. She is interviewed by researcher Paul Redford (Zimbalist). They fall in love, and she is frigid no more once she beds him."

Cukor's direction to Jane was "to look frigid cold with a tight lip and to speak with an upper-class accent. When you smile, make it country club."

The movie was based on the best-selling novel by Irving Wallace released in 1960 about researchers conducting anonymous sex surveys of American women.

After helming Jane, Cukor said, "She has a lot of talent, but her main problem is her tendency to overact."

Stanley Kaufman in *The New Republic* wrote that "A new talent is rising—Jane Fonda. Her light is hardly under a bushel, but as far as adequate appreciation is concerned, she might as well be another Sandra Dee."

The Chapman Report was unsuccessful at the box office, although one critic hailed it as "the sexiest mainstream movie ever made."

At the end of the shoot, in May of 1961, a call came in for Jane from the French director, Roger Vadim, who wanted to meet her for lunch at the Beverly Wilshire Hotel. "I was terrified," she told friends. "Based on his reputation alone, I feared he might rape me if we were ever alone together. I down-dressed in blue jeans and wore no makeup. However, I found him kind and considerate."

Later, she told George Cukor, "Under no circumstances will I work with Mr. Vadim."

MAJOR-LEAGUE TALENTS AS LADIES OF THE BOUDOIR

Four tough, skeptical onscreen survivors of L.A.'s singles scene: Left to right: **Claire Bloom, Glynis Johns, Shelley Winters,** and **Jane Fonda,** each a beneficiary of "sexual therapy" and "sexual healing" in *The Chapman Report.*

Ty Hardin emerged in the late 1950s' era of blonde beefcake when studly male actors began dropping obvious hints of raw meat, hot and throbbing.

Here, he appears in *The Chapman Report* with **Glynis Johns,** noted for her British, sweet-as-honey voice and enormous talent. Their highly confrontational scene was described by some viewers as foreplay.

***

Period of Adjustment (1962)

When it was finished, Henry attended a screening of *Period of Adjustment* (1962), but only because it was by Tennessee Williams. Its plot focused on newlyweds, Jane and Jim Hutton, who arrive at the home of his friend, Anthony Franciosa, finding that he, too, is having marital problems.

"I went expecting another *Streetcar Named Desire* or at least *Suddenly, Last Summer,*" Henry said. "I could not believe that Tennessee wrote this silly little fluff piece. I'm sure it was by Neil Simon."

MGM hired George Roy Hill, who had directed the play on Broadway, to make his film debut with the Williams work. Isobert Nennart wrote the screenplay, which would turn Jane Fonda into a first-rate movie star, and win her a Best Actress Golden Globe Award. Hill rounded out the cast with Anthony Franciosa, Jim Hutton, and Lois Nettleton.

The plot focuses on George (Hutton) and Isabel (Jane), who have just been married, and it's not going well. He drives to the home of his best friend, Ralph Baitz, portrayed by Franciosa, finding that he is estranged from his wife, Dorothea (Nettleton).

On the set, Franciosa warmly greeted Jane with a hug and kisses. She had recently worked with his former wife, Shelley Winters, on filming *The Chapman Report*, and he knew that Shelley had gossiped to her (and a lot of other people, too) about very personal details, including "that one."

A New Yorker, Franciosa had begun his career on Broadway in *A Hatful of Rain*, in which he'd been cast as the brother of a drug addict. He later reprised the role on screen. In time, he would go on to star in such films as *A Face in the Crowd* (1957).

Cast as the alienated wife of Franciosa, Lois Nettleton was a film, stage, radio, and television actress. She was ten years older than Jane.

In 1948, she came very close to winning the title of Miss America. The following year found her on Broadway understudying for Barbara Bel Geddes in *Cat on a Hot Tin Roof.*

She told Jane, "Mostly I've been wandering in and out of TV series, everything from *Gunsmoke* to *The Mary Tyler Moore Show.*"

As Jane's new husband, Jim Hutton was three years her senior but looked even younger than her. His credentials were fairly weak. He is best remembered for his portrayals of Ellery Queen in the 1970s TV series of the same name. He and actress Paula Prentiss co-starred in four movies, the biggest hit being *Where the Boys Are* (1960).

Surprisingly, in an upcoming picture *(Sunday in New York)* starring Jane, he was cast in a brief, uncredited cameo where he's seen in a rowboat listening to his radio.

Hutton would die early, at the age of 45, from liver cancer. His son, Timothy Hutton (born in 1960), also became an actor.

His father married twice yet maintained a 15-year affair with model Yvette Vickers.

Coincidentally, at the time Jane was shooting *Period of Adjustment*, she dined twice with Marilyn Monroe, who at the time was shooting *Something's Got to Give* for Fox. That is, whenever she showed up on the set. (Mostly,

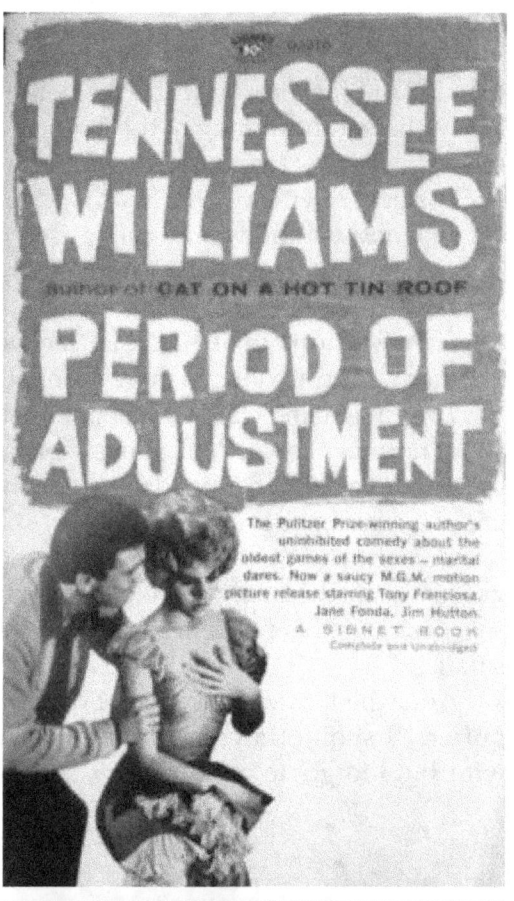

The sexually sophisticated veteran of a six-year marriage, the character played by **Tony Franciosa** tries to guide the newlywed portrayed by **Jane Fonda** into a marital bed with her shy, insecure, and awkward groom, played by Jim Hutton.

During rehearsals for *Period of Adjustment*, the director advised her "to play it like Marilyn Monroe."

she didn't show up.)

At their first dinner, Marilyn had just returned from Palm Springs, where she'd spent a weekend at the villa of Bing Crosby with President John F. Kennedy.

At the end of filming of the Tennessee Williams play, Jane phoned her dad to tell him, "At long last, I've come to realize that making movies is what I really want to do. Good or bad, bring 'em on."

Bosley Crowther of *The New York Times* wrote, "Jane Fonda is appropriately jittery and shallow. Her vague emotions and wispy feelings seem no deeper than her goose pimples. Could it be that Miss Fonda is trying to imitate Marilyn Monroe? The question is, is it worth your money to watch Jane and Hutton fight?"

Stanley Kaufman of *The New Republic* found Jane's performance "full of delights. She plays a nervous Southern bride anxious in more than one scene."

Time magazine claimed, "Shock merchant Tennessee Williams shocked everyone by writing a play about normal people. Well, almost normal. As a marriage counselor, he is somewhat less than convincing, but as a carpenter of situation comedy, he knows his trade. He wrote *Period of Adjustment* with the sly detail of a cannibal devouring a cookie."

One critic wrote, "Jim Hutton played the bridegroom on his honeymoon like a husband afraid to show his wife his penis, fearing she will find it too small."

After the film was released, Franciosa told a reporter, "I should have made Jane Fonda my next wife, but I forgot to propose."

***

In the Cool of the Day (1963)

After the release of her next film, an MGM production, *In the Cool of the Day* (1963), Jane expressed a wish: "I wish I had never made it."

Her co-stars, Peter Finch and Angela Lansbury, echoed the same sentiment.

Shot mostly in Greece, the film was directed by Robert Stevens and produced by John Houseman.

Finch had just made *I Thank a Fool (1962)*, also directed by Stevens, who had also worked on several occasions with Houseman in scattered television productions.

Stevens gave Jane the opportunity to almost direct herself in her scenes. He told Houseman, "Fonda's daughter knows more about movies than I do."

The Connecticut-born director hit his stride in the 1950s and 1960s, and had been a frequent director on the TV series *Alfred Hitchcock Presents*. By the 1970s demand for his work was very sporadic, and he retired in 1987.

Shortly before his death in 1989, he was beaten and robbed in his rented home in Westport, Con-

Two views of **Jane Fonda** with **Peter Finch** from *In the Cool of the Day*.

Unlike many of Jane's later "message films," it had absolutely nothing to do with politics or activism, and a lot to do with soapy drama and unrequited love.

Cast as a tubercular foreigner, Jane falls for a Britisher, Finch, who already has "a bloody wife" (Angela Lansbury).

necticut. He died shortly after from cardiac arrest.

Houseman, a longtime partner of Orson Welles, returned to MGM after a six-year absence to make this film. The movie was based on a 1960 novel by Susan Ertz, which was marketed as "a mixture of high romance and an erotic travelogue."

Houseman had worked with Jane's father on several occasions, including helming Henry when he toured in his one-man stage show, *Clarence Darrow,* a saga of the fabled attorney.

Both Houseman and Stevens agreed that their new movie was "a glorified soap opera" set against the romantic backdrop of the ruins of ancient Greece. The tubercular Christine (Jane Fonda) meets Murray Logan (Peter Finch), and they fall in love, beginning an adulterous relationship. Each of them is involved in a failing marriage: Finch is wed to Sybil (Angela Lansbury); Jane to Sam Bonner (Arthur Hill).

Their affair is doomed because Christine, a tubercular, is dying in a plot device perhaps inspired by Greta Garbo's movie, *Camille.* Near the end of the film, Christine (Jane) warns Murray (Finch) that she does not want him to have to deal with her chronic illness as she nears twilight time.

An Englishman, Finch, deserved better material. He was one of the most celebrated actors in the world at the time, in the same league as Richard Burton, Richard Harris, Rex Harrison, Anthony Quayle, Peter O'Toole, and Laurence Olivier.

AMID THE RUINS

Angela Lansbury, long before anyone ever heard of *Murder, She Wrote*, basks *In the Cool of the Day* beside the Acropolis.

He was married three times, once to Yoland Turnbull, a performer from South Africa. She wrote a memoir, *Finch,* that was subtitled *A Drunkard, a Womanizer, a Genius.* She painted a portrait of him as a "degenerate" pub crawler, Hollywood madman, rubber of elbows with the High and Mighty, a whoremonger, insomniac layabout…in other words, a holy terror."

Finch's most famous love affair was with the mentally disturbed Vivien Leigh. Some of his other "dollybirds," as he called them, included actresses Kay Kendall and Mai Zetterling.

Yolande's final summation of her former husband was as a "piss-pot and hell-raiser."

Author Mart Martin summed up Finch's other conquests: "Lots of other women, including a Sabena Air Lines stewardess, a German princess, the daughter of an African chieftain, a professor of Greek, and many hookers and starlets."

Houseman summed up Finch's appeal as a screen actor: "He was one of the best in the business, conveying a sense of world weariness punctuated with a deep sensitivity."

The very talented Lansbury also did not look with favor on *In the Cool of the Day*, especially having to portray Sybil Logan, Finch's wife. Lansbury described the character she played as "surly, spiteful, sarcastic, and sadistic."

Years later, when asked what it was like to work with Fonda and Finch, Lansbury said, "It is too awful to recall, and I have erased it from my memory."

The Canadian actor, Arthur Hill, was assigned the role of Jane's overly protective husband, Sam Bonner. There was a certain irony in his working with Jane. The role of George in the Broadway production of *Who's Afraid of Virginia Wolff?* had originally been offered to her father, but before Henry's agents didn't inform him

Jane found herself on screen with older, vastly more experienced actors who included **Constance Cummings**, a revered *grande dame* of the British stage.

Here's Cummings as she appeared with **Rex Harrison** in *Blithe Spirit* (1945), a romantic comedy in which a man and his second wife are haunted by the ghost of his first wife

of that until it was too late.

The role of George in the original Broadway production of *Virginia Wolff* went to Hill. He won a Tony Award for Best Dramatic Actor for his portrayal opposite Uta Hagen.

In the year Hill worked with Jane, he also starred with Marlon Brando in *The Ugly American*.

Constance Cummings, as Mrs. Nina Gellert, played Jane's nagging mother. Early in her career, Cummings headed south from Seattle to Los Angeles, where she was cast as a whore in the 1926 production of *Seventh Heaven*, but she went on to loftier roles. Samuel Goldwyn discovered her in New York and brought her to Hollywood. Between 1931 and 1934, she made an astonishing 20 films, including *Movie Crazy*, in which she played opposite Harold Lloyd.

In 1933, Cummings married the English playwright, Ben Levy, and moved to London, where she sustained a praiseworthy career as an actress. One of its highlights involved her starring on stage with Laurence Olivier in *Long Day's Journey Into Night*. She also originated the role of the harridan, Martha, in Edward Albee's *Who's Afraid of Virginia Woolf?* on the London stage.

In January of 1974, she was elevated to the rank of Dame Commander of the Order of the British Empire for her contribution to that country's entertainment industry.

In spite of its array of talent, *In the Cool of the Day* bombed at the box office. In *The New York Times*, Stanley Kaufman wrote that "Jane Fonda struggled in her role, whereas Finch safely slept throughout the movie."

However, he would go on to greater glory in such films as *Sunday, Bloody Sunday* (1971), in which he played it gay. He would also win a posthumous Best Actor Oscar for *Network* (1976).

He later referred to *In the Cool of the Day* as "that god damn stinker. I did it just for the money, and to see what it was like banging Jane."

It was never proven that Finch and Fonda ever sustained an actual affair, and his statement should be taken with more than a grain of salt.

As late as 2018, Jane recalled that *In the Cool of the Day* "was the worst movie I ever made. I wish that it had never been filmed. In fact, I don't even know if it were ever released."

***

Sunday in New York (1963)

This sex comedy had first played to Broadway audiences in 1961. It was the creation of playwright Norman Krasna, who was known for his screwball comedies, often centered on a case of mistaken identity.

After its success as a play, MGM and Seven Arts purchased its screen rights for $150,000, envisioning it as a vehicle for Natalie Wood and Warren Beatty. Both of these off-screen lovers rejected it. An aspiring young actor, Robert Redford, who had played the male lead in its Broadway production, wanted to reprise his role in the play's movie adaptation but was rejected.

Producer Everett Freeman hired the relatively untested Peter Tewksbury as the film adaptation's director. After serving as a U.S. Army Captain in the Pacific theater during World War II, he had returned to civilian life in the U.S. intent on finding a niche in the entertainment industry.

In the 1950s, he worked in television, directing *Father Knows Best*, which earned him an Emmy.

In spite of his success in television, it came as somewhat of a surprise when he was hired to direct a feature film like *Sunday in New York* with an all-star cast.

Jane Fonda was assigned the female lead—a 22-year-old virgin from Albany, freshly arrived in Manhattan.

The script called for the casting of three handsome young men. Tewksbury joked to the producer, "I'll have a lot of fun putting all these good-looking mother fuckers on my casting couch."

"You're too late," Freeman warned. "Maybe you might have gotten lucky a few years ago, but now, none of these guys has to go that route. All of them are stars in their own right."

Cliff Robertson was assigned the lead role of Adam Tyler, an airplane pilot, who is the older brother of Eileen Tyler (Jane Fonda).

In his private life, Robertson had been married to actress Cynthia Stone, the former wife of Jack Lemmon. By 1966, he would marry another actress, the heiress Dina Merrill of the Post Cereals dynasty. She had owned Mar-a-Lago before selling it for a bargain basement discount to Donald Trump.

Shortly before working with Jane, Robertson had played a young naval lieutenant, John F. Kennedy, in *PT-109*. By 1968, he would win a Best Actor Oscar for his performance in *Charly*.

A little-known incident in the life of Robertson occurred on September 11, 2001. Two days after his 78th birthday, Robertson, as a skilled pilot, was flying 7,500 feet above Manhattan's World Trade Center.

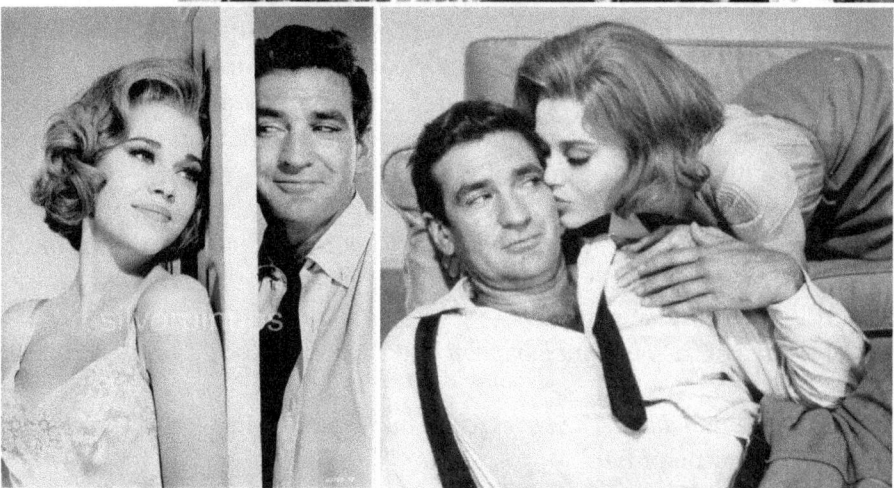

Jane Fonda, as Eileen Tyler, and **Rod Taylor** managed to showcase every phase of an unexpected romance during a swinging and highly sexual *Sunday in New York*. Those phases included an argument *(upper photo)* that ends behind locked doors and between the sheets.

Tyler was only one of the coyly flirtatious, sexually alluring hipsters Jane would become adept at portraying.

Suddenly, as he looked down, he saw a commercial plane crash into one of the Twin Towers. With something approaching panic, air traffic control ordered him to land his private Beechcraft Baron at the nearest airport, which turned out to be in New Jersey.

After safely landing, he learned of the unfolding terrorist attack on the skyscraper over which he had just flown.

He later appraised it as "a day to remember…and how!"

Rod Taylor was a studly, good-looking actor born in New South Wales, Australia. In *Sunday in New York*, he played Mike Mitchell, a Philadelphia music critic, who will ultimately win the prize—that is, Jane herself. He and Jane's character are powerfully attracted to each other, but a series of misadventures will have to occur before they hop into the sack together.

Taylor had morphed into tabloid fodder during the early 1960s thanks to his fling with the Swedish sex symbol, Anita Ekberg. At the time he met Jane, on the movie set, he had already married his second wife, model Mary Hilem.

As a young man, he'd first wanted to become a commercial artist like his mother. At college, he took art classes and occasionally posed frontally nude as a model.

However, after seeing Laurence Olivier on a tour of Australia in a production of *Richard III*, Taylor decided that he, too, wanted to be an actor.

Before starring with Jane, Taylor had received renown for some of his movie roles, notably *The Time Machine* (1960); *One Hundred and One Dalmations* (1961); and Alfred Hitchcock's *The Birds* (1963).

Cast as Russ Wilson, Robert Culp played Jane's former boyfriend, a handsome, athletic, and thoroughly self-absorbed scion of the richest family in Albany.

At the time Jane worked with Culp, he had just been cast in the upcoming role of Kelly Robinson on TV's *I Spy* (1965-1968). Both he and his co-star, Bill Cosby, would play secret agents.

Before joining Jane on the set, Culp had played Ensign George Ross, a Naval officer and friend of Lt. JFK in *PT-109* starring Cliff Robertson. Jane later referred to Culp as "the marrying kind" because he had had a total of five wives and five kids.

The script called for Jane to arrive at the chic Upper East Side apartment of her elder brother Adam (Robinson). She admits to him that she's still a virgin, and he more or less suggests that he, too, does not sleep around. Of course, the arrival of his girlfriend, Mona Harris (Jo Morrow) seems to disprove that.

One afternoon while he is away, Jane meets Mike (Taylor) and they get soaked in a rainstorm, hastily retreating to Adam's apartment. Adam, witnessing them together after returning unannounced and unexpectedly, instantly jumps to all the wrong conclusions.

The plot becomes more complicated with the arrival of the estranged boyfriend (Culp), but it all works out in the end when, many months later, he learns that Jane has married Mike (Taylor), and is now living in Tokyo with their three daughters.

Although *Sunday in New York* was not a success at the box office, it did not put the studio into debt either. Made for a budget of $2 million, it took in that same amount in Canada and the U.S. combined.

In their review of this minor sex comedy, *Newsweek* reviewed Jane as "the loveliest and most gifted of all our new young actresses."

The boys at the *Harvard Lampoon* had a different point of view: "Jane Fonda is still the year's worst actress."

Stanley Kaufman at *The New York Times* said, "Miss Fonda has wit even if Krasna doesn't. I wonder what will become of her?"

Time magazine found that Jane's "winking wickedness turns out to be mostly eyewash. The plot is more to be pitied than censored."

During her filming of *Sunday in New York,* Jane had a reunion with her father, who was shooting *Fail Safe* (1964). Around the same time, her brother, Peter, was in the city co-starring with Warren Beatty in *Lilith* (1964).

In 2018, Jane said, "I'm surprised that many people told me over the years how much they loved *Sunday in New York.* For God's sake, why?"

Her only reward for starring in the film was a paycheck of $100,000. Otherwise, for her, at least, it had been just another *ingénue* romp.

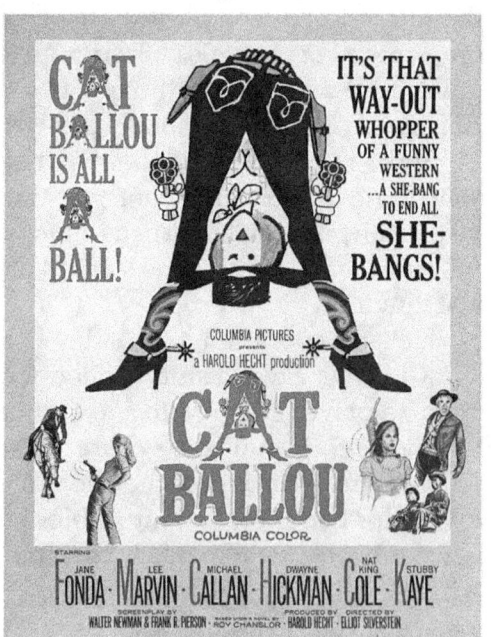

***

Cat Ballou (1965)

A Bostonian and Yale graduate, director Elliot Silverstein, thought he had discovered the ideal Western yarn when he read the screen treatment of *Cat Ballou.*

Walter Newman and Frank Pierson had turned the original (rather serious) novel by Roy Chanslor on which it was based into a cinematic spoof.

Before *Cat Ballou*, Chanslor had written the novel on which was based the film version of *Johnny Guitar* (1954). In it, Joan Crawford starred wearing Western garb. Off screen, she seduced both of her leading men, Sterling Hayden and Scott Brady.

Silverstein decided that *Cat Ballou* would make the perfect vehicle for Ann-Margret in the title role, and with Kirk Douglas cast in a dual role playing both a boozy gunfighter named Kid Shellen and also a character known as Tim Strawn. The script called for Strawn to wear a silver *schnozz*, a metal "shield" to cover the mangled remains of what had once been his nose, bitten off in a brawl.

Ironically, Douglas rejected the dual role, and the agents for Ann-Margret did not even tell her of the film producers' offer. She later claimed that she would have loved playing Cat Ballou.

Silverstein had directed a small but notable output of films during the mid-20th Century. In addition to *Cat Ballou*, they included *The Happening; A Man Called Horse; Nightmare Honeymoon; The Car;* and *Flashfire*. The casting choices he made for *Cat Ballou* would shoot both its male and female leads into international stardom.

After wrapping *Sunday in New York,* Jane had flown to France, where she was living with the French director, Roger Vadim. While abroad, she made two films, *Joy House* (aka *Les Félins,* aka *The Love Cage,* 1964) and *Circle of Love* (aka *La ronde,* 1964), each of which will be previewed in an upcoming chapter.

At first, she was reluctant to star in such an offbeat film (*Cat Ballou*) in such an offbeat role, but Vadim talked her into it, even going so far as to travel from France to California to be with her during the shoot. They'd be living together in a rented villa in Malibu.

Interiors for the Western spoof would be shot in Los Angeles, the outdoor scenes near Colorado Springs.

Silverstein later admitted that when he first met Jane, he was physically attracted to her and intended to invite her out on a date. But when Vadim showed up on the set, he dropped that plan. "I heard this French director was 'a sex nut,' but he turned out to be a nice guy."

Marvin was introduced to Vadim on the first day of shooting. Almost immediately he told him, "I hate the French, and I hear you're part Russian. I loathe Russians even more than I hate frogs."

Writer James Brough said, "After playing 'Girl Next Door' roles, tarts and prostitutes, Jane Fonda was ready for some boisterous sex in *Cat Ballou*. It was a burlesque of every shoot-'em-up ever filmed since the reign of Bronco Bill. The titillating formula devised for her appearance mixed wide-eyed innocence and hot-lipped sex appeal, skin-clinging jeans, and plunging spangles. Jane was off to a galloping start as Hollywood's fastest and hottest Impossible Dream labeled as an 'American sex kitten.'"

As the killer, Ted Strawn, Lee Marvin was flashily dressed in snaky black, accented with the bizarre complement of his silver nose plate.

In his portrayal of the other personality (Kid Shelleen) he played in the film, Marvin was a

In *Cat Ballou*, a Western-themed "spoof," **Jane Fonda** (who appears as the title character in each of the photos on this page) plays a schoolmarm morphed into a "sexual outlaw."

Lee Marvin *(with Jane in the photo above)* portrays an evil gunslinger with an artificial *[i.e. prosthetic]* silver nose. According to many viewers, he "stole" the picture. For his efforts, he hobbled home with an Oscar.

drunken bum on a horse which seems to have as much personality as he does.

When Kid Shelleen comes to the aid of Cat Ballou, he is a drunken cowpoke whose pants fall down whenever he draws his gun. He is unable to hit a barn until he gets completely drunk, at which time he turns out to be a crack shot. He proves useless until Strawn kills Frankie Ballou (Cat's father).

When the town refuses to bring Strawn to justice, Jane morphs from a schoolmarm into a gun-totin' Annie Oakley-style sharpshooter.

Lee Marvin, noted for his prematurely gray hair and rasping voice, was the most bizarre actor with whom Jane had ever been cast. Before *Cat Ballou*, he had appeared for the most part in supporting character roles.

Marvin had been named after one of his ancestors, General Robert E. Lee, who led Confederate forces against Northern armies during America's Civil War. He was also directly descended from both Thomas Jefferson and George Washington.

As a youth, he'd gotten kicked out of one school after another for his bizarre behavior. During World War II in the Pacific theater, "I was shot in my ass by a Jap on Saipan. My ass was fucked up for all time, and the bullet severed my sciatic nerve."

"After my discharge, I headed west with my severed buttocks to play villains in movies. Unlike some actors in upcoming pictures, I would not be required to show my ass—say, like Jon Voight."

Reporters found that he could always be good for a quotable quote. When asked about Jane Fonda, he said, "She looks like a gal who's getting fucked a lot."

"As for John Wayne, he's the kind of guy who walks around yelling, 'Bring on more Japs!'"

"What does being a movie star mean? They engrave your name on Hollywood Boulevard, and some hound dog comes by and decides to shit on it," he said.

Marvin was one of the first stars to come out for gay rights. "Why should we care what someone free, white (or black) and 21 loves? If a gal wants to get off by having a guy shove a coke bottle in her ear, then let her have her sexual pleasure."

Marvin missed out on some roles that became classics. Originally, he and Marlon Brando had been cast together as co-stars in *Deliverance* (1972). But then something happened, and the co-starring roles went to Burt Reynolds and Jon Voight.

Marvin also rejected an offer to play General Patton "because I hate war."

Right after *Cat Ballou,* he attacked Vivien Leigh aboard *The Ship of Fools* (1965), a film based on the novel by Katherine Anne Porter. Yet off-screen, Leigh and Marvin became friends. Some said they were more than just friends.

Cat Ballou opens with a pair of troubadours, Nat King Cole and Stubby Kaye, singing "The Ballad of Cat Ballou."

Cole was "The Sunrise Kid" and Kaye "Sam the Shade." In the film's opening scene, they regale their audiences by singing about that gun-totin' gal who went from schoolmarm to a cowgirl hell-bent on avenging the murder of her father.

In *Ship of Fools* (1965), **Vivien Leigh** beats the hell out of a drunken and impertinent **Lee Marvin** after he attempts to rape her.

Years later, he said, "That beating was not play acting. She actually whipped me. For revenge, I visited her dressing room later and actually raped her. It wasn't rape, exactly. She asked me to go for a second round."

At one point, Jane dresses up as a prostitute for a rendezvous with Sir Harry Percival (Reginald Denny) and attempts to lure him into confessing that he was "the varmint" who ordered the slaying of her father. As they tangle, she kills him. In the aftermath, she's arrested, tried, and sentenced to be hanged.

Then "Uncle Jed" (Dwayne Hickman) appears, pretending to be a preacher. He cuts the rope from around her neck and opens a trap door. Just as she is slated to die, Cat falls through the trap door into a wagon, which her fellow gangsters use to rescue her. As a reunited team, they flee.

Denny, a noted English thespian, was perfectly cast into his role. Once the amateur boxing champion of Great Britain, he had broken into the flickers in 1911 and in time would migrate to Hollywood, where he starred with such legends as Katharine Hepburn and Greta Garbo. In 1920, he had appeared onstage with John Barrymore in *Richard III*. From there, the two actors became close friends and would work together in screen adaptations of Shakespeare's plays.

Dwayne Hickman was known in the 1960s as the title character in the hit TV sitcom, *The Many Loves of Dobie Gillis*. He was often confused with his younger brother, Darryl Hickman. As a child actor, Darryl had starred with Henry Fonda in John Steinbeck's *The Grapes of Wrath* (1940). The troubadours, Nat King Cole and Stubby Kaye, set the mood and tone for the action that was about to unfold on the screen. This would be Cole's last picture. During the shoot, he was on the road to death from lung cancer. A chain smoker, he died four months before the release of *Cat Ballou*.

Kaye was a singer and comedian who had originated the role of Nicely Johnson in both the stage and screen versions of *Guys and Dolls*.

Character actor Jay C. Flippen was cast as Sheriff Cardigan. During the filming of *Cat Ballou*, he suffered a minor injury in a scrape against a car door. It evolved into something major. His condition was complicated with a bad case of diabetes. The injury didn't get better, and his leg became afflicted with gangrene, which led to its amputation. He finished the Western in great pain.

[The amputation did not end his screen career, and he carried on until the final curtain in 1971. Until then, he was assigned to roles where he did not have to hide his disability, appearing in wheelchairs, for example.]

Bruce Cabot was assigned the minor role of Sheriff Maledon. He'll be forever remembered for his performance as Jack Driscoll in *King Kong* (1933), co-starring with Fay Wray and the Ape.

He would go on to make more than 100 movies, often starring with John Wayne, and later becoming known as one of the Duke's "regulars."

In 1939, he co-starred with Errol Flynn in *Dodge City*, and the two actors became close friends. In the 1940s, they were known for hostings of (or participation in) orgies at various private homes in Hollywood.

It was Lee Marvin who won the Best Actor Oscar that year, thanking his trusty horse, whom he claimed deserved half the credit.

Jane suddenly found herself in the enviable position of having starred in a hit picture. The fee she was paid for her subsequent movie shot up to $400,000, a lot of loot back then.

Cat Ballou became the seventh highest-grossing film of 1965. In time, the American Film Institute ranked it as the tenth-greatest Western of all time.

A reviewer for *The Monthly Film Bulletin* wrote, "The jokes in *Cat Ballou* are uneven, but the mood behind the film is happily

In his later years, with his career in decline, **Bruce Cabot** *(left)* took whatever movie role he could get.

His career highlight had come in 1933 when he rescued **Fay Wray** from the clutches of a monster ape in *King Kong*. By doing so, Cabot's place in movie history is assured.

Bruce Cabot, as Sheriff Maledon, *right*, appears here in *Cat Ballou* with **Dwayne Hickman** as a bible-toting preacher.

consistent."

Philip K. Schener of the *Los Angeles Times* weighed in, too: "I'm not in the majority, apparently. *Cat Ballou* is being hailed as a cowboy *Tom Jones*, or something of that sort, but it seems to me about as funny as a soundtrack burp."

Judith Crist in *The New York Herald Tribune* claimed, "Jane Fonda is marvelous as the wide-eyed Cat, exuding sweet feminine sex appeal every sway of the way. This *Cat Ballou* is just a honey."

Variety noted that "the film emerges maddingly successful, sparked by an amusing way-out approach and some sparkling performances, especially from Jane and Lee Marvin."

Bosley Crowther of *The New York Times* called it "a corny little film which does have flashes of good satiric wit. But under Elliot Silverstein's direction, it is mostly just juvenile lampoon."

Richard Coe of *The Washington Post* praised the movie as a "springy saga. What makes this fun is its style."

Pauline Kael in *The New Yorker* wrote that "Two Lee Marvins playing good and bad gunfighters is enough to suffice. Wasn't Nat King Cole enough? Do we really need Stubby Kaye? The movie is uneven, lumpy, coy, obvious, and self-consciously cute."

In *Cat Ballou*, **Jane Fonda** appears in lacy "virginal white" for her hanging for crimes she committed as a female outlaw. Don't worry: She gets rescued at the last minute.

The New York Times wrote, "Jane Fonda is a big-eyed, big-hearted grown-up child, a veritable Little Mary Sunshine who takes to gunning and robbing a train with the *gee-whiz* excitement of a youngster confronted with a huge banana split."

Although admitting that it was Marvin's picture, *Time* magazine heaped praise on Jane. "Actress Fonda does every preposterous thing demanded of her with a giddy sincerity that is at once beguiling, poignant, and hilarious. Wearing widow's weeds over her six-guns, she romps through one of the zaniest train robberies ever filmed, a throwback to Pearl White's hilarious heyday. Putting the final touches on a virginal white frock to wear to her own hanging, she somehow suggests that Alice in Wonderland has fallen among blackguards and rather enjoys it."

JANE FONDA, LADY OF CONTRADICTIONS AND MISTRESS OF THE UNEXPECTED

Here's Jane emulating a woman in the process of sexual awakening in *The Chapman Report*. America noticed.

CHAPTER SIX

JANE & HER FRENCH INVASION

JANE FONDA

aka "America's Answer to Brigitte Bardot" Moves to France and inaugurates an affair
with the French actor voted, prior to their meeting, as
"The Handsomest Man in the World" (Alain Delon)

ROGER VADIM

The Sexy French Director (Bardot's Ex), Enters Jane's Life.
"He was my new Svengali, and my life would never be the same."

Vadim, not God, Created Her:

BRIGITTE BARDOT

A Cinematic Icon, Gallic and Blonde, She Became Known as "France's Sex Kitten"

CATHERINE DENEUVE

"The Most Beautiful Woman in the World"

LA RONDE (aka CIRCLE OF LOVE)

Its Producers Rent a Mammoth Billboard Above Times Square.
It Features her Nude Effigy—Until Jane Sues.

THE CHASE

Back in California, Jane's Co-Stars are
MARLON BRANDO & ROBERT REDFORD
Despite a Spectacular Cast, Critics demolish it.
"Who will get lucky first?" asks a Columnist

In September of 1963, Jane flew to Paris, perhaps to establish roots there, as she was tired of the Hollywood scene. She met with French reporters and felt confident enough to address them in their native language.

MGM had dispatched her to Paris to star in *Joy House* (aka *Les Félins*, aka *The Love Cage*), to be directed by René Clement.

Her perception was that its script seemed unfinished, but she trusted Clement because he was one of the most distinguished directors in France, the winner of numerous awards. His star-studded epic, *Is Paris Burning?* (1965), written by Gore Vidal, would soon go over big in his native country. In the U.S., however, it bombed.

She told reporters that she had fallen in love with Paris when she was a student there studying art and working for *Paris-Match*.

She also spoke of her excitement at what was happening with the French film industry and how delighted she was to be in a film helmed by the distinguished Clement.

She also seemed familiar with some of the works of such New Wave names as Jean-Pierre Melville, Jean-Luc Godard, Louis Malle, and such Italian directors as Luchino Visconti and Michelangelo Antonioni. "I hope in my near future I will get to work with all of them."

She was also asked what she felt about working with Alain Delon. She had seen him in such movies as *Purple Noon* (1960) and *Rocco and His Brothers* (also 1960). "I can only play love scenes when I'm in love with my leading man. Alain is a beautiful young man, easy to fall in love with. I can't wait until his lips are on my own, followed by…whatever."

Vivien Leigh had rejected him for the role of the Italian gigolo in Tennessee Williams' *The Roman Spring of Mrs. Stone* (1961). "I don't want to work with a leading man who is prettier than I am."

***

Joy House (*aka Les Félins, aka The Love Cage;* 1964)

Even before Jane's arrival in France, René Clement had defined his upcoming movie as "a French mystery thriller in the style of Alfred Hitchcock." The director himself had written part of the script based on a novel by Day Keene.

Alain Delon was cast as Marc, a petty gangster on the run from crooks he had double-crossed.

Lola Albright, an American actress known for her brief affair with pre-presidential Ronald Reagan, had the third lead, playing Barbara.

The women meet Delon in a soup kitchen and move him into Albright's Gothic mansion. The Albright character is a bit weird, keeping a shrunken head in a jar. Her lover threatens to poison him.

The role of the wealthy widow had first been offered to Jeanne Moreau, who rejected it. Jane was cast as Melinda, the niece of Barbara. Marc (that is, Delon) suddenly realizes that he'll have to perform double boudoir duty.

The remainder of the plot, at least according to Stanley Kaufman of the *New Republic,* was not worth mentioning.

Throughout the shoot, Jane continued to face the fast-spreading comparison of herself as "America's answer to Brigitte Bardot."

At first, *Variety* had announced that the female lead had been assigned to Natalie Wood, but when she dropped out, she was replaced by Jane.

In discussing her first movie shot in France, Jane recalled, "There was chaos, rain, last-minute script changes. I fought sixty battles and won all of them. I was desperately trying to learn French, but I shot the movie in English. My voice was dubbed into French.

Acid-tongued Judith Crist in *The New York Herald Tribune* rated *Joy House* as one of the worst films of that year. She also claimed that Jane, as Melinda, was "impersonating *Baby Doll, The Mad Woman of Chaillot*, and Henry Fonda."

Jane's fling with Delon began almost at once and from all reports was rather torrid, enough so that it led to his breaking up with his mistress, Romy Schneider.

At the end of the shoot, Delon and Jane were photographed on the French Riviera toweling one another off.

Their romance ended during his filming of *The Yellow Rolls-Royce* (1964), when Shirley MacLaine entered Delon's life.

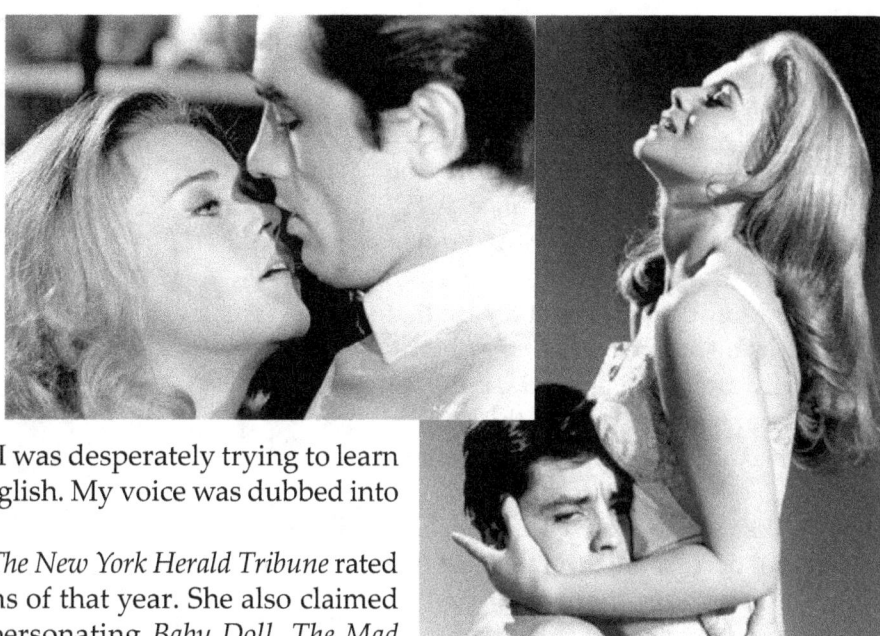

Two views of **Alain Delon** romancing **Jane Fonda** in *Joy House*.

She was being hailed more for her sex appeal than for her acting. At the peak of his sullen beauty, he was labled 'the biggest heartthrob in Europe."

***

Jane Fonda had first met Roger Vadim when she was an 18-year-old student studying in Paris. She was on a date with Christian Marquand, an actor, screenwriter, and director. He was often cast as a heartthrob in French films of the 1950s. Between his other affairs and marriages, he was also the longtime lover of Marlon Brando.

Marquand's first film appearance had occurred in 1946 when he portrayed a footman in Jean Cocteau's *La Belle et la bête (Beauty and the Beast)*. Marquand eventually ended up on that French author's casting couch. He would eventually be helmed by Vadim in *Et Dieu... créa la femme (And God Created Woman; 1956)*.

By that time,

Jane, by luck or through charm and her connections, fell into the cream of the *avant-garde* postwar arts universe of France: *Left to right,* three arts industry powerhouses, **Jean Cocteau, Christian Marquand,** and **Roger Vadim.**, all of whom maintained complicated and deeply intertwined personal, sometimes sexual, histories.

Vadim, Marquand's former roommate, had become his best friend. They would remain so for the rest of their lives.

Marquand had invited Jane on a date and decided to take her to Maxim's, the most famous restaurant in France. All of the legendary names of Paris had dined there, as had visiting movie stars from America. Marquand was not aware that Vadim was also dining there that night. But shortly after they arrived, an invitation was transmitted through the staff for Marquand and his "young schoolgirl date" to join Vadim at his table.

The historic meeting between Jane and Vadim occurred within the next five minutes. The young, *ultra avant-garde* director would change her life forever.

He was seated with an aspiring young actress, Annette Stroyberg, whom he would marry in 1958. At the time, she was pregnant by him. Soon, she would give birth to Nathalie Vadim. *[Ironically, one day Jane would become Nathalie's stepmother.]*

Although Jane had heard of Vadim, she was not impressed with him, having been told that he was "cynical, rotten to people, especially women, a *devoté* of teenaged girls, and a modern-day and dangerous kind of Svengali."

Vadim was not impressed with Jane, either. After she danced with Marquand, Vadim told his friend, "The Fonda girl has fat ankles."

The next day, Jane boarded a flight to Los Angeles. She would not encounter Vadim again until three years later.

By 1962, Vadim was entrenched within Hollywood's film community. At one point, it was suggested that Jane might be ideal as an American in a movie being considered for him to direct. During his final days in California, he phoned her agent and arranged for a meeting with her at the Beverly Hills Hotel, where he had rented a suite.

She agreed to the meeting, but with trepidation. "Considering Vadim's reputation," she recalled, "I feared that I might be raped." Therefore, she made herself anything but sexy and alluring.

Her agent had told her, "Try to look hot, promote yourself as a kind of American Brigitte Bardot, and show a lot of cleavage."

Jane did just the opposite and decided to make herself unattractive, showing up in a pair of blue jeans and a blouse described by Vadim as "rather masculine. In other words, Jane could have played a dyke."

She wore no makeup and looked as if she'd just come from running a mile on a southern California beach. Her windblown hair was a mess.

"Try as I might, I can't remember one god damn word of what we talked about," Vadim said. "Obviously, it was not about casting her in one of my upcoming films. That didn't happen, at least not at the time.

Stylish, fashionable, and connected, **Maxime's,** 3 rue Royale, Paris 8e. was the venue for Jane Fonda's *entree* into the stratosphere of the very stylish world of French arts and letters.

Here's a scene that emulates Maxime's from *Gigi* (1958) where **Louis Jourdan** guides **Leslie Caron** through the gastronomic labyrinth of what's been cited as one of the most breathtaking art nouveaux restaurant venues—polished, of course, for the cinematic lens—of France.

Se og Hør ("See and Hear") is a TV guide and celebrity journalism magazine published in three independent versions in Denmark, Norway and Sweden

On the front cover, **Annette Stroyberg**, a daughter of Denmark, poses with her husband, the ultra-avant-garde French-Russian filmmaker, **Roger Vadim.**

Yet I remembered her. There was something about the little vixen, but I didn't know what it was. Of course, I was impressed that she was the daughter of Henry Fonda. At the time, he was a legend."

Three years would pass before they met again.

In the meantime, she was hearing more and more about this "roving rake" named Roger Vadim, "seducer of the innocent, deflowerer of maidenheads, and all-around sex maniac who sometimes impregnated his beautiful captives."

She'd heard that he was not a *bona-fide* Frenchman, but actually the son of a libidinous White Russian military officer and pianist. Born in Paris on January 26, 1928, his birth name was Roger Vadim Plemiannikov.

But just who was this provocative and daring screenwriter/filmmaker who turned out lavish films with erotic qualities?

***

As Jane learned later, Vadim was of mixed blood, tracing his ancient ancestry back to the days of that great Mongol conqueror, Genghis Khan. Vadim's father, Igor Nikolaevich Plemiannikov, had emigrated from Imperial Russia before becoming a citizen of France. He was later appointed as France's Vice-Consul in Egypt and stationed in Alexandria. Later, he was posted to Turkey.

He met and married a French actress, Marie Antoinette Ardilouze.

When his father died, Vadim was nine. He and his mother returned to France, where she settled in the French Alps, where she ran a way station for fleeing Jews, refugees from Nazi Germany.

Vadim's mother later married Gerald Hanning, a much younger man who was an engineer, an urban planner, and a collaborator of Le Corbusier. It was later revealed that Hanning was a secret British agent.

After studying journalism at the University of Paris (but not graduating), Vadim was nineteen. He went to work as an assistant to film director Marc Allégret. Vadim and Allégret had met during Vadim's stint at the Théâtre Sarah Bernhardt. Allégret maneuvered the then-teenager onto his casting couch and was pleased with him, giving him a job that granted close contact and taking him home with him at night.

Born in Basel, Switzerland in 1900, Allégret had emigrated to Paris as a young man, hoping to study to become a lawyer.

There, he met the great French writer, André Gide, who became his lover.

In 1927, Gide and Allégret visited the Congo in Africa, and the young Vadim, who accompanied them, documented their trip on film.

That experience changed his mind about his career path. Dropping his intention of becoming a lawyer, and with Gide's encouragement, he aimed to become a film director.

In that new goal, he succeeded "beyond my wildest dreams," helming some fifty movies during the course of his career.

He also became known as a key player in the careers of not only Vadim, but Simone Simon, Michèle Morgan, Jeanne Moreau, Brigitte Bardot, Louis Jourdan (whom he seduced), Jean-Paul Belmondo, Gérard Philipe, and Odette Joyeux.

Vadim was one of the screenwriters who worked on *Maria Chapdelaine (The Naked Heart*; 1950), which had starred Michèle Morgan in both the French and English-language versions. She became the first leading lady Vadim would seduce, setting off a pattern that extended throughout the rest of his career as a director. *[He also managed to seduce many French actresses he did not direct.]*

Elegant and beautiful, Morgan was between marriages at the time. After she met Vadim, who was eight years her junior, she'd go on to become known as one of the great French actresses of the 20th Century.

Inspired by a turn-of-the-20th century novel, **Maria Chapdelaine** *(1950)* was a tragic tale of unrequited and misguided love in a logging town of French-speaking Québec.

With a script co-authored by Roger Vadim, It starred **Michelle Morgan,** (whom Vadim seduced), a star beloved by postwar French audiences.

Allégret helped launch her career by casting her in *Gribouille* in 1937.

When the Nazis invaded France in 1940, Morgan fled to Hollywood, where she signed with RKO. Her career never shot up in Tinseltown, though she did get cast in *Joan of Paris* (1942). She made *Higher and Higher* (1944) with Frank Sinatra and had a brief fling with him. Her great disappointment came when she lost the female lead opposite Humphrey Bogart in *Casablanca* (1942), the part going instead to the Swedish actress, Ingrid Bergman. She eventually worked with Bogie in 1944 when they co-starred in *Passage to Marseille*.

She returned to Paris, where her career blossomed as she succeeded in one critically received role after another in such films as Carol Reed's *The Fallen Idol* (1948) and *Marie-Antoinette Reine de France (Shadow of the Guillotine)* in 1955.

In 1969, when France awarded her the *Legion d'Honneur*, Vadim sent her a note: "Thanks for the memory."

RAREFIED LIONS OF THE FRENCH AVANT-GARDE

Long-time companions and partners, **Marc Allegret** (a mentor of Roger Vadim) and the then-impossibly famous **Andre Gide** in 1920.

After Morgan, Vadim drifted into a brief affair with a beautiful young American woman living as an expatriate in Paris. Years later, he claimed, "There have been so many girls, so I don't remember her name. However, there is one thing I recall. She was also getting fucked by an aging Ernest Hemingway."

One night she invited me to dine with him, and I was afraid to do so. But I went anyway. It was a horrible evening. She spent most of the night telling him what a terrible lover he was, even though he was a symbol of a macho man."

"What did Papa do with this assault?" Vadim asked.

"He just looked sad and tugged, on occasions, at his beard."

Vadim was one of the writers who turned out the script of *Loves of Three Queens* (1954). It starred Hedy Lamarr in an anthology where she was cast in three roles—Helen of Troy, Empress Joséphine of (Napoleonic) France, and Geneviève of Brabant.

Like most educated people, Lamarr was familiar with the sagas of Helen of Troy and Joséphine, but had to be told who Geneviève was.

[Geneviève of Brabant was the heroine of a medieval legend, a virtuous wife falsely accused of infidelity. Her story gained wide popularity in the 17th Century, and has, over the years, been a frequent subject for drama, both on the stage and on the screen. Operas by Robert Schumann, Jacques Offenbach, and Giacomo Puccini drew upon her saga.

Her legend was also referenced in Marcel Proust's A la recherche du temps perdu (In Search of Lost Time (1913-1927). *As late as 1964, José Luis Monter filmed* Genoveffa di Brabante, *an Italian-Spanish movie.*

In the 1940s, Lamarr was hailed as "the world's most beautiful woman." On the third day of the shoot of *Loves of Three*

Michelle Morgan in the title role of *Marie-Antoinette Reine de France (Shadow of the Guillotine;* 1955).

In the film, the character she played lost her hat and also lost her head.

Queens, Vadim received a summons from her to visit her dressing room. "When I got there, she was ready and waiting. All I had to do was undress slowly before her, as she commanded."

He knew he was following in a trail blazed by Charles Boyer, Clark Gable, Charlie Chaplin, Errol Flynn, John Garfield, David Niven, Howard Hughes, Otto Preminger, and George Montgomery before he fell in love with Dinah Shore.

"But did she really, at the urging of her husband, Fritz Mandl, the munitions king, go to bed with both Mussolini and Hitler?" Vadim asked his friends.

***

The next time Jane met Vadim was on her twenty-sixth birthday, December 21, 1963. She had been deeply saddened by the assassination of then-President John F. Kennedy, about a month before.

Her French agent, Olga Horstig, had invited Vadim to a party at the Armenonville Pavilion in the Bois de Boulogne. It was a masquerade party, and she came as Charlie Chaplin wearing a bowler hat and a fake mustache. Vadim was smartly dressed as an officer in the Soviet Army.

As she remembered him, "He seemed funny and sweet in an offbeat, old shoe kind of way. By god, he was handsome. Not in some perfect way—his teeth were too big, face too long—but the way the whole thing came together made him startlingly attractive. It was a fun party, and he sang ribald marching songs from the French-Algerian War."

"I would soon meet him again, this man with the green, slanted eyes above high Slavic cheekbones, eyes that seemed filled with mystery and promise."

"I think Jane's opinion of me changed after that night," Vadim said. "Before, she knew my reputation as a womanizer and seducer, and seemed to want to stay clear of me. To her, in the beginning, I was a cynical *débauché* lusting after virgin flesh. I was also thought of as a diabolical magician who, unlike alchemists, could transform precious metals into lead, or else I could turn roses into thorns."

Brigitte Bardot had met Vadim at a time when he was part of a *ménage à trois* with his best friend, actor Christian Marquand and Marlon Brando.

After a big success in Tennessee Williams' *A Streetcar Named Desire,* Brando had escaped to Paris for a vacation. At a sidewalk café, Marquand and Vadim had met the handsome American actor and invited him to come and live at their apartment.

Bardot had been reared by prosperous but very strict Catholic parents in a luxurious, seven-room apartment in the chic 16th *arrondissement* of Paris. For years during her girlhood, she had studied ballet.

In 1949, when she was 15, she appeared as a model on the cover of *Elle,* which brought her an offer from Marc Allégret to

French film-goers were understandably confused by **Hedy Lamarr**'s success navigating the political chasms between her early life as the wife of a wealthy Austrian Nazi (Fritz Mandl). and later, as a Hollywood mega-star.

After years of Hollywood promotions, everyone was interested in how she'd portray seductive figures from French history.

Heeeere's Hedy in a "frock flick" (*Loves of Three Queens;* 1954) as Napoleon's Empress, Josephine.

Its script was partially written by Roger Vadim:

JAILBAIT A young, *bourgeoise*, sometimes suicidal **Brigitte Bardot**, scion of a devout Catholic family, at the beginning of her spectacularly *risqué* movie career

test for a part for a film he had conceptualized (but never made), entitled *Les Lauriers sont coupés*. *[It was inspired by a then avant-garde novel originally published in 1887 by the French author Édouard Dujardin. It's cited today as an early version of the stream of consciousness techniques later amplified by James Joyce in Ulysses.]*

Although her family strenuously opposed Bardot's becoming an actress, her grandfather said, "If this little girl is to become a whore, cinema will not be the cause."

There's confusion today as to whether Bardot was assigned or not assigned the role she auditioned for, and the film, as noted above, was never made, but Allégret left it up to his assistant, Vadim, to break the news to her that the movie had collapsed. Later, according to Vadim, "From the moment I met her, I fell in love with her."

Bardot married Vadim on December 20, 1952. Her family had strongly objected to the marriage until Bardot very seriously threatened suicide.

She had denounced their objections to their future son-in-law as "bourgeois snobbery."

Her parents financed their honeymoon in the French Alps and purchased a small motorcar and an apartment for them in the suburbs of Paris.

From the very beginning, their marriage was turbulent. Some brutal fights were followed by passionate love-making. "She often held up a mirror so she could see me plunging in and out of her," Vadim claimed.

Associates called Vadim a child molester, al-

INFAMOUS VIVIEN, FAMOUS MARLON

Here, Scarlett O'Hara (the immortal **Vivien Leigh**) interacts with her brother-in-law, ("that brutal Polack") portrayed by **Marlon Brando** in the 1951 film adaptation of Tennessee Williams' A *Streetcar Named Desire*.

When its filming was over, Brando "escaped" from the theater and filmmaking world for a holiday in avant-garde Paris, and quickly became a scandal-soaked and very intimate friend of Christian Marquand and Roger Vadim.

Erotic postcard, discovered in Istanbul and later posted on the web, of the voluptuous French star, **Brigitte Bardot**, whose very name elicited powerful reactions, both moral and biological, from critics and fans.

This alluring "jailbait" photo of a very young and very delectable **BB** is still used to promote the sybaritic charms of the French resort (**St-Tropez**) that Bardot adopted, endorsed, and promoted during the zigzagging course of her hugely popular career.

According to promotional materials distributed by one of the resort's five-star hotels, "Experiencing Brigitte Bardot's Saint-Tropez means appreciating all that the star has seen and done in, and for, the resort. It's truly *art de vivre* in action!"

"Although she has not appeared onscreen since 1973, **Brigitte Bardot** remains an absolute star; a paragon of triumphant femininity. **Saint-Tropez** celebrates its icon as much as it protects her and invites you to experience everything that she found so enchanting here."

though she was eighteen at the time of her wedding. Marquand said, "Whereas Bardot invented herself and that body of hers, Vadim created her myth."

Allégret did not want her, but other directors did.

[In 1952, director/producer Jean Boyer cast her in a small part in Le Trou Normand (Crazy for Love), *followed by director/producer Willy Rozier's* Manina, la fille sans voiles. *Filmed in Paris, Nice, and Cannes, and making ample use of footage of the then-17-year-old Bardot in the then very controversial bikini, it was eventually released in the United States in 1958* as Manina, the Girl in the Bikini *and in 1959 in the U.K as* The Lighthouse-Keeper's Daughter.

Bardot's father had demanded a clause in his daughter's contract specifying that the film would not include "indecent images." When, before the film's release, some "highly suggestive" publicity photos of his daughter were released, he accused the producers of not respecting the contract and demanded that scenes including his daughter be cut from the film. He lost the suit.]

Also in 1953, in California, Bardot was assigned a small role in the American film Act of Love, *during the filming of which Kirk Douglas allegedly raped her as he had a young Natalie Wood.]*

Finally, Allégret changed his mind and cast Bardot as the female lead, a flirtatious (underaged) student, in *Futures Vedettes (aka Joy of Living or School for Love in the U.S.; Sweet Sixteen in the U.K. and Reif auf jungen Blüten in West Germany; 1955)*. Her co-star was Jean Marais, the lover of Jean Cocteau.

After that, Bardot had a sizable English-speaking role (her first) in the British comedy, *Doctor at Sea* (1955) as the love interest of the gay English actor, Dirk Bogarde.

After three more films, she was cast in the Italian movie, *Mio figlio Nerone (aka Nero's Weekend and Nero's Mistress; 1956)*. Its director asked her to "abandon" her naturally brunette hair and dye it blonde. So pleased was Bardot with the result that she remained a blonde for the rest of her life.

Cette sacrée gamine (aka Mam'zelle Pigalle; aka Naughty Girl; 1956) was a big hit co-written by Vadim. In it, Bardot played a troublesome schoolgirl. That was followed by *Plucking the Daisy* (1956), written by Vadim and directed by Allégret, followed by the French comedy *La mariée est trop belle (aka The Bride is Much Too Beautiful; aka Her Bridal Night; 1956)*, in which she co-starred with Louis Jourdan.

At last, events coincided to allow Vadim to emerge as a director in his own right, and to morph Bardot into an international star.

Et Dieu…créa la femme (aka And God Created Women; 1956), was co-scripted by Vadim and Raoul Lévy, who was also the producer, and who had chosen Vadim as its director. Bardot was cast in the female lead as the "sex kitten," Juliette Hardy.

MANINA, LA FILLE SANS VOILES

Poster, conceived for the U.S. and British market of the Bardot hit that Vadim, as a film insider, launched during the early days of their marriage. The press and PR slogans were quick to point out that she was only 17 during the filming of this movie.

MAM'ZELLE PIGALLE
(aka Cette sacrée gamine, aka Naughty Girl)

Some Bardot fans viewed her protective interchange with the bird in this poster as an advance preview of **Brigitte Bardot's** deeply commited "late in life" status as a strident defender of animals, their well-being and their rights.

The French-language title of this film Vadim "invented" for the "invention" later known to the world as **BB** was soaked with implications: The **Place Pigalle** ("Pig Alley' to many American GIs after the Liberation of Paris) was known throughout most of the 20th Century as a working class district with LOTS of prostitutes. Many of whom were politely referred to as "Mam'zelles (aka "Mademoiselles.)

To the horror of her very strict parents, Bardot herself never fully "outgrew" the reputation bequeathed to her as a teenager in the aftermath of this film.

Its leading men were Curd Jürgens, Jean-Louis Trintignant, and Christian Marquand. The story centered on two brothers, both in love with Bardot. By the end of the film, the younger one marries her.

At first, Bardot had objected to the casting of Trintignant. "Why don't you find me a handsome boy?" she asked Vadim. "Jean-Louis is too odd-looking."

After he'd made love to her on screen (and soon was making love to her off-screen, too), she changed her mind.

"The last thing I ever expected was for her to fall in love with this boy from Nîmes in Southern France," Vadim said. "I'm sure Brigitte didn't expect to fall in love with him, either. But she did."

As filming progressed, with Vadim frequently screaming "CUT!," their love-making continued.

Raoul Lévy claimed, "Vadim became an accomplice to his wife's adultery by writing and directing those torrid love scenes."

On December 6, 1957, Bardot divorced Vadim in a French court. The judge ruled that both of them had been "seriously guilty of insulting each other."

Bardot later said, "I have always lived for passion. That's why I went through four husbands but was never faithful."

She and Trintignant lived together for less than two years but never married. *[Actually, he was already married (1954-1956) to actress Stéphane Audran.]*

Bardot's friendship with Vadim would continue, and they would work together and socialize in the future, even after his marriage to Jane Fonda.

Vadim later recalled that "One night with Brigitte is worth a lifetime."

Bardot had a different point of view: "If Vadim had been jealous, our marriage might have worked."

***

Prior to his marriage to Jane Fonda, Vadim one night, at a Left Bank *boîte* named Epi-Club, dropped in after dinner at the nearby *La Coupole,* known as a favorite of Hemingway and Gertrude Stein.

In the poster (upper photo) a slogan translates from the French as **"And God Created Woman...but the Devil invented BB."**

In an era when American actors were forced to suggest lovemaking ONLY in twin (not double) beds—remember Ozzie and Harriett?—French filmmakers, including Roger Vadim, inserted *l'amour* defiantly positioned between the sheets,.

Here's **Brigitte Bardot** and her (eventually) real-life lover, **Jean-Louis Trintignant** in *"Et Dieu créa la femme."*

American censors were outraged. So was Vadim when Bardot left him for Trintignant.

He arrived at Epi-Club and immediately spotted two young women, each beautiful, dancing together. At first, he thought they were lesbians and lovers. Later, he learned that they were sisters, out together for a night on the town.

When they finished, he recognized one of them as the actress Françoise Dorléac, who later changed her name to Catherine Deneuve after she, too, became a film actress famous for her portrayal of icy, aloof, and mysterious beauties for such directors as Luis Buñuel, Francois Truffaut, and Roman Polanski. Deneuve had made her film debut in 1957, but would not come into her glory until she shot Jacques Demy's 1964 musical romance, *Les Parapluies de Cherbourg* (aka *The Umbrellas of Cherbourg).*

She went on to star in Roman Polanski's British psychological horror classic, *Repulsion* (1965), in which she portrayed "an ice maiden, cold and erotic."

When he met her, Deneuve was only seventeen years old, and Vadim was in his thirties. "I was mesmerized by her finely drawn, classically perfect lips that concealed her deep sexuality," Vadim later said.

"She was the very image of a poster girl for a classic beauty."

After a brief chat, Françoise had to excuse herself and her sister, telling Vadim that she had an early call at the Billancourt Studios, where she was shooting scenes for a film.

Vadim took Catherine's hand, telling her he'd like to meet her there the following afternoon.

"You are most welcome to come by," she said, trying to retrieve her hand, which he was reluctant to release.

"After Catherine left, I could not wait for tomorrow to come, when I'd visit her at the studio," Vadim said. "When I got home, my wife, Annette Stroyberg, was packing for a trip to Rome, where she'd make a film. Our divorce would come through in March of 1961. Before flying to Italy, she left me with our three-year-old daughter, Nathalie."

THE FACES OF LOVE, POSTWAR AND "À LA FRANÇAISE"

Left photo: **Brigitte Bardot** with **Jean-Louis Trintignant**, her co-star and real-life lover in *And God Created Woman*, and

Right photo: Between takes and on the set of *And God Created Woman* **BB** acknowledges her camera-savvy, perhaps voyeuristic director (and husband), **Roger Vadim** with a dazzling smile

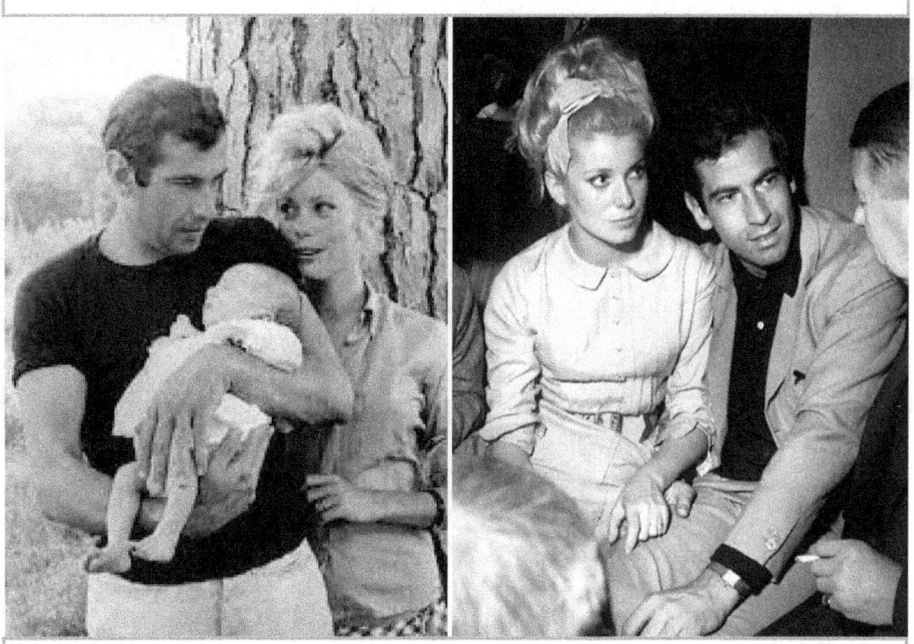

Two views of what was, at the time, one of the most talked-about and *oooh-la-laaahed* about, celebrity affairs in Europe, **Roger Vadim** and the *Belle de Jour* star, **Catherine Deneuve**. In the *left photo*, Roger holds Christian Vadim, the child they produced in 1963.

Deneuve—gorgeous, charming, elegant, and as *bon chic* and *bon genre* as the great nation of France can produce—opted not to marry him. Christian went on to become an actor, too.

That afternoon, Vadim met and sat with Catherine at a small café within the Billancourt Studio, where her sister was facing the cameras. "Catherine was drinking vodka with tonic, but I stuck to Perrier to cure the previous night's hangover."

After bidding the sister goodbye and remaining with Catherine for a while in the café, Vadim realized he'd lost the keys to his car. He'd also left his wallet behind, in his apartment.

"It's all right," Catherine assured him. "I have some francs."

He decided not to take her to the bed he'd shared with both Stroyberg and Bardot, so he invited her instead to the studio apartment of Christian Marquand, his best friend. *[He knew where Christian hid his door keys during that era of "lightened" security.]*

So in the same bed where he'd made love to Christian, he took Catherine's virginity.

He later recalled the event, noting that "She had the world's most beautiful breasts."

In the days and weeks to come, their affair would deepen, much to the regret of her family. Vadim also began to find out what existed "beyond her mask of serenity and beauty."

Deneuve was born in 1943 during the Nazi occupation of Paris. She'd made her film debut at the age of twelve.

In spite of her family's objections, the teenager went to live with Vadim, although she never married him. They lived together in a luxurious ninth-floor apartment on the Avenue Ingres in Paris' fashionable 16th arrondissement.

Many rumors about the young couple were spread around at the time. But did Brigitte Bardot really come by one night for a game of "strip billiard" *(a derivation of strip poker)*?

"Under Catherine's cold exterior, I found a passionate heart," Vadim claimed. "Brigitte was in the past, Jane Fonda in my future. What little White Russian boy gets to seduce three of the most desirable women on the planet? Each one of them, in their unique way, changed me forever. Oh, I left out one thing. This trio of stars were not only beautiful, they were talented, too."

Catherine gave birth to their son, Christian Vadim, on June 18, 1963. He, too, would grow up to become an actor, working first with his father on the movie *Surprise Party* (1963). His parents had gone their separate ways when he was only six months old.

Without meaning to, Vadim admitted that he had caused the break-up. "She had been very supportive of me and my career goals while moving ahead as an actress herself."

"In a search for her next leading man, I felt the role would be perfect for Johnny Halliday, the French version of Elvis Presley. But as the filming progressed, Catherine and Johnny seemed to be falling in love. The same thing happened with Brigitte and her leading man when I shot *And God Created Woman*."

Deneuve and Halliday led a cast of European actors in *Tales of Paris*, a 1962 "comedy drama anthology" consisting of four different episodes. Marc Allégret was one of four directors, and Roger Vadim was one of five scriptwriters. The Halliday/Deneuve segment was entitled "Sophie." In France, the 105-minute movie attracted two million viewers.

Born the same year as Deneuve, Halliday had a career that spanned 57 years, including 79 albums, selling more than 110 million records worldwide, mostly in the French-speaking world. He sang 1,154 songs, working with 187 artists. In the English-speaking world, he was dubbed "the biggest rock star you've never heard of."

According to Vadim, "After the filming was over, I came home one day and found Catherine packing her bags. She didn't tell me where she was going, but I knew it was to hook up with Halliday in Lyons, where he was appearing in concert."

Later, Deneuve would have an extended affair with Marcello Mastroianni, following the breakup of his longtime affair with Faye Dunaway. Although they never married, they had a child, Chiara Mastroianni, who became an actress, too.

THAT GODDESS, CATHERINE DENEUVE, LEFT ROGER VADIM FOR WHO?

Upper photo: France's answer to Elvis Presley, **Johnny Hallyday**, and

Lower photo: the "Ultimate Italian," **Marcello Mastroianni,** as he appeared as a "bathtub cowboy' in *8 1/2*, the very *avant-garde* film by Franco Fellini, in 1963.

Over the course of her film career, Deneuve would also sustain affairs with Burt Reynolds, Dean Martin, Roman Polanski, and Omar Sharif, among others.

She had one husband, David Bailey, the British fashion photographer, to whom she was married from 1965 to 1972. She wore black at her wedding, at which Mick Jagger served as best man.

What did she think of all her lovers who came and went? "All men are Arabs," she said.

***

Vadim's next meeting with Jane was when he showed up at Studios Éclair, where she was starring in that MGM film, as mentioned, being shot in Paris and directed by René Clement, co-starring Alain Delon. Vadim had arrived there to meet with Jean André, a production designer of movie sets.

She was 26 years old. She later admitted that as soon as she was free, she rushed breathlessly across the lot for an encounter with him. She entered the room where he was, in her words, "Breathless, flushed, and clearly excited."

She had been shooting a love scene with Delon and had hastily put a raincoat over her see-through nightgown. Suddenly, the trench coat opened, and Vadim got a preview of coming attractions.

"Her chest was heaving, and I knew at that very instance that I was in love again with a new girl."

Within two hours, he was inside her hotel room at the Relais Bisson, whose windows opened onto the River Seine.

It didn't take very long for that raincoat to come off, and soon, he was passionately kissing her and fondling her assets on the sofa. "I was so worked up and so was she, and she had most of her clothes off. I was about to strip down myself when she rose from the sofa and headed to the bathroom. She returned soon thereafter, completely naked."

"Then something happened to me that had never occurred before," he said. "In spite of my inner desires, my erection stayed hidden. I had read that a man can be so much in love he can't experience an erection, but I never thought it would happen to me, with my forever reliable love-making tool. But it was. I felt blocked, humiliated, and reduced to total impotence."

"Maybe her action was too aggressive. I don't really know."

Jane herself later said, "Instead of blaming Roger, I blamed myself. Was something wrong with me? He'd been so attracted to me at first, with all those passionate kisses."

"My impotence lasted for three long weeks, in spite of everything she did to break through to me, or to my hidden erection. But instead of kicking me out of her bed, she seemed to care for me more as if being vulnerable made me human—and not the sex machine of my reputation."

Finally, the spell was broken. As Vadim later admitted, "We stayed in bed for two days and nights making love. My virility was restored…and how!"

Suddenly, she announced she was flying to Geneva to meet with a producer who wanted to cast her in a new movie.

"It was an uncertain time in my life," Vadim claimed, "and the ever-faithful Christian Marquand came to comfort me, as he always did."

When Jane returned, she admitted she'd had a brief fling with the producer in Geneva. "But when he was making love to me, I realized how much I wanted you, needed you, loved you."

Their life together had begun, but at first, she didn't realize how many other people they would have to share

Roger Vadim with **Jane Fonda** in Rome in 1967, three or four years after the debut of their affair in Paris.

"The first time I saw her, I knew I was in love. I had to have her!"

it with. One gossipy Parisian tabloid picked up on their liaison, headlining an exposé with FRENCH RAKE SEDUCES AMERICA'S SEX KITTEN.

***

Jane rented an apartment at rue Séguier no. 12. Vadim remembered it as having a loggia, a fireplace, and craggy old beams on the ceiling.

"It had been built by an eccentric Frenchman, who, according to legend, entertained a lot of partners of both sexes," Vadim said.

Vadim lived there while working on the script of his upcoming film, *La Ronde (Circle of Love, 1964)*. The apartment proved too small when Nathalie, his six-year-old daughter, moved in with her nanny.

Through a friend (Commander Paul-Louis Weiller), Vadim arranged larger lodgings within the very grand Hôtel les Ambassadeurs de Hollande, a 17th century mansion in the historic and very central Marais district.

Soaked with aristocratic references from the *ancien régime*, including ownership, in 1711, by the private secretary of King Louis XIV, it was known as a haven for artists and the beautiful women they attracted. Roland Petit, the director of Les Ballets de Paris, was in residence within one of its units, and Charlie Chaplin was also said to have had an apartment there, even though Jane never encountered him.

A STRANGER IN A STRANGE LAND

September 7, 1963—Media Buzz: **Jane** hits the cover of *Paris-Match*, the biggest circulation weekly news and lifestyle magazine in the French-speaking world.

It was in this exotic and ponderously historic *atelier* that Jane made a home for Vadim and their family, to which she would later contribute a daughter.

To amuse Jane one night, Vadim told her how, on a spring day in 1944, he lost his virginity when he was 16 to a more experienced woman who had recently turned 21.

"We were in a hayloft in a barn in Normandy. I had taken up with this farmgirl. Her husband was in the French Resistance. We had sex in the hayloft. Just as I shot off inside a woman for the first time, the ground trembled, the walls of the barn rattled. Never in my life had I ever imagined that a climax in a woman could be this powerful."

As it turned out, it was zero hour on June 6, 1944. The world's greatest armada, the Allied Invasion of Normandy, had begun to rid France of the Nazis. Vadim and his girlfriend were among the first to receive the reverberations of a British bomb which had been dropped nearby.

One night, Vadim announced that Bardot was coming over for dinner. In a panic, Jane rushed to the market. She was no cook, but at the meat market, she bought a length of blood sausages which, although they looked repulsive, she carried home anyway.

The meal was cordial, and Bardot even complimented her on the blood sausage. *[Bardot didn't know her way around a kitchen either.]* "She didn't have any sex kitten aura, but was quite amusing and down to earth," Jane said. "My only sense of anxiety came when I pictured her in the arms of Roger Vadim."

Later, when their respective schedules allowed it, Vadim and Jane opted to visit the country of origin of his father. He booked tickets for them on a Soviet plane heading from Paris to Moscow. Their arrival there was on the last day of April in 1964. The entire city was preparing for the May Day (May 1) Parade—a celebration of the Russian defeat of the Nazis in World War II.

The next day, Jane and Vadim witnessed the greatest parade of their lives as armies of Russian soldiers and, scores of Russian tanks marched or rolled through the city's streets and fighter planes flew in formations overhead.

In spite of all this showmanship of military might, Jane was welcomed by the Russian people. Unknown to her at the time, Henry Fonda movies were popular in Russia, especially *The Grapes of Wrath* (1940), which many Russians believed was an accurate depiction of how America treated its poor and downtrodden.

***

La Ronde (aka *Circle of Love*, 1965)

Producers Raymond and Robert Hakim had a grand ambition when they decided to remake *La Ronde*, which the great German film director, Max Ophüls had first filmed in 1950.

The cast Ophuls enrolled was one of the most spectacular of the postwar years: Danielle Darrieux, one of France's great movie stars, with a career that spanned eight decades; Gérard Philipe, Jean-Louis Barrault, Anton Walbrook, and both Simone Signoret and Simone Simon.

Darrieux had achieved international notoriety during her ill-fated marriage to Porfirio Rubirosa, a native of the Dominican Republic, known for his marriages to the tobacco heiress, Doris Duke, and later to the Woolworth heiress, Barbara Hutton.

Set in *belle-époque* Vienna, the play it was based on was entitled *La Ronde,* written by Arthur Schnitzler in 1897. It had scrutinized the sexual morality of class ideologies of its day, with commentary on how sexual intimacies transgressed the class boundaries of its era.

It was not performed until 1920 in Berlin, when it was billed as *Reigen*. Its opening elicited violent criticism for its sexual overtones. Schnitzler came under virulently anti-Semitic attacks and was labeled "a Jewish pornographer."

Above, left, is a photo of the 8-story tall billboard on Broadway at 47th Street, over which **Jane Fonda** sued. It derives from the archives of the "Book of Record" for all things New York, **The NY Public Library.**

When Roger Vadim was named director of its film adaptation, he hired Jean Anouilh to fashion a screenplay set in 1913. For its release in the United States, *La Ronde* was retitled *Circle of Love.*

Vadim was selected in part because the producers were in awe of his 1959 film, *Les Liaisons dangereuses,* starring Jeanne Moreau, Gérald Philipe, and Annette Vadim (aka Annette Stroyberg), the director's wife from 1959-1961.

The producers certainly didn't select Vadim because of the commercial success of *Les Liaisons dangereuses.* It had cost the U.S. equivalent of $4.3 million dollars to produce, and it had generated only $4,325,000 at the box office—a modest profit, at best.

Anouilh had earned a distinguished international reputation for a writing career that had survived five decades. His plays ranged from absurdist farce to high drama. His *Antigone,* an adaptation of Sophocles classic, a drama, had been produced throughout Europe and the United States. He characterized his later plays as "rather Molièresque."

During the filming of *La Ronde,* Thomas Quinn Curtis of the *International Herald Tribune* visited the set, later claiming, "I felt I was watching Josef von Sternberg direct Marlene Dietrich, not Roger Vadim directing Jane Fonda."

Vadim told Curtis, "When I make a picture about relations between people, something erotic comes through. I can't help it. Sex has been an inspiration, the greatest inspiration, since art has existed. I don't mean pornography. It is very difficult in France to talk about anything but sex."

Circle of Love was not the first picture in which Jane was offered a chance to work with Vadim as her director. Producer Francis Cosne had once recommended that Jane be cast in *Angélique, Marquise des Anges,* a film based on a best-selling French-language novel. He wanted Jane to portray the adventurous, passionate Marquise.

She was sent the script, and her agent responded within a few days: "Jane Fonda is not interested in a costume drama. She also asks me to tell you that she will never make a film with Roger Vadim."

Cosne then signed an unknown actress, Michel Mercier. When it was released, it became a big hit.

On the first day of *Circle of Love's* filming, Jane told Vadim, "I came to Paris to escape my reputation as "just Henry Fonda's daughter. I feel I am more than that, and I want you to help me change my reputation by directing me in this very different drama from what I've done before. I want to establish a new identity. I also hope to discover who I really am. "I'm glad to be out of Hollywood, a town I detest."

One reason Jane had rejected the offer to work with Vadim is that she had gone to see *Et Dieu Créa...la femme,* that 1956 erotic movie that launched Brigitte Bardot as "The French sex kitten."

"I am not impressed," was Jane's brief review.

Circle of Love featured a cast of strong supporting players such as Anna Karina, an *avant-garde* Danish actress, who, in the

Maurice Ronet appears as an 18th century rake in this commemorative postcard from the former DDR (East Germany).

Jean-Claude Brialy *(right),* cast as a sophisticate, with **Gérard Blain,** playing a country lad, in *Le Beau Serge* (1958), a film about decadent students in Paris. Film historians assessed it as the first of *La Nouvelle Vague.*

Catherine Spaak with **James Franciscus** in the Italian "murder, suspense, and slasher film," *Cat O' Nine Tails (aka Il gatto a nove code;* 1971)

1960s, was a collaborator of Jean-Luc Godard, the French New Wave director, performing in several of his films. They included *Vivre sa vie (My Life to Live,* 1962*). The New York Times* called her "one of the screen's great beauties.

Maurice Ronet was an actor, director, and writer, a native of Nice. At the time he worked with Jane, he was one of the most prolific actors in European cinema, often portraying characters who are in conflict with themselves or with society. In 1959, he made his international box office breakthrough as Julien Tavernier in Louis Malle's first feature film, *Elevator to the Gallows* (1958), co-starring Jeanne Moreau.

Born in Algeria, Jean-Claude Brialy was both an actor and a movie director. By the late 1950s, he had become one of the best-known actors of the French *nouvelle vague*, working with such directors as Louis Malle, François Truffaut, Jean-Luc Godard, Jean Renoir, and Luis Buñuel. Godard defined him as "the French Cary Grant."

In a memoir, he revealed that he was the gay love of his longtime partner, Bruno Finck.

Cast as "La midinette" was Catherine Spaak. Although French, she starred mostly in Italian films, and her career was aided greatly by Sophia Loren. Spaak co-starred with Marcello Mastroianni in *The Man, the Woman, and the Money* (1965) at around the time she was appearing with Jane.

She noted that during filming, "Vadim had little time for the rest of us, since he was so devoted to Fonda."

The plot is complicated, as one of the characters seduces another, who then seduces another—and so it goes.

The story begins in Vienna, as a sentimental prostitute (Marie DuBois) offers herself to a handsome soldier (Claude Giraud) because he resembles her true love. Seeking to take advantage, the soldier seduces Rose (Anna Karina), a lonely housemaid.

Returning home, Rose allows her employer's son, Alfred (Jean-Claude Brialy), to make love to her. He then seduces Sophie (Fonda), a married woman. Refreshed by her seduction, Sophie then makes bold overtures to her stuffy husband, Henri (Maurice Bonet).

When the picture was released in Italy, authorities charged Vadim, Jane, and five other stars of *Circle of Love* with obscenity. Jane's nude scene was the first ever to "showcase" a leading American actress in a foreign film.

A scandal blew up when Walter Reed opened *Circle of Love* at a movie theater (the DeMille) near Times Square. He publicized it with an eight-floor billboard of a provocatively nude Jane Fonda. It (and she) quickly became the gossipy talk of the town. Columnist Dorothy Kilgallen wrote, "Leave it to Jane Fonda to indulge in this cheap stunt."

Actually, Jane had nothing to do with it, and was horrified at the display, filing a $3 million dollar lawsuit. The sign came down, and a settlement was reached out of court.

The movie had been shot in French and dubbed into English. One reviewer found Jane's French accent "*á la* Laurel and Hardy."

In spite of that, *Circle of Love* was nominated for a Golden Globe as Best Foreign Language Film of the Year.

Brigitte Bardot went to see it and later told a reporter, "I liked the woman they called 'the American Bardot.'"

Samedi et Dimanche claimed that "Jane Fonda is America's gift to France. She may be the next actress Vadim molds into a child-woman of universal appeal. She would have had a flourishing career even if she had not been the daughter of Henry Fonda and

Jane Fonda's *Circle of Love* (1965) was conceived by her husband, Roger Vadim, as a remake of a French classic *(La Ronde;* 1950) which had originally starred the fabled French socialite and movie star, **Danielle Darrieux** *(photo above)*.

Darrieux continued acting in A-list (usually European) films until she was in her 90s. During the course of her eight-decade career, she starred in "indelible incarnations of *ingénues, coquettes, femmes fatales,* and *grande dames*" and lived for exactly one century.

After their divorce, one of her husbands, (the charming, well-hung, and internationally sought-after Dominican playboy, Porfirio Rubirosa) famously married two of America's richest women. (Their names? Doris Duke and Barbara Hutton.)

had never set foot in France."

The London Movie Express found that "the only time Jane Fonda seemed natural in the film was when she was in bed with Jean-Claude Brialy. She is more at home there with her illicit lover than she is in bed with her film husband, Maurice Ronet."

The Guardian praised the film's color and production values but wrote, "There is a vulgarity about Vadim's frequent fleshy close-ups. Anouilh and Vadim stick closely to Schnitzler's original, but the film is obviously embroidered with the imagery of Vadim's creation—a visual superfluity."

The famously acerbic critic Kenneth Tynan called the film "a master of colour photography. This is the nearest approach to a work of art that Vadim has yet directed."

Eugene Archer, critic for *The New York Times*, defined *Circle of Love* as "a total debacle, a dull, pointless, ineptly acted vulgarization of a distinguished play, with nothing to recommend it beyond some attractive color photography."

***

Jane had met Bardot but not Vadim's second wife (1958-1961), Annette Stroyberg. That union had produced a daughter, Nathalie Vadim. *[Jane later became Nathalie's stepmother, with especially close contacts during the months they lived together, en famille.]*

Jane was in bed with Vadim one night when an urgent phone call came in from Stroyberg's apartment.

Jane answered the phone to hear Stroyberg confess in a barely audible voice that she had overdosed on Veronal, a barbital sedative and hypnotic. "Roger and I will be right over," she said.

She awakened Vadim, and within thirty minutes, they arrived at Annette's apartment.

In the bathroom, Jane induced her to vomit, with the (in this case, correct) belief that the pills hadn't yet been fully ingested into Stroyberg's system.

Meanwhile, Vadim remained in the kitchen making black coffee.

In a weakened condition, Stroyberg returned to bed, where she revealed the reason for her attempted suicide. She had fallen in love with the Egyptian actor, Omar Sharif. However, after a torrid affair during which she had expected him to propose marriage, he had dumped her.

Vadim was a friend of Sharif, and he knew how fickle he could be. "He was a serial seducer, going from one boudoir to the next. He never intended to marry Annette. Actually, he was rarely romantic, his interest focused only on one part of a woman's anatomy."

For the first time, Vadim, in the days ahead, spoke of his ill-fated marriage to Annette.

Born in Denmark, she launched her career, as so many actresses do, posing for commercials—in her case, Tuborg beer ads.

She moved to Paris, where she met and fell in love with Vadim. He tried to turn her into a big-time *vedette*, casting her in a film he directed, *Les Liaisons dangereuses* (1959) with co-stars

Annette Stroyberg is depicted with **Roger Vadim** and their child. But this scene of domestic bliss was doomed to fail. Lurking in her future was Omar Sharif. "The fact that I entertain many girls is only because I'm searching for the right one."

A KNACK FOR BEAUTIFUL ACTRESSES

Roger Vadim appears with his **Annette Stroyberg** on the cover of the Danish weekly magazine, *Billed-Bladet*'s edition of April 20, 1957, shortly before their marriage in 1958.

Jeanne Moreau and Gerard Philipe.

In a minor role, Vadim cast Louis Trintignant. Bardot would later fall in love with him and leave Vadim for his arms.

Les Liaisons dangereuses became a massive hit in France, the most successful domestic film since 1954. When it was shown in America, some police commissioners shut down the theaters that screened it. The Catholic Church denounced it as "unfit for viewing," citing some of the scenes that had featured Annette.

Vadim also cast Stroyberg in *Blood and Roses,* a 1960 erotic horror movie, set in 19th century Italy. Her co-stars included Mel Ferrer and Elsa Martinelli. Also included in a small role was Serge Marquand, an actor he'd hire again, later, in future pictures. *[Serge was the brother of his best friend, Christian Marquand.]*

Stroyberg recovered quickly from her suicide attempt and later dated Warren Beatty, lived for a time with the Italian matinee idol Vittorio Gassman, and had sexual liaisons with Alain Delon.

By 1967, she met and married Guy Senouf, a French Moroccan hailed as the "Sugar King of Morocco" because of his ownership of sugar refineries near Casablanca. They produced a son, Yan, born in June, the year of their marriage.

In 1974, after a divorce, she wed Gregory Callimanopulos, a Greek shipping magnate, in New York, with whom she produced another son, Pericles.

[Callimanopulos made headlines again in 2011, at the age of 74, based on allegations of sexual harassment brought by his 24-year-old assistant, Adelheid (Heidi) Waumboldt, of Manhattan, who filed a lawsuit.]

Although Stroyberg would die in 2005, she had one final marriage in 2001 to Christian Lillelund, an attorney. She ended up in her native Copenhagen, and was often seen with Queen Margrethe II of Denmark and her husband, Prince Henrik.

***

Vadim, in Jane's admission, was the first man she ever really loved. But there were problems right from the start. She still had $150,000 of the money she'd inherited after her mother's suicide. She came to realize that Vadim was a compulsive gambler, fully capable of ripping through her inheritance, often at casinos and racecourses. His addiction to gambling was equivalent, in its power, to alcoholism, anorexia, or bulimia.

Even before their wedding, and very clearly in the presence of his friends, he advocated sexual freedom. "Even if a guy gets married, he and his wife should agree to an open marriage," he often proclaimed.

She had learned to cook reasonably well, but sometimes, when she prepared dinner for him, he would fail to show up, arriving home the following morning.

Then one night, it happened.

As relayed by biographer Patricia Bosworth, "Vadim brought home a beautiful red-haired woman who turned out to be a prostitute employed at Madame Claude, the most elegant bordello in Paris, catering to movie stars, moguls, and politicians.

As Jane herself confessed, "I took my cue from him and threw myself into the threesome with skill and enthusiasm like the actress I am."

Sometimes Jane herself was sent out to do the soliciting, although she later claimed, "I never got much pleasure from these arrangements. Invariably, the women fell in love with me."

Roger Vadim was one of the patrons of the infamous **Madame Claude (Fernande Grudet)**, administrator of the most elegant (and many said, ('tasteful') call girl ring in Paris.

It attracted world leaders (John F. Kennedy), playboys (Porfirio Rubirosa) actors (Sinatra, Brando, and Rex Harrison), world-class artists (Marc Chagall and Pablo Picasso), and heads of state (Muammar Gaddafi).

She referred to her girls as "swans," as she found the world prostitute "degrading and revolting."

Reportedly, JFK famously asked Madame Claude for a girl who looked just like his wife Jackie, '"but hot."

Brooke Hayward, one of her best friends, said, "Jane and Roger enjoyed a lot of sexual freedom. They were banging other people and not afraid to admit it."

In the early stage of his affair, Vadim made it clear to Jane that he considered monogamy "unnatural, a sign that one is bourgeois. To hell if I'll follow bourgeois morality, like some fat banker from Lyon."

***

If there was anything that Vadim liked to do, it was to go on vacation, not just to the ocean and its beaches, but also to the French Alps. He took Jane to the Alpine chalet where he and his widowed mother had lived after his father's death, when she was searching for a new husband.

Even though Vadim was married to Jane at the time, Catherine Deneuve had a mutual friend deliver a secret love letter to Vadim, inviting him to a secret rendezvous at her own (rented) chalet.

As he later reported, "The night was heaven, truly divine. But later that morning, we launched our war of words. We were only compatible in bed, not forging a life together."

Vadim believed that "sex from the outside can keep a marriage alive, avoiding the divorce courts. I want to convert Jane to my hedonistic philosophy. I don't want her to follow some Puritan ethic. That went out of date with knee-length bloomers and corsets."

"For God's sake, we're moving into the last 50 years of the 20th Century. Time to get on with the modern agenda for a man and a woman, and that includes a husband and his wife, facing a more liberated life, often bringing in others to share their joy of sex."

Sandy Whitelaw, who worked at United Artists' branch office in Paris, got a preview of the Vadim/Fonda relationship during one of his visits.

Jane hosted a dinner party to which he was invited. Warren Beatty arrived with his current "hottie," none other than Brigitte Bardot.

"We had a lot to drink, and finally Jane served *hors d'oeuvres*. Beatty seemed to enjoy them, announcing "There's only one thing that I find that tastes better." Then he looked over at Bardot.

"Brigitte is, indeed, a morsel," Vadim chimed in. "Jane here is not in the same class."

Disgusted, Jane quickly left for the kitchen, later telling Whitelaw, "Roger considers me a watered-down version of Bardot."

Patricia Bosworth reported on another invitation that some would consider shocking. Susan Blanchard, Jane's former stepmother, came to visit. With her was her new husband, actor Michael Wager. To show their sexual liberation, Vadim invited both of his guests to join Jane and him in the bedroom. Wager politely declined for both his wife and himself.

"Jane and I were in the vanguard of a new movement toward sexual freedom," Vadim claimed. "How did I know at the time that this freedom would eventually lead to her escape from me?"

***

Back in France, Jane decided that the time come to end her nomadic lifestyle with Vadim. They had moved from apartment to apartment, some of which had been badly furnished.

She began scouring the Île de France for a farmhouse on about an acre of land, and eventually found what she was looking for 37 miles west of Paris. It was near the village of Saint-Ouen-Marchefroy, three miles from the town of Houdan.

The village, with its limited shopping, had a market but little else for its 100 inhabitants. It was so close to Paris that they'd be able to visit, efficiently and frequently, returning easily to their idyllic retreat.

Beech and oak trees dominated the landscape. In the distance stood tall poplars, over which partridges flew. Hare and wild boar still roamed the forests.

Her life began to revolve around restoring the circa-1830 farmhouse. She searched for antiques for the house and arranged for the construction of a badminton court, a henhouse, and a winter conservatory.

After Jane had completed *Cat Ballou*, she'd been given a pony. The animal was shipped to France and housed in its own private stable. Vadim's daughter, Nathalie, not only rode it to the little schoolhouse she attended, and to the nearby village, bringing back fresh milk and cheese for Jane and her father.

Jane planned to do a lot of entertaining, so guest rooms were upgraded. A former granary was adapted into an indoor swimming pool, and a projection room was added for screenings, mostly of the latest New Wave French films.

Unlike Hollywood, with its sprawling urban mass, film production in France at the time was far more limited. "Vadim knew every filmmaker in Paris, including major actors and actresses. Many of them were his friends, and some of them even became her friends, too.

It's amazing that they had enough money to finance all this restoration, since Vadim made only one movie every two years. To help pay some of the costs, Jane borrowed $40,000 from her father, Henry.

In Jane's opinion, the terrain around her house didn't match the lush surroundings of other properties nearby, so she ordered truckloads of trees to be planted near and around it. They included a gracefully branched Cedar of Lebanon.

When he finally surveyed the many additions to his landscape, Vadim stole a phrase from Oscar Levant: "If God had a bank account, he would have created Jane's forest, where beech and birch grew along with pines and flowering bougainvillaea."

In a cottage on the grounds lived their helpers: Two Italian parents with their son and daughter. The matriarch of that family was experimenting with new culinary styles and developed a specialty: turkey with pineapple.

When spring came, the property's hundreds of sunflowers grew so fast that Vadim feared that they'd take over the house.

The local villagers had no idea that Jane Fonda was a movie star. She was referred to as "the American girl."

Jane had always wanted a menagerie of animals. She ended up with five dogs, four cats, two rabbits, and four ducks.

The farmhouse, with its honey-colored stone walls, evoked an Andrew Wyeth painting.

She later planted maple and cherry trees around the farm. She wore blue jeans, but when she went to the city, she became Parisian chic and sported Cardin or Dior.

She continued to receive scripts, later admitting, "I made a mistake when I turned down a film offer from David Lean."

Doctor Zhivago (1965) would require a nine-month shoot in Spain, and the cast had been selected, all except for the character (the female lead) of Lara, which Lean had hoped Jane would accept, opposite Omar Sharif, Tom Courtenay, Rod Steiger, Alex Guinness, and Geraldine Chaplin. After Jane's rejection, Lean cast Julie Christie.

For the most part, Jane avoided reporters. However, perhaps since she had once worked for *Paris Match*, a woman reporter was driven from Paris by Vadim to interview her.

During the course of a long conversation, the reporter asked Jane an explosive (explosive to Vadim, at least) question: "Why do you present so much flesh in your films?"

Without answering, Vadim rose to his feet and went into the bathroom. When he emerged, he was completely naked and shook his penis at her. "That," he said, "is too much flesh."

Earlier in the day, Jane had been told, "Your brother, Peter Fonda, claimed that you're prostituting yourself by working with Vadim."

"If my brother said that, it must be true," Jane said, sarcastically.

Bardot was a sometime visitor, and she and Jane could talk

Yves Montand and **Simone Signoret**, both actors, indulged in one of the great romances (later marriage) of France.

Of course, as time went by, she had to forgive him for falling into the "honey trap" (her words) of Marilyn Monroe.

Montand and Signoret met and fell in love one sunny afternoon in the resort town of Saint-Paul-de-Vence on the French Riviera.

Actually, this "hot-blooded Frenchman" had been born in Italy. As a very young man, he was spotted by the legendary Edith Piaf and became her lover.

freely about a number of subjects that usually centered on Vadim. Jane wanted to understand him better, and she felt that quizzing Bardot would provide insights that would help her to more effectively evaluate him.

Front cover of *Le Figaro's* obit edition of **Valerie Giscard d'Estaigne** (also known simply as Giscard or VGE) served as President of France from 1974 to 1981.

He visited Roger Vadim and Jane Fonda at their farmhouse outside Paris.

***

The political side of Jane developed slowly, as she spent many weeks with some of Vadim's leftist friends, notably Yves Montand and his wife, the French actress Simone Signoret.

Slowly, Jane began to develop a political awareness of her own. In the beginning, she listened but did not have much to contribute. Originally, she complained, "Some of those guys sitting in our living room talk like they had just read *Pravda* that morning."

As weekends went by, she became more sympathetic to their leftist leanings.

Vadim noticed this change in her, telling Christian Marquand, "Right before my eyes, I am witnessing the birth of a political radical."

For the first time in her life, she watched endless coverage of the war in Vietnam on the French-language TV news. She was horrified that American planes were bombing churches, schools, even hospitals. She also heard refugees deliver eyewitness accounts of torture and enforced starvation by the invading Americans.

One report claimed that the U.S. Air Force had dropped a million pounds of bombs, more than they had during their invasion of the South Pacific during World War II.

This became evident when one weekend, the President of France, Valérie Giscard-d'Estaing, came to visit their farmhouse.

When she rose to answer a phone that was ringing in another room, the President of France turned to Vadim and asked. "But who is Jane talking to? A Maoist? Perhaps a terrorist? Or perhaps the president of the Trotskyists?"

Week after week, Vadim noticed Jane becoming, in his view, increasingly strident. He feared that he would have no part of this new world emerging before his eyes. As he related to Marquand, "Week by week, I am assuming the role of her wife in our marriage."

Vadim also noticed an increasing sexual liberation permeating Jane's value system. "The sexual freedom of the era led to a focus on women's rights," Vadim said. "That would become one of Jane's pet causes for the rest of her life. The old rules were under fire, notably that a woman's place was in the kitchen or else in the bedroom. Old walls were crumbling down."

"However, no one knew how to rebuild them, especially Jane and me. She and I were guinea pigs of a new

Two views of **Merle Oberon**, *above* with **Laurence Olivier** as Heathcliff in *Wuthering Heights* (1939).

Left photo: Press coverage during her Hollywood heyday as an object of near-veneration by her movie fans.

world which was unstable. But for a while, we did not know that."

***

The offers from Hollywood were becoming increasingly tempting, and Jane needed the money, so she flew back to her native land to collect some big paychecks—the kind that only American studios were providing at the time.

The offer was made more tempting when Vadim agreed to go to America with her.

In their search for housing, she and Vadim decided to spend most of the summer among the Hollywood colony whose homes were scattered along the beachfront at Malibu. They rented a villa from the actress, Merle Oberon, who had achieved international fame during her movie gig opposite Laurence Olivier in *Wuthering Heights* (1939).

When Vadim met Oberon, he was enthralled by "her ageless beauty" and her legend.

Oberon's sexual aggressions and indiscretions seemed to play out almost daily. The "objects of her affection" ranged from carpenters on a film set during daylight hours to actors, perhaps Rex Harrison, at night. They were aimed at, among many others, James Cagney or David Niven, Clark Gable, Ronald Colman, or Gary Cooper.

During one of his visits to Mexico, Prince Philip enjoyed her charms, too.

The photographer, Cecil Beaton, defined Oberon as a nymphomaniac. Marlene Dietrich called her "a real common piece."

After arranging the details of the rental of her villa to the Vadims through her agent, Oberon visited it later to collect some personal belongings. Vadim was there, but Jane had not yet arrived.

It was later reported that she left the villa five hours later. Reports circulated that Oberon, an older woman born in 1911, seduced the younger Vadim.

***

The Chase (1966)

For a while, Marlon Brando showed up for some of the weekend "open houses" Jane staged with Vadim at their rented villa in Malibu. Sometimes, he brought a male lover like Wally Cox or the French actor, Brando's friend, Christian Marquand.

Ever since she had met Brando at the Actors Studio in Manhattan, Jane had admired his talent and hoped that one day they might co-star together in a film.

One morning, as Jane read *Variety*, she came across the announcement that producer Sam Spiegel had cast Brando as the male lead in his upcoming film, *The Chase* (1966).

Its screenplay, a saga about racism, wife-swapping, megalomania, and murder, had been written by Lillian Hellman. Taking place all in one day, it was set in a small town in Texas.

Jane asked Brando to use his influence with Spiegel to get her cast as his leading lady. He promised that he'd try.

Unknown to her at the time, Faye Dunaway was also auditioning for the role, but was rejected. Ironically, when Jane was offered the title role in an upcoming crime drama, *Bonnie and Clyde*, Jane rejected the part. The role went instead to Dunaway. It launched her into a stellar career as a motion picture star.

Brando was grateful that Siegel had cast him, twelve years previously, in *On the Waterfront* (1954). For that picture, Siegel had

Marlon Brando as he appears in *The Chase*, where he was cast as a small-town, Deep South sheriff. Even his star power, plus that of his co-stars, Jane Fonda and Robert Redford, could not rescue it from what emerged as a disaster at the box office.

Time magazine said that Jane "made white trash seem altogether first class." She was cast as "the trollop wife" of a fugitive (Redford).

carried home an Academy Award for Best Picture of the Year. For the Best Actor Oscar that year, Brando won, beating Humphrey Bogart, James Mason, and Bing Crosby.

Spiegel was a Jew who had fled from Nazi Germany in 1933 with his life at stake. When he reached Hollywood, he decided to change his name to S.P. Eagle "to avoid anti-Semitism." He used that name until 1954, eventually becoming one of the best producers in town, known for such box office triumphs as *The African Queen* (1951) with Katharine Hepburn and Bogart; *The Bridge Over the River Kwai* (1957), with William Holden, and *Lawrence of Arabia* (1962) with Peter O'Toole.

Brando welcomed the idea of signing Jane, and Vadim also urged her to make the picture.

Spiegel didn't want to keep the secret, so he held a press conference. "Our screenplay was written by Lillian Hellman, one of the great playwrights of our day. She has written many great roles for women. A good example is *The Little Foxes,* which Tallulah Bankhead played on Broadway and Bette Davis portrayed on the screen."

Because of her "left-wing beliefs," Hellman had been blacklisted in the early 1950s during the McCarthy era. But she had bounced back. On an ironic note, Jane, within a few years, would portray Hellman herself in the movie, *Julia* (1977).

According to Spiegel, "I now believe that Ms. Hellman has written her finest role for a woman in the person of Anne Reeves, to be played by Jane Fonda, one of Hollywood's best actresses, who is fast shooting to super stardom. The role of Anne is the most exciting and sexiest any Hollywood actress has ever played."

"Such hype!" Jane said. "How can I live up to that advance billing?"

The next day, she got the final version of Hellman's screenplay, a drama based on a 1956 novel by Horton Foote, a Texas-born playwright and screenwriter best known for his film script for *To Kill a Mockingbird* (1962). Late in his presidency, in 2000, President Bill Clinton presented Foote with the National Medal of the Arts, saying, "He is the nation's most prolific writer for stage, film, and television."

Brando liked to shock. On his first day working on the set with Jane, he told her, "You don't have to worry about the casting couch with Spiegel. To him, you'd be in the grandmother category. He choice would be a 13-year-old girl. Fifteen would be entering old age for him, and sixteen would be just too ripe for him. He told me that gals of thirteen and younger, taste sweeter, and that after the age of sixteen, they lose their special flavor."

Before shooting began, Jane met with the director of *The Chase,* Arthur Penn, who had once helmed her father, Henry Fonda, and Anne Bancroft on Broadway in *Two for the Seesaw* (1958).

[Penn had also directed Bancroft in her Oscar-winning performance in The Miracle Worker (1962).]

Jane, perhaps jokingly or with touches of irony, told him, "Under your direction, I, too, expect to bring home the gold for *The Chase."*

For *The Chase,* Penn assembled a gold-plated cast of supporting players: Robert Redford, E.G. Marshall, Angie Dickinson, Janice Rule, Richard Bradford, Robert Duval, the English actor, James Fox, Henry Hull, and Bruce Cabot, who had appeared with Jane the year before in *Cat Ballou* (1965).

Although Penn was supportive of Jane and respectful of her talent, he had a mixed reaction to Brando. After seeing the first rushes of the mega-star, he said, "Marlon looks like a baby version of Orson Welles."

Early in its development, Brando had high hopes for *The Chase.* He told Penn that he was counting on it to restore some of his reputation after the critical mauling he'd received in 1962 after reprising Clark Gable's performance of 1935 in *Mutiny on the Bounty.*

Brando's acting in *The Chase* received its highest praise from Jane herself. She stopped a scene with him to tell him, "You're the best fucking actor in the world."

As shooting continued, and Spiegel (as producer) kept interfering, Penn (as director) told Brando and Jane, "Our producer is really letting me know what it's like to get fucked in Hollywood. He interferes in *everything."*

Brando had gone to Spiegel and asked him to cast his older sister, Jocelyn, in one of the roles. In response, Spiegel offered her a choice of two. She selected the small part of Mrs. Briggs. Later, her brother warned her that she'd probably chosen the wrong part: "Your Mrs. Briggs has a good chance of ending up on the cutting-room floor."

One afternoon, the director, Stanley Kramer, visited Brando for lunch. He later reported that by then, Brando's high hopes for the artistic viability of *The Chase* had crashed and burned.

"Fuck 'em," BRANDO said. "If they're going to be so stupid, I'll just take the money and run. Let them do whatever they want with this dud. On my last day, I'm fleeing. I don't give a damn about anything that happens after that."

"Many things," Kramer claimed, "contributed to the debacle, but the consensus seems to have been that the various creative forces were overwhelmed by Spiegel, who had rigid ideas about what he wanted filmed. Hellman, who had been absent from films for twenty years, was finally subjected to the kind of strong-arm bullying that had marked the screen careers of F. Scott Fitzgerald and William Faulkner. She joined the army of prominent writers who had given their names and their talents to a costly bomb."

***

The Chase would be the first star role Jane made with a handsome son of California, Robert Redford, who was only a year older than her. In the late 1950s, he struggled for a niche as an actor, mostly in television. His Broadway debut had been in *Tall Story* (1959), whose film adaptation (1960) had paired Jane with Tony Perkins as the leads. In that same film, ironically, Redford had been cast in a minor role.

On Broadway in 1961, Redford would star in *Sunday in New York*, a play that was later adapted into a movie pairing Jane with Cliff Robertson and Rod Taylor.

Redford's first big success on Broadway came when he was cast as the stuffy husband of Elizabeth Ashley in Neil Simon's *Barefoot in the Park* (1963). He would be asked to repeat his role in that play's film adaptation. For the film adaptation, Ashley was replaced by Jane Fonda.

Before working with Jane on the screen, Redford would make two movies with Natalie Wood. In *Daisy Clover*, he played a bisexual actor who marries Wood with disastrous results. He reteamed with Wood to make *This Property is Condemned* (1966) by Tennessee Williams.

In *The Chase*, Redford worked with Brando for the first and only time.

A latter-day critic of *The Chase* wrote, "A Robert Redford character could possess certain unwholesome characteristics. Indeed, he could be an out-and-out villain without losing the sympathy of the audience. And that is a very neat trick."

Brando as Sheriff Calder tries to maintain order and justice in a town filled with hate and violence.

In *The Chase*, Angie Dickinson played Ruby, the loving and supportive wife of Calder (i.e., Brando). This daughter of North Dakota became known in such films as *Rio Bravo* (1959) and sustained a career

Two views of then "lesser than Brando" stars from *The Chase*.

Upper photo: **Marlon Brando** with **Jane Fonda** appear in a tense scene where they're about to face a town of vindictive rednecks.

Lower photo: Marvelous Marlon leading **Robert Redford** not to a hotel—as the neon sign implies—but to jail.

spanning six decades and 50 movies.

As the doomed prisoner, Bubber Reeves, Robert Redford escapes from jail and foolishly heads back into town with the intention of reuniting with his wife, Anna, a sexy vixen portrayed by Jane. Alas, during his time in jail, she had begun an affair with Jake Rogers (James Fox), the son of Val Rogers (E.G. Marshall), the richest and most powerful man in town.

Cast into minor roles in *The Chase*, Janice Rule played the town flirt, Emily Stewart. In front of her husband, Edwin Stewart, she openly flirts with Damon Fuller (Richard Bradford), who is married to Mary (Martha Hyer). Bruce Cabot, in the minor role of *Sol*, had recently worked with Jane on *Cat Ballou*.

Nearing the end of a distinguished film career, Miriam Hopkins, semi-retired, returned to the screen to play the shrill and clinging Mrs. Reeves, the mother of Bubber (Redford).

Bubber sneaks into town after his escape from prison, hiding in a junkyard where he hopes to have a rendezvous with Anne, his wife.

The townspeople, conflicted about his guilt or innocence, drink heavily. When they learn that Bubber is hiding out, they drive to the site of the junkyard and—with the intention of flushing him out, set it on fire.

Bubber manages to escape from the fire, but is arrested by Brando, the sheriff. As Brando leads Bubber up the steps of the courthouse and into jail, one of the vigilantes fatally shoots him. By that time the sheriff has been beaten and bloodied by the mob.

Then, with his wife, Ruby, Brando heads out of town forever.

The dangerously racist and psychotically violent town in Texas envisioned by Lillian Hellman was "created" on the backlot of a studio in Hollywood. A critic defined it as "a visit to Peyton Place with a side detour to Gary Cooper's *High Noon* Western outpost."

"Poor Mr. Brando," wrote Bosley Crowther of *The New York Times*. "His latest picture, *The Chase*, has continued his downward spiral of film roles. He just rides around in his patrol car, perhaps thinking of the *good ol' days* when he was the toast of Broadway playing Stanley Kowalski in *A Streetcar Named Desire*. Mr. Brando cannot make his role anything other than a stubborn, growling cop. *The Chase* is a phony, tasteless movie."

Judith Crist in the *New York Herald Tribune* wrote, "The big name performers like Brando and Jane Fonda offer professionalism with their accomplished polish. But *The Chase* is a series of shameless clichés and stereotypes hailed up with such skill you roll along with them to a smashing conclusion. But you'll hate yourself an hour later for having been hooked."

A review from *Time* magazine interpreted *The Chase* as "a shopworn message film expertly exploiting the violence, intolerance, and mean provincialism that it is supposed to be preaching against. Jane Fonda conquers a casting error as Bubber's faithless and trollopy wife, making trashy seem altogether first class."

Writing in *Life* magazine, Richard Schickel said, "*The Chase* is no longer a minor failure. Thanks to the expenditure of a great deal of time, money, and talent, it has been transformed into a disaster of awesome proportions."

Rex Reed in *The New York Daily News* found *The Chase* "the worst thing to happen to movies since the year Lassie played a war vet with amnesia. Out of style, out of fashion, out of date, Lillian Hellman has written about the most *wife-swappin'est, blackhearted'est, gun-totin'est, nigger-hatin'est town* in Texas."

Jane Fonda, re-adjusting to life in the US, after her interludes in France, and pushing her "vulnerability boundaries" through small-town rancor in *The Chase* (1966).

CHAPTER SEVEN

JANE FONDA IN
BARBARELLA
JANE GETS MORPHED INTO THE SEX KITTEN OF THE 22ND CENTURY

A CELEBRITY SHINDIG
JANE AND ROGER HOST THE BEACH PARTY OF THE DECADE
STARS (BRANDO! BEATTY!) EMERGE FROM THEIR LAIRS FOR THE MOST WIDELY PUBLICIZED BEACH BASH EVER ORGANIZED IN THE HOLLYWOOD COLONY OF MALIBU

ANY WEDNESDAY
AUDREY HEPBURN REJECTS THE FEMALE LEAD. SO DOES NATALIE WOOD.
DEBBIE REYNOLDS GOES FOR IT. BUT THEN JANE SNATCHES IT AWAY

WEDDING BELLS RING FOR THE THIRD WOMAN (JANE FONDA) TO BE IDENTIFIED AS
MRS. ROGER VADIM
AFTER A BIZARRE CEREMONY IN LAS VEGAS, THE GROOM DEMANDS AN "OPEN MARRIAGE"

THE GAME IS OVER
A "SECRETLY SNAPPED" NUDE PHOTO OF JANE ENDS UP IN HUGH HEFNER'S *PLAYBOY*

HURRY SUNDOWN
OTTO PREMINGER CASTS JANE IN THIS RACIAL SAGA. SET IN REDNECK LOUISIANA WHERE THE KKK TAUNTS AND THREATENS THE FILM CREW. JANE IS FORCED TO PERFORM FELLATIO ON A SAXOPHONE

BAREFOOT IN THE PARK
FOR YEARS AFTER ITS FILMING, JANE IS ASKED BY FANS:
"WHAT'S IT LIKE TO KISS ROBERT REDFORD?"

MYRA BRECKINRIDGE
"Jane would make the perfect transsexual."

—Roger Vadim

At their rented villa in Malibu, Roger Vadim and his new wife Jane entertained lavishly. Every weekend became something that evoked an "open house," where no one knew who might show up.

Perhaps Mia Farrow and Frank Sinatra; Dennis Hopper and Brooke Hayward; Larry Hagman in a bikini that revealed more than it concealed; or Lauren Bacall who arrived with (of all people) Andy Warhol.

Even Henry Fonda showed up on occasion with his devoted Shirlee, or Peter Fonda might arrive with an entire rock band.

With enormous fanfare, Jane had recently completed *The Chase* and *Cat Ballou*. In the interim before the debut of another project, she decided to throw what became known as "the Beach Party of the Decade."

Peter (Fonda) with his friends, members of the rock group "the Byrds," provided the music.

Vadim commissioned the erection of a mammoth tent directly on the beach. Henry Fonda volunteered to set up a spit and spent a good part of the day roasting a pig. Although he had reservations about his daughter's involvement with Vadim, he managed to keep silent about their liaison.

Peter had spent time evaluating Vadim. He didn't trust him at first, although he eventually came to like him. "At first, I compared Roger to my Dad. As I got to know him better, I realized he came in a better package than dear old Dad."

Peter's familiarity with recreational drugs was well-known in Hollywood, and it was having a negative effect on his film career.

During the months ahead, he would lobby for certain choice roles, getting rejected because of his reputation. He wanted to star in the upcoming *The Sand Pebbles* (1966) but was rejected in favor of Steve McQueen. He also tried out for a role as one of the killers in Truman Capote's *In Cold Blood* (1967), but lost the part to Robert Blake.

The guest list of the Malibu party contained a mixture of Old Guard Hollywood with the more liberated and cutting-edge younger generation. Ironic pairings cropped up everywhere: George Cukor found himself near a hippie girl who later joined the Charles Manson gang. Oblivious to the guests around her, she prominently began breast-feeding her hungry infant. Danny Kaye, also standing nearby, improvised a schtick in which he mimicked a baby in need of breast feeding.

Darryl Zanuck showed up with an unknown starlet, mingling with Sam Spiegel. William Wyler—who had directed Merle Oberon in *Wuthering Heights,* and who had for a while been married to Margaret Sullavan, Henry Fonda's first wife—was also an honored guest.

Other guests included Jack Lemmon, Gene Kelly with a beautiful male dancer, Sidney Poitier,

Here's a mid-1950s view of the fabled cluster of beachfronting houses in Malibu, a nostalgia-soaked enclave dating back to Old Hollywood and its yearnings to get away from the madding crowds and insanity-inducing studios.

In 1965, Jane Fonda and her then-husband, Roger Vadim, rented one of these beach houses in Malibu for $200 per month. Adjusted for inflation, that would be about $1,800. In the early 2020s, that same 1930's era house, since renovated, is currently available for rent for $125,000 per month.

Where's the beef? Sadly, it costs a lot more money in the 21st century to live like a bohemian than when "Jane and Roger," the entertainment industry's most sought-after hipsters, were throwing legendary beach parties for the drug-soaked, uber-promiscuous *cognoscenti*.

and Jules and Doris Stein. Warren Beatty showed up with what Paul Newman labeled as "his latest piece," Miss Natalie Wood herself.

The doomed Sharon Tate was a guest, seen dancing with the French novelist Romain Gary. Standing on the sidelines, looking on, was his wife, the also doomed Jean Seberg.

The party was touted as the highlight of that summer at Malibu.

Throughout the summer, other guests came and went, notably Marlon Brando, who had completed *The Chase* (1966) with Jane. He was with his male lover, Christian Marquand, Vadim's dearest friend. Brando continued to visit, sometimes with another male lover, Wally Cox, or perhaps Rita Moreno, even on one occasion, Ursula Andress.

Larry Hagman, son of Mary Martin, visited several times. For some reason, when not in "that bikini," he liked to parade up and down the beach in a gorilla suit.

Jill Schary Robinson, the daughter of MGM's Dore Schary, had an experience she'd never forget. She attended a Sunday afternoon open house at the Vadim/Fonda home and had too much to drink.

She wandered down the beach, where she encountered some tough surfers. They practically dragged her back to their rented house where collectively, they assaulted her.

Hours later, she returned to the Vadim household with her clothes half torn off, shaken and sobbing.

Jack Nicholson, who had co-starred with Peter Fonda, visited the Vadims, sometimes with Jerry Hall or perhaps model Lauren Hutton.

***

Any Wednesday (1966)

This American Technicolor comedy featured a top-billed Jane Fonda with Jason Robards Jr. and Dean Jones cast as her leading men. Each of the characters they played wanted exclusive rights to her.

Julius J. Epstein was both its producer and writer. He based the screenplay on a play written by Murial Resnik that had run on Broadway for 984 performances from 1964 to 1966.

That production had starred Sandy Dennis., Don Porter, Gene Hackman, and Rosemary Murphy.

Dennis was at the peak of her career and had hopes that she could repeat her stage role on the screen. She had won the Best Supporting Actress Oscar for the film adaptation of Edward Albee's *Who's Afraid of Virginia Woolf?* (1966).

Jane was not Epstein's first choice as his female lead. He later admitted that he had had Audrey Hepburn in mind for the lead, but she rejected his script, calling it "a bit of fluff."

Natalie Wood told Epstein that only a week before, she'd been offered three far superior scripts. "Your *Any Wednesday* seems on life support," she said.

In contrast, Debbie Reynolds was most willing to do it, telling Epstein, "If shooting starts Monday morning, I'll be there at 5AM."

When Jane became available, Epstein didn't bother to tell Debbie that she didn't have the part.

Julius J. Epstein was the twin brother of Philip. They had immortalized themselves with the screenplay for Warner Brother's classic, *Casablanca* (1942), which brought them an Academy Award. It also earned its stars, Humphrey Bogart and Ingrid Bergman, a place in film history, since it's often cited as the best

Thanks in part to the international notoriety she'd attracted in France, **Jane** was now a noted celebrity in Italy, too.

Here's a promotion for **Any Wednesday**, Italian-style, showing a hip and sexually liberated American fox provocatively dangling the oversized keys to her boudoir.

movie ever made, competing with Orson Welles' *Citizen Kane* (1941) for that honor. Two years later, the twins were both designated as the writers of *Mr. Skeffington*, a box office success that brought Oscar nominations for its stars, Bette Davis and Claude Rains.

The brothers often feuded with Jack Warner. He became so furious with them that he turned their names over to the House Un-American Activities Committee, but they were never investigated.

When Julius was asked if he were ever part of any subversive organization, he admitted that he was: "Warner Brothers" he answered.

CARRIE FISHER & DEBBIE REYNOLDS
Princess Leia & Unsinkable Tammy in Hell

ANOTHER OUTRAGEOUS TITLE IN BLOOD MOON'S BABYLON SERIES
DARWIN PORTER & DANFORTH PRINCE

Debbie Reynolds, shown here with an early version of her real-life daughter, **Carrie Fisher** (aka Princess Leia from *Star Wars*) urgently wanted the *Any Wednesday* role later awarded to Jane.

Did you know? That Debbie Reynolds is one of this writing team's most unsinkable icons, and that its members are hard-core fans? For more about this survivor of the Great Depression who started her career as **Miss Burbank of 1948** and later as **Tammy** (with or without her Bachelor), check out Blood Moon's award-winning overview of her life story.

The director, Robert Ellis Miller, was fairly new to filmmaking. But by 1968, he would helm the film adaptation of the Carson McCullers' classic, *The Heart Is a Lonely Hunter,* hailed as one of the best American novels ever written. The 1940 book depicted a deaf man's relationship with a teenaged girl in the 1930s in Georgia.

It starred Alan Arkin and introduced the then-unknown Sandra Locke to the screen. Each of them received Oscar nominations for their roles.

After helming Jane Fonda, Miller would go on to direct such stars as Cicely Tyson, Peter Ustinov, Omar Sharif, and Goldie Hawn. Many of these actors also remembered Miller for doing the best Bette Davis imitation ever known, beating out an array of drag queens across the country.

As the movie opens, Ellen Gordon (Jane) is about to turn thirty, and no man has ever placed a wedding ring on her finger. She's living in luxury in an apartment with rent paid by the married John Cleves (Jason Robards). He is an executive who lives with his wife, Dorothy (Rosemary Murphy) in New Jersey. Every Wednesday, he stays over in the city "on business."

[Actually, that is the night he schedules for regular visits to his mistress, portrayed by Jane.]

The plot gets complicated when the secretary to Cleves sends a business client from Akron, Cass Henderson, (Dean Jones), who cannot find a hotel room, to live in the suite during his stay in New York. *[The secretary is mistaken in her belief that Jane's apartment is a sort of executive suite for housing clients from out of town.]*

When Jones meets Ellen, he mistakenly assumed that she has been hired to entertain him.

The attraction between Cass and Ellen quickly blossoms. Eventually, Dorothy learns what her husband has been up to, and she leaves him. During their parting scene, she cynically tells him that he can come and visit her "any Wednesday."

Robards was a very talented actor who, in time, would win an Oscar, a Tony, and an Emmy, one of two dozen actors to take home that "triple crown." At the time he worked with Jane, he was married to Lauren Bacall, who was becoming disillusioned with him for his alcoholism.

Jane and Robards would have far more chemistry together when they teamed up again in *Julia* (1977) and in *Comes a Horseman* (1978).

A son of Alabama, Dean Jones, in the words of one critic, "was the epitome of a wholesome, family-oriented, nice guy with a bright but quavering voice." He became synonymous with lightweight comedies for Walt Disney, although he did co-star with Elvis Presley in *Jailhouse Rock* (1957).

In 1973, he became a devout "Born Again" Christian. As he recalled, "One night I got down on my knees and prayed that God would free me from the miserable moods I suffered. In an instant, my prayer was answered, and I felt peace and joy flooding my heart."

Later, after Jane had received tsunamis of press notoriety, Jones was asked what it had been like working on a movie with her. "She's led a wicked life," he answered, "and I have prayed to God to spare her from Hell's fire."

Suffering from Parkinson's disease, Jones died on September 1, 2015 at the age of 84. His body was cremated.

Many reviewers cited Rosemary Murphy, as the wife of the cheating husband, as performing better than the film's three big-name stars. Born in Munich, Germany, she had been nominated for three Tony Awards for her stage roles. But most of America came to know her when she portrayed Sara Delano Roosevelt in the TV miniseries, *Eleanor and Franklin* (1976).

The *Monthly Film Bulletin* defined *Any Wednesday* as "a moderately entertaining film version of the Broadway stage production. It could have been much more so if director Robert Ellis Miller had a lighter touch."

Richard Coe of *The Washington Post* found Fonda miscast because "she is simply not the sort of girl who doesn't know what she is doing."

Variety called it "an outstanding sophisticated comedy with solid direction and excellent performances."

Philip K. Scheuer of the *Los Angeles Times* wrote, "Neither Jason Robards nor Jane Fonda strike me particularly as a natural comedian (whatever that may be), and the timing of both of them seems off. Robards is a superior actor, and I was surprised that he was willing to waste his time and talent on such a contrived and cinematically weak affair as this."

Rex Reed in the *New York Daily News* gave the most scathing review: "Simply everything is wrong with this loud-mouthed movie that is boring and vulgar. The story of the thirty-year-old mistress gets all but stomped on by the cleated boots of Fonda. She is about as funny as a manic-depressive having her first nervous breakdown. She screams, weeps, beats the furniture, picks at her cuticles and, when she has no lines, she just pouts and fusses with her fright wig."

Richard F. Shepard of *The New York Times* wrote: "Jane Fonda's eyes widen appropriately, she gets hysterical, she pouts and goes through these exquisite changes of mood like a barometer in an area of rapidly changing pressures."

Time magazine summed it up best: "Sex ought to seem less work, more fun."

***

 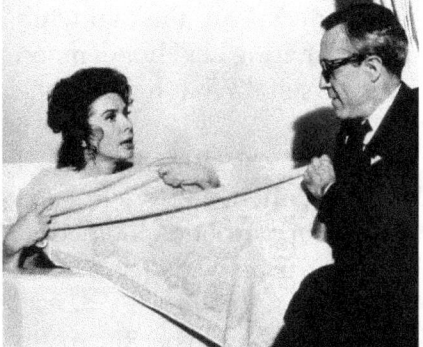 

SEXUAL AND OFFICE POLITICS AT THE FORTUNE 500
WEDNESDAY, as the film's title implies, is HUMP DAY

Left photo: **Jason Robards** kissing his secretary, played by **Jane**
Middle photo: **Rosemary Murphy**, the "locked up" wife in the suburbs, playing defensive with her cheating husband (Robards), and
Right photo: **Dean Jones**, a youngish exec on the make, kissing his boss's disillusioned playmate, Ellen (**Jane Fonda**).

In Los Angeles, before the autumn leaves started to fall, Jane and Vadim were packing to return to Paris, where she was to begin shooting *The Game Is Over,* to be directed by him.

Their final visitor was Christian Marquand, who was also returning to Paris. He later said, "Roger was open about his seductions of other women. He liked threesomes. Jane may not have known this, but, for variety's sake, he sometimes topped a pretty young man who might have hoped to get cast in one of his movies. Vadim assured her that although he fucked around, she was the one true love of his life. Before the summer was over, he married her, promising to be faithful forever. Yeah, right!"

***

The wedding of Jane Fonda to Roger Vadim took place on August 14, 1965 in their six-room suite at the Dunes Hotel on the Las Vegas Strip. It was officiated by Justice of the Peace James Brennon, who, only a month before, had married Cary Grant to actress Dyan Cannon.

Jane and Vadim, with such friends as Brooke Hayward and Dennis Hopper, flew to Nevada in a chartered plane from Los Angeles. Henry Fonda could not attend since he was on Broadway and about to open in a play.

Peter Fonda, who was also aboard that flight from California, came with his wife, Tina Aumont, to whom he was married from 1963 to 1966. She was the daughter of the famous French actor, Jean-Pierre Aumont. When Peter married her, she was only 17 and he was 36.

Vadim's mother, Marie Antoinette, was designated as matron of honor.

When it came time for Vadim to place a wedding band on Jane's finger, it became flagrantly clear that he had forgotten to buy one. Hurriedly, Marquand removed his own wedding band and handed it to Vadim. It didn't fit Jane's slender finger, of course, but it had to suffice as a means of finishing their final vows.

She signed the marriage register as "Lady Jane Seymour Brokaw Fonda Plemiannikov."

Peter, on his guitar, provided the wedding music. He was accompanied by a half-dozen women vocalists, each attired in skintight, sequin-covered evening gowns.

After a lavish buffet dinner, the Vadims and their guests visited a nightclub for a burlesque stage show, a so-called "re-enactment of the French Revolution."

The actress portraying Marie Antoinette (the name of Vadim's mother) was topless during her "beheading" on the guillotine.

Jane's wedding night did not go as planned. After the nightclub act Vadim headed for a casino. Jane ended up sharing her "honeymoon night" with his mother. She bitterly asked herself, "What have I done in marrying this compulsive gambler?"

The next day, as dawn broke over Nevada, the by-now-disheveled wedding party returned to Los Angeles aboard their chartered plane.

Jane had begun her married life. Two other husbands loomed in her future: Activist Tom Hayden and later, television tycoon and CNN founder Ted Turner.

Numerous lovers would also play important roles in her future. In the years to come, she'd be rumored take as lovers Alain Delon, Kris Kristofferson, Jimmy Smits, Mick Jagger, cinematographer Sven Nykvist, TV host Geraldo Rivera, columnist Robert Scheer, slain hairdresser Jay Sebring, Donald Sutherland, and members of the Black Panthers.

With his marriage to Jane Fonda, **Roger Vadim** brought to fruition the triptych of women who collectively built his image as the ultimate Pygmalion of the 20th Century.

Here's the cover of **his** (some said shameless) **memoir,** published in 1986, about a decade before his death.

Despite his brilliant career as a filmmaker, it was ironic, writers at *The Guardian* said, that his role as a Svengali to international sex symbols was the only guise in which he would eventually become known.

Vadim was quick to trade, as he aged, on his own tabloid reputation.

***

The Game Is Over (aka *La Curée*; 1966)

Back in France, Vadim was both the director and the producer of Jane's next picture.

The plot, updated to modern times, was very loosely based on Émile Zola's 1871 novel, *La Curée* (released in England as *The Kill)*. His saga dealt with the lives of the *nouveaux riches* of France's Second Empire, set against the backdrop of Baron Haussman's reconstruction of Paris in the 1850s and 1860s. Vadim worked with screenwriter Bernard Frechtman on a new version of the old story.

The film co-starred Michel Piccoli and Peter McEnery. In the role of Jane's older husband, Piccoli was not only an actor, but at times a producer and director in a career that spanned seven decades. He could play a seducer, a policeman, a gangster, even the Pope, roles he portrayed in 170 movies.

Six of his films were directed by Luis Buñuel, including *Belle de Jour* (1967). He was also Bardot's husband in Jean-Luc Godard's *Le Mépris (Contempt; 1963)* and the main antagonist in Alfred Hitchcock's *Topaz* (1969). From 1966 to 1977, he was married to the fabled French singer, Juliette Greco.

Peter McEnery was an English actor three years younger than Jane. One of his best-known films was *Victim*, a 1961 British *neo noir* suspense film. He was cast as a young, working-class gay man who falls prey to blackmailers. In contrast, McEnery was known for giving Hayley Mills her first grown-up screen kiss in *The Moon Spinners* (1964).

FATHERS AND SONS

"**WHAT SHOULD A GIRL DO AFTER MARRYING THE FATHER?**" Asks the character played by **Jane Fonda** in a film adaptation of a turn-of-the-century French potboiler by Emile Zola, *La Curée*.

Left photo: Jane gets down with the veteran French actor **Michel Piccoli**, her (older than she) husband and also *(right photo)*. with his biological son from an earlier marriage, as portrayed by **Peter McEnery.**

The setting is Paris. Maxime Saccard (McEnery) visits his rich industrialist father, Alexandre (Piccoli). Here, he meets his father's beautiful Canadian wife, Renée (Fonda). Alexandre had fathered Maxime years ago in a prior marriage.

Renée confides to Maxime that she married Alexandre when she was pregnant, following an unhappy affair. The child was stillborn and whatever passion they existed between them is long gone.

Renée and Maxime, as might have been predicted, fall in love. Renée wants a divorce, but it comes at a price. Alexandre agrees to let her go, providing she will leave her fortune (and any claim to his money) behind.

Maxime faces a dilemma: He can run off with a now-penniless Renée or become engaged to Anne Sernet (Tina Aumont), the daughter of a wealthy banker. Maxime goes for the money. Before the film's release, Vadim told the press, "I am making no attempt to give the wide sociological picture that Zola did. I am not a naturalist or a moralist. The Zola characters were hardly everyday. There was something fantastic about them, though they have their counterparts today, as I hope to show."

"I loved working in French," Jane said. "You feel a certain freedom and can say things you wouldn't dare say in English."

Once again, Jane starred in some nude scenes. Some unauthorized black market "souvenir" shots were snapped of her, showing her topless and, in some cases, views of her rear. These were sold to *Playboy*, which published them. She filed a lawsuit, which led to nothing for her.

The movie was a hit in France but attracted only a small audience in America. According to *Playboy's* publisher, Hugh Hefner, "The photos of her in my magazine caused it to sell like hotcakes."

When *La Curée* was released in Italy, government authorities seized all copies on the grounds that it was obscene. Vadim and Fonda were not charged, but its producer, Mario Sarago, and 23 others associated with it were booked.

Roger Ebert of Chicago's *Sun-Times* defined *The Game Is Over* as "tedious and ridiculous, but a film of great physical beauty."

The critic for the *Washington Post* found it "a deliciously false and phony picture."

Bosley Crowther of *The New York Times* wrote, "*The Game Is Over* has absolutely nothing in it but fancy clothes and décor."

Judith Crist in the *New York World Journal Tribune* said "Roger Vadim firmly establishes himself as Ross Hunter of the *Nouvelle Vague* and Jane Fonda is Miss Nude of 1967. The movie will firmly set the cause of cinema back some 40 years."

Dale Monroe of the *Hollywood Citizen News* had a very different view: "*Game* is Vadim's best picture to date and is unquestionably Miss Fonda's finest screen portrayal."

Kevin Thomas of the *Los Angeles Times* found "*The Game Is Over (is)* the finest film so far in Jane's career. She creates a comprehensive portrait of a woman in love—her joys and sorrows, hopes, and fears."

Rex Reed, in the *New York Daily News* counted seven full bare-breasted scenes of Fonda. "Her father must be purple-faced with embarrassment. Vadim handles her as if she were the Venus de Milo. However, all that half-hearted upper-class sexual depravity is enough to make one long for the dear departed ways of Walt Disney."

***

Roger Vadim stayed in Paris, working on the script for their upcoming movie *Barbarella*. Its producers had offered its lead female role to Brigitte Bardot and then to Sophia Loren, each of whom had rejected it. Vadim was working to turn it into a vehicle for Jane.

But first, Otto Preminger wanted her to star in *Hurry Sundown*, which meant she had to fly to New Orleans.

***

Hurry Sundown (1967)

Otto Preminger was given a copy of the novel *Hurry Sundown* before it was officially published. In 1965, the 1,100-page book sold 300,000 copies. Its author was listed as "K.B. Gilden," which turned out to be a pseudonym of a married writing team, Bert and Katya Gilden.

After acquiring its film rights for $100,000, Preminger proclaimed, "I'm going to make a movie to outshine *Gone With the Wind*."

Preminger was in London at the time, shooting *Bunny Lake Is Missing* (1965). He moved screenwriter Horton Foote and his family into a home in the city, and

Michael Caine attempts to expose **Jane Fonda**'s breasts as a prelude to sex, but she seems reluctant.

the screenwriter stayed there for three months, at the director's expense, adapting the novel into a script. He had been hired because of his success he'd had in the film adaptation of Harper Lee's *To Kill a Mockingbird* (1962).

Regrettably, Preminger didn't like Foote's final manuscript, but he paid him off, flying his family back to the United States. He had wanted far more melodrama than Foote had inserted into his script.

He then hired Thomas C. Ryan because he'd liked his adaptation of Carson McCullers' *The Heart Is a Lonely Hunter*. Ryan was a very troubled writer, a homosexual who had made several suicide attempts.

When Preminger was given an acceptable script, he set about casting the roles with both white and African American actors.

For the male lead—that of the bigoted, draft-dodging, gold-digging racist, Henry Warren—Preminger made an odd casting choice: the London-born Michael aine, who still maintained a distinctive Cockney accent. Caine claimed that he could "talk Southern," but one critic claimed that his mock accent "out-Remuses the old Uncle Remus himself."

Preminger had seen *The Chase* (1966) in which Jane had co-starred with Marlon Brando and Robert Redford. He thought she would be ideal as Caine's wife, a land-owning heiress. They are determined to sell the land to the owners of a northern canning factory, which wants to move South to take advantage of the cheap labor.

In the most controversial scene in *Hurry Sundown*, **Michael Caine** suggestively holds a saxophone between his legs. Later, **Jane Fonda** simulates fellation on the instrument.

The scene was so tasteless that it was removed from showings on television.

The deal rests on selling two adjoining plots, one owned by Henry's cousin, Rad McDowell (John Philip Law) and his wife, Lou (Faye Dunaway).

The other plot of land is owned by a black farmer, Reeve Scott (Robert Hooks), who lives with his dying 54-year-old mother, Rosa (played by Beah Richards). They are not interested in selling their land, and they form a kind of interracial partnership with the McDowell family.

Here, the plot thickens and trouble is on the way as the rednecks pierce a dam and flood the disputed farmland.

When the floodwaters roar over the farmland, the crops and homes of both the McDowell and Scott families are ruined, and the youngest son of the McDowells is drowned.

Henry (Michael Caine) disputes the Scott's ownership of their land. However, a black school teacher, Vivian Thurlow (Diahann Carroll), searches the town records and finds that the Scott's ownership is valid.

Other key supporting roles were played by George Kennedy as Sheriff Coombs; Burgess Meredith as Judge Purcell; Madeleine Sherwood as Eula Purcell; and Jim Backus as Carter Sillens.

Preminger was careful in the choices he made for the casting of every role.

Law, born the same year as Jane, was a child of Hollywood itself. From an early age, he always wanted to be an actor, and his breakthrough role came when he was cast as a Russian sailor in the comedy, *The Russians Are Coming, the Russians Are Coming* (1966).

It is said that for months after Jane saw him emerge clad only in a skimpy bathing suit from their motel's pool, she remembered his "pretty boy" looks and played a major role in getting him cast as the blind and winged angel in her upcoming sci-fi drama, *Barbarella.*

As Dunaway was involved with the filming of her a minor role (Lou McDowell) in *Hurry Sundown,* she got "the break of my life" when Jane Fonda rejected the female lead in *Bonnie and Clyde* (1967) opposite Warren Beatty. Dunaway stepped in and shot to overnight fame. Her portrayal of Bonnie Parker put her on the Hollywood map, and she received her first Best Actress Oscar nod.

In her future career, she worked with some of the most famous directors in Hollywood, including

Women of **Hurry Sundown**, left to right: **Beah Parks; Madeleine Sherwood; Jane Fonda** (in a sun hat) with **Diahann Carroll;** and **Faye Dunaway.**

Elia Kazan and Roman Polanski.

Opinions in the film industry varied. Bette Davis labeled Dunaway "the worst person I ever worked with." In contrast, director Sidney Lumet defined her as "a selfless, devoted, and wonderful actress."

Almost immediately after working with Jane on *Hurry Sundown,* Dunaway made *A Place for Lovers* (1968) and fell in love with her co-star, Marcello Mastroianni, a married man. He had to break it off after 2½ years, but later told reporters, "Faye was the love of my life."

Here's **Faye Dunaway** (*left photo*) pouring poison in the ear of her ethical, kind-hearted sharecropping husband (**John Philip Law**) in *Hurry Sundown*, and (*right photo*) after her "in a hurry' migration to bigger roles in bigger films—in this case, as serial crimester **Bonnie Parker** in *Bonnie and Clyde*.

Diahann Carroll was an actress, singer, model, and activist who rose to fame appearing with black casts in such films as *Carmen Jones* (1954) and *Porgy and Bess* (1959).

Although she was married four times, she was more famous for her affairs, including an almost decade-long relationship with the married actor Sidney Poitier. For four years, she lived with David Frost, the British TV host and producer.

Beah Richards, an African American actress who rose from the cotton fields of Mississippi, became a star of stage, screen, and television, and also a poet, playwright, and author.

In *Hurry Sundown,* she portrays Rosa Scott, the dying mother of Reeve Scott (cast with Robert Hooks). They are trying to save their homestead from land-grabbers.

When she was a baby, Julia (Jane) was wet nursed by Rosa. But now, the land deal is tearing at the core of their longtime friendship.

Beah Richards' acting career didn't really begin until 1955, when she was cast in mother or grandmother roles. Her early Broadway roles were in the stage versions of *The Miracle Worker* and *A Raisin in the Sun.*

She received a Best Supporting Actress Oscar Nomination in 1967 for playing the mother of Sidney Poitier in *Guess Who's Coming to Dinner* with Spencer Tracy and Katharine Hepburn.

From the 1930s till the late 1950s, Richards was a member and organizer of the Communist Party in Los Angeles, working in close collaboration with Paul Robeson.

A daughter of Québec, Madeleine Sherwood was widely known for her portrayals of Sister Woman and Miss Lucy, each both on Broadway and in the film adaptations of Tennessee Williams' *Cat on a Hot Tin Roof* with Elizabeth Taylor and Paul Newman. She also appeared in *Sweet Bird of Youth* (1962) with Geraldine Page and again, with Paul Newman.

During the McCarthy era, Sherwood was blacklisted, in part because of having worked with Martin Luther King, Jr.

Jim Backus was a familiar face, especially for his portrayals of Thurston Howell III on the 1960s sitcom *Gilligan's Island;* and as the father of the James Dean character in *Rebel Without a Cause* (1955). Children usually knew him as the voice of the nearsighted cartoon character, Mr. Magoo.

Arriving late in court is Backus in his role of attorney for the defense. In this small role, he was cast against type from his by then "usual" comedic characters.. Judge Purcell regards him with contempt, because in his court, he prefers that blacks defend themselves—and not hire lawyers.

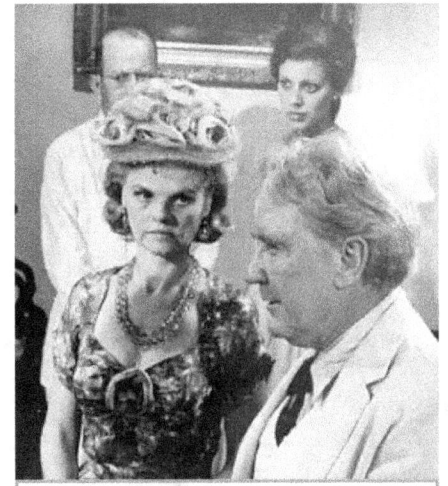

There's no southern comfort in *Hurry Sundown:* **Madeleine Sherwood,** left, as the petulant and socially ambitious daughter of the petulant and probably sociopathic judge, as played by **Burgess Meredith.**

In *Hurry Sundown,* **Jim Backus** (right) played against the grain of his usually high-eccentric type. Here, he appears with **Natalie Schafer** as out-of-step socialites, Mr. and Mrs. Thurston Howell III in *Gilligan's Island.*

Burgess Meredith delivers a performance as a redneck Southern judge that is without equal in cinema history. One critic defined him as "the most disgusting judge who ever appeared on screen."

Jane had long known Meredith, as he was one of her father's best and oldest friends. When Henry got married to Frances Seymour Brokaw and no longer roomed with James Stewart, Meredith took his place as Stewart's roommate. He would later marry Paulette Goddard after her marriage (1936-1942) and divorce from Charlie Chaplin.

George Kennedy was known to Jane, since he had co-starred with Henry in the Otto Preminger-directed World War II drama, *In Harm's Way* (1965), and again with Henry in *The Boston Strangler* (1968), starring Tony Curtis as the psychotic killer.

Preminger originally planned to shoot *Hurry Sundown* in the rural bowels of redneck Georgia, but found the locals hostile, deeply mired in the racial prejudices of the Old South. Word quickly spread that the plot dealt with "niggers gettin' the best of whites" and "noble blacks scoring points on white trash."

Finally, Gene Callihan, who had already won two Oscars for art direction, suggested that instead of in Georgia, they should film in the area around Baton Rouge, about 70 miles north of New Orleans, beside the Mississippi River.

"The locals tolerate us better, I think. Besides, the landscapes will photograph better than those in Georgia."

Preminger arrived with a crew and set about altering some of the local terrain, even constructing a dam that would hold the almost 18 million gallons of water that were needed for the dramatic flood scene. He also ordered the construction of some "sharecroppers shacks."

Dozens of rooms were reserved at the Bellmont Motel, the second-largest in the United States. However, when it was discovered that some of the rooms would be occupied by blacks, a controversy arose, especially when one of the African Americans actually took a swim in the heretofore all-white swimming pool.

The local branch of the KKK issued death threats, and the cars of cast and crew were often vandalized, their tires slashed. Once, Caine was walking down Baton Rouge's main street where he encountered a local policeman. The cop warned him, "You'd better get your nigga-lovin' ass out of this town."

Jane and Diahann tried to dine at Brennan's Restaurant, the best in town, but were refused a table. As a champion of civil rights, Jane flew into a screaming rage.

Sometimes, when members of the crew were driving to various filming locations, shots were fired at them.

For the most part, Preminger was kind and supportive of both Caine and Jane, although in the scalding heat of a Louisiana summer, Jane and Preminger sometimes lost their respective tempers and went into screaming fights.

Their relationship ended when he told her, "Little girl, you were the single factor holding this damn movie together."

Caine later told a reporter, "Otto is only happy when he has made everybody else miserable."

Throughout the shooting, the director's fury was for the most part aimed at Faye Dunaway and John Philip Law. In one scene, he even had to show Law "how to kiss a woman."

Reportedly, Dunaway later said, in reference to Preminger, "I detested the swine."

Upon the release of *Hurry Sundown,* critical attacks were laced with acid. The Legion of Decency condemned it, citing its portrayal of both blacks and of sex. One scene with Jane and Caine was so controversial that it was actually cut in some showings.

"Never before and never again would I be called upon to perform saxophone fellatio," Jane said.

Critic Richard Schickel called the scene "one of the most embarrassing moments in the history of cinema." Sitting at the feet of her husband, she uses the saxophone to suggest how good she might be at fellatio. She knows the saxophone "symbolically and seductively."

"That scene was difficult to perform," Jane later said. "I also detested another scene where I had to slap the face of Diahann Carroll because she came into a restroom reserved for white ladies."

Roger Ebert of the *Chicago Sun-Times* wrote, "The trouble with this film is not that it's racist and tasteless, but that it is naïve and dull."

Bosley Crowther of *The New York Times* found the movie "pure pulp fiction, an offense to intelligence."

Rex Reed cited what he mockingly called Jane's best line. "I was ten years old before I learned that *Damn* and *Yankee* were two words."

He also claimed that at the screening he attended, members of their audience threw popcorn at the screen.

Channel 4 noted that "Preminger wears a liberal heart on his sleeve and then blows his nose on it as a heavy-handed sentimentality and nobility dominate the story. Good sex, class, guilt, moralizing, and Negro spirituals are all thrown into the stew. You'll come away feeling that although it's worthy in its ideals, it could have been done with a touch less overblown melodrama."

In the *New York World Journal Tribune,* Judith Crist didn't hold anything back in her review: "Gather roun', chillum, while dem banjos is strummin' out. *Hurry Sundown* and ol' Marse Preminger gwine tell us all about de' South. He has provided us not only with soap opera plotting that gives *Peyton Place* Dostoievskian stature, but also with cartoon characters and patronage of Negroes that are incredible in 1967. Jane doesn't even melt when Caine grabs her by the breast. The movie stands with the worst films of any number of years."

HURRY IT UP, ALREADY!

After savagings from critics everywhere, moviegoers hoped that sundown for this film, would indeed, hurry.

***

Flying in from Paris, Vadim took time off from his work to visit the set of *Hurry Sundown* for one week. He not only claimed "husband's rights" with Jane in her rented room, but spotted John Philip Law one day around the hotel swimming pool. He saw the handsome young actor emerge from the pool like a piece of sculpture. It was at that very moment that he offered him the role of the blind angel in *Barbarella.*

Law later said, "I thought he was a gay Frenchman trying to pick me up for sex."

After she finished her work for Preminger, Jane was rushed almost immediately into the film adaptation of Neil Simon's *Barefoot in the Park.*

***

Barefoot in the Park (1967)

After Henry Fonda had seen his daughter emote in *A Period of Adjustment,* he said, "I can't believe that was not a Neil Simon play. Surely Tennessee Williams didn't write this silly romantic comedy!"

[Actually, Tennessee Williams DID write A Period of Adjustment, *although it was hardly in the same class as* A Streetcar Named Desire *or* Cat on a Hot Tin Roof.*]*

***

As it came to be, deep into her marriage to Roger Vadim, Jane was selected as the female lead in a film adaptation of a Neil Simon play, *Barefoot in the Park.*

As a play, it had opened to success on Broadway in 1963, starring Elizabeth Ashley and a young Robert Redford.

Simon was on hand and available for consultation during the production of the film, and Jane, indeed, got to meet him. He was in the early stages of his career. In time, he would go on to receive more Oscar & Tony award nominations than any other writer. During the course of his career, he wrote scripts for 30 plays and almost as many movies, many of them screen adaptations of his own plays.

Right after *Barefoot*, he would write *The Odd Couple* (1965), which in its various adaptations would generate millions of dollars. By then, he was widely acknowledged as "the hottest playwright on Broadway."

Hal B. Wallis, who acquired the film rights to *Barefoot*, saw the film as a vehicle for Troy Donahue and Natalie Wood, but Natalie was too expensive. At the time, the handsome and blonde Donahue was being (successfully) marketed as "the new Tab Hunter," taking over as a Hollywood heartthrob. Wallis later rejected him and agreed to give the role to Redford, who had performed it frequently and reliably on Broadway. Wallis didn't believe that Elizabeth Ashley had enough name recognition, so he decided to award the part to Jane Fonda.

Redford and Jane had previously co-starred in *The Chase* with Marlon Brando, but they didn't become good friends until more than a year later, when they made *Barefoot* together. She predicted that Redford would morph into a big Hollywood star, as he combined good looks with talent.

In the years to come, Jane and Redford would often battle for the same political causes. Over the years, he watched as she became a notorious figure in American politics. As he recalled, "Jane is like the phoenix who keeps rising from the ashes."

She said, "There is something about Bob (Redford) that's impossible not to fall in love with. I was smitten, utterly twitter-pated. Nothing ever happened between us except that we always had a good time working together. I have never seen women react to a man the way they do to Bob. Of all the male stars I've worked with,

In a sexually provocative scene in *Barefoot in the Park*, a pantie-less **Jane Fonda** tries to lure her somewhat stuffy husband, **Robert Redford**, out of not only his overcoat, but his pants and jockey shorts, too.

Bob is the only one about whom women ask me, 'What's it like to kiss him?' The reality is a little different: Fabulous for me, not fabulous for him. He hates filming kissing scenes."

Mildred Natwick asked to repeat her stage role as Jane's mother, Ethel Banks. She'd made her Broadway debut in 1932 in Frank McGrath's play, *Carry Nation*, about the famous Temperance crusader, whose name in some historic records is spelled "Carrie" Nation.

For years, Natwick had been a favorite of Josh Logan, the actor/director/playwright, who had been instrumental in the early careers of both Henry and Jane.

Natwick appeared in a number of John Ford classics such as *The Quiet Man* (1952) starring John Wayne and Maureen O'Hara. In *Barefoot*, she would be Oscar nominated for Best Supporting Actress. Many critics said she stole many scenes from Redford and Jane.

AN ODD COUPLE: Character actress **Mildred Natwick** manages to steam up **Charles Boyer** in this restaurant setting from *Barefoot in the Park*. Jane Fonda is Corrie, the daughter of Natwick.

Just for fun, Corrie arranges a romantic date for her old-fashioned mother, who ends up spending the night in the Frenchman's apartment.

In the twilight of his career, Charles Boyer, cast as Victor Velasco, plays the bohemian neighbor of the Bratters. He has to cross through their apartment to get to his lodgings in the attic.

A Boyer biographer, Larry Swindell, claimed, "Boyer seemed out of his element as the seedy upstairs neighbor dodging creditors while leering at Miss Fonda."

Between 1920 and 1976, Boyer would star in about eighty movies, most notably in *Algiers* (1938), *Love Affair* (1939), and *Gaslight* (1944).

Boyer had been an early friend of Henry Fonda, and he shared memories of that relationship with Jane.

Sadly, on August 26, 1978, he committed suicide by overdosing on Seconal during his visit to a friend in Scottsdale, Arizona.

The director of *Barefoot in the Park*, Gene Saks, was both an actor and a director. As a director, he would, in time, be nominated for seven Tony Awards, winning three times.

Saks was married to Bea Arthur from 1950 to 1978, and had helmed her in the 1974 film adaptation of *Mame* alongside Lucille Ball.

Redford was cast as a conservative and a bit stuffy young lawyer recently married to Corie (Jane), who is vivacious and spontaneous. They have moved into a fifth-floor walk-up in Greenwich Village.

Huffing and puffing after that steep climb, Ethel Banks (Natwick) pays her daughter Corie a visit.

Corie, who fears that her mother is lonely, fixes her up as a date with Victor Velasco (Charles Boyer), and they embark, as a foursome date, with the Bratters to an Albanian restaurant on Staten Island. The fun is just beginning.

The young couple go through what Tennessee Williams might define as "a period of adjustment." At the end of the film, Corie chases after her drunken spouse as he wanders "barefoot in the park."

Love wins out in the end.

Made for a modest budget of $2 million, *Barefoot in the Park* earned $30 million at the box office.

Bosley Crowther of *The New York Times* wrote, "If it's romantic farce you delight in—old-fashioned romantic farce loaded with incongruities and snappy verbal gags—then you should find the movie version of *Barefoot in the Park* to your taste. But if you're in for a certain measure of intelligence and plausibility in what is presumed to be a take-out of what might happen to reckless newlyweds today; if you expect a wisp of logic in the make-up of comic characters, which is, after all, what make them funny, instead of sheer gagging it up, then beware."

Charles Champlin of the *Los Angeles Times* stated: "High glass, low-density comedy requires a special touch and Robert Redford and Jane Fonda handle themselves with a fine, deft charm."

Time magazine claimed that "Jane's performance is the best of her career: a clever caricature of a sex kitten who can purr or scratch with equal intensity."

Arthur Knight in *Saturday Review* weighed in with "Jane Fonda, who hitherto seems to have had difficulty with which note to hit in her various roles, at last displays that she in in fact a charmingly fey, disturbingly sexy, light *comedienne* with an instinct for the timing and intonation of lines that should keep her busy for many years to come."

"After filming *Barefoot*, director Mike Nichols tested Redford for his upcoming film project, *The Graduate* (1967). His vision included co-starring Redford with Doris Day as Mrs. Robinson.

But after Redford's screen test, Nichols decided, "No one would believe that you had any trouble attracting women."

He gave the role instead to Dustin Hoffman, and Doris Day rejected the female lead. That became a lucky break for "Mrs. Robinson" (Anne Bancroft).

***

Around this time, many of Roger Vadim's dreams of directing scripts he'd written fell through. He worked on a script for *Paris by Night*, in which he wanted Frank Sinatra to star with Brigitte Bardot. She was willing, but the deal collapsed when Vadim flew to the Eden Roc Hotel on Miami Beach. Sinatra agreed to star, but only if the film were made in Hollywood, not in Paris. Since at least half of the film's scenes involved the landscapes and buildings of Paris, Vadim abandoned the project.

***

Myra Breckinridge (1968)

Abandoning Hollywood, at least for the moment, Vadim and Jane flew to Rome where *Barbarella* was to be shot at the De Laurentiis Studio. They rented a villa, part castle, part dungeon, on the city's outskirts.

From their bedroom, they looked out at a tower, parts of which had been built two centuries before Jesus Christ.

One of their first overnight guests was the controversial and spectacularly outspoken Gore Vidal. Vadim had a motive for entertaining him.

While dining, a "grey bundle" suddenly dropped onto Vidal's dinner plate. It turned out to be a baby owl.

Immediately, Vidal jokingly asked, "May I have the recipe?" Then a trio of other baby owls, testing their wings, flew around the Vadim's dining room, having each emerged from a hole in one of its stone walls.

In 1968, Vidal had published his most controversial satirical novel, *Myra Breckinridge*, an assault on the norms of gender and sexuality, which swept the western world with themes of transsexuality, feminism, machismo, patriarchy, and deviant sexual practices. The controversial book was high camp. Within its pages, the protagonist (Myra and/or Myron) undergoes a "gender re-assignment."

In Vadim's view, it was a major cultural assault on the "assumed norms of gender and sexuality," and he felt the work called for him to direct it.

Vadim had read the novel three times, interpreting it as ideal material for Jane as Myra.

Originally, after MGM had acquired the rights, they suggested Jane as

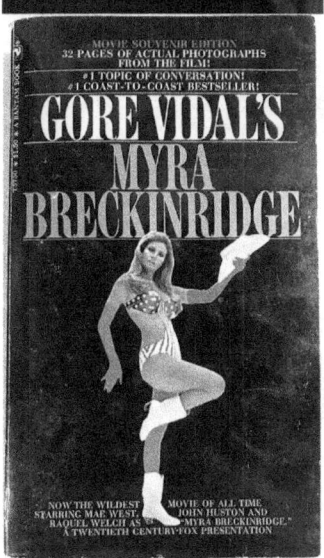

It was first suggested that Jane Fonda, not **Raquel Welch**, should portray Myra Breckinridge, based on **Gore Vidal's** most notorious novel.

In the plot, Myron becomes Myra after a gender re-assignment.

131

Myra with the understanding that she'd play opposite the football star, Joe Namath. But that deal had fallen through.

Vidal promised he'd support Vadim with any maneuvering he could manage, but later sold the movie rights to his novel for $750,000 to producers David Giler and Robert Fryer for a release in 1970. Then, in *lieu* of Vadim directing the picture, the unknown Michael Sarne was assigned to the job. When it was finished, he would never be asked to helm a film ever again.

The role of Myra went to Raquel Welch, being hailed at the time as Hollywood's latest sex symbol. Mae West, who had not appeared on the screen since 1943, signed on to play the talent agent, Leticia Van Allen. She insisted on writing her own dialogue.

When she meets a young man who wanted her to represent him, she was told he stood 6 feet, 7 inches. As a response, she tells him, "Let's forget the six feet and talk about the seven inches."

Rex Reed was cast as Myron Breckinridge, the male embodiment of Myra before her gender reassignment.

Other key roles went to John Huston as Buck Loner and to Farrah Fawcett and Mary Ann Pringle.

Rounding out the cast were Jim Backus, John Carradine, Andy Devine as "Coyote Bill," and Tom Selleck as "The Stud."

Myra Breckinridge received ferociously negative reviews and was a box office flop. *Time* magazine called it "about as funny as a child molester. It represents the nadir in the history of American cinema."

Herb Kelly of *The Miami News* nominated it "as the worst film ever made."

Its author, Gore Vidal dismissed his novel's film adaptation as "an awful joke."

Roger Vadim went to see it, claiming, "I could have pulled it off."

Since its initial release, *Myra Breckinridge* has acquired a cult following.

***

Barbarella (1968): Camping it up in Outer Space

Directed by Roger Vadim, the sci-fi film, *Barbarella*, would make Jane "the most fantasized female on the Planet Earth," no doubt because of its excessive nudity.

As the film credits roll, Jane is floating nude in a weightless (gravity-free) environment.

"To do the scene, I got drunk on vodka," she later confessed. "As a young woman, I hated my body and suffered from bulimia. Every morning I woke up in fear that Vadim would realize he'd made a terrible mistake casting me as Barbarella."

Actually, Jane was not the director's first choice, as he had originally offered the role to Virna Lisi, who rejected it. He then presented it to Sophia Loren, who told him, "I'm pregnant."

Finally, he turned to his wife.

Vadim expressed his goal in making the film to its producer, Dino De Laurentiis: "Here is my chance to depict a new, futuristic morality. I want to make something

The Sex Kitten of the 1960s made the cover of *Life* with her sensuous sex exploits in *Barbarella*. Her performance was hailed as "a hell of a lot more than a naughty, naked actress."

Critics hailed her mammary glands as being in excellent shape for this sexy sci-fi film.

beautiful out of eroticism."

With Vadim's permission, Jane phoned her father and asked him if he would appear in a cameo as President of Earth. "Will I have to take off my clothes?" he asked before rejecting the part.

He later said, "It's a shame that my daughter has to survive so many bad movies."

The script for *Barbarella* was penned by several writers, including Terry Southern.

It's about a space traveler of the United Earth Government who's sent to locate "Dr. Durand-Durand" (Milo O'Shea). He is the inventor of a laser-powered super weapon, which, it's feared, will fall into the wrong hands and threaten Earth.

Jane's wardrobe was often skimpy, even virtually nude. In some scenes, she wore a *cache-sexe [aka "modesty plate," aka "G-string"]* with barely enough fabric to cover her vagina. She sometimes appeared in Nancy Sinatra-style go-go boots and shiny, clingy metallic fabrics and/or furs. All of this entrenched her designation as "The Sex Kitten of the 21st Century."

Physically, at least, some of Jane's scenes were almost impossible "nightmares."
As expressed by Christopher Andersen, "At various points, she is gnawed by piranha-toothed dolls; swung about by a mechanical arms; hung upside down over a vat of oil and dry ice (to give the impression of boiling); and strapped into an 'excessive pleasure' machine that blows up when Jane overloads it. For that, they rigged the machine with smoke bombs and flares."

Along the way, Barbarella meets Pygar, a blind angel with big wings, who has lost the will to fly. He has an affair with Barbarella.

Sex-crazed males may have gone for Jane, but John Philip Law, semi-nude as Pygar, quickly developed an international gay cult following. Hailed as a "major league" male beauty, he had a trim physique and sky- blue eyes like those of Henry Fonda himself.

Jane had worked with Law during the filming of *Hurry Sundown* and had recommended him to Vadim.

[Actually, the director had already encountered Law when he emerged from a motel swimming pool wearing only a cache-sexe.*]*

After the completion of *Barbarella*, Law was offered the role of Joe Buck in *Midnight Cowboy* (1969) but rejected it. It went instead to Jon Voight. After its release, *Midnight Cowboy* was voted Best Picture of the Year.

Most of *Barbarella* was shot at the Cinecittà Studios outside Rome. Vadim and Jane lived in a rented villa on the Appian Way, and Law was invited to live with them.

John Philip Law as a blind angel, ascending with Barbarella (**Jane**) into heaven.

Some critics, especially the gay ones, found the semi-nude "angel" sexier than Jane herself. A critic for *After Dark* magazine said, "John Philip Law, in that loincloth, is a sodomite's dream."

Scion of an aristocratic German family, **Anita Von Pallenberg**, groupie and associate of *The Rolling Stones*, appears as the "Black Lesbian Queen' in Vadim's film.

There's a larger-than-life suggestion of an orifice built into the lower part of her costume.

The actor later admitted to De Laurentiis, "Roger sodomized me several times. He is very sexy."

Anita Pallenberg portrayed the lesbian black queen who, in her dream chamber, can make fantasies take form. *[Known as the "It" girl of the 60s and 70s, Pallenberg was a muse of the Rolling Stones, a member of the inner circle at Andy Warhol's factory, an oft-involved actress in the experimental film scene, and a seminal figure in the arts and drug scenes of NYC of her era.]*

Upon its release, *Barbarella* became a sensation, generating massive controversy. The National Catholic Office for Motion Pictures urged that it be banned, "since it is a sick, heavy-handed fantasy of nudity and graphic representations of sadism."

Andrew Sarris, film critic at *The Village Voice,* noted its "comic-strip conceits and Playboy-Bunny-in-

Disneyland décor."

Rex Reed, in the *New York Daily News* labeled it as "sci-fi trash."

Pauline Kael in *The New Yorker* found that Jane's *Barbarella* evoked "a saucy Dorothy in *The Wizard of Oz*."

Barbarella has survived the tests of time to become the most famous sci-fi cult classic of all time.

***

Spirits of the Dead (aka: ***Histoires extraordinaires***, aka *Tre passi nel delirio*, aka ***Tales of Mystery and Imagination***; 1969)

In the United States, *Variety* was the first to announce that Brigitte Bardot, the former wife of Roger Vadim, and Jane Fonda, his present wife, would co-star in a movie helmed by the director himself.

The film, based on stories by Edgar Allan Poe, would be an anthology with three different sub-sections, or episodes directed, respectively, by Roger Vadim, Louis Malle, and Federico Fellini.

As it turned out, Bardot and Jane would not appear together in any of the sequences. Jane's co-star would be none other than her brother, Peter. This would mark the one and only time they would ever co-star together in a film.

In the Bardot segment, directed by Louis Malle, her co-star would be the French heartthrob, Alain Delon.

The English actor, Terence Stamp, as directed by Federico Fellini, would star in the third and final episode.

Reviewers would speak of the Fonda episode, entitled "Mertzengerstein" without actually explaining what that meant. *[The word evokes orgies, bisexuality, lesbianism, hints of bestiality, and other so-called "perversions."]*

Countess Fréderique Metzengerstein, at the age of 22, inherits an estate where she devotes her life to debauchery and promiscuity. One day, in a forest, her leg is caught in a trap. She is later freed by Baron Wilhelm (Peter Fonda), her neighbor and cousin. She has never met him before because of long-standing family feud. She becomes enamored with him, but he rejects her because of her wicked ways. In an act of revenge, she sets his stables on fire. He dies during attempts to save his prize stallions.

A mysterious black stallion later appears on the Metzengerstein estate, and the Countess (Jane) tries to tame him.

Here, the plot grows a bit muddled. Is he the reincarnation of Wilhelm? She soon becomes obsessed with him. During a violent thunderstorm, Fréderique is carried off by that spooked horse into a blazing fire caused by a lightning strike.

Many American critics later brought up the subject of incest in their critiques. Jane objected to this, claiming, "When the day comes that I want to depict incest on the screen—say a brother-sister relationship—we will do so openly and honestly. We'll meet this taboo subject head-on."

Ironically, it had been Peter himself who had pitched the subject of a movie about incest to Vadim after he landed in Paris. *[At the time, he was toying with a plot wherein a brother and sister are sexually involved and in the business of making porn movies. Vadim, as a director, rejected the idea.]*

Once again, in a Vadim picture, Jane shows a lot of flesh, her Renaissance-inspired costumes each seemed to have aspects of "peek-a-boo." She keeps her vagina covered, but not much else.

One reporter suggested that what Peter did in his advocacy of pot and LSD, Jane did in her promotion of the undraped form. *[In certain films from around the same era, Peter, too, at least shows his ass, usually as he jumps out of bed, supposedly after a night of sex.]*

In Jane's episode, the landscapes of Brittany, brilliantly captured by the cinematographer Claude Renoir, deserve star billing. Scenes range from heather-covered moors to black granite cliffs. "The landscapes of Brittany evoke the end of the world," Vadim claimed.

Jane had co-starred with Alain Delon before and had enjoyed a brief fling with him. She was well aware that, although he remained a box office star in France, he had bombed in America, despite many attempts to make him a Hollywood legend.

[Delon had started out in a small role in the all-star anthology, The Yellow Rolls-Royce *(1965), co-starring Shirley MacLaine. He later co-starred with Ann-Margret in* Once a Thief *(1965). The following year, he appeared with Anthony Quinn and Claudia Cardinale in* The Last Command.

Unexpectedly, Universal used him in a Western, Texas Across the River *(1966) with Dean Martin.]*

In episode two, ("William Wilson") Delon is an army officer during the early 1900s in Northern Italy. He confesses to a priest that he has committed murder. He later tangles with a courtesan, Giuseppina (Bardot), his *doppelgänger*. Wilson later commits suicide by jumping from the tower of the Palazzo della Ragione.

Louis Malle directed the Delon/Bardot segment. The French director was also a producer and screenwriter. Over the course of his career, he would be nominated multiple times for an Academy Award. He was equally at home in French or Hollywood films. By 1980, he would marry actress Candice Bergen.

After completing his work on *Spirits of the Dead,* Malle told a reporter, "I did not like working with Delon, and I think Miss Bardot was miscast."

"Toby Dammit," the film's third and final segment, starred the English actor, Terence Stamp as Toby Dammit. He plays a Shakespearean actor losing his career because of his alcoholism. He agrees to work on his final film, shot in Rome, where he is given a new Ferrari.

He continues to drink and has nightmarish visions of a macabre girl with a white ball. He slowly begins to lose his mind.

Outside of Rome, driving recklessly, he's involved in a violent crash. The girl from his vision picks up his severed head as the sun rises.

This segment (the most critically acclaimed of the three) was directed by Federico Fellini, one of the greatest and most influential directors of all time, noted for such international hits as *La Dolce Vita* (1960). He was known for blending fantasy with baroque images and earthiness. During the course of his career, he was nominated for twelve Academy Awards, winning four.

[The talented Terence Stamp launched his acting career in 1962 and, in time, became the "master of the brooding silence." His performance in the title role of Billy Budd *(1962) earned him an Oscar nod for Best Supporting Actor.*

In the 1960s, he was known for his numerous romances. He became tabloid fodder for his affairs with film star Julie Christie and supermodel Jean Shrimpton.]

Spirits of the Dead came under heavy fire from critics. Vincent Canby of *The New York Times* found the Vadim episode "overly decorated and shrill as a drag ball."

Enrico Zanghi asked a question: "How long can Jane Fonda be popular in America or elsewhere if she make any more films like this?"

John Simon also weighed in: "There may be worse filmmakers than Vadim, but no one can surpass his spiritual rottenness. His is a megalomaniacal interior decorator's world inhabited by campy marionettes. His orgiasts have sawdust in their heads, veins, and glands. For all his sexual shadow-boxing, Vadim can't even rise to that nadir of eroticism, dishonest titillation."

***

After the wrap of *Spirits of the Dead*, Vadim and Jane flew for a ski vacation in Megève in in the French Alps. She would remember what happened there a week after she turned 30, no longer feeling young: On December 28, 1967, Vanessa was conceived.

It was a difficult pregnancy. At one point, she bled a lot and was confined to bed for a month, hoping to prevent a miscarriage.

She came down with the mumps. Her gynecologist recommended an abortion, fearing that the child might be born with either a deformity or a brain impairment. But after discussing it with Vadim, Jane decided to take the risk and bring the baby to term. At the time, Vadim was convinced that it would be a boy.

Vanessa Vadim entered the world on September 28, 1968, and she was born healthy. Susan Blanchard, Jane's former stepmother, flew in to help Jane during the early weeks of her motherhood. Jane also read every page of some of Dr. Benjamin Spock's books on child care.

Jane took her role of mother very seriously. "I can't believe I got through the miracle of giving birth to another human being. It almost seems a miracle. I want more children."

It was assumed that Jane named her daughter after her favorite actress, Vanessa Redgrave. *[In the future she would co-star with Redgrave in* Julia *(1977).]*

Hearing of the birth of Vadim's daughter, Bardot sent Jane a cabbage. At first, Jane didn't understand such a gift. But a note explained it: "In America, babies are delivered by the stork, but in France, they come in a cabbage."

In Paris, Vadim had become a friend of Sargent Shriver, who at the time (May of 1968 to March of 1970) was the U.S. Ambassador to France.

A diplomat, politician, and activist, he was the husband of Eunice Kennedy, sister of President John F. Kennedy. Shriver had married her in 1953.

A graduate of Yale Law School, he had served in the South Pacific during World War II, fighting the Japanese.

During JFK's election bid, he had worked hard for his campaign and later helped to establish the Peace Corps.

After the assassination of JFK, Shriver worked with Lyndon Johnson on anti-poverty programs.

In 1972, he ran for vice president of the United States after Thomas Eagleton resigned from the ticket. (Shriver replaced him.) He and the presidential candidate, George McGovern, lost in a landslide to Richard M. Nixon and Vice-President Spiro Agnew, both of whom would later be forced to resign in disgrace.

Vadim and Shriver became good friends, often dining together. Vadim designated him as the godfather of Vanessa.

Sargent Shriver, who became a very close friend of Jane's husband, Roger Vadim, was famous for his status as brother-in-law to both JFK and RFK.

He appears here with his wife, the former **Eunice Kennedy,** in a rally in Detroit in 1972 during his run for U.S. President in the election of 1976.

***

Gerald Jones, in *The New York Times,* noted the contrast between Jane's American-made films and those shot abroad. "The actress who appeared with Tony Perkins in *Tall Story,* or with Robert Redford in *Barefoot in the Park,* had little resemblance to *Barbarella.* In America, she appears in the film dressed like the roommate of the girl you dated in college. In her early career in Hollywood, she was thought of mainly as Henry Fonda's daughter."

"In France, she sounds like the girl you eavesdropped on in a Paris café. She undresses like Brigitte Bardot, and everyone knows she is the wife of Roger Vadim."

Meanwhile, Peter Fonda, after the release of *Easy Rider* (1969), had become a popular symbol of the new Hollywood. "A poster of him on a motorcycle became the best-selling example of this new media form," wrote Thomas Kiernan. "All the long-accepted barriers of guilt and shame were coming down, and curiosity about drugs and uninhibited sexuality were given full reign. The time was ripe for a film that would repudiate the Christian sense, celebrate and legitimatize the new eroticism, and depict a futuristic morality that would make the current cover of present-day morality absurd. *Barbarella* was the ideal vehicle."

CHAPTER EIGHT

"THE ENCHANTED COUPLE"
Roger and Jane Fascinate and Charm France's New Wave Directors and Actors

THE VAGARIES OF VADIM
Cultural Giants Jean Cocteau, André Gide, and Jean Genet each solicit sex from Vadim, but he'd prefer a three-way with Marlene Dietrich and Edith Piaf

JEAN MARAIS
One of France's Greatest Male Stars, and the Lover of Jean Cocteau, Was also a Star in Various Gay Boudoirs

JEAN-PAUL BELMONDO
With a Gauloise Dangling from His Lips, He became France's Answer to Marlon Brando, Humphrey Bogart, and James Dean

LOUIS JOURDAN
What did "The Handsomest Man in the World" And Vadim do during their week together in the *Île de France*?

LUCHINO VISCONTI
He became sexually intimate with women when they were famous: Anna Magnani, Maria Callas, Marlene Dietrich, and Princess Grace. But for his casting couch, he preferred handsome young men—especially **Helmut Berger**

GUNTER SACHS
This Playboy of the Western World Was the kind of guy "That Harold Robbins Got Rich Writing About."

"I may be the father of 100 children, perhaps double that. You see, I never use protection. I find it dims the sensation."
—Omar Sharif to Roger Vadim

MARCELLO MASTROIANNI, THAT YUMMY ITALIAN
After Catherine Deneuve dumps Vadim, she falls into bed with him.

"He's the man every woman wants."

—Federico Fellini

JEAN GABIN
France's greatest male star claims:
"I don't know why, but when I meet a woman, she immediately starts undressing."

JEAN-LOUIS TRINTIGNANT
Vadim cast him opposite Bardot in *Et Dieu…Créa La Femme*, during which he shot erotic scenes with the director's wife. After doing so, she dumped Vadim, preferring the love-making of Jean-Louis instead

ROMAN POLANSKI
Years after Charles Manson's gang stabs Polanski's pregnant wife, Sharon Tate, sixteen times, He's convicted of raping a 13-year-old in Los Angeles. Before his sentencing, he flees from the United States and is re-defined as "a fugitive from the American justice system."

In Paris, as a young director, Roger Vadim had spent a lot of time hanging out in literary Left Bank cafés that attracted figures from the art world. He made friends with André Gide (who wanted to go to bed with him), Jean Cocteau (who wanted to go to bed with him), and Jean Genet (who also wanted to go to bed with him.)

He also became friends with the surrealist artist, Salvador Dalí, and with the chanteuse Edith Piaf, who often showed up for socializing with Marlene Dietrich. The American author of *Tropic of Cancer*, Henry Miller appeared with the diarist Anaïs Nin, his mistress, who had a husband waiting at home.

For a while, Vadim shared a mistress with Ernest Hemingway. He also visited Colette—who wanted him to adapt one of her short stories into a film and direct it— in her apartment.

Vadim introduced Jane to many of these literary icons, and her life was enriched. Her knowledge of films and filmmakers, especially the French ones—broadened. As Vadim's officially designated wife, Jane's actual years of marriage ranged from 1965 until their divorce in 1973.

On looking back on those times in her own memoir, she said, "I could write a version in which Vadim could come across as a cruel, misogynistic, and irresponsible wastrel. I could also write of him as charming, lyrical, poetic, and tender. Both versions would be true."

What follows is just a preview of some of the exciting artists who came and went from the Vadim-Fonda association. Most of them centered around Vadim, who had the knack of moving in on a famous person and charming him or her in less than an hour.

***

JEAN MARAIS
Simultaneously, France's Errol Flynn and its James Bond

Perhaps there was no figure in French cinema as talented and versatile as Jean Marais. A poet, playwright, novelist, designer, filmmaker, visual artist, and critic, he starred in more than a hundred films.

Marais eventually morphed into one of the foremost creative forces of the surreal, *avant-garde*, and Dadaist movements. He was also, from 1937 to 1947, the muse and lover of the celebrated author and director, Jean Cocteau. In 1996, two years before his death, he was awarded the French Legion of Honor for his contribution to French cinema.

His first screen role was uncredited: a brief appearance in *Dans les rues (Song of the Streets;* 1933). The future matinée idol, Charles Boyer, took more than a fatherly interest in him and cast him in *Sparrowhawk* (1933) and *Happiness* (1934), in which Boyer was the star.

Cocteau first spotted Marais in the stage production of *Oedipe* in 1937 and invited him to live with him as his lover. Cocteau began casting Marais in his plays such as *Les Parents terribles* (1938), which was a great success.

Marais secretly fought for the Free French Forces during World War II, later receiving the Croix de Guerre for his involvement.

Jean Marais in a photo sometimes interpreted as a kind of narcissistic self-love, in *Orphée* (1950), and (*right*) a later-in-life photo when he reigned as one of the unofficial patriarchs of French cinema, arts, and letters.

Even during the occupation of France by the Nazis, Marais starred in *L'Éternel retour* (1943), a re-telling of the *Tristan & Isolde* fable, this one set in 1940s France. It was so popular, it made Marais a star. His role in the 1944 film production of *Carmen* helped morph it into one of the most popular movies in France during the bleak years of World War II.

In spite of his involvement as Cocteau's lover, Marais had a two-year affair beginning in 1942 with the actress Mila Parély, eventually becoming her business partner in a startup company that manufactured pottery.

During the course of her movie career, Parély starred in films directed by Jean Renoir, Robert Bresson, Fritz Lang, and G.W. Pabst.

In 1947, she married racing car driver Taso Mathieson, and when he was seriously injured for life, she retired from acting to take care of him. For the last fifty years of her life, she lived in obscurity

Jean Marais (*left*) preferred to sunbathe in the nude, but his lover, **Jean Cocteau** remained carefully robed. The handsome French heartthrob was Cocteau's life-long passion.

In his memoirs, he admitted that as a teenager, he first saw a fresh farm boy "bathing naked and fainted in ecstasy of joy and fear at the sight of his penis in the midst of its dark patch of pubic hair."

in the city of Vichy, dying there in 2012 at the age of 94.

After the war, in the waning days of his love affair with Cocteau, Marais starred in the famous *La Belle et la bête (Beauty and the Beast; 1946)*, written and directed by his lover. Even after their separation, Marais and Cocteau maintained their friendship and worked together in other films together, including *L'Aigle à deux têtes (The Eagle with two Heads; 1948)*.

He made other movies with major female stars in French cinema, including Jeanne Moreau and Michèle Morgan. His *Le Comte de Monte-Cristo (The Count of Monte Cristo; 1954)* was hugely popular.

Marais once asked his mentor, Cocteau, if he could trust a script by "this young playwright, Roger Vadim, Marc Allégret's boy."

The great Cocteau answered, "Indeed, with your eyes closed."

The film was called *Futures Vedettes (School for Love; 1953)*, and it starred Marais with Bardot. Seen dancing in that film was an American, George Reich, who had become Marais' lover (1948-1959).

Reich became well known in Vadim's world, partly because of his dance performances at the Moulin Rouge, the Olympia Music Hall, and the Ballets de Paris. He directed and choreographed shows for such stars as Edith Piaf, Marlene Dietrich, and Josephine Baker.

By the time Marais starred in *Elena et les Hommes* (aka *Elena and Her Men*; aka *Paris Does Strange Things: 1956*) with Ingrid Bergman, he had become an international star. By the late 1950s, he had evolved into a swashbuckler, hailed as "The Errol Flynn of French cinema."

The success of James Bond films diverted his career into spy films and at the same time, he also scored one of his all-time box office triumphs with *Fantômas* (1964), playing both the villain and the hero. By 1970, he was co-starring with Catherine Deneuve in *Peau d'âne* (aka *Donkey Skin* aka *Once Upon a Time*; aka *The Magic Donkey; 1970*).

In the 1960s, Marais adopted a young man, Serge Ayala, a singer and actor, who, in 2012, at the age of 69, committed suicide.

Marais' autobiography, partially set in the French theater world during Paris' Nazi occupation, later influenced the storyline and direction of FrançoisTruffaut's film, *Le Dernier Métro (The Last Métro; 1980)*.

***

Romain Gary (1914-1980)
A SUICIDAL NOVELIST IN LOVE WITH A SUICIDAL ACTRESS

Originally a native of Lithuania, Gary is hailed as a major writer of French literature during the second half of the 20th Century. He was a novelist, diplomat, film director, and World War II aviator.

In American pop culture, he became famous for his marriage (1962-1970) to the doomed actress Jean Seberg.

During the summer of 1964, he was entertained by Roger Vadim and Jane Fonda at St. Tropez. After a sleepless night, he pulled back the shutters of his window to watch the sunrise. In the distance, as he later relayed to Vadim, "I saw Jane on the beach

Two doomed lovers, novelist **Romain Gary** and the American actress **Jean Seberg** were caught on camera in 1971, a year after their divorce. A major writer of French literature, he once challenged Clint Eastwood to a duel after he learned of his affair with his wife. Eastwood declined.

at dawn. She was a glorious, naked pagan goddess, followed by a nymph and two fauns. It was an image of the beginning of the world. It was youth, boldness, and freedom."

What he saw was both Vadim and Jane naked, with two friends, a handsome young man with his wife, whom Vadim described as having "the proportions of a Rodin sculpture and eyes sparkling with life—the kind of beauty that causes a person to look, even if his back is turned."

Gary was to die of a self-inflicted gunshot wound on December 2, 1980, in Paris. He left a note that stated that his suicide had no relation to Seberg's suicide of the previous year. He also revealed that he was the real Émile Ajar, a pen name he had used for some of his work. He had been the only French author to win the Prix Goncourt for works attributed to both his real name (Romain Gary) and to his pseudonym (Émile Ajar).

***

Gérard Philipe (1922-1959)
His Early Death Helped Make Him a Legend

Born in Cannes and eventually morphing into a film icon of postwar France, Gérard Philipe became a legendary actor during his short life, appearing in 32 films between 1944 and 1959, the year of his death. His image was both romantic and youthful.

Vadim's own mentor, Marc Allégret, discovered the handsome young actor and arranged for his film debut in *Les Petites du quai aux fleurs* (1943), about a bookshop owner with four daughters with romantic troubles. It was shot during the Nazi occupation.

He was on the way to super stardom after he starred in *L'idiot* (*The Idiot*; 1946), an adaptation of the popular novel by Fyodor Dostoevsky.

Two more movies brought Philipe even greater fame—Claude Autant-Lara's *Le diable au corps* (*Devil in the Flesh*; 1947) with Michelle Presle, and an even bigger hit, *La Chartreuse de Parme* (1948) for director Christian Jacque. In 1950, Philipe was also a member of the star-studded cast of Max Ophüls *La Ronde*.

He later worked with international stars and directors who included Gina Lollobrigida, Michèle Morgan, Valerie Hobson, and Danielle Darrieux, and with directors ranging from Luis Buñuel to René Clément.

Vadim cast Philipe as Valmont in his modern-day version of *Les Liaisons dangereuses* (1959) with Jeanne Moreau.

Philipe's death from lung cancer shocked his fans. He was just a few days short of his 37th birthday. He requested that he be buried in the costume of Don Rodriguez from *The Cid*.

He died at the peak of his popularity and enjoys a kind of mythic status in France today, with streets, postage stamps, theaters, awards, and festivals named in his honor. Even a cultural center in Berlin is named for him.

Gérard Philip with **Jeanne Moreau** in *Les liaisons dangereuses* (1959), directed by Roger Vadim. The film was denied an export license because it was "unrepresentative of French film art."

Nonetheless, New York censors allowed the film to be released after two "objectionable nude scenes" were deleted.

***

Jean-Paul Belmondo (1933-2021)
A FRENCH-SPEAKING IMAGE OF SUPER COOL

During his career, Jean-Paul Belmondo was marketed as the French version of James Dean, Marlon Brando, and Humphrey Bogart, often appearing with a Gauloise dangling from his lips. Linked with the French New Wave of the1960s, he has been called "an integral part of the history of French cinema—and of France itself."

He refused to learn English, despite heavy demand in Hollywood. Directors there thought he could be morphed into another Charles Boyer or Maurice Chevalier.

Belmondo became famous outside of France after the release of *Breathless* (1960) in which he had co-starred with Jean Seberg. The role had first been offered to Vadim's wife, Annette Stroyberg.

Belmondo and Vadim often talked of his being directed in one of Vadim's movies, but nothing ever made it before the cameras.

During the course of his 50-year career, some 160 million viewers (most of them French) watched Belmondo perform in such hits as *L'Homme de Rio* (*That Man from Rio*, 1964); *Cent mille dollars au soleil* (*Greed in the Sun*, 1965); and *Borsalino* (1970). He was mostly noted for his portrayals of police officers in action thrillers. He was married (1952-1968) to Elodie Constantin, with whom he had three children.

He was better known for his long-time affair (1965-1972) with Ursula Andress, the Swiss-born international sex symbol.

After Belmondo's death at the age of 88 in 2021, President Emmanuel Macron celebrated him, defining him as "a national hero."

Jean-Paul Belmono in a scene with **Jean Seberg** from Jean-Luc Godard's *film Breathless.*

One of the best examples of French New Wave cinema, it was Godard's first feature-length film and the breakthrough role for Belmondo. The legendary French actor, who refused to learn English, was hailed as "the epitome of cool."

***

Louis Jourdan (1921-2015)
THE EPITOME OF THE SUAVE CONTINENTAL

Born in Marseille, the son of a hotel owner, Jourdan, early in his youth, decided that he wanted to become an actor.

Vadim's future mentor, Marc Allégret, who had

Perpetuating the image of the very suave Frenchman: **Louis Jourdan** in a publicity pic for Gigi with **Leslie Caron.**

Based on a novel by Colette, *Gigi* became Jourdan's most celebrated role, winning nine Academy Awards, including Best Picture. It's often reviewed as the last of MGM's great movie musicals.

"a talent for discovering talent," spotted him in a stage role and hired him to work as an assistant camera operator on *Entrée des Artistes* (*The Curtain Rises*; 1938)

He was struck by the Jourdan's male beauty, and was rumored to have maneuvered him on a casting couch.

In 1939, he set out to star Jourdan with Charles Boyer in *Le Corsaire*, but filming was interrupted by the coming of World War II, during which the Nazis occupied (directly or indirectly, depending on the region) France.

Too young for army service at the time, Jourdan was hired by Marcel L'Herbier to appear in *La Comédie du bonheur La Comédie du bonheur* (*The Comedy of Happiness*; 1940) in Rome. He was there when Italy declared war on France, and he fled back to France, where he co-starred with Danielle Darrieux in *Premier Rendezvous* (1941).

When the Nazis took over, he spent a year on a work gang. Later, when he was ordered to appear in Nazi propaganda films, he fled, joining his family in Vichy, France, where the German occupation was less obvious and somewhat less onerous. .

He started making movies again, including several for Allégret, who still found him "sexually desirable," casting him in several of his movies, including *La Belle aventure* (*The Beautiful Adventure*; 1942).

Jourdan joined the French Resistance, working to distribute propaganda leaflets. In 1946, he married his childhood sweetheart, Berthe Frédérique (aka "Ouique").

Spotted by a talent scout for David O. Selznick in the spring of 1946, Jourdan was offered a Hollywood contract. His first American film was *The Paradine Case* (1947), a *film noir* starring Gregory Peck. Many critics could not decide on "which actor was more beautiful." Actually Hitchcock did not want Jourdan cast as the valet in that movie.

Opposite Joan Fontaine, Jourdan starred in the Max Ophüls movie, *Letter from an Unknown Woman* (1948). John Houseman, the film's producer, felt he lacked sex appeal, but thousands of his fans disagreed.

At the time, in an unofficial survey, Jourdan was voted "the handsomest man in the world."

Regrettably, all of Jourdan's films lost money, and he eventually bought out his contract with Selznick for $50,000.

During his career "post Selznick," one of Jourdan's biggest hits was *Three Coins in the Fountain* (1954), which was followed by his Broadway debut in the lead role of André Gide's *The Immoralist*, in which he co-starred with the young James Dean.

Jourdan also starred in *The Swan* (1956) with Grace Kelly, her last movie role and a dud at the box office.

Vadim became very friendly with Jourdan when he returned to France to co-star with Brigitte Bardot in *La mariée est trop belle* (*The Bride is Much Too Beautiful*; 1956).

Vadim spent a long week with Jourdan at a friend's château in the Île de France, and rumors spread among gossips in the Parisian film world.

Jourdan's biggest hit was *Gigi* (1958), the film adaptation of the novella by Colette.

The major fan of that movie, in England, was John Gielgud, who saw the film three times "just to get

Louis Jourdan evolved into the image of France and the handsomest man, some said, in the world. '

He shocked his fans when he was cast against type in the BBC's television production of *Count Dracula* in 1977

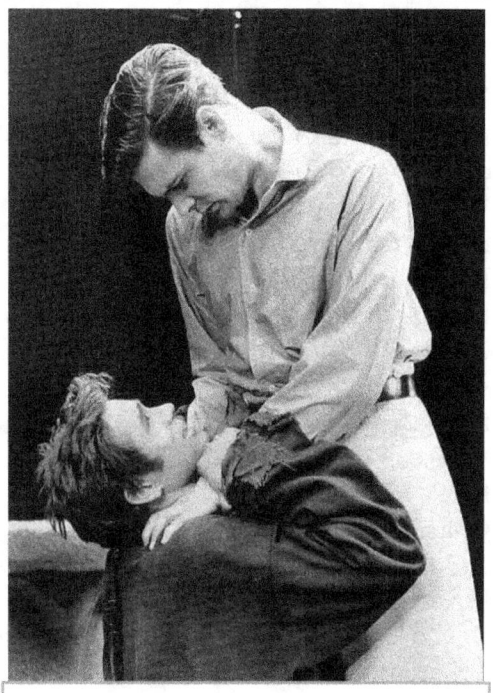

Jourdan strangling **James Dean**, onstage on Broadway, in *The Immoralist*, a play by André Gide . It's permeated with simmering homosexual lust and intrigue. Dean, ironically, was miscast as an Arab hustler.

a look at that big basket Jourdan was showing in those tight pants."

After that, many of Jourdan's films were shown around the world, with wide releases in the United States. In the musical *Can-Can* (1960), he co-starred with Shirley MacLaine, Frank Sinatra, and Maurice Chevalier. Another hit was made for MGM. Called *The V.I.P.'s* it starred Jourdan with Richard Burton and Elizabeth Taylor.

As Jourdan's career sagged, he ended up playing Dracula in the 1977 television production of *Count Dracula.* He also appeared in the James Bond thriller, *Octopussy* (1983), despite the fact that he interpreted its title as "vulgar."

***

Marcello Mastroianni (1924-1996)
THE UNDISPUTED SUPERSTAR OF ITALIAN CINEMA

In 1962, Vadim got to know Mastroianni when he co-starred with Bardot in *Vie Privée* (*A Very Private Affair*). Vadim had anticipated a torrid affair between the French sex symbol and the Italian heartthrob, but that did not happen. If anything, Bardot seemed rather indifferent to him off-screen, because she was involved at the time in her own tangled web of affairs.

At the time, Bardot was divorcing her second husband, actor Jacques Charrier (1959-1962). Bardot's only child, a son named Nicholas-Jacques Charrier, was born on January 11, 1960. At the time she worked with Mastroianni, Bardot was also embroiled in an affair with the American actor, Glenn Ford.

The undisputed superstar of Italian cinema, **Marcello Mastroianni** emotes with "sexpot" **Anita Ekberg** in *La Dolce Vita (The Sweet Life)*. This masterpiece is hailed as one of the greatest films of all time. Fellini originally wanted Paul Newman for the role, but found him "too beautiful."

Whatever happened to Ekberg, the once-ravishing Swedish movie star? As her beauty faded, she became a saleswoman of used cars in Rome.

Louis Malle, the director of *Vie Privée,* complained to Vadim when he showed up one day on the set, "There is just no sexual chemistry between Bardot and Marcello."

Mastroianni may not have been subdued by Bardot, but in 1970, he began an affair with Catherine Deneuve, Vadim's former girlfriend (1961-1964).

The Italian actor would never marry Deneuve, but their affair would last for four years. (He'd had another affair with Faye Dunaway that lasted from 1968-1970). Mastroianni told Vadim, "Faye is the only woman I've ever really loved, but she sent me packing when I would not marry her and become father of her babies."

On July 18, 1963, Deneuve had given birth to Vadim's son Christian. On May 28, 1972, she also gave birth to a daughter named Chiara Mastroianni. As she grew older, Vadim claimed, "Chiara is the prettiest girl I've ever seen."

At one point, Vadim was invited to dine with Deneuve and Mastroianni in a Left Bank Bistro in Paris. Later, Mastroianni confessed to Vadim, "I felt like the odd man out. You two were laughing and talking together and having so much fun. I felt not wanted. I was a bit jealous. I thought Catherine might be planning to leave me to hook up with you again, but that following night in my bed, she convinced me that she was staying around for a while."

Mastroianni even today remains a towering figure in the history of 20th Century Italian cinema. Federico Fellini brought Mastroianni world acclaim when he cast him in *La Dolce Vita* (1960), in which he portrayed a disillusioned and self-loathing tabloid gossip columnist who spends his nights exploring

Rome's decadent high society. That was followed by Fellini casting Mastroianni in *8½* (1963).

Great success came to the Italian in films in which he co-starred with Sophia Loren, movies such as *Yesterday, Today, and Tomorrow* (1963) and *Marriage Italian Style* (1964).

In an admission one night when Mastroianni and Vadim had had too much wine, the Italian admitted, "I'm not such a great fucker. Just ask Catherine."

Of course, Vadim didn't ask.

One night, Catherine made a surprise admission of her own: "It's an amazing thing, but you and Marcello have virtually the exact penises. I can't tell one from the other."

Loren weighed in with her opinion of Mastroianni, too: "Marcello is a man who thinks like a man, talks like a man, and is a man! He has such magnetism. He brings out the very soul of a woman."

When a reporter asked him about Fellini, hoping to get a statement about his opinion of him as a director, Mastroianni made a surprise revelation: "The one thing both Fellini and I have in common is that we have to keep our socks on while having torrid sex."

Before his death in 1996, the Italian actor shared one final secret related to his success in films. "One must be in love with one's co-star. Otherwise, who in the audience will believe it?"

***

Jean Gabin (1904-1976)
France's First Very Famous International Star

After Vadim's marriage to Bardot fell apart, they remained friends. He visited her on the set of *En Cas de malheur* (*In Case of Adversity,* aka *Love Is My Profession;* 1958).

Bardot had been hired as the co-star of Jean Gabin, the star of the picture and one of the leading figures in French cinema. Vadim received a luncheon invitation from the film's director, Claude Autant-Lara, and he accepted, eventually joining Autant-Lara at table with Gabin and Bardot.

The critics were already reveling in the idea of France's pretty little doll (Bardot) being swallowed by the French ogre (Gabin), but they were disappointed. Gabin's talent did not smother Bardot's spontaneity. For the first time, they spoke not only of Bardot's charm, but of her abilities as an actress, too.

Gabin specialized in the portrayal of criminals, murderers, thieves, and anti-heroes.

The plot of the film with Bardo tells the story of a married lawyer who rigs a trial to acquit a young female criminal with whom he has become obsessed.

Bosley Crowther of *The New York Times* defined Autant-Lara as one of the best directors in France, but found Bardot's performance "falling far short" and Gabin "missing, too."

Born in Paris to a café owner and a cabaret entertainer, Gabin found work in the music halls imitating Maurice Chevalier. Director Julien Duvivier

Lovers in real life, sultry **Marlene Dietrich** co-starred with **Jean Gabin** in *Martin Roumagnac* (aka The Room Upstairs; 1946). Whereas she is elegant and refined, he is macho tough, drinking only Pernod and chain-smoking Gauloises.

A building contractor in a small town, he falls for the glamourous but treacherous *femme fatale* with tragic results for both of them.

helped establish him as a major star in such films as *Pepe le Moko* (1939). He also starred in Jean Renoir's *La Grande Illusion* (1937), an anti-war film that ran for six months in Manhattan. Renoir's major work, *La Bête Humaine (The Human Beast,* aka *Judas Is a Woman; 1938),* a *film noir,* was another major success.

After the Nazi occupation of France, Gabin fled to Hollywood, where he began a highly publicized romance with Marlene Dietrich that lasted until 1948.

During his affair with her, he was said to be "insanely jealous" often pounding her with his fists when he suspected she'd had an affair (including one with Greta Garbo) outside their home.

Gabin was unhappy in America, and finally left to join General Charles de Gaulle's Free French Forces in North Africa. Dietrich was also anxious to entertain Allied soldiers abroad.

After a postwar slump, Gavin made almost fifty more films, most of which were successful, including the one with Bardot.

***

Omar Sharif (1932-2015)
THE EGYPTIAN ROMEO WHO DEFLOWERED HIS LEADING LADIES

A phone call at around three in the morning awakened Jane and Vadim in bed at their farmhouse.

It was a frantic call from his second wife, Annette Stroyberg, whom he had divorced in 1961. At first, Jane thought the call might be an emergency concerning Annette's daughter with Vadim, Natalie. But it wasn't.

Annette was threatening suicide because she'd been dumped by her lover, the Egyptian actor, Omar Sharif.

Jane and Vadim dressed hurriedly and drove to Annette's apartment. There, Jane was especially helpful in comforting the dumped lover. She had thought Sharif was going to propose marriage. "Omar is a charming man and an excellent friend," Vadim said, "but he had a particular style with women. In spite of the passionate lover he played on the screen, he was not romantic in private life…he was a 'love them and leave them' kind of guy."

Jane spoke with Annette for hours, trying to convince her that she should never be just a plaything, existing just for the pleasure of any man.

Sharif had admitted, "I like sex, wine, and food in that order."

The greatest male star to emerge from Egypt, **Omar Sharif** appears with **Julie Christie** in *Dr. Zhivago,* David Lean's epic based on the 1957 novel by Boris Pasternak. Because the book was banned in the Soviet Union, it had to be shot somewhere else—in this case, in Spain.

Its producer, Carlo Ponti, originally intended it as a vehicle for his wife, Sophia Loren.

Annette recovered quickly from her suicide attempt, and in two weeks, she called Vadim to tell him she had fallen in love again. This time with "the sugar king of Morocco," who owned sugar factories outside Casablanca. They were soon to be married.

The greatest actor to emerge from Egypt, Sharif became an internationally sought-after movie star, his career encompassing more than 100 films over a half-century. He played opposite Peter O'Toole in the David Lean epic, *Lawrence of Arabia* (1962), which earned him an Oscar nomination. He had also played the title role in Lean's *Doctor Zhivago* (1965).

As he told Vadim, "The fact that I entertain many girls is only because I'm searching for the right one."

Sharif had become known for seducing his leading ladies. When he co-starred with Vadim's former girlfriend, Catharine Deneuve, in *Mayerling* (1968), the couple also had an affair that lasted from 1970 to 1974.

Ava Gardner was also in *Mayerling*, and Sharif seduced her, too.

Others of his conquests included Ingrid Bergman, his co-star in *The Yellow Rolls-Royce* (1964); Julie Christie in *Dr. Zhivago* (1965); Sophia Loren in *More Than a Miracle* (1967); and Barbra Streisand, his co-star in *Funny Girl* (1968).

When a photo was released in Egypt that showed him kissing Streisand, a Jew who had raised money for Israel, it caused a furor in his native land. Sharif was denounced as a traitor, and many of his countrymen demanded that he be stripped of his citizenship. Fortunately, that never happened.

***

Luchino Visconti (1906-1976)
THE DECADENT FATHER OF CINEMATIC NEOREALISM

Vadim made a friend of the aristocratic Visconti, a major figure of Italian art and culture in the mid-20th Century, when each of them lived in separate apartments at the Hôtel des Ambassadeurs de Hollande, the converted 17th Century *monument historique* in the Marais district of Paris.

Visconti remembered the first time he ever saw Jane, who was leaving the building at the time. He told a friend, "She is beautiful—that is, if you like girls. I don't. I prefer male beauty—young, endowed, and handsome."

"I saw most of the Visconti output, and of course, he had an impact on me and my own work," Vadim said. "His themes were those of beauty, decadence, death, and the history of Europe, especially the decay of the nobility and the bourgeoisie."

Born to a noble Milanese family, he launched his career working as an assistant director to Jean Renoir. His 1943 directorial debut, *Obsessione*, was condemned by Mussolini's Fascist government for its depiction of working class characters resorting to criminality.

Burt Lancaster was the star of *Il Gattopardo* (*The Leopard*; 1963). He later said, "Visconti is a man who loves little boys. It's as simple as that, a throwback to the old Roman emperors. He often put his leading man on the casting couch."

Lancaster was referring to Farley Granger in *Senso* (1953) and to Alain Delon in *Rocco and His Brothers* (1960), and especially to Helmut Berger (whom Visconti defined as "the love of my life") in *The Damned* (1969).

Lancaster ignored the fact that Visconti had enjoyed a few female seductions with some of the most celebrated women on earth—notably Coco Chanel, opera diva Maria Callas; Marlene Dietrich; Anna Magnani (whom he directed in *Bellissima* (1951); even Princess Grace of Monaco. Visconti also had an affair with his fellow director, Franco Zeffirelli.

Luchino Visconti (*upper photo*) liked to make sweeping film epics dealing with beauty, decadence, and death.

The love of his life was **Helmut Berger** (*left figure in lower photo*), his partner from 1964 to 1976.

Berger also seduced Marisa Berenson, Rudolf Nureyev, Britt Ekland, Ursula Andress, Tab Hunter, Linda Blair, Anita Pallenberg, Jerry Hall, and both Mick and Bianca Jagger.

John Philips (1935-2001)
THE PAPA OF *THE MAMAS & THE PAPAS*

When Jane and Roger Vadim lived in a villa on the beach at Malibu, a frequent visitor to their home was John Philips, the singer, songwriter, and guitarist of *The Mamas & the Papas.*

He was often seen at Vadim-hosted parties that attracted Jack Nicholson, Larry Hagman, Mia Farrow, Marlon Brando, and Jacqueline Bisset, among many others. Vadim served his classic Provençal fish soup for both lunch and dinner, and never seemed to prepare enough.

Philips wrote many hits, notably "San Francisco (Be Sure to Wear Flowers in Your Hair)" He also wrote "Me and My Uncle," a favorite in the repertoire of *The Grateful Dead.*

From 1942 to 1946, Philips attended Linton Hall Military School in Bristow, Virginia, a place he hated. "Four nuns watched me take a shower every day, and I put on a real display for them."

After many involvements in the music industry, he finally achieved the fame he sought with *The Mamas & the Papas*, with whom he released such *Billboard* classics as "California Dreamin'" and "Monday, Monday." The rock vocal group was a sensation from 1965 to 1968. It featured the overweight Cass Elliot, Michelle

CALIFORNIA DREAMIN'

Promotional photo of "Popsters We Loved," **The Mamas and the Papas**. *Clockwise from top,* **John Philips, Cass Elliot, Michelle Philips,** and **Denny Doherty**

Philips (married to John), and the Canadian Denny Doherty. The group sold more than forty million records worldwide.

For most of the 1970s, John was lost in heroin addiction, which led to his arrest and conviction in 1980, when he spent a month in jail.

John had married Michelle on the last day of 1962, living with her until their divorce in May of 1969.

In 1970, Michelle (the voice described by *Time* magazine as "the purest soprano in pop music") married Dennis Hopper.

Friends jokingly said, "Their marriage didn't even survive the honeymoon." They divorced the year of their marriage.

[In September of 2009, eight years after her father's death, John's eldest daughter, Mackenzie —born 1959, the product of John's first marriage (1957-1962) to Susan Adams—claimed that she and her father had had a decade-long sexual relationship that began when she was nineteen. She also maintained that he had frequently injected her with cocaine and heroin. The sexual abuse, according to her, ended when she became pregnant and had an abortion. "I never let him touch me again," she claimed.]

Actually, Michelle's marriage to Hopper lasted only a week before she fled back to John Phillips. She cited Hopper's abuse: "At one point he called me a witch and handcuffed me. He terrified me when he started firing guns inside the house."

Finally, Hopper got in touch with her, urging her to come back. She asked him if he had ever considered suicide.

***

Count Gunter Sachs von Opel (1932-2011)
The Playboy of the Western World

Gunter Sachs was that rare breed of millionaire who takes pleasure in spending money, especially on beautiful women. He also married a rich and famous woman, Brigitte Bardot, and he had more money than she did.

He was known as a handsome sex symbol in European high society, and his reputation of seduction and promiscuity matched hers.

His mother, Eleanor, was the daughter of Wilhelm von Opel, co-founder of the automaker Opel. His father, Willy Sachs, a former friend of Hermann Göring and Heinrich Himmler, was a leading manufacturer of ball-bearings. The American army arrested him after World War II for his Nazi links, but let Willy go.

His son, Gunter, was tabloid fodder for years, beginning with a romantic link to Soraya, the former Empress of Iran. After his first wife, Anne-Marie Faure, died in 1958 during surgery, he courted Bardot by flying over her villa on the French Riviera in a helicopter and dropping hundreds of roses.

They were married on July 14, 1966 in Las Vegas but divorced in 1969. During those years, he gave her "a hell of a ride."

Even before his marriage to Bardot, he and Vadim had become friends. Both of them agreed that women are the most divine creatures on earth, but they had to be controlled.

"I face one challenge with Brigitte," he confessed to Vadim. "I had to convince her that the best way to live is to spend fortunes, large piles of money, at one time."

"Gunter is a strong man," Vadim told the press. "Bardot needs a man like that."

Without Jane's knowledge, Vadim suggested that he would be available if Sachs ever wanted to invite him to visit his marital bed with Bardot. "You and me together could really satisfy the vixen," he said. It is not clear if Sachs accepted the offer.

For a "cozy" dinner, Sachs would invite 150 guests to dine with him and Brigitte at Maxim's in Paris.

"Brigitte told me that she felt that the marriage was doomed almost from the beginning," Vadim said. "But she would carry on for two or so more years. "I think money removes humanity from a man," she told her ex-husband, Vadim.

Months before a divorce, both Brigitte and Sachs

The handsome, sophisticated, German-born, and very wealthy **Gunter Sachs**, pictured above with his third wife, **Brigitte Bardot**, was hailed as "the Playboy of the Western World." He gained international fame as a documentary filmmaker, photographer, purveyor of fabulous and fabulously expensive parties, and hedonism. Some matchmakers considered him the most desirable man in Europe.

Known for his savvy investments in contemporary art, especially the fast-appreciating works of Andy Warhol, he once headed an institute devoted to the research of astrology and the accuracy of its forecasts.

were involved in a number of secret romances.

Vadim remembered visiting his former wife, Bardot, in Rome, where she was living with Sachs (that is, when he was home) in a villa rented to them by Gina Lollobrigida.

"I'm bored, bored, and more bored," she lamented. "Every night, I have to entertain. What is more boring than guests like the ex-King of Greece, Ava Gardner, Paul Newman, Visconti, the Duke of Savoy, and a husband who thinks that showing his wife a good time is showering her with expensive gifts such as Bulgari jewelry? I want to wear blue jeans. He wants me to dress in Chanel or Dior."

Leaving for a flight going out of Mallorca, Sachs met a reporter who asked him about the status of his marriage. "When you open an international magazine and see your wife naked with a naked man, don't you think that is grounds for a divorce?"

One day, a call came in for Vadim. As he told Jane, "I expected it. It was from Bardot."

"I'm divorcing him. I've refused all the money he offered, and I've returned all the jewelry."

On hearing of her divorce, Vadim said, "Bardot exists mostly in the imagination of others. She has become a true myth. In the sun, she is without a shadow. You cannot reach out and hold her. She is a night thought."

[On May 7, 2011, press associations announced the news: Gunter Sachs had died at the age of 78 in Gstaad, Switzerland. He had committed suicide by putting a gun to his head and pulling the trigger. The suicide note claimed he was escaping "a hopeless illness," which was Alzheimer's.

The note concluded, "The loss of mental control over my life is an undignified condition which I decided to counter decisively."]

During their marriage (1966-1969), **Brigitte Bardot,** the French "sex kitten" and the very wealthy sybarite, **Gunter Sachs,** became the most publicized couple on the planet.

"It was difficult being married to the one woman that was the most desired on the planet. I had a lot of competition—namely Roger Vadim, Sean Connery, Louis Jourdan."

***

Françoise Dorléac (1942-1967)
France's Answer to Katharine Hepburn

Had Dorléac, the older sister of Catherine Deneuve, lived, she might have been the longtime lover of Roger Vadim. Although Deneuve became one of the most celebrated beauties to grace the screen, Dorléac herself was also stunning.

He had first spotted her at a *boîte* on the Left Bank of Paris, Epi-Club, where she was dancing with her younger sister, an actress who later became known worldwide as Catharine Deneuve.

In his memoir, Vadim made the claim that it was Catherine, not Françoise, who attracted him. In reality he fell for both of the sisters, but always managed to keep his involvement with Françoise a secret except to close friends like Christian Marquand.

Vadim boasted, "I was the only man in Paris who found Catherine more beautiful than her sister." Actually, according to his best friend, Christian Marquand, "Roger moved in on Françoise faster than he did on Catherine, but their liaison was carefully concealed."

In her early films, the French press made reference to Françoise's ability to evoke a younger Katharine Hepburn, especially as she looked in *Morning Glory* (1933), one of Hepburn's first films.

Vadim did admit, however, that "the charm and fame and intelligent personality of the older sister at first was greater than Catherine's. When Deneuve launched her own career, some in the Parisian press claimed that the older sister "overshadowed the younger one, who was but a pale reflection."

Vadim's assistant, Jean-Michel Lacor, was an eyewitness to his boss getting sexually involved with both beauties, although keeping it a secret for years. "Apparently, the sisters never confided to each other exactly what was going on," Lecor claimed.

At the time of her involvement with Vadim, Françoise was rumored to have had another beau named Jean-Pierre Casel.

When Vadim started secretly dating Françoise, she was sharing a bunk bed with Catherine in a crowded apartment on the Boulevard Murat near Paris' Porte de Saint-Cloud. Six members of the family, including a third sister, Sylvia, were "living on top of each other."

Although the parents had been actors themselves, they were rather strict about Catherine getting involved with Vadim. Apparently, they never learned he was also fornicating with Françoise.

Françoise, a slim, beautiful blonde, had made her film debut in *Les loups dans la bergerie* (*The Wolves in the Sheepfold*; 1960), directed by Hervé Bromberger. She made a number of other films before Vadim cast her as one of the French stars in *La Ronde* (*Circle of Love*; 1960), a drama that generated much controversy because of Jane Fonda's nude scene.

Circle of Love did nothing for Françoise's career, but during the same period, she leapt to international stardom as the female lead in *L'Homme de Rio* (*That Man from Rio*; 1964). Françoise co-starred with Jean-Paul Belmondo in this adventure spoof of all those James Bond movies. At the 37th Academy Awards, it was nominated for an Oscar as Best Original Screenplay. This was the first film to be made by the French subsidiary of United Artists, and it became the fifth highest-earning movie of the year in France.

When not slipping around for *rendezvous* with Vadim, Françoise was engaged in an affair with Jean-Paul Belmondo. She followed *Rio* with *La peau douce* (*The Soft Skin*; also 1964), a Franco-Portuguese romantic drama directed by François Truffaut. It was the story of a married publisher who falls for a beautiful "air hostess."

Françoise teamed with Belmondo again in *The Gentle*

La brune et la blonde
(aka "Sister Act à la française")

Françoise D'Orléac (*left figure in both photos above*) with her (internationally, at least) better-known sister, **Catherine Deneuve** in 1967, in these publicity photos for *Les Demoiselles de Rochefort*.

Art of Seduction (1964) that also starred Jean-Paul Brialy and her younger sister, Catherine.

Both Vadim and Françoise were surprised at her next film offer, in which she would play the female lead in *Genghis Khan* (1965), distributed by Columbia. Henry Levin, the director, lined up an impressive cast of male actors, led by Omar Sharif and featuring James Mason, Stephen Boyd, and Eli Wallach.

Sharif was a friend of Vadim, who listened patiently as the Egyptian actor told him of his sexual exploits with Françoise. *[Vadim apparently did not confide that he, too, was one of her lovers.]*

Genghis Khan was shot over the course of several months in Yugoslavia. Vadim's affair with Françoise, when filming ended, began to wind down.

Val Guest, a director well-known to Jane and Vadim, cast her in her next film, the British comedy-adventure, *Where the Spies Are* (1966). In it, she played the love interest of her co-star, David Niven, portraying a Parisian high-fashion model named Vikki. Its release in Canada and the United States brought disappointing results, taking in only $1.2 million.

Back in France, Françoise's love affair with Vadim, although they remained friends, had come to an end. She told him she was going to work with Gene Kelly and her sister, Catherine, in *Les Demoiselles de Rochefort* (*The Young Girls of Rochefort;* 1967), an homage to big-budget Hollywood movie musicals. Vadim told her that she'd be safe with Kelly "because he is mainly gay."

Jacques Demy, a well-known director in French cinema, would helm the movie with such co-stars as Danielle Darrieux, Michel Piccoli, and George Chakiris.

The movie was a hit at box offices in France, but it did not perform well in the United States.

Vadim may have been instrumental in recommending Françoise to his friend, filmmaker Roman Polanski. Deeply impressed, he cast her in his second English-language film, a thriller named *Cul-de-sac* (1966). It follows two injured American gangsters who take refuge in a remote island castle of a young British couple in Northern England.

Like Polanski's previous film, *Repulsion* (1965), *Cul-de-sac* explores the themes of horror, frustrated sexuality, and alienation.

Françoise's farewell to the screen occurred after she was cast opposite the English actor, Michael Caine, in *Billion Dollar Brain* (1967), a Technicolor espionage movie. Caine starred as a British secret agent, Harry Palmer. The "brain" of the title was a sophisticated computer that controls an anti-Soviet network of spies.

Caine and Françoise were backed up by some well-known supporting players—Karl Malden, Eli Wallach, and Oskar Homolka.

Jane Fonda's future lover, Donald Sutherland, made a brief appearance as a computer technician.

The film crashed at the box office. Caine later told the press, "We had a lunatic genius, director Ken Russell, on our hands. He was the least ideal man to direct a thriller. What he has is this passion for making thundering great messes. He really wanted to make a film about Nijinski, starring Rudolph Nureyev."

Vadim was outside the borders of France when news reached him that on June 16, 1967, Françoise had been killed while speeding to the Nice airport. Late for boarding a flight, she lost control of her rented Renault 10 and hit a signpost ten kilometers from Nice at the Villeneuve-Loubet exit of the autoroute La Provençale. Her car flipped over and burst into flames. She could not free herself from her safety belt and died in the ensuing fire.

"Although we were no longer lovers, Françoise had a soft spot in my heart," Vadim said. "Catherine loved her very much, so I could only imagine the sorrow of her death. I think she never really recovered from the loss."

***

Jean-Louis Trintignant (1930-2022)
The Quiet Frenchman Who Stole Bardot from Roger Vadim

When Vadim directed Bardot in *Et Dieu…créa la femme* (*And God Created Woman;* 1956), he ordered her to perform nude love scenes with an actor he was promoting, Jean-Louis Trintignant, born the son of a rich industrialist. At the age of 20, he moved from Piolenc, near Avignon in Provence, to Paris, where he would fulfill his dream of becoming one of the most gifted of French New Wave actors.

His first meeting with Bardot, arranged at a luncheon orchestrated by Vadim, had been a disaster. After he left, Bardot told Vadim, "He's a clod."

But after filming some nude love scenes with him, she changed her mind. Their making "realtime love" continued that night after they left the studio together without Vadim. Before filming ended, she had fallen in love with Jean-Louis. She later told Vadim that their marriage was over.

Jean-Louis Trintignant with a dumure-looking **Brigitte Bardot** at their onscreen wedding in *Et Dieu Créa la femme*. Although at the time, they were real-life lovers, in legal terms, they never married.

Vadim remembered standing outside Jean-Louis' apartment building, gazing up at its fifth floor, fully aware that his wife was inside, making love. He later recalled that he was so jealous that he almost committed suicide. But in time, he recovered, defining jealousy as "a bourgeois conceit."

His standing outside her apartment building evoked a similar incident in the life of Henry Fonda, when he did the same thing in the early 1930s: In Henry's case, that involved looking up at the apartment windows of Broadway producer Jed Harris, knowing that Henry's first wife, Margaret Sullavan, was up there making love to him.

Even though Jean-Louis was married at the time to actress Stéphane Audran, his affair with Bardot lasted for about two years. It came to an end when he was drafted into service with the French Army and stationed in Algeria.

Back on his home turf of Paris, Jean-Louis returned to screen acting, scoring a big success in the film *Un homme et une femme (A Man and a Woman; 1966)*. Director Claude Lelouch cast him opposite Anouk Aimée playing a young widow and a widower who meet by chance, waiting for their respective children at a boarding school, and fall in love.

The movie was a commercial success, and even earned $14 million after its release in the United States.

Jean-Louis also starred in *L'Homme qui ment (The Man Who Lies, aka,* in Slovak, *Muž, ktorý luže; 1968)*, for which in Berlin, he won the Silver Award as Best Actor of the Year.

Jean-Louis was on his way, and became so popular that he was cast in both Italian and English-language films. In Italy, Bernardo Bertolucci cast him in *Il conformista (The Conformist; 1970)*.

Throughout the 1970s, Trintignant starred in a number of films in England, beginning with *The Outside Man* (1971), in which his leading ladies were Ann-Margret and Angie Dickinson.

By 1973, he starred in *Under Fire,* in which Nick Nolte and Gene Hackman took the leads. It was the saga of the last days of the Nicaraguan Revolution that brought the downfall of the Somoza regime, the corrupt family which had ruled Nicaragua for the previous forty-three years.

That was followed with Trintignant's involvement the last film of François Truffaut, *Vivement dimanche! (Confidentially Yours, aka Finally, Sunday!; 1983)*. Jean-Louis played a realtor suspected of murdering his wife and her lover.

As late as 1994, Jean-Louis starred with Irene Jacob in a notable film, *Three Colors: Red* by a notable director, Krzystof Kieslowski. It was released to critical acclaim and was nominated for three Oscars, including Best Picture.

Jean-Louis never married Bardot, but he was famously wed (1960-1976) to Nadine Trintignant, a multi-talented director, producer, screenwriter, and novelist. She was the sister of Christian Marquand, Vadim's best friend.

Following the death of her nine-month-old daughter, Nadine wrote and directed *Ça n'arrive qu'aux autres* (*It Only Happens to Others; 1971*), starring Catherine Deneuve and Marcello Mastroianni as a couple coping with the death of their infant daughter.

Roman Polanski (1933-)
"I REALLY HATE WHAT THE PRESS WRITES ABOUT ME."

Roman Polanski, the Polish film director and producer, helmed such pictures as *Rosemary's Baby* (1958).

He faced two horrific tragedies in his life: 1) In 1969, his pregnant wife, Sharon Tate, was murdered by members of the Charles Manson gang, and 2) In 1977, he fled the United States to avoid a prison term based on his controversial conviction for the rape of a teenage girl.

After Jane finished *They Shoot Horses, Don't They* (1969), Vadim wrote that he felt his marriage to her still had a chance.

However, at a party at the home of Roman Polanski in Benedict Canyon, he saw her (as described in his memoir) disappear for more than half an hour with a very handsome man.

"When she appeared again, her hair was disheveled, and her skirt slightly crumped."

As he recalled, "the butterfly had emerged from its chrysalis and was spreading its wings."

At the end of June, the house at Malibu was returned to its owners after Vadim and Jane moved on.

"If I compare myself to Roman Polanski, all my troubles seem petty," Vadim claimed. "Roman seemed destined to lead a tragic life, even as a kid in Poland."

Polanski entered the world on a hot summer day in August of 1933 in Paris. But by 1937, his Polish-Jewish parents moved back to Krakow in Poland, a terrible mistake. Within two years, the Hitler-ordered Nazi invasion of Poland launched World War II. The Polanski family found themselves trapped in the Krakow ghetto, and his mother and father were later carted off in a raid by Nazi soldiers.

The young son they left behind grew up in foster homes, later identifying himself as a survivor of the Holocaust.

He turned to making films, beginning with the highly rated *Nóż w wodzie* (*Knife in the Water;* 1962), which was Oscar nominated as Best Foreign Film of the Year.

Leaving Poland, Polanski emigrated to London, where he helmed a trio of movies beginning with *Repulsion* (1965); *Cul-de-Sac* (1966); and *The Fearless Vampire Killers* (1967).

Moving then to Hollywood, he launched himself by directing the horror film *Rosemary's Baby* (1968) with

Roman Polanski with **Sharon Tate** in *The Fearless Vampire Killers* (1967). Set deep in the heart of Transylvania, this British comedy horror was also known as *Pardon Me, but Your Teeth Are in My Neck.*

Mia Farrow.

From 1959 to 1962, Polanski was married to an actress with the "marquee unfriendly" name of Barbara Kwiatkowska-Lass.

The murder of his second wife, Sharon Tate, and his unborn son devasted his life. "I was in London at the time of the slaughter by the cult followers of Charles Manson."

He later wrote, "Sharon's death is the only watershed in my life that really matters. Her murder changed my personality from a boundless, untroubled sea of expectations and pessimism—eternal dissatisfaction with life."

More troubles loomed in his future. Once, when he had recovered enough, he made *Macbeth* (1971) in England, returning to Hollywood to film the highly successful *Chinatown* (1974) with Jack Nicholson.

In 1977, he was arrested and charged with raping and drugging a 13-year-old girl. As a result of a plea bargain, he pleaded guilty to a lesser offense of unlawful sex with a minor.

In 1978, he learned that a judge planned to reject his plea and sentence him to jail. He fled from California to Paris, becoming a fugitive from the American justice system.

From abroad, he turned out such movies as *The Pianist* (2002), which earned him an Oscar for Best Director. He also made such films as *The Ghost Writer* (2010); *Venus in Furs* (2013); and *An Officer and a Spy* (2019).

In 1989, he married actress Emmanuelle Seigner, and they had a daughter, Margane, and a son they named Elvis.

In May of 2018, the Academy of Motion Picture Arts and Sciences voted to expel Polanski from their membership.

***

Sharon Tate (1943-1969)
Stabbed Sixteen Times When 8 ½ Months Pregnant

Through Vadim's friend, director Roman Polanski, Vadim and Jane Fonda entertained Sharon Tate at their villa that summer in Malibu. A beauty from Dallas, Texas, they found her charming and talented.

She'd been nominated for a Golden Globe as "New Star of the Year" for her performance in the 1967 film adaptation of Jacqueline Susann's best-selling novel, *Valley of the Dolls*. Tate's career was beginning to accelerate.

However, she became pregnant at the end of 1968. In February of 1969, she and Polanski moved to 10050 Cielo Drive in Benedict Canyon in Los Angeles. The house had been previously occupied by Terry Melcher (son of Doris Day) and Candice Bergen.

Polanski was in London finishing work on *The Day of the Dolphin*. He hoped to return to Los Angeles in time for the birth of his baby with Tate.

On August 8, 1969, Tate had dined at El Coyote Café with hairdresser Jay Sebring, Wojciech Frykowski, and Abigail Folger. They returned to Tate's home around

Press and PR photo of **Sharon Tate** and **Roman Polanski** at their widely publicized and very stylish California wedding in 1968.

In one of the greatest and most brutal of all murders, their unborn child was stabbed to death in his mother's womb.

10:30PM.

Shortly after midnight, all of them were murdered by members of "the Charles Manson family." The pregnant Tate was stabbed sixteen times, many of the knife wounds deliberately aimed at her pregnant belly.

The dead bodies were discovered the morning after their deaths by the housekeeper. When the police arrived on the scene, they found Steven Parent shot dead in his car in the driveway.

On the front lawn lay the bodies of Frykowski and Folger. Inside, Tate and Sebring were discovered in the living room, each with one end of the same rope tied around each of their necks and interconnecting them.

The murder became one of the most notorious crimes in American history.

Hollywood celebrities seemed, collectively, to go into shock, and security guards were hired by one household after another, some of them hiring guards procured from and flying in from Florida.

Dominick Dunne recalled, "The shock waves that went through the town were beyond anything I had ever seen before. People were convinced that the rich and famous of the community were the most in peril. Children were sent out of town. Steve McQueen packed a gun when he attended the funeral of his friend, Sebring."

Those shock waves extended to Vadim and Jane Fonda, who feared for their own lives, while grieving over the death of a friend.

No one was more shocked or had experienced as many emotional agonies as Polanski. He later claimed, "In moments of unbearable personal tragedy, some people find solace in religion. In my case, the opposite happened. Any religious faith I had was shattered by Sharon's brutal murder and the butchering of my unborn son. It reinforced my faith in the absurd."

***

Jeanne Moreau (1928-2017)

(JEANNE MOREAU IS) "THE GREATEST ACTRESS IN THE WORLD."

—Orson Welles

In post-war France, there was no more captivating actress than Moreau, a Parisian whose trademark was a downcast mouth "and the haunting and suggestive gaze of her eyes that made her the reigning queen of that smoldering European sensuality that caused the art house circuits to light up in those days," according to one film critic.

She and Vadim moved in the same social circles, and may have been intimate on more than one occasion. She could be the role model to which Jane Fonda would aspire.

She appeared on the stage but beginning in 1949, she found small roles in films.

Director Louis Malle was one of the first to recognize Moreau's talent on the screen. He cast her in *Ascenseur pour l'échafaud (Elevator to the Gallows; 1958)*.

Moreau was teamed with Maurice Ronet in this crime thriller of illicit lovers and murderers. Their alibis unravel after one of them become entrapped in an elevator.

After working with Jean Cocteau for several years, this was Malle's first feature film.

Moreau was cast after Malle saw her on the stage in Paris, performing in Tennessee Williams' *Cat on a Hot Tin Roof*.

The career of the sultry French actress **Jeanne Moreau** spanned half a century. Product of a French father and an English mother, she was a favorite actress of such notables as Orson Welles, Joseph Losey, Luis Buñuel, Louis Malle, Michelangelo Antonioni, and François Truffaut.

Miles Davis' musical score became "the model for sad-core music ever since," in the words of one critic.

In *Time* magazine, Barry Farrell wrote: "Forget about those twenty films Moreau made before Malle brought her into cinematic realism and revealed the face behind all those heavy cosmetics in her previous movies. Malle, so we heard, was falling in love with her both on and off the screen."

Based on a story by Marguerite Duras, *Moderato cantabile* **(***Seven Days…Seven Nights;* 1960), as directed by Peter Brook, teamed Moreau with Jean-Paul Belmondo. Brooke had directed Moreau in a French-language stage production of *Cat on a Hot Tin Roof* in Paris, and wanted to work with her again, this time in this romantic suspense caper.

Raoul Lévy, the producer, had wanted Simone Signoret as the female lead, but Brooke convinced him to use Moreau instead.

His original co-star, before Belmondo was assigned to the part, had been Richard Burton, who had agreed to the director's stipulation that he'd be speaking in French. "It is for art, not for the money," Later, Burton told the press that he'd had to withdraw from the project.

After he sat through the film, Belmondo told the press, "It's very boring."

Ironically, for her performance—and despite Belmondo's pronouncement—Moreau won the Best Actress Award at Film Festival in Cannes—her first major success.

Franco-British Lioness of the New Wave

Jeanne Moreau was one of the most celebrated actresses in film history, known for her strong character roles, her sensual features, her expressive face, and her enigmatic air of mystery that captured men as wide-ranging as Lee Marvin and Marcello Mastroianni.

Then along came Michelangelo Antonioni who cast Moreau in *La Notte (The Night;* 1961*),* starring Marcello Mastroianni. Filmed on location in Milan, the movie depicts the collapsing relationship between a disillusioned novelist and his frustrated wife as it follows a single day and night in which they confront their (respective) alienation.

Before its release in Italy, that nation's Committee for Theatrical Review demanded several cuts, including a scene in which Moreau displayed her naked breasts.

"Many men fall in love with her," claimed Mastroianni. "Jeanne loves you until the end of the filming."

Orson Welles fell madly in love with Moreau and cast her in a trio of films, beginning with *The Trial* (1962). Based on the posthumously published novel by Franz Kafka, the movie also starred Anthony Perkins, Romy Schneider, and Elsa Martinelli.

Although lambasted by some reviewers after its release, *The Trial* is viewed in the eyes of some critics as a masterpiece. Welles said, "It's the best film I have ever made."

Critic Devin Rhodes asked: "Has Welles forgotten *Citizen Kane?"*

Moreau had come to the attention of many New Wave *avant-garde* directors in France. François Truffaut cast her as the lead in *Jules et Jim (Jules and Jim;* 1962). Partly as a result of its magnetic casting, she became known internationally.

Set around the time of World War I, it depicts a tragic love triangle with her male co-stars, Henri Serre and Oskar Werner. *Time* magazine later put it on its list of 100 *Best Movies of All Time. [Editors' note: This list was compiled in 2005.]*

Moreau continued to be helmed by some of the top directors of her era, including Louis Buñuel in *Diary of a Chambermaid* (1964), a French-Italian crime drama that cast her with Michel Piccoli. It depicted a saucy social saga of corruption, violence, sexual obsession, and perversion.

Vadim became fascinated when Louis Malle teamed his former wife, Brigitte Bardot, with Moreau in *Viva Maria!* (1965). In South America, two sexy women meet and become revolutionaries during the early years of the 20th Century. It also starred George Hamilton as Flores, a socialist revolutionary. Moreau and Hamilton were alleged to have had an affair during the shoot.

The characters played by Bardot and Moreau are each named Maria. Maria II (Bardot) accidentally invents striptease on stage.,

Malle's idea was to make a "buddy" movie, but, in this case, showcasing female, rather than male, bonding. For inspiration, he drew upon Burt Lancaster and Gary Cooper as they had emoted together in *Vera Cruz* (1954).

Time magazine defined the film as "jaunty but slipshod farce. Malle rides to the rescue with more anti-state, anti-church, antedated spoofery than he can handle."

Although Pierre Cardin received credit for the costumes, it was also suggested that Bardot and Moreau appear onscreen whimsically dressed like creatures invented by Toulouse-Lautrec or Degas.

Viva Maria! was a huge commercial and artistic success in France. In Texas, the film was banned for its anti-Catholic content. Later, the U.S. Supreme Court struck down the Texas ban.

Orson Welles later cast himself as the male lead to Moreau in *Falstaff (aka Chimes at Midnight;* 1966) based on *Falstaff* by William Shakespeare. Welles said that the story was about "the betrayal of friendship." He even got John Gielgud to play the English king, Henry IV, and Margaret Rutherford to essay the role of "Mistress Quickly."

At one point during filming, Welles had to shut down production because he ran out of money and had to find a new "angel" to invest additional funds.

He later said, "If I wanted to get into heaven on the basis of just one film, *Chimes at Midnight* would be the movie I would show to God."

Moreau's final film with Orson Welles was *Une histoire immortelle* (*The Immortal Story;* 1968), a French movie in which the corpulent star operated as both the male lead and also the film's director. Based on a short story by the Danish writer, Karen Blixen (aka Isak Dinesen), and with a running time of only one hour, it was the shortest movie Welles ever made.

The setting is 19th Century Macao. Dr. Clay (as portrayed by Welles) is a wealthy merchant nearing the end of his life. One night, his constant companion relates a story he'd been told during an ocean crossing about a rich old man who offers a sailor money to impregnate his young wife.

Clay becomes obsessed with the legendary tale, and he dispatches his aide to find a sailor and a young woman who dramatize and "act out" the roles defined by the dimly recollected tale. Tapped for the role of Virginia Ducrot was Moreau. The part of Paul, the young "sailor for hire" was cast with Norman Eshley.

In the mid-1970s, Elia Kazan cast Moreau in *The Last Tycoon* (1976), an adaptation of F. Scott Fitzgerald's last and uncompleted novel. Never before had she appeared with such an array of famous male stars: Robert de Niro, Tony Curtis, Robert Mitchum, and Jack Nicholson. The plot was based on the short life of Irving Thalberg, who virtually ran MGM in the 1930s. De Niro was cast as the Thalberg-inspired character.

The screenplay by Harold Pinter turned it into a Hollywood story of frustrated ambition and unattained love of the young and beautiful in Hollywood.

In the 1980s, the German director, Rainer Werner Fassbinder, teamed Brad Davis with Moreau in *Querelle* (1982), adapted from Jean Genet's 1947 novel. It was Fassbinder's last film before his sudden death.

The plot centers on a handsome Belgian sailor, Georges Querelle, a thief and a murderer. Moreau, as Madame Ysiane, runs a bar and brothel for sailors. The movie had a strong homosexual theme.

CHAPTER NINE

They Shoot Horses, Don't They?
Jane, as an Embittered "Endurance Competitor,"
at a Depression-Era Dance Hall, Can't Ask for Anything but Death

Pretty Maids All in a Row
Rocking and Rolling with **ROCK HUDSON**,
Who's Cast as a Serial Killer Specializing in Nymphettes and Co-Eds

"There is no role in my film for Jane Fonda, and no role for her in my life."
—Roger Vadim

Klute
Jane Portrays an Endangered Prostitute Seeking Therapy
Later, She goes to bed with an Oscar
Donald Sutherland Comes into Jane's Life In Many Different Ways

Steelyard Blues
Cast Again as a Whore, Jane, wearing an Afro Wig, Joins a Coven of Misfits Who Hope
that their Junkyard Airplane Will Somehow Fly into the Wild Blue Yonder

Tout Va Bien
La crème de la Nouvelle Vague (**JEAN-LUC GODARD**) Casts Jane with Child Molester
and Serial Seducer **YVES MONTAND** (MM's Former Boyfriend)

In Ibsen's Feminist Drama,
A Doll House
Jane Stars in the "Most Performed" Play from the 19th Century

The Blue Bird
Even such accumulated talent as Ava Gardner, Elizabeth Taylor, George Cukor, and Jane Fonda
Can't Rescue the USSR's Sloppy, Confusing, and Murky remake of Shirley Temple's Classic

Fun with Dick and Jane
To Pay their Mounting Bills, They Turn to Crime

Julia
Although Jane probably Deserved an Oscar for Diving into the film adaptation of a hotly litigated *novella* by "Hellish Hellman," Another Actress, for another Film, Wins the Gold

Jane ended the turbulent 1960s, career-wise, on a high note, starring in the existentially grim *They Shoot Horses, Don't They?*. It became one of her most critically acclaimed movies, and in the aftermath of its release, she was acknowledged as one of America's foremost actresses.

Ironically, for the moment, at least, she did not successfully perpetuate that triumph, and instead, veered off into a string of politically themed movies of little interest to the general public.

An example of her "up to her neck" involvement in this genre was *Introduction to the Enemy*, in collaboration with her newest husband, a fellow activist named Tom Hayden. *Introduction to the Enemy* (1974), a documentary about the Vietnam War, did not go into general release. It was the first production of her new company, IPC (Indochina Peace Campaign Films).

Months later, when she received her first Oscar nomination for *They Shoot Horses, Don't They?*, she told the press, "When young audiences see how people in the Depression pulled out of it, perhaps it will give them inspiration to pull out of the mess we're in now."

Her performance as Gloria, the marathon dancer in *They Shoot Horses, Don't They?* did nothing to help her failing marriage to Roger Vadim. In his memoirs, he wrote, "At home, she was living the role of Gloria with morbid intensity. A cold barrier was coming between us. I felt I was living in a waking nightmare."

In her immediate present, at least, she was very selective (some said "misguided") about the films being offered to her. As noted before, she rejected the female leads in both *Bonnie and Clyde* (1967) and *Rosemary's Baby.* (1968).

By 1970, she began to receive some of what later became massive publicity when she championed the cause of how the country treats its Native Americans.

Until this point in her career, Jane's biggest career triumph had involved her performance as a prostitute in the critically acclaimed *Klute* (1971).

But *Klute* was followed by a series of films that did not perform well at the box office.

One reporter for *Variety* claimed, "Jane Fonda was not blacklisted like communist sympathizers in the 1950s. She was 'graylisted.'"

Movies that performed poorly included *A Doll's House* (1973); *Steelyard Blues* (1972) in which she co-starred with her lover, Donald Sutherland; and *The Blue Bird* (1976) with Elizabeth Taylor and Ava Gardner.

[*Her involvements in political activism and her marriage to fellow activist Tom Hayden will be explored in a chapter coming up.*]

A hit at the box office, *Fun with Dick and Jane* (1977), co-starring George Segal, was marketed (more or less accurately) as her "comeback picture."

***

They Shoot Horses, Don't They? (1969)

It all began with Horace McCoy's Depression-era novel, *They Shoot Horses, Don't They?*. It was a bitter story, set in the 1930s, published in 1935, as many Americans were starving. Its focus was on a disparate group of young men and women desperate to win a dance marathon for a $1,500 prize. Goaded on by an opportunistic emcee, hopefuls are urged to dance until they drop, winner take all, even if it leads to death.

At first, the novel did not sell well in America, perhaps because its citizens were living through those hard-nosed days and didn't later want to go to the movies to see how awful that era really was.

However, the novel proved a success among French intellectuals such as André Gide, Jean-Paul Sartre, Simone de Beauvoir, and André-Georges Malraux.

Director Roger Vadim labeled it as "the first" existential novel to come out of America. For a while, the young director considered acquiring the rights and turning it into a film vehicle for his lady love at the time, Brigitte Bardot. He later claimed, "That was my moment of insanity."

The author of the novel on which it was based, Horace McCoy, knew how hard it was to make a living during the Depression. He had had a series of odd jobs he performed for his survival. They included washing cars, harvesting lettuce in the Imperial Valley, and working as a bouncer at the Santa Monica pier, where he witnessed marathon dances up close. From that evolved his masterpiece, *They Shoot Horses, Don't They?*

Another of his novels, *Kiss Tomorrow Goodbye* (1948) was adapted into a movie (1950) starring James Cagney. McCoy also wrote several Westerns and crime melodramas, and was employed by such directors as Nicholas Ray, Raoul Walsh, and Henry Hathaway.

In 1951, Charlie Chaplin purchased the screen rights to *They Shoot Horses, Don't They?*, hoping to adapt it into an Oscar-winning film. He wanted it to star his son, Sidney, as the male lead alongside Sidney's

THE MADDING CROWD. Here's an up close and personal view of one of the posters used to market and define the sweaty desperation of Jane's then-newest film.

blonde-haired girlfriend, Marilyn Monroe, then involved with each other in a torrid affair.

Norman Lloyd launched its pre-production. In the meantime, Chaplin sailed to England for the London premiere of his latest film, *Limelight* (1952).

All of this occurred at the time of Senator Joseph McCarthy's witchhunt, whose intention involved finding (and destroying) alleged Communists, both within the U.S. government and in the nation's film industry. "The Little Tramp" himself was accused at the time of being a subversive. J. Edgar Hoover, the chief of the F.B.I. and a closeted homosexual, made a deal with the Immigration and Naturalization Service to revoke the re-entry permit of Chaplin. That marked the death of Chaplin's dreams for his "Marathon Dance movie."

It took until 1969 before interest in making the Depression-era film was revived. Its film rights were acquired again, this time by Palomara Pictures, presided over by Edgar Scherick. He turned the project over to the producing team of Irwin Winkler and Bob Chartoff. They hired James Poe to write the script, and he told them he also wanted to direct it, but after he submitted a filmscript, the two producers were terribly disappointed. In the aftermath, they fired him and hired Robert E. Thompson to drastically rewrite it.

The original plan involved shooting the film for a modest budget of $900,000, but that estimate was later raised to a more realistic $4.86 million.

It might have seemed like an odd casting call, but Warren Beatty and Mia Farrow were originally, as a team, considered for the leads.

It is not known if Beatty even read the script that was sent to his agents, but Farrow did. She agreed to play the female lead, but for $500,000, which was beyond the budget of the (then) production crew.

Eventually the lead roles went to Jane Fonda as Gloria, and Michael Sarrazin as Robert.

As its early-stages director, Poe was fired after only a week. Three other candidates were considered as his replacement, each with his own price tag—Jack Smight for $250,000; William Friedkin for $200,000; and Sidney Pollack for $150,000. Pollack became their man.

Pollack, who had begun his directing career in television dramas, used *They Shoot Horses* as a vehicle to switch to film direction, where he had great success. In time, his films would receive forty-eight Oscar nominations, and he'd win eleven. Many actors he directed would also win Oscars, not only Jane, but Barbra Streisand, Dustin Hoffman (in drag) for *Tootsie* (1982), Meryl Streep, Holly Hunter, and Paul Newman.

Pollack used the unusual technique of flash-forward—that is, glimpses of the future, which some movie-goers found confusing, having been attuned, in their film-loving pasts, to flash-backs but not flash-forwards.

Jane later said that she was not impressed with *They Shoot Horses* final script. However, Vadim, who retained his position, despite their marital differences, as her mentor, urged her to sign for the role because he found similarities between the ideas expressed in the script and those of the French existentialists.

She was somewhat apprehensive about working with Pollack but was put at ease when he visited her home to discuss the script. "It was a germinal moment for me," she recalled. "This was the first time in my life as an actor that I was working on a film about larger societal issues. Instead of my professional work feeling peripheral to life, it felt relevant."

She was going through a troubled time in her marriage to Vadim, and she drew upon her own personal problems to help

Here's then 32-year-old director **Sidney Pollack** in 1966, at the Oscar ceremony that recognized him for his directorship of an episode of *Bob Hope Presents the Chrysler Theater*—the last of TV's drama anthologies, a genre that had *drawn* huge audiences in the 1950s.

Itching to get into feature filmmaking, he was part of a generation that learned its trade in TV.

After that, his reputation as a hard-hitting director who wrung the best out of actors and scripts became more deeply entrenched.

with her characterization of Gloria.

Vadim said, "Jane was living her private life like the ravaged Gloria. She was moody and depressed. She didn't come home but slept in Mae West's old dressing room. The shadow of Gloria was coming between us. I felt I was walking through a dark nightmare. The erosion of love is a sordid thing. It's a cancer that eats out pieces of your heart, taking away not only your body, but your mind. No one ever completely recovers from the loss of a major love."

The sound track of the movie included several standards that were played across the country during the 1930s. These included "Brother, Can You Spare a Dime?"; "I Found My Million Dollar Baby in a Five-and-Ten Cent Store;" and "The Best Things in Life Are Free."

A strong supporting cast was lined up. Susannah York was cast as Alice LeBlanc; Gig Young as Rocky Gravo; Red Buttons as Harry Kline; Bonnie Bedalia as Ruby Bates; and Bruce Dern as James Bates.

Jane later claimed that she had a good reason to accept the role, other than because of its artistic merits. In France, she and Roger Vadim had purchased a farmhouse and spent a lot of money on renovations. In addition, Vadim owed back taxes. Their outstanding debts at that point totaled around $400,000. That was the exact amount the studio was offering Jane to play Gloria.

In the plot, Robert Syverton (Michael Sarrazin) has high hopes of becoming a movie director. He wan-

Here's an exhausted actress, **Jane Fonda.** portraying an exhausted "endurance dancer." Desperately committed to remaining in the contest, she's physically supporting her dance partner, played by **Michael Sarrazin.**

But They Shoot Horses, Don't They? During the Depression era of the 1930s, cruel and grueling "marathon dances" were organized. They attracted young men and women desperate for money to live on. Many of them evolved into graphic depictions of hopelessness and poverty.

Albert Camus hailed the book on which the film was based as "the first existentialist novel to come out of America."

ders into a days-long dance marathon in the shabby, gone-to-seed La Monica ballroom, which opens onto the Santa Monica pier jutting out into the Pacific. He soon finds himself recruited by Rocky Gravo (Gig Young), the sleazy emcee. He hooks Robert up as a dance partner with Gloria (Fonda). As a team, they compete for that $1,500 prize.

Susannah York had been cast as Alice Le Blanc, a would-be actress who will probably never make it. In her emotionally fragile state, she partners with Joel Girard (Robert Fields), who is also an aspiring actor.

An impoverished farmer, James Bates (Bruce Dern) dances with his pregnant wife Ruby (Bonnie Bedelia). Of all the contestants, with a baby soon due, they need the cash more desperately than their competitors.

In the tragic role of Harry Kline, a middle-aged and retired sailor, Red Buttons gave a winning performance for a character who is later carted off the dance floor, dead.

In one of the most dramatic scenes in the movie, Harry has a heart attack during one of the "dance races." Undeterred, his partner lifts him onto her back and staggers across the finish line. It becomes quickly apparent that Harry has died in the aftermath of being dragged across the floor. Rocky assures the stunned audience that he is merely suffering from heat exhaustion, and the unknowing crowd cheers for him as medics remove his corpse.

Robert and Gloria make it across the finish line, with both of them in a state of exhaustion. Then they learn that expenses will be deducted from the prize they hope to win, leaving them with nothing. Shocked, newly embittered, and betrayed, they drop out of the marathon. Together, they leave the shabby dance hall and stand on the pier overlooking the ocean. She removes a pistol from her purse and tells him she wants to die but is too afraid to pull the trigger. In desperation, she pleads with him to kill her. Obligingly, he shoots her in the head. Later, when questioned by the police, he answers, "They shoot horses, don't they?"

At the end of filming, Jane visited her hairdresser, telling him, "I grew tired of my Gloria look and wanted her out of my system. I told him to give me a marcelled bob and then to dye my hair a dark brown. Later, when I confronted my image in the mirror, I thought I looked like dear old Dad with my new look, except that I was prettier. As a young girl, I wanted to be a boy. Now I was one."

WHO WAS WHO IN THE CAST OF *THEY SHOOT HORSES*

A Londoner, Susannah York became a familiar figure on the movie screens of the 1960s, appearing in such box office smashes as *Tom Jones* (1964) starring Albert Finney in the title role. *The Telegraph* called her "the blue-eyed English rose with the china-white skin and cupid lips, who epitomized the sensuality of the Swinging Sixties." She was also cited as "an actress of extraordinary emotional range." She received a Best Supporting Actress nomination for her role in *They Shoot Horses, Don't They?*

She shocked her fans when she told the press," I don't think much of this film or myself in it. I found working with Miss Fonda a drag. She was very aloof. I think she spoke no more than eight words to me during the entire shoot."

[At the Academy Awards ceremony that year, the Best Supporting Actress Oscar went to Goldie Hawn for her

Susannah York, "an English Rose." as she appeared with **Albert Finney** on this British lobby card for the 1963 film adaptation of Henry Fielding's picaresque and very bawdy novel, first published in 1749, *The History of Tom Jones, a Foundling*.

performance in Cactus Flower.*]*

Over the span of her career, York co-starred with leading men who included Alec Guinness, John Mills, Kenneth More, William Holden, George C. Scott, and Peter O'Toole. But more of the movie-going public saw her playing Superman's (biological) mother, Lara, on the doomed planet, Krypton, in *Superman* (1978). She also starred in two of its sequels, *Superman II* (1980) and *Superman IV: The Quest for Peace* (1987).

A Canadian from Québec, Michael Sarrazin, three years younger than Jane, would never again top the visibility of his performance as Robert Syverton in *They Shoot Horses, Don't They?*.

In Montreal, the actor landed his first professional job when he was only 17. He later worked in TV dramas before migrating to Hollywood.

Right before emoting onscreen with Jane, he had filmed *Gunfight in Abilene* (1967) and *The Flim-Flam Man* (also 1967) with George C. Scott. At Universal, he had been cast in *A Man Called Gannon* (1968) with Anthony Franciosa, Jane's previous co-star in *Period of Adjustment* (1962).

Michael Sarrazin, depicted above with **Jane Fonda** in *They Shoot Horses*, never scored a role as visible when it was wrapped

Sarrazin also made *Journey to Shiloh* (1968) starring James Caan, Jane's future romantic interest in *Comes a Horseman* (1968). "During my emoting with Jane on and off the screen," Sarrazin recalled, "I saw her becoming Gloria. It was like Jane and Gloria had developed the same personality. She walked like Gloria. Off-screen, she talked like Gloria, too, even mumbling like her. She lost weight, growing thinner and thinner, or so it seemed. Both Sidney Pollock and I agreed that Jane was delivering the performance of her life. She was holding nothing back in reserve, but giving it her all. I don't want to sound jealous, but I feared that in my scenes with her, no one would know I existed. I did learn one thing: She told me she was tired of being written up as a sex symbol."

A native of Chicago, Bruce Dern first met Jane at the Actors Studio in Manhattan. Formerly married to the actress Diane Ladd, he was often cast in supporting roles of a villainous nature.

Bruce Dern was gifted at portraying angry, "borderline crazy" white males. Here he is in *The Cowboys (1972)*, where the psychotic character he played was noted for killing a character played by John Wayne.

During the course of his career, he won several accolades. His big moment would come when he teamed with Jane and Jon Voight in *Coming Home* (1978) for which he was nominated for a Best Supporting Actor Oscar.

In *They Shoot Horses*, he had a sympathetic role as an impoverished farmer dancing with his pregnant wife, trying to make enough money to afford a child when they could barely support themselves.

***

Cast as Bruce Dern's wife, Bonnie Bedelia portrayed an equally pathetic figure, trying to survive not only for herself and her husband, but for the infant growing inside her.

It was a sad, endearing role for this New Yorker who had begun her career in the theater in the 1960s when she was very young, having been born in 1948. She'd made her film debut in *The Gypsy Moths* (1969) when she was 21.

She also worked in television, earning two Emmy nominations.

Bedelia would get a lot of attention when she played the wife of Bruce Willis in *Die Hard* (1988).

Although never gaining any super stardom, her talent was widely recognized, and she worked steadily, even until 2019 when she was guest starring in the Netflix series *What/If*.

Bonnie Bedelia, as life-threatened by evil mastermind **Alan Rickman** in *Die Hard* (1988).

***

Born to Jewish parents in New York City, Red Buttons was both an actor and a comedian. His real name had been Aaron Chwatt until he got a job as an entertaining bellhop at Ryan's Tavern on City Island in the Bronx.

His combination of red, big, shiny buttons on his bellhop uniform led to orchestra leader "Dinty" Moore nicknaming him "Red Buttons." He used that name for the rest of his career, which began in New York's Borscht Belt with Robert Alda "enrolled" as his comedic counterpart.

On December 8, 1941, Jose Ferrer had planned to open with Buttons in *Vickie* on Broadway. However, that Sunday, the Japanese attacked Pearl Harbor and the show never opened. Not many theatergoers wanted to see a farce whose plot took place in Oahu, Hawaii. Buttons did make his debut on Broadway in September of 1942 with Ferrer and Uta Hagen.

Later that year, Buttons was starring in a production of "Minsky on Broadway" entitled *Wine, Women, and Song*. In the middle of his act, the police, as ordered by Mayor Fiorello La Guardia, raided the theater and shut it down. This was the last classic burlesque show ever performed in New York City.

Red Buttons doomed to an early heart attack and death from exhaustion and heart failure in *They Shoot Horses*.

Later, Buttons co-starred with Marlon Brando in *Sayonara* (1957). As a dramatic departure for him, he portrayed airman Joe Kelly, stationed in Japan. He marries a Japanese woman but is barred from bringing her back to the United States. For his performance, he won an Oscar as Best Supporting Actor.

Arguably, Gig Young was the most mentally disturbed actor Jane ever worked with. In *They Shoot Horses*, he starred as Rocky Gravo, the almost sadistic emcee of the marathon dances, where he urges the dancers to go on and on until they nearly die of exhaustion. For this effort, he would win a Best Supporting Actor Oscar.

Winning an Oscar, as Young told columnist Louella Parsons, "can be a kiss of death. Many Oscar winners end up tragically." That was certainly true for him as he ruined his career with his increasingly obvious alcoholism.

Young, who emerged from St. Cloud, Minnesota, in 1913, was quite charming and rather handsome on the surface.

He developed a passion for the theater when appearing in school plays. After school, he got a job hawking seemingly worthless (but very cheap) used cars. A friend offered him a ride to Hollywood if he would pay for half the gas. There, he trained at the Pasadena Playhouse.

Using his original name of Byron Barr, he made his film debut in *Misbehaving Husbands* (1940), in which he played a floor walker. One of his most prestigious parts came when he was cast in *Old Acquaintance* (1943) as the love interest of Bette Davis.

In 1947, he was cast as Errol Flynn's rival for Eleanor Parker in *Escape Me Never*. That set a pattern for his usual roles, cast as a second lead to the star, who got the girl before the end of the final reel.

During the course of his career, Young worked with an impressive array of leading men: Gregory Peck, Glenn Ford, Van Johnson, Clark Gable, Richard Widmark, David Niven, Cary Grant, Elvis Presley, Kirk Douglas, Charles Boyer, and Rock Hudson.

Young had five wives, his most famous marriage, his third (1956-1963), being to actress Elizabeth

Montgomery.

His fifth and final marriage became one of the most widely publicized (and most horrifying) tragedies in Hollywood. On September 27, 1978, at the age of 64, he married Kim Schmidt, a 31-year-old magazine editor.

Three weeks after the wedding, the newlyweds were found dead at his apartment in the prestigious Osbourne Apartment House (Seventh Avenue at 57th Street in Manhattan, near Carnegie Hall) The police determined that he fatally shot his wife before committing suicide. A motive was never agreed upon.

***

Gig Young, an unbalanced actor portraying the ultimate sleazeball MC in *They Shoot Horses*.

Upon its release, *They Shoot Horses, Don't They?* Earned $12.6 million at the box office and for the most part got favorable reviews.

John Mahoney in the *Hollywood Reporter* wrote: "Miss Fonda is the embittered Gloria, who knows that life was rigged before she got there, longs for death and yet is incapable of executing the sentence she has cast... While all other lines bespeak of her longing for death and her weary and angry regard for life, so much of the film is conveyed through an unspoken subsurface, the unspoken response that reveal the soul of the tormented creatures of the arena, and it is on this level that Miss Fonda reveals the longing, the vulnerability, the momentary hopes and capacity for further injury which enrich the role and the film."

The often acerbic John Simon wrote: "As Gloria, the fine little actress, Jane Fonda, graduates into a fine big actress. She gives an antipodal (*i.e.,* "*relating to or situated on the opposite side of the earth*") performance. There is none of the glitter, kittenishness, or jollity that have been her specialties in the past. There is something about her very toughness that repeatedly moves us."

Pauline Kael of *The New Yorker* wrote: "Fortunately, Gloria, who is the raw nerve of the movie, is played by Jane Fonda, who has been a charming, witty nudie cutie in recent years and now gets a chance at an archetypal character. Sharp-tongued Gloria, the hard, defiantly masochistic girl who expects nothing and gets it, is the girl who thinks the worst of everybody and makes everybody act it out, the girl who can't ask anybody for anything except death, is the strongest role an American actress has had on the screen this year. Jane Fonda goes all the way with it, as screen actresses rarely do once they become stars. She doesn't try to save some ladylike part of herself, the way even a good actress like Audrey Hepburn does, peeping at us from behind "vulgar" roles to assure us she's not really like that. Jane Fonda gives herself totally to the embodiment of this isolated, morbid girl who is determined to be on her own, who can't let go and trust anybody, who is so afraid of being gullible chat she can't live."

Many Hollywood insiders thought Jane's performance was a sure-fire bet that would carry off the Best Actress Oscar that year. However, the prize went to Maggie Smith for her portrayal of the eccentric schoolmarm in *The Prime of Miss Jean Brodie* (1969).

James Stewart, still Henry Fonda's best pal, later admitted, "I think that Jane truly deserved that Oscar, but I did not vote for her. I feared she would embarrass Hank when accepting the award, turning the moment into a political vessel, spouting all that antiwar rhetoric."

Jane's greatest tribute came from her father: "My daughter as an actress has finally come into her own. *They Shoot Horses, Don't They?* is her *Grapes of Wrath.*"

***

Pretty Maids All in a Row (1971)

With his marriage to Jane Fonda sputtering and at risk of dying, Roger Vadim announced that he was going to shoot his first American film, *Pretty Maids All in a Row* in California. It was to star Rock Hudson, who was still a big box office attraction at the time.

When MGM had originally acquired its film rights in 1968, it was announced that the new movie would star football's Joe Namath teamed up with (and co-starring with) Jane Fonda.

When Roger Vadim was named director of his first film shot in America, he told the press, "There is no role in it for Jane Fonda. Actually, there is no role in my life for Jane Fonda."

He offered the female lead to Brigitte Bardot, but she had another film commitment. He then presented the role to Angie Dickinson, and she signed on to play Betty Smith.

He was later so pleased with his choice that he told the press, "Angie has more sex appeal than any actress I've ever worked with." *[That pronouncement was obviously not designed to appeal to either Brigitte Bardot or to Jane Fonda.]*

Throughout the course of her six-decade career, Dickinson, born in North Dakota in 1931, appeared in more than fifty films. In 1966, she had co-starred with Jane Fonda, Marlon Brando, and Robert Redford in *The Chase*. One of her most notable movies was Brian De Palma's erotic crime thriller, *Dressed to Kill* (1980), for which she received a Saturn Award for Best Actress.

Her greatest exposure came on television from 1974 to 1978, when she starred as Sergeant Pepper Anderson in the NBC crime series *Police Woman,* for which she won a Golden Globe Award as Best Actress in a Television Series.

Dickinson's love life has been the source of tabloid fodder, notably her alleged affair with John F. Kennedy. Rumor has it that she has an autographed photo of the former president inscribed: "Angie, to the only woman I've ever loved."

CALIFORNIA DREAMING: Dripping with visual references of the "blonde-and-amiable' nymphettes for which California at the time was famous—especially in Europe—Roger Vadim's *Pretty Maids All in a Row* seemed permeated with underaged nymphettes, each of them pretty, sexually available, and curious. The photo above was included in a press and PR campaign that would, by today's standards, seem to encourage sex with minors.

Who's on top? That's **Rock Hudson** portraying an unlikely (but "California Cool' and very charming) serial killer.

At Oceanfront High School, a married faculty adviser and sports coach (Hudson) beds his female students and eventually has to kill several of them to keep them quiet. Shocking at the time of its creation--the dawn of the sexual revolution--and perhaps even more unthinkable today in this era of heightened rigor, it was written by Gene Roddenberry, creator of *Star Trek*, and directed by Roger Vadim.

In the final throes of his marriage to Jane Fonda, he was by now, one of the film world's most legendary erotic kings and quick to profit from his association with his trio of glamourous wives.

She has also been romantically linked to Frank Sinatra, Johnny Carson, and actor David Janssen. She told one reporter, "I dress for women, but undress for men."

[Perhaps they were just tabloid fantasies, but Dickinson's name has also been linked to Eddie Fisher, William Shatner, Marlon Brando, Dean Martin, and Richard Burton.]

Her most famous marriage was formalized in 1965 to composer Burt Bacharach. Technically, they were married for fifteen years, although they separated during the latter years of that span. The union produced a daughter, Nikki, who led a tragic life.

In 2007, Bacharach announced that his daughter had committed suicide, presumably to escape from the ravages to her brain brought on by Asperger's Syndrome.

Pretty Maids All in a Row is set within a fictitious American high school where female students are being targeted by an unknown serial killer. Vadim carefully selected six beautiful wannabe actresses as the "pretty maids."

Rock Hudson was cast as the high school's football coach and guidance counselor, Tiger McDrew. According to the plot, he has already sustained sexual encounters with a number of female students.

Telly Savalas, cast as Police Chief Sam Surcher, suspects that handsome and charming Tiger is the serial killer, but can't prove it.

As the film's director, Vadim worked smoothly with Hudson until he called for the star to appear full-frontally nude.

Hudson adamantly refused: "Not that I have anything to be ashamed of. If Vadim wants to see my cock, I'll whip it out privately for him and let him suck me off. But there is no way in hell I'm gonna flash Jumbo to worldwide audiences."

The April 1971 issue of *Playboy* carried an article written by Vadim, plus a nine-page pictorial of actresses in the movie, including Ms. Dickinson.

The movie bombed at the box office. Critic Roger Ebert defined it as "embarrassing." However, Quentin Tarantino selected *Pretty Maids* as one of his choices in *Sight & Sound* magazine's 2012 edition as one of the *Top Ten Greatest Films of All Time.*

Roger Vadim crafted his movie within a classroom environment that seemed to indulge subliminal sexuality, in class, between (good looking) teachers and their breathlessly horny students.

Left photo: **Rock Hudson** and (right photo) **Angie Dickinson,** each cast as teachers it would be fun (and easy) to get down and low with between homework assignments.

The ad campaign that accompanied the film's release made abundantly clear that it that celebrated the then-prevalent stereotype of (underaged) beauties nurtured by the sun, surf, and sexuality of California.

***

Klute (1971)

In her second motion picture (*Walk on the Wild Side*; 1962) Jane Fonda had played a prostitute in New Orleans with co-stars Laurence Harvey and Barbara Stanwyck. Now, once again, director Alan J. Pakula called upon her to portray a whore: Bree Daniels, a high-priced call girl in Manhattan opposite her leading man, Donald Sutherland as John Klute, a detective.

Although her character is at first suspicious, she eventually falls in love with him.

Klute was the first installment in what became known as Pakula's "paranoia trilogy." It would be followed by *The Parallax View* (1974), starring Warren Beatty in a post-Watergate thriller involving political assassinations.

The trilogy would conclude with Robert Redford and Dustin Hoffman cast as Bob Woodward and Carl Bernstein as the investigative reporters who were key figures in exposing the secrets of the Watergate break-in that led to the resignation of Richard M. Nixon. Pakula would follow with one of his most lauded movies, *Sophie's Choice* (1982), starring Meryl Streep.

Pakula could bask in the prestige of having produced the 1962 film adaptation of Harper Lee's novel, *To Kill a Mockingbird*, but the only movie he'd ever directed was *The Sterile Cuckoo* (1969) starring Liza Minnelli.

"One of my major achievements was to get Jane to play a prostitute again," Pakula recalled. "I practically had to force her to accept the role. She did not think she had it in her to pull off the role of Bree—in fact, she recommended that I offer it to Faye Dunaway. Faye was her main rival for parts in Hollywood. Jane foolishly gave her the female lead in *Bonnie and Clyde* (2013) with Warren Beatty."

A tough kid who grew up on the streets of the Bronx, Pakula was born to Polish Jews. His "polish" derived partly from his years at Yale, where he majored in drama, although some of his more athletic male classmates viewed men who studied drama as "faggots." He was almost thrown out of Yale for fistfighting, attacking his detractors.

During his direction of *Klute*, Pakula was often depressed, since he was going through a divorce proceeding with the actress Hope Lange, whom he had married in 1964.

A half-dozen years later, Pakula would re-enter Jane's life when he directed her in *Comes a Horseman* (1978), co-starring James Caan and Jason Robards.

One of Jane's chief concerns was that as a nascent feminist, she should not be playing a prostitute, selling her wares to any John who could meet her price.

While living in France, she had met Madame Claude, infamous for running the most elegant bordello in the French capital.

The madame told her that nearly all of her girls had been sexually abused when young, often at the age of eight or nine. Jane also learned that a majority of the women for rent were junkies and were often drugged during intercourse.

Sutherland and **Fonda** in *Klute*.

Is the film about a detective and his protectee?

Is it about a hooker and her john?

Or is it about a psychiatrist and her patient?

Only the scriptwriters (and the audience) knew for sure.

In some cases, there was no intercourse, the madame confessed. She cited the manager of a large department store who came every week to have three young women urinate on him, calling it a "golden shower." Another client requested that a needle be used to jab into his testicles. Many of the clients wanted to be beaten by women dressed in leather. A very rare John flew in once a month from Frankfurt. He wanted to eat the feces of a call girl who had been put on a special diet of his choosing for three days before his arrival in Paris.

To prepare herself for the role, Jane, in Manhattan, became acquainted with madams and their "girls for rent." She wanted an intimate preview of the life of a whore, and to that effect, she hung out in pick-up bars and had long talks with hookers. Some of them were paid $1,000 a night for intimacies with Johns who included a U.S. senator and a visiting CEO of a company in Chicago.

When news of her rehearsal methodologies leaked out, it was rumored that Jane herself turned a few tricks. However, this appears to have been just "tabloid fodder" and unconfirmed gossip.

Of course, Jane didn't really have to go to Manhattan to learn about prostitution. She once said, perhaps ruefully, "Working in Hollywood does give one a certain expertise in the field of prostitution."

Despite Jane's reservations about accepting the role, she needed the money.

She worked with the studio's wardrobe department to come up with the appropriate garb. She did not want to appear like a flashy, vulgarly dressed whore as depicted in countless *films noirs*. Her hairdresser gave her a shag cut and depending on the scene, she wore either a miniskirt or a longer skirt held up with a brass-buckled belt. She carried a large, fringed bag. On occasion, she also wore above-the-knee leather boots and stretchy sweaters without a bra.

Originally, the script had focused on Klute, the character played by Sutherland, but as filming continued, Pakula was so impressed that he expanded her role. *[She would not succeed at persuading him to change the title of the film from* Klute *to* Bree.*]*

As the character of Bree unfolds, she seems to feel safer as a prostitute than she would be facing true intimacy with a man.

Bree, to her therapist, reveals the emptiness of her life and searches for an answer to why she became a prostitute in the first place.

At first, a male actor was tapped to play the psychiatrist until Jane objected, demanding that a woman fill the role. Actress Vivian Nathan was assigned the part.

Jane became so wrapped up in how a prostitute lived that she even got involved with the set decoration of her character's apartment. While she was investigating the lives of high-priced hookers, she came across a beautiful young woman who had made herself up to look like Marilyn Monroe as she'd been in 1952.

About once a month, she was flown to Washington to spend a night with President John F. Kennedy. After learning that, Jane asked the set decorator to place a photographic portrait of JFK within (her character's) apartment.

Klute's most memorable scene occurs near the end of the film, when Bree is trapped by her sadistic tormentor, who forces her to listen to a tape recording of a desperate woman minutes before her life is snuffed out. Tears flow from Bree's eyes, mucus from her shapely nose.

Jane's leading man was a Canadian actor, Donald Sutherland, portraying John Klute. His job is to investigate the disappearance of Tom Gruneman, CEO of a chemical company in Pennsylvania. The police find an obscene letter inside his home addressed to Bree.

Klute rents an apartment in the basement of Bree's building, taps her phone, and follows her as she turns tricks. At first, she refuses to answer Klute's questions. But in time, they develop a romance, al-

QUESTION:
Who is a Working Girl's Best Friend?

ANSWER:
Her Shrink

Vivian Nathan, a prominent woman of influence within the Actors Studio and a long-time member of its board of directors, was assigned the small but pivotal role of Bree's (aka Jane Fonda's) psychiatrist in *Klute.*

With quiet authority and sensitivity, the character she portrayed helped to stabilize the character Jane played (a working prostitute) throughout her murderous onscreen ordeals.

Some viewers remember Nathan's counseling sessions with Bree, decades later, as one of *Klute's* most interesting sideshows.

though she confesses to her therapist that she wished she could go back to "just feeling numb while servicing a John."

Jane had nothing but praise for her leading man, finding Sutherland brilliant as an actor and appealing as a sexual partner. She described him as "rangy, with a hangdog quality and droopy pale blue eyes which were especially appealing, a real gentleman."

For more details about their relationship, see below.

Roy Scheider was cast as Bree's pimp, Frank Ligourin.

Charles Cioffi was cast as Peter Cable, a colleague of the missing man, Tom Gruneman (Roger Mill).

Scheider had nothing but praise for Jane's performance, remembering a scene where she is praising a John as she's having sex with him, but glancing frequently at her wristwatch with hopes that her ordeal with him will soon be over.

Scheider found working conditions on the set rather tense. Members of the Black Panthers sometimes showed up, requiring time and attention, and Jane was often busy on the phone in attempts to raise money for various political causes.

"There was a hell of a lot of antiwar rhetoric," Cioffi claimed. "Many members of the crew were very patriotic. One morning, shortly after Jane arrived on the set, she "discovered" an enormous and prominently positioned Stars and Stripes dominating the scenery.

In minor roles was a trio of soon-to-be famous stars: Jean Stapleton ("Edith" in *All in the Family*) played a secretary. In a bar scene, patrons included an uncredited Sylvester Stallone during his pre-Rocky days. Also in the bar was Candy Darling, a transgendered person who would achieve fame in the *avant-garde* film repertoire of Andy Warhol.

After the release of *Klute,* Pakula claimed, "I would not have made the film without Jane. Her inspired characterization of Bree as an intelligent, nervous, ambitious, sad, manipulative, frightened, and vulnerable young woman elevated the picture from an average crime thriller to a classic study of a certain kind of woman in our society. She was brilliant in her portrayal of the psychological terrors she has both within and without. Her terror is both interior and exterior."

Roger Greenspan in *The New York Times* wrote, "The acting in *Klute* seems semi-improvisatory, and in this, Jane Fonda, who is good at confessing, is generally successful. Everyone else merely talks a lot, except for Sutherland, who scarcely talks at all. A normally inventive actor, he is here given precisely the latitude to evoke a romantic figure with all the mysterious intensity of a youthful Calvin Coolidge."

Pauline Kael of *The New Yorker,* wrote, "She disappears into Bree, the call girl, so totally that her performance is very unadorned by acting. She gives herself over to the role, but doesn't get lost in it, remaining in full control. There isn't another young actress in American films who can touch her. Henry Fonda has given filmdom an amazing talent."

On *Rotten Tomatoes, Klute* holds an approval rating of 93% based on forty reviews. That website's critical consensus reads: "Donald Sutherland is coolly commanding, and Jane Fonda is a force of nature in *Klute,* a cuttingly intelligent thriller that generates its most agonizing tension from its stars' *repartée.*

Roger Ebert of the *Chicago Sun-Times* weighed in, too. "While the thriller elements were poorly executed, the performances of Sutherland and especially Jane Fonda carry the film. It should have been entitled *Bree* after her character, since she is the soul of the movie. She avoids the hooker with the heart of gold stereotype."

Ebert continued: "What is it about her that makes her such a fascinating actress to watch? She has a sort of nervous intensity that keeps her so firmly locked into a film character that the character actually seems distracted by things that come up in the movie."

Enrico Zanghi in *Oggi* claimed, "Jane Fonda dominates the rest of the cast. She gives the best portrait of an American prostitute ever, infinitely more real than Shirley MacLaine in *Irma la Douce.* But there is no excess of vulgarity, no sensationalism, and no nudity, though there is suggestiveness, humor, and a successful effort by the producer-director to introduce the audience to Bree and her story."

On the night of the 44th annual Academy Awards presentation, Jane showed up chicly dressed with Donald Sutherland as her escort. She wore a Mao collar with a black pants suit designed by Yves Saint

Laurent. She was running a fever, and the night dragged on for her as she sat through endless presentations. "I think the Academy even gave an Oscar to the janitor," she said.

Charles Chaplin made a rare appearance to accept his second honorary Oscar. *[Ironically, he had once tried to acquire the film rights to* They Shoot Horses, Don't They?.*]*

Before the ceremony, Henry had warned his daughter not to make a prolonged speech, and she did not, graciously accepting the Oscar and thanking the Academy. She used Henry's actual line: "There's a lot to say, but tonight is not the time."

Earlier, Henry had said, "I did not vote for my daughter because I do not believe in the Oscars. How can you compare performances—say, Laurence Olivier vs. Jack Lemmon?"

Backstage, Jane held up her Oscar and asked reporters, "Why hasn't Henry Fonda won one of these?"

Within three months of that Award ceremony, Jane would travel to Hanoi and into notoriety.

***

JANE'S LOVER (BOTH ON AND OFF THE SCREEN) IN *KLUTE*

Donald McNichol Sutherland was born on a rare very warm day (July 17, 1935) in Saint John, in the Canadian province of New Brunswick. His *alma mater* was Victoria University in Toronto. With the intention of becoming an actor, he later enrolled at London's Academy of Music and Dramatic Art.

His ultimate aim involved becoming a movie star in Hollywood, and in that endeavor, he went over big, launching a film career that lasted more than fifty-five years.

He starred in *The Dirty Dozen* (1967), a movie about murderers, rapists, and other criminals who redeemed themselves in World War II. In that film, Lee Marvin, Jane's co-star in *Cat Ballou* (1965), headed a cast that included not only Sutherland, but Ernest Borgnine, George Kennedy, Ralph Meeker, John Cassavetes, Robert Ryan, Telly Savalas, and Clint Walker.

Donald Sutherland and **Jane Fonda** began an affair on the set of *Klute*. The lanky Canadian actor was propelled to stardom in 1969 in the role of Trapper John in Robert Altman's smash hit, *M*A*S*H*.

Sutherland gained even greater exposure in *M*A*S*H* (1970), where he "ate up the scenery" in his interpretation of "Hawkeye" Pierce. It was based on an Oscar-winning screenplay by Ring Lardner, a black comedy dealing with the wild and sometimes surreal exploits of a medical unit during the Korean War.

Before working with Jane in *Klute* (1971), Sutherland starred in *Kelly's Heroes* (1970). Clint Eastwood and Telly Savalas were among the co-stars in that far-fetched wartime story about a heist behind enemy lines during World War II.

Before co-starring with Sutherland, Jane, on occasion, visited with him and his then-wife, Lois Hardwick, in Malibu, where they had been neighbors during the course of that marriage (1959-1966), Sutherland's first. Jane found that at their home, cocktail hours—during which they were said to regularly divide a quart of Scotch between them every day—began early.

By now, both Jane and Sutherland were coming to an end of their respective marriages. Jane was encountering Roger Vadim only on occasion, and Sutherland would soon file for divorce from his second wife, Shirley Douglas (married 1966-1970).

Whenever Jane visited Sutherland during his Shirley Douglas period, the conversations were invariably about politics. Douglas was the daughter of Tommy Douglas, a well-connected Canadian politician (a Social Democrat) hailed as the father of Canada's universal health care system. Shirley and Sutherland had produced twins, Rachel and Kiefer.

Shirley was a firebrand, and she encouraged Jane to articulate some of her more notoriously left-wing political stances. All three of them were opposed to the Vietnam War, and Shirley also persuaded Jane and Sutherland to support the Black Panthers and also to become advocates for better treatment of Native

Americans.

As they got to know each other better and became more public with their politics, both Jane and Sutherland ended up on the National Security Agency's watchlist, in part because of their very visible antiwar stances.

The affair between Jane and Sutherland didn't begin until they started filming *Klute* in Manhattan. He lived in a small suite at the fabled Chelsea Hotel, which often catered to actors and writers. To save money, she stayed at the Fonda brownstone. At first, they kept their affair secret, but it was eventually leaked to the press.

She gave greater clarification in an interview for *The New York Times* magazine. "I will never again be a wife. Donald and I are friends. We think the same things. When we are together, it is delightful. But he is not indispensable to me. I am not indispensable to him. Our attraction involves learning and respect, and we don't intend for our relationship to continue forever."

The affair continued during the making of their next two films. But inevitably, considering Jane's previous romance record, she would wake up one morning convinced that "the time has come for me to move on."

Jane later claimed that getting involved with Sutherland influenced her portrayal of Bree in *Klute*. "My role was deepened and even my voice registered lower. No long the girlish sound in *Period of Adjustment*, my voice came from my gut. My affair with Donald was passionate. I transferred my love for him onto the screen."

Sutherland later gave his own impression of his affair with Jane to *Playboy* magazine. "It was a time when we were both experimenting—emotionally, politically, personally—it was like being in one big bowl of soup together. It was terrific. You couldn't ask for a more generous, exciting, funny, sensuous woman than Jane. I loved her with all my heart. She provided me with the basis of what I guess will be with me for the rest of my life. Jane helped me come out of an intellectual and emotional closet."

***

During the final months of her marriage to Vadim, Jane was often on the move, criss-crossing America to appear at various protests and demonstrations. "For most of the time, I had to be both father and mother to our dear little daughter, Vanessa, whom I love very much."

Nathalie, the daughter Vadim had produced with Annette Stroyberg, asserted that "Jane Fonda was the true love of my father's life."

Jane's salary from *Klute* quickly disappeared, often to pay bills. Vadim seemed to be perpetually in debt but refused to give up his gambling.

To raise much-needed cash, they sold the farmhouse at St-Ouen and moved, simultaneously but separately, back to Los Angeles.

Whereas Vadim stayed at a villa in Malibu, entertaining a parade of starlets, Jane—for a while at least—rented a house for $1,000 a month. It was furnished with pieces from the Salvation Army. Jane slept on an air mattress on the floor.

When reporters asked Jane if she were giving up her film career, she denied it. "In the future, I'll make films that have some social or political significance. I'm not going to star in any movie that exploits women."

To cut costs even more, she moved into a dingy apartment in a low-rent district of Los Angeles off the Hollywood Freeway. She shared the apartment with five other girls, turning it into a sort of female commune. Her new wardrobe consisted of two pairs of jeans, two blouses, and a sweater or two. She accessorized her wardrobe with a (then very chic, then very expensive) Louis Vuitton handbag.

This new wardrobe placed her as Number One on Christopher Blackwell's "Worst-Dressed Actresses of the Year" list.

Long before her divorce, Jane had started to break away. She ushered in what she called "my feisty period," in which she had an adulterous romance, "but out of discretion, I won't name him." She admitted that she did not feel any guilt about that because "I knew that Vadim was playing around."

When Vanessa turned one year old, Jane confronted Vadim, telling him that she didn't think either of them could save their doomed marriage. "A callus had formed around my heart," she claimed.

***

F.T.A (Fuck the Army; 1972)

It was called "The Show the Pentagon Couldn't Stop."

A documentary, it reteamed Jane Fonda with Donald Sutherland and it follows an anti-Vietnam road show for GIs, with stopovers in Hawaii, the Philippines, Okinawa, and Japan. Part of the film included candid conversations with the servicemen themselves as they expressed their anger about the presence of United States forces in Indochina.

Directed by Franchine Parker, *F.T.A.* was sometimes referred to as Jane's "spit-and-a-prayer production."

Parker was a TV and film director, one of the first female members of the Directors Guild of America. She knew her movie would have a very limited release and that most theaters would not show it. Of course, the *Fuck the Army* title had to be altered to *Free the Army*. Regrettably, insofar as its distribution potentiality was concerned, its final cut was riddled with profanities.

F.T.A.'s preview occurred simultaneously with Jane's visit to Hanoi. It was rumored that Richard Nixon himself, an avowed foe of Jane, was behind the shutdown of the documentary. The movie just disappeared one night.

It has since been screened on rare occasions during the 21st Century, including at a viewing in 2005 attended by Jane herself. She was later quoted as saying, "I must say, looking at it now, it's no wonder the film was shut down."

At the time of its original release, *F.T.A.* was interpreted as "the opposition's" answer to Bob Hope's patriotic and pro-war USO tours. Hope's tours were dimming in popularity with the young GIs of the 1970s.

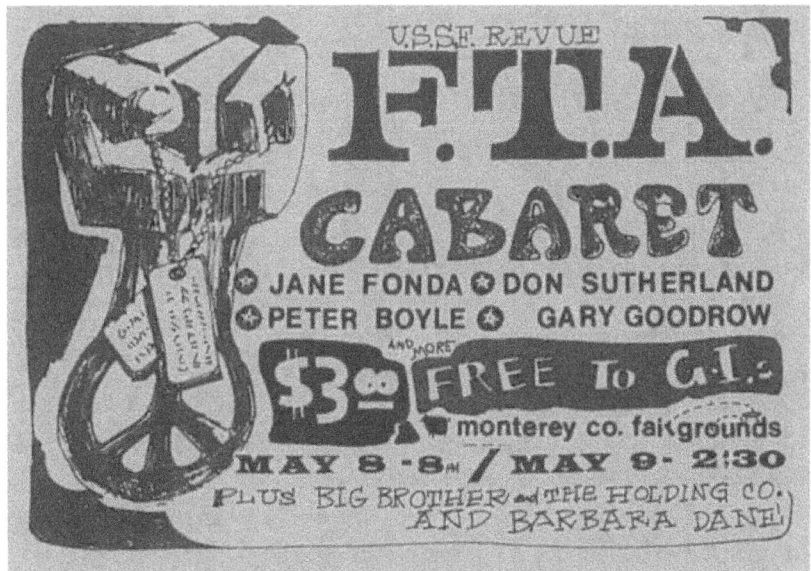

One of the brightest sequences in *F.T.A.* was when Jane teamed with performer Holly Near to dance in the style of the *Folies Bergères* to the tune of "Bomb Another City Today."

One aspect of *F.T.A.* drew a fervently strong reaction from the Right. Black marines discussed racism in the military and at home. One marine said, "I didn't want to fight the people of Vietnam because I have a feeling for them as oppressed nonwhite people."

The *F.T.A.* in the title was a direct response to the Army's recruitment slogan, "*Fun Travel, and Adventure.*" In a song, Jane warbled, "Tired of Bastards Fucking Me Over." In another line that described the male-dominated military brass, she said, "They whistle like a dog and make noises like a hog."

LIFE IS A (SOMETIMES INTENSELY POLITICIZED) CABARET

Sutherland and **Fonda** singing together at a performance of FTA, as captured in a photo which in later years they'd have liked to forget:

Sometimes, pro-Vietnam war hecklers tried to hoot and holler to interrupt the show. One pro-Vietnam soldier on tape admitted, "I wanted to go to Vietnam because I like to kill people. I also get an extra $65 buck in combat pay.:

F.T.A. ends with Sutherland reading from Dalton Trumbo's 1938 novel, *Johnny Got His Gun*.

From 1969 to 1973, Sam Jaffe, then a young man, was Jane's personal press agent. He later recalled "This was a lady who was unjustly accused of being anti-American. To my way of thinking, what could be more pro-American than putting her money and her job at risk for her beliefs? I knew she was digging deep into her cash reservoir to finance hundreds of antiwar protests."

***

Steelyard Blues (1973)

Jane Fonda was just a girl during the infamous McCarthy witch hunt of communists in the film industry. Therefore, she was never blacklisted like so many others. However in the 1970s, when she became a movie star and supported antiwar and other civil rights protests as mentioned before, she was more or less "graylisted." Film roles became scarce.

Along came a starring role in *Steelyard Blues*, where, once again she would be cast as a part-time prostitute named "Iris Caine."

Cast as Jesse Veldini, Donald Sutherland was the star of the movie, rebelling against the norms of society, an ex-con with passion for demolition derbies. He has wrecked almost every car he ever sat be-

After her spilt from Vadim, who by now was hyping his three marriages as exploits of a stylish lothario, Jane might have felt shamelessly "marketed" once again by distributors eager to find another "angle" for hawking her films.

Here's a poster for **Steelyard Blues**, in which, once again, Jane was pigeonholed as a smart hooker with strong survival skills.

hind the wheel of.

He violates his parole when confronted with a 1950 Studebaker.

In the movie, Jane maintains him as an on-again, off again sex partner, perhaps a reflection of what was going on between her and Sutherland in real life.

In pre-release publicity, Warners claimed, "*Steelyard Blues* is a wacky, anti-establishment comedy about a band of misfits who outwit the law in the merry and sympathetic tradition of *Bonnie and Clyde*," that movie whose female lead Jane had rejected.

Their motley gang tries to get a World War II-era, now-vintage flying machine up into the wild blue yonder so that all of them can flee from their troubles. They come across the plane in a scrapyard and have to steal parts to make it airborne once again. They want to go away to a place where there are no laws to break.

As a hooker, Jane appears in an Afro fright wig. Any emphasis on sex is played down. Even though she's cast as a whore, Jane perhaps was trying to create a new image.

However, scenes of vulgarity were not overlooked. She charges $100 a night for her services.

At one point, she is beaten up by the police at the direction of the district attorney, Frank Veldini (Howard Hesseman), who just happens to be the brother of Jesse Veldini, as portrayed by Sutherland.

Several members of the cast, including the film's director, Alan Myerson, were veterans (some said "refugees") from the *F.T.A.* filming. These included Peter Boyle, who in this new movie was cast as Eagle Thornberry, described as a "jolly schizoid," and as a former (now unemployed) circus performer.

A highlight of the film is his impersonation of Marlon Brando. Jane and Boyle had become friends, and he joined her in her political protests.

After *Steelyard Blues*, Mel Brooks would hire Boyle as the comical monster of *Young Frankenstein* (1974). In vivid contrast, right before working with Jane, Boyle had starred in *The Candidate* (1972) with Robert Redford.

Boyle recalled that during the filming of *Steelyard Blues*, Jane was not as friendly as she had been. "She was always sitting in a corner reading some revolutionary newspaper. She had adopted a dour and forbidding attitude that suggested all of us were male chauvinists because we didn't laugh at her jokes."

Its director, Alan Myerson, claimed, "Jane had this dour anxiety, as if haunted by time. She was into feminism and anti-elitism, but actually unaware of the contradictions in her own life."

Cast members of *Steelyard Blues* who had also appeared in *F.T.A.* expressed their belief that Jane was moving from her anti-war stance into a militant form of feminism.

"All of a sudden, or so it seemed," Boyle said, "she was promoting sisterhood. She seemed ashamed at the former exploitation of herself as a nudie sex kitten. Other than Marilyn Monroe, she had been the sexiest gal on the screen, not ashamed to take off her clothes and flaunt her goodies."

"I don't want to be a sex symbol anymore," she told Boyle. "I'm ashamed of some of my former films."

"Jane had begun to look elsewhere for love, or at least an affair," Boyle claimed. "She told me her greatest regret was not to have seduced Che Guevara. By the end of filming, her once-torrid affair with Suther-

The producers of **Steelyard Blues** released this press and PR photo of **Donald Sutherland** slugging **Jane Fonda** with a caption that headlined: "NO WAY TO TREAT A HOOKER".

Had Jane reached, at this point in her sexually *avant-garde* career, "beyond the point of no return" in terms of being perennially cast as a hooker and/or slut?

land had wound down. For Jane, it was time to move on. I think she broke Donald's heart. She was heading back to France to make another bomb.

In terms of ticket sales, *Steelyard Blues* fast-evolved into a total disaster, earning less than a million dollars in the U.S. and Canada. Very few movie goers saw it during its initial release. Greater numbers of consumers saw it on TV in 1979 when it was re-configured with the title of *Final Crash*.

Pauline Kael of *The New Yorker* aimed her ire at its director, Alan Myerson, evaluating him as "amateurish and erratic. The film never gets a rhythm going and doesn't draw us in." She also interpreted it as "almost embarrassing to watch Sutherland and Fonda emote."

The *London Movie Express* stated that "Jane Fonda watchers will be disappointed by her relative modesty and conservative attire."

Vincent Canby of *The New York Times* focused on Sutherland: "He plays a gloomy but gentle demolition derby driver, working on plans to wreck every vehicle manufactured in the United States between 1940 and 1960, not just passenger cars, but dump trucks, school buses, pick-up trucks, delivery vans, trailers, campers, and, at the finale, mobile homes."

The reviews in *Motion Picture* magazine were cruel but accurate: "Miss Fonda, who has played happily amoral kooks in the past, now seems obsessed with hookers, as if some kind of symbol of oppressed womankind, and that role is getting tiresome. After her significant portrayal in *Klute*, why repeat herself in a role that isn't even worth watching? *Steelyard Blues* is almost as big a bomb as *F.T.A.*, if that is possible."

***

Tout Va Bien (All's Well; aka Just Great; 1972)

Jane never really wanted to make this propaganda film but was talked into it. On Christmas Day in 1971, she flew from Tokyo to Paris to begin shooting it.

Separated from Vadim, she occupied a seedy Left Bank apartment with five other women. "I felt homeless," she said. "Not only that, but hopeless, structureless, loveless, and bulimic."

She'd finally agreed to shoot the film where she would be cast as "She," with Yves Montand playing "He."

Ever since she had seen Godard's *À bout de souffle* (*Breathless;* 1960) with the doomed Jean Seberg, she had admired the work of Godard. Most of his films reflected his political views, which were heavily influenced by existential and Marxist philosophies.

Godard was a Swiss-French director who rose to fame in the 1960s during the French New Wave. He became the most influential French movie producer of the post-World War II era.

According to *AllMovie,* his work "revolutionized the motion picture through its experimentation with narrative, continuity, sound, and camerawork."

In 2022, a *Sight and Sound* poll ranked Godard third in its assessment of the top ten film directors of all time.

But after the second week of shooting, Jane soured on her director. "He hates people, especially women. A true revolutionary cares about people. After a few days, I wanted to leave, but he threatened me with physical violence."

Her leading man, Yves Montand, was one of the alltime most famous French actors. Actually, he wasn't French at all, but Italian. The son of a broom maker, he and his family, in 1923, left Italy for France because of his homeland's Fascist regime.

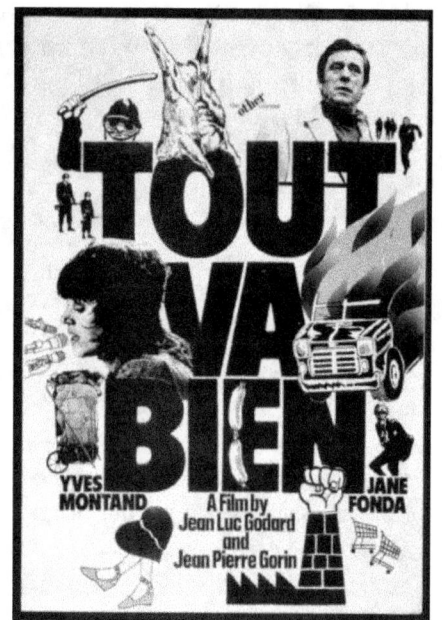

Other than being filtered through a very French lens, and being peppered with urban French humor and argot, what was this movie about?

An idealistic, hard-driving, and perky American news correspondent (**Jane Fonda**) gets mixed up with both a wildcat strike in Paris and in a love affair with **Yves Montand**.

As a young man, he'd grown up on the tough streets of Marseille, where he had a series of jobs ranging from an assistant in his sister's beauty salon to a dockworker.

Eventually, he broke into show business as a singer in a music hall. There, he was discovered by Edith Piaf, who seduced him and then made him a part of her own cabaret act.

In time, he became an international star, not only in France, but in America, too, even in the Soviet Union.

In 1951, he met and married the French actress, Simone Signoret, and they made films together. She overlooked his many adulterous affairs over the years.

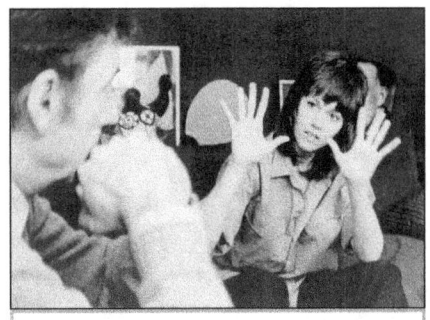

The Actors Studio (in the form of **Jane Fonda**, shown here in some aspect of Method Acting) communicates with a then-lion of the French film world, **Yves Montand**.

When he made *Let's Make Love* (1960) with Marilyn Monroe (one of her last films), news of their affair made headlines. Signoret remained ever-forgiving of her errant spouse.

In 2004, Catherine Allégret, Signoret's daughter from her first marriage to director Yves Allégret, made headlines when her autobiography was published. She claimed that Montand, her stepfather, had sexually abused her since she'd been five years old.

According to Jane, "During the making of our film, Montand, almost every day, perhaps more than once a day, was cheating on his wife," Jane claimed. "It seems that every little girl in Paris wanted to sample the dick that had plowed Marilyn Monroe. I adore Simone and felt sorry for her."

Years later, Montand was asked by a reporter if he had seduced Jane herself during their joint venture: "I certainly meant to seduce her, but I don't recall getting around to it," he answered.

Before filming began, the not-yet-completely-written script was explained to Jane as "part Marxist soap opera, part Brechtian agit-prop."

Its script had been written by Godard himself along with his collaborator, Jean-Pierre Gorin. The Godard/Gorin collaborations would continue with a film featurette called *Letter to Jane,* a postscript to *Tout Va Bien.* It was shown at some film festivals.

At least a decade before his involvement with Jane Fonda, that dashing and romantic Frenchman, **Yves Montand**, was already known to the American entertainment industry's *cognoscenti*.

Here's the front cover of the playbill associated with his one-man show that opened on Broadway in 1959.

***

The plot of *Tout Va Bien* centers on a wildcat strike at a sausage factory. It's witnessed by Jane, cast as a news reporter from the United States, and her French husband, who is a director of commercials for television. Godard was inspired to make the film in the wake of the massive civil unrest in Paris in May of 1968.

The movie had a strong political message—too strong and too overstated for some viewers—and it outlines the logic of the class struggle. It also examines the "social destruction caused by capitalism."

While working on the film, Jane met privately at night with agents of North Vietnam to discuss details of a possible trip to Hanoi.

Vincent Canby of *The New York Times* wrote, "Although I find Jane Fonda most appealing (and very funny) as a solemn American political correspondent who becomes radicalized after being trapped overnight in a strike in a Paris sausage factory, I suspect that most people who go to movies would prefer to see her as the unhappy hooker for which she won an Academy Award." *[Of course, he was referring to Klute.]*

Roger Greenspun, also writing for *The New York Times* claimed, "Both Montand and Miss Fonda (speaking her own French) are expressive and energetic actors. They provide *Tout Va Bien* with a measure of articulate brightness that is its pleasantest quality as a film."

[*On September 13, 2022, Jean-Luc Godard died at his home in Rolle, Switzerland, at the age of 91. Those around him claimed that he died "from assisted suicide suffering from multiple disabling pathologies."*

A spokesperson claimed, "He wanted to die with dignity, and so he did."

In the aftermath of his death, French President Emmanuel Macron called Godard "a national treasure."]

***

A Doll's House (1973)

In this film adaptation of Henrik Ibsen's play, *A Doll's House*, written in 1879, Jane Fonda became one of dozens of distinguished actresses or thousands of college drama students who tackled the role of Nora Helmer. In Jane's film version, she plays the wife in a broken, loveless marriage and the mother of three small children.

Her tyrannical husband, Torvald Helmer (David Warner), dominates the household, although constantly criticizes what he calls her "careless and childlike nature."

He refers to her as his "doll." The plot thickens.

When he became seriously ill, and the family almost destitute, she secretly borrows money from Nils Krogstad (Edward Fox), one of his co-workers at the bank.

After his recovery, Torvald is named director of the bank and fires Krogstad, who attempts to blackmail Nora for repayment of the secret loan. Matters become more complicated when the elderly Dr. Rank (Trevor Howard) develops a love interest in Nora.

At the end, Nora asserts her independence and sets out on her own, deserting her family.

The film was directed by Joseph Losey, who was also a producer and screenwriter. He had been blacklisted in the early 1950s because he had joined the Communist Party.

He relocated to England, where he developed professional associations with both Charles Laughton and Bertolt Brecht. He also produced plays written by Harold Pinter, notably *The Servant* (1963). He had a history of feuding with his leading ladies—and Jane was no exception. She felt he was building up the male roles at the expense of Nora. She also objected to anti-feminist remarks he had made to the press.

"The director's efforts to deal with a strong woman did irreparable harm to the film," Jane said. "I was never able to penetrate the paranoia or snobbery he possessed in great abundance."

To retaliate, Losey claimed, "Fonda has no sense of humor and spent most of her time working on political speeches instead of trying to learn her lines. Compared to Fonda, Elizabeth Taylor and Richard Burton were angels."

The cast and crew divided into warring camps between women and men. "These super-machos considered us as either dykes or bitches," Jane claimed. "They were chauvinistic pigs. The movie should have been retitled *Sturm und Drang.*"

Jane found an ally in Delphine Seyrig, the French actress cast as Kristine Linde. "Jane and I shared the same views and supported the cause of feminists."

Born in Manchester, England, David Warner later studied at the Royal Academy of Dramatic Art before becoming a star in film, television, and stage. He was skilled at playing romantic leads or villains. Although honored for his dramatic roles, he achieved his greatest name recognition when he appeared in *Star Trek,* the TV franchise.

Another son of England, Edward Fox, also built up a reputation in films, television, and on the stage. He was known for such movies as *Brief Encounter* (1945) and *The Third Man* (1949) with Orson Welles.

Critics claimed that the movie's failure to find a studio release should have been blamed on Jane's political activism at the time.

Rex Reed said that "Fonda's star personality undercut her performance in an otherwise admirable production. One never believes her as that macaroon-munching bird-brain or the charming coquette or the abused wife. She comes more alive in her grand scene at the end, walking out on her family to pursue an independent life."

The New York Times attacked the great liberties taken with Ibsen's script. "It has been fattened with feeble lines and short scenes that the old genius (Ibsen) didn't write."

Filming had taken place in the old Norwegian town of Røros, where many of the townspeople served as extras

In lieu of a general movie house, *A Doll's House* was sold to ABC for a telecast on December 23, 1973.

To make it even harder to find an audience, another filmed version of *A Doll's House* was released at the same time, this one starring Claire Bloom and Anthony Hopkins.

***

The Blue Bird (1976)

The announcement in *Variety* hit Hollywood like a big news break. The 1940 Shirley Temple movie, *The Blue Bird*, would be remade, this time co-produced between Hollywood and Soviet movie studios. Arthur Penn initially was announced as the director of this exciting new adventure in filmmaking until the Soviets nixed him as "too liberal."

The 76-year-old George Cukor was announced as his replacement. He was to helm an all-star cast that consisted of Marlon Brando, Katharine Hepburn, Shirley MacLaine, and James Coco. As fate would have it, none of these stars made it into the picture.

The new cast selected by Cukor starred Elizabeth Taylor, Jane Fonda, (Cukor had previously helmed her in *The Chapman Report*), Ava Gardner, Cicely Tyson, Will Geer, and Nadezhda Pavlova as "The Blue Bird."

[After his direction of The Blue Bird, *Cukor would go on to direct his last movie,* Rich and Famous *in 1981. It was based on* Old Acquaintance *(1943) which had starred Bette Davis and Miriam Hopkins. This new version (it co-starred Jacqueline Bisset with Candice Bergen) of that impossibly successful classic ended Cukor's career with a box office dud.]*

Before filming of *The Blue Bird* began, Cukor attended a screening of the original, Shirley Temple version, mainly to highlight, in advance, how different the original and updated (Soviet) versions would be.

Even the original, 1940 version of *The Blue Bird* with Temple and directed by Walter Lang, had been a box office flop. Fox had conceived it as their answer to MGM's *The Wizard of Oz* (1939), starring Judy Garland as Dorothy, which had been released the previous year.

Temple was almost assassinated when she performed in a 30-minute presentation of *Bluebird* in December of 1939 for CBS. Her radio co-star was Nelson Eddy.

At one point, as Temple sang "Someday You'll Find Your Bluebird," a woman rose from her seat, bran-

Filmed through an international coalition of filmmakers, and spearheaded by a bureaucracy of the then-Soviet Union, *The Blue Bird* ran into snafus that seemed almost inconceivable to the American actors who consented—usually to their regret—to appear in it.

Here's **Patsy Kensit**, an adolescent heroine of the film, with the magical bird.

DIVAS WHO'VE SEEN BETTER DAYS

Here's **Elizabeth Taylor** (*left*), "dolled up and dragged out" with an equivalently overdressed **Ava Gardner**, in this publicity still for the film everybody in it hated, *The Blue Bird*, ridiculed later as "a commie flop."

And here's **Jane Fonda**, gamely clad but almost unrecognizable as "Night," a character virtually no one understood, in *The Blue Bird*.

dishing a handgun and pointing it directly at Temple. She froze just long enough for the police to stop her.

Police later discovered that the woman's daughter had died on the day she had (mistakenly) believed Temple had been born. She thought the child star had stolen her daughter's soul.

Before the filming of Shirley Temple's version of *The Blue Bird* had even begun, two different silent screen versions had also been released. Each of these three film adaptations had derived from an Edwardian-era play, *l'Oiseau bleu* (1908) by Maurice Maeterlinck. For Cukor's re-adaptation, writers Hugh Whitemore and Alfred Hayes were ordered to devise a very different version from what had gone before.

As the producer of Cukor's 1976 remake of *The Blue Bird*, Paul Maslansky seemed an odd choice. He had played jazz for a living while briefly attending law school in New York City. Although his career as a producer and writer had begun relatively late (in 1964) it would in time climb to 41 credits. As a producer, his most notable movies eventually included such films as *Race with the Devil*; *Damnation Alley*; *The Villain*; and *Love Child*.

Maslansky's great financial success would come after *Blue Bird*. He had a breakthrough hit with *Police Academy* in 1984. From a budget of $4 million, the film grossed $65 million and spawned at least six movie sequels, a television series, and an animated film.

Robert Redford had once compared Jane to "a phoenix rising from the ashes."

"Well, in May of 1975, I was still that bird in those damn ashes," Jane said, with irony. "That's why I accepted what turned out to be a minor role in *The Blue Bird*. What a mistake. Many critics predicted that it would be the end of my Hollywood career. Elizabeth Taylor *[who was in it too]* got an even worse press. Nearly all the gossip columnists predicted that this would be her last motion picture."

After arriving in Leningrad right before filming began, Jane learned that most of her previous pictures had never been released in the Soviet Union, because censors had rejected them as "too sexually explicit." In vivid contrast, however, *They Shoot Horses, Don't They?* had been a big hit, perhaps because of its socialist overtones and because it presented America in such a dark light.

Cukor was the first to arrive on location, and he was booked into a hotel suite which he shared with a handsome young Hungarian man he had met in Budapest. "This guy captivated my heart," he would later tell Elizabeth.

After Ava Gardner flew in and surveyed the scene, she quipped, "George spent more time salivating over this Adonis than he did directing Elizabeth (Taylor), Jane (Fonda) and me."

Many of the actors who appeared in *The Blue Bird* had been, until then, unaware of the bizarre aspects of the U.S.S.R.'s film industry.

Here's a replica of a postage stamp first issued in 1950 as a commemoration of 30 years of Soviet filmmaking. It quotes Stalin, who defined cinema as "the greatest medium of mass agitation."

Who was the most fussed-over diva on the set of *The Blue Bird*? It was **Nadezhda Pavlova**, the Soviet ballerina who danced her way through most of her scenes in "this awful movie" that got many of the biggest names in Hollywood hot, bothered, and ultimately, furious.

In 1984, she was designated as a "People's Artist of the USSR," (aka "National Artist of the USSR"), a coveted cultural honor.

Hired as "everybody's errand boy," Ivan Balova eagerly awaited the arrival of Elizabeth and her lover, Henry Wynberg, an automobile salesman. Elizabeth quickly explained to Cukor why she had brought him along: "He fucks better than Burton."

At last, Ivan laid eyes on the Hollywood goddess, Elizabeth Taylor, and by his own admission, he was bitterly disappointed. He later told the press, "Miss Taylor is this frumpy, pot-bellied, triple-chinned damsel with short legs and a big mop of hair. She was also drunk at ten o'clock in the morning. I looked into her famous violet eyes. They were a fiery bloodshot red. I turned to Cukor and said, 'So, this is America's Catherine the Great?'"

Every star salary was low, although Taylor was allocated $5,000 in weekly expenses. She spent thousands of her own money to have her wardrobe re-designed for the four characters she played—"Queen of Light," "Mother," "Bitch," and "Maternal Love."

In her characterization of the character she portrayed ("Night"), Jane appeared for the most part in "black velvet and midnight furs."

Vincent Canby of *The New York Times* took a jab at her. "Night sounds as if she has been moonlighting in the America of the Nixon administration, linking her with her most despised political foe."

"'Tricky Dicky and I had a mutual hatred society," Jane said.

Many film critics felt that Jane was too much of a modern woman to be cast as a 19th-century queen, "Night," in black furs and velvet.

Cukor said, "Although aging, Elizabeth Taylor and Ava Gardner, at least in the Soviet Union, still had the reputation of Hollywood love goddesses. However, I learned that if given a choice, most of the Soviet crew would prefer to haul off Jane Fonda instead."

The health of the cast became a major problem during filming. Often, Cukor had to shoot around a star because he or she was in sick bay. James Coco had been cast as "The Dog." Several of the stars had animal roles, most notably Cicely Tyson as "The Cat."

Coco had arrived in Leningrad with a handsome young man he'd met in London.

Early, on location and attempting to film, Cukor learned that the stars of his film found the Russian food repulsive. Coco was celebrated as one of the best (amateur) chefs in Hollywood until he became "deadly ill" with a gall bladder attack. He and his companion bowed out and flew back to London.

Cukor replaced him with actor George Cole as "Tylo the Dog."

Elizabeth's health suffered the most. Cukor often had to juggle his shooting schedule to compensate for her medical crises. She contracted a terrible case of the flu, and later, was plagued with "a severe cast of amoebic dysentery."

Gardner detested everything about Russia—"the gawking people following me around, the wire-tapping of my bedroom, the hidden camera in the bathroom, the horrible foot that tasted like what I supposed Russian soldiers ate as rations in the darkest days of World War II."

"I was forced to share a bathroom with Elizabeth Taylor, who was always stealing all the toilet paper, a hard item to buy in Leningrad. Of course, Elizabeth and I had shared before—namely lovers, and notably, Frank Sinatra."

Gardner had refused to drink the tap water, but nevertheless became "deadly ill" and was flown to London to recuperate because she did not trust Russian doctors.

According to *The Blue Bird's* script, a sister and her brother with the unlikely names of Mytyl and Tylyl, set out to find "the Blue Bird of Happiness." The "Queen of Light" (Elizabeth) gives them a hat with a magic diamond that allows them to call forth the souls of all things both living and inanimate. The roles of Mytyl and Tylyl were cast with Patsy Kensit and Todd Lookinland.

Robert Morley played Father Time, and Will Geer was cast as Grandfather. Other characters were named "Bread," "Sugar," "Milk," and "Water." The children visit the "Queens of Night" (Fonda) and "Luxury" (Gardner). In time, they discover that "The Blue Bird of Happiness" has been living in their own back yard.

Cicely Tyson, cast as "The Cat" often portrayed strong African American women onscreen. She enjoyed a career that spanned seven decades. In 1972, in the role of Rebecca Morgan in the film *Sounder,* she was nominated for a Best Actress Oscar.

[Tyson's most famous love affair and later marriage was with jazz trumpeter Miles Davis in the 1960s. They were eventually married in 1981 at the home of Bill Cosby, but divorced in 1988, two years before Davis' death.]

English-born Robert Morley was described as "recognizable for his ungainly bulk, bushy eyebrows, thick lips, and double chins." As such, he was frequently cast as a pompous windbag, usually representing "The Establishment."

Morley had his highs and lows. His major disaster occurred when he appeared on Broadway in a musical adaptation of *East of Eden,* the 1955 classic film starring James Dean. The play closed immediately after its opening night, but in 1969, Morley bounced back in another Broadway play, Neil Simon's *The Last of the Red Hot Lovers.* Simon had written that play specifically with Morley in mind.

Will Geer, born in Indiana in 1902, was an actor, musician, and social activist. Blacklisted in the 1950s, he was the longtime lover of Harry Hay, a gay activist who became a member of the Communist Party in 1934. Geer's favorite movie had been Henry Fonda's *The Grapes of Wrath* (1940). He was one of the organizers of *The Grapes of Wrath Rally.* Organized in 1940, it was conceived as a declaration of support for migrant farm workers.

As the Blue Bird, the film's title role, Nadezhda Pavlova was a Russian ballet dancer who showed spectacular promise at the age of seven. By the age of 15, she'd already won many awards from the Soviet ballet regime, and later toured Europe, the United States, Japan, and China. One of her greatest roles was in Prokofiev's ballet, *Romeo and Juliet.* During the course of her spectacular career, she appeared onstage with most of the top male dancers of the Bolshoi Ballet.

A Londoner, George Cole had an acting career spanning 75 years. He starred on stage and screen with actors who included Laurence Olivier.

When *The Blue Bird* was finally released as a 99-minute film by Twentieth-Century Fox, it generated only $3.5 million at the box office in the United States and Canada.

It had been budgeted at $15 million but cost many millions beyond that. The movie nearly bankrupted Fox in the same manner that *Cleopatra* had in the 1960s.

Fortunately for Fox, they'd persuaded some outside backers to chip in, notably J. Cornelius Crane, a manufacturer of mobile homes.

The *London Express* evaluated it like this: "*The Blue Bird* is a mixture of Soviet ineptitude and the American belief that the grotesque expenditure of dollars can set anything right."

Upon its release in the late spring of 1976, most critics attacked it. *Time Out New York* called it "desperately pedestrian and a hideously glitzy version of Maeterlinck's delicate fantasy. You'd never believe that Cukor directed it."

Gene Siskel of the *Chicago Tribune* gave the film one star out of four and said that its production problems "show on the screen. Elizabeth Taylor has never looked uglier than she does portraying the spirit of light. She wears a '50s-spangled gown topped by a lava-like tiara. The Russians in the cast appear as interlopers, their speeches badly dubbed. The two starring children are as disingenuous as most movie children. Artistically grotesque moments abound. The film couldn't have its heart in a more right place, but what's up on the screen makes this 'The Blue Bird' one of unhappiness."

Variety wrote, "Nobody's going to laugh in ridicule at any of it. (It's that good.) But nobody's going to be strongly moved. (It's that bad.)"

Vincent Canby of *The New York Times* described *The Blue Bird* as "two films that want to compete but don't, everyone being polite, accepting compromise, effectively neutered. One of these films is blandly American, like the sort of processed cheese sold in jars that can later be used as water glasses. The other is dimly Russian but without any real Russian character, except for the sets, which aren't great. They look like stuff left over from the Bolshoi Opera's last road tour. Spectacle for spectacle's sake no longer is the rage in this country. It can still work sometimes if it's put on a large patch of ice, but the romantic notions that motivate *The Blue Bird* are enough to send most American children, to say nothing of the ancients who may accompany them to the film, into antisocial states beginning with catatonia and ending in armed rebellion. Mr. Cukor seems to have had less chance to direct in this case than to act as the goodwill ambassador who got his actors on and off the sets on time. None of the English-speaking actors can do much but behave as if he or she were in a very unlikely pageant. The Soviet cast members, who speak in badly dubbed English, are no better except when they are given a chance to dance."

***

Fun with Dick and Jane (1977)

After all those flops, Jane desperately needed a box office bonanza, and she found it when director Ted Kotcheff co-starred her with George Segal in this comic film that was caustically critical of the "anarchy" of the American way of life.

Its title came from the Dick and Jane series of children's educational books. The title was used for one of the books in the series, and did not relate to Fonda.

The cast was rounded out by Ed McMahon, Johnny Carson's sidekick, and Dick Gautier as "Dr. Will."

Many well-known actors rejected the male lead, but George Segal went for it.

As the director, Ted Kotcheff was a Bulgarian/Canadian producer and director. Mostly he worked in British and American television productions, such as *Armchair Theatre* and *Law & Order.* His best-known action movie was *First Blood*, which didn't come along until 1982. It starred Sylvester Stallone.

Three years older than Jane, Segal was well established as an actor, comedian, and musician. He became acclaimed for such films as *Ship of Fools* (1965), and *King Rat* (also 1965), and the classic *Who's Afraid of Virginia Woolf?* (1966) with Richard Burton and Elizabeth Taylor. For his role in that Edward Albee play, he was nominated for a Best Supporting Actor Oscar. He jokingly said, in reference to the hellish harridan Elizabeth portrayed, "Liz found me a lousy lay in that movie."

Throughout the 1970s, Segal popped up on the screen many times, as he did in *The Owl and the Pussycat* (1970) with Barbra Streisand.

In a nutshell, as stated by one writer, "Some director or producer just had to make either a serious movie or else one with comic overtones that dealt with the American way of life—that is, a family living far beyond its means and running up credit card debt. Not only that, but the plot dealt with the recession, where many workers were either laid off indefinitely or else not to return."

Dick's boss, Charlie Blanchard (McMahon), abruptly fires him. Dick and Jane have no income and are $70,000 in debt. He searches for work but as an aerospace engineer, his is overly qualified. Jane enters the workplace and gets a job modeling fashion in an overcrowded restaurant, but that evolves into a humiliating disaster. Dick applies for unemployment, and the family goes on food

It wasn't the first film where Jane had to conform to a venue where arguments were just another variation of foreplay. Here's comedic **Jane Fonda** with funny man **George Segal,** involved in an altercation that every movie fan knew would end up in bed.

American audiences seemed relieved to see "their Jane" back to her old tricks as an adorable ingenue. After years of appearing in underachieving avant-garde films from Europe, *Fun with Dick and Jane* did very well at the box office.

stamps.

In a surprise move, Dick and Jane turn to crime, even robbing the telephone company.

After several robberies, they agree to retire from a life of crime after one more big heist.

Dick is aware that Blanchard keeps a $200,000 slush fund in his safe to pay off crooked politicians. They decide to go for the loot, but security guards overtake them and arrest them.

Dick admits to his former boss that he has stolen his slush fund. Knowing that a police investigation will expose his crooked dealings, Blanchard lets them go free.

When the police arrive, he claims that no crime was committed, as it was a false alarm.

At the end of the movie, Blanchard has resigned, and the new president of the company is Dick himself.

"I wanted to prove I could be funny and pretty, but I also needed the money in real life," Jane said. "I got $100,000 to star in the film, not my usual $400,000."

Robert Redford, who had previously commented on her comeback skills, said, "The phoenix has now risen from the ashes."

Many moviegoers hailed Jane for "being funnier than she was in *Cat Ballou*."

The studio advertised *Fun with Dick and Jane* with a banner headline—AMERICA LOVES JANE FONDA AGAIN.

Roger Ebert of the *Chicago Sun-Times*, said, "The stuff is funny enough, but somehow, it's too easy. It's situation comedy, when the movie's earlier moments seemed to be promising us a hard-boiled commentary."

London Movie Express noted that, "Jane Fonda appears to be trying to change from stern *tragedienne* to bouncy *comedienne* and is ill at ease in the latter role. She does well enough, but the brittleness shows. After the demanding roles she has weathered, she should hold out for more challenging material now that she is one of America's leading thespians."

The critic for *Motion Picture* wrote: "Jane Fonda is excellent playing herself, and she gets the chance to sport several changes of a snappy wardrobe, plus different wigs and hairstyles. One scene in the john should have been left on the shelf, but apart from that, *Fun with Dick and Jane* is a comedy for the whole family, as long as the ending isn't taken too seriously."

Vincent Canby of *The New York Times* weighed in too: "I never have trouble remembering that Miss Fonda is a fine dramatic actress, but I'm surprised over and over again every time I see her do comedy with the mixture of intelligence and abandon she shows here. One sequence in particular in which she makes a botch of an attempt at fashion modeling in a crowded restaurant at lunchtime is a nearly priceless piece of modern slapstick."

Shot for a budget of $4.5 million, the movie made $13.6 million at the box office in the U.S. and Canada.

Columbia released the 99-minute comedy on February 9, 1977, and it became the studio's third-highest-grossing movie of that year, despite the mixed reviews it received from critics. For Jane, it represented her first financially successful movie in seven long years.

***

Whether her enemies liked her or not, **Lillian Hellman,** depicted here as part of an ad campaign for The Great Lakes Mink Association (*aka* Blackglama), was every inch a celebrity..

Ferociously protective of her reputation, even though it sometimes had holes in it, she was involved in endless litigation associated with the historic character of **Julia** and how Hellman knew (or didn't know) her.

Julia (1977)

For this drama, Jane Fonda tackled one of her most difficult roles when she was cast as the controversial playwright Lillian Hellman opposite Vanessa Redgrave as the mysterious Julia. The movie was based on a chapter from Hellman's widely debated 1973 memoir, *Pentimento: A Book of Portraits*.

That particular chapter—allegedly drawn from the pages of Hellman's private life—showcased an anti-Nazi activist named "Julia," and later became the core and foundation of a film presented as non-fiction. But did Julia ever really exist?

Hellman was accused of inventing the story. Its publication led to a legal battle between Hellman and fellow author Mary McCarthy that received nationwide publicity from the libel suit that ensued. *[More about that later.]*

Jane Fonda (as a perhaps partially fictitious version of Lillian Hellman), meets the elusive Julia (played by **Vanessa Redgrave**) in a scene defined by the script as the last time they'll ever meet.

Hellman's (aka Jane's) **striking fur hat** plays a prominent (later, disputed) role in the script.

In the early stages of its pre-production, a trio of talent devoted itself to the film adaptation of Hellman's story and its subsequent casting. Richard N. Roth, the producer, hired Fred Zinnemann as director. Each of them agreed that Alvin Sargent was the writer who could best adapt Hellman's "statement" about Julia who, in reality, may have been simply a figment of Hellman's imagination, despite having been presented as a historical figure.

Most critics and the movie-going public were impressed with Roth's *The Way We Were* (1973), which had starred Barbra Streisand and Robert Redford.

In engaging Jane and Vanessa, Roth said, "Why not? The casting was perfect symmetry. The two most famous left-wing women of the 1970s playing two left-wing women of the 1930s. Of course, the fact that Jane and Vanessa were both terrific actresses didn't hurt either. Not to mention that both of them agreed to work cheap."

[Richard N. Roth went through his career constantly being confused with another producer, Richard A. Roth. Ironically, both of these men produced Oscar-winning movies in the 1970s.]

At first, Zinnemann opposed the casting of Jane as Lillian Hellman. "She still had the stunning beauty on full display of Barbarella. I feared that was wrong for the character of Hellman, who was plain-faced."

The composer, Leonard Bernstein, once claimed, "Lillian Hellman has the face of a droopy-eyed basset hound."

Jason Robards (as Dashiell Hammett) comforts **Jane Fonda** (as the neurotic and ferociously ambitious literary lioness, Lilliam Hellman) after a nightmare

Roth insisted, however, on casting Jane, and she later won the director's confidence, although she personally was said to have found him "indifferent and dictatorial."

During the first week of the shoot, Zinnemann changed his mind about Jane. "Jane Fonda did an extraordinary job with the role of Lillian Hellman in *Julia*. She is a splendid actress with a strong analytical mind, which sometimes gets in her way. She has an incredible technique and control of emotion. She can cry at will, on cue, mere drops or buckets, as the scene demands. I thought Jane deserved another Best Actress Oscar for *Julia*."

No one disputed the casting of Vanessa Redgrave in the supporting role of Julia. In 2010, a poll conducted by *The Stage* rated her as number nine of the greatest stage actresses of all time. She also had a distinguished history of film roles, with *Julia* about to be added to her string of triumphs.

Born in a northern tier of the Austro-Hungarian Empire (now Poland) in 1907, Fred Zinnemann entered the world two years after the birth of Henry Fonda. He had an amazing and varied career, turning out 25 films over half a century. These ranged from thrillers, Westerns, *films noirs,* and adaptations of plays first seen on Broadway.

He was best known for *High Noon* (1952) that starred Gary Cooper with his "child bride," as portrayed by Grace Kelly. Some critics cited *High Noon* as the greatest Western ever made.

Zinnemann followed that in the following year with the release of another mega-hit, *From Here to Eternity* (1953) that was set at the time of the Japanese attack (December 7, 1941) on Pearl Harbor.

It starred Burt Lancaster, Montgomery Clift, Deborah Kerr (after Joan Crawford dropped out), Donna Reed, Ernest Borgnine, and Frank Sinatra in his "comeback" role of Maggio.

Zinnemann was the first director to bring Marlon Brando to the screen in *The Men* (1950). In *Julia*, he would introduce Meryl Streep, who quickly rose to become one of the greatest screen actresses of the 20th Century.

Those actors were not the only ones he introduced. On the list, in other films, were Rod Steiger, Pier Angeli, Julia Harris, and Shirley Jones.

He directed 19 actors to Oscar wins, including Sinatra and Clift as well as Jane, Vanessa, and Jason Robards, Jr. Zinnemann's direction of Gary Cooper would bring him a Best Actor Oscar. Not only that, but he would helm many other actors who won Oscar nominations: Audrey Hepburn, Paul Scofield, Wendy Hiller, Maximilian Schell, Robert Shaw, and Glynis Johns.

In Hollywood, Zinnemann was viewed as a maverick, willing to take chances, filming many stories about lone and principled souls tested by tragic events. Instead of sound stages, he preferred location shooting, mixing stars with civilians to give his motion pictures more realism. One film historian wrote, "Zinnemann's style demonstrated his sense of psychological realism and his apparent determination to make worthwhile pictures that are nevertheless highly entertaining."

Julia would bring an Oscar for Alvin Sargent for Best Adapted Screenplay. He was given a similar Oscar for *Ordinary People* (1980) helmed by Robert Redford in his directorial debut and starring Donald Sutherland (Jane's former lover) and Mary Tyler Moore.

[Actually, Sargent's writings received their greatest exposure when he collaborated on the 2004 screenplay for Spider-Man 2 *(2004) and the 2007 screenplay for* Spider-Man 3. *He also worked on the screenplay for that series' 2021 reboot*, The Amazing Spider-Man.*]*

Before shooting began, Jane visited Hellman at her vacation home on Martha's Vineyard. There, Jane rode out a hurricane with her, boarding up the windows and hunkering down.

The two women never mentioned *The Chase* (1966), that film scripted by Hellman that had flopped at the box office, even though it had starred Marlon Brando, Robert Redford, and Jane herself.

Before meeting Hellman face to face, Jane read up on her career.

Hellman had been born in New Orleans in 1905, the same birth year as Jane's father. In time, she gravitated to New York, where she had several hits on Broadway, notably *Watch on the Rhine; The Autumn Garden; Toys in the Attic, Another Part of the Forest, The Children's Hour,* and *The Little Foxes* starring Tallulah Bankhead on Broadway, and Bette Davis in its film adaptation.

Hellman became notorious for her communist sympathies and political activism. After her appearance before the House Un-American Activities Committee, she was blacklisted. Although Hollywood dropped her, she continued to write plays for the stage.

Hellman became the first female screenwriter to receive, for her work on *The Little Foxes* (1941), a separate Oscar for Best Adapted Screenplay.

As *Julia* clearly depicted, Hellman was also romantically linked to the fellow activist and writer, Dashiell Hammett, who was blacklisted for a decade. He was the author of such classic detective novels as *The Maltese Falcon,* in which Humphrey Bogart starred in 1941. One of Hammett's biggest hits on the screen involved the amateur detective "The Thin Man," as portrayed by William Powell in a number of screen adaptations.

Although Jane was known for leftist views, she found it dangerous to talk politics with either Hellman or with her future co-star, Vanessa Redgrave. To Jane, both of them had extremist (and passionate) views.

After one particularly "stormy" meeting with Hellman, Jane said in an interview, "Lillian is a homely woman, yet she moves as if she were Marilyn Monroe. She sits with her legs apart with her satin underwear partially showing. She's very sexy and sensual. That's fine for Lillian, but not for me. I plan to play her in *Julia* more ascetic than she really is."

Her comments "pissed off" Lillian. That was how she expressed it in the blistering response she sent to Jane.

In 1976, as the autumn leaves were falling in Manhattan's Central Park, Jane flew to France, where filming of *Julia* would begin.

Never again in her career would Jane work with an actress who had the electrifying appearance of Vanessa Redgrave. Even though both of them were (frequently) referred to as "left wing,", Vanessa was far more "leftish" than Jane. *[All this in spite of the fact that Jane's most publicly offensive political statement (i.e. her press and public relations tour of Hanoi) was still in her future.]*

Some observers felt that at the time, Jane was softening some of her most extreme political stances and moving discreetly toward the middle. In her words, "My political positions seemed right at the time, but today, some of my statements might appear to be a bit much. I have no intention of becoming the next Vanessa Redgrave in the press because of my politics."

※※※

Jane was very pro-Israel, and throughout her life, had been a champion of Jews.

In contrast, in 1977, the year she made *Julia*, Vanessa had produced and starred in an anti-Israel documentary film, *The Palestinian,* which focused on the Palestine Liberation Organization (PLO). She financed it by selling her house. In the interviews, Yasser Arafat, the chairman of the PLO, was quoted as saying that the only solution to the Middle East problem was "the liquidation of the State of Israel." Of course, Jane interpreted that statement as horrifying.

Julia was hailed as the first female "buddy" film. Prior to that, male/male buddies dominated the screen, films such as Paul Newman and Robert Redford in *Butch Cassidy and the Sundance Kid* (1969).

Many viewers interpreted *Julia* as a film about loyalty, love, self-doubt, and "coming of age," a tale of two women involved in a deep friendship. At one point, Jane, as the Hellman character, says, "I love you, Julia."

Many in the audience interpreted that to suggest a lesbian love affair. Throughout her life, Hellman had often been accused of lesbian affairs. Tallulah Bankhead, going so far as to call her "that miserable dyke."

In the movie, when a gossipy character portrayed by actor John Glover flippantly and drunkenly suggests a lesbian link between Hellman and Julia, Jane (as Hellman) slapped him so hard during the scene's filming that she knocked him unconscious. Zinnemann rushed to his actor's aid to help him regain consciousness.

Sometimes relayed in flashbacks, the characters of Julia and Lillian Hellman have been friends since their respective adolescence. According to the script, years, later, Julia becomes a medical student at the University of Vienna.

Lillian, according to the filmscript, is frantically trying to write a play and living with her mentor and sometimes lover, Dashiell Hammett, who, both in the film and in real life, was celebrated for his "hard-boiled" detective novels.

One day, Lillian learns that Julia's medical school in Vienna has been overrun by Nazi thugs who beat her up and seriously wound her. By then, Lillian has become a noted author of Broadway plays. From a base in Paris she meets Johann (Maximilian Schell), an associate of Julia's, from whom she learns about her condition and the danger she's in. He asks Lillian to smuggle some $50,000 in cash into Nazi Germany. It will enable, the script tells us, some 500 to 1,000 Jews to obtain exit visas.

Lillian is informed that her fateful meeting with Julia will occur in a public place. She is instructed that at the meeting, she should unobtrusively relinquish the cash she's been entrusted with. She arranges for it to be sewn into the lining of a large fur hat that she wears.

Lillian agrees to cross borders with the money. The Cossack-style fur hat seems so expensively obvious that Lillian feels than no smuggler would conceal money there.

She is allowed a tender farewell meeting (it occurs in a *bierhalle* near a railway station) with Julia, during which she learns that her beating by the Nazis was so severe that she'd had to have one of her legs amputated.

Later, Lillian learns that Julia has been murdered by Nazi agents in Frankfurt.

The film ends with an image of the real Lillian Hellman seated in a boat, alone, on a lake. A voice-over reveals that she continued to live with Hammett for another thirty years, perhaps with the memory of the doomed Julia constantly with her.

During the shoot, Jane developed great respect for Vanessa as an actress. As for Vanessa, the activist, Jane labeled her politics as "Trotskyite."

According to Jane, "Her (Vanessa's) voice seems to come from some place that knows all suffering and all secrets. Watching her work is like seeing through layers of glass, each layer painted in mythic watercolor images—layer after layer until it becomes dark. Even then, you know you haven't come to the bottom of it."

Since there was a charge of subtle but focused lesbianism in the film, many critics mockingly suggested that the film's title should have been changed to *Reds in Bed*.

Jane was paid $250,000 for her performance. Many of her interior scenes were filmed at Elstree Studios outside London.

The film held its premiere on October 9, 1979. It cost $8 million to shoot and generated $21 million at the box office. Reviews ranged from high praise to sharp criticisms. Critic John Simon cast a negative vote: "Very little of what happens in *Julia* is interesting."

TV Guide found it "beautifully crafted," but then continued with, "It was nominated for eleven Academy Awards, yet it is a dramatic dud. If you like red nail polish, *faux* cynicism, painfully brave smiles, and European train stations, *Julia* may be your kind of cocktail."

Jack Kroll, writing in *Newsweek*, gave Jane hope for the future of her films. "Julia supposedly signals a new deal for women in movies: Hopefully, they will no longer be satellites to men, but suns and stars in their own right."

Roger Ebert of the *Chicago Sun-Times* found Julia "a fascinating story, but I feel it suffers from

As if it were possible, **Vanessa Redgrave** was an even more committed (some said "ultra left-wing') social activist than Jane Fonda. It was said that Vanessa consistently wore her Marxist politics on her sleeve.

In 1978, just a few weeks after winning her Best Supporting Actress Oscar for her portayal of Julia, she stood for election as a candidate for the far-left Workers' Revolutionary Party in a working-class neighborhood of Manchester in the rust-bound Midlands of England,

Although she didn't win, with resiliency, she morphed herself into a prominent campaigner, like Jane Fonda, in the anti-Vietnam War effort.

Like Jane in the U.S., British ultra-conservatives never forgave her.

being told by Lillian Hellman's point of view. The movie never really establishes a relationship between the two women. It's awkward, the way the film has to suspend itself between Julia—its ostensible subject—and Hellman, its real subject.

In *After Dark,* Norma McLain Stoop wrote, "*Julia* is a courageous film about courage of which human beings are capable. Jane Fonda is so good as Lillian that it's almost embarrassing to watch her—one feels like a trespasser in the privacy of a life."

Stoop recalled dramatic moments where Jane, as Lillian, throws her typewriter out the window of a Long Island beach cottage in despair at her lack of progress on her latest play. She is at her most loving when she holds the hand of a bandaged-swathed Julia in a hospital in Vienna after she has been beaten by the Nazis.

At the Academy Awards ceremony, *Julia* was nominated for eleven Oscars, winning three—Best Supporting Actor (Jason Robards); Best Supporting Actress (Vanessa Redgrave); and Best Adapted Screenplay (Alvin Sargent). Jane was nominated as Best Actress but lost to Diane Keaton for *Annie Hall.*

Jane was apprehensive when Vanessa was presented with her Oscar. Before the ceremony, pickets formed representing both the Jewish Defense League (JDL) and counter-protestors waving PLO flags.

In her acceptance speech, Vanessa thanked Academy members for "standing firm and refusing to be intimidated by the threat of a small bunch of Zionist hoodlums, whose behavior is an insult to the stature of Jews all over the world, and to their great and heroic record of struggle against fascism and oppression."

Minutes before heading to the podium, Vanessa learned that extremists in the JDL had offered a bounty to have her assassinated. Many members of the audience booed her.

In the year of *Julia's* release, Vanessa sold her home to finance a 66-minute documentary called *The Palestinian,* a movie perceived to be anti-Israeli. The film depicted children training with guns under a banner saying, "Kill the Enemy!"

The most criticized segment of the film was an interview with Yasser Arafat, the head of the PLO. He claimed that the only solution to the Middle East problem was the liquidation of the State of Israel. In the most controversial (and widely publicized) response of her life, Vanessa responded with "Certainly."

After the release of that documentary, Vanessa was damned as an anti-Semite for years into the future. At 4:26 AM on June 15, 1978, a bomb exploded in front of the Doheny Plaza Theatre in Los Angeles, where *The Palestinian* was scheduled to open later that day.

It would be seven years before Vanessa filmed another Hollywood movie, *The Bostonians* (1984), which also starred Christopher Reeve. Vanessa was perfectly cast as Henry James' 19th Century feminist heroine.

After shooting *Julia,* Jane felt that her reputation was on the road to recovery. The American Film Institute invited her to appear on a nationally televised tribute to Bette Davis. She had co-starred with Henry Fonda in *Jezebel* (1938).

"My father had to leave *Jezebel* before shooting was finished. In some places, Bette in close-up is seen talking to my father, but he was airborne, *en route* to Manhattan to celebrate my entry into this crazy world."

Jane was also quoted as saying, "Ingrid Bergman, Vanessa Redgrave, and one Jane Fonda know about comebacks!"

***

BUT DID JULIA REALLY EXIST??

The question is still debated today: Lillian Hellman went to her grave asserting that Julia had been a real woman, but her detractors alleged she made everything up, just so that she could add another enticing, self-serving chapter to her controversial memoir, *Pentimento* (1973).

When *Julia* was still in pre-production, Hellman wrote to its producer, Richard N. Roth with the following rather tricky statement:

Julia is not a work of a fictional character. I did not make her up. Your major difficulty in my view is the treatment of Lillian Hellman—that is, myself—as the leading character. The reason is simple: No matter what she does in the movie—and I do not deny the danger I was in when I took that money into Nazi Germany—my role was nonetheless passive. Nobody and nothing can change that unless you write a fictional and different story. Isn't it necessary to know that I am a Jew? That, of course, is what made my entry into Hitler's Germany all the more dangerous. If arrested for bringing in the illegal cash to save fellow Jews, I could have been sent to a concentration camp where I'm sure I would have faced my ultimate death."

Shooting of the film transpired in France and England between September 8 and December 15, 1976. By then, the filmmakers began to hear and believe stories that Julia was a fictional character. Nonetheless, Hellman continued to stridently deny that she created the character from her imaginative mind.

Three years after the film's release, director Fred Zinnemann weighed in with his own belief: "Lillian Hellman in her own mind owned half of the Spanish Civil War, while Ernest Hemingway owned the other half. She would portray herself in many dramatic situations that were not true. I think all of her so-called 'non-fiction' is riddled with made-up events. As a writer, she is talented and brilliant, but she is a phony character. I'm sorry to have to say that. My relations with her were very guarded and ended in pure hatred."

In 1979, author Mary McCarthy, long a critic of Hellman, brought the behind-the-scenes controversy over *Julia* into the homes of millions when she appeared for an extended interview with Dick Cavett on his television talk show.

McCarthy was a respected novelist, critic, and political activist not given to fanciful, made-up stories. She always called herself a "seeker of truth," regardless of how painful that truth might be.

From the beginning in her debut novel, *The Company She Keeps*, she created a *succès de scandale* depicting the social milieu of New York intellectuals of the late 1930s with unreserved frankness.

Her greatest popular success came with her 1963 novel, *The Group*, which remained entrenched on *The New York Times* best-seller list for two years. Unlike Hellman, McCarthy knew how to combine autobiography with fiction.

With fanfare, *The Group* was adapted into a movie. In 1966, Sidney Lumet turned it into a popular film starring Candice Bergen in her film debut. It was actually the saga of eight undergraduates in a high-class soap opera. Their college evoked Vassar.

McCarthy's feud with Hellman did not begin that night on the Dick Cavett Show. It had been simmering since the late 1930s over ideological differences, particularly the questions of the Moscow Trials and Hellman's support for the "Popular Front" of Stalin.

[*Notorious in their day, the Moscow Trials were actually "show trials" organized and choreographed by Stalin between 1936 and 1938 at the dawn of World War II. Most of them were conceived as an excuse to round up (or "purge") "Trotskyists."*

For the most part, the defendants were top officials within the Soviet secret police and former Bolshevik Party leaders. The most serious charges were that these officials had conspired with agents of Western democracies to restore capitalism to Russia and its annexed territories, and to assassinate Stalin.

Many former Soviet leaders, especially those who disagreed with or who competed with Josef Stalin, were sent to the electric chair.

The trials and executions should have been an embarrassment to left wing activists throughout Western Europe and the United States. Yet advocates who included Lillian Hellman denounced critics of the Moscow Trials, much to the fury of many liberals, who were horrified by what seemed like support by her of blatant grabs for power by Josef Stalin and a flagrant disregard for human rights.

The New York Times summed it up in an editorial on March 3, 1938: "It is as if twenty years after Yorktown, somebody in power in Washington found it necessary, for the safety of the State, to send to the scaffold Thomas Jefferson, James Madison, John Adams, Alexander Hamilton, and most of their associates. The charge against them would be that they conspired to hand over the American government to George III.]

Based in part on these long-festering rancors, decades of betrayals on every level, and in front of millions of American television watchers, McCarthy attacked Hellman, claiming that "Every word she writes is a lie, including 'and' and 'the.'"

Hellman responded by filing a $2.5 million defamation lawsuit against McCarthy, Cavett, and PBS.

McCarthy countered by producing evidence that proved that Hellman lied in accounts of her life. Novelist Norman Mailer attempted, without success, to mediate the dispute through an open letter he published in *The New York Times*, but that came to nothing. At the time of her death in 1984, Hellman "bequeathed" the still-pending lawsuit to her estate. Eventually, Hellman's executors dropped the litigation.

***

In the wake of the Jane Fonda/Vanessa Redgrave film released in 1977, Muriel Gardiner, a psychiatrist based in Manhattan, came forth with the tantalizing claim that she'd been at the core of the Julia character as interpreted by Vanessa.

Hellman had never met Gardiner but she had read about her exploits. Hellman denied Gardiner's claim, but she never came forth with a real-life alternative. Coincidentally, Hellman and Gardiner retained the same attorney, Wolf Schwabacher, who had been privy to a draft of Gardiner's then-unpublished memoirs. Some people believe that Hellman acquired a copy of them, too. *[They were eventually published, but not until 1983, under that title of* Code Name Mary.*]*

Author Samuel McCraken investigated the allegations made by McCarthy and published his finding in *Commentary* magazine in June of 1984. He investigated and concluded that the funeral home in London where Hellman allegedly claimed Julia's body did not exist. Also, there was no record that Hellman ever made the transatlantic crossing at that time.

More importantly, he could find no evidence that an actual Julia ever lived or died. Additionally, McCracken concluded that "It was highly unlikely that so many people in the anti-fascist underground would have helped Hellman smuggle that $50,000 to Julia."

After Hellman's death, her own attorney publicly questioned Hellman's veracity, specifically referencing her chapter on Julia in *Pentimento*. "I believed there might have been a real Julia, but Hellman most likely heavily dramatized her and invented a lot of plot devices and incidents that never really happened. After all, she wrote drama."

So what did Vanessa, who portrayed Julia, think? "I knew that Julia was a true story before Lillian Hellman confirmed it. Every line in her book told me that."

Dan Callahan, who wrote one of Vanessa's biographies, said, "Hellman's tall tale worked on the screen, but it was a fastidiously arranged, obscure, phoney movie. Not even Redgrave's full iconographic impact and Jane Fonda's most Bette Davis-like exertions as Hellman can do anything to enrich the material."

For a long time, it was said that Jane admired Vanessa Redgrave so much that she named her daughter Vanessa Vadim after her. That claim was disputed in some quarters.

Jane later compared working with Vanessa to her experience co-starring with Marlon Brando in *The Chase* (1966). "Like Vanessa herself, Brando always seemed to be in another reality, working off some secret, magnetic, inner rhythm."

***

WHO WAS WHO IN THE CAST OF JULIA?

As the mysterious Julia, Vanessa Redgrave was a Londoner born the same year (1937) as Jane. As a couple on the screen, they were in perfect harmony. Even today, Vanessa is often called "Our greatest living actress." She was not only known for her stage and screen roles, but for her political stances, especially her support of the PLO (Palestine Liberation Organization).

The year she made *Julia* with Jane, she also produced and starred in the anti-Israel documentary film, *The Palestinian*. She even sold her home to finance this documentary.

"Half the world came down on her head," said Fred Zinnemann, who had directed her in *Julia*.

The most controversial moment in her documentary came during an interview with the PLO's chairman, Yasser Arafat. He said, "The only solution to the Middle East problem is the liquidation of the State of Israel."

Vanessa responded to him with the phrase, "Certainly."

Throughout her life, Vanessa had been called "fearless, daring, perverse, and always unpredictable." She was also called a lot of other X-rated names, too.

The Jewish Defense League warned Fox that it would picket theaters showing her documentary. They meant it, releasing cages of white mice into movie houses that screened *The Palestinian*.

On June 15, 1978, the Doheny Plaza Theatre in Los Angeles was bombed during a screening of *The Palestinian*.

Vanessa later claimed that Jane and herself had done their best work in *Julia*.

***

Vanessa's career spanned six decades and brought numerous accolades, including an Academy Award, two Golden Globes, two Screen Actors Guild Awards, plus many honorary citations.

From 1962 to 1967, she was married to film director Tony Richardson, but he dumped her for Jeanne Moreau, the French actress. From 1971 to 1986, Vanessa also maintained a romantic relationship with actor Timothy Dalton. Their affair began when they co-starred together (along with Glenda Jackson) in *Mary, Queen of Scots* (1971).

Vanessa told a reporter, "Perhaps at the end of my life, people will say, 'That old girl certainly tried doing a bloody hell of a lot, didn't she?'"

On the set of *Julia*, Jane had a reunion with Jason Robards, Jr. with whom she had previously co-starred in that silly comedy, *Any Wednesday* (1966). Since she was aware of his life and career, they spent time together discussing the relationship they were acting out together on screen, that of lovers Lillian Hellman and Dashiell Hammett.

Hammet had been well-known for his "hard-boiled" detective novels and short stories. Today, he's remembered as one of the finest mystery writers of all time, noted for creating such enduring characters as Sam Spade in *The Maltese Falcon*.

That novel was adapted twice into movies: First in 1931 with Ricardo Cortez, and again in 1941 with Humphrey Bogart. Hammett became even better known for creating Nick and Nora Charles in *The Thin Man*, starring William Powell and Myrna Loy.

As a youth, from 1915 to 1922—except for time off for service in World War I—Hammett worked for the Pinkerton Detective Agency.

By 1931, he had embarked on a 30-year romantic relationship with Hellman.

Much of his life was as a left-wing activist, and in 1937, he joined the Communist Party. Other members included Clifford Odets and Arthur Miller, who would later marry Marilyn Monroe.

In 1942, he wrote the screenplay for Hellman's *Watch on the Rhine*. For that, he received an Oscar nomination for Best Adapted Screenplay. However, that Oscar went to *Casablanca*.

In 1951, Hammet was blacklisted for his outspoken communist leanings, but he refused to cooperate with Federal investigators. He was sent to a Federal Penitentiary in West Virginia, where he was assigned the job of cleaning the foul toilets.

Hellman later said, "Jail had made a thin man thinner and sicker. I knew he would now always be sick."

Hammett died in 1961 of lung cancer.

Meryl Streep made her film debut in *Julia*. She had been born in 1949 as a Baby Boomer in the bowels of New Jersey, rather gawky with glasses and frizzy hair.

Her scenes with Fonda played in flashback. She portrayed a snobby, meddling, Southern flirt, Anne Marie.

Most of her scenes ended up on the cutting room floor. "I had to wear a big, bad, black wig. They took my words from one scene I shot with Jane and put them in my mouth in a different scene. I thought

I'd made a big mistake appearing in a movie and not on the stage. I vowed 'no more film roles for me.' I hated the business."

Streep's rise into super stardom was rapid. Eventually, she was hailed as the greatest actress of her generation. Her versatility was unequaled in Hollywood, with characterizations ranging from TV chef Julia Child to the "Iron Lady" herself, Margaret Thatcher, Britain's former Prime Minister.

Over the course of four decades, Streep would garner twenty-one Oscar nominations, winning three, plus a record-breaking number (32) of Golden Globe citations.

Jane was deeply impressed with Streep's talent. "I had not seen such talent since Geraldine Page."

Jane wanted to appear with her again in her upcoming film project, *Coming Home*, but Robert De Niro had already run away with her to play his girlfriend in *The Deer Hunter*.

"Jane should be credited with opening many doors for me, more than I knew about," Streep said. In *Kramer vs. Kramer* (1979) she won a Best Supporting Actress Oscar for her portrayal of the troubled wife. She was stunning as a Holocaust survivor in *Sophie's Choice* (1982), and also had a big success in *Out of Africa* (1985).

Writer George Mills claimed, "Early in her career, Jane Fonda was called 'The next Bette Davis.' Then along came Meryl Streep, who made such an impression in her film debut in *Julia* that she was labeled 'the next Jane Fonda, even a latter-day Bette Davis.'"

When Jane heard that comment, she said, "Oh, Hollywood. When Meryl makes a few more pictures in a few years, some new actress will come along and be called 'the next Meryl Streep.'"

Born in Vienna, Maximilian Schell was cast in *Julia* as "Johann," a refugee who wants Hellman to smuggle $50,000 in U.S. dollars to rescue some Jews being held by the Nazis.

His sister, Maria Schell, also became an actress.

In 1938, after the *Anschluss*, when Austria was annexed to Nazi Germany, the Schell family fled to Switzerland. At the end of World War II, in 1945, Maximilian moved to Germany.

In 1961, he won an Oscar for his performance in *Judgment at Nuremberg*, in which his character defended former Nazi leaders against charges of war crimes. In the cast with him were Burt Lancaster, Spencer Tracy, Marlene Dietrich, Montgomery Clift, and Judy Garland.

[Before that, Maximilian had worked with Clift when they'd co-starred in the World War II drama, The Young Lions *(1958) alongside Marlon Brando and Dean Martin.]*

Maximilian could play more than German characters. He was also convincing as Simón Bolivar of Venezuela; the Russian Emperor, Peter the Great; and physicist Albert Einstein. He also played Vladimir Lenin in the TV film *Stalin* (1992).

On stage, he appeared in any number of plays. Critics hailed him as "one of the greatest Hamlets ever performed on stage," ranking him alongside Laurence Olivier.

Dorothy Parker, married at the time to Alan Campbell, was Hellman's best friend. In *Julia*, they were portrayed by Rosemary Murphy cast as Parker, with Hal Holbrook cast as Alan.

Murphy had co-starred with Jane in *Any Wednesday*, stealing many of the scenes from the other actors. "Jane and I were friends back then," she recalled. "On the set of *Julia*, she was very aloof."

As Alan Campbell, Holbrook had made his film debut in *The Group* (1966), based on that Mary McCarthy novel. He later gained international fame for his performance as "Deep Throat" in *All the President's Men* (1976), a film that also featured Robert Redford and Dustin Hoffman.

Holbrook was known for his one-man stage show in which he performed as Mark Twain. He executed that signature role beginning in 1954 and continued it for more than sixty years, dropping off in 2017 because of failing health. *[He died in 2021.]*

Dorothy Parker and her husband, Alan Campbell, were such a fascinating couple that they deserved a stage treatment of their own. Parker was a poet, writer, and satirist, best known for her wit, wisecracks, and sharp eye for 20th Century urban foibles. She often wrote for *The New Yorker* and was a founding member of the Algonquin Round Table. There, members of New York's literati gathered for lunch, including Robert E. Sherwood, Robert Benchley, and Alexander Woollcott.

In 1932, Parker met Alan Campbell, an actor with aspirations of becoming a screenwriter. They married two years later, but she soon discovered that he was "as queer as a billy goat." He had numerous affairs, and in the late 1930s, fell in love with Desi Arnaz, a bandleader from Cuba.

Parker's marriage to Campbell was tempestuous, beset with fallout from his outside affairs and her increasing addiction to alcohol.

Parker and Hellman began a friendship in the 1930s that endured for years to come, although Hellman detested Campbell, and Parker did not like Hellman's boyfriend, Dashiell Hammett.

Hellman often encountered members of groups that Parker regularly hung out with, including, one night, a coven of lesbians. One of them advocated the position that lesbians should have the right to marry, legally.

Hellman concluded that her friendship with Parker was "a tangled fishnet of contradictions." Parker was often broke and borrowed money from Hellman.

"Poor Dottie," Hellman said. "She and the world didn't move in the same orbit."

Cast as Grandmother in *Julia*, Cathleen Nesbitt was the oldest member of the cast, having been born in England way back in 1888. Her stage debut in London occurred in 1910. A year later, she joined the Irish Players when they made their debut on Broadway in their production of *The Playboy of the Western World*

Everyone's favorite caustic English wit: **Cathleen Nesbitt** onstage in 1956 in *The Sleeping Prince*

[Interpreted today as a masterpiece of the Irish literary renaissance, this comedy in three acts by J.M. Synge, was first produced in Dublin in 1907. During its first-ever run on Broadway, Nesbitt and her fellow players were pelted from the outraged, mostly Catholic and Irish-American audience with fruits and vegetables.]

The English poet, Rupert Brooke, fell in love with Nesbitt and wrote love sonnets to her. Because he was killed during World War I, they never married.

In 1916, Nesbitt became John Barrymore's leading lady in John Galsworthy's *Justice*. It was the first dramatic stage role for the American actor who was celebrated for decades after that as "The Great Profile."

Nesbitt also became a film actress, starring in Anita Loos' adaptation of *Gigi* in 1951. In 1956, she played Mrs. Higgins in *My Fair Lady* opposite Rex Harrison on Broadway. In *An Affair to Remember* (1957), she was Cary Grant's mother, despite the fact that she was only sixteen years older than Grant.

Nesbitt also portrayed the mother of Richard Burton in *Staircase* (1969), a British comedy about an aging gay couple who own a barbershop in the East End of London.

After starring with Jane in *Julia*, Nesbitt died in 1982, ending a career that spanned eight decades, one of the longest acts in show business.

CHAPTER TEN

TOM HAYDEN

Barbarella Becomes Hanoi Jane
And Weds a Presidential Candidate

Jane Settles into a Life with a Political Activist
Likened to Napoleon and Machiavelli

"Wherever there is a political rally, my sister Jane will be there."
—Peter Fonda

In Her New Role (That of an Crusading Housewife)
Jane is Likened to Marie Antoinette
Playing a Milkmaid at Versailles

Quotes from "Revolutionary Jane"

— *"Jesus Christ was the greatest revolutionary of them all."*
— *"Fidel Castro's Cuba is the finest example of a near-utopian society."*
— *"There's a new kind of soldier fighting in Vietnam: He is no John Wayne freak."*
— *"If I don't vote, the answer is revolution. I fear it's going to be bloody."*

It would take at least two or three more volumes to describe the life of Jane Fonda as she turned 85. She accurately entitled her autobiography, published in 2005, as *My Life So Far*.

It is not only her life as an actress, but her role as a political activist that would fill page after page.

Volume II of this two-part project is focused mainly on the film careers of Henry, Jane, and Peter Fonda.

We will only review some of the highlights of her marriage to another political activist, Tom Hayden, and her controversial role in opposing American intervention in a war against the communist regime of North Vietnam.

At the same time she was doing that, taking one controversial (some said "career-killing") stand after another and earning the notorious title of "Hanoi Jane," she was also championing the rights of Native Americans, the Black Panthers, and feminism.

Actually, she began to turn against the Vietnam War while still married to Roger Vadim. He often entertained such leftists as actor Yves Montand. Their dinners and meetings usually turned to politics in which America was portrayed as an aggressor against, and murderer of, innocent women and children.

***

In April of 1970, Jane and her then-lover, Donald Sutherland, along with another of her lovers, Fred Gardner, formed the FTA. Its initials, officially at least, stood for "Free the Army," although insiders usually referred to it as "Fuck the Army."

The FTA tour of key cities within North America was conceived as a deliberate contrast to Bob Hope's patriotic USO tours. Jane referred to the FTA as "political vaudeville." Unlike Hope's tours, almost anything associated with FTA was not allowed to appear in South Vietnam.

Jane also raised money for the Vietnam Veterans Against the War (VVAW) and she toured college campuses attacking America's role in the conflict. Sometimes, she met with loud boos, and, on occasion, received death threats, most of them through the mail.

At Michigan State University, she began her speech by saying, "I would think that if you understood what communism was, you would hope, you would pray on your knees, that all of us would soon become communists."

Before she delivered that speech, Henry Fonda warned her, "If I hear you have become a communist, I will be the first to turn you in."

"I was shocked that he threatened me like that," she said. "Henry Fonda, my own father, who had played Tom Joad, that crusading attorney Clarence Darrow, and even young Abe Lincoln."

The Vietnam War, and **Jane Fonda's** role as a protester within its context, remains a political lightning rod. Even though Gallup polls usually list her as one of the most admired women in the country,

"Hanoi Jane" became a reviled figure among conservatives for her highly publicized trip to North Vietnam in 1972, as documented in intricate detail in this book by Mary Hershberger.

Today, millions of Americans continue to link Fonda's name, often unfavorably, to Vietnam.

The FBI took an especially keen interest in her involvement, eventually amassing a file on her that was, it was said, in the years before computerization, more than twenty-feet -thick

***

TOM HAYDEN:
A Life that Collided Head-On with History

Jane Fonda was deep into her fling with actor Donald Sutherland when she first met Tom Hayden, a highly publicized political activist. Among his other sexual and romantic conquests, he was involved with a student at Berkeley at the time.

Both Hayden and Jane had been booked to appear on stage at a rally of the "Winter Soldier Investigation," a media event sponsored by Vietnam Veterans Against the War.

The title of the group came from Thomas Paine, the 18th Century political philosopher who wrote about soldiers during America's Revolutionary War: "A sunshine patriot fights only when the weather is good. A winter soldier is dedicated to his cause regardless of rain or shine."

After listening to Jane speak for the first time, Hayden said, "Her urgency was real, and the audience was moved."

The protest group organized this rally early in 1971 to publicize war crimes which American armed forces had committed in Vietnam. Both Jane and Hayden addressed 109 veterans and other protesters gathered at Ann Arbor, Michigan.

Tom Hayden, a voice of youthful anguish, at a news conference in 1973. Despite the later acceptance of many of his then-radical ideas, he was often denounced as a traitor

[A filmed documentary, Winter Soldier, based on the rally's premises, would be released in 1972.]

Jane was vaguely familiar with Hayden's reputation as an activist and seemed pleased to meet him. For the most part, she held a favorable view of him without knowing much about him.

She was soon to learn just how controversial he was, even suffering criticism from many of his supporters. He was referred to as "two faced," "controlling," and "Machiavellian." Some critics accused him of having a "Bonapartist" streak."

After the rally, Hayden and Jane agreed to meet for breakfast at the Howard Johnson Motor Inn in Detroit, where she was staying. He would have preferred to have met with her alone, but she came with a female French writer who dominated the conversation, attacking the United States as a "warmonger."

On stage the night before, he had found her "skinny and taut, nervously fingering a purple shirt pulled over her blue jeans."

He didn't have the good looks of some of her previous beaux or leading men. He had "close-set eyes, a bulbous nose, and a moonscape of pock marks," in her evaluation.

At the time of that breakfast, he had already launched in 1962 Students for a Democratic Society (SDS). This was a national student organization dating from 1960. It stood for "participatory democracy" and had branches at around three hundred universities.

He had seen three of her movies, including *Barbarella*, during which, he admitted, "I became sexually aroused."

He'd also seen *They Shoot Horses, Don't They?* for which he'd praised her acting, and not just her body. He'd also gone to see her Oscar-winning performance in *Klute* (1971), in which she was cast as a prostitute.

In the words of the French author, Simone de Beauvoir, "Jane Fonda in *Klute* became the invalidation of all the official virtues."

The scene of the "Second Coming" of Hayden with Jane was at the Embassy Theater in downtown Los Angeles. It occurred in April of 1972 when she was appearing on stage showing American atrocities in the war in Vietnam.

"The first time I saw Tom (Hayden), he looked like a young Lenin in black," she said. "This time around, he'd morphed into an Indian, with braided hair. He wore moccasins and a bright Apache shirt."

After her presentation, he invited her to dinner, where they lingered and talked for hours before he walked her back to her car.

The next day, she told a friend, "I think I might be spending the rest of my life with Tom Hayden."

Tom Hayden with **Jane Fonda** at the Democratic National Convention in NYC, July 1976

As an authentic and deeply committed political activist, **Tom Hayden's** credentials were blue-ribbon impeccable. He appears in the photo, above, seated, the victim of an assault by a "morally offended" local, **Carl Hayes** in McComb, Mississippi, in October, 1961.

Hayes pulled Hayden, who was involved at the time in a local protest, out of a car and began beating him. The photo captured the event before it was flashed around the world.

In the photo below, police officers poised outside a civil rights protest in the Mississippi town of Clarksdale make their feelings abundantly **clear.**

Hayden would have a tremendous impact on Jane's life as a political activist. Born on December 11, 1939, he was slightly younger than her. Growing up in Royal Oak, a suburb of Detroit, he came from parents of Irish descent. His father was a former U.S. Marine who worked as an accountant for Chrysler in Detroit. He was labeled "a violent alcoholic," which led to a divorce when Hayden was ten.

After that, he was reared by his mother, Genevieve Garity. "I could never remember her without a cigarette dangling from her lip," he later said.

She sent him to a Catholic elementary school, where "I learned to fear hell." As a schoolboy, he had many clashes with the nuns, later claiming, "The horny bitches spied on us when we showered after working out on the sports field."

He later attended the University of Michigan, where he was the controversial editor of the school paper.

After graduating, Hayden became a political journalist. It was Martin Luther King Jr. who urged him to go from being an observer reporting on political events to an active participant in causes, notably so-called "leftist activities."

He started out by being a "Freedom Rider" in the Deep South, getting involved in racial strife. Once, he was severely beaten by a gang of redneck thugs, who called him "a commie fag."

Later, he was arrested at a political rally and jailed in Albany, Georgia.

By 1965, most of his attention was focused on protesting America's entry into the war in Vietnam. He took a controversial trip to North Vietnam, where he toured bombed-out villages and met with America POWs whose planes had been shot down.

The communist government in Hanoi agreed to release unspecified numbers of American prisoners to return to the United States.

Back on his home turf, Hayden made a number of speeches attacking "Pig Amerika."

He attended the 1968 Democratic Convention in Chicago that nominated Vice President Hubert Humphrey as the candidate to challenge Richard M. Nixon that year in which Robert Kennedy and Martin Luther King Jr. were both assassinated.

At the "Festival of Light," the mob turned ugly, when the protesters called the police "Mother Fuckers," and the cops shouted "Kill the Commies" back at them.

Tom Hayden was never shy about wading into police confrontations like the one above. Things got even more contestatorial at the Democratic National Convention in Chicago (1968). See photos below.

Tom Hayden was also deeply involved in protests in Chicago in 1968 during that city's hosting of the notorious Democratic National Convention. The upper photo shows the near-chaos on the convention floor. The lower photo shows the absolute chaos on the streets outside.

From the safety of their homes, viewing the blood and carnage on TV, much of the nation was horrified.

The police fired tear gas into the mob and even beat up news reporters and photographers covering the event. As one of the leaders of the SDS, Hayden was arrested.

He was released on bail the next day. He attended an event known as the "unbirthday party" for President Lyndon Johnson. Constable Ralph Bell recognized Hayden and severely beat him before re-arresting him for violating his bail conditions.

Released once again Hayden joined the Chicago Police Riot in Grant Park on August 28, 1965. The angry mob pelted cops with bottles, rocks, even chunks of concrete, charging that "Pigs are Whores."

The police attacked the mob violently, using tear gas. The word they used most frequently to describe the young male protesters was "cocksuckers." Scenes involving the burning of the Stars and Stripes and raising of the Viet Cong flag were flashed around the world.

After four days and nights of violence, 668 protesters were arrested, 425 demonstrators were treated at medical facilities, and 200 were treated on the spot by medics. In addition, 400 were given first aid for exposure to tear gas, and 110 were hospitalized. A total of 192 cops were injured, a few of them suffering permanent brain damage, especially those hit with chunks of broken concrete blocks.

Six months after the convention, Hayden and seven others were arrested and became known as "The Chicago Eight." Hayden joined Abbie Hoffman, Jerry Rubin, Bobby Seale, and David Dellinger, among others. The Chicago Eight became the Chicago Seven when Seal's case was declared a mistrial. Defendants were convicted of crossing state lines to incite a riot, with jail terms ranging up to four years.

In 1972, after an appeal, the convictions were reversed and the government declined to bring the case to trial again.

Hoffman later called Hayden "Our Nixon," not a flattering comparison. Hayden was also denounced as a radical communist, but he described himself to *The Guardian* as "I'm Thomas Jefferson in terms of democracy, Thoreau in terms of environment, and Crazy Horse in terms of social movements."

***

Jane Fonda and the Black Panthers

In the early 19760s, Jane was an avid supporter of the Black Panthers. "Revolution is an act of love. We are children of revolution. Born to rebels. It runs in our blood. We must support the Black Panthers with love, money, propaganda, and risk."

The Black Panther Party was a Marxist-Leninist Black Power political group founded in October of 1966 in Oakland, California by the African Americans Huey P. Newton and Bobby Seale.

Chapters of this militant organization spread to major cities throughout the United States. Party members were often engaged in gunfire with police officers. Newton issued a controversial statement: "Only without guns will black masses be denied their victory. But we learned from Malcolm X that with the gun, we can recapture our dreams and bring them to reality."

Of course, the history of the Black Panthers went beyond battles with the police and the F.B.I. Survival programs included legal advice, seminars, clothing banks, housing cooperatives, free breakfasts for children, and even ambulance service.

Black Panther party members and founders **Bobby Seale** and **Huey Newton** brandishing a Colt 45 and a shotgun during the peak of their notoriety.

It's possible that Jane first learned about the behind-the-scenes story of the Black Panthers in talks with Marlon Brando, her former co-star. He was an avid supporter. He told her that the Panthers would resort to violence if that is what it took to achieve their goals. "How else can they get justice for the oppressed?"

Another admirer of the group, Shirley Sutherland, wife of the actor Donald Sutherland (also Jane's co-star), introduced Jane to leaders of the Black Panthers. She met its members at the home of actress Jean Seberg, who was rumored to be sexually involved with some of its leaders, especially Hakim Jamal, described as "handsome, charismatic, and possessing burning eyes."

At the Seberg home, Jane talked with Paul Newman, an early supporter. She also encountered a very pregnant Vanessa Redgrave.

Jane reportedly became captivated by party leader Huey Newton, who was charismatic too. His posed photograph was prominently displayed. With his flair for the dramatic, he was seated in a wicker peacock chair wearing a black beret. In his left hand, he held an upright spear, and in his right, a rifle.

Biographer Patricia Bosworth wrote: "Jane enjoyed seeing the Panthers at Dalton Trumbo's parties, attended by a wild mix of dropouts, visionaries, hustlers, lawyers, activists, therapists, and movie stars." Jane met novelist James Baldwin at the Seberg home. Angela Davis was also in attendance."

Jane went public with her support of Newton: "He is the only man I've ever met who I would trust to be the leader of my country."

When Henry Fonda heard that, he said, "If my beloved daughter continues to make statements like that, I'll have to send her off to a psycho ward. Hers is not my way of life, and hers is not my way of thinking. But I love her. I respect her right to say what she thinks. She seems to feel it deeply."

Jane later issued another statement about Newton that elicited controversy, even ridicule. "Huey Newton is the only person I've ever known who approaches sainthood."

The complete roster of details about the complicated relationship between Newton and Jane may never be known. James Baldwin ventured an opinion: "Maybe Jane finds him as handsome as Harry Belafonte."

FBI Director J. Edgar Hoover had his own opinion of the Black Panthers: "They are the single greatest threat to the internal security of the United States."

Hayden recalled attending a party for the Black Panthers at the elegant Manhattan apartment of composer Leonard Bernstein: "I had to go real bad, but the hallway john was occupied. I opened a door that led to Bernstein's bedroom, which was dimly lit. I hurried across his carpeted floor and opened the door to his bathroom, eager to take a piss. To my surprise, Bernstein was on his knees fellating Newton. Newton saw me, but Bernstein was too engrossed to notice. I quietly slipped back out. Fortunately, the hall john had become free."

Here's a replica of **Jane Fonda's** mugshot after her arrest in Cleveland. Some people said her *sang-froid* in front of hostile cameras was something that could only have been mastered by a cinematic pro deeply familiar with the high-tech aspects of the film industry, and a woman comfortable with a bifurcated life.

These photos were snapped in 1970 after she was arrested for "drug smuggling" in Ohio. The charges were dropped when it was discovered that the "drugs" were merely vitamins. Decades later, Fonda told an interviewer at *Harper's Bazaar*, "It was like I had Richard Avedon in that jailhouse taking my mug shot; it's a beautiful mug shot."

Another roadshow on the protest circuit. Here's **Jane Fonda** at a protest in Holland in 1975. It was by now a venue with which she was very very familiar.

The next day in a speech, Hayden called the Black Panthers "America's Viet Cong."

From Paris came an unlikely supporter in the form of Jean Genet, the French novelist, playwright, and political activist. In 1970, the Black Panthers invited him to visit with them in America, and he accepted, staying for three months. He gave lectures and even attended the trial of Huey Newton.

Before returning to Paris, he told his friend, Jean-Paul Sartre, "I'm going to suck as many cocks of Black Panthers that I can fit into my mouth."

Later, in Paris, he confessed to Sartre, "I carried out my goal, and not a one of those black boys turned me down. I have nothing but praise to heap on African American genitalia."

[Throughout the course of his adult life, Huey P. Newton was accused of murder but somehow managed to escape getting prosecuted for it. In 1967, he was involved in a shoot-out which led to the death of Police Officer John Frey. The following year, he was convicted of manslaughter and sentenced to from two to fifteen years in prison. In May of 1970, the conviction was reversed. Two subsequent trials ended in hung juries.

Later in life, he was accused of murdering Kathleen Smith and Betty Patter, although he was never convicted.

He was schooled in the works of such men as Malcolm X, Che Guevara, Karl Marx, and Lenin.

His time finally ran out on August 22, 1989 in West Oakland, California. He had stolen 14 "rocks" of cocaine from a crack house. This was said to be the property of Terry Robinson who trailed Newton and mowed him down. Robinson was later sentenced to 32 years to life in prison. Today, a statue of Newton stands on the corner where he was fatally shot.

One of Newton's best-known quotes was: "If the white devil does not give us the freedom we deserve, he will face a potentially destructive force."]

Huey Newton, as archived by the Library of Congress.

***

At the time of Hayden's first visit to Jane's home to show her his slides of Vietnam, she was having an affair with Robert Scheer, the editor of *Ramparts* magazine.

Ironically, Robert was involved at the time in an affair with Anne Scheer, his ex-wife. "Coincidences in love affairs like ours were very commonplace in La La Land," he claimed.

At one point, Jane was reduced to tears when Hayden showed her slides of grotesque young Saigon prostitutes. "They had undergone drastic plastic surgeries in both breasts and eye operations performed on them to make them ostensibly more alluring to American soldiers. Their eyes became round, instead of slanted and their breasts were enlarged in the tradition of Marilyn Monroe."

"Suddenly, I understood why Jane was shedding tears," Hayden said. "She, too, had promoted her own image of superficial sexiness, a reputation she was now trying to shake to become a more serious actress. This sensitivity caused me to look at her in a new way. Maybe I could love someone like that."

Hayden's first night of sex with Jane was interrupted by the sudden appearance of little Vanessa. She had wandered from her bedroom and opened the unlocked door to her mother, seeking comfort after a nightmare.

Concealing his erection, Hayden got out of bed and befriended her, later taking her back to her room and putting her to bed.

Then he returned to Jane's boudoir to link "my plumbing with hers."

Somehow, novelist Gore Vidal was one of the first to hear of this new Hollywood mating. He took a cynical view: "Jane is a millionaire, and Hayden is piss poor. The only thing going for him is his charisma as a public speaker and his ability to incite left-wing protesters. I also heard a rumor that his always-reliable weapon has taken the virginity of many a college girl at some of his rallies. Of course, I can't verify that from any personal experience with me."

News of the mating of Hayden with Jane reached the tabloids, and the couple became known as "The Beauty and the Beast" the same label that would be applied to Mel Brooks and Anne Bancroft.

It was soon reported that Hayden had become Jane's "friend, mentor, lover, savior, pillar of support, and an example of what she hoped to become as a political activist."

Peter Fonda took a dim view: "Hayden hooked up with my sister and that was to advance himself politically with the money he got from her and all the press publicity he would get from being her lover and potential husband. The fucker gives opportunism a bad name."

Image was especially vital to Hayden, and he felt that Jane's residence, with its swimming pool, was too luxurious for the political activism he envisioned for themselves.

Reacting, she purchased a ramshackle $45,000 house in the working class district of Santa Monica. Its previous occupants had included a hippie commune of at least eight—maybe a lot more, depending on circumstances. Its members had painted its walls in psychedelic colors.

Jane's Oscar from *Klute* served as a book end for Hayden's collection of political works by Mao Zedong, Émile Durkheim, Franz Fanon, Plato, and Donald Ward (who later changed his name to Khalid Abdullah Tarig Al-Mansour).

Furniture from the Salvation Army filled the living room. Peter noticed that there was no bed in the Jane Fonda/Tom Hayden bedroom, only a dirty mattress on the floor, perhaps left over from the former occupants. At the entrance hung a portrait of Ho Chi Minh.

After a visit from Henry Fonda, he told his wife Shirlee, "If a studio remakes *Tobacco Road,* Jane can rent her home."

"I never knew what my sister was going to say or do next," Peter said. "Her new boyfriend, Tom Hayden, is a difficult dude to understand. Does he really believe that his supporters should burn New York City and Washington? Back in 1968, he called Robert Kennedy a 'little Fascist,' yet he was one of the pallbearers at his funeral after his assassination in Los Angeles."

Hayden later told Peter, "The lure of violence and martyrdom are powerful subterranean forces in my makeup."

Jane spent so much money on political activities that she and Hayden one night sat out in the moonlight trying to conjure up some money-making schemes. That night marked the birth of Jane's workout empire.

***

They Called Her "Hanoi Jane"

When Jane made her controversial trip to North Vietnam in 1972, she was following not only in the footsteps of Tom Hayden, but in those of pastors and professors from American churches and universities, all of them antiwar activists.

At Orly Airport in Paris, Jane was running late to catch her plane to Moscow. As she rounded a corner, she slipped on a polished floor. In her fall, she re-fractured the same foot that had been broken the previous year. She had to make a quick decision: continue with the trip or use her injury as an excuse to abandon her plan.

By the time of her arrival in Moscow, her foot had swollen drastically and the skin around it had turned blue. Since there was a four-hour delay before the continuation of her trip, she had time to taxi to a local hospital, where her foot was X-rayed. Indeed, it was fractured. Her injured foot was encased in a plaster cast and she was given a pair of crutches. During her ongoing flight, she admitted, "All that the Vietnamese need is a disabled American descending on them."

With her on her trip to Hanoi were two hundred letters given to her by the families of young American soldiers being held captive at the time in North Vietnamese prison camps.

Her hosts in Hanoi met her at the airport. They seemed aware of the propaganda victory that her presence might generate. In the next few days, they invited her on a tour of civilian targets—including schools and hospitals—which had been bombed by American aircraft,.

She was shown damage to the vital system of dikes that held back the raging waters of the Red River (*aka* Hong River) Delta, the most densely populated region of what was then known as North Vietnam. If not for the dikes, the rice fields that fed 15 million people would be flooded. She declared that those rice fields should never have been defined as a military target, because destroying them would lead to massive starvation.

During the two weeks of her controversial tour, she visited bombed-out villages and factories. Then she took what became her most controversial "statement." She was photographed seated astride the barrel of an anti-aircraft battery used to shoot down American planes. From that moment forward, she would forever after be known (and often reviled) as "Hanoi Jane" even as late as 2023.

She compounded what was later viewed as a mistake by making ten propaganda broadcasts over Radio Hanoi, defining American military and political leaders as "war criminals."

She began her broadcasts by saying, "This is Jane Fonda speaking in Hanoi, and I'm speaking privately to U.S. servicemen who are stationed in the Gulf of Tonkin."

During one broadcast on July 21, 1972 she stated, "Nixon is continuing to risk your lives and the lives of prisoners of war under a last desperate attempt to keep his office come November."

In another broadcast, she told the servicemen, "If they told you the truth, you wouldn't fight, you wouldn't kill. You were not born and brought up by your mothers to kill. You have been told lies so that it would be possible for you to kill."

Her broadcasts were later compared to the pro-Japanese propaganda voice of Tokyo Rose during World War II.

During Jane's visit, she also visited camps housing American prisoners of war (POWs), giving them letters

Here, as published within the *New York Post*, was one of thousands of editorials condemning **Jane Fonda** for treason.

from their families back home. Her aide gathered letters from them with the understanding that they'd be forwarded to their families upon Jane's return.

Many lies and distortions emerged from her encounters with these American prisoners. Many claimed she was warmly received; others stated that some of the servicemen spat on her. A story spread that the prisoners who refused to appear with her were later tortured, especially Colonel George Day, the ranking military officer at what was mockingly called "the Hanoi Hilton."

At the time of Jane's arrival, Day had already spent thirty-seven months in solitary confinement. For refusing to appear with Jane, it was said that "his buttocks were flogged with a fan belt until they were turned into hamburger."

Back in the States, Jane would later denounce these charges of torture as "coming from hypocrites and liars. The POWs I met were not tortured. Nor were they starved."

At the end of her tour she boarded a plane flying from Hanoi to Paris. There, at Orly Airport, she transferred to an ongoing flight to New York.

She arrived at Kennedy Airport "wearing black Viet Cong pajamas and a coolie hat."

A group of protesters greeted her at the moment of her return to her homeland. They screamed at her, calling her every name from "Red Pinko!" to "Hanoi Rose." *[Later, of course, that reference was changed to "Hanoi Jane."]*

On some radio stations, a previous broadcast of hers was played over and over, listeners hearing her claim that American soldiers were "cannon fodder for U.S. imperialism."

After Jane's return to her home turf in California, rumors swirled between New York, Washington, D.C., and Los Angeles, deeply upsetting Henry Fonda. At one point, after a barrage of hostile questions from reporters, he became so angry, he said, "Daughter? I don't have a daughter!"

One of the most vicious rumors spread about her was that any American POW who refused to appear with Jane for a "press and PR photo op" later faced a firing squad.

Back in Washington, Secretary of State Henry Kissinger defined her trip as "immoral." Several congressmen urged that she be tried for treason.

Jane accused Nixon of "slaughter." Patricia Nixon, his wife, later spoke out about that charge: "Miss Fonda should have gone to Hanoi and on her knees begged those communists to end their aggression and killing."

Jane had created two powerful enemies, Richard Nixon and J. Edgar Hoover of the F.B.I. Eventually, her secret dossier was said to have included several thousand pages referencing every embarrassing detail of her past. Her mail was secretly opened, and her phones tapped.

When Nixon was forced to step down from the presidency because of the Watergate scandal, Jane said, "The people who wanted to send Tom and me to jail are going to jail themselves, especially some of the former president's chief aides. The only thing that kept Tricky Dickie out of jail was that pardon from Gerald Ford."

When asked about Jane's trip to Hanoi, Tom Hayden told the press, "It was the case of a sex symbol turned against macho men who are killing or wounding innocent men, women, and school kids."

After she was back in Los Angeles, Jane was besieged with death threats. A typical one read: "John F. Kennedy, Martin Luther King, Robert Kennedy…You're next!"

Years later, in a 1988 interview with Barbara Walters, Jane expressed regret for some of her comments and actions, stating:

In their very diplomatic coverage of **Jane Fonda's** involvements in many of the protest movements then galvanizing America, *Life* magazine's edition of April 23, 1971 was restrained.

Their coverage did not reflect the rage generated among vets and conservatives, whose bumper stickers, pins, and armbands were a LOT more vulgar that the ones displayed immediately above.

> *"I would like to say something, not just to Vietnam veterans in New England, but to men who were in Vietnam, who I hurt, or whose pain I caused to deepen because of things that I said or did. I was trying to help end the killing and the war, but there were times when I was thoughtless and careless about it, and I'm very sorry that I hurt them. And I want to apologize to them and their families. I will go to my grave regretting the photograph of me in an anti-aircraft gun, which looks like I was trying to shoot at American planes. It hurt so many soldiers. It galvanized such hostility. It was the most horrible thing I could possibly have done. It was just thoughtless ..."*

Critics, however, pointed out that her apology came at a time when a group of New England veterans had launched a campaign to disrupt a film project she was working on, leading to the charge that her apology was motivated at least partially by self-interest.

***

After the Viet Cong overran Saigon in April of 1975, Jane and Hayden needed a new political issue. They formed the Campaign for Economic Democracy (CED). Some of its stated goals involved promoting solar energy "to save the climate:" and to curb the political power of large corporations "who bought and sold politicians."

To house the staff of the CED, Jane shelled out $700,000 of her own money to buy a 160-acre ranch north of Santa Barbara. She also financed the construction of a dozen modest little homes to house staff members. In summer, they ran a camp for underprivileged children "imported" from the inner cities.

***

Jane Marries Tom Hayden

At the time of Tom Hayden's marriage to Jane Fonda, many movie-goers, fans of Jane, had never heard of this new man in her life, even though he was increasingly well-known in political circles.

Nicholas Lemann, correspondent for *The Atlantic*, claimed, "Tom Hayden changed America. He was the father of the largest mass protests in U.S. history."

Richard N. Goodwin, speechwriter for both JFK and LBJ, said that Hayden, "without knowing it, inspired the Great Society."

The Reverend Richard York of the Berkeley Free Church, on January 23, 1973, married Jane to Tom Hayden in the backyard of her home in Laurel Canyon in Hollywood. About three dozen guests attended the ceremony. Her wedding cake was inscribed with the word PEACE.

Noting her pregnancy, she claimed, "Tom and I will start a revolutionary family of our own."

Jane Fonda with **Tom Hayden** and their son, **Troy Garrity,** *en route* to the polls near their home in Santa Monica, California, in June, 1976

Their wedding was attended by some Vietnamese students, some Vietnam U.S. Army veterans, and some Irish priests and balladeers. Shirlee and Henry Fonda showed up to look after daughter Vanessa. Peter Fonda also sang seven "sweet songs."

Hayden recalled, "Our wedding was hardly Norman Rockwell."

Photographer Sam Jaffe attended Jane's wedding, reporting that a number of guests were Vietnamese living in America. At the end of the ceremony, they sang songs from their native land. Hayden then led the dancing of Irish jigs.

Jane was three months pregnant when she married. It was a tumultuous union that lasted until 1989.

She gave birth to their son, Troy Garity, on July 7, 1973, in Los Angeles.

Instead of leaving their infant boy with a nanny, they preferred to take him on the road. He was "assigned" to a series of open dresser drawers, each functioning as a crib, in one dreary motel room after another.

Garity grew up to become a producer and actor, starring in such pictures as *Soldier's Girl* (2003), its plot centered around a young soldier who falls in love with a transgendered performer.

Henry Fonda told a reporter, "I admire Tom Hayden very much, in spite of many of our political differences. Jane seems happy being married to him, and I wish them all the best."

Hayden and Jane later unofficially adopted a teenaged African American foster daughter, Mary Luana Williams (nicknamed Lulu), the daughter of members of the Black Panthers.

On their first visit to Paris, Jane and Hayden called on Roger Vadim to pick up their daughter, Vanessa. There, they met Vadim's new bride, Catherine Schneider whom he'd married in 1975, the union lasting two years.

In the words of her new husband, "She was 28 years old. She was tall, elegant, and had a great deal of charm, her blue eyes irresistible. But she had a very cruel sense of humor. She was renowned for her beauty and the way she played with men's hearts."

They produced a son named Vania.

Jane found them living in an apartment overlooking the Champs de Mars on which stood the Eiffel Tower.

Schneider's cousin (Valéry Giscard d'Estaing) sometimes dropped in for afternoon tea. Otherwise, he was occupied with his duties as President of France.

***

In 1976, Hayden announced that in the Democratic Primary, he was going to challenge Senator John V. Tunny for his seat as U.S. Senator from California. "The radicalism of the 1960s has become the common sense of the 1970s," he told *The New York Times*.

Jane herself became Hayden's biggest political contributor, and he drew support from many figures in the entertainment world.

Jane even got her father to stage a fundraiser for her husband in his Bel Air mansion. She also got him to agree to sell some of his paintings, but she found no buyers for them. Secretly, she purchased the works of art herself.

Jane herself helped finance Hayden's run for the Senate, putting up half a million dollars. *[That would be worth $4 million in 2023 currency.]*

Other supporters included Jerry Brown and his girlfriend, Linda Ronstadt, as well as Groucho Marx, Arlo Guthrie, Lucille Ball, Danny Kaye, Jon Voight, and Red Buttons.

Hayden was a bit nervous, fearing that he might be labeled "the Hollywood candidate," especially after he received the backing of such powerful men as Norman Lear, the TV producer.

As the campaign got rougher, Jane accused Tunny of "dating teenagers," which seemed to be true.

As Hayden rose in the polls, Tunny brought in some "heavy guns" to attack him and his "movie star wife."

Tunny had been a former boxing champion and the Harvard roommate of Ted Kennedy. He was known as an "Old School Liberal" and had a loyal list of supporters.

On election night, Jane and Hayden eagerly awaited the outcome, surrounded by supporters. By midnight, Hayden was forced to concede, although the final tally gave him forty percent of the vote. "Some 1.2 million people of California voted for Tom," Jane said.

However, that autumn, in the general election, Tunny lost to S.I. Hayakawa, president of San Francisco State University.

Insiders reported that Tom Hayden, with Jane at his side, had ultimately wanted to make 1600 Pennsylvania Avenue his address, with Jane as the nation's First Lady. He often talked about running for President.

Peter Fonda said, "I can imagine my sister becoming another Dolley Madison, but not another Eleanor Roosevelt. That is a bridge too far."

Hayden was furious when Ronald Reagan won the presidency in 1980 by unseating the peanut farmer from Georgia, Jimmy Carter.

"Reagan was just a two-bit B-picture actor,"

Jane Fonda with **Tom Hayden, Troy Garrity**, and **Vanessa Vadim** in 1976.

Whereas Troy was their shared biological son, Vanessa came from Jane's previous marriage to film director Roger Vadim.

Hayden said, "and that little starlet, Nancy Davis, in the 1940s, was known as the fellatio queen of Hollywood. George Cukor told me that he'd be rich if he had a nickel for every Jew Nancy was under."

Of course, all of the financial support Jane provided to Hayden brought criticism, especially from Max Palevsky, who, along with Peter Bart, was producing *Fun with Dick and Jane,* a 1977 movie in which Jane co-starred with George Segal.

"Hayden is shamelessly using Jane…exploiting her, really," Palevsky claimed. "She's a smart gal but seems taken in by him as if he has her under some spell. Maybe he has a big dick…I don't know. Sometimes he's been known to mock her to his friends."

As time went by, and according to Peter Fonda, "my sister's marriage to Tom became less a marriage and more of a political and business union. He even had an apartment in Sacramento where he had a number of affairs. On weekends, he often commuted to a much better home that Jane had acquired. It was a spacious, solar-heated home in Santa Monica."

Tom Hayden on the floor of the California Legislature in 1986.

When he ran for office, he was sometimes reviled as "The Second Coming of Lucifer."

He was also denounced as a "traitor, a communist, and a diablolical revolutionary." Campaigning against him were such high profiles as President Gerald Ford and actor Charlton Heston.

Hayden was preparing to aid in the 1988 campaign of Michael Dukakis during his run for U.S. President.

Rumors reached Jane that he was involved with Morgan Fairchild and/or Margot Kidder. Actually, he was spending his nights with Vicky Rideout, a sexy Harvard graduate who was two decades younger than Jane. She was the chief speechwriter for Dukakis. To complicate matters, Hayden was frequently showing up drunk.

Eventually, whenever Jane was invited to a party or some gathering, she showed up alone. "No Tom," said one of her friends.

Time was moving on for Jane. Nothing seemed to dramatize that more than when she accompanied Vanessa to enroll her at Brown University in ways that evoked Jane's enrollment at Vassar. Her daughter's adult life was about to begin.

To top it all, Vadim had recently written and released his memoir, *Bardot, Deneuve, Fonda,* an intimate (some said "embarrassing") overview that detailed "three-in-a-bed romps." *[Jane, prior to its release, managed to persuade him to remove some of the more "controversial" sexual revelations.]*

During the closing days of December 1988, Hayden and Jane faced reality and agreed to separate, although delaying for a long time any public announcements about it. By then, he'd moved on to Vicky Rideout, the previously referenced speechwriter for Massachusetts governor Michael Dukakis

Hayden admitted to Jane, "I've fallen in love with another woman." He'd chosen Jane's 51st birthday to admit what she had suspected for a long time.

Jane snapped, "I hear she's so young you have to change her diapers."

News of the impending Fonda-Hayden divorce made headlines around the world.

Jane avoided reporters until one from *Newsweek* finally reached her. He asked her, "How do you feel?"

"I've been on my exercise bike," she answered, "for the last five hours pedaling away. I stopped when my butt started bleeding. The physical pain is nothing to what I feel emotionally. I'm breaking apart."

Hayden later served, from 1982 to 1992, in the California State Assembly, and, from 1992 to 2000, in California's State Senate. He also mounted a failed bid in the Democratic Primary for Governor of California but lost in 1994.

In 1997, he ran for Mayor of Los Angeles, losing to incumbent Richard Riordan.

With the passage of time, Hayden's dream of becoming President of the United States became a distant memory.

In 1993, three years after divorcing Jane, he married Barbara Williams. They adopted a son, Liam, in 2000. Williams stayed with Hayden until his death on October 23, 2016.

Jane would marry one final time, in 1991, to Ted Turner, the cable television tycoon and CNN founder. They divorced in 2001, and she never remarried.

Today, as she confessed as she nears the age of 86, she's also given up "dating."

Some of her fans agree that the barely suppressed rage catalyzed by her social protests helped **Jane Fonda** as an actress.

Here, she appears with **James Caan** in a scene from *Comes a Horseman*, released in 1978, around the time when her activisim had "calmed down" a few notches. In it, she portrays a rancher who's cheated out of her land by greedy railroad barons and cattle kings.

Her director at the time, Alan Pakula, told the press, "In most westerns, the woman is either in a calico dress, running after the hero on the horse saying, 'Nothing is worth dying for,'" or portraying a gun-toting Calamity Jane."

Behind the scenes, Jane assessed her role in the film like a dyed-in-the-wool activist and revolutionary: "What should have happened," she said, "is that all the small ranchers in the valley should have organized and banded together. Then, maybe, we would have won."

CHAPTER ELEVEN

JANE AGES GRACEFULLY

COMING HOME
The Judgment of Paris: Falling in Love with a Paraplegic Army Veteran
(He's Jon Voight, the Former Midnight Cowboy)
For Her Performance, Jane Wins a Best Actress Oscar

COMES A HORSEMAN
Jane Plays a Hard-Bitten, Post World War II Rancher Who's Ready for a Fight
(Her Ally and Love Object is James Caan)

CALIFORNIA SUITE
Portraying a Tough-As-Nails NYC Editor,
Jane Engages in a Custody Battle with Her Laid-Back Ex-Husband.
At the Age of 40, She Appears in a Micro-Bikini

THE CHINA SYNDROME
The Son (Michael Douglas) of a Famous Movie Star (Kirk Douglas),
and the Daughter (Jane) of another Famous Movie Star (Henry Fonda)
Avert the Catastrophic Meltdown of a Nuclear Power Plant

THE ELECTRIC HORSEMAN
Jane Re-Unites in "A post-modern Western" with Robert Redford

9 TO 5
Jane, Dolly Parton, and Lily Tomlin Plot a Terrible Revenge
for their Sexist, Arrogant Boss.
And Guess What? It's a **MEGA-HIT!!**

Jane Fonda's reputation as "Hanoi Jane" would remain, forever, as part of her epitaph. And although the Vietnam war ended in 1975, three years later, almost as a catharsis for the American public, it re-emerged as the subject of intense discussion, in part because of her film, *Coming Home* (1978).

Partially produced by her own newly established film company, she was cast as Sally Hyde, a perplexed woman whose macho Marine husband, Captain Bob Hyde (Bruce Dern), has been deployed to Vietnam. While he's away, Sally volunteers to work in a veteran's hospital that specializes in the rehabilitation of paraplegic war veterans who had been seriously injured in combat.

Without meaning to, she falls in love with one of the patients, Luke Martin (Jon Voight).

[Jane's company was called IPC Films, an abbreviation of "Indochina Peace Campaign," although it was later changed.]

Many male stars (including John Wayne, Burt Lancaster, Humphrey Bogart, and Clint Eastwood) had already formed their own production companies. Other than Mary Pickford in the Silent Era, the most famous female producer in Hollywood history had been Lucille Ball, who, with her then-husband Desi Arnaz, had purchased RKO and reconfigured it as Desilu Productions. After their divorce, Lucille bought out the interests of her husband.

Of course, Jane as a film producer would be miles behind the "industrial scale" output of the former star of the *I Love Lucy* TV series in the 1950s.

During the production of *Coming Home*, Jane's associate producer was Bruce Gilbert, with whom she had formed a friendship during their antiwar protests. A decade younger than Jane, Gilbert had gone to Berkeley but dropped out after the campus was tear-gassed from helicopters flying overhead and some students had been shot. He would run the business side of IPC throughout the production of several of Jane's upcoming movies, such as *The China Syndrome* and *Nine to Five*.

Gilbert had been introduced to Jane by her husband, activist Tom Hayden. A son of privilege in Beverly Hills, Gilbert had later joined Hayden's "Red Family" of activists and protesters.

He told Jane that he was most impressed with *Easy Rider*, the star vehicle for her brother, Peter Fonda. But he promised her that together, they could produce films that were even more provocative.

"I agree with Samuel Goldwyn about message pictures," he said. "If you want to send a message, call Western Union."

Jane had worked in political drama before, especially documentaries. *Julia* (1977) had been a political drama of sorts, but—as she relayed to Gilbert—she wanted a new style of political drama that would be antiwar "but not preachy."

She preferred a story line that would transcend the individual tastes of whatever movie-goer opted to see it. In other words, she wanted human drama to win out over anyone's individual political stance.

In part because of her "revised"(and less strident) priorities, by the late 1970s, Jane was no longer viewed as "box office poison." To some insider's surprise, and once again on the comeback trail, she began evoking "money in the bank" to other, sometimes envious, producers.

***

212

Coming Home (1978)

The inspiration for *Coming Home* began when Jane met Ron Kovic, a paraplegic Vietnam veteran, at an anti-war rally. A native of Wisconsin, Kovic had been born one year after the end of World War II.

In December of 1965, he volunteered for military service and was sent to Indochina. There, he participated in long-range reconnaissance patrols into enemy territories. His tour of duty lasted for thirteen months. When it was over, in January of 1967, he "came home" to the U.S., but later volunteered to return to Vietnam for a second tour of duty.

Tragedy struck on January 20, 1968 during his command of a battalion of scouts. His men came into contact with elements of the Viet Cong, a ferocious battalion in the process of besieging a village.

While leading his rifle squad across some open terrain, Kovic was shot—first in the right foot, which tore out the back of his heel, and then again with bullets that entered through his right shoulder. He suffered a collapsed lung and a spinal cord injury that left him paralyzed from the chest down. The first U.S. Marine who tried to save him was shot through the heart and died instantly Under heavy fire, another Marine carried Kovic to safety.

The book that started it all: Displayed above is a first edition, with sales and promotional photos, of the brave and tenacious veteran whose memoir touched off an avalanche of public support and public grief.

From his base he was rushed to an intensive care unit which at the time was filled to overflowing with other Marines wounded by the Viet Cong. For his bravery at the front, Kovic was later awarded both the Bronze Star and the Purple Heart. For the rest of his life, Kovic would remain confined to a wheelchair.

Back in the States, Kovic became one of the best-known activists among Vietnam veterans, most of whom had been permanently wounded. During the course of his protests, he was arrested by the police at least a dozen times, including when he attended the Kent State shootings. At one antiwar rally in Levittown, Long Island, his address to the crowd was interrupted by a bomb threat.

In 1976, Kovic published his memoirs. They were entitled *Born on the Fourth of July*. It was this book that inspired Jane to begin pre-production on what eventually emerged as *Coming Home*.

"I wanted to share with people as intimately as possible what I and others had gone through, what I had endured," Kovic said. "I wanted them to know what it really meant to be in the middle of a war, to be shot, to be wounded, to be fighting for your life in intensive care—not the myth we have grown up believing."

Kovic's *Born on the Fourth of July*, was adapted into a movie in 1989, thirteen years after its publication, and had nothing to do with Jane Fonda. It starred Tom Cruise and highlighted the life of Kovic over a twenty-year period. Its director was Oliver Stone, his second installment in a trilogy of films beginning with *Platoon* (1986) and ending with *Heaven & Earth* (1993).

Born on the Fourth of July became a cinematic mega-hit, generating $165 million worldwide and receiving eight Oscar nominations, including Best Actor for Cruise; Best Director for Oliver Stone, and Best

Picture for the film itself.

[Originally, Al Pacino had been offered the role of Kovic, but he rejected it. Sean Penn wanted to star in it, as did Charlie Sheen and Nicolas Cage, but Stone rejected them.]

When Kovic saw the final cut, he presented his Bronze Star to Cruise for his "heroic performance."

Bruce Springsteen wrote the song "Shut Out the Light" in honor of Kovic's memoir.

Kovic summed up his life by saying, "I may have lost my body, but I've gained my mind."

***

Jane's idea for her movie about a veteran (or veterans) of the war in Vietnam would focus on two men: "I hadn't decided yet what my role would be. Since I wanted to present the movie through the lens of a woman, I hired Nancy Dowd to write the first draft."

Dowd's other screen credit was *Slap Shot* (1977), inspired by her brother's experience playing hocky in the minor leagues.

Bruce Gilbert worked on the script with Dowd. The original title for what became *Coming Home* was *Buffalo Ghost*. When Jane read its script, she was disappointed, finding it "much too dark and rather unsettling—not the story I had in mind."

Jane had been impressed with Waldo Salt's script for *Midnight Cowboy* (1969), which had won an Oscar as Best Picture of that year. It derived from an adaptation of a novel about a handsome but not too bright dishwasher from Texas who dons a cowboy outfit and heads to Manhattan to sell his sexual services, ostensibly to women, as a stud.

On the brutal streets of Manhattan, he forms a bond with a larcenous and sleazy character named Ratso Rizzo, portrayed by Dustin Hoffman after Sal Mineo was rejected by the casting director.

For his efforts, Salt won an Oscar for Best Adapted Screenplay, and both Hoffman and Voight received Best Actor nominations.

Jane referred to Salt as "an old lefty who had once been blacklisted."

Salt, who had endured a tormented past, read the Dowd script and did not like it. He began working on a new version.

In part because nudity, beginning in the late 60s, had made recent inroads onto the New York Stage and to a lesser degree, onto the screen he activated several daring press and P.R. ploys and some ultra-avant-garde scenes, some so provocative they had to be removed from the film's final cut.

[One of them called for a block of 42nd Street in Manhattan to be roped off by the police. Voight as Joe Buck in a dream sequence, was to run frontally nude for one full block of cityscape. That was just too much for the producer, who nixed it, partly because of the expense and difficulty of getting it filmed.]

Salt turned to director John Schlesinger and to producer Jerome Hellman to help him get the movie launched. A New Englander, Hellman became the recipient of a Best Picture Oscar for *Midnight Cowboy*. Nine

Hollywood was on the dawn of the 1970s when the controversial **Midnight Cowboy** was voted Best Picture of 1969.

It became the first X-rated film to win a Best Picture Oscar, beating out such hits as *Hello Dolly; Butch Cassidy and the Sundance Kid;* and *Anne of the Thousand Days*.

Jane was impressed with the writing skill of its scriptwriter, Waldo Salt.

years later, he'd be nominated for the same award for *Coming Home.*

During the eventful course of his twenty-five years in film production, he'd turn out *A Fine Madness* (1966) with Sean Connery; *The Day of the Locust* (1975) with Donald Sutherland; and *The Mosquito Coast* (1986) with Harrison Ford.

In all, Hellman's seven feature films would garner seventeen Oscar nominations and win six.

Hellman took Salt's pre-production treatment of *Coming Home* to Arthur Krim, the head of United Artists. The executive held out little hope for such a grim tale, but finally agreed to put up "a barebone five million," which was barely enough.

A Londoner, Schlesinger was known for a variety of stories about both America and his British homeland. He'd been instrumental in the career of Julie Christie, casting her in *Darling* (1965), a corrosive portrait of an amoral woman who changes professions (model, actress, countess) as often as she changes lovers.

For *Darling,* Christie won a Best Actress Oscar; Schlesinger was nominated for Best Director, and the movie itself was nominated for Best Picture of the Year.

Schlesinger later awarded Christie the female lead in *Far From the Madding Crowd* (1967), based on the epic novel by Thomas Hardy.

The early stages of trying to launch Jane's *Coming Home* proved too much for Schlesinger. Late one morning, he told her he was moving on. "I'm not the bloke to direct a film about wounded vets and piss bags. You don't need a British fag for this one."

Jane's need for a director was quickly solved by the arrival of Haskell Wexler, her favorite cinematographer, who had performed, in her opinion, brilliantly during the filming of her documentary, *Introduction to the Enemy* (1974).

He had just worked with Hal Ashby on *Bound for Glory* (1976), and a meeting was arranged between Ashby and Jane.

Like Jane, he had been adamantly opposed to the Vietnam War. Wexler predicted, "You guys will work together like clockwork."

When Ashby and Jane met, she encountered a director who looked like a hippie descended from some commune left over from the 1960s. As a pot smoker, he was stoned, wore love beads, and had long, gray, and stringy hair.

Jane had made it a point to have seen some of his best work before their meeting.

As a director, Ashby's notable films had included *Harold and Maude* (1971), a coming-of-age black comedy permeated with existential drama. In it, Harold Chasen (Bud Cort) develops a romantic relationship with 79-year-old Maude (Ruth Gordon), who teaches him about living life to the fullest.

Jane had already seen an earlier film Ashby had directed, *Shampoo* (1975,) starring Warren Beatty, Julie Christie, Goldie Hawn, and Lee Grant. A satire of late 1960s sexual and social mores, it follows a promiscuous Los Angeles hairdresser as he juggles affairs with several women.

Ashby had also directed *The Last Detail* (1973). It had starred Jack Nicholson in a story about two sailors assigned to escort a young, emotionally withdrawn recruit from a military base in Virginia to a Naval prison in Maine. Later, it was nominated for three Oscars. The word "fuck" was articulated in that movie sixty-five times. For his performance, Nicholson was nominated for a Best Actor Oscar.

Ashby told Jane that one of the reasons he wanted to direct *Coming Home* was because it would be the

Critics had been impressed with the directing skill of John Schlesinger. Not only had he directed *Midnight Cowboy,* he had helmed the controversial *Darling* that brought fame to **Julie Christie.**

Alas, as it turned out, Schlesinger himself concluded that he was not the man to helm Jane's upcoming movie, *Coming Home.*

first to deal with a disabled vet's sexuality. Even though the budget was limited, he demanded (and received) $400,000. As such, he was the highest-paid person working on the production.

Around this time, both Ashby and Jane suspected that something was wrong with Salt. When they met with him they found that he had written only thirty-six pages of dialogue. He looked frail and in a very weakened condition. He assured them that, even though he'd been ill, he had recovered and soon would be turning out at least five pages of the script every day.

That never happened. The following day, Salt suffered a massive heart attack. Hellman and Jane wanted to keep that a secret, for as long as was feasibly possible, from their financial backer, United Artists.

Ashby then brought in Robert J. Jones, who had been the film editor of *Midnight Cowboy*.

To everyone's frustration, the script for *Coming Home* just never seemed to come together as a united whole. Everybody, including Jane, contributed something until the script looked like a pasted-up mess.

Then a young novelist, Rolf Wurlitzer, who had previously worked for the famous author Robert Graves on the island of Majorca off the coast of Spain, was hired "to fix it." He was a descendant of the legendary founder of the Wurlitzer jukebox empire that had brought music to every dive in America. He was the same age as Jane.

Although he contributed mightily—"and out of respect for Salt"—whom he admired, Wurlitzer did not allow his name to be used as the scriptwriter, allowing the others to take all the credit.

The script was still being written as the roles were cast. When Al Pacino turned it down, its male lead was offered first to Jack Nicholson and then to Sylvester Stallone. Both of them rejected it. Also considered were Paul Newman, Steve McQueen, and Clint Eastwood. Finally, the decision was made to star Bruce Dern as the wounded vet (Luke Martin), with Jon Voight cast as Captain Bob Hyde, the husband of Sally Hyde (Jane Fonda).

Jane had recently worked with Dern on the set of *They Shoot Horses, Don't They?*, in which he had portrayed an impoverished farmer marathon dancing with his pregnant wife, hoping to earn a little money for the expenses associated with the upcoming birth of their child.

Like Jane, Dern had been a graduate of the Actors Studio in Manhattan, working with Lee Strasberg and Elia Kazan. Dern had starred on Broadway in the original production (1959) of Tennessee Williams' *Sweet Bird of Youth*.

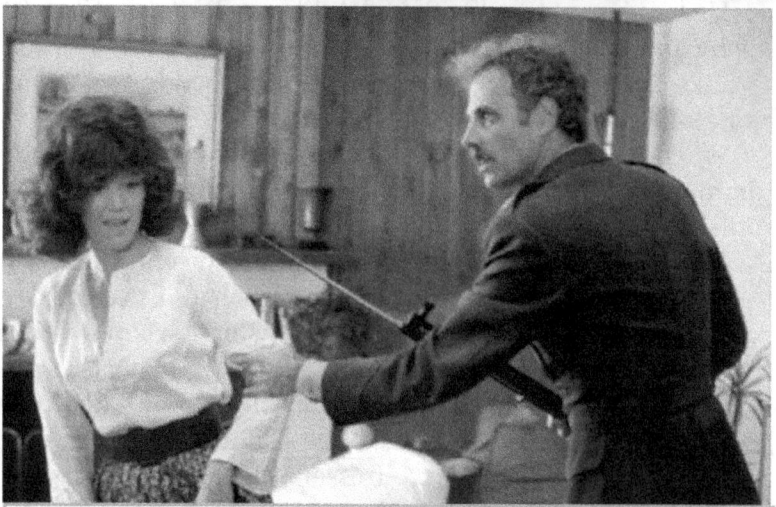

It was a tense marriage between the characters played by **Jane Fonda** and **Bruce Dern** in *Coming Home*.

A Marine Corps captain, Dern returns home to find his wife having an affair with a paraplegic played by Jon Voight.

Before signing with Jane's film company, Dern had also had a minor role in *Hush…Hush, Sweet Charlotte* (1964) starring Bette Davis and Olivia de Havilland.

Dern had also co-starred with John

Wayne in *The Cowboys,* a 1972 Western in which he had played the mysterious "Long Hair" Watts, the cowboy who kills Wayne in the end.

[For any movie starring John Wayne, it was very rare for him to be fatally shot at the end of the picture. Wayne warned Dern, "The public will hate you."

Dern shot back, "But they'll love me in Berkeley."]

He also appeared as the husband of Mia Farrow in the film adaptation of F. Scott Fitzgerald's *The Great Gatsby* (1974) starring Robert Redford. Before working with Jane, Dern had also starred in John Frankenheimer's thriller, *Black Sunday* (1977).

Dern's godfather was none other than Adlai Stevenson, who had run twice for President of the United States in the 1950s, losing to General Eisenhower.

Many times during the pre-production of *Coming Home,* Voight beseeched Ashby to let him switch roles with Dern. "I'd be perfect as the wounded vet," he said. Finally, just three days before the beginning of shooting, Ashby agreed to the change in casting.

According to the script, the "*gung-ho* and macho" character played by Dern (Sally's husband) was said to have never given his wife an orgasm. He believes that a woman's place is in the home and that she should always look like Jacqueline Kennedy at her best.

Voight had emerged into the world in Yonkers, New York, a year after Jane was born. He rose to fame in the late 1960s when he starred as the hustler, Joe Buck, in *Midnight Cowboy,* for which he was Oscar-nominated. To today's Generations X and Z, he is better known as the father of Angelina Jolie.

He had another good role in *Deliverance* (1972) with Burt Reynolds, although neither actor was the producing team's original choice.

After those hit movies, in the aftermath of the films that followed, Voight's career sagged because of low box office sales. These "lesser" films included *The All American Boy* (1973); *Conrack* (1974); *The Odessa File* (also 1974); and *End of the Game* (aka *Der Richter und sein Henker;* 1976).

Voight was married twice, both times to actresses—first to Lauri Peters and later to Marceline Bertrand. Since his second divorce, he never remarried, but over the years, he dated any number of women, most notably Barbra Streisand and Diana Ross.

Voight was eager to play Luke, telling Jane, "I can identify with him, with all his pain and suffering."

In contrast to Kovic, the "paralyzed from the neck down" real-life paraplegic whose memoir inspired the movie, the Voight character is paralyzed only in the legs, meaning that (albeit with difficulty) he could react (and perform) sexually.

Fortunately for the plot, Voight's character can not only perform sexually, but he gives Jane's character, Sally, her first-ever orgasm.

The sex scene took some time to shoot, and Voight lay "buck naked" on top of Jane for extended periods, waiting for crew members to set up the shots. Rumors spread among the cast that during some of those interims, he actually penetrated her.

Jane had originally wanted the sex scene to be exclusively oral but was overruled.

Later, Henry Fonda arrived on the set, expressing his wish to witness the filming of the sex scene that involved

In *Coming Home,* **Jane Fonda,** married to a tense and macho superpatriot, plays Sally Hyde, a volunteer in a veterans' hospital. There, she meets and falls in love with the character played by **Jon Voight.**

Despite his handicap (he's a paraplegic), he can satisfy her sexually. That is something her own husband cannot do.

his daughter.

He claimed that he'd been offended by it, and that he'd urged Ashby to cut it, which the director refused to do.

Later, when Henry saw the entire film, he applauded Jane for her brilliant performance. "It makes a father proud."

Jane's husband, Tom Hayden, on another occasion, sat through one of the takes of the filming of the sex scene. At the end, he got up and left the room without speaking to Ashby or Jane. At the door, he murmured, "nice try."

When Johnny (in this case, the character played by Dern) came marching home again, he learns of his wife's affair with Luke.

He loses control and confronts the lovers with a loaded rifle. Ultimately, he backs down. His life ends tragically as he goes to the beach and strips off his dress uniform. He removes his wedding ring, places it atop his uniform, then swims naked into the ocean to drown.

The suicide scene evokes James Mason's death in *A Star Is Born*, the picture he made with Judy Garland in 1954.

For access to a hospital location, Jane was rejected by the National Guard, the Marines, the Navy, and the U.S. Army because both the Pentagon and the Veterans' Administration were opposed to the filming of *Coming Home*. [*It was speculated at the time that many of the administrators of those organizations still remembered—and hated—Jane from her "Hanoi Jane" period.*]

Eventually, a civilian hospital that specialized in the treatment of spinal injuries in Downey, California, gave the cast and crew permission to shoot.

"I was hoping that my character would find an audience sympathetic to me," Jane said. "At the time, thousands of people viewed me as a traitor. I was hated. I'm sure people wanted me dead."

The film's background music borrowed heavily from the rock music of the 1960s. The soundtrack included "Strawberry Fields" by the Beatles; "Manic Depression" by Jimi Hendrix; "Just Like a Woman" by Bob Dylan; and "Ruby Tuesday" from the Rolling Stones.

Before *Coming Home* went into general release, Ashby arranged for it to be shown to a group of Vietnam veterans, some of whom had been wounded. He expected their reaction to be hostile but did not find that so. Nearly all of them approved of the picture.

Critic Pauline Kael claimed that whereas Bette Davis had dominated movies of the 1940s, and that Marilyn Monroe did so in the 1950s, "Now, Jane is the major film actress of the 1970s." [*Kael left out the 1960s.*]

Stephen Farber of *New West* magazine cited Jane as "the finest actress now working in America. In spite of a garbled conclusion, the relationship between Fonda and Voight made the most moving love story of the year."

Jack Kroll in *Newsweek* claimed: "Jane Fonda's character undergoes the greatest transformation. Starting out as a do-good volunteer at the hospital, she winds up angrily lecturing the other military wives who'd rather write sports items for the base newspaper than write about the problems of the soldiers. She falls in love with Voight, lets her hair go curly, and has her first satisfying sexual experience despite his paralysis."

On Oscar night, **Jon Voight** and **Jane Fonda** carry home the gold, each winning for Best Actor and Best Actress for *Coming Home*.

Jane had feared that her antiwar protests over Vietnam would harm her chances of winning an Academy Award.

But those smoldering resentments against her, a stinging backlash, seemed to have been forgiven.

At the Academy Awards ceremony that spring, Voight and Jane won for Best Actor and Best Actress. Nancy Dowd, Salt, and Robert C. Jones won as scriptwriters.

From the podium, Shirley MacLaine announced Jane as the winner. Both actresses feared she might face boos. Jane gave a rather tender acceptance speech, simultaneously rendering it into American sign language, which she had recently learned. She did that as a tribute to millions of her fellow citizens who suffer from deafness.

As Best Picture of the Year, *Coming Home* lost to *The Deer Hunter* with Robert De Niro.

Prior to the Oscar ceremony, Jane was said to have denounced *The Deer Hunter* as "racist…the Pentagon version of the Vietnam War." Later, or so it was reported, she told a reporter that she had not seen it.

Many Hollywood insiders asserted, with irony, that Jane as a producer made far more money than she ever did as an actress.

She later changed the name of her film production company to *International Pictures Corporation*. Later still, it became *Fonda Pictures*.

***

Like all Hollywood actors, many of Jane's film projects never materialized. She and Barbra Streisand wanted to produce a film in which, as seamstresses, they'd be trapped during a fire on the tenth floor of a sweatshop during the early 20the Century in Greenwich Village in Manhattan. The historic "inspiration" for this project was the Triangle Shirtwaist Factory Fire of Saturday, March 25, 1911, one of the deadliest industrial disasters in U.S. history.

Brooklyn-born Herb Gardner was hired to write the script. *[He was best known for his 1962 play,* A Thousand Clowns, *which ran on Broadway for 428 performances. When he was instrumental in writing its screen adaptation, he received an Oscar nomination for Best Screenplay. His biggest success came with the script of* I'm Not Rappaport *(1985), a play which ran on Broadway for two years, eventually winning a Tony Award for Best Play.*

Gardner claimed that he sometimes met and talked with the two superstars (Fonda and Streisand) for long periods of time. "Their combined energy was enough to propel a moon launch."

The fire killed 146 garment workers, 123 of whom were women, many of them low-income recent immigrants. Many of them jumped to

141 MEN AND GIRLS DIE IN WAIST FACTORY FIRE; TRAPPED HIGH UP IN WASHINGTON PLACE BUILDING; STREET STREWN WITH BODIES; PILES OF DEAD INSIDE

154 KILLED IN SKYSCRAPER FACTORY FIRE; SCORES BURN, OTHERS LEAP TO DEATH.

The Triangle Shirtwaist Factory Fire in Greenwich Village New York City, on Saturday, March 25, 1911, was one of the deadliest industrial disasters in U.S. history.

Most of the workers who died were women and girls, most of them recent immigrants to the United States, all of them working for wages which were, even at the time, substandard, in working conditions that were abysmally unsafe.

A creative team spearheaded by Jane Fonda and Barbra Streisand struggled to adapt it into a movie that focused on the tormented history of labor relations. Alas, like many dreams in Hollywood, it was never meant to be.

their deaths from the building's upper floors. Some were as young as 14. Most of the building's stairwells and exit routes had been locked, a common custom at the time as a means of preventing workers from taking unauthorized breaks.

Accompanied by Gardner (the scriptwriter), Jane visited the site of the fire, at 23–29 Washington Place, between Greene Street and Washington Square East. She alarmed him at one point by moving to an open window and climbing outside onto its sill, as if she were about to jump off.

He cried out to her, but she remained there, teetering on the edge for a long minute. When she came in from outside, she said that she wanted the experience of how those girls must have felt when faced with the choice of either being burned alive or falling ten floors to their deaths.

She asked Gardner what he would do, but he had no answer. Finally, she admitted what she would have done: "I'd jump, praying that a net is waiting for me."

The picture was never made, although Gardner worked on the script for a full two years. Streisand moved on to *Yentl* (1983) and Jane switched to working instead on *The China Syndrome* about a near-meltdown of a nuclear plant.

***

Comes a Horseman (1978)

At the wrap of *Coming Home*, Jane Fonda had turned forty and vowed to take better care of herself. Her next film would be a Western drama but not a typical Old West saga. This one would take place at the end of World War II in Colorado, where she fights with a cattle baron and oil tycoon to hold onto her ranchland.

She was looking forward to being directed again by Alan J. Pakula, who had helmed her in her Oscar-winning *Klute* (1971), the story of a prostitute.

This Western was remarkably different from her other more famous and more successful cowgirl picture, *Cat Ballou* (1965) This time around, Jason Robards Jr. is not her lover (as he'd been in both *Julia* and in *Any Wednesday* but her enemy, a land baron trying to take over her ranch.

In this new picture, Jane would play Ella Connors whose family had owned it for two generations.

Her leading man and fellow

Jane Fonda and **James Caan** indulge in a high plains romance in *Comes a Horseman*. In it, Jane battles a greedy cattle tycoon who is trying to take her land.

Caan comes to her rescue, although in the end, they lose to an oil company.

In most westerns, men fought the battles, but in this one, Jane emerges as the more tenacious, a strong yet vulnerable woman of the West.

rancher was James Caan, cast as Frank ("Buck") Athearn. He joins her in her fight. During the course of the film, her character falls in love with him.

Norman Jewison described Caan as "having football-field shoulders, blue eyes as bright as those of Paul Newman, tight-knit fair hair receding from a tanned forehead. The scars above his nose and above his right eyebrow are not from rodeo riding but from taking a stab at bullfighting."

Caan's signature happened when Francis Ford Coppola, his former college mate, cast him in the role of Sonny Corleone in *The Godfather* (1972) starring Marlon Brando. Caan was nominated for a Best Supporting Actor Oscar.

Coppola had also cast Caan in *The Rain People* (1969), starring Shirley Knight. At the time that it was made, Caan was living with fellow actor Robert Duvall. They were making some films together, so the director decided to give Duvall the third lead.

Jane may have found that her favorite role starring Caan was *Cinderella Liberty* (1973), in which he plays a sailor who falls in love with a prostitute and becomes a surrogate father to her 10-year-old mixed-race son. Marsha Mason played the prostitute mother.

Caan's big hit was *Funny Lady* (1975), playing vaudeville impresario to Barbra Streisand's Fanny Brice.

Ironically, in Hollywood, Caan developed a kind of notoriety for the roles he rejected: *M*A*S*H; The French Connection; One Flew Over the Cuckoo's Nest; Close Encounters of the Third Kind; Kramer vs. Kramer* ("middle class bourgeois baloney" he called it); *Apocalypse Now;* and *Superman* ("I didn't want to wear a cape").

Dry heat, as the character Jane played learned, is bad for a girl's skin. Here's **Jane Fonda**, unafraid to fully look her age, in a worn-out moment in *Comes a Horseman*.

Her director, Alan Pakula, had advised her to play it "rawhide tough," and Jane acquiesced.

Jane Fonda and James Caan were miles apart politically. In 2016, as a "very conservative," he voted for Donald Trump as President. "The only news channel I watch is Fox," he said at the time.

In her portrayal of a woman engaged in a fight against land barons and oil tycoons, Pakula advised Jane to play it "rawhide tough. I want you to show as much passion as Gary Cooper did in *High Noon* (1952) or John Wayne in anything."

Another menace for ranch-owning Ella (Fonda) was Neil Atkinson, a rich oil company executive played by George Grizzard. He and Jane in 1961 had appeared together on stage in W. Somerset Maugham's *A String of Beads*. On Broadway, Grizzard had starred in the original production of Edward Albee's *Who's Afraid of Virginia Woolf?*

Mark Harmon was cast as Billy Joe Meynert, a fellow vet and partner to Buck (Caan). In 1986, the former college football player would become *People* magazine's "Sexiest Man Alive."

In the role of "Dodgers," Richard Farnsworth is an assistant to Ella (Jane) on her ranch. For his work on the film, he would receive an Academy Award nomination for Best Supporting Actor.

At 16, he was working as a stable boy on a polo field in Los Angeles, and he later became a stuntman in the Kirk Douglas picture *Spartacus* (1960). Years before that, Farnsworth had had an uncredited role in *Gone With the Wind* (1939).

Like so many actors who worked with Jane, Farnsworth would commit suicide in 2002 when he was suffering from terminal cancer. His last words were, "I was not made to play a role in the 21st Century."

Comes a Horseman was hyped as THE WEST WAS WON BY MEN BUT CHALLENGED BY A WOMAN. At the box office, it did not fare as well as some of Jane's other "comeback films," but it did earn a respectable $9.5 million.

Richard Greier in *Cosmopolitan* noted: "Here, we are in a grim, stark world of deep hatreds, primitive living conditions, and desperate economics. The dialogue of *Horseman* is sparse, hard-bitten and so laconic that it can be hard to follow."

The critic for *McCall's* magazine cited "the tender relationship between Fonda and Caan almost redeems the dull and draggy post-World War II Western about Fonda's fight to keep her ranch. It's refreshing to see a movie in which sexual attraction depends upon more than good looks or a fast line."

Time magazine wrote, "Alan Pakula seems incapable of visual sloppiness or vulgarity. He also coaxed a performance from Fonda superior to her rather saintly appearances in *Julia* and *Coming Home*. Her face is as weather beaten as her Dad's in *Grapes of Wrath*. This beautiful woman manages to capture the essence of frontier toughness in the film's first half. When she finally melts for a man, her blushing radiance almost melts a movie that long since congealed."

In the *Washington Post,* Gary Arnold wrote, "Pakula may claim he reveres Westerns, but his form of respectful imitation is lifeless, strictly token respect for the dead. By the time *Comes a Horseman* wheezes to an anticlimactic fadeout, Robard's depredations have begun to resemble Gothic camp."

In *Variety's* review, it was stated that the movie is "so lethargic that even James Caan, Jane Fonda, and Jason Robards can't bring excitement to this artificially dramatic story of a stubborn rancher who won't surrender her land to a local land baron."

***

California Suite (1978)

Jane's previous trio of films—one of which was an Oscar winner—had restored her image in Hollywood as an actress of beauty, talent, and charisma.

As a change of pace, she agreed to take on a small role, and a rather unsympathetic one at that, in *California Suite*. In it, she would play Hannah Warren, a tough-as-nails editor at *Newsweek* in Manhattan—or, in the words of Fonda herself—"a bitch."

Neil Simon based its filmscript on his play that had opened on Broadway two years before. Similar to another of his hits, *Plaza Suite,* the movie version consisted of black and white actors divided into different segments, each with a subplot of its own, a sort of mixed stew of humanity all arriving at the Beverly Hills Hotel.

At the time, Simon was the hottest playwright on Broadway, burying other writers with his Oscars and Tony awards. Along with Robert Redford as her stuffy husband, Jane had co-starred in an earlier work by Simon, *Barefoot in the Park* (1963).

Still sexy in a bikini at the age of 40, **Jane Fonda** in *California Suite* appears in a beach scene with her character's former husband, played by **Alan Alda**, not usually marketed as a male bathing beauty. "My waist is smaller now than it was when I was 20," Jane told the press.

Soon, her workout regimens would be publicized across the country.

California Suite was produced by Herbert Ross, who by 1988 would marry Lee Radziwill, the sister of Jacqueline Kennedy Onassis. The son of Russian Jewish immigrants, he was also a choreographer, having turned out such productions as *On a Clear Day, You Can See Forever* (1965). He'd made his directorial debut with the musical version of *Goodbye, Mr. Chips* (1969) starring Peter O'Toole. For his second feature as a director, he starred Barbra Streisand in *The Owl and the Pussycat* (1970).

Ray Stark was the producer of *California Suite*. Stark would produce eight films with Ross, and he'd also sustain an 18-year partnership with Neil Simon. Stark's hits include *West Side Story* (1961) and *Funny Girl* (1968) starring Streisand as Fanny Brice. All in all, Stark was the most successful and prolific independent producer in postwar Hollywood.

Simon, Ross, and Stark hired eight of the most talented actors in Hollywood to perform in the different "playlets" about guests arriving at a (Californian) luxury hotel.

In Jane's segment, (it was entitled "Visitors from New York"), she would play Hannah, a Manhattan workaholic who wings into Los Angeles to retrieve her daughter Jenna (Dana Plata) from her ex-husband, Bill Warren (Alan Alda).

Before the end of their bickering, both parents will have to decide which environment is better for Jenny, New York or California.

Alda, the actor, director, screenwriter, and comedian, had just made *Same Time, Next Year* (1978) co-starring Ellen Burstyn.

While working with Jane on *California Suite,* Alda was still under contract to the hit TV series, *M*A*S*H* in which he played Hawkeye Pierce.

The most lauded member of the movie's cast was Maggie Smith, a Londoner, star of stage and screen. Since the mid-1950s, she had appeared in sixty films and seventy plays. In 1969, she'd won the Best Actress Oscar for *The Prime of Miss Jean Brodie*. She would also win the Oscar that spring as Best Supporting Actress in *California Suite*.

According to the plot, her character was flying into Hollywood because she'd been nominated for a Best Actress Oscar, although she had no hope of winning. As the movie progresses, she switches from hope to panic to despair.

She is married to Sidney Cochran (Michael Caine), a closeted gay antique dealer with a fondness for handsome young men. He is becoming more and more indiscreet about his homosexual hookups.

Over the course of her career, Smith was usually typecast as impeccably and relentlessly British. On stage, she had been hailed as "the finest living Lady Macbeth." She had also starred in another Neil Simon film, *Murder by Death* (1976) opposite David Niven.

While working in Los Angeles, she gave an interview: "I didn't have any scenes with Jane, but we had numerous conversations. She's willing to endure certain hardships and criticism from several quarters to better the country she was born into."

"I told her that if I were a bit younger—and sexier—I would adore working with some of these American machos—most notably with Warren Beatty, Ryan O'Neal, and Robert Redford. I adore films that team American men with the women of England—take *Yanks*, for example, with Vanessa Redgrave and Richard Gere."

On the set, Jane had a reunion with Caine, who'd been her co-star in *Hurry Sundown (1967)* in which he'd played her husband in a doomed marriage.

In another segment, "Visitors from Philadelphia," a middle-aged businessman, Marvin Michaels (Walter Matthau), wakes up in bed with a prostitute whose services had been arranged as part of an unexpected "gift" from his brother, Harry (Herb Edelman). There is trouble on the way. Marvin's wife, Mille (Elaine May), is heading for his suite.

On Broadway, Matthau had originated the

This photo, one of a batch of several promotional pix issued by Columbia Pictures for *California Suite*, describes its subjects, **Michael Caine** and **Maggie Smith**, as "looking very much married." It wasn't true.

He was cast as a homosexual.

role of Oscar Madison in *The Odd Couple,* also by Neil Simon. He'd received a Best Actor Tony for that performance. He would also star in ten films with Jack Lemmon, critics viewing them as "the perfect couple."

A comedian, Elaine May made her initial impact in the 1950s with her improvisational comedy routines with Mike Nichols. May had also directed the black screwball comedy, *A New Leaf* (1971) in which she also had starred opposite Matthau.

Right before working on *California Suite,* May had received a Best Adapted Screenplay Oscar for her screenplay of *Heaven Can Wait* (1978) starring Warren Beatty.

In yet another of *California Suite's* subdivisions ("Visitors from Chicago"), Dr. Chauncey Gump (Richard Pryor) and Dr. Willis Panama (Bill Cosby) and his wife Bettina (Sheila Frazier) arrive at the hotel for their vacation, but everything seems to go wrong. The two husbands must resolve their differences, not in a brawl, but in a tennis match.

Cosby, a son of Philadelphia, started out as a stand-up comedian. After appearing in *California Suite,* he would become "America's Dad" because of his starring role in his hit TV sitcom, *The Cosby Show* (1984-1992).

At the time, he was a beloved figure, but during the years after that, he'd morph into a national disgrace because of accusations of rape, sexual assault, sexual battery, child sexual abuse, and general misconduct.

In 2016, his attorneys revealed in court that Cosby is legally blind.

Pryor, hailing from Illinois, is widely regarded as one of the greatest and most influential stand-up comedians of all time. In 2017, *Rolling Stone* ranked him Number One on its list of best comedians.

He never worried about being politically correct, releasing such recordings as the 1974 "That Nigger is Crazy" (1974); and "Bicentennial Nigger" (1976). Pryor continued working steadily until his death in 2005.

AN EVENING WITH MIKE NICHOLS AND ELAINE MAY

Women We Love and/or **Comedy Acts We Remember**

One of the co-authors of this book remembers, how, when he was eight years old, he heard a recorded, "on vinyl" recording of ***An Evening with Mick Nichols and Elaine May*** and never forgot some of the gags, gigs, and punch lines.

Woody Allen defined Nichols and May like this: "Individually, each one is a genius, and when they worked together, the sum was even greater than the combination of the parts—the two of them came along and elevated comedy to a brand-new level"

The playbill from their stage debut, which opened on Broadway in October of 1960, is displayed above.

At the age of 40, Jane was told that for a beach scene, she would have to wear a very brief bikini. To prepare herself for the role, she underwent many strenuous workout regimes.

At the end of filming her segment, Jane gave her review of life in California. "I can't wait to get out of here. It's like paradise with a lobotomy."

She also asserted that she enjoyed working with Alda. "He's the only man I ever met who calls himself a feminist."

For the most part, reviews were favorable, although with the inevitable attack. *Cue* magazine found that Jane as a performer "did so with flair and feeling." Stephen Farber of *New West* magazine thought that "Fonda's Hannah Warren is tough, testy, and snobbish, in contrast to her ex-husband (Alda), a model of laid-back California casualness."

Vincent Canby of *The New York Times* praised Ross and others for "having assembled a dream cast, especially Jane Fonda and Maggie Smith."

Time Out New York found that the picture suited Neil Simon's "machine gun gag-writing. Jane Fonda provides the film's center, giving another performance of unnerving sureness."

Channel 4 claimed, "*California Suite* is expertly crafted, a slick movie that sets up each of its coconuts and knocks them over with a sure eye, but ultimately it's emotional sushi rather than a satisfying catharsis."

California Suite made *The New York Times* list of the "Best 1000 Movies Ever Made."

***

The China Syndrome (1979)

Jane's next movie was a disaster film about the meltdown of a nuclear power plant. After a number of working titles were proposed, it was eventually entitled *The China Syndrome*. Before it morphed its way through several rewrites, the projected picture began its life as a fictionalized story about the doomed Karen Silkwood.

Jane started working on Silkwood's tragic story with Bruce Gilbert, her business partner at her IPC film production company, which operated outside the control of any major studio.

A native of Longview, Texas, and born in 1946, Silkwood became a chemical technician and labor union activist whose main concerns involved corporation-sanctioned health and safety issues at a nuclear facility.

She was employed by the Kerr-McGee Cimarron Fuel Fabrication Company near Crescent, Oklahoma. She soon discovered what she believed to be numerous violations of health regulations, including exposure of workers to nuclear contamination.

In the summer of 1974, she testified before the Atomic Energy Commission (AEC). A few months later, she discovered that her body contained almost 400 times the legal limit for plutonium contamination.

On the morning of November 13, 1974, when she was 28 years old, while driving to the site of a pre-arranged rendezvous with a reporter (David Burnham) from *The New York Times*, the car she was driving crashed under mysterious circumstances and she was killed.

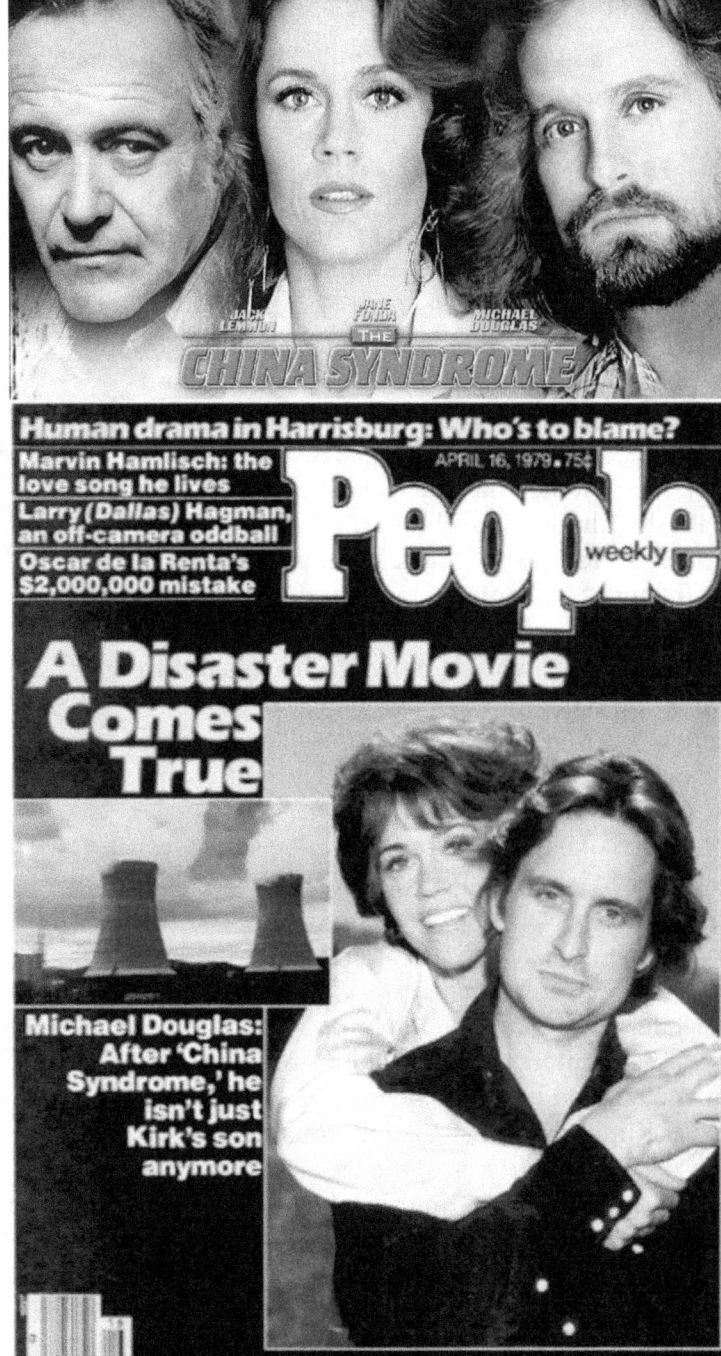

In *The China Syndrome*, **Jane Fonda** found a script and a role that combined her penchant for activism with filmmaking. Then, with the breakout of nuclear contamination from Three Mile Island near Harrisburg, Pennsylvania, fiction became reality.

In the *upper photo*, she appears between her co-stars Jack Lemmon (*left*) and Michael Douglas. In the *lower photo*, *People* magazine seems poised to both report horrifying news and also to publicize the film.

With her, she carried documentation to substantiate her claims. Her intentions involved publicizing the ineffective worker safety policies of Kerr-McGee, especially as they applied to exposing its workers to contamination.

When the police found her wrecked car with her dead body inside, all the documentation she'd carried had been removed. It appeared that another vehicle had rammed into hers in an act of sabotage that resulted in her death.

After lawsuits from her family, the company finally paid out $1.38 million without admitting liability.

When a screen treatment about Silkwood's life and death was ready, Jane and Gilbert met with David Begelman at Columbia, finding him mired in his own problems, many of them related to his embezzling of company funds. She also learned that Michael Douglas had submitted a script about a nuclear meltdown. She and Michael had something in common: Each was the daughter or son of a major-league movie star, Henry Fonda and Kirk Douglas.

Karen Silkwood

Jane and Michael lunched together and worked out an agreement to pool their projects into one script. What emerged was *The China Syndrome*. At the time, Michael had great success with the film he'd produced, *One Flew Over the Cuckoo's Nest*, starring Jack Nicholson.

Douglas had gone so far as to sign Jack Lemmon for the important role of Jack Godell, a plant manager whistle blower who sets out to expose his corrupt bosses at a nuclear-powered generator. Michael had cast himself as Richard Adams, a cameraman who inadvertently captures, on film, a nuclear meltdown.

Much of it had focused on a television news reporter in a role to be interpreted by Richard Dreyfuss. He had recently scored a big success in the mega-hit, *Jaws* (1975). Based on that, he was demanding that his salary be tripled. Michael refused and let him go.

Jane wanted to star in the film, hoping to turn what had been a male role into the character of Kimberly Wells, an ambitious reporter of *exposés* that would reveal the true story of what was going on at a technically flawed and very dangerous nuclear plant.

The alleged murder of **Karen Silkwood**, a whistleblower at a plutonium extraction unit of Kerr-Mcgee, has mystified researchers and activists since her unexplained death in 1974. Immediately above is a photo of the wreckage of the car she died in.

Widespread newspaper coverage at the time of her death, and later, Meryl Streep's performance in the film *Silkwood* (1983), alerted the public to the dangers of nuclear contamination and the steps that miscreants will take to conceal them.

The very existence of *The China Syndrome* derived from a collaboration of Jane Fonda with Michael Douglas. Each was a fervent activist, and each was the by-product of parents who had been A-list actors in Golden Age Hollywood.

Michael agreed to replace Dreyfuss with Jane. He also reached out to Mike Gray to direct the picture.

Since Gray had actually studied to become a nuclear engineer, he seemed to be the most qualified to unwind the plot. He'd been a producer of minor documentaries, as well as a writer, director, and cinematographer. Jane did not want him as her director, yet parts of his script would be used, although with many pages added by the new director, James Bridges and T.S. Cook. She told Gray that he was just too unknown. *[Ironically, Bridges himself wasn't that well known either.]*

She had been impressed with his direction of *The Paper Chase* (1973), a film that had starred Timothy Bottoms, Lindsay Wagner, and John Houseman. *[Houseman had won a Best Supporting Actor Oscar for his performance in it as a Harvard law professor.]*

When Jane met with Bridges, she found he was also preparing a script called *Urban Cowboy*. Scheduled for a release in 1980, it would star John Travolta and Debra Winger. The action would revolve around a football-themed honky tonk in Pasadena, Texas, a citadel of country music.

The director (Bridges) was gay and had been in a long-term relationship with Jack Larson, the former lover of Montgomery Clift, since 1959. Larson was an actor, librettist, screenwriter, and producer. Most TV addicts knew him for his portrayal of cub reporter Jimmy Olsen in the TV series, *Adventures of Superman*.

A lot of people didn't understand the title. *The China Syndrome* was a fanciful term that described the theoretical aftermath of a nuclear meltdown in which superheated components of the reactor would melt through their containment structures and sink deep into the earth in a sea of molten lava "all the way to China."

[At this point, Jane and Bruce Gilbert had long-ago abandoned their script documenting the experiences of Karen Silkwood. Mike Nichols, however, would direct the biographical drama named Silkwood *(1983). It starred Meryl Streep as the twenty-something protagonist, along with Cher in her first serious work, with Kurt Russell as the male lead. Its script was by Nora Ephon.]*

At the 56th Academy Awards presentation, Silkwood *received five Oscar nominations, including Streep as Best Actress; Cher as Best Supporting Actress; and Nichols as Best Director.]*

Most critics cited Jack Lemmon as the nuclear plant's manager for giving the best performance in *The China Syndrome*. The talented actor was adept at both drama and comedy, although he would be forever celebrated for his performance in drag with Tony Curtis (also in drag) in *Some Like it Hot* (1959) with Marilyn Monroe. *[In that movie, Lemmon is pursued by Joe E. Brown. When he learns Lemmon's true sexual identity as a man, he is still willing to carry on with their affair. "Nobody's perfect," he exclaims just before THE END appears on the screen. Perhaps he knew all along that Lemmon was no lady.]*

Mostly, Lemmon was known for all those pictures in which he co-starred with Walter Matthau.

Some of his most notable works include *The Apartment* (1960) with Shirley MacLaine, and *Days of Wine and Roses* (1962) with Lee Remick.

Jane had met him when he'd played Ensign Pulver in *Mister Roberts* (1955), the movie Lemmon had made with her father. Jane admitted to him that she'd had a big crush on him at the time.

"Why didn't you tell me?" he asked. "We could have done something about that."

Michael Douglas, who was seven years younger than Jane, having been born in 1944, was as good an actor as he was a producer. For having produced *One Flew Over the Cuckoo's Nest* (1975), based on the Ken Kesey novel, he'd won the Academy Award for Best Picture.

Many more awards and acclaimed motion pictures lay in his future, movies such as the musical *A Chorus Line* (1985) and the psychological thriller, *Fatal Attraction* (1987).

Douglas even played the campy Liberace in the HBO film, *Behind the Candelabra,* in which his faked gay love scenes under the

Bad, Belligerent, and Handsome

Upper photo: **Scott Brady,** as he appeared as The Dancing Kid in *Johnny Guitar*, had seen better days by the time he appeared in *The China Syndrome* with Jane Fonda.

Lower photo: As promoted by this poster for screenings of *Johnny Guitar* at a California "drive-in and make-out" movie theater in 1954, he was ***"Crawford's kind of man."***

sheets with a nude Matt Damon as his lover.

He was famously married to Catherine Zeta-Jones.

In *The China Syndrome,* the "hot, hell-raising hunk" Scott Brady had the fourth lead as Herman de Young.

Brady was the brother of "Bad Boy" actor Lawrence Tierney, who often got arrested for his drunken brawls. Brady had been a star football player before enlisting in the U.S. Army during World War II. He'd also been a boxer and a lumberjack. His reputation in Hollywood quickly spread, and he was sought out by gay directors and horny women. When, as the "Dancin' Kid," he'd appeared with Joan Crawford in *Johnny Guitar* (1954), she'd demanded at least two intimate encounters per day from him, usually in her dressing room. Among his many lovers were Anne Bancroft and Merv Griffin.

***

In his role of Jack Godell, the nuclear facility's manager, Lemmon portrays an honest man who comes to realize that the nuclear plant poses a deadly threat to the surrounding region and its inhabitants. He also learns that his corrupt bosses have been falsifying their safety reports, most of them insisting that the plant is "not a menace at all."

When Godell tries to come forward with the truth, he is ultimately killed by the company's "hit man." Before dying, he feels, once again, the unusual vibrations of the nuclear plant—a sign of impending disaster.

Kimberly Wells (Jane) witnesses an accident at a nuclear power plant. As a hard-nosed reporter, she wants to go public with news of the disaster, but she soon becomes locked into a sinister conspiracy to keep it under wraps. Her cameraman, Richard Adams (Michael Douglas), had surreptitiously filmed the incident, although security had not granted him permission. It was concluded that the plant had come perilously close to meltdown...in other words, "The China Syndrome."

As a girl, Jane had read comic strips devoted to Brenda Starr, girl reporter. For *The China Syndrome,* she demanded that her hairdresser give her the same red-hair treatment as displayed in the comics.

During the final weeks of filming, Jane had an accident that fractured her right foot, forcing her to wear a cast and to walk on crutches. As her director, Bridges was able to camouflage her infirmity.

Jane was reported to have suffered through many anxious nights during the filming of *The China Syndrome.* As she told Bridges, "I kept dreaming that my husband (Tom Hayden) left me. When not plagued by that, I dreamt of my poor dogs drowning."

During her filming of *The China Syndrome,* Hayden appeared on television as the subject of an interview by Barbara Walters.

"What is it like for your family to have such a famous actress as Jane Fonda as a wife and mother in your household?"

"It turns out that the kids and I are mere props," was his off-putting reply.

Lemmon later made three TV documentaries about air pollution, nuclear power, and other issues. For doing that, George Murphy, the U.S. Senator from California and a former film star, called him "a son of a bitch."

Hundreds of letters attacked Lemmon. "I was called a commie, a pinko, and a perverted fag bastard," he said. "Even before the release of *The China Syndrome,* a lot of pressure was brought on Columbia to not release it. Some of the executives there were scared shitless."

The China Syndrome premiered at the 1979 Cannes Film Festival, where it competed for the Palme D'Or. Lemmon walked off with the Best Actor of the Year honor. Its theatrical release was on March 16, 1979. It became a critical and commercial success, although many critics found the plot unbelievable, calling it "gross fiction."

Richard Schickel, the chief reviewer for *Time* gave his opinion: "The movie depicts the utility company that owns the plant and the contractor that built it resorting to lies, corruption, and violence to prevent the public from discovering how narrowly a disaster was averted, how large is the potential for similar incidents in the future—and never mind the sizable body of scientific opinion about the improbability of a chain of accidents anything like that proposed in the film."

A reviewer in Kansas City wrote, "The entire plot of *The China Syndrome* is not only bizarre, but a conceit of Lemmon and Fonda. It might be okay as sci fi, but as a realistic event, it is pure claptrap. Nearly all advocates of nuclear energy felt that 'these phony theatrics' will alarm the country and perhaps endanger its pursuit of desperately needed energy sources."

The nuclear power plant at Three Mile Island, near Harrisburg, Pennsylvania (*left photo*) and this image (*right photo*) of **Michael Douglas** with his co-star, **Jane Fonda**, in The China Syndrone seemed to eerily juxtaposition a real-life event with its cinematic advance preview.

Critics of the film, however, were deeply embarrassed twelve days after its release when the Three Mile Island nuclear accident near Harrisburg, Pennsylvania, burst onto the news scene. The film's subject matter became an unexpected prescience, and lines at the box office at many theaters stretched around the block.

At 4AM on the morning of March 28, 1979, the most significant accident in U.S. commercial nuclear power plant history (at Three Mile Island) took place. It began with failures in the non-nuclear secondary system followed by a stuck-open pilot-operated relief valve in the primary system that allowed large amounts of nuclear reactor coolant to escape.

Jane was later told that a major explosion of the plant could lay to waste the entire land area of the State of Pennsylvania.

In the *Chicago Sun-Times,* Roger Ebert called the movie "a terrific thriller that incidentally raises the most unsettling questions about how safe nuclear power plants really are. The movie is well-acted, well-crafted, scary as hell. The events leading up to the 'accident' in *The China Syndrome* are indeed based on actual occurrences at nuclear plants. Even the most unlikely mishap (a stuck needle on a graph causing engineers to misread a crucial water level) really happened at the Dresden plant outside Chicago. And yet the movie works so well not because of its factual basis but because of its human content. The performances are so good, so consistently, that *The China Syndrome* becomes a thriller dealing in personal values."

Movie reviewers in London wrote, "The power of this movie is more than just acting, although Lemmon is superb. It is that this scenario could really happen. The atmosphere produced in the plant's control room is heart-stoppingly intense, and the characters are uniformly well-acted. I recommended *The China Syndrome* as an example of the dangers of money and corruption."

John Simon called the film "taut, intelligent, and chillingly gripping until it turns melodramatic at the end. The ending is both false and bathetic."

For her services as an actress, Jane was paid one million dollars. However, since the movie grossed more than $52 million at the box office, her real money derived from her status as head of IPC Films, *[It had cost $6 million to produce.]* In the final tally, IPC took in $350 million from the five films it released.

After the release of *The China Syndrome,* Hayden and Jane began to lobby against the use (and existence) of nuclear power plants.

At the 52nd Academy Awards ceremony, both Lemmon and Jane were nominated as Best Actor and Actress. Jane lost to Sally Field for *Norma Rae.*

***

The Electric Horseman (1979)

Beginning in 1973, Robert Redford, Jane's former co-star, experienced an amazing four-year run of box office triumph. His winning streak began to cool only after his Western, *Jeremiah Johnson* (1974), became that year's number two highest-grossing movie.

Competitors included Barbra Streisand's *The Way We Were* (1973), which morphed into Number Eleven among that year's box office hits. The crime caper with Paul Newman, *The Sting* (1973), became the top-grossing film of 1974. The film adaptation of F. Scott Fitzgerald's novel, *The Great Gatsby* (also 1974) was Number Eight that year, too.

By the mid-1970s, Redford had morphed into Hollywood's top box office star. *All the President's Men* (1976), in which he'd co-starred Dustin Hoffman in a film about the Watergate scandal, was the Number One box office hit of that year.

Finally, Redford took a two-year hiatus from the movies before returning to film an adventure romance, *The Electric Horseman* with Jane Fonda. She had previously co-starred with him in *The Chase* (1966) alongside Marlon Brando as the lead, and also in the film adaptation of Neil Simon's *Barefoot in the Park* (1967).

The Electric Horseman brought together reoccurring collaborations among cast and crew. It marked the fifth film in which Sydney Pollack had helmed Redford. The others included *This Property is Condemned* (1966); *Jeremiah Johnson* (1972); *The Way We Were* (1973); and *Three Days of the Condor* (1975).

Pollack and Redford would go on to make two more movies together—*Out of Africa* (1985) and *Havana* (1990).

In *The Electric Horseman*, Redford was cast as Sonny Steele, a former championship rodeo rider who is now reduced to making public appearances hawking a brand of breakfast cereal. At a promotional appearance in Las Vegas, he discovers that the $12 million champion thoroughbred, Rising Star, has been drugged and injured.

He decides to kidnap the horse and travel cross-country to release him into the wilderness, a remote canyon where he can join other wild horses.

Once again, as in *The China Syndrome*, Jane is cast as a television reporter, Hallie Martin. Sensing a hot story, she trails Sonny into the countryside. This leads to a romance before they part at the end.

Cynics and wits quipped that this shot of **Jane Fonda's** *derrière* was a tacit agreement that she had—by her own admission—always considered her backside one of her greatest assets.

Here it is on ample display as a come-on for a country-western parable about a lonesome cowboy on a voyage of self-discovery and the rehab of a broken-down racehorse.

[This was the second film for Jane to appear in a film with the word "Horseman" in its title. For a 1978 release, she had previously starred with James Caan in Comes a Horseman.*]*

Redford, who would receive payments totaling $3.5 million, requested Jane as his leading lady. For her involvement, she was paid a million dollars.

Ray Stark was brought in as its producer, and he arranged for most of the movie to be shot in Utah and outside Las Vegas within the Red Rock National Conservation Area.

The most difficult shot was a kissing scene involving Redford and Jane. Although the final scene lasted for only twenty seconds on the screen, its filming was frequently interrupted because of traveling thunderstorms. It ended up requiring 48 takes, and cost $280,000. The film went over budget, costing $12.5

million. That figure was easily offset by the $62 million it took in at the box office.

Unlike most of the crew, Jane was not a devotee of Las Vegas, referring to it as "a place built on greed, representing the worst of our culture."

On two different occasions, both Redford and Pollack had rejected the script of *The Electric Horseman* before finally accepting it. They had wanted to film a script with the title of *A Place to Come To*, but that had not worked out. They returned to the *Horseman* script but kept little of its original plot. It was vastly rewritten.

Pollack claimed, "For *Electric Horseman*, I literally ended up writing half of it every night before the next day's shoot. We made jokes about my saying, 'Let's pick the most remote location possible, 'cause I'll have time to write the scene by the time we get there.' That was literally true. There were yellow pads all over the place. We were writing the script on the way to work every morning."

Another key role was cast with Willie Nelson (see below). Valerie Perrine was cast as Charlotte, the estranged wife of Sonny; and John Saxon as Hunt Sears.

Singing star Willie Nelson, born during the Great Depression in Texas, wrote his first song at the age of seven. In time, after service in the U.S. Air Force, he became one of the major figures in "the outlaw country," a subgenre of country music that developed during the late 1960s as a reaction to the restrictions of the Nashville sound. He later was one of the major advocates of the legalization of marijuana.

Robert Redford appears above as part of his character's rodeo act.

As reviewed by Vincent Leo in 2007, "In *The Electric Horseman*, Redford plays a former rodeo champion who has spent his retirement years shilling boxes of cereal that he doesn't eat and making public appearances for a corporation called Ampco, riding in rodeos adorned with glowing light bulbs. He's often late, drunk, and depressed, but finally wakes up from his stupor when he makes a Vegas appearance in a publicity event that would have him riding a former thoroughbred champion racehorse, Rising Star. After finding out the horse is injured and injected full of steroids, Sonny decides to snatch the $12 million horse and make the long trek to set it free in horse country."

Jane Fonda, as seen with Redford in the photo below, once again plays a scrappy reporter, this time one who's interested in the human aspects of what she hopes to craft into a feature article. Naturally, as part of the film's "feel-good" dynamic, she falls madly in love.

One success followed another after the release of his first album, *Shotgun Willie* in 1973. Many of his songs became country standards, including "Funny How Time Slips Away."

In 1990, the IRS seized his assets, claiming that he owed $32 million in back taxes. The auction of his assets cleared the debt. Over the years, he continued to work in musical genres that included reggae, blues, jazz, and folk.

The Electric Horseman marked his film debut. In it, he portrayed "Wendell." According to Pollack, Nelson improvised most of his dialogue. Pollack later became the executive producer of Nelson's 1980 starring vehicle, *Honeysuckle Rose*.

Nelson teamed with Redford again in *The Natural*.

In *The Electric Horseman*, Nelson sang five songs, including "Midnight Rider" and "Mammas Don't Let Your Babies Grow Up to be Cowboys."

Valerie Perrine emerged from Galveston, Texas, to play Charlotta Steele, the ex-wife of rodeo champion Redford in *The Electric Horseman.*

After working with Redford and Jane, her career became uneven. For her role in *Can't Stop the Music* (1980), she was nominated for a Razzie Award as Worst Actress of the Year. She had better luck in 1982, playing Marcy, the wife of a corrupt police officer in *The Border,* starring Jack Nicholson.

In *Lenny* (1974), she played Honey Bruce, the wife of the controversial comedian. At the time she worked with Jane, she was cast in *Superman* (1978) and also in its sequel, *Superman II* (1980).

In Kurt Vonnegut's *Slaughterhouse-Five* (1972), she played soft-core porn actress Montana Wildhack. That same year, Hugh Hefner persuaded her to pose nude for a layout in his May 1972 issue of *Playboy.* She became the first actress to appear nude on television by showing her breasts during a May 1973 broadcast of Bruck Jay Friedman's *Steambath* for Hollywood Television Theater.

In the minor role of Hunt Sears, the handsome actor, John Saxon would star in film and television in some 200 projects before his death at the age of 83 in the summer of 2020. He often played police officers or detectives and was frequently seen in horror films and Westerns.

Once, he migrated to Italy to find work. Studios in Rome employed him throughout the 1970s and '80s. "I was a hunky leading man in the 1950s, but my career in Hollywood dwindled down to drive-in junk."

"Occasionally, I got to bed one of my leading ladies, Sandra Dee and an older Lana Turner come to mind. However, Audrey Hepburn turned me down."

Starring opposite Marlon Brando in *Appaloosa* (1966), Saxon was nominated for a Golden Globe Award as Best Supporting Actor.

The Electric Horseman was released in the United States on December 21, 1979, and became the 11th highest-grossing film of that year.

Jack Kroll of *Newsweek* wrote, "Will we ever see Jane Fonda and Robert Redford playing people with no virtue? Those on the wrong side of great issues, scurvy meanies, wrongos instead of rightos. Don't bet on it. That's too bad, because we need Lady Macbeths as well as Cordelias, Iagos as well as Othellos. You'd think that high-voltage actors like Fonda and Redford would want to transmit both negative and positive electricity as human beings."

Roger Ebert of the *Chicago Sun-Times* claimed that *The Electric Horseman* "is the kind of movie the film colony used to make. It's a love story about a guy and a girl and a prize racehorse, and it has a chase scene, some smooching, and a happy ending. In the old days, it could have starred

Whatever Happened to Valerie Perrine, Centerfold Goddess of the 80s?

Long ago and far away, after her appearance with "Jane and Bob," in *The Electric Horseman,* and back when disco was king, **Valerie Perrine** made news at least twice, once (*upper photo*) when she co-starred with Steve Guttenberg (left) and a bare-midriffed **Bruce Jenner** (*right*) in the cult artifact and "Discosploitation" film, *Can't Stop the Music; (1980),* a pseudo-biography of *The Village People.*

In the *lower photo* she appears as the cover girl and centerfold star of the August, 1981 edition of *Playboy* in a t-shirt that evokes her appearance in *Superman* (1978).

Since then, Bruce changed his gender to female, and his name to Caitlin.

Perrine, born in Galveston, Texas in 1943, won a lot of awards during the course of her highly visible career in Hollywood. For her role as Honey Bruce in the 1974 film *Lenny* (1974), she won the BAFTA Award for Most Promising Newcomer to Leading Film Roles; the Cannes Film Festival Award for Best Actress; and was nominated for the Academy Award for Best Actress. She is also viewed as an early advocate of "tasteful bare-breastedness" in other, earlier, film roles and magazine spreads.

Katharine Hepburn and Spencer Tracy, perhaps Clark Gable and Claudette Colbert."

Gene Siskel of the *Chicago Tribune* defined the film as "a nicely polished piece of entertainment with genuine chemistry between Redford and Fonda."

Vincent Canby in *The New York Times* wrote, "Miss Fonda, in addition to being a fine dramatic actress, is a first-rate comedienne, whether she's stumbling over a Utah mountain in her chic, spike-heeled patent leather boots or suddenly becoming shy after a night well spent in the cowboy's sleeping bag."

Another reviewer pointed out that "In their love scenes, Redford and Fonda actually make you believe that pure virtue is the strongest of aphrodisiacs."

***

9 to 5 (1980)

Jane claimed that "the nugget of an idea" for *9 to 5* began in Paris when she worked for the *Paris Review*. "I was fired when I refused to sleep with my boss."

Before its filming began, she conducted a series of private interviews with dozens of secretaries, hearing their tales of sexual harassments from their bosses.

She met with female clerks at banks whose wages were so low that they were sustained by food stamps. Often, women were bypassed in favor of men they had trained.

"My ideas for films always come from things I hear and perceive in my daily life," Jane said. "A very old friend of mine started an organization called 'nine to five,' about an association of women office workers. I heard them talking about their work, and they had some great stories to relay. I've always been attracted to those 1940s films with three female stars."

Part of Jane's research would focus on women who had begun their careers late in life, owing to being widowed or divorced. Indeed, in *9 to 5* she would play a woman entering the work force after she divorced a husband with a cheating heart.

"What I found was that secretaries know that the work they do is important, is skilled, but they also know they're not treated with respect. They're called 'office wives.' That means they're on the coffee run to bring the boss coffee. They know how much cream or sugar he takes. They put gas in his car. They even go shopping for a present for his wife's birthday or anniversary. They also have to buy presents for his mistress."

Jane Fonda (*left*), **Lily Tomlin**, and busty **Dolly Parton** show what rebellious secretaries can do to a sexist boss played by **Dabney Coleman**.

At first, *9 to 5* was envisioned as a drama. "Any way we did it, it seemed too preachy, too much of a feminist line," Jane said. "I'd wanted to work with Lily Tomlin for some time. Suddenly, it occurred to me and my producing partner, Bruce Gilbert, to turn the script into a comedy. We hired Patricia Resnick to write the first draft."

Jane herself, along with Gilbert as her producer, cast the lead roles, not only awarding one to Tomlin, but hiring Dolly Parton in her screen debut.

A relatively unknown Colin Higgins was brought in to direct, but first, he was needed to rewrite the script "to create three equal female roles."

He came up with a shootable script and worked smoothly with his "unholy" trio of stars. "Colin is a very nice, low-key type of guy," Parton said. "I don't know what I would have done if I'd had one of those mean directors on my first film."

"I expected a lot of tension, especially working with three famous females, but all of them were totally professional, great fun, and a joy to direct," Higgins said. "I just wish that everything would be as easy."

"Colin and I agreed on most things with only a minor difference here and there," Jane said. "We took out a lot of stuff that was shot. I was super sensitive to anything that smacked of the soapbox or appeared to be a lecture to the audience."

The film's theme song, "9 to 5" was written and recorded by Parton, and became one of the biggest hits of the decade. During the shoot, Parton found that she could use her long acrylic fingernails to simulate the sound of a typewriter. She wrote the song on the set by clicking her nails together to establish and define the beat. The song morphed into Number One for two weeks on the *Billboard Hot 100*. It also topped country singles charts, and was later nominated for several awards, including an Oscar for Best Original Song.

The director of *9 to 5* was the relatively unknown Colin Higgins. Born in New Caledonia, (*a* sui generis *collectivity of* overseas France in the Indian Ocean) to an Australian mother and an American father. For the most part, Higgins grew up in Sydney before migrating to California.

Eventually, he settled in New York, where he "hung out" at the Actors Studio. "Once I introduced myself to Jane Fonda, but I don't think she remembers that."

Not finding work as an actor, he enlisted in the U.S. Army, where he was sent to Germany, where he worked as a reporter for *Stars and Stripes*. Secretly, he became known for "servicing" a lot of young servicemen, but there was no scandal, as he was very discreet.

Back home in the U.S., he enrolled at Stanford University and performed in small theater productions. After finishing school, he became what he called "an able-bodied seaman sailing the South China Seas."

When he returned to the States, he took whatever jobs he could find—pool cleaner or part-time chauffeur. It was a long, hard struggle, but he finally made it to the big screen thanks to a script he had written for *Harold and Maude* (1971), starring Ruth Gordon and Bud Cort. In time, he earned a million dollars for *Harold and Maude*.

"I could not believe it when I was assigned to direct such stars as Jane Fonda, Dolly, and Tomlin in *9 to 5*. I expected trouble from them, but we worked smoothly together, enough so that I also got to helm Dolly in that *Best Little Whorehouse in Texas* film (1982).

During the final months of his life, Higgins was working on a script for a project tentatively entitled *Washington Girls* with the hope of bringing together and directing "that trio" [*Fonda, Parton, and Tomlin*] again. Sadly, he died from an AIDS-related illness on August 5, 1988 at the age of 47.

Dolly Parton needs no introduction, as she is today a legend. Born into poverty in Pittman Center, Tennessee, in 1946 (the first year of the Baby Boomers), she rose to an amazing level of success. She is a singer, songwriter, multi-instrumentalist, actress, author, and businesswoman.

In 1967, she made her album debut, *Hello, I'm Dolly*, eventually evolving into one of the greatest recording artists of all time, selling more than 100 million records.

More than a dozen of her songs hit No. 1 on *Billboard's* country music charts. She has also composed some 3,000 songs, including such memorable hits as "I Will Always Love You."

She hit the big screen with *9 to 5*, and two years later starred with Burt Reynolds as the female lead of *The Best Little Whorehouse in Texas* (1982).

Nobody does kleig lights, bustiers, big hair, big smiles, and *razzmatazz* better than **Dolly Parton,** who "poured herself a cup of ambition" every day during the filming of *9 to 5*. Although she'd been a celebrity on the country-western music scene for years, it was her debut appearance in a feature film.

She was also the author of the movie's theme song, which became something of an anthem for office workers in the U.S.

It earned her four Grammy Award nominations, an Academy Award nomination, and awards for Best Country Vocal Performance Female, and for Best Country Song.

It's one of the few *Billboard* chart songs to feature the clacking of a typewriter.

Today, she co-owns the Dollywood Company, which managed a number of entertainment venues, mainly the Dollywood Theme Park near Knoxville, Tennessee.

Lily Tomlin excels as an actress and writer. In the 1960s, she became increasingly well-known as a stand-up comedian, her breakout role coming from the variety show, *Rowan & Martin's Laugh-In* (1969-1973).

Her feature film debut occurred in 1975, when she starred in Robert Altman's *Nashville.* Earning her an Oscar nomination as Best Supporting Actress of the Year.

On Broadway, her signature role came when she starred in *The Search for Intelligent Life in the Universe* (1985). Her role was written for her by her then partner (now wife) Jane Wagner.

In 2015, Tomlin began starring as Frankie Bergstein with Jane Fonda on the Netflix series, *Grace and Frankie.*

As *9 to 5's* male lead, the horrible boss, Frank Hart Jr., as portrayed by Texas-born Dabney Coleman, has a lusty eye for secretaries, especially one as well-stacked as the Dolly Parton character. To their on-going fury, he refers to his secretaries (Fonda, Parton, and Tomlin) as "my girls."

In time, Coleman would appear in sixty feature films. He'd had a number of roles, but it was not until involvement in *9 to 5* that he became established as the character type for which he became best known—a "comic relief villain."

In 1981, he had a key role in *On Golden Pond* alongside two Fondas (Jane and Henry), and a year later, he played the arrogant, sexist, trivializing soap opera director in *Tootsie* (1982) alongside Dustin Hoffman in drag.

The office workers live out their fantasies of wreaking vengeance on their autocratic boss, whom they refer to as "a sexist, egotistical, lying, hypocritical bigot."

Jane portrays Judy Bernly, who after divorcing her husband, is forced to get a job. She makes friends with Tomlin and Parton.

Parton plays the sexy, attractive, and married character of Doralee Rhodes. Her boss flirts with her and sexually harasses her. He spreads the rumor that he and Doralee are having an affair, which is not true.

Tomlin, as Violet Newstead, is a working woman with four kids. She trains young men in the ways and means of the company they work for, but she's always passed over at promotion time.

In conversations fueled with marijuana, the women decide what fate should await their boss. Violet wants to put rat poison in his coffee; Doralee would hogtie him and roast him over a slow fire; and Judy would shot him like a hunter does a deer.

Sterling Hayden in *9 to 5.*

In the 1940s, a poll of movie-goers voted "The Viking God" as the most macho man in motion pictures.

A fading star of yesterday, Sterling Hayden, plays Russell Tinsworthy, the chairman of the board at Consolidated. He's so impressed with Frank's work that he assigns him the task of supervising a project in Brazil, where he's kidnapped by a tribe of Amazons, never to be heard from again.

The role was a comedown for Hayden, a handsome, masculine A-list acting veteran of classic Hollywood. A former Marine Corps officer, he migrated to Hollywood where he became a leading man in post-war Westerns and *film noir.* He had notable roles in John Huston's *The Asphalt Jungle* (1950) and in Nicholas Ray's *Johnny Guitar* (1954). Off screen, during filming of *The Asphalt Jungle,* he seduced Marilyn Monroe, and off screen in *Johnny Guitar,* he made out with Joan Crawford.

He shot to international fame for his memorable performance as General Jack D. Ripper in Kubrick's *Dr. Strangelove: How I Learned to Stop Worrying and Love the Bomb* (1964).

He later played the Irish-American cop in Francis Ford Coppola's *The Godfather* (1972).

He was known for his "rapid fire baritone" voice and for standing 6 feet 5 inches tall. He liked to brag, "Those five inches in my height measured ten inches if you traveled south."

Made on a budget of $10 million, *9 to 5* grossed $105 million at the box office.

Roger Ebert in the *Chicago Sun-Times* wrote: "I liked it despite its uneven qualities and a plot that's almost too preposterous for the material. Dolly Parton is a natural-born movie star who contains so much energy, so much life and unstudied exuberance that watching her do anything in this movie is a pleasure."

In the rival *Chicago Tribune,* Gene Siskel wrote, "The most pleasant surprise is the appearance of Dolly Parton, who with this one film establishes herself as a thoroughly engaging movie star. The biggest disappointment is that this Jane Fonda comedy about a trio of secretaries out to get their boss doesn't have more bite. Instead, getting darker and darker, it gets lighter and lighter until it loses most of the energy it established earlier."

In *Newsweek,* David Ansen claimed, "If Oscars were given for the casting coup of the year, *9 to 5* would win hands down. Fonda has the least appealing role, playing straight woman to her antic cohorts."

Meri Lyndon in *Hollywood Studio* felt that *9 to 5* was "one of the sharpest, funniest, most dazzling comedies of the year. It is the brainchild of Jane Fonda and her increasingly busy production company. As a feminist and creative filmmaker, she is doing more for actresses, female characters, and humanist entertainment than most of the studios put together."

Gerald Nachman of the *San Francisco Examiner* suggested a different title. "It could be called "The Dead End Kids Meet Gloria Steinem."

Variety stated, "Although it could be argued that the script at times borders on the inane, the bottom line is that the picture is a lot of fun."

In the *Washington Post,* Gary Arnold thought the move "runs a merely weak comic premise into the ground with course, laborious execution."

At the end of filming, Jane was notified that the Gallup Poll listed her among the ten most admired women in America.

By now, no one—not even her father or any of her previous husbands—could deny that *Jane Fonda* had "arrived" as a major power broker in "the New Hollywood."

The editors at *Life* magazine agreed, issuing this special edition in May of 1986 listing her among the the five most powerful women in Tinselfown. She appears in the photo on the lower right.

Her colleagues, competitors, and frenemies on the same cover included *(left to right, upper tier), Jessica Lange, Sally Field, Barbra Streisand,* and *(on left in lower tier) Goldie Hawn*

***

POSTSCRIPT

Jane Fonda continued to work in films during the 1980s after scoring such a hit with her father and Katharine Hepburn in *On Golden Pond.*

In 1985, she co-starred with Anne Bancroft in a *neo-noir* mystery thriller directed by Norman Jewison. In *Agnes of God,* the plot swirls around a novice nun who gives birth and insists that the dead child was the result of a virginal conception.

A psychiatrist (Jane) and a mother superior (Bancroft) clash during the resulting investigation. Bancroft was nominated for a Best Actress Oscar. Made for $7.5 million, *Agnes of God* took in $26 million at the box office.

Sidney Lumet cast Jane in *The Morning After* (1986) in which she played a washed-up alcoholic actress who wakes up on Thanksgiving next to a murdered man, a sleazy photographer. She feels sick and remembers nothing from the night before. Jane received a Best Actress Oscar nomination.

For the first time, in *Old Gringo* (1989 she co-starred with Gregory Peck. It unfolds as an action thriller during Pancho Villa's revolution in Mexico in 1913.

In the 1990s, she co-starred with Robert De Niro (again, for the first time) in *Stanley and Iris* (1990) a romantic drama. It was marketed with the tagline, "Some people need love spelled out for them."

After its release, Jane disappeared from the screen for fifteen years, returning in 2005 to star in *Monster-in-Law.

She continued with an occasional film, but her greater success came with her exercise videos, beginning with the *Jane Fonda Workout* exercise video in 1982. Extroverted, sweat-inducing, and buoyant, they helped launch the fitness craze for Baby Boomers at the dawn of middle age. They eventually sold 17 million copies and collectively inspired a best-selling publishing phenomenon, *Jane Fonda's Workout Book.* She would go on to release nearly two dozen more workout videos, plus five more workout books.

She reteamed with her former co-star Robert Redford to make a drama about an older couple falling in love in *Our Souls at Night* (2017).

Her final big hit was when she and Lily Tomlin starred in the hit Netflix series *Grace and Frankie*. They played aging women whose husbands reveal that they are in love.

The show premiered online in May of 2015.

As she moved into the 21st Century, a detailed view of Jane Fonda after her filming of *On Golden Pond* (1991) would require a volume of its own. Her marriage (1991-2001) to TV mogul Ted Turner and her subsequent move to Georgia would itself be worthy of a detailed and illustrated saga.

Shortly after her divorce from Turner, Jane claimed she had become a Christian. However, she is opposed to bigotry, discrimination, and dogma, which she believes are promoted by only a minority of Christians. On *Charlie Rose* in 2006, she claimed that her newfound Christianity may have played a part in her divorce from Turner, who is known to be a critic of organized religion.

Modern Psychiatry vs. the Tenets of Faith

Upper photo, **Jane Fonda** with **Meg Tilly.**

Lower photo, **Anne Bancroft** with **Jane Fonda**

In *The Morning After,* **Jane Fonda** played a washed-up alcoholic actress who wakes up in a stranger's loft with a dead body beside her.

Seasoned Media Pros in Love: To entertainment industry insiders, the wedding of **Jane Fonda** to **Ted Turner** (founder of TNT, TBS, and CNN) was one of the genuinely interesting romantic venues of the year.

More madcap high-jinx with the already proven, perhaps formulaic, sidekick of **Lily Tomlin** in Grace and Frankie.

J. Lo and **Jane Fonda**: No one could have imagined two more formidable and intimidating divas on the same movie set.

Stanley and Iris. It was the last film **Jane** would appear in for fifteen years until 2005's Monster-in-Law. **Robert De Niro** was her co-star.

Her **Exercise Videos:** Making millions in leg warmers and leotards.

Old Gringos and Seasoned Pros play-acting at being deeply in love. Here's **Jane Fonda** with **Gregory Peck**.

Part Three
PETER

Henry Fonda (*left*) looks on as his two movie star children, **Jane** and **Peter,** review their latest film scripts. Bennett Cerf, the publisher at Random House, had told Henry that a shocking novel was about to be published that was clearly based on all three of them.

"I have long grown accustomed to lies written about me and my talented kids, especially Jane. Peter has had his hits, too. Frankly, my dear, as Rhett told Scarlett, I don't give a damn anymore."

The family's own favorite tagline was "The Fabulous Fondas."

HERE'S PETER!

As he appeared in incidents, episodes, and films highlighted in VOLUME ONE (*Henry Fonda, He Did It His Way*) of this two-part triple biography.

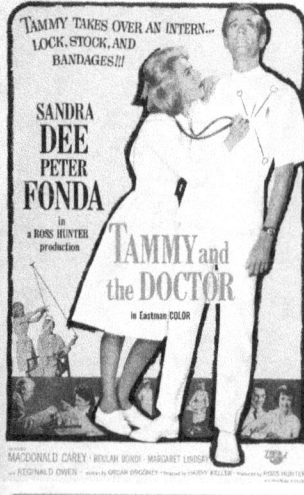

CHAPTER TWELVE

PETER FONDA

Entitled Child of Hollywood, Iconoclastic Rebel, and "Resentfully Royal" from Birth

Tammy and the Doctor
After His Film Debut in this Harmless, Pre-Hippie Romance,
Peter Fonda Is Defined as "A Poor Man's James Stewart," and a "Brooding Baby Boomer."
His Fast-Fading Co-Star, Sandra Dee, Confides,
"You're a better kisser than my husband, Bobby Darin"

Sinking *PT 109*
After Peter Auditions for the role of Lt. John F. Kennedy in *PT 109*
Jack Warner Sees his Screen Test and says "NEVER," defining Peter as
"a silly son of a bitch and a smug little asshole."

The Victors
In this WWII Drama, Peter, cast as an American GI,
helps liberate Europe from the Nazis.
Henry Fonda asks his friend and Peter's co-star, George Peppard,
to hang out with his son and "Make a Man Out of Him"

DOES UNCLE SAM REALLY NEED PETER FOR THE U.S. ARMY?
During a Medical Exam, Peter Physically Threatens an Army Doctor,
Denouncing Him and Refusing to let him "Stick a finger in my rosebud."

Lilith
During the peak of the "Swinging Sixties," Peter stars with Warren Beatty and the doomed, nymphomaniacal American Actress **Jean Seberg**. She manages to "service" both of her co-stars, But later, mysteriously commits suicide in Paris. **Joan Collins** spreads the word that Peter's co-star, Warren Beatty can orgasm "Twice, three, four, even five times a day."

[Enquiring Minds Wanted to Know: Did Beatty maintain that performance record with Jacqueline Kennedy?]

WARREN BEATTY

Peter learns that Warren Beatty is "Heavy Dating" His former stepmother
[Henry Fonda's Fourth Wife, Afdera Franchetti,]
And that Beatty had known Peter's sister, Jane, "as David knew Bathsheba"

GETTING HIGH WITH JAMES MITCHUM

The Eldest Son of Robert Mitchum turns Peter onto "The Joy of Bhang."
[PSSST: Some call it "Weed"]

GETTING COSTUMED WITH ADAM WEST

"Batman" confides to Peter a Wardrobe Policy that Studio Executives Spent a Lot of Time Debating before they'd Approve his Batman Costume for TV:
["Should the outline of my cock and balls get revealed in that skintight suit—Or not?"]

Shaking It with
TOM JONES

In Las Vegas, Peter hangs out with the sexy Welsh singer. His onstage "Schtick" includes very tight pants that accentuate his heavy equipment. Jones confesses that he seduces 250 of his "groupies" every year. *"Coming from Wales I'm a Celt, anyway, so I thought it would be interesting,"* Sir Tom said.

Sunbathing with
GEORGE HAMILTON

Peter puts a question to his sun-tanned co-star:
"When you dated Lynda Bird (LBJ's daughter), did you ever get lucky?"

STARRING CHUCK CONNORS

Peter's co-star—famous for his blockbuster TV series, *The Rifleman*—
Shows Peter a secret Porn movie he made as a young man.
In it, he sodomizes a male.

***

Editor's Note: Whereas the boyhood and adolescence of Peter Fonda were explored in detail in Volume One of this two-part series, his peak years as a movie star are detailed in this and in the following chapters.

***

When he reached his full height, Peter was actually an inch taller than his father, Henry, and he was even thinner Nonetheless, he had his father's slow drawl and his loose-jointed walk.

By 1960, he was determined to follow in his father's footsteps, although it was widely believed in advance that he was highly unlikely to reach the pinnacle of international fame that his *"dear ol' Dad"* had achieved.

Peter made it to Broadway in 1961 when he opened in *Blood, Sweat, and Stanley Poole*, a drama about life in the Marine Corps.

During the run of that play, he married Susan Brewer, the stepdaughter of Noah Dietrich, who for years was the right-hand man of Howard Hughes, the bizarrely erratic billionaire movie mogul and aviator.

During their union, they became parents of the future actress, Bridget Fonda, and a son Justin, who has kept a low profile.

Throughout most of his life, **Henry Fonda** was accused of being a distant father. In this candid snapshot, he gently holds baby **Peter** in his arms and looks lovingly at **Jane**. They would miss their dad when he went off to fight in World War II.

In the months that followed the closing of that play, Peter popped up on TV sets in living rooms across America, guest-starring in such hit TV series as *Naked City*. Major stardom would elude him for many years. As he put it—realistically but perhaps with a touch of bitterness—"I never expected to fill my living room with Oscars."

Peter made his film debut in a "piece of fluff" (his words) entitled *Tammy and the Doctor* (1963), co-starring with Sandra Dee. Blonde, perky, and misleadingly virginal-looking, she was not so much an actress as a token of the bland 1950s that by then was quickly devolving into a then-scorned memory that was being bulldozed by the explosive power of the Swinging Sixties.

"I'm not going to see it," Henry said about *Tammy and the Doctor*. "Sandra Dee?" What a joke!"

Peter fared much better when Ross Hunter cast him in the star-studded World War II drama, *The Victors* (1963). Somehow, in this cast of deeply talented actors, Peter managed to stand his ground, even winning a Golden Globe as "Most Promising Newcomer of the Year."

It was back to the television screen for Peter, as he starred in such telecasts as *The Alfred Hitchcock Hour* and *Twelve O'Clock High*, based on a former feature film that showcased Gregory Peck.

Peter lost out on the coveted (and laudatory) film portrayal of Lt. John F. Kennedy in *PT 109* (released in 1963, before the President's assassination), but he rallied from his disappointment when he got third billing in the darkly pessimistic *Lilith* (1964), emoting opposite Warren Beatty and Jean Seberg.

After that Peter carried on, accepting whatever roles were offered to him, even though he was hardly excited by any of their scripts. In his only directorial effort, Samuel Goldwyn Jr. cast Peter as the lead in *The Young Lovers* (1964), about an out-of-wedlock pregnancy.

Much to the horror of his father, Henry, Peter, along with a few million other young Americans, turned to recreational drugs, especially LSD, in the 1960s. He grew his hair long and became a motorcycle-riding hippie. Movie producers claimed, often with derogation, that he'd developed "a solid reputation as a dropout."

In ways consistent with the social upheavals blowing Hollywood apart at the time, Peter developed friendships with other young drug users, very visibly with members of the rock band, *The Byrds*.

In 1965, he visited the Beatles at their rented home in Benedict Canyon. At one point, while smoking a joint with John Lennon, Peter said, "I know what it's like to be dead."

[Lennon was so impressed with that remark that he used it as a phrase in his song, "She Said She Said."]

In 1966, Peter signed a contract with American International Pictures to make low-budget movies. He wouldn't be well paid, but, as extra compensation, he would be given a boat.

As Peter said, "That studio was the refuge for starving actors whose heyday had come and gone."

Here he met Roger Corman, "The King of the Bs," who profoundly influenced some of the values that later became forever associated with Peter's career and filmmaking.

[Corman produced and directed an outlaw biker film, The Wild Angels (1966), which, as a box office smash, opened the motorcycle genre of 1960s movies. Filmed on location in southern California, it was the first film to associate Peter with Harley-Davidsons and the counterculture 1960s.]

During these experimental entrepreneurial days, Peter saw seven screenings of Gary Cooper's *High Noon* (1952). He secured the money for a pilot to be made entitled *High Noon: The Clock Strikes Noon Again*, but no sponsor could be found to allow it to be enlarged into a TV series.

Peter had become a counterculture movie star, especially when he starred in Corman's *The Trip* (1967), a saga of his experiences with LSD.

Its script had been written by Jack Nicholson and it starred Susan Strasberg, daughter of Lee Strasberg of the famed Actors Studio where Jane had studied.

Peter flew to Paris to co-star with his sister Jane in *Spirits of the Dead* (1968), directed by her then-husband, the French director Roger Vadim. Some reviewers found Jane and Peter together on the screen distasteful and "incestuous."

Peter had not expected to like his brother-in-law, Roger Vadim, but at the end of the picture, he appraised him as "a better version of my father."

Brigitte Bardot also appeared in a separate episode of that film. Before leaving Hollywood, Peter told Dennis Hopper, "My one goal in France is to seduce Bardot." He flew back to Hollywood without accomplishing that lofty ambition.

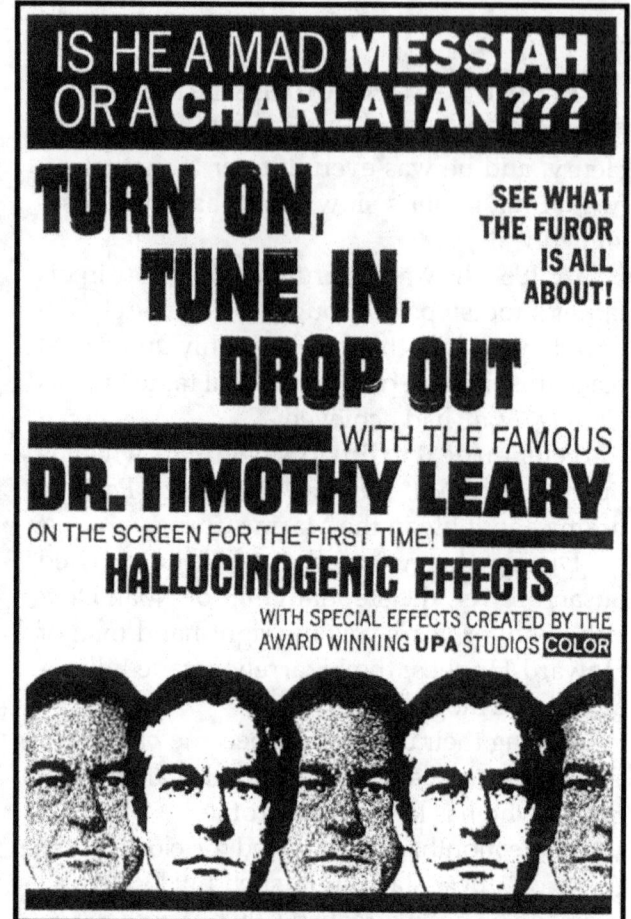

Despite his cinematic origins as a mild-mannered intern in a fluff romance, *Tammy and the Doctor*, **Peter Fonda** evolved into a poster boy for the psychedlic drug subculture. Here's a poster for a 60-minute film, released in 1967, that was briefly popular in urban centers like NYC and San Francisco around the time Peter began his widely publicized promotions for an illegal substance which many Americans at the time found horrifying.

Reviewers of the film (including film critic Steven Puchalski) advised movie-goers, "To prepare, you should smoke a little weed, or better yet, drop a tab (of acid)."

The producers of the film were quick to disclaim that they were not promoting the recreational use of LSD, but that "we should all go out of our minds to get to our senses."

Today, this film and the theories it espoused is interpreted as an artifact of the age of LSD, an artifact which Peter Fonda —a scion of one of Hollywood's most "royal' families—will forever carry as an indelible part of his legacy.

The highlight of Peter's film career, never to be equaled again, was when he and Dennis Hopper teamed to make what became a mega-hit, *Easy Rider* (1969).

It was the story of two long-haired, disaffected hippies traveling on their motorcycles through the southwest and into redneck Louisiana, where they are assassinated.

In this, his most memorable (and profitable) role, Peter was cast as Wyatt, a laconic but charismatic hippie cruising the highways on his "Captain America" Harley-Davidson. His leather jacket has a large American flag prominently displayed on its back.

In the screenplay by Terry Southern, Jack Nicholson had the third lead as an alcoholic civil rights lawyer. He stole every scene in which he appeared and was nominated for a Best Supporting Actor Oscar.

From then on, Peter's film career, in his words, "drifted down a never-ending slope, although I continued to get roles," even for the first two decades of the 21st century.

As a director, Peter's "druggie" friend, Dennis Hopper, cast him in *The Last Movie* (1971). Peter co-starred in it with Michelle Phillips, a singer with *The Mamas and the Papas.*

Peter himself was both the director and the male lead of *The Hired Hand* (1971), a 1971 Western that drifted into obscurity after its release, but which has benefitted from critical praise in a recent revival.

Minor movies followed until Peter co-starred with Susan George in *Dirty Mary, Crazy Larry* (1974), a movie about NASCAR hopefuls who pull a heist to finance their jump into bigtime racing.

An oddity occurred with Peter both directed and starred in *Wanda Nevada* (1979) opposite "jailbait," Brooke Shields, who was only 13 at the time. In his only film appearance with his son, Henry Fonda played a bearded, grizzled old man.

Peter summed up his relationship with his father and his sister: "I dig my father. I have a great deal of compassion for him. I wish he could open his eyes and dig me, too. I also dig Jane… probably a great deal more than she digs me."

Before his death in 2019, as he moved deeper into his 70s, Peter often looked back: "What did Jane and I do that caused us to be so hated? How come everybody didn't just love us? I asked myself, what did two little innocent kids do to get fucked up this much? The worst that I could say about my life is that nobody told me anything. I had to go and find out everything for myself. My father could have been more helpful."

"As Dad aged and mellowed, I reconciled with him," Peter said. "I love him dearly. I forgive him for his neglect in my past."

Peter never became as ardent a political activist as his sister, Jane, but a year before his death, he expressed strong disapproval of Donald Trump, whom he loathed. In fact, he made the most controversial pronouncement of his life about him: "We should rip Barron Trump from the arms of First Lady Melania Trump and put him in a cage with pedophiles."

His remark met with a massive backlash from Mike Huckabee, the former governor of Arkansas, who claimed that Peter's statement about Barron violated Federal Criminal Law.

His statement about Barron was uttered shortly before the release of Peter's farewell to the big screen. In 2018, he played a secondary character in *Boundaries,* starring Christopher Plummer. Before releasing it, Sony Pictures, on June 22, 2018, told the press, "Peter Fonda's statements about Barron Trump are abhorrent, reckless, and dangerous, and we condemn them completely." In a clear attempt to disassociate them-

Barron Trump appears with his parents on the lawn of the White House in August 2019.

One of late-in-life Peter Fonda's most widely publicized *faux pas* involved an off-color condemnation of the then-president's son in terms shocking enough to offend even most moderates. Of course, everyone knew that the object of Peter's famous outspokenness wasn't the then-13 year old, but his later twice-impeached father, the President himself.

Like his very famous father, Henry, **Peter Fonda** was never a great male beauty, even at his physical peak.

Here's how, as a diminished shadow of his heyday as a drug-ingesting motorcycling roughneck, he appeared in 2010 at the Toronto Film Festival.

Ironically, despite strenuous efforts to escape from the perceived oppression of his status as a child of Hollywood royalty, he never really escaped his past. What was the title of the autobiography he released in 1998? ***Don't Tell Dad.***

selves, they made it clear that they would neither edit the film nor change its release schedule but noted that Fonda "plays a very minor role."

During the course of his life, Peter would take three wives. He divorced Susan Brewer in 1974 after thirteen years of marriage. He married Portia Rebecca Crockett in 1975, a union that lasted for 36 years until their divorce in 2011.

Shortly after that divorce, eight years before his death, he took a third wife, Margaret DeVogelaere, in 2011, that union lasting until his death.

At the age of 79, Peter expired on August 16, 2019. He died at his home from respiratory failure brought on by lung cancer.

In the wake of his death, Jane said, "I am very sad. He was my sweet-hearted baby brother. The talker of the family. I have had a beautiful time with him in his last days. He went out of life laughing."

***

Then 22, an insecure but wholesome-looking **Peter Fonda** was assigned his first stage role on Broadway as the second lead in *Blood, Sweat, and Stanley Poole*. After lukewarm (and sometimes scathing) reviews, it was not particularly helpful to his career as an actor.

Blood, Sweat, and Stanley Poole (1961).

Peter Fonda made his debut on Broadway in this play by the Goldman Brothers, William and James, who, in 1955, had served together in the U.S. Army as part of the 101st Airborne division.

From their memories of time served, they teamed to write a play that eventually, in 1961, made its way to Broadway: *Blood, Sweat, and Stanley Poole* (1961). It dealt with a supply sergeant who served at a U.S. Army post in the Deep South.

Its original production starred Peter with actor Darren McGavin, with Jerome Chodorov directing. A relatively unknown actor, James Caan, was in the cast, too. *[In 1978, Jane Fonda would co-star with him in* Comes a Horseman.*]*

The play cost $100,000 to produce but brought in only $85,000. To win the second lead, Peter had to compete with two hundred other actors who showed up to audition.

Howard Taubman of *The New York Times* did not like the play, giving it a bad review. "The plot is spaced out as mechanically as if it were to run forever on the home screen."

Peter's performance, however, won him a New York Drama Critic's Award.

After Broadway, the production was transferred to Los Angeles, where the *Los Angeles Times* called it "a routine military service comedy."

***

Peter Fonda Doesn't Get to Star as Lt. John F. Kennedy

Through a connection, Peter got an interview to test for the role of a young Naval officer, Lt. John F. Kennedy for *PT 109,* a

Upper photo: **THE REAL DEAL: John F. Kennedy** as he appeared in 1943 around the time he skippered his "plywood coffin" (the name he gave to the minor torpedo boat—PT 109—during World War II in the Pacific.

Lower photo: Actor **Cliff Robertson**, who was chosen above Peter Fonda as JFK's impersonator in the trumped-up "promotional film" (*PT 109)* crafted in Hollywood as a celebration of Kennedy's alleged prowess under duress.

reference to his vessel which was torpedoed by the Japanese during World War II.

JFK had called his boat "a plywood coffin."

For the actual screen test, Peter worked on his best "Irish Catholic from Boston" accent.

Its director was Raoul Walsh, who wore a black patch over one eye. Coincidentally, he was the director who had helmed Henry Fonda in his first screen test.

Peter's screen test was later watched as "one of the dailies" by the tyrannical mogul of Warner Brothers, Jack Warner himself.

After seeing Peter emote, Warner shouted, "That silly son of a bitch. I'll see that he never works another day in this town. NEVER! I'll squash him like a little bug, that smug little asshole!"

The next day, the *Hollywood Reporter* and *Variety* each used the same headline: PETER FONDA FLUNKS SCREEN TEST.

With no immediate prospects after that, Peter took a three-week gig at a theater in Mineola on Long Island in New York. For it, he was paid $2,500 a week for starring in *Under the Yum-Yum Tree*. His co-stars were Hugh O'Brian and the former child star, Margaret O'Brien.

Under the Yum Yum Tree had originated on Broadway as a play starring Gig Young. In 1963, Jack Lemmon and Carol Lynley turned it into a romantic comedy for the screen.

**Network TV in the Early 60s.
Cattle calls and daily grinds**

Here's **Peter Fonda** (*left*) in an episode of *Naked City* with **Martin Sheen** (*right*).

Peter Fonda as a "Transient" Guest Star during the Peak Years of Network American Television [*Naked City, Wagon Train*, etc.]

In reference to the "Television centric" period of his career as an occasional guest star during the early 1960s, Peter said, "Appearing on anthology shows in 1962 was good training for me. Each episode featured a new star. An actor drew from $7,000 to $11,000 a week. Of course, I longed to make it on the big screen."

One of Peter's earliest appearances in TV drama occurred when he was cast as Jody Selkin in an episode of *Naked City*, a crime series broadcast on ABC from 1958 to 1962. Formatted as a "semi-documentary" it was inspired by the 1948 release of the feature film, *Naked City*, starring Barry Fitzgerald, Howard Duff, Don Taylor, and Dorothy Hart.

Peter's debut on *Naked City* starred him in an episode named "The Night the Saints Lost Their Halos," first broadcast on January 17, 1962.

The plot was relatively simple: When the son of a close friend is involved in a robbery, a woman doctor tries to shield him from the police. His co-star (the doctor) was Jo Van Fleet.

Elliot Silverstein was its director. This Bostonian had previously helmed Jane Fonda in her hit feature film Western, *Cat Ballou* (1965) with Lee Marvin.

Peter had seen Van Fleet emote brilliantly in *East of Eden* (1955) starring James Dean. For her portrayal of Dean's character's estranged mother (the madam of a local bordello), she had won an Oscar for Best Supporting Actress.

Each segment concluded with a somber narrator intoning the iconic line: "There are eight million stories in the *Naked City*. This has been one of them."

James Franciscus, Jane Fonda's former boyfriend, starred in the series in 1958 and 1959.

What kept viewers tuned in were the guest stars, who changed with every episode: Orson Bean, James Caan, Diahann Carroll, James Coburn, Gene Hackman, Dustin Hoffman, Dennis Hopper, Leslie Nielsen, Carroll O'Connor, Eddie Albert, Claude Rains, even Robert Redford.

Another TV series, hot on the footsteps of and inspired by *The Naked City*, was *The New Breed*. Its producers cast Peter as Ronnie Bryson in an episode entitled "Thousands and Thousands of Miles."

Leslie Nielsen, then 35 years old and very handsome, headed the cast of *The New Breed*, which was telecast on ABC from October of 1961 to June of 1962. He starred as Lt. Price Adams, who worked on "the Hot Shot Detail" of the Los Angeles Police Department.

It, too, kept changing its array of guest stars as a means of keeping viewers "second guessing" and tuned in. Stars on the show came and went almost as quickly as television audiences could switch channels—Eddie Albert, Peter Falk, Anne Francis, Gloria Grahame, Joan Hackett, Jack Klugman, and Cloris Leachman. Even the future superstar, Robert Redford, starred in one of the episodes.

For a while, *Wagon Train* was the top-rated series on TV, according to the Nielsen ratings. It was aired on NBC from 1957 to 1962 and on ABC from 1962 to 1965. Its regular stars included Ward Bond, Robert Horton, and John McIntire. The entire series was inspired by the 1950 feature film *Wagon Master*, directed by John Ford and starring Ben Johnson, Harry Carey Jr., and Bond himself.

The series chronicled the adventures of a massive wagon train leaving St. Joseph, Missouri, making its way across the Midwestern Plains and into the Rocky Mountains. Destination: Sacramento, California.

Big Skies, Big Wagons, Small Roles

The lower photo shows **Peter Fonda** cast as a youthful but embittered outlaw in a 1962 episode of *Wagon Train*.

In 1962, Peter Fonda was the guest star on an episode entitled "The Orly French Story," with him cast in the title role. Like the other series, the telecasts were enlivened by a series of guest stars, perhaps Bette Davis, Ronald Reagan, Jane Wyman, Lee Marvin, Ernest Borgnine, or Joseph Cotten.

All in all, *Wagon Train* would be telecast for a total of 284 episodes. Once, John Wayne spoke from the shadows, but in a voice that was clearly recognizable. However, he was billed as "Michael Morris."

***

Tammy and the Doctor (1963)

If given his choice, Peter Fonda might not have chosen *Tammy and the Doctor* for his screen debut. This was the third of four Tammy films which had originated with Debbie Reynolds, who had starred in *Tammy and the Bachelor* (1957), the first (and many say, "the best") of the Tammy quartet.

A romantic comedy directed by Joseph Pevney, *Tammy and the Bachelor* teamed Debbie as Tammy with her Grandpa, cast with Walter Brennan. They live in a houseboat on the Mississippi River, where "Nan" is her best friend. (Nan is a goat.)

Tammy's life is about to change when a small plane crashes in the nearby swamp. In it, Tammy and her Grandpa find an unconscious pilot, Peter Brent (Leslie Nielsen). After nursing him back to consciousness and good health, she falls in love with him.

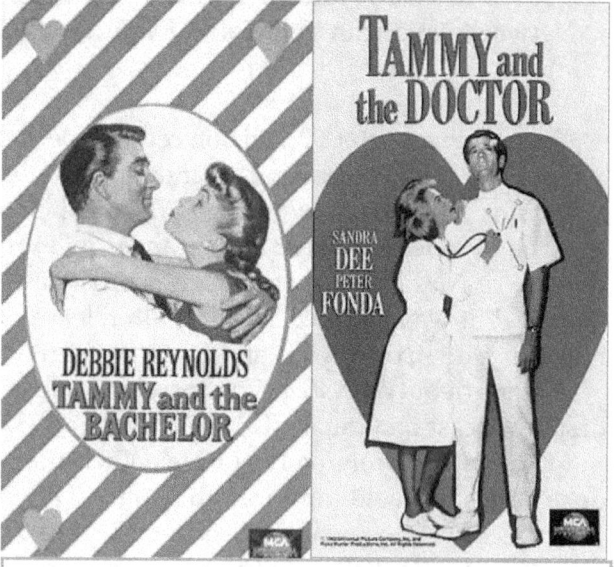

When **Debbie Reynolds** and **Leslie Nielsen** met, fell in love, and co-occupied his ancestors' grand antique house in the bayou, fans of *Tammy and the Bachelor (1957)* fell in love with both of them and cried out for more.

Four installments and six years later, **Peter Fonda** and **Sandra Dee** repeated the theme (a perky ingénue meets a sophisticate) but with less charming results. By now, the theme had grown corny and the actors seemed moderately irritated and way too jaded.

Tammy and the Doctor, as the final installment of a four-film series, crashed, burned, and sent both of its co-stars scurrying to update their images.

The film was so successful that it spawned three movie sequels. Reynolds did not want to continue as Tammy, so producer Ross Hunter offered the role to Sandra Dee.

Few insiders in Hollywood viewed Sandra Dee as the next Sarah Bernhardt, but she was good at playing the quintessential sweet, perky, all-American girl, although she was anything but. But whereas that type of girl was popular in the late 1950s and early 60s, Dee enjoyed only a brief reign before her kind of *character [i.e., perky, All-American, flirtatiously provocative, and coyly virtuous]* went out of style in the counterculture 1960s.

Producer Ross Hunter was said to have discovered Dee, a child model, as she was walking along Park Avenue in Manhattan at age 12. By 1957, she was in Hollywood making the MGM picture, *Until They Sail,* directed by Robert Wise and starring Paul Newman, Jean Simmons, and Joan Fontaine.

Louella Parsons announced that Dee was "the next Shirley Temple." The columnist got it wrong.

Dee was assigned the lead role in *The Restless Years* (1958) with John Saxon. Her third film for Hunter was a remake of *Imitation of Life* (1959), starring Lana Turner. It grossed $50 million, the highest box office success that Universal had ever had.

That was followed by *Gidget* (also 1959), in which Dee was cast with Cliff Robertson and James Darren. The Darren role of "Moondoggie" Matthews had been intended for Elvis Presley, but he was drafted into the U.S. Army.

Dee found herself at the center of a massive hit when she appeared opposite the blonde heartthrob Troy Donahue in *A Summer Place* (1959).

Like Dee, Troy Donahue, "the replacement for Tab Hunter," would also have a short reign on the screen. *[Both Dee and Rock Hudson later complained that "his penis is too small."]*

In *Tammy Tell Me True* (1961), Dee assumed once again the original Debbie Reynolds role.

That same year, she made *Come September* in Portofino, Italy, starring Rock Hudson. There, she met singer Bobby Darin, with whom she entered a tumultuous and widely publicized marriage.

In *Tammy Tell Me True* (1961), John Gavin was cast as Sandra's leading man, although he was eleven years (born in 1931) older than she (born in 1942). Gavin later claimed that "that film haunts the tube like a permanent miasma."

Gavin was later cast with leading ladies who were better-suited for him. They included Doris Day, Sophia Loren, and

Two actresses, both blonde, both ferociously competitive, one in training to replace the other.

Here's sexpot and screen pro **Lana Turner** (left) playing a concerned mother to **Sandra Dee** in *Imitation of Life*. Although 'Luscious Lana" emerged as one of the grandest and most durable divas in the history of Hollywood, Dee—something of an anachronism even in her heyday, never really survived the debut of the Sixties.

A Summer Place (1959) focused on puppy love and teenaged anguish between teen idol **Troy Donahue** (who some fans thought eerily resembled Peter Fonda), and a coyly virginal **Sandra Dee**. Today, it's considered an antiquated and harmless artifact of the Age of Sputnik. Everything about it roared out of style within a few months of its release. Its co-stars never survived.

Here's **Peter Fonda** with **Sandra Dee**—who was by far the more successful actor at the time. As a cobbled-together duo marketed aggressively by the studio, they made wholesome, family-friendly puppy love in *Tammy and the Doctor*—just before the Swinging Sixties made their romantic presuppositions look old-fashioned and quaint.

Susan Hayward.

Producer Ross Hunter promoted him as "the next Rock Hudson," and, according to rumor, managed to get him to drop his jockey shorts early in his career.

Gavin, a former U.S. Naval intelligence officer, also starred in *Spartacus* (1960) with Kirk Douglas and in *Psycho* that same year with Anthony Perkins.

He later became President of the Screen Actors Guild (1971-1973) and, during the Presidential Administration of his friend, Ronald Reagan, the U.S. Ambassador to Mexico (1981-1986).

Hunter tapped Dee once again for the role of Tambrey ("Tammy") Tyree in the third installment of the Tammy series, *Tammy and the Doctor*, released in 1963. This time, her male co-star was Peter Fonda in his film debut. By now, the "Tammy" premise, and its plotlines, were wearing thin.

The storyline by Oscar Brodney was relatively simple: Mrs. Call (Beulah Bondi) requires surgery in Los Angeles. She is accompanied there by her young companion, Tammy (Dee), a country lass from Mississippi. She lands a job with the hospital staff.

She is soon attracted to Dr. Mark Cheswick (Fonda).

Mark's superior, Dr. Wayne Bentley, and his head nurse, Rachel Coleman (Margaret Lindsay), have serious doubts about the viability of this romance.

Tammy and the Doctor was hardly a prestige assignment for its director, Ross Hunter. He had produced previous box office hits that included a remake of *The Magnificent Obsession* (1954), co-starring Jane Wyman and Rock Hudson. Another big hit was *Pillow Talk* (1959) with Doris Day and Hudson. In part by collaborating with Hunter on a casting couch, Hudson had risen fast to major stardom.

"Hunter never put me on the casting couch," Peter Fonda claimed. "I guess I just didn't measure up to Hudson."

Based on popular perception, at the time that Hunter signed Peter, the young actor was perceived as "a sort of poor man's James Stewart—tall, gangly, the boy next door, all-American and virginal."

Again, Hunter opted for Harry Keller as the director of this, the newest version (and third installment) of *Tammy*. Keller had started in films in 1939, working as a film editor. The most famous movie on which he'd ever worked was Orson Welles' *Touch of Evil* (1958), starring Marlene Dietrich.

Keller rounded up a cast of well-known actors to

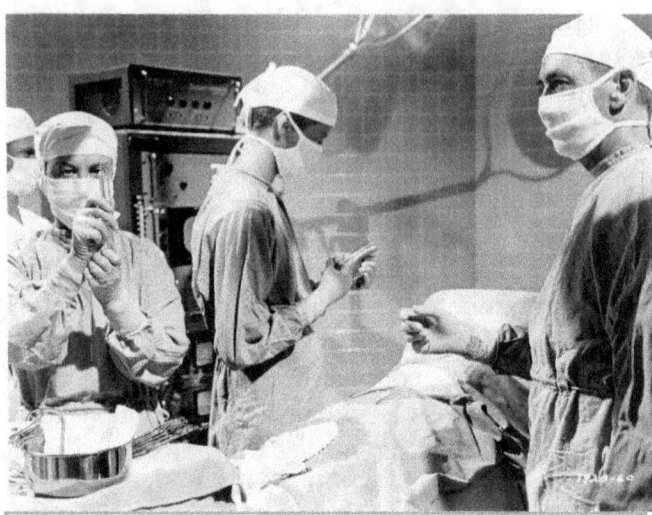

Tammy and the Doctor: At the time of its release, daytime TV was loaded with high-drama medical scenes like this with **Peter Fonda** (*center*) and **Macdonald Carey** (*right*) preparing for heart surgery on Beulah Bondi, a specialist at the time in grandmother roles.

In the words of one detractor, "virtually any actor, if he was reasonably clean cut, affable, and well-spoken, could have faked their way through an surgical drama—on-screen at least."

That is precisely what Peter did.

He'd Seen Better Days: in the publicity photo above, **Macdonald Carey** (*right*—this time not wearing a surgical mask) emotes with **Paulette Goddard** in *Hazard* (1948).

Character actress **Beulah Bondi**, (*right photo*) veteran of dozens of films from the golden age of Hollywood, as she appeared around 1950.

But what did she really think of Peter Fonda and Sandra Dee?

back up Dee and Fonda. As Dr. Bentley, Macdonald Carey also cast as a doctor, perform heart surgery on Tammy's grandmother, Mrs. Call (Beulah Bondi). For decades, Bondi specialized in mother or (later) grandmother roles.

According to Peter, "Mac and I uttered surgical jargon while clipping hemostats *[surgical clamps]* onto each other's surgical gowns," Peter said.

Before hitting TV's big time (in his case, in *Days of Our Lives*, a daytime soap opera), Carey had reigned as "King of the Hollywood Bs." *[In contrast, at around the same time, Lucille Ball was often referred to as "Queen of the Bs."* He had worked alongside some of the biggest names in Hollywood—Claudette Colbert William Holden, Betty Grable, Maureen O'Hara, Ray Milland, Alan Ladd, Paulette Goddard, Betty Hutton, Anne Baxter, and Jane Wyman.

His sagging career as an actor was salvaged by *Days of Our Lives*. *[Airing almost every weekday from 1965 to 2022, it became one of the longest-running scripted television programs in the world.]* At the beginning of many episodes, Carey's voice intoned the series' tag line and slogan, "Like sand through the hourglass, so are the Days of Our Lives."

"I took the gig because I couldn't find any film roles," he told Peter. He starred as one of the show's perennial patriarchs, Dr. Tom Horton.

On the set of *Tammy and the Doctor*, Peter met Beula Bondi. Years earlier, she had appeared with his father, Henry, in *The Trail of the Lonesome Pine* (1936), co-starring with Sylvia Sidney. She told the press, "Young Peter has much of the same aura as his father, a kind of sensitive lad who is most alluring."

Cast in it as a nurse, Margaret Lindsay had been praised for the quality of her supportive roles in successful films of the 1930s. Critics regarded her portrayal of Nathaniel Hawthorne's Hepzibah Pyncheon in *The House of the Seven Gables* (1940) as her standout career role. She reminded Peter that she had been Henry Fonda's love interest in *Jezebel* (1938), in which she had stolen him from Bette Davis.

Reginald Owen as Jason Tripp was a British actor who'd made his acting debut in 1905. He'd worked on Broadway but was more successful in Hollywood, where he appeared in a string of motion pictures. Today, he is best known for playing Ebenezer Scrooge in Charles Dickens' *A Christmas Carol* (1938). He also was one of several actors—none better than Basil Rathbone—who appeared onscreen as Sherlock Holmes.

[SHOWBIZ TRIVIA: In 1964, Owen rented his mansion in Bel Air to the Beatles, since no hotel in Hollywood would take them, fearing that the premises would be overrun with crazed and hysteri-

Margaret Lindsay (*right figure in photo above*) had a link to Peter Fonda's father **Henry** (*see above*) that Peter might not have remembered.

In *Jezebel*, (1938), she played the demure and restrained "Yankee gal" that **Bette Davis** (*left figure, above*) **competed with for the affections of Henry Fonda.**

Notes from Lavender Hollywood

Shown above is **Margaret Lindsay** (*left*) with **Janet Gaynor,** her friend and lesbian companion, during their shared holiday at the Desert Inn in Palm Springs in 1934.

Two views (right) of **Reginald Owen** as Louis XV in the then-very-risqué pre-code historical drama, *Madame du Barry* (1934).

In the far right photo, the foot he's kissing belongs to **Dolores del Rio.**

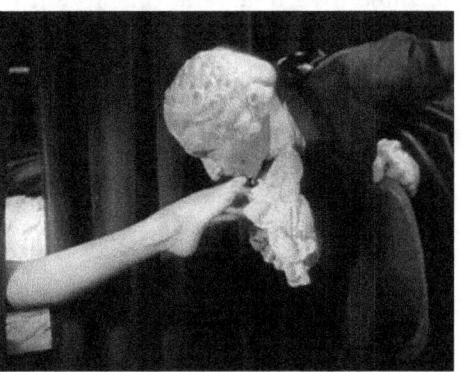

cal fans.]

Alice Pearce as "Millie" had been lured to Hollywood by Gene Kelly to reprise her Broadway performance in the film adaptation of Thornton Wilder's play, *Our Town* (1949). She became household famous when she was cast as Samantha Steven's nosey neighbor, Gladys Kravitz, in the television series *Bewitched* in 1964.

Peter's most difficult day on the set of *Tammy and the Doctor* occurred during a kissing scene with Dee. "Sandra was a great little kisser—in fact, she told me I was better than Bobby Darin—and we really got into it until the director (Keller) yelled 'cut.'"

"You had your mouth open." Keller said. "So did she. There was way too much tongue—none of it suitable for a chaste *Tammy* movie. We pleased him by giving one another a reprise of chaste kisses. However, I turned her on."

"When filming of the scene ended, and we were finished for the day, she invited me for a visit to her dressing room. It took three hours to satisfy her. She complained that Bobby (Darin), as a lover, was in and out too quickly."

During the filming of *Tammy and the Doctor*, Peter bonded with actor Adam West, cast as Dr. Eric Hassler. From Walla Walla in Washington State, West drifted south. Although he had a number of film roles, he became a household name for his portrayal of Batman in ABC's campy 1960s TV series.

Batman was based on the comic book character. West played Bruce Wayne/Batman with Burt Ward as Dick Grayson/Robin. Each portrayed a crime fighter who defended Gotham City from archvillains. The series was known for its campy style and its intentionally humorous morality aimed at a largely teenaged audience.

Cesar Romero as "The Joker' was one of the recurring villains and Batman's arch enemy. He leaves clues at the scene of each of his crimes, each configured as a joke.

Burgess Meredith as "The Penguin" was a gentleman thief who commits crimes using multi-purpose umbrellas.

The Cat Woman character was a jewel thief known for her form-fitting costumes and for her complicated love/hate relationship with Batman. She was portrayed by Julie Newmar in Seasons 1 and 2 and by Eartha Kitt in Season 3.

Of the various other characters who sparkled and faded from *Batman's* lineup was Milton Berle as "Louie the Lilac," a gangster with a fondness for flowers.

Years later, at a party, West told Peter Fonda that "wardrobe had a problem fitting me for my costumes in *Batman*. The debate involved either showing or not

Adam West during his deadpan, gag-soaked heyday as *Batman*.

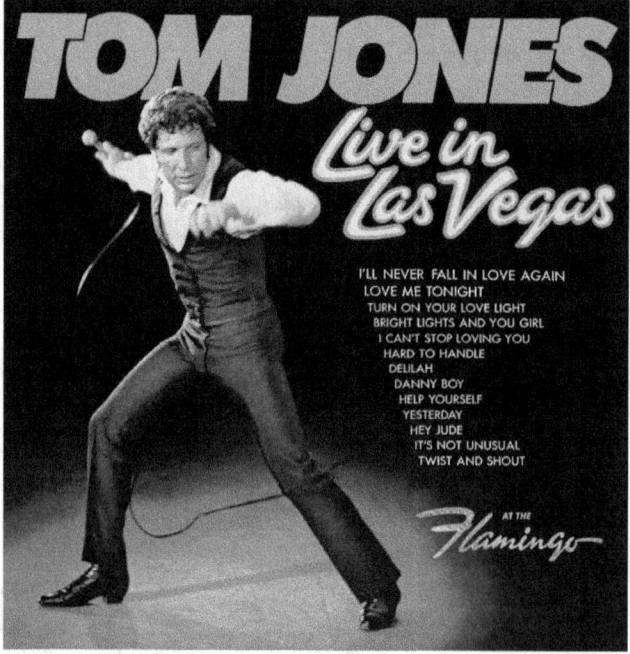

Tom Jones, in his unexpected role as the biggest draw in Las Vegas, did more than any other Welshman to promote the glories of Celtic studliness.

"I never competed with those pretty boys like Troy Donahue and Tab Hunter. They have their following of lovesick teen girls. From my experience, I find that my groupies prefer a real man—rugged, macho, and packing a powerful weapon. Sometimes, I wore a jockstrap; at other times, I didn't, causing orgasmic screams in the audience."

showing the outline of my junk behind that blue and gray outfit: Should they show the outline or should they make it appear as if I had no dick at all?"

"Everyone who saw the series," Peter told him, "thought that you (as Batman) and Burt Ward (as Robin) were lovers."

After the release of *Tammy and the Doctor, Variety* wrote, "Peter Fonda, sprig of Henry Fonda, is a cross between his dad and a lean Fred Astaire. *Tammy and the Doctor* is, unfortunately, an inane role for a film debut."

The 88-minute film was released on May 29, 1963, but did not perform as well as the previous pair of Tammy movies. It generated only $2 million at the box office.

At the end of its filming, Sandra Dee invited Peter and his wife, Susan Brewer, to fly to Las Vegas with her to hear Bobby Darin, her husband, perform in his nightclub act at the Tropicana Hotel Casino.

Before Darin came on stage, a then-relatively-unknown Welsh singer, Tom Jones, was scheduled to go on as his "warmup" act. Jones was introduced by the sometimes cruel "slash-and-burn" comedian Don Rickles, who said, "Tom wears pants designed to show off his big dick. His pants, in fact, are so tight that you can tell he's uncircumcised."

Later, at a gathering, Peter and the rest of the party got to meet the Welsh singer, whose voice was described as "a full-throated robust baritone." In time, Jones became one of Peter's favorite singers, in part because of songs that included "What's New, Pussycat?" and "It's Not Unusual."

Even at that early stage of his career, Jones became known as a consistently reliable, some said "obsessive" seducer of his "Groupies." On the night Peter met him, he was surrounded with girls. Jones later admitted that at the peak of his career, he was sexually intimate with an astounding 250 groupies per year, despite his marriage to the former Linda Trenchard since 1957. Sometimes, he dated famous women, such as Mary Wilson of *The Supremes.*

Beginning that night in Las Vegas, Peter and Bobby Darin became "buddies" in a friendship that endured for the remainder of Darin's short life. Peter tried to attend any performance of Darin that he could and would listen for hours to his recordings. He was constantly amazed at how Darin could go from jazz to pop to rock 'n roll or swing, even country music.

Peter had followed Darin's career since he first heard him sing "Splish Splash" in 1958. That was followed by two of his other favorites, "Dream Lover" and "Mack the Knife."

One night in Las Vegas, Darin asked Peter if they could go somewhere alone, because he had something to tell him. Peter noticed that he was nervous and looked confused. "I just found out yesterday that the woman I thought was my sister was actually my mother."

In the years that remained, Peter would sometimes meet with Darin just to talk. He confessed that his health was failing because of the damage to his heart he'd sustained during a childhood bout of rheumatic fever.

"The doctor told me I'll never live beyond forty," Darin confessed. "So I'm trying to live life to the fullest in whatever time remains for me."

Darin faced heart surgery in January of 1971, when two artificial heart valves were implanted into his chest. Even so, before and after future stage performances, he was administered oxygen.

On the evening of December 19, 1973, four surgeons worked for six hours to repair Darin's damaged heart. He never regained consciousness after his operation, dying later that night

The sudden marriage of **Bobby Darin** to **Sandra Dee** reigned briefly as the hippest, most talked-about union in show-biz. Teenaged hearts stayed aflutter for months.

Here's how it was handled on the cover of the March, 1961 edition of *Photoplay*.

in the recovery room. He was only 37 years old.

Peter took the news of his death very hard, plunging into a deep depression. "Bobby was so talented, such a good and loving friend. I cannot replace him in my life."

He had divorced Sandra Dee in 1967, as their widely publicized marriage had steeply declined. Emotionally unstable, even at her best, Dee had became haunted with memories of her stepfather, who had abused her sexually during her childhood. She also suffered from drug abuse and alcoholism, never getting over her *anorexia nervosa*. Once a widely emulated teen idol, her persona had gone out of style, as new stars with radically different demeanors and styles emerged in the "Swinging Sixties."

Sandra Dee, otherwise known as *Gidget* and/or *Tammy*, died in 2005.

***

The Victors (1963)

For his next feature film, a black-and-white British-American wartime drama, Peter Fonda found himself lost within an all-star cast that featured Vincent Edwards, Albert Finney, and George Hamilton.

Having cast a blend of European and American actresses, its director, Carl Foreman, chose a half-dozen actresses whose images appeared often on posters: Elke Sommer from West Germany; Romy Schneider and Senta Berger from Austria; Melina Mercouri from Greece; Jeanne Moreau from France; and Rosanna Schiaffino from Italy.

Previously blacklisted, Foreman told the press, "I want to make a personal statement about the futility of war. Both victor and vanquished are the losers."

He'd been a member of the Communist Party from 1938 to 1942. "The idea at the time was just in the air," he later claimed.

During World War II, he served in the U.S. Army Signal Corps making training films for director Frank Capra.

After his return to Hollywood, he formed an alliance with producer Stanley Kramer. One of their biggest hits involved the boxing tale, *Champion* (1949) starring Kirk Douglas. Foreman received an Oscar nod for the script.

Kramer and Foreman had worked on Marlon Brando's debut film, *The Men* (1950). One of their greatest triumphs was marked by shared collaboration on *High Noon* (1952), starring Gary Cooper and Grace Kelly.

The Victors was based on an anthology of short stories entitledl *The Human Kind*, a saga of the wartime experiences of the English author, Alexander Baron. The British characters in the novel were changed to Americans to attract U.S. audiences.

Peter read one of Baron's novel, *Strip Jack Naked*, and lobbied to star in a movie adaptation of it, but the project never got off the ground.

The rambling plot of *The Victors* follows a group of soldiers in World War II, beginning in war-torn London in 1942.

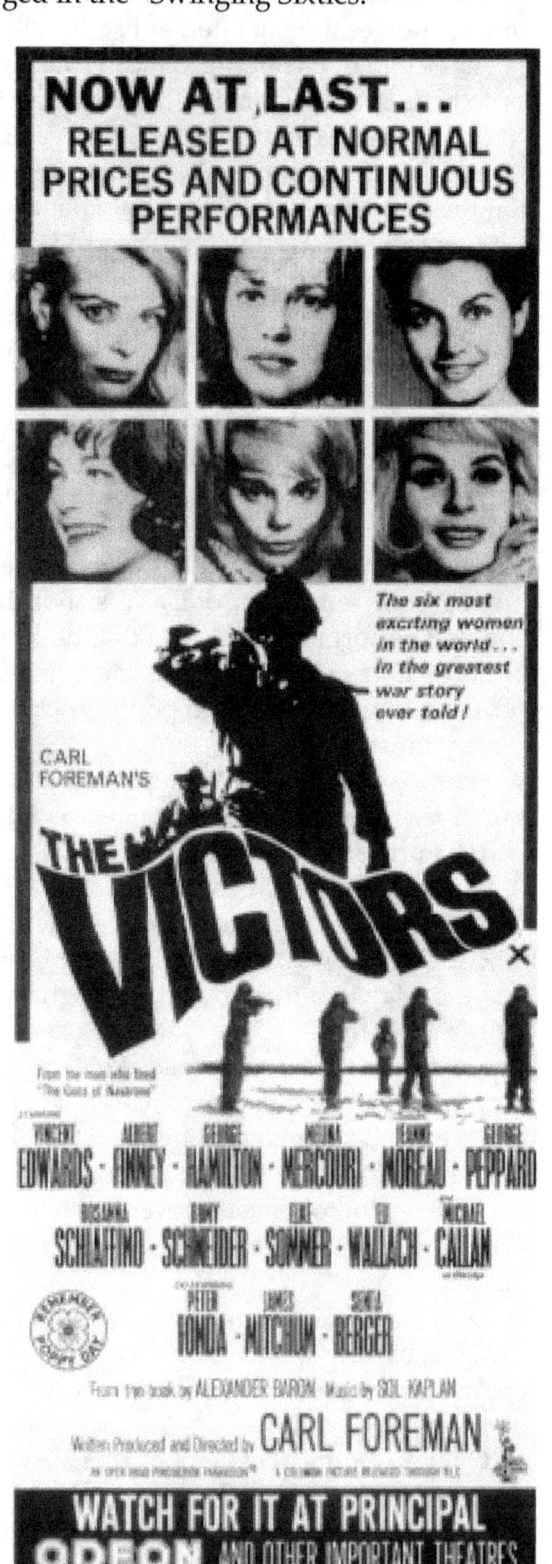

It goes through the fierce fighting in Sicily and Southern Italy before finally landing on the beaches of Normandy in June of 1944 to begin the liberation of France and ultimately, of Western Europe. Episodes even take the viewer to the uneasy occupation of war-torn Berlin in 1945.

Peter was cast in the small role of Weaver, whose character *Variety* defined as "an exasperatingly juvenile newcomer to the squad."

Brooklyn-born Vince Edwards, a former collegiate swimming champion, had the lead role of Baker. In the 1950s, he'd been a contract player at Paramount in minor roles. His big break came when he appeared as *Ben Casey*, a medical drama that aired on ABC from 1961 to 1966. In the role of Dr. Casey, Edwards was young, idealistic, and intense. According to the plot, he develops a romantic relationship with Jane Hancock (Stella Stevens), who has emerged from a coma after fifteen years.

Filmed at Desilu Studios, the series was produced by Bing Crosby Productions. Crosby liked Edwards' light tenor voice and recorded half a dozen albums with him for Decca. One of them, *Vincent Edwards Sings*, remained for several weeks on the top *Billboard* LP charts in 1962.

In *The Victors*, Baker strikes up a relationship with Maria (Rosanna Schiaffino), a young mother and resident of a small Sicilian town. Her soldier husband is missing.

Peter Fonda, cast as an "exasperatingly juvenile" newcomer to the platoon. Some of his colleagues, on a personal level, agreed.

The English actor, Albert Finney, was miscast as a Russian soldier in Berlin. On the screens of the 1960s, he'd made his debut in *The Entertainer* (1960) and followed that with another hit, *Saturday Night and Sunday Morning* (also 1960). When he worked on *The Victors*, he was enjoying the success of his massive hit, *Tom Jones* (1963), in which he'd been cast in the title role.

A son of Tennessee, George Hamilton rose to fame in the 1960s in such films as *Home From the Hill* (1960), *By Love Possessed* (1961), and *Light in the Piazza* (1962). He would later portray country singer Hank Williams in *Your Cheatin' Heart* (1964).

In 1966, he would become quite famous when he was the boyfriend of Lynda Bird Johnson when her father, Lyndon, occupied the White House. He later struck up a bond with Imelda Marcos, the widow of the former dictator, Ferdinand Marcos, of the Philippines.

Elke Sommer, who, decades later sued Zsa Zsa Gabor for slander, with **George Hamilton,** later notorious for his friendship with Imelda Marcos, multi-millionairess co-dictator of the Philippines, in *The Victors*.

Hamilton was known for his debonair style and his perpetual suntan. He often competed with John Derek as to who was the more deeply tanned.

In *The Victors*, he played Trower, who meets and falls in love with Regine (Romy Schneider), a violinist. During the course of the film, she dumps him for a sleazy pimp, Eldridge (Michael Callan).

George Peppard was cast as Chase, who had a relationship with Magda (Melina Mercouri). She wants him to desert and join her in the black market. He refuses and rejoins his unit. Later, in a battle, he's wounded in the leg.

Peppard, a close friend of Henry Fonda, also became—at least during the shoot—a companion of Peter. Henry told his wife, "Hanging out with George will make a man out of Peter. At times, my son comes off a bit effeminate."

Peppard's good looks, elegant manners, and acting skills had won him the sought-after role of Paul Varjak in *Breakfast at Tiffany's* (1961).

George Peppard in *The Victors* was once married to actress Elizabeth Ashley, who called him "a Viking god."

Truman Capote had written his *novella* (*Breakfast at Tiffany's*, published in 1958) with Marilyn Monroe in mind, but Audrey Hepburn beat her out for the part. Director Blake Edwards did not want Peppard in film adaptation, "but he was forced on me."

Peppard, too, didn't like working with Hepburn or Patricia Neal, the latter referring to him as "cold and conceited."

Peppard went on to star in *The Carpetbaggers* (1964), in which he played a ruthless aviator and film mogul, a character obviously inspired by Howard Hughes. The novel had been a best-seller for Harold Robbins.

Its cast included Elizabeth Ashley, with whom Peppard fell in love. She described him at the time as "some kind of Nordic god—six feet tall with beautiful blonde hair, blue eyes, and a body out of every high school cheerleader's lust fantasy."

Eli Wallach was cast as Craig. When he is visited at the military hospital, it is discovered that most of his face has been blown off.

Wallach was married to actress Anne Jackson and the two of them often appeared together on the stage, jointly hailed as one of the most notable acting couples in America.

Beginning with his Broadway debut in 1945, Wallach would go on to garner ninety film credits over the course of his life.

Women We Love: Melina Mercouri as she appeared in *The Victors*.

In her later years, as minister of Culture for Greece, she lobbied hard for the return from the British Museum of the Elgin Marbles, which she maintained had been illegally removed from the Acropolis at Athens.

On the set of *The Victors*, he amused the cast by telling them what went on during the making of *The Misfits* (1961), the last complete film of the mentally disturbed Marilyn Monroe, co-starring at the time with Clark Gable and Montgomery Clift.

Before his final cast of "the women," Foreman offered roles to Sophia Loren and Simone Signoret. Both of him rejected the parts.

When the Greek actress, Melina Mercouri, showed up, she had already shot her most celebrated movie, *Never on Sunday* (1960), in which she played a prostitute. For that performance, she received a Best Actress Oscar nomination. Born in 1920, she was the oldest of the glamour girls in *The Victors*.

In France, Mercouri introduced Peter to Julius (aka Jules) Dassin, who had directed her in *Never on Sunday*. The character she'd played was that of a self-employed, free-spirited prostitute living in the port of Piraeus in Greece. There, she meets Homer, an American tourist and classical scholar who is enamored of all things Greek.

Dassin, an American-born native of Connecticut who spent many of his years as an expatriate in France and in Greece, had been put on the Hollywood blacklist during the McCarthy era.

In 1981, Mercouri would become the Greek Minister of Culture, the first woman to hold that post. During her term, she kept putting pressure on Queen Elizabeth II of England to return the Parthenon Marbles (aka The Elgin Marbles) on display in the British Museum in London.

Peter expressed a seductive interest in Romy Schneider. Born in Vienna in 1938, she was two years older than him. She'd begun her career as an actress in the early 1950s, when she was only 15. From 1955 to 1957, she played the central character of Elizabeth of Austria (the oft-estranged wife of Franz-Joseph) in the film trilogy *Sissi*.

In France, where she ultimately moved, she became critically acclaimed for many other films, too.

In *The Victors*, Foreman had cast her in the role of Regine. He later said, "Peter, on at least three occasions, spent quite a bit of time in her dressing room, but I have no knowledge of whether he got lucky or not."

A Berliner, Elke Sommer, cast as Helga Metzger, was known in the

Born in Vienna, but raised in Germany, actress **Romy Schneider** joined the cast of *The Victors*. She was one of the European beauties imported to spice up U.S. films, but she actually had talent as an actress.

Her beauty captivated Peter Fonda.

1960s for her performance in the second installment (*A Shot in the Dark*; 1964) of *The Pink Panther* series. In time, she was hailed as a sex symbol and moved to Hollywood, where she became a pin-up girl and posed for *Playboy*. One of the world's top film actresses, she made nearly 99 films for TV and the big screen.

[In latter-day, widely publicized moments of bitchy notoriety, Sommer sustained a long-running feud with Zsa Zsa Gabor. In 1993, Zsa Zsa allegedly told two German-language newspapers in Europe that Sommer was a financially strapped Hollywood has-been. Sommer successfully sued Gabor and Gabor's then-husband, Frederick von Anhalt, in a California court for libel and was awarded $3.3 million in damages.]

In *The Victors*, the French actress, Jeanne Moreau, played "a Frenchwoman" (no name given). Orson Welles was lavish in his praise for her, calling her "the greatest actress in the world."

Though less well-known in the U.S., Moreau, born in Paris in 1928, was already "impossibly famous" in France. While still in her 20s, she'd become one of the leading actresses at the *Comédie-Française*. By the late 1950s she was working for an emerging generation of new French filmmakers, such as Louis Malle in *Elevator to the Gallows* (1958) and *The Lovers* (1959). In time, she would work with France's "New Wave" of avant-garde directors, including a leading role in François Truffaut's *Jules and Jim* (1962), her biggest success internationally. Other notable directors who hired her included Michelangelo Antonioni, Luis Buñuel, Elia Kazan, and Rainer Werner Fassbinder.

Sultry **Senta Berger** added "sex and spice' to *The Victors*. Before working in Hollywood, she became known in German films. The question is: Did such co-stars of hers as Dean Martin, Frank Sinatra, or James Caan get lucky?

Moreau also was a favorite of the literati, hanging out with Jean Cocteau, Jean Genet, Henry Miller, and Marguerite Duras. Director Tony Richardson left his wife Vanessa Redgrave to be with her, but the couple never married. She was known for having affairs with many lovers, not only with Malle and Truffaut, but with fashion designer Pierre Cardin.

Senta Berger in the role of Trudi Metzger, was an Austrian-German actress who worked in films in Europe before coming to Hollywood in 1962. There, she starred with such actors as Charlton Heston, Frank Sinatra, Dean Martin, Richard Widmark, John Wayne, Tom Tryon, Harve Presnell, James Caan, Robert Wagner, and George Segal.

Moreau did not like her time in Hollywood and got her revenge in 2006 when she published her autobiography, entitled *I Knew That I Could Fly* in English. She wrote about Darryl F. Zanuck's attempt to put her (or force her) onto the casting couch, and "all the shallow people, both men and women, I met in my Hollywood career."

Rosanna Schiaffino, a daughter of Genoa, was cast as Maria. She was billed as Italy's answer to Hedy Lamarr," once widely billed by publicists as "the most beautiful woman on earth."

Her chief competitors for Hollywood film roles, (and the actresses to whom she was most often compared) were her Italian compatriots, Sophia (Loren), Gina (Lollobrigida), and Claudia (Cardinale).

By the 1980s, Schiaffino abandoned her film career and became a highly publicized "jet setter," especially during the course of her affair with Giorgio Enrico Falck, the handsome playboy and steel industry ty-

Jeanne Moreau with **Eli Wallach** in a scene from *The Victors*. It's signed by the film's director, Carl Foreman.

Her trademark downcast mouth and the haunting but suggestive gazes of her eyes lit up the screen.

coon. Eventually, they married, although their union seemed doomed from the start.

During the filming of *The Victors*, Peter met and bonded with James Mitchum, who was cast in it as Grogan. James Mitchum was the oldest son of Robert Mitchum, to whom he bore a striking resemblance. His first major role had been in *Thunder Road* (1958), a part intended for Elvis Presley until Presley's manager, "Colonel" Tom Parker, demanded too much money. Young Mitchum went on to work with actors who included Henry Fonda,. Kirk Douglas, John Wayne, and Mickey Rooney. Critics pointed out that Mitchum had his father's "sexy, sleepy eyes and taciturn good looks."

During the time in the early 1960s when Mitchum lived with Peter and his wife in London, he may have contributed to, or encouraged, Peter's frequent use of *Bhang*. Peter might not have been familiar with that specific term until Mitchum explained: "Fucking *Bhang,* man, you know, pot, grass, marijuana—whatever you want to call it."

Mitchum had learned to smoke weed from his father, the most famous "pot pioneer in Hollywood."

James Mitchum never came even close to replacing his father, Robert Mitchum, on the screen, although the young man did inherit some of his father's looks.

On many a night, he and Peter Fonda privately indulged in getting "marijuana high."

"In smoking pot," James said in an interview, "I found the new magic potion in my life. I became a regular user of it. I even put more flesh on my skinny bones, and I'm sure I made my Dad proud of me. Pot helped me become a man—not a skinny boy."

The premiere of *The Victors* was configured as part of a command performance in London, where Peter was introduced to Queen Elizabeth, the Queen Mother, Prince Philip, and Princess Margaret Rose.

In anticipation of the event, Peter checked into the deluxe Dorchester Hotel with George Peppard and George Hamilton. As he admitted, "We went out on the town, raising hell."

The reception of *The Victors* in the United States did not go well. Distributors demanded cuts, citing as a particularly offensive scene as the one wherein an eleven-year-old boy, a character defined in the script as "Jean-Pierre," is seen propositioning American soldiers for sex in exchange for money or food.

Foreman was very disappointed by the public's disinterest and by his film's low sales at the box office. In the U.S. and Canada, it generated only $2,350,000, despite the high cost of its production.

George Hamilton said, "Our movie was way, way, way too dark, foreshadowing the paranoid films released later in the decade. All these bad days in films seemed to begin right after the assassination of John Kennedy in Dallas in November of 1963."

In spite of its negative reviews, Peter was nominated for a Golden Globe as "Most Promising Newcomer."

Bosley Crowther in *The New York Times* did little to increase business. He reviewed the film with this: "What's wrong with most of this picture is that it is specious, sentimental, and false to the norm of a soldier and the realities of war. Foreman's direction is generally artless, highly romanticized, and there is not really one good performance—or strong characterization—in the whole film."

For some, the most disturbing scene involved a truckload of GIs being pulled out of a convey as a means of supplying witnesses to the execution, by firing squad, of a GI deserter. This cinematic scene had clearly been ripped from the real-life tragedy of Private Eddie Slovik, a deserter during the closing days of World War II.

In a confusing transgression still noted in military history books today, real-life Eddie Slovik was executed in a snow-covered field near a château in eastern France at Sainte-Marie-Aux-Mines (in German, *Markirch*; in Alsatian, *Màrkìrisch*) on December 31 (New Year's Eve) of 1945. As the incident was presented in *The Victors*, Frank Sinatra was heard on recordings singing "Have Yourself a Merry Little Christmas," the sound of the shots that killed Slovik was followed by a chorus of "Hark, The Herald Angels Sing."

The New York Times' review noted that this ghastly scene within the film "stands out in stark and sobering contrast to the other, gaudier, incidents in the film."

[Actually, the story of Eddie Slovik, born in 1920, would make a fascinating movie all by itself. Sinatra considered

doing just that.

He hired screenwriter Albert Maltz, who had been part of the blacklisted "Hollywood 10," to draft a screenplay about it. At the time, Sinatra was campaigning for John F. Kennedy, and, with the belief that it might negatively affect the outcome of the vote, Robert Kennedy asked Sinatra to drop the project—and he did.

Slovik was the first U.S. solider to be court martialized and executed for desertion since the Civil War. More than 21,000 American soldiers were charged with desertion during World War II. Forty-nine of them were convicted and sentenced to death, but only Slovik paid the ultimate penalty.

Facing death by firing squad, Slovik made a last-ditch appeal to General Eisenhower to save his life. However, desertion had become a systemic problem with the Allies in France after the Battle of the Bulge. There were many desertions at the time.

Eisenhower refused Slovik's plea for his life, claiming that his death was necessary to discourage further desertions.]

***

After filming The Victors, Peter and his wife flew to Los Angeles. Peter had been ordered to report to the U.S. military's induction center in Los Angeles.

At the time, as the war in Vietnam raged, America's Selective Service System (aka the military draft or conscription) required almost all male U.S. citizens and immigrants, ages 18 through 25, to register with the government for possible induction into the U.S. military. A lottery system allocating who was first and last in line, was in effect at the time.

At the induction center, he was herded into a large room filled with about thirty other young men. Each of them was given a questionnaire to fill out. One of the questions really upset Peter: "Have you ever thought about suicide, or has anyone in your family ever committed suicide?"

After that, the men were herded into a locker room, where they were told to strip completely naked, and to stash their belongings in a locker.

"As is natural in a gym, all of us were looking around, comparing our junk to other guys," Peter said. "Two or maybe three guys were winners in the competition, but most of us were 'regulars.'"

Everyone's eyes were tested, and the soles of their feet were examined to see if they were flat.

Later, Peter was directed to a private room, where a young medical examiner, a graduate of Harvard, awaited him. "This is where guys were told to bend over and spread their cheeks. A check for hemorrhoids. The guy put on a rubber glove with a greased finger for the probe."

"I stood right up to him, facing him almost nose to nose," Peter said. "I told him that if he touched my ass, I'd knock his front teeth to the back of his head."

The medic backed off and wrote something cryptic on his examination report.

Next, Peter was ushered toward a room where a Marine major sat behind his desk: "I refused to go into his office, claiming I was a civilian and could not be ordered around. I yelled out to him, 'How did you get your fucking job? Sucking some general's dick? You're nothing but a sadistic commie faggot ass-

The real **Eddie Slovik**. This unfortunate young man had been a deserter from the U.S. Army during World War II.

It seemed cruel and unusual punishment to execute him on New Year's Eve in 1945, months after the conflict ended. Thousands of other deserters were allowed to live.

Join the Army? Peter said No. His enraged (some said "unhinged") rejection of everything to do with the military at his induction process remains a part of his legend.

hole.'"

The major rose from the desk as if he were about to strike Peter, but changed his mind. Peter was dismissed and directed to the office of a psychiatrist for a final review.

"He wanted to grill me about my mother's suicide, but I wasn't into it," Peter said. "I was jaybird naked, but I fled from the building. Then a Marine guard reminded me that I was naked and could be arrested for indecent exposure. I went to my locker and put on my clothes and headed home.

Three weeks later, he received notification of his draft status. He had been rejected from military service, having been diagnosed as "mentally incompetent."

"On looking back years later," he said, "as time went by, I learned to control my temper better and to check all those foul words emerging from my mouth."

***

The Defenders and *Channing* (1963)

Peter Fonda was hired to perform in an episode of the TV series *The Defenders* entitled "The Brother Killers."

Like Perry Mason, this was a courtroom drama series that was telecast on CBS from 1961 to 1965. A total of 132 episodes were produced and aired.

It starred E.G. Marshall and Robert Reed as father-and-son defense attorneys specializing in legally complex cases involving neo-Nazis, civil rights demonstrators, conscientious objectors, pornographers, mercy killers, and a school teacher fired for being an atheist.

Many topics had never been dramatized on TV before—"no-knock" searches, custody rights of adoptive parents, capital punishments, insanity defenses, immigration quotas, the Hollywood blacklist, and Cold War visa restrictions. One episode in particular, "The Benefactor," was the most controversial, as the father-son legal team defended an abortionist. Because of it, three regular sponsors of the show, including Lever Brothers, withdrew their sponsorship, and the Canadian Broadcasting Company refused to broadcast it.

Another episode, originally entitled "The Gentle Assassin" for a December 1963 telecast, was revised and reworked after the assassination of John F. Kennedy in Dallas that November.

The creator of the series, Reginal Rose, told the press, "We were not interested in producing a 'who-done-it' like *Perry Mason*, showing a flashy courtroom battle of wits. The law was our subject—not crime, not mystery. Also, unlike Perry Mason, victory was far from certain in *The Defenders*.

Although Peter appeared briefly (and with an utter lack of consequence) in only one of its 132 episodes, *The Defenders* evolved into a controversial and widely popular courtroom drama during its heyday in the early 1960s.

Here are its two stars, **E.G. Marshall** *(left)* and **Robert Reed.**

***

In yet another TV series that was popular at the time, *Channing,* Peter was offered the lead role in an episode named "An Obelisk for Benny."

Broadcast between September of 1963 till April of 1964, *Channing* depicted life at the fictitious Channing College, with Jason Evers cast in the lead role of Professor Joseph Howe and with Henry Jones as Fred Baker, the college dean.

Rounding out the cast were some well-known actors of that era: Keir Dullea, Leslie Nielsen, Suzanne Pleshette, Joey Heatherton, and Leo G. Carroll.

To spice up ratings, Peter joined a list of guest stars such as Agnes Moorehead, George Segal, William

Shatner, Ralph Meeker, James Caan, James Earl Jones, Forrest Tucker, and Telly Savalas.

***

Warren Beatty and Jean Seberg in Lilith *(1963)*

Warren Beatty had gotten launched as a movie star because of scripts written by two gay playwrights and one gay novelist.

As a writer of award-winning Broadway plays, William Inge at the time was a rival of Tennessee Williams. He had scored big with his play *Bus Stop* (1956), which had been adapted into a hit movie with Marilyn Monroe, then the reigning blonde goddess of the 1950s.

Inge admitted that he had fallen "madly in love" with the then-relatively-unknown Warren Beatty: However, that didn't do Inge much good because Beatty was not only straight but he constantly seduced beautiful women, many of them stars.

"Sex was my brother's hobby," said his older sister, Shirley MacLaine.

Beatty had sustained an early affair with the English actress and sexual bombshell, Joan Collins, who said, "Warren would proposition a chair if it looked at him sideways. Three, four, even five times a day was not unusual for him."

Over the course of Beatty's career, even Jacqueline Kennedy Onassis would fall for him; also her ravenous sister, Lee Radziwill.

A book could be written devoted to Beatty's conquests. To name only a few, they included Julie Christie, Leslie Caron, Cher, Jane Fonda, Bianca Jagger, Diane Keaton, Mary Tyler Moore, Christina Onassis, Vanessa Redgrave, Diana Ross, Barbra Streisand, Natalie Wood, and Madonna.

Inge had written a play, *A Loss of Roses* which, although it had a short lifespan, had starred Beatty. Inge had become so enamored of Beatty that he wrote a screenplay, crafting it specifically with Beatty in mind. It was entitled and eventually produced as *Splendor in the Grass* (1961), co-starring Natalie Wood as his young lover growing up in Kansas in 1920.

Tennessee Williams also fell under Beatty's seductive spell. That playwright became instrumental in getting him cast as a Roman gigolo in *The Roman Spring of Mrs. Stone* (1961), co-starring Vivien Leigh as a fading stage actress.

During the shoot, rumors circulated that Beatty was bedding Leigh, impossibly famous at the time as the actress who interpreted the screen roles of both Scarlett O'Hara and Blanche DuBois.

Around the same time, the gay novelist, James Leo Herlihy, the future author of *Midnight Cowboy,* had written and released his first novel, *All Fall Down,* which came to Inge's attention. Inge was so intrigued by Herlihy's first novel that he agreed to adapt it into a screenplay specifically intended as a vehicle for "the object of his affection," Warren Beatty.

Warren Beatty and the doomed **Jean Seberg** in *Lilith*. She joined Peter Fonda in her dislike of Beatty. He gets a job working inside a mental hospital, but ends up seeking admission as an inmate.

Peter Fonda with **Jean Seberg** in *Lilith*.

During the context of the film, the mentally unstable character played by Peter becomes obsessed with Lilith and commits suicide. As an actor. it almost certainly stirred memories of the suicide of his mother

In the resulting screen adaptation by Inge, also entitled *All Fall Down* and released in 1962, one of the female leads, played by Eva Marie Saint, falls in love with the character portrayed by Beatty. It quickly becomes clear that the Beatty character's mother, portrayed by Angela Lansbury, is also in love with him (i.e., her son).

After that, Beatty was offered a different script almost weekly from producers or directors throughout Hollywood. Beatty, however, had, for the moment at least, lost interest in movie-making, preferring instead to travel the world, seducing beautiful women (lots of them), and having fun.

Within two-and-a-half years, by now $10,000 in debt, it was time for Beatty to return to work. As such, he accepted the male lead in *Lilith*, a film that had been written by, and was being produced and directed by Robert Rossen.

Rossen was known primarily for producing films, *All the King's Men* (1949) and *The Hustler* (1961).

All the King's Men, based on the life of Huey Long, the corrupt governor of Louisiana, was voted Best Picture of the Year. Although Rossen lost the Oscar for Best Director, Broderick Crawford, the star of the picture, won the Best Actor of the Year Oscar. Mercedes McCambridge, as one of the film's female leads, won the Best Supporting Actress Oscar.

More than a decade later, Rossen also had great success with his casting of Paul Newman and Jackie Gleason in *The Hustler* (1961).

Rossen's reputation, however, was still tainted. The House Un-American Activities Committee had blacklisted him after it was revealed that he'd been a member of the Communist Party. Early in the investigative process, at a hearing, Rossen had pleaded the Fifth Amendment, a stance which led to his placement on the blacklist.

To rid himself of that stigma, he named 57 other members of the communist party, a betrayal which made him very unpopular in certain circles.

Selecting an actress to portray Lilith was a difficult choice for Rossen. At first, he thought either Samantha Eggar or Yvette Mimieux might be right. Then he opted for Diane Cilento, the then-wife of Sean Connery. She'd won a Best Supporting Actress Oscar for her performance in *Tom Jones* (1962), starring Albert Finney.

Peter Fonda had read the novel *Lilith* by J.R. Salamanca and thought it worthy of adaptation into a feature film. He soon learned that Rossen had acquired its film rights, and he met with him, seeking a role. Peter knew that he was not right as the male lead, so he lobbied instead for the role of a suicidal mental patient, Stephen Evshevsky. Rossen thought he might be perfect for it and assigned it to him.

Peter would remember Rossen as a man of thinning gray hair with the figure of a barrel. When he spoke, it sounded like sandpaper.

Casting the title role of Lilith was a difficult choice for Rossen. Peter told him that his older sister, Jane, should accept the role and "probably walk off with a Best Actress Oscar," but Rossen was not convinced.

Finally, he decided that Jean Seberg would be the best of all of them.

Seberg, who would live half of her young life in France, had actually been born in Marshalltown, Iowa, in 1938. She had burst onto the scene when Otto Preminger cast her as the star of *Saint Joan* (1947), a role for which she beat out 18,000 other hopeful candidates. The picture, when it was released, was a colossal failure.

On looking back at the casting choice, Peter said, "Preminger cast a martyr to play a martyr."

Beatty and Rossen flew to Paris to meet with Seberg. They were directed to a Left Bank café where she was having a late-morning coffee. "Jean had an air of mystery and also a sense of doom about her," Rossen said.

Her first question to the men was, "Which one of you to I have to fuck…maybe both of you at the same time? That would hardly be a first for me."

"We want you as an actress, not as our whore," Rossen said. She agreed to become Beatty's co-star, admitting that she found him "very attractive."

On March 29, 1963, all three of them flew together to New York on a "redeye flight" from Paris, which almost killed them. Lightning struck their Boeing 707 shortly after takeoff. The plane made an emergency landing with no one injured.

Back in Hollywood, Rossen distributed the final draft of his screenplay to all of the film's principals and supporting players,

Vincent Bruce (Beatty) a troubled ex-soldier, applies for a job as a trainee at a posh mental institution, Chestnut Lodge, in Rockville, Maryland. After a while there, he becomes dangerously obsessed with the seductive, artistic, and schizophrenic Lilith Arthur (Seburg). She has been diagnosed as "emotionally nymphomaniacal." Soon, Lilith is sleeping with Bruce, but he soon catches her trying to seduce another patient, this time, a female.

Bruce later triggers the suicide of another patient, Stephen (played by Peter Fonda), based on that patient's jealousy of Lilith.

In the aftermath, Lilith goes on a destructive rampage of her room and winds up in a catatonic state. Bruce himself goes to his superiors, seeking psychiatric help for himself.

In the movie's final scenes, Bruce's own fate seems bleak.

Peter Fonda in a "second fiddle," supporting role in *Lilith*. He's a suicidal patient in a mental ward jealously obsessed with Lilith.

Before shooting began, Peter was offered the chance to visit a mental hospital, but he refused to do so. He called it "the local looney bin." He talked to both Rossen and Beatty about why he rejected the idea. "Once the doctors met me, I'm sure they would have locked me up. I'm nutty enough. I don't need to visit a nuthouse."

Rossen thought Peter and Warren Beatty might bond during the shoot, as both of them had something in common. Each of them had sisters who were already movie stars: Jane Fonda and Shirley MacLaine. "But I found him protected by this steely reserve," Peter said about Beatty. "It was hard to break into him."

It didn't help matters to learn that Beatty was also dating Peter's former stepmother, Afdera Franchetti, Henry Fonda's ex-wife. "Not only that, but I'd heard that he'd fucked my sister, Jane."

Beatty's seduction of Seberg came early in the shoot. Before the end of filming, she had turned against him and transferred her sexual favors to Peter.

Peter had seen Seberg's performance in the 1960 French film, *Breathless* (1960) and was quite captivated by her as an icon within the New Wave of French cinema.

Actually, at the time that Seberg was romantically involved with Romain Gary, the French aviator, resistance fighter, novelist, and diplomat. He was 24 years her senior. She'd given birth to his son, Alexandre Diego Gary, in Barcelona in July of 1962. The child's birth to Seberg was kept a secret, in part because Gary had not yet divorced his wife at the time, Lesley Blanch by the time of the child's birth.

[After Gary's divorce from Blanch, he married Seberg on the French island of Corsica in October of 1962.]

Married or not, Seberg was known for sleeping around, not just with Fonda and Beatty, but with such stars as Clint Eastwood during their co-filming of *Paint Your Wagon* (1960).

She also had an affair with Sammy Davis Jr., and another with Dennis Hopper, a close friend of Peter.

Many of her lovers came from exotic backgrounds, as was the case with Fabio Testi when the co-starred in *Camorra (Gang War in Naples; 1972).*

Seberg's other lovers included the ski champion Jean-Claude Killy, Carlos Navara, a Mexican revolutionary; Masai Hewitt, a Black Panther leader; Hakim Jamal, a black nationalist; and Kader Hasni, an Algerian soccer player. One of her lovers was actor John Maddox, who was said to have disappeared into the Bermuda Triangle.

Seberg's other, "random" lovers, in the words of one author, included "lots of musicians, exchange students, outright bums she picked up on the streets of Paris, long-haired hippies, and an assortment of blacks and Algerians.

Yves Boisset, the French film director, said, "It was important to Jean to feel, well, excuse the term, 'fuckable.' In her depression, she'd turn to men for assurance. Jean could have sex in an elevator, between the third and fourth floors."

In *Lilith,* Kim Hunter, as Dr. Bea Brice, hires the Beatty character. This talented Detroit-born actress was forever remembered for creating the role of Stella Kowalski in the original stage production, on Broadway, of *A Streetcar Named Desire* with Marlon Brando. She reprised that role in the 1951 film adaption with Vivien Leigh playing her sister, Blanche DuBois. Hunter won a Best Supporting Actress Oscar that year.

Later, in 1968, she was cast as the chimpanzee Zira in *Planet of the Apes.*

Gene Hackman played the minor role, in *Lilith,* of "Norman," but in 1967 he'd fare much better when he was cast opposite Beatty in *Bonnie and Clyde.*

At first, Beatty had high hopes for his role in *Lilith,* but soon realized that he'd been "trapped in a bad picture." He constantly annoyed Rossen by asking him, "What is my motivation in this scene?"

Finally, in exasperation, Rossen fired back, "Your motivation is a paycheck."

Rossen told Peter, "You're fine in your role, but Beatty was miscast. I should have offered the role to Anthony Perkins. If I die before the end of the shoot, have Beatty indicted for murder."

Kim Hunter as Stella, arguing over the contents of her sister's jewelry and makeup case with **Marlon Brando**, in Tennessee Williiams' *A Streetcar Named Desire.*

Anne Meacham, a very talented actress, was cast in the role of Mrs. Yvonne Meaghan. She became famous for her roles off Broadway, most notably in plays by Tennessee Williams, a close friend. Williams later told *The New York Times*, "There is nothing Anne won't say or do onstage without any sign of embarrassment, even feeling a man's crotch."

Meacham won a Best Actress Obie for playing "Catherine Holly" in the original 1958 stage play version of Tennessee Williams' *Suddenly, Last Summer.* [*That character was more famously interpreted a year later (in 1959) by Elizabeth Taylor in its film adaption.*]

Meacham also appeared in Williams' *The Gnädiges Fräulein* in 1966, and *In the Bar of a Tokyo Hotel* in 1969.

Beatty was disappointed when he sat impatiently through the rushes, blaming any failures on Rossen. "A couple of my movies didn't have them lined up at the box office. I can't afford to be in another turkey if I hope to have a film career."

When Rossen could take no more of Beatty's "suggestions," he turned on him. "Why should I listen to a wet-behind-the-ears, snot-nosed jerk like you?"

Rossen got along far better with Seberg, telling her, "I want you to have the face of an angel but the soul of a devil."

"As for Peter, he played it like an emotionally disturbed young man," Rossen said. "All of it was typecasting on my part."

Seberg told Peter, "Other than my hatred of Otto (Preminger), I have only two memories of *Saint-Joan*. One, when I was burned at the stake, the other when the critics crucified me."

In spite of their differences and the views of the critics, Preminger awarded her the lead in *Bonjour Tristesse* (1958), the following year, even though the money people wanted Audrey Hepburn. "That's when I fell in love with France and its people," she told Peter.

"I would have gone into oblivion if Jean-Luc Godard hadn't cast me in *Breathless (aka Á bout de souffle; 1960)* She co-starred with Jean-Paul Belmondo. Her screen performance caused François Truffaut to hail Seberg as "the best actress in Europe."

"I've been in a lot of shit since then," Seberg said, "but I'm hoping my role in *Lilith* will signal the critics that I'm a serious actress."

Columnist Norma Sloane wrote that Beatty wanted to disassociate himself as a movie star from the other "pretty boys" dominating the screens of that era.

She went on to cite John Gavin as "the handsomest male star on the planet." Others of her pretty boys included Tom Tryon, Troy Donahue, Tab Hunter, Tony Curtis, Robert Wagner, and George Hamilton. "With an exception here and there, you might say that the hearts of these stars are "young and gay," she wrote.

Arthur Penn, who directed Anne Bancroft in her Oscar-winning performance in *The Miracle Worker* (1962), had a positive view: "Warren Beatty is going to be the biggest male movie star since Clark Gable, Rhett Butler himself."

***

In reference to *Lilith,* Bosley Crowther in *The New York Times*, wrote, "A gauzy, opaque work of clever camera trickery that suggests the eerie, abnormal realms of mental aberration into which the heroine often goes. A muddy performance by Warren Beatty doesn't help. He does not help to clarify matters. Nor does he create sympathy."

Judith Crist in *The New York Herald Tribune* wrote: "It's a muddle of Americana and schizophrenia, sex, and sophistry, with a ludicrously lubricious plot and enough fuzzy-wuzzy incoherent camera work to turn it into an unwillingly parody of 'festival' films at their worst. Beatty cannot deliver a line until counting to ten."

Lilith collapsed at the box office, generating slightly more than one million dollars, although Columbia tried to book it into more than the usual number of movie houses, beginning with its opening in New York on October 1, 1964.

During the shooting of *Lilith,* Rossen had been in ill health, and he broke out in liver spots. All the feuds he'd had, especially the one he'd had with Beatty, had taken a serious toll on his body. Disillusioned and ailing, he died two years after the release of the film. He was 57 years old.

On September 9, 1979, Paris police officers found Jean Seberg's decomposing body on the back seat of her Renault, parked in a location near her apartment in the 16th arrondissement. It was wrapped in a blanket.

In the Renault, the French police also found an empty bottle of barbiturates and a note, written in French, to her son: "Forgive me, I can no longer live with my nerves."

Her death was ruled a probable suicide, but that was later changed, in 1980, after additional charges were leveled against "persons unknown for non-assistance of a person in danger."

Her partner at the time, Ahmed Hasni, told police that in July of that year, she had attempted suicide by jumping in front of a Parisian subway train, but was rescued almost at the last second.

The subsequent police report determined that Seberg had such a high level of alcohol in her blood that she would have been too comatose to get into the Renault, and to have taken all those pills, without assistance.

The Ironies and Tragedies of Fame
Who could have known at the time this photo was snapped how horribly **Jean Seberg**'s life would go?

It appeared in her Iowa home town's local paper on the occasion of her 18th birthday. The text that accompanied it made this announcement:

BACK HOME, A CELEBRITY

Jean Seberg of Marshalltown stands beside a poster proclaiming her triumph in being chosen in an international contest to play the role of Saint Joan. Jean returned Thursday and received a big hometown welcome from 3,000 who braved cold weather to greet her. She will leave next week for London to begin work on the picture after celebrating her 18th birthday at home on Tuesday....

Although he'd divorced her in 1970, Romain Gary held a press conference, blaming the FBI for driving her to suicide. At that press conference, Gary claimed that Seberg "became psychotic" after the media reported the false story that the FBI had planted. It claimed that she was pregnant with a child fathered by a Black Panther in 1970.

The FBI's campaign against Seberg was similar to its attack on Jane Fonda. It was further explored by *Time* magazine in a front-page article, "The FBI *vs.* Jean Seberg."

Ironically, Gary himself committed suicide in December of 1980, leaving a note. He claimed that his own death was not to be blamed on the suicide of Seberg, but on his own failure. "I felt I could no longer produce literary works and did not want to go on living."

The legacy of the doomed expatriated American actress lives on. In 1986, Madonna, inspired by Seberg's film, *Á bout de souffle (Breathless)*, released a music video called "Papa Don't Preach." The pop singer wore a pixie blonde wig, a striped jersey shirt, and black Capri pants, her outfit inspired by Seberg's performance as an *ingénue* in *Breathless*.

In 1991, Jodie Foster purchased the film rights to a biography of Seberg but canceled the project two years later.

Actress **Jean Seberg** with **Romain Gary** had one of the most ill-fated marriages in the world of celebrities. Both of them were tragic figures who each committed suicide. "Talented but tormented" was how the French press called their mental states.

One Parisian wrote: "They had everything, including fame and money. What they lacked was the will to live."

***

Arrest and Trial (1964)

In the 1960s, there were good years and lean years for Peter and his career. Thanks in part to two feature films and three major television roles, 1964 had been a good year.

Before he appeared in those feature films, *Lilith* and *The Young Lovers*, he was cast in an episode of *Arrest and Trial* as Alex Bakalyan in "A Circle of Strangers."

The telecast was a 90-minute crime and legal drama that ran on ABC-TV once a week at prime time (8:30pm, Eastern) during the 1963-64 season.

The first part, "The Arrest," trailed detective Nick Anderson (Ben Gazzara) and Dan Kirby (Roger Perry) of the Los Angeles Police Department as they pursued and captured criminals, sometimes very dangerous ones.

Born to Italian immigrants in New York City, Gazzara already knew one Fonda (Jane), from the Actors Studio.

His breakthrough role had come on Broadway in Tennessee Williams' *Cat on a Hot Tin Roof* (1955), which earned him widespread acclaim for his portrayal of a closeted homosexual.

That was followed by another memorable performance as a soldier on trial for murder in Otto Preminger's *Anatomy of a Murder* (1960).

Right after Peter worked with him, Gazzara would become

Handsome, studly, and GREAT choices for a crime and courtroom television drama: **Ben Gazzara** *(left)* and **Chuck Connors**.

the star of a television series, *Run for Your Life* (1965-1968), for which he would be nominated for two Emmys and three Golden Globes.

Roger Perry, a native son of Iowa, had been an intelligence officer for the U.S. Air Force in World War II. In the early 1950s, after military service, he became a widely recognized figure on television.

In 1960, he co-starred with James Coburn in *The Texan*.

After working with Peter, Perry got his greatest exposure when he was cast as a U.S. Air Force pilot in an episode of ABC's *Star Trek*.

In the second segment of *Arrest and Trial's* "Circle of Stangers," young lovers escape from their feuding families, but become fugitives from justice when they're suspected of murder. Apprehended, they are suspects defended in court by criminal attorney John Egan (Chuck Connors).

Handsome and studly, Brooklyn-born Chuck Connors was one of only thirteen athletes in the history of American professional sports to have played in both Major League Baseball (with the Brooklyn Dodgers and the Chicago Cubs) and with the National Basketball Association.

But despite his success as a professional athlete, Connors is best remembered for his five-year gig as Lucas McCain in the highly rated ABC TV series, *The Rifleman* (1958-1963). In the series, which had ended by the time he worked with Peter, he played a widowed father raising a young boy.

"I was riding high in the Nielsen ratings until the fuckers put me into the same time slot as that bitch, Lucille Ball, on *The Lucy Show*," he said.

He also revealed that his greatest fan was Leonid Brezhnev, the leader of the Soviet Union. At a party that Richard Nixon hosted at the White House, Connors presented him with a pair of Colt "signed six-shooters." Later, just before Brezhnev's departure for Moscow, he and Connors were photographed together in a bear hug.

Privately, Connors met with Peter, telling him of his fear that his acting career might soon come crashing to an embarrassing end. During the permissive 1960s, in a movie house on Broadway, a porn film entitled *Hollywood Blue*, narrated by Mickey Rooney, had opened. In a film clip, Connors, who was not identified, is clearly seen sporting an enormous erection from a ten-inch penis and sodomizing a young man.

As it turned out, that exposure did not harm his career. Actually, it gained him a new legion of fans among gay men.

"I knew that Connors used to be a baseball player, but I didn't know that he carried around a bat that big," wrote one reviewer in *The Village Voice*.

Hollywood Blue came and went. By 1977, Connors portrayed a slave owner in two episodes of the television miniseries *Roots*.

***

Alfred Hitchcock Presents (1964)

"I was thrilled when I got a call from the office of Alfred Hitchcock, where I learned that he wanted me to star in an episode of his anthology series," Peter said. The hit TV series had been telecast on CBS and NBC between 1955 and 1965. Peter would appear in it in 1964 in the title role of a segment named "The Return of Verge Likens."

When he was presented with the actual script, with the understanding that he'd be paid $11,000 for his involvement, he was not impressed. "I was to play a Tennessee hillbilly who scares a man to death by shaving him too close in revenge for the death of my father."

He was also disappointed to learn that he had to speak with

a Tennessee accent. He immediately called on Dean Hargrove, a voice coach and Hollywood expert on Southern vernacular accent. Hargrove began to train Peter, noting that a true Tennessee accent differed from the typical "southern" accent. In just a few days I pulled it off," Peter claimed. "I was speaking as if I had grown up eating cracklin' bread and fried possum."

The Hitchcock series always began with the camera flashing on a sketch of the director himself, a pen-and-ink profile that he had personally crafted. His opening words, delivered with his distinctive British accent, were always "Good evening…"

In a total of 381 episodes, Hitchcock starred many famous guests: Robert Redford, Sir Cedric Hardwicke, Steve McQueen, Bruce Dern, George Segal, Claude Rains, Joan Fontaine, Roger Moore, Teresa Wright, and (in 1959), Miss Bette Davis.

After Peter completed the terms of his contract, Hitchcock talked to him, sharing behind-the-scenes memories of his having directed his father, Henry Fonda, in one of his classics, *The Wrong Man* (1956).

"That darling boy, your father, had only one problem," Hitchcock asserted: "He cannot give a bad performance."

"I wish I had his problem," Peter said, ruefully.

***

12 O'Clock High (1964)

Peter's last star turn on television in 1964 was in the series *12 O'Clock High,* a military drama set during World War II. It had originally been telecast on ABC-TV from September of 1964 to January of 1967.

The series was based on the hit feature film, *Twelve O'Clock High* (1949). *[Unlike the TV series, the movie's title spelled out the world Twelve]* that had starred Gregory Peck.

The TV plots focused on the U.S. Army's Eighth Air Force, which flew dangerous daylight bombing missions over Nazi Germany and Occupied France during the early days of the American involvement in World War II.

Their B-17 bombers, called "Flying Fortresses," were heavy aircraft taking off from an airfield in the eastern sector of England. For the first season, many of the actors who had appeared in the Peck movie were retained.

Peter had been an avid watcher of the series since its inception. New to the series, he was cast as Lt. Andy Lathrop in an episode called "The Sound of Distant Thunder."

Peter got tanked up one afternoon on margaritas before the beginning of shooting, and decided to go on a solo motorcycle ride along Hidden Valley Drive, in the posh, high-altitude regions of Beverly Hills.

Along the way, he faced an oncoming car that seemed like it was out of control and was about to crash into him. Veering off the road, he hit a speed bump and was thrown onto the asphalt, where "I bounced along like a ball."

Later, after being rushed to the hospital, doctors discovered that "my back looked like ground hamburger." He also suffered from a deep wound to his

Still closely resembling TV Land's fantasy of a cleancut "matinee idol," young **Peter Fonda** appears here with **Jill Haworth** in an episode of *12 O'Clock High*, "The Sound of Distant Thunder."

Very few viewers at the time could have imagined that throughout its filming, he was numb from painkillers and mangled from a "wipe out," the result of a recent very serious motorcycle accident.

left hip.

His face, however, was not injured. Since he needed the money, he reported for work on the set of *12 O'Clock High* in agony but "soaked" with painkillers. He managed to get through the five-day shoot, later thanking his co-star, Jill Haworth, for giving him "pills and tenderness."

Five years younger than Peter, Haworth, who was English, had been born on V-J Day *[August 14, 1945, the day the Allies declared victory over Japan]*.

The daughter of a textile magnate and a mother who was a ballet dancer, Haworth came to America and appeared in many films during the 1960s. She originated the role of Sally Bowles in the Broadway musical *Cabaret* (1966) that Liza Minnelli later made famous on film.

Otto Preminger put her under contract for five years and cast her in *Exodus* (1960), where she played an ill-fated Danish refugee in love with the character named Dow Landau (played by Sal Mineo). As Haworth told Peter, "Off screen I fell in love with Sal. Otto didn't tell me he was gay and sleeping with Peter Lawford."

After working with Peter Fonda, she was cast in *In Harm's Way* (1965). "On screen, I got raped by Kirk Douglas, but off screen, he was a real gentleman. However, I detested another cast member, John Wayne. He was one nasty creep, the meanest bastard I ever worked with."

In their episode of *12 O'Clock High*, Peter and Haworth were guest stars operating in conjunction with "regulars" who included Robert Lansing, Frank Overton, and Paul Burke.

Lansing had a long career, spanning five decades, but he's best remembered for portraying the authoritarian Brigadier General Frank Savage in *12 O'Clock High*. His rugged good looks, commanding presence, and stentorian voice assured him ongoing stage work in such plays as Tennessee Williams' *Suddenly, Last Summer*, and in August Strindberg's *The Father*, where his "mannered, tortured, and racked portrait of the Captain" was lauded by critics.

At the end of its first season, studio executives decided that a younger-looking lead actor was needed as the male lead of *12 O'Clock High*. Therefore, for the series' second season, Lansing was fired and replaced with Paul Burke in the role of Colonel Joe Gallagher.

Ironically, Burke, although he looked younger, was actually two years older than Lansing. The decision to replace Lansing with Burke proved unpopular with TV audiences, and ratings nosedived.

For his performance as Major Harvey Stovall, Frank Overton was also praised. He had joined the cast at the series' inception, having previously starred in *To Kill a Mockingbird* (1962).

The year he worked with Peter, he also starred with Henry Fonda in *Fail Safe*, in which he was cast as General Bogan.

PETER VS. THE POLICE
SEX, DRUGS, ROCK AND ROLL, AND LOTS OF BAD PUBLICITY

Police move in among crowd during Sunset Strip demonstration. (Associated Press Wirefoto)

Sunset Strip—Long Hair and Fuzz

Bored, perhaps, with too many cattle calls and tryouts for minor, time-consuming parts in television series and nerdy movies, then-26-year-old **Peter Fonda** began to act out his frustrations and rages in altercations with the police. In the photo above, he appears in white jeans on the photo's far right. Here's the nationally syndicated text that accompanied it:

Nov 27 (1966): It's sort of a gas," one of the kids said. It was a feeling Los Angeles city and county police didn't share today after another round of what has become the favorite teen-age sport here—the Saturday night riots on the once-glittering, now run-down Sunset Strip.

The cops swept up 67 persons as they battled 1,500 long-haired and short-skirted youngsters last night. Among them were actor **Peter Fonda,** 26, who was released after explaining that all he was doing was taking pictures for a documentary on teenagers.

In Court

Actor Peter Fonda leaves a Los Angeles court building today after his attorney asked that marijuna possession charges against him and three other men be dismissed.

Other, widely publicized disagreements with the police followed, as noted in the headlines *left* and *right*.

Peter's horrified father, **Henry Fonda,** did what he could to persuade judges to be lenient with his errant son, and worried that the negative publicity would adversely affect his desirability as a matinee idol and emerging movie star.

Cynics countered that Peter had shrewdly concluded that his marketability was waning within the television venues he'd been pursuing, and that perhaps he consciously decided to revise his image to coincide with the enraged, drug-fueled rebellions breaking out nationwide.

In the aftermath, considering the limitations of both the movies and his talent, Peter's decision to become an "Easy Rider" seemed like a smart and logical choice..

Peter Fonda Arrested

Actor Peter Fonda (foreground) son of Henry Fonda, is restrained by deputies at the scene of a Sunset Strip disturbance in Los Angeles. Fonda later was arrested after telling officers he was filming a documentary on teen-agers. Fonda was a close friend of Eugene F. (Stormy) McDonald and was a witness at the inquest into the Feb. 3, 1965, death of McDonald. McDonald, an heir to Zenith Radio millions, was found dead of a gunshot wound in his Tucson home. The death was ruled not a suicide.

Sunset Strip Youths, Motorcycle Club Spark New Los Angeles Riots

CHAPTER THIRTEEN

PETER FONDA VS. HOLLYWOOD'S OTHER "HEARTTHROBS OF THE MOMENT"

*How **Nick Adams**—the cheerfully resourceful but doomed young actor, the rumored former lover of both James Dean and Elvis Presley—solicited Peter as "My Next Motorcycle Buddy"*

*Why **Tommy Kirk**, Peter's co-star, confessed: "I used to be summoned to the office of Walt Disney, where I had to drop Trou."*

*What **Brandon deWilde** did with Peter during their LSD Trip in the desert outside Palm Springs: Peter later confessed to Dennis Hopper, "Brandon and I did unspeakable things."*

Michael Pollard: *a short and stubby character actor known mostly for his performance in* Bonnie and Clyde *asks Peter to help finance his run for President of the United States*

THE YOUNG LOVERS
(ABORTION? YES OR NO.)
PETER FONDA CO-STARS WITH "THE NEXT ELIZABETH TAYLOR"
IN A FILM ABOUT AN OUT-OF-WEDLOCK PREGNANCY

HOW THE KING OF B-LIST FILMMAKING,
ROGER CORMAN,
INVITED PETER TO STAR IN A MOTORCYCLE FLICK, *THE WILD ANGELS*.
ACCORDING TO CORMAN, "IT WILL DO FOR THE '60S WHAT MARLON BRANDO'S *THE WILD ONE* DID FOR THE 1950S."

THE WILD ANGELS
PETER GETS HIGH AND "REHEARSES" WITH MEMBERS OF THE HELL'S ANGELS FOR THIS FEAR-INDUCING CINEMATIC SAGA ABOUT LIFE ON THE ROAD: GANG RAPES, ORGIES, SADISM, RECREATIONAL DRUG HIGHS, AND THE COMMERCIALLY PROVOCATIVE FLAUNTING OF MAINSTREAM CONVENTIONS

FALLEN CHERUBINI?
FRANK SINATRA AND HIS DAUGHTER, NANCY
How Ol' Blue Eyes wanted Peter "To keep it zipped up when he's working with 'MY LITTLE GIRL.'"
Peter obeys but Elvis doesn't.

"When I divorced Nancy Sinatra, every door in Hollywood slammed shut on me."
—Tommy Sands

THE TRIP
Roger Corman tries to recruit Peter to star in the film industry's first major movie about the mind-bending effects of LSD.

Mr. Universe to the Rescue
[CORMAN HIMSELF, AFTER ACID TRIPS OF HIS OWN, CONFESSES THAT IN HIS FANTASIES, HE WAS BRUTALLY RAPED BY STEVE REEVES]

Re the Unclothed Derrières of Male Actors:
"I became the first male actor to show my bare ass in a major, non-porno motion picture. Soon, Marlon Brando and Jon Voight did the same."
—Peter Fonda

"Be warned: I might get an erection."
—What Peter Fonda said to Susan Strasberg about the upcoming filming of their nude scenes together.

As the 1960s progressed, Peter deepened his allegiance to his counter-culture, rebellious, somewhat angry image. Still struggling for recognition as an actor, but swept up in the "sex, drugs, and rock 'n roll" movements of his times, he seemed increasingly aware of the futility of trying to match the creative output of either his father or his sister, Jane. The wholesome, all-American image he'd established in *Tammy and the Doctor* and some of his TV appearances, seemed outdated and almost quaint—images and projections that hadn't been pertinent in years. Now, his film *persona* seemed realistically focused on experimental, edgy projects specifically aimed at the counterculture. They included the following films:

The Young Lovers (1964)

In the same year that he completed *Lilith* (1964), Peter accepted the male lead, and completed, *The Young Lovers,* the sole directorial effort of its young-ish producer, Samuel Goldwyn Jr.

An inside, sometimes indulged, member of Hollywood Royalty, Goldwyn Jr. told Peter, "My father is a legend in movie history. I will never come within miles of being his equal, so why even try?"

Born in Los Angeles in 1926 to movie mogul Samuel Goldwyn Sr. (1879-1974), and Frances Howard, Goldwyn Jr. had served in the U.S. Army during World War II. Later, in London, he was a theatrical producer before joining Edward R. Murrow at CBS in Manhattan. Following in his famous father's footsteps, he later founded productions companies which included Formosa Productions, the Samuel Goldwyn Company, and Samuel Goldwyn Films.

The Young Lovers had a long gestation period. It was based on a novel by Julian Zimet, who published it under the pseudonym of Julian Halavey, since he was blacklisted at the time because of alleged communist affiliations.

It was first optioned as a play that never made it to Broadway. Goldwyn read it early in 1957 and thought it would make "a hell of a movie," eventually buying the rights from Zimet.

Robert Dozier wrote the first of several scripts for it. Goldwyn Jr. then launched a search for 100 "young lovers," with the intention of using them as extras.

For the next few years, he rejected script after script, claiming that "no writer came up with a screenplay that captured the spirit and attitudes and idiom of the young people."

Finally, he met and hired George Garrett, an assistant professor of English whose prose Goldwyn admired. He directed the movie himself "because I want complete control."

As director, he set about casting the movie, deciding that Richard Beymer would be perfect in the lead role of Eddie Slocum.

This native son of Iowa had been a sensation in the role of Tony in the film version of *West Side Story* (1961) opposite Natalie Wood. Before that, he had starred as Peter in *The Diary of Anne Frank* (1959). Some critics hailed him as "the next Gary Cooper, "although Beymer himself was reported to be unhappy with his acting. He rejected many film roles, including one associated with *The Young Lovers.*

SONS OF FAMOUS FATHERS
Making Noise in 1964's "New Hollywood"

Samuel Goldwyn, Jr., *(left)* with **Peter Fonda**, during the conceptualization of their then provocative and avant-garde film, *The Young Lovers.* Plagued by dilettantism, long delays, and many reworkings of a confusing script, it didn't really work.

[The role Beymer really wanted, he didn't get. It was eventually awarded to Sal Mineo for the character he played in Rebel Without a Cause *(1954), starring James Dean.]*

With Beymer out of the picture, Goldwyn turned to Peter Fonda, whose Broadway stage performance in *Blood, Sweat, and Stanley Poole* he had liked.

Since Goldwyn had not included a major star in his cast, he found it difficult to arrange financing. Eventually, however, in September of 1963, he and his partner, Doug Netter, raised enough money to begin shooting.

Later, Goldwyn Jr. signed a distribution deal with Metro-Goldwyn-Mayer that would begin in May of 1964. He noted with a sense of irony that the studio still carried the name of his father who had parted, in his son's words, "centuries ago."

It was Goldwyn Jr. who devised the tagline of his film: "THERE IS A MOMENT WHEN THE REST OF THE WORLD CEASES TO EXIST."

Here, in a nutshell, is the storyline of *Young Lovers:* At college, Eddie Slocum (Fonda) shares a modest apartment with "Tarragoo" (Nick Adams). Eddie's girlfriend, Debbie, (Deborah Walley) is a frequent visitor, often with her friend, Pam Burns (Sharon Hugueny). Pam, who wants to become a teacher, lives with her widowed mother, played by Beatrice Straight.

Eddie and Pam become lovers, and she finds herself pregnant. However, Eddie is not exactly ready for fatherhood. First, he barely has enough money to support himself, and he is also afraid of losing his scholarship. She rejects the idea of an abortion.

The rest of the film deals with the young lovers having to work out these "untidy" complications.

Despite its low budget, Goldwyn assembled a rather remarkable coterie of talent beginning with its two female leads: Sharon Hugueny and Deborah Walley.

A daughter of Los Angeles, Hugueny had previously appeared in James Leo Herlihy's *Blue Denim*, another film about teen pregnancy. She had made her debut opposite Troy Donahue in *Parrish* (1961)

[Hugueny became more famous for her marriage to future Paramount mogul Robert Evans than she did for any role she ever played. Evans had met her on the set of Parrish *in the era when she was being publicized as Warner Brothers "Next Elizabeth Taylor."*

"She was being protected like the Hope Diamond, and I felt guilty even kissing this virgin," Evans said. "Of course, with me after her, her virginity would have a short life span. I married her even though she was only three months past her 17th birthday. There should be a state law against marrying a virginal teenager."

At their wedding in Beverly Hills, Eddie Fisher

Richard Beymer (left in photo above) rejected the role that was later awarded to Peter.

Here's Beymer with **Natalie Wood** in his greatest, most oft-remembered performance as Tony in the 1961 (original) movie production of Leonard Bernstein's *West Side Story*.

Peter Fonda, presumably on the verge of impregnating his character's girlfriend, played by **Sharon Hugueny**. She was cast into the role when she was 24, three years after her widely publicized divorce from Paramount Studio's Chief Executive, Robert Evans.

Gossips rushed to lacerate her previous nuptials. She was only 17 when she had married for the first time. It had also been the first marriage for Evans, his first of what eventually morphed into a total of six unhappy marriages.

Actually, Hugueny at the time was a lot more famous than Peter Fonda, who didn't generate a lot of onscreen heat. Casting directors complained that he looked out of shape and scrawny.

was there. So was Elizabeth Taylor, who came to see the actress that Warners was promoting as her replacement. Kirk Douglas showed up, too, as did Jack Lemmon. But what entranced Hugueny was the appearance of the handsome Robert Wagner with Natalie Wood. Hugueny whispered to Taylor, "This guy they call 'R.J.' is the one I should be marrying."

"After our marriage, I took the girl, no longer a virgin—I really made her bleed—to New York," Evans confessed. "It was like turning loose a Persian cat in the Amazon. She was a fragile flower. Our marriage was not a success, to put it mildly. One of our problems was that I was never at home. I admit it, with half the girls on Broadway to seduce, I was just too busy."

It wasn't until 1964 that Hugueny got around to divorcing Evans. She would later marry a 21-year-old freelance photographer and later, a 45-year-old writer, the founder of Mid-America Pictures.

In 1977, she decided to try to relaunch her film career, with the understanding that she had made only four feature films, including The Young Lovers. En route to sign a contract with a new management team, she was nearly killed when a police car in hot pursuit of an escaping crook plowed into her car. She was injured for life and never fully recovered. She was still suffering some form of pain when she succumbed to cancer at the age of 52.

Robert Evans with **Sharon Hugueny** in 1961, the year of their marriage. Her resemblance to Elizabeth Taylor was one of her strongest assets.

Evans began his adult life selling women's apparel in Manhattan in 1956 before migrating to Hollywood for a brief career as a film actor. He played the bullfighter in The Sun Also Rises (1957) based on the celebrated novel by Ernest Hemingway.

Deserting acting, he began a meteoric rise in the film industry, becoming head of Paramount Pictures in 1967. The studio's fortunes were at low tide until he released one hit after another: Rosemary's Baby, Love Story, The Godfather, and Chinatown.

After dumping his first wife (Sharon Hugueny), he'd take another six wives. His most famous bride was actress Ali MacGraw (1959-1973). A later marriage to Catherine Oxenberg was annulled after nine days.

In May of 1998, Evans suffered a stroke while delivering a toast in public. Rushed to Cedars-Sinai Medical Center, he, in time, recovered. However, the patient in the adjoining room did not. Frank Sinatra's death made headlines internationally.]

Nick Adams with **Deborah Walley** in Young Lovers.

The film's other leading lady, Deborah Walley, cast as Debbie, was born in Connecticut to ice-skating stars and choreographers. "Debbie, as they called her in real life, made her first appearance at Madison Square Garden when she was three years old.

She tried to become a serious actress, appearing in a stage production of Chehkov's Three Sisters, but fate had a different career for her. She was cast in Gidget Goes Hawaiian (1961), and it was a big hit, sealing her immediate future. In fact, Photoplay designated her as "The Most Popular Actress of 1961."

Walley followed that with a performance in Beach Blanket Bingo (1963) with Frankie Avalon and her then-husband, actor John Ashley. That led to a series of other "beach party" movies. A highlight for her was when she was cast in Spinout (1966). During a break in its filming, Elvis Presley invited her to his dressing room, where he removed his jockey shorts, promising "I'm gonna give you some enjoyment for being so cooperative on our movie."

That same year, after working with Elvis, Walley was cast opposite Tommy Kirk in Ghost in the Invisible Bikini (also 1966).

From Elvis to Kentucky-born Tommy Kirk was a big jump for Walley. Kirk was best known for family-friendly films made by Walt Disney. His "wide-eyed, gangly, keen, and immensely likable look became a familiar face on both television and in feature films. He even worked with Sarah Churchill.

Old Yeller (1957), an adventure story about a boy and his heroic dog, became one of Kirk's biggest hits.

Kirk got along with Walley, but some of his co-stars resented him. "I wanted a father figure when I met Fred MacMurray," Kirk confessed. "I also wanted to be incestuous with him, but he hated me. Jane Wyman was a real bitch to me. She was a god damned homophobe."

Kirk eventually became box office poison when he was exposed as gay and arrested for drug possession. "I was fired by Disney in 1963, but Walt hired me back for a final movie, *The Monkey's Uncle*. Walt was in the closet himself, and he always liked it when I visited his private office. Behind locked doors, I would drop trou for him."

In his post-acting career, Kirk became a waiter, a chauffeur, and a carpet cleaner. :"I made a lot of money and spent it all. No bitterness. No regrets. I'm human. I was not Francis of Assisi."

Tommy Kirk with **Cheryl Sweet** in this publicity photo for *Pajama Party* (1961). He shocked Hollywood when he claimed that as a child actor, Walt Disney had seduced him.

He was reported dead in Las Vegas in September of 2021 at the age of 79.

In *The Young Lovers,* Beatrice Straight, cast as Pam's (Sharon Hugueny's) mother, had the most distinguished résumé of any of the other actors. She had trained at the Actors Studio, spending time with Marlon Brando and Montgomery Clift.

Her most awarded performance would come during her gig as William Holden's devastated wife in *Network* (1976) when she confronted him about his infidelity. Her appearance on the screen lasted only five minutes and two seconds, yet she won an Oscar as Best Supporting Actress of the year, the shortest performance of any actress who ever won an Academy Award.

As for *The Young Lovers,* she dismissed it as "a piece of fluff."

Kent Smith, cast in it as Dr. Shoemaker, had known greater days as a movie star. During its making, he had several talks with Peter about the days on Cape Cod when he starred in productions with Henry Fonda and James Stewart. "At the time, they were my best friends, and I saw a lot of them. I also saw a lot of Hank's first wife, Margaret Sullavan."

"This sounds conceited, but I thought back then that I would be the bigtime movie star, and Hank and Jim would be my supporting players. How wrong I was."

He also spoke of having been one of the

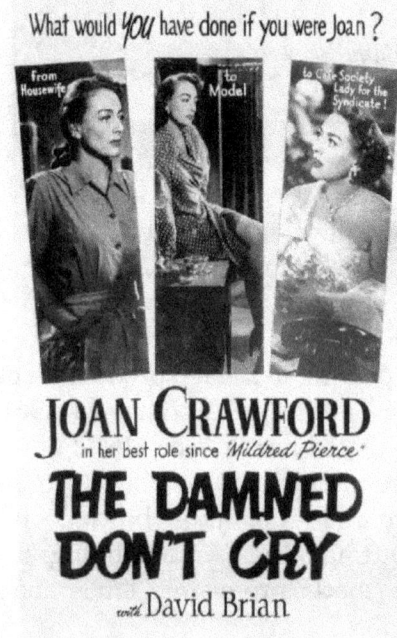

WHAT WOULD YOU HAVE DONE IF YOU WERE JOAN? Fed up with poverty and a dull husband, Ethel Whitehead (**Joan Crawford**) schemes and works her way up to champagne buckets and Palm Beach swimming pools.

Kent Smith (*right*) played a meek, colorless accountant. He later said, "Crawford didn't even try to seduce me. Sexy 'cocksman' Steve Cochran and David Brian kept her busy."

founders of the Harvard University Players.

During the Golden Age of Hollywood, Kent appeared in several classic movies as a supporting player to celebrated stars. They included *Old Acquaintance* (1941) with Bette Davis and Miriam Hopkins; *My Foolish Heart* (1949) with Susan Hayward; *The Fountainhead* (also 1949) with Gary Cooper; and *The Damned Don't Cry* (1950) with Joan Crawford.

"No one noticed me," Smith confessed to Peter, "but I was also in *Bus Stop* (1956) with Marilyn Monroe."

"I once saw you on TV in *Curse of the Cat People* (1944)," Peter said.

"You *would* bring that up," Smith replied. "As a struggling actor, you need to eat. Sometimes, you take what comes your way. That's why I appeared in *Hitler's Children* (1943).

Joseph Campanella, cast as Professor Reese in *The Young Lovers*, is a relatively forgotten figure today, but was well known to viewers of daytime TV. He achieved a certain fame when he played Joe Turino on *Guiding Light* (1959-1962). He went on to appear in the detective series *Mannix* (1967-1968) and the legal drama *The Bold Ones: The Lawyers* (1969-1972).

Hooray for Hollywood and for one of its daytime TV and soap opera icons, **Joseph Campanella.**

He is best remembered for the soap opera *The Days of Our Lives* (1987-1992).

"Yes," as he later admitted, "I was the voice of "The Lizard" on *Spider Man: The Animated Series* (1994-1997)."

Variety reviewed *The Young Lovers* with "It has a lot of things going for it even though it's an uneven production with awkward spots and a slow build-up. While the story is no longer the shocker it would have been a generation ago, the talk is frank and the switch to the unwed father, rather than the mother, will stir more than the usual interest and controversy. Peter Fonda's overall portrayal fits the character, and he delivers key bits of dialogue well."

Steven H. Scheuer described the movie as "pangs of first love, Hollywood style. As usual, the principals are more dopey than romantic."

The New York Times called the film "A tasteful, occasionally interesting and tentative little drama that seems decorously light years away from today's campus realism. But even on its own terms, it disappointedly beats a retreat from reality. Best of all are Nick Adams, Fonda's roommate, and Deborah Walley as his peppery, virtuous little quarry."

***

Most critics agree that the controversial Nick Adams stole *The Young Lovers* from Peter Fonda, but apparently, that did not make Peter jealous.

If anything, he formed a close bond with Nick during the shoot, a relationship that continued for weeks after filming ended. Sometimes, on their motorcycles, in a style akin to how Peter had played it on the screen, they'd head out together into the countryside of Southern California.

In a 2007 interview, Peter (rather elliptically) commented on his life on motorcycles: "The bike takes you on a free road. There's no fences on the road I ride, since I don't ride freeways. That's as much as I can tell you, because there are more lands waiting for this little Christian boy. That's not true. I'm an atheist, but what the heck."

Dennis Hopper, another of Peter's friends, knew more of the details about the burgeoning friendship of Peter with Nick Adams than anyone else.

"Peter found Nick intoxicating in the beginning," Hopper said. "I don't think he'd ever had a friend like that. The stories he told about James Dean and Elvis Presley, to cite only a few, were riveting. He didn't make it up either. He actually knew those two guys."

"I think what happened to the friendship came when Peter suspected that Nick was falling in love with him," Hopper claimed. "That was not Peter's scene. Though he had enjoyed his times with Nick, Peter felt it was time to go, for him to move on. Nick had this way of working himself into the lives of famous people, none more notable than Elvis and Jimmy Dean."

"Peter was well aware of that. When he saw Nick trying to make more of their relationship than a conventional friendship, Peter bolted. He was no longer home when Nick called."

Nick Adams re-entered Peter's life, at least his memory did, at the time of his death of February 7, 1968.

That was when Hopper and Peter got together and, as filmmakers, decided that the turbulent life of Nick Adams should be the focus of a movie they wanted to produce themselves, with the belief that they'd later persuade a studio such as Columbia to distribute it.

The two actors, according to Hopper, even speculated endlessly about who to cast in it. At first, Peter toyed with the idea of playing Nick himself, but finally decided that Hopper would be more convincing. Peter preferred, instead, to direct the movie.

With Hopper as Adams, both of them agreed that the actor Christopher Jones would make the ideal James Dean. In fact, at the dawn of his career, the handsome actor was being hailed in the press as "The Next James Dean."

Nick Adams (*left*) confronts **Peter Fonda** in *The Young Lovers*. Offscreen Nick and Peter became great buddies until Nick began to fall in love with him. Peter bitterly rejected his advances.

Peter and Hopper met with Jones to discuss the offbeat role. Like Dean himself, Jones had been a hellraiser. He'd joined the U.S. Army but was later sent to prison for going AWOL.

Back in New York, Jones decided to become an actor, and (some said "as part of the process") he seduced both Shelley Winters and Tennessee Williams, each of them instrumental in casting him in the Broadway debut of Williams' *Night of the Iguana* in 1961.

Nick Adams (*left*) as he appeared on TV in *The Rebel* (1959-1961), *and* (*right*) in a snapshot with bare-chested **Elvis Presley**.

He not only turned Elvis onto "speed," but he may have introduced him to homosexual sex, according to a book written by Elvis's associate, close friend, and cousin, Earl Greenwood.

It was Winters who introduced Jones to Susan Strasberg, whom he married in 1965. But when he met with Peter Fonda and Dennis Hopper, he was in the process of divorcing her.

Both actors had seen him on the ABC television series, *The Legend of Jesse James* (1965-1966) and had found him charismatic.

At the meeting with Peter and Hopper, Jones had completed that cult film, *Wild in the Streets* (1968) with Winters. He would soon be working with Yvette Mimieux in the hit sex comedy *Three in the Attic* (1968).

At one point, Peter asked Jones, portraying James Dean at the time, if he'd do a nude love scene with Hopper as Nick Adams. "Hell yes, I would, even frontally, if requested."

The casting of Elvis, both of them agreed, would be much harder. Nearly all of the Elvis impersonators, especially those in Las Vegas, "were pieces of shit," in Peter's vocabulary.

Finally, they settled on morphing Ricky Nelson into Elvis.

Nelson seemed delighted at being offered the role of Elvis. He and Peter had been born the same year (1940), and Peter had grown up watching Ricky and his family on the hit TV sitcom, *The Adventures of Ozzie and Harriet*. That series had also starred Ricky's older brother, David.

Over lunch, Ricky told them that it was Elvis who had inspired the crafting of his first recording. He was dating a teenager named Diana Osborn. "She was crazy about Elvis, and I was jealous, so I told her I was going to make a record myself. It turned out to be that Fats Domino standard, 'I'm Walkin', and that's exactly what I did, walking to a singing career."

"In the spring of 1957, I was *rock 'n rollin'* on TV like a maniac and enjoying being a teenage heartthrob."

Ricky had no objection playing a gay love scene as Elvis with Hopper as Nick Adams. "I'm a straight shooter and have had plenty of girls. But if Elvis ever called for me, I would have come running with clean underwear."

In case the two actors didn't know it, Ricky reminded them that in 1958 and 1959, he had twelve hit records on the charts, compared to eleven for "The King."

"For a while there, I was getting more teen fan adulation from both girls and boys, mostly girls. In May of 1960, six teenagers tried to fling themselves under the wheels of my motorcycle, so that I'd run over them. That's frightening stuff.

"Peter and I would also replicate scenes from *Rebel Without a Cause*," Hopper said. "That meant we'd need a Natalie Wood and a Sal Mineo."

Without telling friends or family, Peter Fonda and Dennis Hopper labored for weeks on and off trying to come up with a workable Nick Adams script. It is not clear why they abandoned it. There was speculation that they might face legal challenges from persons still alive.

But both of them agreed that the untold story of Nick Adams "would make a hell of a movie."

The title of their move would have been *Live Fast. Die Young.*

Christopher Jones would have been ideal cast as James Dean in a movie that Peter Fonda wanted to make about the traumatic life and suspicious death of Nick Adams.

Jones had recently been voted "the sexiest man in Hollywood."

Susan Strasberg expressed doubts about marrying him: "After all, you don't want to wake up in the morning with a man prettier than you are. He was dazzling, lean and tightly coiled, skin glowing with energy, strong, masculine, and self-assured."

Ricky Nelson in *Rio Bravo* (1959).

As a means of escaping from the innocent image he'd developed through TV's *The Adventures of Ozzie and Harriet*, **Ricky** was asked to pose for a sexy photograph without his shirt.

Later that night, at the photographer's studio, he even posed nude, and with an erection, "for special collectors only."

***

The Wild Angels (1966)

Roger Corman was a trail blazer in independent filmmaking who was frequently hailed as "The Pope of Pop Cinema" and "The Spiritual Godfather of the New Hollywood." He both produced and directed *The Wild Angels,* a film which inspired the biker film genre of the 1960s. He was known for a stream of low-budget movies adapted from such works as *The Tales of Edgar Allen Poe,* and for helping to launch the careers of Peter Fonda, Dennis Hopper, William Shatner, Jack Nicholson, Sylvester Stallone, Bruce Dern, and Diane Ladd.

Corman had seen Marlon Brando in *The Wild One* (1954) three times. The original motorcycle gang movie, it showcased Brando as the leader of a group of cyclists who terrorize a small town.

Corman felt that Hollywood sagas about motorcycle gangs needed a 1960s update. Originally, he hired Charles B. Griffith to write a screenplay, but Corman wasn't pleased with it and ordered it to be redone. The director wasn't pleased with the rewrite either, so he hired Peter Bogdanovich, a film journalist at the time, to create a new version.

Corman liked the Bogdanovich rewrite and set about to cast it. His original ensemble was to have starred George Chakiris as the ringleader of the gang, with Peter Fonda as the second male lead, the character of "Loser" Kearns.

But when Corman was told that Chakiris could not ride a motorcycle, he dismissed him and asked Peter to play the lead instead.

[Confusingly, Bruce Dern had previously been offered (and had accepted) the role of "Loser" that was later re- assigned to Peter. Oddly, in advance of filming, Peter made only one demand from Corman: that his character's name be changed from "Loser" to "Heavenly Blues."

That made no sense to Corman until Peter explained the meaning of "Heavenly Blues" aka "Pearly Gates": Consisting of pulverized Morning Glory seeds mixed with water into a paste, it had gained notoriety at the time as a mild hallucinogenic.]

Peter Fonda with **Nancy Sinatra** in *The Wild Angels (1966).*

"She and I were already friends when we co-starred together," Peter said. "For accommodations, we shared a duplex log cabin during the shoot. One day, Father Frank visited the set to check up on Nancy. I assured him that nothing bad would happen to her. Hell, she not only could take care of herself, but Tina, Frankie Jr., even Ol' Blue Eyes himself."

Roger Corman *(left)* directing **Dennis Hopper** *(center)* and **Peter Fonda** in *The Wild Angels.*

The director said, "I decided to make a movie about Hell's Angels, since they were in the headlines, and they were something new and different. I chose Fonda because he was not only a good actor, but he was a hell of a bike rider. Think Marlon Brando in *The Wild One.*

Corman agreed to the change in the character's name and then, almost in the same breath, informed him that bike-riding Nancy Sinatra would be his girlfriend, playing a character named "Mike."

Instead of hiring extras, Peter suggested that two actual motorcycle gangs, "Hell's Angels" and "The Coffin Cheaters" be hired. They came cheap. On the first day of the shoot, the leader of the Hell's Angels gang gave Peter a generous supply of "grass soaked in opium."

***

Before working with Peter, Nancy Sinatra and her father, Frank, had each appeared in *Marriage on the Rocks* (1965), a comedy. Nancy's collaboration with Peter in *The Wild Angels* came at around the time of her greatest triumph, the success of her recording "These Boots Are Made for Walkin,'" a mega-hit heard around the world. For some reason, it was very popular with American soldiers.

Nancy would soon be joining Elvis Presley in the filming of the musical drama *Speedway*, and there were rumors about her possible affair with "The King." Daddy Sinatra, of course, had plenty to say about that.

When Nancy went to work on *The Wild Angels*, she had just emerged from the throes of divorcing her first husband, Tommy Sands.

To Peter, Tommy Sands was a symbol of how precarious a career in show business could be. He'd worked as a performer since he was a child but became an overnight sensation and teen idol when he appeared on *Kraft Television Theatre* in January of 1957 as *"The Singin' Idol."* He was only fifteen when Col. Tom Parker, the manager of Elvis, signed him to a contract with RCA Records.

Sands excited female fans with his similarities to Elvis. His *schtick* included a guitar, tight pants, and hair arranged into a glossy pompadour.

By 1958, Sands landed a film contract with 20th Century Fox. He worked with such stars as Fabian Forte and Annette Funicello. He married Nancy Sinatra in 1960. Frank Sinatra offered him a role in his film, *Come Blow Your Horn* (1963), but Sands turned it down, a decision that angered Sinatra, *père*.

In 1965, Sands landed a role in the feature film, *None But the Brave*, starring and directed by Sinatra. At least in part because his marriage to Nancy was falling apart, Ol' Blue Eyes was "tough as nails" with Sand throughout the course of the filming.

After his divorce from Nancy, "Doors throughout Hollywood seemed to slam shut for me," Sands said. "I could not get acting roles, and my singing career on TV and in film ended."

Sands later ran an outlet for clothing and eventually left Hollywood to settle in Fort Wayne, Indiana.

It was a poster advertising *The Wild Angels*, but its promoters thinly disguised it as an "FBI's MOST WANTED" notice.

That added to the notoriety of the film, and to the rage of **Nancy Sinatra's father, Frank**.

When he read the caption the press and PR department had associated with her photograph (*"MIKE: She's too much in love to care what she does—or with whom..."*) he emphatically (some said "violently") objected.

Tommy Sands (*right*) with **Nancy Sinatra** in 1962 on the TV program *Stump the Stars*

Speculation throughout the movie industry was that Sinatra had arranged for the "blacklisting" of Sands.

"I don't want that to happen to my career," Peter said. "I plan to treat Nancy with the same respect I'd show the Queen of England herself."

In *The Wild Angels*, Bruce Dern as "Loser" looked like the lowest bum on Skid Row, but he was happy to be working with his wife, Diane Ladd.

Dern had previously played a minor role as a dance marathoner with Jane Fonda in *They Shoot Horses, Don't They?* (1969). His most memorable role, also with Jane, lay in his future when he was cast as a military husband in *Coming Home* (1970). For his performance, he was nominated for a Best Supporting Actor Oscar.

Ladd had risen from the bowels of Mississippi, the daughter of a veterinarian who sold food products for poultry and livestock. She was a relative of Tennessee Williams.

She and Dern became the parents of another actress, Laura Dern.

During the course of her career, Diane would appear in 120 movies, either feature films or on television. For the 1974 *Alice Doesn't Live Here Anymore*, she was nominated for a Best Supporting Actress Oscar.

The Gang's All Here! This scene from *The Wild Angels* made anxieties surge and survival instincts roar, especially among parents who feared for the safety (and morals) of their children. **Peter Fonda** appears as the second figure from the right.

Diane Ladd posed for this picture in 1975. During the shooting of *The Wild Angels*, she was married to co-star Bruce Dern. "This Belle of Mississippi should have become better known," Roger Corman said. "Hell, she appeared in tons of movies but never really hit the big time."

Michael Pollard immortalized himself when he appeared in *Bonnie and Clyde* with Warren Beatty. Critic Roger Ebert said, "There is something about Pollard, an actor short of stature, that is absolutely original and that strikes audiences as irresistibly funny. It's easy to become addicted to him."

As a character named Pigmy, Michael J. Pollard had seventh billing. Descended from Polish parents in New Jersey, he would be forever remembered for his performance as C.W. Moss in *Bonnie and Clyde* (1967), starring Warren Beaty and Faye Dunaway. For his part in that gangster flick, he would be nominated for a Best Supporting Actor Oscar.

Rising to a height of only 5' 6", and looking younger than his years, he specialized--late into his 30s--in playing characters who were simultaneously silly, scary, and creepy.

In 1968, Pollard ran as part of a "joke campaign" for President of the United States. The winner, Richard Nixon, wrote to him the day after the election, with "Sorry about that, boy."

Although the cast of *The Wild Angels* was riddled with "some good-looking bike chicks," Peter Fonda, according to reports, did not make out. However, he flirted a lot with Polly Platt, the lovely wife of "the other Peter," Peter Bogdanovich.

The movie rides along, a wild spew of sex, drugs, rock 'n roll, bongo drums, fistfights with Mexicans, and the loud revving of motorcycle engines.

The ending is tragic, when Loser (Dern) is shot by the police as he rides to escape on one of their bikes.

He initially survives, but when gang members, in a frantic attempt to help him avoid incarceration, remove him from his hospital bed, they inadvertently disconnect him from his life support machines, hastening his death.

The ending is sad. At Loser's funeral, the survivors learn that the police are on the way to make arrests. Mike (Nancy Sinatra) pleads with Peter to leave with her, but he refuses.

With "nowhere to go" in the final scene, Peter stands defiantly alone, shoveling dirt over the coffin of Loser, which is draped with the Nazi flag.

Although Peter Bogdanovich went uncredited, he later said that he wrote eighty percent of the script for *The Wild Angels*.

After that, he started directing his own films, none more notable than *The Last Picture Show* (1971), which brought eight Academy Award nominations. That was followed by *What's Up, Doc?* (1972), a big hit.

Peter Bradshaw of *The Guardian* defined Bogdanovich as "a loving cineaste and fearless genius of cinema."

The Wild Angels established Peter Fonda as a "counter-culture star," and earned $7 million at the box office, the highest-grossing low-budget film at that time.

Reviews were often scathing, none more amusing than the one by film critic Leonard Maltin, who suggested "go see *The Wild Angels* after about 24 beers."

***

The Trip (1967)

By the early 1960s, Americans who had never heard of LSD (lysergic acid diethylamide, aka "acid") were intimately familiar with its hallucinogenic side-effects. They were said to intensify thoughts, emotions, and sensory perceptions. On occasion, the drug could also cause mystical experiences and ego dissolution.

It was adopted by users of recreational drugs and psychedelics, and soon became synonymous with the counterculture. Viewed by many as a cultural threat to the American way of life, it was defined as illegal in 1968. In some cases, it could spark mental disorders, acted out as "bad trips."

The film producer and director, Roger Corman, was an odd choice as producer of the world's first major film about LSD. It would star Peter Fonda.

LSD had first come to Corman's attention when he saw the poet, Alan Ginsberg, who had converted to Buddhism, blow into a conch shell before chanting meditative verses in Hindi. Ginsburg then urged all Americans over the age of fourteen to try LSD. But it was Timothy Leary who popularized LSD across

the country with his slogan of "Tune In, Turn On, and Drop Out."

Before making *The Trip*, Corman decided that he, too, should take some LSD, following in the footsteps of such established actors as Cary Grant.

For his "first time" sampling of LSD, Corman drove north from Los Angeles to Big Sur and found an isolated redwood forest. There, he swallowed the acid-laced sugar cubes. "I spent the next seven hours lying face down in front of this towering tree. I don't think I even moved. Strange visions raced through my mind. I was the king of a harem of 30 beautiful young women. But in another (this one horrible) scene, I was raped by Steve Reeves."

[*At the time, Montana-born Reeves was a professional bodybuilder and actor who became internationally famous in sword-and-sandal flicks, playing such muscular characters as Hercules, Goliath, or Sandokan.*

For a time, he was the highest-paid actor in Europe, and by 1960, he was ranked as the number one box office draw in 25 countries around the world.

Reeves reigned as Mr. America in 1947, Mr. World in 1948, and Mr. Universe in 1950.

He could have broken out of those musclemen movies or spaghetti Westerns had he made wiser career choices. Ironically, he had rejected the role of James Bond in Dr. No (1962), *the part going to Sean Connery. Reeves also rejected* A Fistful of Dollars (1964), *the lead role of which went to Clint Eastwood.*]

As Corman admitted, "I was more Arrow Shirt than love beads. I was the big square in a group of long-haired hippies like Peter Fonda and Dennis Hopper. Those two always seemed on something—and not just weed but experimenting with the next drug sensation. For a good part of the time, they were wandering in Outer Space, at least in their heads."

Back in Hollywood, he had heard that actor Jack Nicholson had experimented with LSD, and he contacted him about writing a script whose name Corman proposed as *The Trip*. Nicholson seemed eager to begin work on it.

At the time, Nicholson wasn't the red hot movie star he was soon to become. He'd started out with appearances in such low-rent flicks as *Cry Baby Killer* (1958) and *The Raven* (1963) with Vincent Price and Peter Lorre. That was followed by *The Terror* (also 1963) with Boris Karloff. Before working with Corman, Nicholson had filmed *Rebel Rousers* (1970) alongside co-stars Bruce Dern (his chief rival) and Dern's wife, Diane Ladd.

THE TRIP was a strange cinematic interlude that most critics found hard to understand and easy to dislike In the *upper photo*, **Bruce Dern** (*left*) coaxes **Peter Fonda** down from a high that's either about agony or ecstasy. (The confusing dialogue led viewers to interpret both options as simultaneously true.).

In the *middle photo*, **Peter**, during an LSD high, demonstrates—either intentionally or not—something approaching a tripped-out, catatonic version of existential anguish.

And in the *lower photo*, two undressed, acid-soaked twenty-somethings with undeniably aristocratic show-biz bloodlines (**Susan Strasberg**, *left*, and **Peter Fonda**, *right*) appear covered with blood.

Why were they covered with blood? Cynics said it was a cheap theatrical trick tacked into the script as a metaphor for acid-induced horror.

In the end, no one who wasn't already tripping really knew for sure. But for Strasberg, at least, and certainly as it affected her own theatrical future, *The Trip* was probably a horrible idea.

Nicholson had a positive feeling about writing a script for *The Trip*, and he worked hard to produce something worthy of being filmed. He referred to the project as a "mental roller coaster ride to hell and back."

Meeting with Corman before filming began, Peter recalled his own experiences with LSD. He claimed that taking the drug had originally been suggested to him by a doctor in London, who recommended it as a cure for his recurring bouts of depression.

***

Before taking the drug, Peter had chartered a plane and flown to Las Vegas to attend the wedding of his sister, Jane, to the French director Roger Vadim.

For the trip, he invited Dennis Hopper and Hopper's wife, Brooke Hayward, the daughter of Henry Fonda's agent and his first wife, Leland Hayward and Margaret Sullavan.

In the left photo, above, **Roger Vadim** and **Jane Fonda** face a justice of the peace during their marriage ceremony in Las Vegas in 1965

The photo on the right, although not derived specifically from their wedding, shows Vadim gallantly simulating the act of carrying Jane across a threshold during a rehearsal for one of their movies, *La Ronde*.

"In Las Vegas, LSD was the big thing, and Dennis and I were anxious to tune in and turn on, but not drop out."

When he returned home from his sister's wedding, Peter wrote about his introduction to LSD: "I remember I started to hallucinate like mad, and the images were beautiful. At first, I neither felt worried or fearful. I just watched the world spin forward in front of my eyes, changing considerably along its pathway with different flashing pictures."

"Among the mind-blowing experiences I had was giving birth to my daughter Bridget. But then the images became more gruesome. In the kitchen, I consumed an oatmeal cookie but found it full of creepy, crawling worms. Out in my backyard, I crawled around the lawn with my dog, Basil. Suddenly, out of a large hole emerged a mammoth frog that looked like a slimy boulder."

Peter always remembered one particularly frightening moment when he bit into a large ripe plum. "The thing came alive and seemed to be growing rapidly until it tossed it away."

Jack Nicholson also had memories of his first experience with LSD. "The drug arose fears in me of homosexuality. I also had the feeling that my prick was going to be cut off."

Peter had known Jack Nicholson before but got to know him a lot better during the production of his next two films. "If Jack is to be remembered for just one thing, it should be for his shit-eating grin. When he spoke, his eyebrows seemed to dance. Of course, he knew how attractive he was to women. When the subject came up, he said, 'So I'm sexy. Is there a law against that?'"

"Jack had talent," Peter said. "He had charisma. Over time, he joined the pantheon of the greats like Marlon Brando followed by Robert De Niro, Al Pacino, and Dustin Hoffman.":

"Jack was also shrewd with the dollar. In time, he became one of the highest paid stars in the history of the movies. Whatever role he played, even in a piece of crap, he was always compelling. How I envied him."

The sexual history of Jack Nicholson as a babe magnet is well documented. He had long-lasting affairs with Michelle Phillips, Angelica Huston, and with dozens of unknown starlets and assorted women from various fields.

On occasion, he would seduce legendary figures, including Princess Caroline of Monaco, Catherine Deneuve (hailed at the time as the most beautiful woman in the world), Jessica Lange, shipping magnate Christina Onassis, Madonna, and Margaret Trudeau, the wife of the prime minister of Canada.

"I've balled all the women," Nicholson told Peter. "I've done all the drugs. I've drunk all the drink. But when bigtime stardom came, I couldn't go around as easily as before, devouring every pussy."

"Jack had such a strange childhood," Peter said. "He grew up thinking his big sister was his big sister until he discovered that she was his mother."

"One night I talked sex with your father," Nicholson told Peter. "When both of us started out as young men in the sack, each of us was a premature ejaculator. But we learned to hold back."

***

For *The Trip,* Roger Corman had already cast Peter Fonda in the leading role of Paul Groves, a director of television commercials. At the beginning of the film, he is sampling his first hit of LSD during the heartbreak and ambivalence of a looming divorce from his adulterous wife, Sally.

The role of Sally was cast with Susan Strasberg, the daughter of Lee Strasburg of the Actors Studio.

Through the Actors Studio, she'd become friendly with Jane Fonda, and she was also one of the closest friends of Marilyn Monroe, in part, perhaps, because of the strong influence of Susan's parents, the Strasburgs, Marilyn's acting coaches. In the movie *Stage Struck* (1958) the older character played by Henry Fonda fell in love with Susan's character onscreen.

"I didn't like my role with Peter," Strasberg later said. "I felt I was mere window dressing. I was shocked when Corman was told the film was running too long. At random, he started ripping out some pages, seemingly not even reading them."

In the script he'd written, Nicholson had crafted the character of John for himself. John, in the movie, becomes Paul's "guide" into the world of LSD, although he later runs away and abandons him out of fear.

Nicholson "was seriously pissed off" when Corman gave the role that Nicholson had so carefully crafted for himself to Bruce Dern, who had previously co-starred with Nicholson in *Rebel Rousers* (1967). Corman had been impressed with the box office receipts generated by the combination of Dern with Peter in *The Wild Angels.*

In *The Trip,* a bearded Dern comes off evoking the image of a young Francis Ford Coppola.

Dennis Hopper was assigned the role of Max, a drug pusher who becomes the hippie High Priest of Paul's hallucinations. His dialogue was defined as "stoned apocalyptic ramblings." [*Actually, Hopper spontaneously ad libbed much of the dialogue himself.*]

In some amazing photography, the script dramatizes the LSD-induced scenes churning through Paul's mind. He is seen running across beach sands, escaping hooded figures riding black horses. What emerges is a kaleidoscopic *mélange* of abstract images flashed across the screen in nightmarish colors.

Figures as diverse as Sophia Loren and Che Guevara appear on the screen, each of them flashing through Paul's festering, feverishly overactive brain.

Nubile, semi-nude women, many ornamented with body paint, bring to vivid life the nightlife along Sunset Strip.

The band, The Electric Flag, provided most of the film's background music.

Peter clashed with Corman at several points during the shoot. Corman refused to finance it, but Peter and Hopper hired a cameraman and went with him to an isolated location in the desert.

"I was running up and down sand dunes like a wild man," Peter said. "When Corman finally saw our footage, he used it in the film, even though he refused to pay for it."

Other than that, *The Trip* was mostly shot in and around Los Angeles, including in Laurel

In this publicity photo from Roger Corman's *The Trip*, **Dennis Hopper**—portrayed as a shaman and mystic—appears partly undressed and "ready to make it a three-way" as **Salli Sachse** kisses **Peter Fonda** as he hallucinates.

Canyon, although at one point, Corman ordered that certain scenes be shot at Big Sur.

Years later, Peter jokingly said, "In the history of cinema, my reputation will live on as the first non-X-rated actor to appear "bare ass" in a feature film. I also appeared in two raunchy sex scenes with my two leading ladies."

Peter had started a trend. Soon, everyone from Marlon Brando to Jon Voight were showing their asses on camera.

Before his nude scene with Strasberg, Peter warned her that with her body pressing against his, he might get an erection. He rephrased that with "It is predictable that I'll get a hard-on, but I promise not to penetrate you.:

"Things got more explicit in his sex scene with Salli Sachse, cast as "Glenn."

"We were jaybird naked," he said. "My 'Mister Happy' got hard as a rock. She seemed like a furnace, her body temperature rising."

At the end of the scene, Corman ordered the crew off the set so the two nude lovers could rise from the bed.

"Many critics later pointed out how authentic my sex scenes looked," Peter said. "They were authentic all right."

Perhaps he exaggerated a bit.

Peter also had another nude scene with Salli Sachse, cast in the film as Glenn. Before it began, he told her, "I hope you wear clothes during these scenes. You're going to be naked on top of me."

Then, as Corman quoted Peter within Corman's memoir (*How I Made a Hundred Movies in Hollywood and Never Lost a Dime*), "As the scene moved on, I put my hand on her back and then on her rib cage and was moving it toward one of her breasts. That's when my 'little mister' decided to pop up and say, 'Hey, guys! I'm in this film, too.' And was he ever. Sally clamped her legs together to capture it and keep it out of camera range."

Born in San Diego in 1943, Sachse had been both a model and a beauty contest winner. She became a starlet at American International Pictures, which cast her in such films as *How To Stuff a Wild Bikini* (1965), where her minor character was named "Bookend #2."

When Peter was working with her, she was heavy dating David Crosby of the musical group, "The Byrds."

It would be Crosby who would provide Peter with a chance to meet the Beatles.

Peter didn't like the final cut of *The Trip*. "I put my balls on the table, and Corman lobbed them right off."

Peter and Nicholson, certainly Dennis Hopper, and even Roger Corman were not pleased with what American International Pictures did to the ending of their film. They had wanted to highlight the "ups" of LSD, but the brass at AIP feared that they wouldn't be allowed to release their picture with an ending that reflected that point of view. So they inserted an ending of shattering glass to suggest the negative aspects of recreational LSD.

The Trip staged its premiere at the Cannes Film Festival where it played to packed audiences from around the world.

It was released at a most opportune time, that "Summer of Love" back in 1967. Made for only $100,000, it garnered $6 million at the box office, though it was banned in the United Kingdom. Many scenes were cut by censors. The full uncut version would not be seen until the film was released on DVD in 2004.

Although it was praised by LSD advocates, it was ferociously attacked by anti-drug forces. Even those who objected to the film were often amazed by its visual effects, many of them stunning triumphs of camera craft. The film suggested that sex might be enhanced after stimulation from LSD.

Peter's drug hallucinations were likened to "Part Bergman, part Fellini, and part scenes from the Bible."

Actually, some of the footage within the final cut derived from previously unused outtakes from earlier horror flicks produced by American International Pictures.

Judith Crist on NBC's *Today Show* reviewed it like this: "*The Trip* amounts to very little more than a 1½ hour commercial for LSD. It boasts Peter Fonda as a television commercial director who decides to "take a trip" in order to be wiser. It has Susan Strasberg in the nude looking like a Venetian blind, courtesy of op and pop art painting. Neither Fonda nor Strasberg is left with any place to go but up after this movie. The subject matter of *The Trip* enables the director to make a totally incoherent film with erratic repetitions, and fake arty effects that simply nauseate both individually, intellectually, and physically. This is one trip to skip."

The critic for *Time* magazine wrote, "*The Trip* is a psychedelic tour throught the bent mind of Peter Fonda, which is evidently full of old movies. In a flurry of flesh, mattresses, flashing lights, and kaleidoscopic patterns, an alert viewer will spot some fancy business from such classics as *The Seventh Seal*, *Lawrence of Arabia*, even *The Wizard of Oz*. Eventually, in a scene that is right out of *8½*, Fonda perches on a merry-go-round while a robed judge gravely spells out his previous sins and inadequacies. The photographer's camera work is bright enough to suggest the heightened inner awareness so frequently claimed by those who use the drug."

Rotten Tomatoes wrote, "*The Trip*'s groovy effects and compelling message can't overcome the rough acting, the long meandering stretches, the pedestrian plot."

Another critic wrote, "Roger Corman comes off like he's hung up on sadomasochism, and Jack Nicholson comes across like he's high on sex. As for Peter Fonda and Dennis Hopper, they have to punctuate every sentence with 'man.' In one long bit of dialogue, the word 'man' appeared 36 times."

At the end of a career that turned out some 200 low-budget films, Corman said, "*The Trip* was the best of them all."

While promoting *The Trip* in Toronto, Peter spent the night alone in his hotel, after turning down the three women who made themselves available for sex…and for free.

Feeling lonely and depressed, he later admitted that he got tanked up on vodka.

Later, he reported that "a flash of lightning hit me. The thunder was not in the sky but in my head. I bolted upright in bed, tingling with excitement. My brain had come up with my next movie, one I would make with Dennis Hopper."

Not remembering or even caring what time it was in Los Angeles, he put through a phone call to Hopper, finally getting him on the phone.

"I've come up with a great idea for our next movie. It's gonna be a real pisser."

The idea that came from his thunderous brain that night turned out to be *Easy Rider*.

***

In *The Trip*, Brandon deWilde, two years younger than Peter, was assigned an uncredited role as the assistant director to Peter's character, Paul Groves. Groves, it's made clear, is a director of television commercials. Peter Bogdanovich also appeared in the film in an uncredited role—as Groves' cameraman.

At the age of seven, in 1950, Brooklyn-born deWilde made his Broadway debut in Carson McCuller's *Member of the Wedding*. It ran for almost 500 performances.

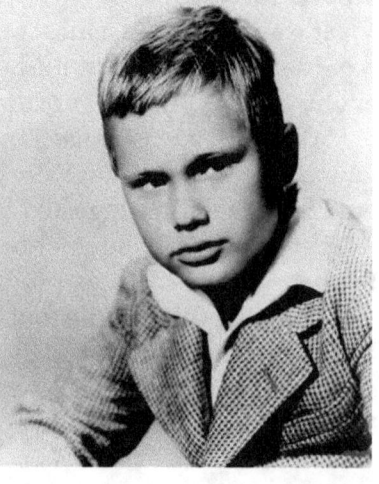

TRIPPING WITH BRANDON deWILDE

(BUT WHEN THEY WERE HIGH ON LSD, DID HE GET IT ON WITH PETER FONDA?)

Upper photo shows **Brandon deWilde** snapped in 1968—four years before his agonizing death—after he began portraying hip young adults familiar with the effects of psychedelics.

His appearance, which reminded some fans of "how Jesus probably looked" was deceptively contrary to his appearance *(right photo)* as a successful—and very endearing—child actor in the early 1950s.

He later starred in its film adaptation (1952), for which he won a Golden Globe award.

He is also well-known for his performance, when he was a boy of ten or eleven, as Joey Starrett in the film *Shane* (1953), starring Alan Ladd and Jean Arthur.

De Wilde quickly moved on from there, working with James Stewart, Lee Marvin, Sidney Poitier, and Phil Harris. At the age of 17, he played an adolescent father in the 1958 stage version of *Blue Denim* and in its 1959 film adaptation, each based on a novel by James Leo Herlihy.

The young star would also appear in the 1962 film, *All Fall Down,* based on a novel by Herlihy that was adapted in a filmscript by William Inge. It starred Warren Beatty and deWilde with Angela Lansbury as their mother. He went from there to co-starring with Paul Newman in *Hud* (1963).

On the set of *The Trip,* deWilde learned that Peter had never taken LSD. The teenager invited Fonda to spend a weekend with him on the periphery of Palm Springs in a rented villa. He was very blunt, confessing to Fonda: "I'm straight, really straight. In the course of 24 hours, I seduced eight teenaged girls. But I'm told time and time again that LSD probes deep into one's psychic, even putting them in touch with their homosexual impulses."

The suggestion was that Peter and him, within this hideaway retreat, would take LSD and see what happened.

As far as it is known, Peter never spoke of that weekend, except what he told to Hopper. All he had to say later was, "Brandon and I both felt it was needed and wanted for us to understand our darker impulses. Society forces us to keep them under wraps. But that miracle drug freed us to do unspeakable things.

Peter was very saddened when news came over his television on July 6, 1972 that deWilde had died at the age of thirty in a car crash. He was in Denver at the time, appearing in a stage production of *Butterflies Are Free.*

***

In *The Trip,* Peter had performed a sexy love scene with Salli Sachse.

In June of 1963, at the age of nineteen, she had married Peter Louis Sachse in San Diego. However, in July of 1966, he was killed while flying a World War II training plane. It crashed offshore while he was making a series of low passes over Windansea Beach near La Jolla in California.

Since then, she had been dating David Crosby of the Byrds, the band that pioneered the musical genre of folk rock in 1965, which seemed to mold aspects of the Beatles with traditional folk music. Peter was said to have "hung out" with members of the Byrds and "done drugs" with them.

When he was still a member of that group, Crosby specialized in rhythm, guitar, and vocals. He formed a friendship with Peter. From it, he extended a genuinely coveted invitation.

The Beatles had arrived in Los Angeles and were mobbed. Since no hotel wanted them because of the hordes of fans they would attract, they had rented a home in Benedict Canyon. A team of 24-hour security guards kept a crowd of semi-crazed fans outside their gates.

As a friend of the Beatles, Crosby arranged for Peter to be admitted through the gates of their rented home.

As it turned out, he would meet the Beatles when some of them were tripping on LSD. In the kitchen, Crosby introduced him to George Harrison, who seemed to be having a bad trip. Although he was in bad shape, he hugged and embraced Peter, saying, "I'm going through hell!" he shouted. "I'm dying!" Then some unknown girl appeared and led him away.

Crosby provided Peter with capsules of LSD so he could "get into the groove" of the party.

Later in the day, he hung out with Ringo Starr and three other musicians. At one point, Peter wandered into the kitchen, then returned to the living room to report, "There's a luscious blonde in the kitchen. I know she's a real blonde because I sniffed her crotch."

He later met Paul McCartney: "Paul seemed the only one sane in the house that day. He was not on LSD."

All day long, songs of the Beatles blasted throughout the rented house and could even be heard on the grounds. They included "Can't Buy Me Love," and "I should Have Known Better" as performed in their 1964 movie, *A Hard Day's Night*.

That evening, the music died down, and the druggies were ushed into a screening room where someone had arranged a screening of *Cat Ballou* starring Jane Fonda and Lee Marvin.

John Lennon, with some unknown girl, sat watching the first half of the film before rising to his feet. Before storming out of the room, he shouted, "I've had enough of the Fondas for one day."

In spite of his hasty exit from the screening of *Cat Ballou*, Lennon and Peter, the following day, had an LSD trip together. The Beatle followed his session with Peter by writing the song, "She Said, She Said."

During their time tripping together, Peter had told him of the incident from his boyhood when he accidentally shot himself in the chest and almost died.

In the Lennon song is the lyric, "I know what it is like to be dead."

Lennon said that for the song's final version, he changed its title from "He Said, He Said" to "She Said, She Said" as a device to "cover up" for Peter. But he also said that that aspect of the song was inspired by Peter after he described how he almost committed suicide, accidentally.

Peter continued to encounter Crosby on occasion, especially when he broke from the Byrds and formed Crosby, Stills, & Nash. Peter attended one of their concerts. There, he met the other members of the trio: Stephen Stills of Buffalo Springfield and Graham Nash of the Hollies.

After making *The Trip* with Peter, Salli Sachse went on to become the personal photographer of Crosby in the late 1960s. She toured with Crosby, Stills, & Nash for two years before disappearing somewhere in Europe to pursue the life of an artist.

After flirtations with LSD and these musicians, Peter returned to the business of making movies, as Dennis Hopper now dominated his life.

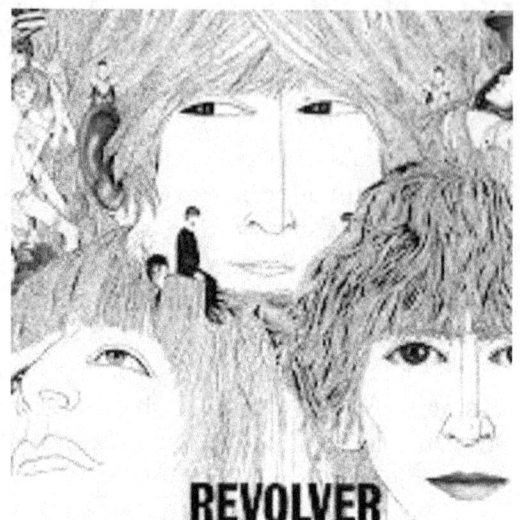

John Lennon cited **Peter Fonda** as his source of inspiration for a lyric within a song that appeared within the Beatle's album, *Revolver*. Released in August of 1966, it was the Beatles' seventh studio album, the first of what critics later defined as "their psychedelic period."

Where and when was the inspiration transmitted? According to Lennon, it derived from Peter's anecdote, relayed to him during an acid trip they shared together in the Beatle's rented home in Benedict Canyon (Los Angeles). Their encounter had been arranged by David Crosby, the musician and man friend of Salli Sachse, Peter's nubile co-star in *The Trip*.

***

At one point, Jack Nicholson told an interviewer that his two favorite actors were Marlon Brando and Henry Fonda. He never got to make a movie with Fonda, but he did co-star with Brando in *The Missouri Breaks* (1976).

He had also co-starred with Peter Fonda, but never with Jane. That was not because he didn't try.

Nicholson originally lobbied his close friend and director, Roman Polanski, to cast Jane in *Chinatown* (1974), which became one of Polanski's most famous movies. It was a Chandleresque murder mystery and story of corruption. Although Jane had wanted to essay the role of Evelyn Cross Mulwray, she eventually rejected the role, saying, "I'm tired of hearing what a great actor Jack Nicholson is." *[At least that is what was reported she said.]*

Jack Nicholson with **Michelle Phillips** at the 1971 Golden Globe Awards.

As rumor had it, no one—and we mean no one—could compete with "Jack in the Sack."

Faye Dunaway took over the role for the bargain price of $100,000, although Nicholson made off with a million dollars.

Jane would also be offered (and also rejected) the female lead in one of Nicholson's most memorable films, *One Flew Over the Cuckoo's Nest* (1975). In it, she would have played Nurse Ratched.

After Jane turned it down, its director, Milos Forman, wanted to cast Anne Bancroft as Nurse Ratched, but she said no. So did Angela Lansbury and Geraldine Page. Even Dunaway turned this one down, the role eventually going to Louise Fletcher. *[For a very brief time, the then-unknown Meryl Streep was considered before it finally went to Fletcher.]*

Directed by Roman Polanski, the psychological horror film, *Rosemary's Baby* (1968), became a classic. Alfred Hitchcock was first offered the chance to direct it, but he turned it down. Finally, Polanski read the Ira Levin novel in one night and called the author the next day, asking if he could both direct it and write the screenplay.

The director had many choices in mind for the character of Rosemary Woodhouse. At first, he envisioned her as a robust, full-figured "girl next door" and thought that Tuesday Weld might be ideal. If not her, then his own fiancée at the time, Sharon Tate.

Polanski would later marry Tate and get her pregnant. He was in London, while she was in an advanced state of pregnancy, when she was murdered by the Charles Manson gang.

Polanski's next choice was Jane Fonda, but he doesn't seem to have made a firm offer. Patty Duke and Goldie Hawn were also considered for the role. It finally went to Mia Farrow, the "child bride" of Frank Sinatra. He didn't want her to do it, and in the middle of filming she was served with divorce papers.

Robert Redford was the first choice for the role of Guy Woodhouse, the husband of Rosemary, but he turned it down.

Nicholson, a friend of Polanski, really wanted the part and was hurt when Polanski considered him only briefly before offering it to John Cassavetes.

Once again, a film starring Jane with Nicholson never made it to the screen.

Jane's final offer to work with Nicholson came from him for a picture that he was directing himself, *Goin' South*, a Western comedy set for a 1978 release.

Jane's reason for rejecting it involved her having already made a Western comedy, *Cat Ballou,* and didn't want "to get trapped" in another one.

The casting of the female role was solved by chance when Nicholson, in the Gulf+Western Building on Columbus Circle in Manhattan, encountered a "curly Magic Pan waitress" named Mary Steenburgen. Although she'd never set foot on a soundstage, the role of Julia Tate Moon was hers.

Later, Jane read the reviews. The one in *Variety* said, "Jack Nicholson playing Gabby Hayes is interesting, even amusing at times, but Hayes was never a leading man, which *Goin' South* desperately needs. The relationship between Nicholson and Steenburgen never jells, as Nicholson continues to sputter and chomp, acting more like a grandfather than a handsome *roué*, out to overcome her virginity."

Peter went to see the movie and later told Nicholson, "Too bad you didn't get Jane. She could have made it jell—and she might have taken your virginity."

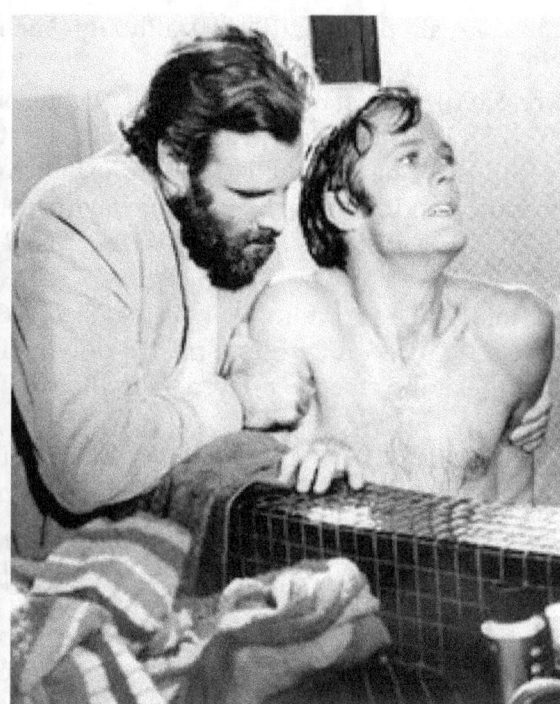

These advertising banners and press photos were released by American International Pictures to promote and publicize their then-radical new film, *The Trip*. In each of them, **Peter Fonda** convincingly conveys the psychic agony and ecstacy of an experience with LSD.

In the *upper center* photo, he's comforted and perhaps guided, by a bearded **Bruce Dern**.

In the *lower photo,* the studio's publicity team used multiple images and multiple exposures of Peter to illustrate the fluidity of time and perception catalyzed by the then spectacularly controversial psychedelic.

CHAPTER FOURTEEN

PETER BITES (AND SWALLOWS) THE ARTISTIC AND COMMERCIAL POTENTIAL OF THE COUNTER-CULTURE

CERTAIN HONORABLE MEN

Peter co-stars in a TV drama as the protégé of a powerful congressman who discovers his boss's corruption.

"I looked like a fag in drag playing Angela Lansbury"

—Peter Fonda

A FILM CONCEPT THAT NEVER MATERIALIZES
THE BEARD

"Its producer had a wild idea: Me, as Billy the Kid, screwing Jean Harlow,"

—Peter Fonda

ANOTHER FILM CONCEPT THAT NEVER MATERIALIZES:
THE QUEEN

PETER FONDA WOULD IMPERSONATE LYNDON JOHNSON, IN DRAG, PLOTTING THE ASSASSINATION OF JOHN F. KENNEDY

Spinning His Wheels:
EASY RIDER

Hailed as "The Touchstone of a New Generation"
And to some, morbidly nihilistic, it morphed into a vastly profitable motorcycle saga
Leaving viewers with a hatred of the Redneck Deep South, and hippies clamoring for more.

ITS DIRECTOR AND CO-STAR
DENNIS HOPPER

REVIEWS HIS CO-STAR, PETER FONDA, WITH:
"THE KID AIN'T NO JAMES DEAN,"

"That piece of crap made my son rich.
In it, Peter is a cross between James Dean and Clint Eastwood."
—Henry Fonda, in reference to *Easy Rider*

PETER'S POSTMODERN WESTERN
THE HIRED HAND
THE BUCK STOPPED WITH PETER, AND THE CRITICS HATED IT

"When I made it, I told all the starlets I seduced that I was a happily married man."
—Peter Fonda

PETER AND THE HEYDAY OF
SEX & DRUGS & ROCK 'N' ROLL

"Peter enticed me to drop some acid with him. As I was tripping, I was menaced by devouring octopuses, their deadly tentacles reaching out for me."
—Larry Hagman

THE LAST MOVIE

"They're druggies, hippies, fags, LSD trippers, panty sniffers, pederasts pursuing nine-year-old Peruvian lads, poon stalkers, and whip lashers"

—Rod Cameron, the former Western film hero, in reference to his director and fellow cast members in *The Last Movie*

TYING THE KNOT

HOW AND WHY DENNIS HOPPER (DRUG-SOAKED COUNTERCULTURE MOVIE STAR) AND MICHELLE PHILLIPS (FORMER LEAD SINGER FOR *THE MAMAS AND THE PAPAS*) GOT MARRIED
(PSSST! The Marriage Lasted for only eight days)

Dennis strips "Jaybird Naked" and confesses: *"I'm a lesbian. I prefer to give head to a woman in lieu of intercourse"*

At this stage of his career, Peter—like millions of his contemporaries—was moving far from the conservative time-tested roles that might have been approved (or at least understood) by his famous father. Though he'd always been something of a rebel, by now, Peter bit and swallowed the potential of the counter-culture herd, moving farther and faster into the psychedelic, drug-fueled aesthetic and lifestyle that tended to horrify members of his father's generation.

Yet despite the cultural *Götterdämmerungs* raging in and around him, Peter continued his allegiance to acting and/or the potential profitability of the entertainment industry…even those that were birthed during the traumas and social upheavals of the 60s.

Certain Honorable Men (1968)

One of the most forgotten of all of Peter Fonda's projects was the 90-minute made-for-television drama, *Certain Honorable Men*. It was part of a series of specials, each sponsored by Prudential, entitled *On Stage*.

Based on a script written by Rod Serling, it starred Van Heflin in a drama loosely inspired by the life and times of Senator Thomas J. Dodd.

Peter was cast as Robbie Conroy, the assistant and "fall guy" for the powerful U.S. Senator. When Peter appeared for location shooting in Brooklyn, he was ordered to cut his long hair. He did so under protest. When he looked at himself in a mirror, he claimed, "I look like a fag in drag, trying to play Angela Lansbury."

Its screenplay was somewhat of a departure for Rod Serling, the 1950s-era playwright, TV producer, narrator, and on-screen host of television dramas. He was especially known for his anthology series, *The Twilight Zone*. His opening remarks at the beginning of every episode became familiar to millions of viewers: "*You're traveling through another dimension, a dimension not only of sight and sound but of the mind, a journey into a wondrous land whose boundaries are that of imagination—your nest stop: The Twilight Zone.*"

CAPITAL CONFLICT—Van Heflin, right, Peter Fonda and Alexandra Isles are starred in Rod Serling's teleplay, "Certain Honorable Men," which will be presented as the initial offering on NBC's new drama anthology series "On Stage," Thursday at 9:30 p.m. on KMJ-TV, 24. Heflin plays a none-too-ethical congressman who finally is unseated through the efforts of his protege (Fonda) and his secretary (Miss Isles).

Serling told Peter that his biggest regret was the December, 1966 made-for-television movie, *The Doomsday Flight*. In it, the pilot of a passenger plane, while it's flying, is warned that a bomb has been placed on board and that it will be detonated unless a ransom is paid.

The Twilight Zone became the most watched series in television history. But, as Serling ruefully relayed to Peter, it also inspired a series of copycats who threatened to blow up airplanes unless "real life" ransoms were paid. "I wish to Christ that I had never written that and instead, had written *Stagecoach*." [*He was referring John Wayne's classic western from 1939.*)

As the male lead of *Certain Honorable Gentlemen*, Van Heflin, cast as Senator Dodd, was not a typical leading man. In 1942, he had won a Best Supporting Actor Oscar for his performance as the boozy attorney in *Johnny Eager*, starring "pretty boy" Robert Taylor and Lana Turner.

"Unlike Bob [*i.e., Robert Taylor*], no one ever accused me of being pretty. I was always second tier," said Heflin.

Katharine Hepburn had selected Heflin to appear on Broadway with her in the stage version of

Van Heflin proved to the world that an actor didn't have to be a pretty boy to get cast as a leading man in Hollywood.

Katharine Hepburn spotted him on Broadway and had RKO cast him in her 1936 movie, *A Woman Rebels*. He played a married man who impregnates her.

She teamed with him again in her Broadway hit, *The Philadelphia Story*, but alas, James Stewart took over his stage role for the film adaptation.

"I was robbed," Heflin said.

The Philadelphia Story (1940). When that play was adapted into a movie, Heflin was tossed aside in favor of James Stewart.

After service in the U.S. Air Force, Heflin returned to Hollywood and to movie making, frequently starring in Westerns, none more notable than *Shane* (1953) co-starring Alan Ladd and Jean Arthur.

Over the years, Heflin's leading ladies included Barbara Stanwyck, Judy Garland, Jennifer Jones, and Joan Crawford. As he told Peter, "Of those ladies, only Crawford demanded that I fuck her."

He also told Peter, "I'll be remembered two-hundred years from now in newsreels of the 1960s. I made a film in 1963 called *Cry of Battle.* The marquee of the movie house advertising my name has been shown in countless newsreels. Why? Because *Cry of Battle* (1963) and *War Is Hell* (1961) were playing side-by-side as a double feature at the Texas Theatre in Dallas in November of 1963, and played an important role in the assassination of JFK."

[After fatally shooting President Kennedy and the Dallas police officer J.D. Tippit earlier that afternoon, Lee Harvey Oswald sneaked into that theater without buying a ticket. The suspicious box office cashier, Julia Postal phoned the police to report it.

At first, within the theater, Oswald attempted to shoot the arresting officer, but was overcome. Two days later, he was gunned down himself by nightclub owner Jack Ruby while being transferred to another jail.]

The real-life protagonist of *Certain Honorable Men* was the then well-known Federal prosecutor and diplomat, Thomas J. Dodd (1907-1971). He had held a number of diplomatic posts in places like Costa Rica and Uruguay, and worked as an assistant to five successive U.S. Attorneys General. As a Federal prosecutor, he had pursued members of the KKK and once exposed a major Soviet spy ring. *[Descendant of four Irish grandparents, Dodd was also the father of former U.S. Senator Christopher Dodd, the longest-serving Democratic Senator (1981-2011) in Connecticut's history.]*

Dodd gained his greatest fame prosecuting high-placed Nazi officials at the notorious Nuremburg war crime trials of 1945 and 1946.

He called these trials "an autopsy of history's most horrible catalogue of human crime."

In one of the most dramatic scenes at the trial, he revealed that Walther Frank of the Reichsbank had a depository of gold teeth ripped from the mouths of victims before or after they were forced into gas chambers. He even introduced as evidence a shrunken head that a Gestapo chief had used as a paperweight.

Why will this minor B picture live on in history? In 1963, after assassinating President John F. Kennedy and Dallas police officer J.D. Tippit, Lee Harvey Oswald (without buying a ticket) walked into a movie house showing *Cry of Battle*. After a gun battle within the theater, Oswald was hauled away.

A few days later, he would be assassinated himself.

A towering figure of moral courage, prosecutor **Thomas J. Dodd** at the Nuremburg Trials (1945-46) attacked leading Nazi officials for committing "unspeakable crimes against humanity. These Nazis killed or tortured more than eight million Jews and others judged as enemies of the Aryan state. They treated their fellow men as less than beasts." That seemed not to have impressed the producers of a TV movie starring Peter Fonda.

In 1967, Dodd (by then a full-fledged Democratic Senator from Connecticut and an active proponent of the war against drugs) was excoriated as part of a highly politicized punishment for what, even at the time, seemed like a relatively minor fiscal indiscretion.

A year later, Peter Fonda, cast in a TV drama as a sanctimonious whistleblower who exposed (or betrayed) the character inspired by Dodd, did not win any friends in high places.

At the Nuremburg Trials, Hermann Göring pleaded not guilty, but Dodd exposed him as having launched the Holocaust, on orders of Hitler.

During the postwar years, Dodd was elected, as a Democrat, to the Senate from Connecticut in 1958 and re-elected in 1964. However, in 1967, charged with pilfering campaign funds to pay his personal expenses, he became the first member of the U.S. Senate to be censured since Joseph McCarthy.

Thomas Dodd's supporters, in editorials throughout the nation, claimed that whereas, in time, his transgressions would be forgotten, those Nuremburg trials would live in public memory forever.

Certain Honorable Men was marketed by the network as a story about "an unethical congressman unseated through the efforts of his protégé and his secretary." It flitted across television sets very quickly, receiving faint praise from *The New York Times*: "*Certain Honorable Men* is far more interesting than the average TV drama."

***

Stage Play: The Beard (1965-1968)

At this point in his counterculture career, Peter had cultivated a friendship with the avant-garde playwright, Michael McClure (1932-2020). Although years later, Peter cast him in a small role in one of his films, *The Hired Hand,* he flew, long before that (in 1965) to San Francisco to attend a performance of McClure's latest and very *avant-garde* play, *The Beard.*

Peter got to know McClure a lot better during his visit to San Francisco.

A native of Kansas, McClure was a poet, playwright, songwriter, and novelist. As a young man, he'd moved to San Francisco, where he became friends with two of the leading figures of the Beat Generation, Jack Kerouac and Allen Ginsberg. McClure is interpreted today as a key member and spokesperson of The Beat Generation.

Lewd, Smut-Ridden Play Given At Cal State Fullerton

Michael McClure, the ultra-avant-garde author of this play, tried to steer Peter Fonda into performing as the male lead in a movie adaptation of a play (*The Beard*) that rocked California.

The headline inserted below the poster was prominently displayed in the local paper (the November 17, 1967 edition of the *Yorba Linda Star*) in reference to its performance on a nearby college campus.

The poster itself, now considered a historically important illumination of the arts scene in San Francisco's Haight-Ashbury district in the late 1960s, was sold at auction at Christies's in 2009 for $2,375.

Disguised as a fictional character, McClure had appeared as a figure in two of Kerouac's works, *Big Sur* and *The Dharma Bums.*

McClure also became a friend of Jim Morrison of The Doors, aggressively promoting him as a mystical poet.

As McClure (who was gay) told Peter, "Jim rewarded me by letting me get down on my knees before him as he unzipped."

McClure wanted Peter to see his stage drama, *The Beard* in hopes that he would option it as a movie with him (Peter) in the star role of Billy the Kid. The Kid would appear on stage with an actress anachronistically cast as Jean Harlow. McClure didn't mind that Harlow and Billy the Kid had lived in radically different historical eras—it was all being done in the name of art and "the *avant garde*."

Always associated with the wide, open landscapes of the American West, the historical figure of Billy the Kid was born on September 17, 1859 in New York City, of all places. He was formally known as either Henry McCarty or as "William H. Bonney," depending on the era, the circumstances, and the location.

Orphaned at the age of 15, he left Manhattan and headed into the tumultuous Old West. Perhaps psychotic, he went on a killing rampage and became "wanted by the authorities" in both Arizona and New Mexico.

His notoriety was widely publicized in various gazettes. Sheriff Pat Garrett captured him in December of 1880, when he was tried for murder and sentenced to hang. But he escaped from jail on April 28, 1881, killing two of the sheriff's deputies. It took two months, but Garrett eventually caught up with him in Fort Sumner, New Mexico, fatally gunning him down on July 14, 1881 and burying him in the town's old military cemetery. At the time of his death, he was only 21 years old.

As his legend grew and became indelibly linked to "the American experience," his character would appear in an astonishing fifty movies, portrayed by actors who included Buster Crabbe, Robert Taylor, Paul Newman, Kris Kristofferson, Val Kilmer, and Jack Beutel.

[*Beutel was the hero of Howard Hughes' controversial film* The Outlaw (1943), *which introduced Hollywood audiences to the bra-less bust of Jane Russell.*]

Like Billy the Kid, Jean Harlow, born in Kansas City, Missouri, in 1922, also became a legendary figure. She rose to fame during the Depression-soaked 1930s, hailed as "The Platinum Blonde" and "the Blonde Bombshell."

"All men want to do is reach up under my dress," she was quoted as saying. She could have been referring to the hands of, among others, Howard Hughes, Lew Ayres, boxer Max Baer, Clark Gable, Chester Morris, William Powell, gangster Bugsy Siegel, author Thomas Wolfe, or even James Stewart, who said, "When it comes to kissing, Harlow is the best."

[*That (short) list of men who wanted to reach up under her dress left out hordes of taxi drivers, salesmen, and delivery boys from Western Union.*]

Harlow also dated MGM's studio executive Paul Bern, an assistant to Irving Thalberg. "I like him," she said, "because he doesn't talk fuck, fuck, fuck all the time." Without having gone to bed with him, she married him, but Bern turned out, on their

Left: **Michael McClure** in 1972. Years later, to the amazement of everyone involved in the Beat Generation and its poetry, the U.S. Postal Service issued a stamp in his honor.

A REAL-LIFE AMERICAN PSYCHOPATH— AND ANYTHING BUT GLAM

Billy the Kid, as captured in a "tintype daguerreotype" in 1878 or 1880 at Fort Sumner, New Mexico.

Later morphed into a tragic folk hero of the Old West, he is alleged to have shot and killed 21 men before he was killed by a shotgun wound at the age of 21.

wedding night, to be impotent. A few months later, he was dead, an alleged suicide.

Harlow's next husband, cinematographer Harold Rosson, made up for Bern's inadequacies. (In Hollywood circles, he was known as "Long Dong.")

Billy the Kid and the Blonde Bombshell (Harlow) were the historically unassociated figures and chronologically impossible characters who interacted together as protagonists in McClure's experimental play, *The Beard*. McClure, as noted earlier, aggressively showcased it to Peter Fonda, in the hopes that Peter would support its adaptation into a film in which he would star.

As a play, McClure's *The Beard* opened at the Actors Workshop in San Francisco on the night of December 18, 1965. It later played at Bill Graham's Fillmore Theatre, a "defiantly counter-culture" venue indelibly bound to the city's fast-emerging psychedelic drug culture, where it was secretly taped by the San Francisco Police Department.

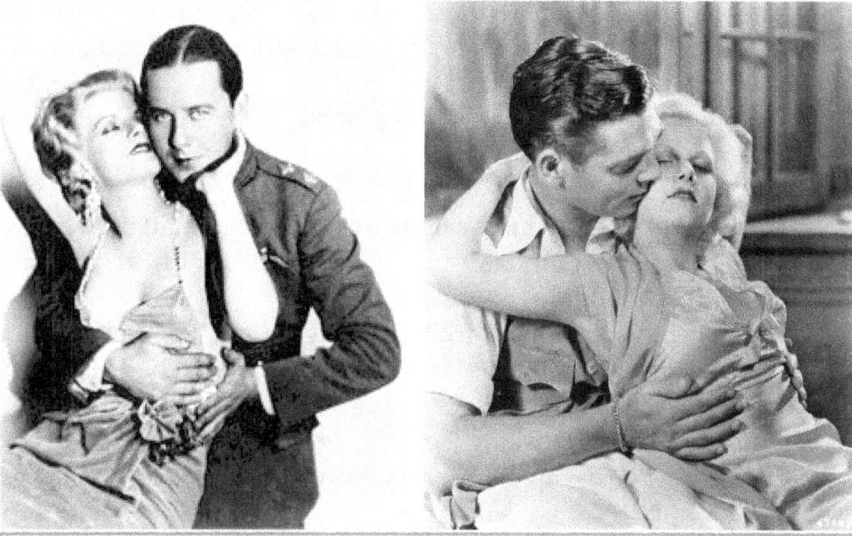

Jean Harlow (aka "the Laughing Vamp" or "the Blonde Bombshell") was the most widely publicized sex symbol of pre-Code Hollywood.

At the age on 19, she appeared "almost bare-breasted' in the *left photo* with **Ben Lyon** in Howard Hughes' *Hell's Angels* (1930), the highest-grossing film of that year.

In the *right photo*, suggestively clad only in boudoir satin, she heats up the screen with **Clark Gable** in *Red Dust* (1932). Swimming in controversy and reviled by morally rigorous censors, she died at the age of 26 in 1937.

In the decades that followed, she evolved into a role model for wannabe celebrities who "lived fast and died young."

[In the mid-1960s, the Fillmore Auditorium under the direction of Graham became a focal point for psychedelic music and the counterculture in general. It was the venue for such acts as the Steve Miller Band, the Grateful Dead, Jefferson Airplane, The Doors, the Jimi Hendrix Experience, Pink Floyd, Santana, and many more. It also staged plays (such as The Beard*) comedy acts (Lenny Bruce) and poetry readings, all enveloped in the counterculture trappings exploding throughout San Francisco and the nation at the time.]*

Having failed in their attempt to suppress Allen Ginsberg's *Howl*, the San Francisco police were determined to nail McClure and, as his associates, the actors portraying Harlow and Billy the Kid in this arty, weirdly unconventional play.

The theater was raided during one of its performances on the evening of August 8, 1966, the fifth time that *The Beard* had been performed in public. Its stars, Billie Dixon (Harlow) and Richard Bright (Billy the Kid) were hauled off to jail.

Lawyers for the American Civil Liberties Union took the case and represented the actors. After months of legal wrangling, the stars of *The Beard*, even the play itself, prevailed in the courts.

What had contributed to the controversy that morphed *The Beard* into a *cause célèbre*, was the very graphic love scene near the end. The actor playing Billy the Kid is seen going down on the actress cast as Harlow. As one reviewer so indelicately put it, "He rips off her panties and eats her out."

The colorful, pugilistic and hot-tempered Norman Mailer later reviewed *The Beard* like this:

"Michael McClure's The Beard *is a mysterious piece of work, for while its surface seems simple, repetitive and obscene, there is an action working which is dramatic and comic at once, and the play emits an odd but intense field of attention, almost like a magnetic field, almost as if ghosts from two periods of the American Past were speaking across decades to each other, and yet at the same time are present in our living room undressing themselves or speaking to us of the nature of seduction, the nature of attraction, and particularly, the nature of perverse*

temper between a man and a woman. Obstinacy face to face with the sly feint and parry all in one, the repetitions serve almost as subway stops on that electric trip a man and a woman make if they move from the mind to the flesh. That mysterious trip, whose mystery often resides in the dilemma of whether the action is extraordinarily serious or meaningless. It is with these ambiguities, these effervescences, that The Beard *plays, masterfully, be it said, like a juggler."*

For its 1967-1968 season, *The Beard* opened in Manhattan, where it won Obie Awards for Best Director and Best Actress. It would later play across America in various locales, and even be staged at the Royal Court Theatre in London.

Optimistically, Peter and McClure thought they could find financial backing for the Harlow/Billy the Kid film adaptation, but that idea sputtered and died when Hollywood's investment community learned about the over-saturation of the Jean Harlow theme within the American film scene. As it happened, two rival studios were each making (separate and unassociated) films, each with the same title (*Harlow*), each scheduled for a release in 1965, and each generating oceans of rage and competitive hatred within the competing camp.

One of them had cast Carol Lynley as Harlow; the other had cast her rival, Carroll Baker. Each was poorly received, and each of them flopped at the box office.

The version featuring Baker, was released by Paramount and starred Peter Lawford as Paul Bern, the studio executive who commits suicide after his wedding night flop. Angela Lansbury was cast as the mother of Harlow. Lansbury's character is married to a historical sleazeball named Marino Bello (Raf Vallone).

The other *Harlow* (the version starring Carol Lynley as the platinum blonde) was produced by Magna Distribution Corporation. The role of the mother was originally cast with a by then increasingly unstable Judy Garland, but she dropped out at the last minute. Garland was replaced by Ginger Rogers as her farewell to the screen. The character she played was "Mama Jean," (Jean Harlow's mother) who's wed to Barry Sullivan as the sponging Marino Bello. Hurd Hatfield was hired to play the impotent Paul Bern.

Believe it or not, Richard Burton was one of the financial backers of this ill-fated movie, the version of *Harlow* distributed by Magna and starring Carol Lynley. It was reviewed as "cheap, lusterless, and excruciatingly dull," and to Paramount's fury, it managed to reach theaters slightly in advance of their version starring Carroll Baker.

***

The Queen (1988)

Before *Easy Rider* began production, Peter and Hopper proposed another project to producer Bob Rafelson, suggesting that the entire film could be made in four days for a cost of $60,000. Entitled *The Queen,* Hopper, Peter, and the other actors would wear ivory-colored off-the-shoulder, beaded gowns. In drag, they would impersonate (male and very forceful) government officials who included Dean Rusk, George Bundy, Robert McNamara, and Lyndon B. Johnson. The script called for those officials, cloaked in the greatest of secrecy, to plot the assassination of John F. Kennedy.

In addition to Hopper and Peter, Rip Torn agreed to play one of the roles, as would Michael McClure.

Rafelson rejected requests for him to finance *The Queen,* citing it as "perhaps the worst idea for a script ever offered in the history of Hollywood."

***

Easy Rider (1969)

After it scored big at the Cannes Film Festival, *Easy Rider* was released in New York on July 14, 1969.

For access to tickets, lines formed around the block—not the typical movie audience, but often long-haired hippies and their girlfriends, many of them barefoot. Within a week, the movie made back its cost of production. It was shot for under $500,000, and in time would generate $60 million, by far the most profitable film Peter ever made.

Easy Rider became more than just another motorcycle movie. It's now viewed as a classic. A landmark counterculture film, it was defined as "a touchstone for a new generation." It also captured the imagination of the country, mostly young people. It was the spark that ignited the "New Hollywood" era of movie making in the 1970s.

Peter Fonda, Dennis Hopper, and Jack Nicholson were the stars. Peter produced it and Hopper directed it from a script created 80% by Terry Southern, with enormous input from both Peter and Hopper

Released by Columbia Pictures, the road drama received two Academy Award nominations, one for Best Supporting Actor (Nicholson), the other for Best Original Screenplay.

A native of Alvarado, Texas, Southern was also a novelist and essayist. He had been part of the post-war literary movement of Paris, and he later returned to America, where he was a figure in the Beat Generation of the 1950s.

It is said that his script for *Easy Rider* was influenced by Jack Kerouac's *On the Road*, published in 1957. That book had been based on his travels across the American landscapes. Critics hailed it as the defining work of the Beat and Counterculture Generation, each with its protagonists living life against a backdrop of jazz, sex, poetry, and recreational drugs.

Southern also landed in the heart of Swinging London in the 1960s, and he would go on to change "the steel and substance" of many American films in the 1970s. His comic novel, *Candy* (1968) was adapted into a film that starred Richard Burton, Marlon Brando, and Ringo Starr.

When *Easy Rider* was released, Southern's previous writings were subjected to a lot of attention. One skeptical critic asked, "Is Southern really trying to tell us that freedom of the road is only another kind of evasion and captivity?"

Peter Fonda had previously starred in such movies as *The Wild Angels* and *The Trip*, but he was never taken too seriously by the Hollywood establishment until the release of the vastly profitable *Easy Rider*.

Both Peter and Hopper had gone to a Hollywood production company called BBS Productions. Bob Rafelson and Bert Schneider had made a lot of money by launching the new musical group, The Monkees. They were also producing *Five Easy Pieces* (1969) starring Jack Nicholson. Their biggest success would come with *The Last Picture Show* (1971).

As seed money for *Easy Rider*, Peter and Hopper wanted more, but

A man went looking for America and couldn't find it anywhere

As expressed by film scholar Steve Chagallon, "The film that launched a thousand road trips, if not countless road movies, was independently produced and ended up as the third highest grossing release of 1969, earning $60 million worldwide, even though it was made for roughly $400,000, a fraction of the budget of its competitors at the box office.

The New York Times reviewed **On the Road** as "The Testament of the Beat Generation."

Called "King of the Beats," **Jack Kerouac** (right) was a controversial anti-hero who loosely presided over the turned-on, dropped-out ecstatic wanderers of the Swinging Sixties. He was a catalyst for a major post-war shift in American values, culture, and literature.

On the left is **Neal Cassady,** who had many affairs with young women.. However, his most enduring sexual relationship was with Beat poet Allen Ginsberg, which lasted twenty years.

Rafelson would only part with $375,000, with the understanding that during its production, cast and crew would have to work for the relatively lean remuneration known as "scale" [*i.e., the minimum pay and work conditions set by the Screen Actors Guild and other actors' unions.*]

***

As both the director and co-star of *Easy Rider*, Dennis Hopper faced a difficult situation.

Born in Dodge City, Kansas, in May of 1936, Hopper had followed the advice of that old maxim, "It was time to get out of Dodge."

In May of 1936, he migrated to New York, where he attended classes at the Actors Studio.

Left photo, **Dennis Hopper** in his breakthrough role as a small-time crook in *True Grit* (1969), and *right photo* as the director of the later-in-his-career highlight, *The Last Movie.*

Early in his Hollywood career, he met and befriended James Dean, appearing with him in both *Rebel Without a Cause* (1955) and *Giant* (1956).

Having virtually worshipped Dean when he was alive, it was said that Hopper never really got over his untimely death in a car crash in September of 1955.

John Wayne would also play a key role in Hopper's career, casting him in *The Sons of Katie Elder* (1965) and later, in *True Grit* (1969).

"Jimmy and I were into peyote and grass when it was something you couldn't even mention to your closest buddies," Hopper said. "I developed a taste for drugs when I was just eight years old and got off smelling the gasoline from my grandfather's truck."

Many of Hopper's days and nights were fueled by drugs. He was also a bit of a wild man. "I don't think there is a starlet around that I didn't have," he told Peter. "I'd rather give head to a woman than plug her."

The reason for that was that his penis did not satisfy many women. Shock jock Howard Stern saw a movie that included scenes of Hopper frontally nude. "His thing is the size of an elevator button," Stern said on the air to widespread audiences.

Hopper was married five times, his first (1961-1969) to Brooke Hayward, who was sixteen at the time. It was troubled. Brooke was the daughter of Hollywood agent Leland Hayward and actress Margaret Sullavan.

Hopper also had relationships not just with starlettes but also with major-league stars who included Ursula Andress, Joan Collins, Jean Seberg, and Natalie Wood.

Before filming began, Hopper announced to the press, "Peter Fonda and I are making a celluloid anthem to macho bravado and to anti-establishment rebellion. We're giving the middle finger to the establishment."

For Hopper, it was a lifetime of triumph and tragedy that spanned 115 movies and four television series.

Although they were friends in private life, Peter and Hopper clashed frequently during the filming of *Easy Rider.*

As Peter recalled, "Dennis often struts around like a god damn fascist, shouting, "It's my fucking movie."

The script of *Easy Rider* had not been finished before its shooting began. Much of it was "birthed" bit by bit as a day's production progressed.

Peter was cast as Wyatt ("Captain America"), the name inspired by Wyatt Earp. Hopper played Billy, a moniker adopted from Billy the Kid.

In a nutshell, *Easy Rider* is about two hip motorcyclists on an odyssey across the often beautiful, often barren landscapes of North America. It is also about their love-hate relationship with the United States, which is returned in kind.

These free-wheeling guys bring cocaine into America from Mexico, and sell it for a large stash of cash. The money will finance their trip all the way to New Orleans in time for Mardi Gras.

The cash is stashed in a plastic tube concealed inside the fuel tank of Peter's Harley-Davidson. They travel through the southwest and southern tier of the United States, where they encounter intolerance and violence.

Fonda as Wyatt is a charismatic but laconic figure whose motorcycle jacket sports a large American flag across its back. Hopper, as Billy, has a more garrulous role.

Along the way, Wyatt picks up a hitch-hiker who invites him to visit his hippie commune, where they remain for the rest of the day in this "free love" camp. As they prepare to leave, the young man gives Wyatt some LSD for him to share "with the right people."

As they cross into New Mexico, still riding their cycles, they join a parade, but are then arrested for "parading without a permit." They're thrown into jail, where they're befriended by George Hanson, a lawyer who works for the ACLU. He has a problem with the bottle.

He helps them get out of jail and agrees to travel with them to Louisiana. Even though he's an alcoholic, he's a bit square when it comes to smoking dope, based on his fear of "getting hooked."

At a roadside diner, the men encounter redneck prejudice from the locals and suffer taunts and denigrating comments. They make camp outside of town. In the middle of the night, one of the psychotic hillbillies attacks them while they're sleeping, beating them with clubs, Wyatt and Billy suffer minor injuries, but George is bludgeoned to death.

Peter and Wyatt continue on to New Orleans, where they go to a brothel and take up with two prostitutes, Mary and Karen. They join the Mardi Gras festivities and end up in a scary, gothic-looking cemetery in the French Quarter where they take some hits of LSD.

The next morning, two Louisiana rednecks in a beat-up pickup truck overtake them on a two-lane country road. One of the truckers reaches for a shotgun and fires at Billy.

The truck passes Wyatt, who rushes back to discover that Billy is covered with blood and dying.

Wyatt then rides down the road toward the pickup, in pursuit. He makes a U-turn, with the intention of confronting its occupants. One of the rednecks aims and fires his shotgun again, this time at Wyatt.

The movie ends as Wyatt's riderless cycle flies through the air, coming apart before landing on the ground, engulfed in flames.

Peter Fonda, riding his motorcycle into fame and fortune in *Easy Rider*.

"My favorite scene," he said, "was when Jack Nicholson, Dennis Hopper, and I were seen pissing together by the side of the road."

MALE BONDING MADE EASY, thanks in part to the nearby accessibility of women, booze, and recreational drugs.

Here, **Peter Fonda,** *left*, chews the fat with **Dennis Hopper** in *Easy Rider*.

***

Originally, the role of George Hanson had been offered to actor Rip Torn, but he wanted to be paid $4,500 a week instead of scale (much less) like everyone else on the crew and in the cast. But something went terribly wrong in a restaurant. There, during their negotiations, Hopper and Torn got into a fight

When it was over, Hopper maintained that Torn threatened him with a steak knife, whereas Torn said it was the other way around.

In the aftermath, Torn was out of the picture.

Peter and Hopper then turned to Jack Nicholson. They had already seen his movie, *Head,* the 1968 satirical musical featuring the boy band, The Monkees.

Before their argument, at least, Hopper had really wanted Torn because he was from Texas and as such, had the requisite accent required. In contrast, Nicholson was from New Jersey. Peter and Rafelson prevailed over Hopper's objections. "Jack is a Hollywood flasher, not a country bumpkin," Hopper protested.

Peter Fonda (*left*) and **Dennis Hopper** (*right*) interact with **Jack Nicholson**, who looks—in this scene at least—like a con artist in a summer suit.

But when Nicholson showed up for work, he looked the part, having selected plain, round glasses and a white seersucker suit held up with suspenders.

With Rafael's approval, Nicholson functioned as a kind of executive producer because he was far better organized than either Hopper or Peter. He hired Laszlo Kovacs as cinematographer as a means of capturing the beauty of the American landscapes.

Nicholson was also instrumental in selecting the film's musical tracks. They originated with artists who included Jimi Hendrix and The Electric Flag, that rock band which had recorded the soundtrack for Peter's film, *The Trip.* The group had been formed only in 1967, and would reach its peak in 1968 with the release of *A Long Time Comin',* a fusion of rock, jazz, and R&B.

One campfire scene featured Peter with Hopper and Nicholson. They are talking and smoking weed, and it required several takes, since all of them were stoned. Peter later estimated that "we smoked 155 real joints of Mexican grass before we had it in the can."

For his New Orleans whorehouse pickup, Hopper wanted the actress Karen Black. A symbol of the New Hollywood, she was known for playing eccentric or offbeat characters. She would rise to greater fame in the 1970s in a career that would span fifty years and include 200 credits. Her greatest performances involved her portrayal of Nicholson's dizzy girlfriend in *Five Easy Pieces* (1970).

As an actress to play his own hooker, May, Peter preferred Toni Basil, and he got his wish. She was a designer, choreographer, dancer, actress, and director. Her song, "Mickey," once topped the *Billboard* charts. She had recently appeared in the Nicholson film, *Head,* working alongside The Monkees.

For the scenes sited at the hippie commune, three uncredited performers included Bridget Fonda (Peter's daughter), Dan Haggerty, and Carrie Snodgrass.

Haggerty became known for playing the title role in the film and TV series, *The Life and Times of Grizzly Adams* beginning in 1974.

Carrie Snodgrass would soon star in her most famous role, the protagonist in *Diary of a Mad Housewife* (1970), for which she was nominated for an Academy Award.

In the minor role of Jack was Robert Walker Jr., a long-time friend of Peter's. Like Peter, himself, he was the son of not one but two movie stars: Robert Walker Sr. and Jennifer Jones (who, after divorcing him, went on to marry both David O. Selznick and mega-millionaire Norton Simon). Walker Jr.'s father had died tragically in 1951 at the end of an affair with Nancy Davis (aka, Nancy Reagan).

Before working on *Easy Rider,* Bob Rafelson had directed Nicholson in *Head* (1968), a showcase for The Monkees, that rock/pop band formed in Los Angeles in 1966. They became one of the most successful bands of the 1960s, selling 75 million records worldwide, including such hits as "I'm a Believer."

The Monkees were outsold only by the Beatles and the Rolling Stones. Rafelson had backed *Easy Rider* based in part on his belief that it would be "carried" on the coattails of the hit it included in its soundtrack, *A Hard Day's Night*. The movie version had starred the Beatles in 1964.

Although cinematically, Peter had moved on from the too-vivid display of effects of LSD that had been so prominent in *The Trip,* acid trips also appear in frames of *Easy Rider.* They include erratic chronological shifts, flash forwards, jump cuts, shots from hand-held cameras, and the fractured (some said "impoverished") narratives and dialogues. Critics pointed out that these effects could be interpreted as direct cinematic translations of the psychedelic experience.

Daniel Bohning wrote, "It is said that *Easy Rider* glamourized drug taking. But if one needed any of the tragic effects of acid, one need only read the obits of Janis Joplin, Jimi Hendrix, and Brian Jones, to name only three fallen idols."

Many critics expressed the belief that Jack Nicholson walked off with the picture, virtually "stealing" it from Dennis Hopper and Peter Fonda. One of them said, "He reeked of bourbon and failure but was richly funny and endlessly sympathetic. His role was one of the consummate pieces of screen acting."

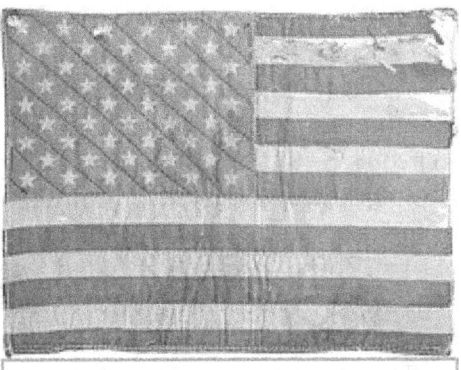

A CRAZY PLANET FULL OF CRAZY PEOPLE

The "Captain America" flag worn on Peter Fonda's leather jacket in *Easy Rider* sold for $89,625 in the Music and Entertainment Auction conducted, October 2007, by Heritage Auction Galleries of Dallas, Texas. The patch measures 14.5" x 11"

After he finished work on *Easy Rider,* William Hayward, its assistant director, said, "The whole thing has been like a Rashomon experience, the entire film, the whole production. Everybody's got a different story to tell about what went on as *Easy Rider* was filmed."

[Editor's Note: The Rashomon Effect is a term used to describe how an event can be described in a variety of ways due to the unreliability of multiple witnesses. The witnesses' unreliability and subjectivity are a result of cultural, social, and situational differences. Since the term was introduced in the 1950s, it has transcended cinema and is now a term that is widely applied to both psychology and law.]

After it was sent back to Los Angeles, the rough cut ran for five hours. Drastic cuts were needed," Nicholson said. "I was allowed to keep my best scenes."

The final cut ran for just 96 minutes.

Some of the scenes landing on the cutting-room floor included an incident where Hopper and Fonda encounter a mostly black and menacing motorcycle gang. Another scene that was removed laid out an elaborate (and expensive to film) chase from lawmen riding on motorcycles and in helicopters.

"In making the movie," Peter told Hopper, "I want to turn out something that will impress both my father and my sister, Jane."

She recalled sitting in a projection room with Henry and her husband, Roger Vadim. They were shown a pre-release version of *Easy Rider.*

"Our Dad didn't know what to make of it," Jane said. "I found it unbelievably audacious that they carried cocaine on their bikes and took acid in a cemetery. I secretly thought it would be too rough to take for most audiences. It was Vadim who better understood that here was a no-holds-barred cinematic breakthrough that would resonate immediately and become a classic."

Henry Fonda, *père,* spoke his mind: "That little bastard. He and that punk, Dennis Hopper, have produced a movie out of nothing and would make more money with this piece of crap than I've made in my entire film career in Hollywood."

***

Easy Rider opened at a time of the greatest disarray in America since World War II. The assassination of Martin Luther King, Jr. and Robert Kennedy; police shoot-outs with Black Panthers; demonstrations against the Vietnam War; the burning of draft cards; flights to Canada where many draft evaders found local brides and never came back.

New leaders on the horizon meant plenty of trouble: Yasser Arafat, leader of the PLO, and Muammar Gaddafi in Libya.

Charles Champlin of the *Los Angeles Times* hailed *Easy Rider* as "an astonishing piece of work, of art, and an overpowering motion picture experience. The talk is spare throughout, and a terse sentence of

Fonda's near the end of their adventure, 'We blew it,' is heavy with implications of his own dawning apprehensions that dropping-out is an inadequate response."

Anthony West of *Vogue* weighed in too: "Three clever chaps (Fonda, Hopper, Southern) get down to a piece of filmmaking so professional, so superbly laconic, and so savagely peaceful as if to lift the picture as a whole into the category of the tragic, and to make it one of the most effective and memorable films that has been produced in the United States. Peter Fonda's austerely convincingly and strangely beautiful performances in the leading role has a lot to do with this."

Howard Smith in *The Village Voice* claimed, "*Easy Rider* will make Peter Fonda an enormous hero-star. He comes across as a combination of James Dean and Clint Eastwood. Hopper, until now, most famous for his frantic pop lifestyle, somehow got his head together to pull off one of the most powerful movies I've ever seen."

Richard Goldstein of *The New York Times* singled out Peter for special praise. "Ultimately, *Easy Rider* is the first real Peter Fonda movie. Nothing heroic like John Wayne at the Alamo. You can't detect any of that charisma-of-the-silver screen in his performance. He's not even trying to resurrect that love-me-I'm-sensitive syndrome of the 1950s. He's just, you know, gettin' his thing together. The cool of acting naturally, that's why you don't get embarrassed watching him turn on."

"Hopper not only starred in the film, but directed it with a steady hand," Goldstein continued. "He virtually helmed himself as Billy, the most vivid evocation of a California 'hip-uptight' you'll ever see on the screen."

The acerbic Rex Reed found *Easy Rider* "an excruciating look at where this country is today, about as strong an indictment of America as I've seen in any medium. The real power of the film lies in the way it turns over the rocks of apple-pie America and reveals the slime. Peter Fonda and Hopper can be proud of a movie which looks not so much photographed but lived."

Archer Winsten in the *New York Post* wrote, "the scenes are great, as are the western roads and landscapes, the little towns and restaurants. What is especially great is Peter Fonda's infinitely patient silence, and Jack Nicholson's flawless, drunken, lawyer-trained flow of pertinent oratory."

***

The Hired Hand (1971)

"Whatever I do next is likely to be a disappointment," Peter said. "*Easy Rider* is a tough act to follow."

The Hired Hand, a 1971 Western drawn from a screenplay by Alan Sharp, was a moody piece. The story spins around Harry Collings (Peter), who returns to the homestead of his wife who he had deserted seven years ago. He finds that she has neither divorced him nor taken up with another partner, but is trying to

As the tagline in the *upper photo* luridly screams,

**"PETER FONDA IS RIDING AGAIN—
To the woman he lost, for the revenge he craves."**

Whether he liked it or not, a lot of critics and film fans compared **Peter Fonda's** portrayals of Western anti-heroes to the bygone Westerns of Peter's father, Henry.

Here, Peter appears with the supporting actor of many cult films, Kentucky-born **Warren Oates,** in what he was quick to define as "a modernized spin" in *The Hired Hand*.

run the homestead herself.

He is accompanied by his fellow "saddle tramp," Arch Harris (Warren Oates). The embittered Hannah, appearing in an unflattering frontier frock without makeup, agrees to take him back, but only as a hired hand. He and Harris are allowed to sleep in the barn but can take their meals in the main house with Hannah and her daughter, Janey (Megan Denver).

Harry and Arch have been traveling with a young companion, Dan Griffen (Robert Pratt). While they're away, member of the McVey gang kill the young man in a shootout. Harry later shoots McVey in the feet, crippling him. Obviously, he will seek revenge.

Larry Hagman, the son of Mary Martin and a friend of Peter's virtually since birth, was cast as the sheriff investigating Griffen's murder.

When the film was wrapped, Hagman was told that his scenes would be removed from the final cut of *The Hired Hand.* His scenes were later restored, however, for the film's release on television.

On the set, Peter renewed his friendship with Michael McClure. In *The Hired Hand,* McClure was assigned the small role of Ed Plummer. Gradually, Hannah's distrust and bitterness over her desertion by her husband fades, and she becomes close to him once again.

Peter Fonda with his then-wife **Susan Brewer** in 1969.

The nearby settlement of "Del Norte" is ruled by McVey (Severn Darden) and his gang of hoodlums.

Later, McVey and his motley troupe of hooligans kidnap Harris and hold him hostage. Harry leaves Hannah once again, this time as part of an attempt to save his friend's life. During an encounter with McVey's gang, he's fatally shot. Harris escapes and returns to the Collings homestead. The movie ends with the lingering suggestion that Arch will become the new man in Hannah's life.

For the most part, *The Hired Hand* was shot in New Mexico in the sweltering summer of 1970 on a relatively modest budget of one-million dollars.

Warren Oates, with whom Peter would co-star in the future, was a Kentuckian best known for his Western roles with Sam Peckinpah, especially *The Wild Bunch* (1969). Before that, he'd won acclaim for his performance as Sam Wood in *In the Heat of the Night* (1967).

Over the years, Oates developed a cult following, especially for his work with Bill Murray in the 1981 military comedy, *Stripes,* in which he played a drill sergeant. That film would turn out to be his greatest success, earning $85 million at the box office.

Oates later co-starred with Jack Nicholson in *The Border* (1982), directed by Tony Richardson.

Critic Richard Linklater gave Oates what is the greatest praise any actor ever received when he wrote: "There was once a god who walked on earth named Warren Oates."

Peter interviewed Verna Bloom for the leading female role of Hannah. During the interview, she asked him, "Will I have to take off my clothes?"

"Not at all," he replied.

Marital discord, misplaced responsibility, and guilt as depicted in the bucolic West of *The Hired Hand.*

Left photo, left to right, **Peter Fonda**, **Warren Oates**, child actress **Megan Denver**, and the deliberately plain-looking wife that Peter's character had abandoned years before, **Verna Bloom**.

Right photo: closeup of **Verna Bloom**

"The only person who shows his ass in a Peter Fonda movie is Peter Fonda himself. When my ass flashes on the screen, you won't believe the fan mail I get from gays who want to fuck me. My ass is off limits to everybody. Even to my wife, and certainly to doctors, even military ones examining new recruits."

Later, he said, "If I were a certain kind of director, I would have ordered Verna to take off all her clothes and lie down on the casting couch. She sure didn't look sexy in our movie, but in her private life, she was a hot tamale."

Bloom had first garnered attention on Broadway when she starred as Charlotte Corday in *The Persecution and Assassination of Jean-Paul Marat as Performed by the Inmates of the Asylum of Charenton Under the Direction of the Marquis de Sade* (1967).

She later co-starred with Clint Eastwood in the film *High Plains Drifter* (1973).

The last Peter ever heard of her was when she was playing Mary in *The Last Temptation of Christ* (1988). Bloom died in 2019 at the age of 80, suffering from dementia.

As producer, William Hayward roomed with Peter on location. The two men had been friends since childhood, as he was the son of Leland Hayward and Margaret Sullavan. They spent most of their evenings smoking pot as they watched the sun set in the West.

Peter could talk freely about his failing marriage to Susan Brewer, the mother of his kids. "I'm gone all the time, and she rightly feels abandoned. She shuns the rock scene and doesn't join me in what I call my 'night moves.' As a movie star, I have my pick. Since the kids came, she no longer joins me on location. I could send her a postcard on the road, but somehow I never get around to that. We are coming apart."

Breaking her usual rule, Susan and the children did show up on location in New Mexico. Hayward planned to move out and get a separate room until Peter told him, "Don't bother. She'll have her own room with the kids. She won't be sleeping in my bed. We don't have that kind of relationship any more."

He always talked about his father with Hayward. He attacked many published reports that he was still intimidated by his father. "He is the one who should be intimated by me. I should write a bio and call it *The Son Also Rises*. Let's face it: I'm a director and an actor, and I make more money than he ever did. Maybe Ill give him a break and cast him in one of my flicks."

"He once asked me how I could be the director and actor in the same picture. My answer? I told him I did so by shadow-boxing with God."

It was during the filming of *The Hired Hand* that Peter told Hayward that he had been offered to star in *Twelve Angry Men* on Broadway, a role his father had made famous in the movies.

"Are you going to accept?" Hayward asked.

"I told those guys, 'Don't hold your breath.'"

In *The Hired Hand*, Peter made some brilliant choices in hiring—and not just the cast of characters. Vilmso Zsigmonds was hired as the cinematographer. Later, he was praised for the high quality of his naturalistic images. "I had a dramatic story to film with good actors," he said, modestly.

Peter chose the relatively unknown Bruce Langhorne as the film's composer. Many reviews signaled him out for special mention for a score that was "unusually expressive and beautiful."

Frank Mazzola, the film editor, in some cases got more praise than Peter. Critics hailed his opening montage as memorable. He was also cited for his elaborate dissolves, his slow motion, and overlapping still photography.

Before the release of *The Hired Hand,* Universal planned to erect a gigantic billboard along Sunset Boulevard. In blaring letters, it would herald: EASY RIDER RIDES AGAIN!

Peter went to the studio and ordered that the billboard be taken down "or else I'll use explosives."

"The boys at Universal paid themselves a hefty fee for distributing our film. I didn't see a pickass dime. At least I got them to take that damn billboard down. I objected to them trying to exploit the fame of *Easy Rider*."

Upon its release, *The Hired Hand* flopped at the box office and drew mixed reviews, most of them negative. For the most part, it was dismissed as" a hippie Western."

The critic for *Variety* wrote, "*The Hired Hand* has a disjointed story, a largely unsympathetic hero, played by Peter Fonda, and an obtrusive amount of cinematic gimmickry which renders inarticulate the confused story subtleties."

Time magazine called the film, "pointless, virtually plotless, all but motionless, and a load of pap."

The critic for *The New York Times* found it "a rather ambitious simple movie, with a fairly elaborate technique and levels of meaning rising to the mystical, which seems so much a part of the very contemporary Old West."

Jack Cocks, another reviewer, found *The Hired Hand* "a fine, elegiac Western."

Universal had clearly called for another "youth hit," but didn't get it. *The Hired Hand* was sold to NBC-TV for telecasts in 1973.

However, it still had life when it was fully restored in 2001 and distributed at some film festivals where, in general, it got good critical responses.

The movie today is regarded as a classic Western, with a *Rotten Tomatoes* rating of 91% favorable.

Critic Bill Kaufman hailed it as "a lovely meditation on friendship and responsibility, one of the least known great movies of that richest of all cinematic eras, the 1970s.

However, the "DVD Savant," Glenn Erickson, still found the film "light in the story department and directed at a mannered crawl by Peter Fonda."

Larry Hagman had been flirting with portraying a character in a cowboy hat long before he got involved in either *The Hired Hand* or the evening soap opera, *Dallas*.

Here, he appears with **Barbara Eden** as a dance hall hostess in this episode from *I Dream of Jeannie* first broadcast in October of 1966.

When his character of the congenial astronaut, Tony, wished for a return to "the Good Old Days," Jeannie used her powers to transform him into a sheriff of a small, disorderly town in the Old West.

***

Peter had arranged for Larry Hagman to play the sheriff in *The Hired Hand*. Although Hagman was nine years older than Peter, the two young men had been boyhood friends in Hollywood. "He was like my older brother," Peter recalled.

Both of them had something in common in their backgrounds. Each was born to a legend in the entertainment business—Peter to Henry Fonda and Hagman to the fabled musical star of Broadway, Mary Martin. His birthplace was Fort Worth, Texas.

Hagman's father was Benjamin Jackson Hagman. He and Martin had divorced in 1936, and Larry grew up under the care of his grandparents. He later moved to Hollywood, where he lived with another grandmother. There, he became the boyhood friend of Peter.

His father wanted him to study law, but Hagman was lured into drama. By 1950, he was acting in productions at Margaret Webster's Acting School in Woodstock, New York. The following year, his mother, Mary Martin, got him cast in *South Pacific*, which ran in London for a year.

That was followed by his being drafted into the U.S. Air Force.

It wasn't until 1964 that Hagman made his film debut in *Ensign Pulver* (1964), a sequel to Henry Fonda's classic, *Mister Roberts* (1955). It also featured a young Jack Nicholson. That same year (1964), he also appeared with Henry Fonda in *Fail-Safe*.

The first big break of Hagman's career occurred in 1965, when he co-starred with Barbara Eden as her "Master" in the wacky hit TV series *I Dream of Jeannie*. It aired for five years. He was cast as Air Force Captain Anthony Nelson, whose love interest is a genie who he has liberated from centuries of incarceration in a bottle.

It was at around this time that Peter designated Hagman as the godfather of his first child, Bridget Jane Fonda. She was born on January 27, 1964 and named after Bridget Hayward, the daughter of Henry Fonda's former wife, Margaret Sullavan, and agent Leland Hayward.

Her mother was Susan Brewer, the woman Peter had divorced in 1974. As a girl, Bridget was reared mostly by Peter's second wife, Portia Rebecca Crockett, previously married to the novelist Thomas

McGuan.

The Fondas lived in the Coldwater Canyon section of Los Angeles as well as in the Paradise Valley, south of Livingston, Montana. As she grew up, Bridget attended Westlake School for Girls in Los Angeles.

She had made her film debut at the age of four in *Easy Rider* (1969), part of a simulated hippie commune visited by her father and actor Dennis Hopper on their motorcycles.

After seeing Peter in *The Trip*, Hagman told Peter that he was inspired to take LSD just to see what it was like.

A few nights after Peter took him to see Crosby, Stills, and Nash, with an after-concert hookup with David Crosby. That night, Hagman was given a handful of "tabs," then the purest form of acid available.

That night, he swallowed them and experienced all sorts of lurid dreams. As he relayed to Peter, he entered a cave guarded by creatures resembling octopuses with long, writhing tentacles.

He was rescued by a vision of his grandmother, who suddenly appeared. "My body was filled with energy, and everything was part of me. Everything was living, dying, and being reborn."

Peter shared similar visions with him. He also invited Hagman to an early screening of *Easy Rider*. He sat through the film feeling wild, dazed, breathless, and in awe.

Hagman was pleased when Peter cast him as the sheriff in the film he was directing, *The Hired Hand*. "There wasn't a bad card in the whole film. We shot the movie in Santa Fe, and I fell in love with the countryside."

Later, he drove to Taos to visit Dennis Hopper, who was more of an acquaintance and rival to Hagman than a friend, having competed in the past for some of the same roles.

"Dennis showed me scenes from *The Last Movie* (1971) that he'd shot with Peter in Peru with some big-name stars.

After a bottle of tequila, Hopper showed Hagman a 20-minute scene from *The Last Movie*. It depicted Hopper, as described by Hagman, "in a long fuck with this Indian girl." He was plugging her with his tiny dick under a waterfall. I was bored, but Hopper thought it his greatest achievement on film. Obviously, this episode didn't make the final cut."

As he later relayed to Peter, "Hopper and I chewed 'peyote buttons' and, as I remember, I took off all my clothes and paraded around jaybird naked. What was my motive? I hate to admit this, but I wanted to show him how a real macho man was hung."

"Later, I got real pissed off at Peter and Hopper," Hagman said. "The fuckers cut my scenes from the movie. But years later, after *Dallas*, when it was telecast, I had become famous, and the network put me back in. Not only that, but a movie theater in Dallas ran the movie for a full week. The marquee read, 'THE MAN FROM DALLAS, LARRY HAGMAN, IN *THE LAST MOVIE*." I got my revenge for his cutting me out of the original. Peter was pissed but we later made up."

Hagman's big break came in 1978 when he was offered the role of the conniving business tycoon, J.R. Ewing in the soap opera *Dallas*. It became a worldwide success, with fans in ninety countries worldwide. It even became a favorite of the Royal Family at Buckingham Palace in London.

By then, Hagman had become one of the best know stars on television. In 1980, the TV special, "Who shot J.R.?" was a cliffhanging phenomenon that attracted speculation world-wide.

Hagman had a problem with alcohol for most of his life. In later life, Hagman suffered through many health emergencies, including, in 1995, a liver transplant. "Peter was always there for me," he recalled. "Through the sunny days and also those filled with clouds of black doom."

When Hagman died, on November 23, 2012 in Dallas at the age of 81, Peter lamented his loss. "He was a dear, talented, loving friend. He cannot be replaced in my life. I will mourn his passing in the time I have left myself."

***

The Last Movie (1971)

Dennis Hopper had a minor role in *The Sons of Katie Elder*, a 1965 Western in Panavision. Directed by

Henry Hathaway, it starred John Wayne and Dean Martin in a plot about how the four sons of a ranch owner, Katie Elder, work to avenge their father's murder and their mother's swindling.

Filmed principally in Mexico, the story revolved around brothers herding a cattle drive from Texas to Colorado. Hopper appeared in the role of Dave Hastings.

Originally, Alan Ladd was to play the oldest brother, John Elder, but he didn't like the role. According to his contract, he still owed Paramount one more picture. For $135,000, he bought his way out of the contract. John Wayne took Ladd's mount in the saddle. The Duke managed to get through most of the shoot of *The Sons of Katie Elder,* although he was suffering, having been diagnosed with lung cancer.

Hopper recalled that during the filming of *Katie Elder*, the idea for a movie began to germinate in his mind. He later called what became the film, *The Last Movie,* "my passion project."

He wanted to explore what happens to natives such as Indians when a film crew shoots a Western on their grounds and then departs, leaving them with the hastily erected sets of memories. Such was the case with the Indians in Peru, where *The Last Movie* was filmed. The native tribes there were stunned to see one of the characters shot dead and then rise from the ground to live again.

Hopper had befriended the scriptwriter Stewart Stern during his authorship of the script for *Rebel Without a Cause* (1955), starring James Dean, with Hopper in a lesser role.

Stern and Hopper became friends, often spending evenings with Arthur Loew Jr. at his lavish home. Loew was dating the British sex symbol, Joan Collins, at the time.

It took some effort, but Hopper eventually talked Stern into writing a screenplay for *The Last Movie.*

A New Yorker, Stern was the nephew of Adolph Zukor, the founder of Paramount Pictures. During World War II, Loew Jr. had fought in the notorious Battle of the Bulge, the war's last major Nazi advance on the Western Front of Europe.

Back in Hollywood, and over a period of years, Stern would have more success with his screenplays for *The Rack* (1965) with Paul Newman; *The Ugly American* (1963) with Marlon Brando; *Rachel, Rachel* (1968) with Joanne Woodward, and *Sybil* (1976) with Sally Field.

The Last Movie would put a severe strain on the friendship of Stern and Hopper. "It became a love-hate relationship, as he seemed to toss Stern's pages into the fire and then improvise dialogue for the actors.

"Dennis the Menace was a man of rage, always cursing God for giving him such a small penis," Stern said. "He had the annoying habit of walking around telling cast and crew that he was a genius."

"Dennis was often stoned, and he spent time hanging out with Peter Fonda and his friend, Robert Walker Jr." Stern said. "As the night wore on, these guys would get stupider and stupider. The butts from their joints would have two or three large ashtrays overflowing."

Stern's first big argument with Hopper occurred over the film's title, as he interpreted the proposed title as weak. His alternative title was *Boo Hoo in Tinseltown.*

Stern always asserted that Peter Fonda was in on a lot of the pre-production details, helping Hopper to finance the upcoming filming of *The Last Movie.*

"Poor, poor Peter," Stern said. "He was always trying to escape from the giant shadow of his father, who was hailed as one of the greatest movie stars in Hollywood history. Compared to his father, Peter could do no more than be a water carrier."

As they searched for financing, Peter and Hopper were still coasting on the prestige and commercial success of *Easy Rider.*

By now, Peter had formed his own small film company, naming it Pando Productions.

The two actors flew together to Manhattan, hoping to meet an "angel" *[a show-biz word for financial backer].* There, they were seen, socially, with everyone from Salvador Dalí to Andy Warhol.

Warhol wanted them to pose frontally nude for a joint photograph, but they rejected his offer.

As part of their campaign, but to no avail, they turned to Timothy Leary, the crown prince of LSD. They were also rejected by Huntington Hartford, the A&P heir.

Back in Hollywood, the actors felt they had come upon their "angel" in the person of Phil Spector, the record producer and songwriter. In the music world, he was hailed for introducing "a Wagnerian approach to Rock 'n Roll." Before his later fall from grace, Spector was riding high in the music world, living in a bubble he referred to as "pop heaven."

During a night of recreational drugs and partying, Spector listened to Peter and Hopper, sketching out their vision of *The Last Movie*. They cast it that night, or at least agreed on who its stars should be. They envisioned Montgomery Clift taking the lead opposite Peter's sister, Jane Fonda. Jennifer Jones and Jason Robards, Jr. would be in supporting roles. [*Regrettably for* The Last Movie, *that particular ensemble fell apart, especially after news broke, in 1966, that Clift had died.*]

After Hopper claimed that he thought it would cost $1.2 million to finance the movie, Spector revealed that he had about $1.5 million, all of it easily convertible into cash, in the bank.

Then Spector made an announcement in the press: "It will be an art movie directed by Dennis Hopper, who was so brilliant in *Easy Rider*. I am an admirer of Truffaut, Stanley Kubrick, and Fellini. *The Last Movie* will be in the tradition of these directors. In my view, Hopper will be our next Kubrick, with a heavy dose of Truffaut and Fellini hovering over his left shoulder."

It was Hopper himself who later rejected Spector's generous offer. "That was all the money he had, and I feared that the picture might flop and wipe him out. I just couldn't take all his cash. Turning him down was one of the most painful things I have ever done."

[*Phil Spector came to a bad end on February 3, 2003 after he shot actress Lana Clarkson in the mouth inside his mansion in Alhambra, California.*

He later presented a weak defense, claiming it was "an accidental suicide" and maintaining that she had kissed the gun from which the fatal bullet was fired into her head.

Amazingly, the murder trial didn't come up until March of 2007, four years after her death. It was later described as a mistrial based on a hung jury: Ten of its members voted for convicting him; two voted "not guilty."]

A retrial in October found him guilty of murder, and he was sentenced to 19 years or life. He died on January 16, 2021, his death attributed to complications from COVID-19.]

With Spector out of the picture, Peter and Hopper searched for "another angel." At a gala party, they met tobacco heiress Doris Duke who, at the time, was widely acknowledged as the richest woman in the world. The plot (and the investment opportunity) of *The Last Movie* did not impress her. According to Peter, "She not only rejected being our angel, but she fled from us, even though we offered to sexually service her."

As it was being shopped around, a plot summary of *The Last Movie* was drafted. The story, such as it was, centered on a young man named "Kansas." He is the stunt coordinator overseeing a stable of horses for a Western being filmed. It was determined that a village deep in the Peruvian Andes would be the setting.

During the shoot, one of the stuntmen would fall from a horse and be killed.

Saddened by the event, Kansas makes a decision to leave the movie business and settle down in this remote location in Peru, living with a native girl.

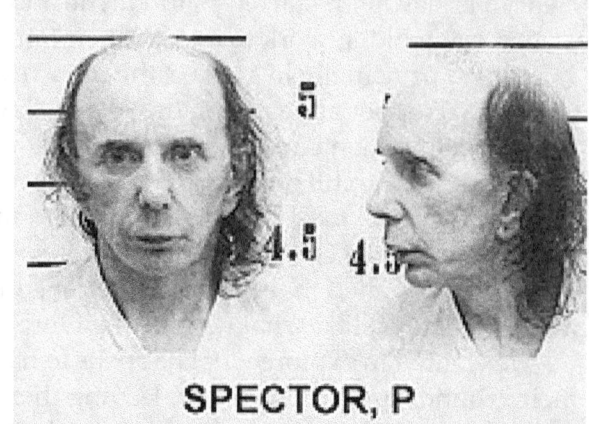

Phil Spector's mug shot (2009). At the time of his murder trial, the press labeled him as "The ugliest man in Hollywood."

He once offered Hopper "all the money I have" to finance his latest movie.

Entire books have been written about **Lew Wasserman**, his well-connected wife, **Edie**, and the grip they maintained on some of the creative projects then evolving in Hollywood.

One of them was Peter Fonda's spectacularly dysfunctional film, *The Last Movie*.

Retirement from the world doesn't turn out happily for Kansas.

After the departure of the film crew, he discovers that the natives, all of them Peruvian, are trying to make their own movie. It seemed that they had taken their perception of the film methodologies too seriously. Instead of having an actor "play dead," they believed that for verisimilitude, he should actually be killed.

Although studio after studio had rejected the premises of the script, at Universal Studios, executives had been instructed to turn out more pictures aimed at "the youth culture." Because of that, it therefore seemed logical for the to at least consider the proposals of the stars of *Easy Rider,* especially if they agreed to come up with a better script.

Hopper and Peter met with Lew Wasserman, the powerful CEO at Universal. He had previously green-lighted such youth-oriented films as the environment-centered science fiction flick *Silent Running* (1972) and the pop-nostalgia soaked *American Graffiti* (1973), as directed by the then-not-very-famous directors Milos Foreman, Douglas Trumball, and George Lucas. Wasserman agreed to give Hopper a million dollars ("and no more than that," he told them very firmly) to launch *The Last Movie.*

Hopper's salary would be only $500 a week, but he would get a percentage of the gross. He immediately set about casting *The Last Movie,* first assigning the role of the young sheriff to Peter.

Rod Cameron as he appeared in *State Trooper* (1957).

In 1960, he divorced his wife and, soon after, married her mother. For that perhaps foolhardy act, director William Witney publicly defined Cameron as "the bravest man he had ever seen."

To the surprise of Wasserman, Hopper rounded up a number of big-name stars. *[Even though they're largely unknown to Generation Z today, they were familiar names and faces on the screens of the 1960s and 70s.]*

Hopper had divorced his first wife, Brooke Hayward, in 1969, and he was now dating Michelle Phillips, whom he cast as the banker's daughter.

Other roles were essayed by Kris Kristofferson as Minstrel Wrangler; Sylvia Miles as a script clerk; Russ Tamblyn as Charlie Bowdre; Dean Stockwell as Billy the Kid; Rod Cameron as Par Garrett; John Philip Law as Little Brother; Don Gordon as Nevill Robey; Julie Adams as Mrs. Anderson; Stella Garcia as Maria; and Jim Mitchum as Art.

Before the plane took off for Peru, Robert Mitchum, the father of Jim Mitchum, put through a last-minute call. Somehow, he had learned that the authorities in Peru were planning to do a drug search of cast and crew immediately after the plane landed. Hopper oversaw a "clean up" campaign aboard the plane so that everyone would arrive drug free. The APSA Boeing 707 then took off, landing at the airport at Cuzco, Peru.

After they settled in, the cast and crew learned that although marijuana was illegal in Peru, cocaine was sold, cheap, on virtually every corner. A packet sold for anywhere from $5 to $8.

Sylvia Miles, shown here with **Tennessee Williams.** Following in the footsteps of Bette Davis (on stage) and Ava Gardner (on film), Sylvia wanted to star on stage in a revival of Williams' *The Night of the Iguana.*

"I'll even do a nude scene with one of those Mexican boys in your play," she promised the playwright.

"Who needs grass?" Peter asked Hopper.

Throughout the shoot, Hopper was in the throes of his romance with Phillips. She had risen to fame as a vocalist for the musical quartet, The Mamas and the Papas, scoring such hits as "California Dreamin."

Kristofferson sang "Me and Bobby McGee" as part of the film's soundtrack. Hopper wanted the makeup staff to give him the "greasy hair" look of Valentino in the 1920s.

A reporter from *Playboy* arrived, later claiming that during his visit to the set, he "attended a mass for James Dean."

Hopper seemed obsessed with his death. *Dean had died in a car crash in September of 1955, killed by the driver—with the name of Turnipseed— of another car.]*

The *Playboy* reporter claimed, "Apparently, Hopper had fallen madly in love with Dean when they made *Rebel Without a Cause* (1955). He showed me a ring that Dean had put on his finger, a bronze silver thing. Was it an engagement ring? Didn't those guys know two men can't get married?"

Don Gordon pops up in the film trying to get help to exploit this Peruvian gold mine he is alleged to have discovered. In a career that began in 1949 and lasted until 1993, he was mostly known for roles in which he appeared with his very close friend, Steve McQueen—*Bullitt* (1968), *Papillon* (1973), and *The Towering Inferno* (1974).

A Texan, Kris Kristofferson, was a singer, actor, and songwriter, releasing such hits as "Help Me Make It Through the Night." As an actor, he would go on to be the co-star of Barbra Streisand in the third remake of *A Star Is Born* (1976).

Julie Adams, star of *Creature from the Black Lagoon* and also a player with Peter Fonda in *The Last Movie*, appears above with **Elvis Presley** in *Tickle Me* (1966).

At the age of 19, Julie Adams was named "Miss Little Rock" in Arkansas. Soon, she was headed for Hollywood to begin a film career that would see her in time play a leading lady or else in supporting roles to such stars as James Stewart, Rock Hudson, Tyrone Power, Glenn Ford, Charlton Heston, Dan Duryea, Rory Calhoun, Joel McCrea, and Elvis Presley.

From 1954 to 1981, she was married to Ray Danton, a rather virile type with dark hair and a prominent cleft chin. His signature performance was as the leading man in *The Rise and Fall of Legs Diamond* (1960).

Stella Garcia, cast as the girlfriend of Kansas, appeared in a few films over the course of her career, including a small role in the Elvis Presley movie, *Fun in Acapulco* (1963). In one of her last films, *Eye for an Eye* (1996), directed by John Schlesinger and starring Ed Harris and Sally Field, she played a very different Maria from what she'd essayed in *The Last Movie*.

Born in Greenwich Village, Sylvia Miles was often cast as a prostitute. A notable achievement was when she was Oscar nominated for a Best Supporting Actress Award in *Midnight Cowboy*, voted the Best Picture of 1969.

She takes Joe Buck (Jon Voight) back to her apartment for sex.

He is selling his services as a stud but thinks this Park Avenue lady is buying him. He finds out that she expects to get paid, since she's a working girl herself.

Miles would also be nominated again for her performance in *Farewell, My Lovely* (1975). She would later work with Peter in *92 in the Shade* (1975).

Russ Tamblyn began his career as a child actor at MGM. He is best remembered for his roles in *Seven Brides for Seven Brothers* (1954) and *West Side Story* (1961), where he portrayed Riff, the leader of the Jets gang.

John Philip Law is still remembered for starring as the blind angel in the Jane Fonda movie, *Barbarella* (1968).

Dean Stockwell would have a career spanning seven decades, beginning as a child star at MGM. As a young man, he would star in the 1959 screen adaptation of *Compulsion*, with Orson Welles. Two of his best performances were in D.H. Lawrence's *Sons and Lovers* (1960) and in Eugene O'Neill's stage play, *Long Day's Journey into Night*.

Clearly the "misfit" in *The Last Movie* was the former Western star Rod Cameron. Born right before

Christmas in 1910, and over the course of his career, he would appear in horror movies, war films, action dramas, and sci-fi spectacles, but was remembered mainly for his sagebrush sagas.

He'd started out as a stand-in for Fred MacMurray, but would go on to co-star with Bing Crosby and Yvonne De Carlo.

He gained a lot of publicity when he divorced his wife and married his mother-in-law.

He would later comment on the cast and crew of *The Last Movie:* "I found myself working with druggies, hippies, lots of fags, LSD trippers, cocaine addicts, pantie sniffers, pederasts preferring nine-year-old Peruvian lads, poon stalkers, and whip lashers."

***

Dennis Hopper and Peter Fonda had long been friends, and Hopper was grateful to him for his collaboration in *Easy Rider.* However, that did not prevent Hopper from filing a lawsuit against Peter in June of 1970, demanding three percent of the profits from *Easy Rider* for his contributions to its script.

It was revealed that Hopper had already made $1.5 million in royalties from *Easy Rider.*

Although he was tied up for months editing and reducing to 108 minutes the vast footage of *The Last Movie,* he nonetheless announced plans for a rosy future.

He was dating Michelle Philipps at the time, and he claimed that they would next co-star together in a movie named *Me and Bobby McGee,* based on the popular song recently recorded by Janis Joplin.
It was promoted as an adventure about lovers hitchhiking through the American Southwest, but it was never made.

The editing of *The Last Movie* went on and on, and during some weeks—especially those interrupted by recreational drugs—very little editing actually happened.

Hopper did make one decision that could only help the movie: In the film's final scene, he had included excerpts from the Mae West and W.C. Fields movie, *My Little Chickadee* (1940). Hopper finally decided that those insertions were inappropriate and unnecessary—and so they were—and eliminated them.

In the middle of all this, Hopper bought a home in Taos, New Mexico, which was in need of repair and refurnishing. He spent a lot of time with visitors passing through New Mexico who popped in to see him and visit, everyone from Nicholas Ray to Ricky Nelson, from Bob Dylan to the Everly Brothers.

Also taking time from Hopper's film editing was his courtship of Michelle Phillips. Finally, on Halloween night, 1970, the couple was wed, the ceremony drawing exactly 213 guests, according to the signature book. In attendance was Phillips' two-year-old daughter, Chynna, the by-product of Phillip's marriage (1962-1969) to John Phillips.

It became known as "the eight-day marriage."

All kinds of reasons were given for the quick dissolution of the marriage. She claimed he called her a witch and, one time at least, handcuffed her. He was also said to have been firing pistols inside the house, raising fears from Phillips about the safety of her daughter.

She may have written a farewell note: "Have you ever considered suicide?"

Finally, she fled with her baby girl. It was later reported that she was seen dating Jack Nicholson and then Warren Beatty.

The editing of *The Last Movie* became a drama unto itself, or so thought L.M. ("Kit") Carson and Lawrence Schiller, who arrived in Taos for about three weeks for the filming of their documentary, *The American Dreamer*. It recorded footage of Hopper both at home and in his studio during the post-production work on *The Last Movie,* a process in which five to six hours of footage had to be cut.

The American Dreamer never achieved a regular theatrical release, but was screened at a few film festivals and on college campuses.

Seven Heller of *The Atlantic* wrote, "The final cut of *The American Dreamer* represents a highly constructed group effort that pushes the limits of documentary."

Peter Bradshaw in *The Guardian* claimed, "*The American Dreamer* tries to be counter-cultural yet the weirdest thing is Hopper's obsession with guns. Nonetheless, it has a certain archival value as a study of Hopper and a footnote of the American New Wave."

Hopper took some dares that few other actors would have risked, including stripping naked for the documentarians. He also revealed a sexual secret that he had confessed to before: That he preferred to "give head" to a woman in lieu of submitting to conventional intercourse. He also confessed to "being a lesbian." Many of the more pornographic scenes filmed for the documentary ended up on the cutting room floor.

A harem of about two dozen girls were brought in and at one point, Hopper drops his jockey shorts to allow the girls to grope his buttocks. That shocked Peter when he saw it. "My ass was always private property," he said. "I would never let any of my wives touch it."

He also admitted that editing *The Last Movie* "was like giving birth to a baby boy and then whacking its little arms off."

Everyone took time off from shooting the documentary or editing *The Last Movie* to get involved with the biggest orgy ever staged in Taos. In the words of screenwriter Stewart Stern, who attended, it was "a field of boobs and buttocks, the phallus, and the vagina."

The American Dreamer was believed to have been lost for some three decades, but in 2016, it was rediscovered, remastered, and released on DVD and Blu-Ray.

***

Finally, the massively edited final cut of *The Last Movie* was ready for public viewing, beginning with a screening for its financial backer, Lew Wasserman at Universal.

He was disgusted with it, telling his associates, "Dennis Hopper will never work in this town again."

It opened at RKO's 59th Street Twin Theater in Manhattan. Immediately, and for the most part, it faced harsh reviews.

It had almost no theatrical release after that, with the exception of being part of a double bill at drive-ins attended by young lovers who spent more time necking than watching the screen.

Time magazine wrote, "The sound you hear is from checkbooks slamming shut in Hollywood, with producers swearing never to finance another Dennis Hopper movie."

Pauline Kael, in *The New Yorker*, asserted, "It's hysterical to blame the violence of the world on films made in the United States. Hopper seems to have worked up a lot of steam about nothing."

Hopper read attack after attack, but had a somewhat off-key reaction, telling a reporter, "I wanted the viewer to keep saying, 'You're really just watching a film.'"

The Last Movie later suffered the notoriety of being documented and ridiculed in the filmmaking textbook, *The Worst Films of All Time*.

CHAPTER FIFTEEN

WINDING DOWN
(AKA *The Slow Goodbye*)
WITH PETER FONDA

PETER FONDA'S WIFE, SUSAN
After she kicks him out of her bed, she suggests he find a girlfriend—maybe more than one.
"If I were your wife, Susan, I would have stabbed you in the back with a large knife."
—an unverified comment from Jane Fonda to her brother, Peter

A Sci-Fi Caper
IDAHO TRANSFER

*"Even though I directed it, I don't think
I ever understood exactly what was happening"*
—Peter Fonda

ALL IN THE FAMILY
The Producer of *Idaho Transfer*, Billy Hayward, fatally shoots himself
after its release and after the earlier suicides of his mother,
Margaret Sullavan, and his sister, Brooke.

TWO PEOPLE
The ferocious Oscar-winning director, Robert Wise, helms Peter,
who portrays a deserter from the Vietnam War hiding out in Morocco

A White Trash Caper
DIRTY MARY, CRAZY LARRY
Peter, at the wheel with Susan George, flees from the cops

Nobody Liked It
OPEN SEASON
Peter is part of a trio of returning Vietnam vets who plan killing sprees
on the American homefront

Peter's flirtation with horror
RACE WITH THE DEVIL
Members of a Satanic Cult, who murder humans as sacrifices to the Devil,
chase after Peter and his mates, hoping to drink their blood.

92 IN THE SHADE

"Who are you impersonating, Lucille Ball?"

—Director/author Thomas McGuane to Peter during a confrontation on the first day of shooting about his henna-colored dye job.

SYLVIA MILES

As a co-star of *92 in the Shade,* she lets Burgess Meredith play onscreen with what he calls "her pussy."

"Offscreen, everybody was fucking everybody else, with so many secret affairs going on I called it 'A sexual swamp meet.'"

—Sylvia Miles

LOVE AND MARRIAGE

PETER MEETS HIS NEXT LOVE, PORTIA REBECCA CROCKETT (A.K.A MRS. THOMAS MCGUANE), THE GREAT, GREAT, GREAT GRANDDAUGHTER OF DAVY CROCKETT, THEN SPENDS THE NEXT 36 YEARS OF HIS LIFE WITH HER.

After *Easy Rider* and the quirky films that immediately preceded or followed it, Peter Fonda never again attained the sales, press coverage, or notoriety of the late Sixties. Here follows a rundown of some of his escapes and movie ventures that followed:

***

Idaho Transfer (1973)

This science fiction film was the only one that Peter Fonda directed but did not star in. Shot for a budget of $500,000, the film was in release for only three weeks before its distributor, Cinemation, went bankrupt.

Many members of its limited audience walked out before the movie was half over. Many others in the audience, those who saw the entire film, didn't really understand it.

An irate sanitation worker told *The Village Voice*, "The best I could tell, it was about using people for fuel. I suspected to find reels of this movie by Peter Fonda in the garbage the following morning."

Peter himself, along with his producer, William Hayward, nicknamed Billy, selected the location for

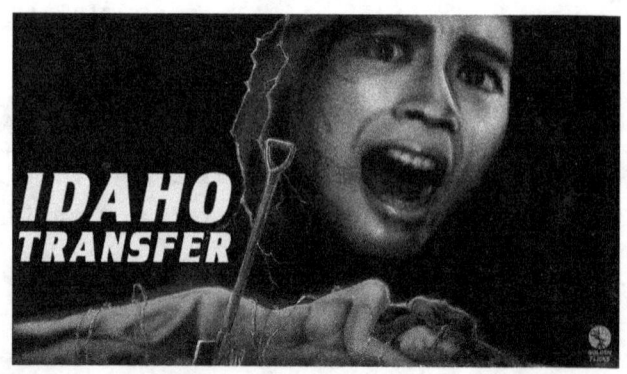

shooting. Most of the movie was filmed near Arco, Idaho, in the Craters of the Moon National Monument and Preserve.

Idaho Transfer spent very little of its budget on the cast of actors who appeared in it. The roles, with one exception, were played by unknowns. Kelley Bohanon, cast as Karen, had appeared in *The Christian Licorice Store* (1971), not much to put on a résumé. Dale Hopkins, who played "Leslie," really earned his living as an agent and publicist before becoming a business executive.

Kevin Hearst, as "Ronald," would later find a few roles in the 1990s—*Star Trek: Generations; Stargate;* and *Darkman.* He seemed drawn to sci-fi projects.

The only known actor in the film was Keith Carradine, who played "Arthur." He was the scion of an acting dynasty, founded by his father, John Carradine. Keith was the only member of the cast who would have a career on both the stage and in feature films and television. One of his most notable roles was as Tom Frank in Robert Altman's film *Nashville* (1975) with an all-star cast that included Lily Tomlin and Geraldine Chaplin.

The bizarre plot by Thomas Matthiesen begins with Karne Braden (Keley Bohanon) being taken from a mental ward by her father and driven to a location near the Crater of the Moon lava fields. A project financed by the government had been greenlighted to develop "matter transference." The mystery of time travel was unlocked.

It was a convenient time to escape the earth, which was about to experience a mysterious ecological catastrophe that would wipe out civilization.

Older time travelers would suffer from negative effects since their kidneys would hemorrhage. Therefore, only teenagers could be sent fifty-six years into the future.

But for some reason, the government shuts down the time travel transfer machines, an act that traps the teens already sent into the future.

In this new, chronologically re-adjusted world, they set out to explore and see where they have landed. Regrettably, one small girl is picked up by a family bizarrely clad in "the fashions of tomorrow." She is forced into the trunk of their vehicle to be used as "fuel."

She asks what will happen when they run out of people who have accidentally arrived here from the past. The driver explains, "We'll have to use each other, then."

"I poured myself into editing *Idaho Transfer,*" Peter said. "When I could take it no more, I sailed the Channel Islands. Bridget, who was 8 and Justin who was 6, my two kids, got to spend Thanksgiving with me."

For the most part, reviews of *Idaho Transfer* were negative, but with an occasional favorable compliment. The critic for *Time* magazine called it "a very deliberate and closely controlled film graced with slow, severe beauty that makes its quiet edge of panic all the more chilling." Jay Robert Nash in *The Motion Picture Guide* declared it "a useless piece of drivel about an obnoxious group of teens."

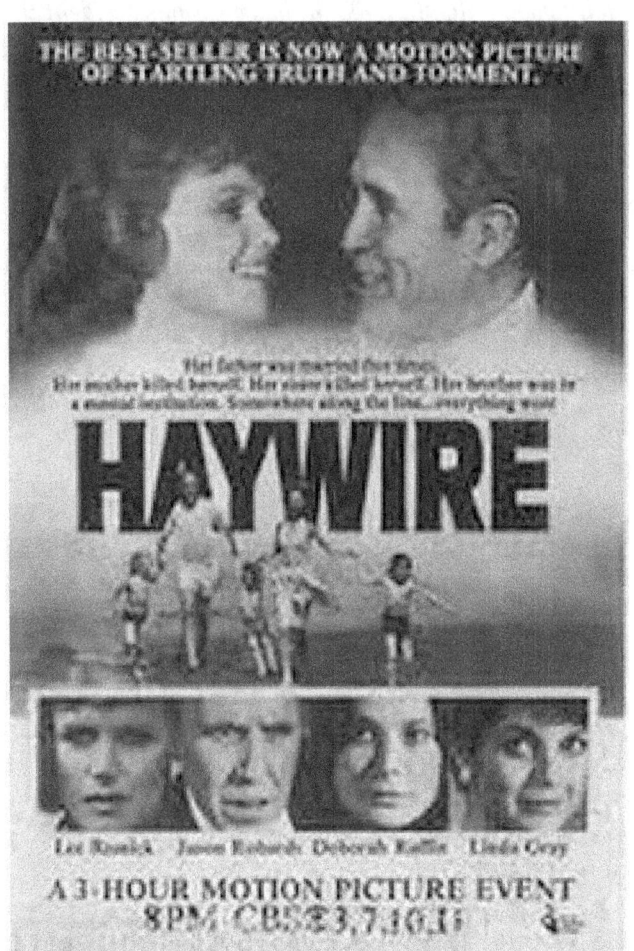

The book that inspired this made-for TV film was based on a tragically dysfunctional family, The Haywards. Important "players" of the upper Hollywood echelon, they became very close to the Fondas, occupying a house nearby. Margaret Sullavan, the matriarch of the Hayward family, had previously been married to Henry Fonda, Peter's father.

The producer of *Idaho Transfer* (and also the associate producer of *Easy Rider*), **Billy Hayward,** was a close personal friend of Peter Fonda. In 2008, BIlly became the third member of his immediate family to commit suicide.

During the shooting and editing of *Idaho Transfer*, Peter's marriage to Susan Brewer was on life support. He was no longer invited into her bed. When he complained of the lack of sex, she reportedly told him, "Get a girlfriend."

That he did, a lot of young women, usually starlets hoping he would cast them in movies. "These birds," as he referred to them, came and went.

"Nothing serious developed," he claimed. "I was concerned about a divorce, not only for what it would cost me, but I faced the possibility of my kids."

[The producer of Idaho Transfer *was Peter's boyhood friend, William L. Hayward, nicknamed "Billy," the son of agent Leland Hayward and actress Margaret Sullavan. He had been the Associate Producer of* Easy Rider.

He would later produce Haywire, *a made-for-television film based on the best-selling memoir by his sister, Brooke Hayward. She wrote about the charmed but tragic life of her Hollywood family. While married to Leland, Sullavan had given him three children, including Billy but also two daughters, Brooke and Bridget. Sullavan had committed suicide in 1960. That was followed by the suicide of Bridget a few months later.*

After the release of Easy Rider, *Billy became addicted to his Harley Davidson and was often seen driving in and out of the Hollywood Hills. In 2003, he had a serious accident that nearly killed him. Severely injured, he also suffered brain damage.*

On March 9, 2008, Billy fatally shot himself in his heart while living modestly in a trailer at Castaic, California. He was 66.

When he heard the news, Peter said, "Billy was a dear friend, and had been so ever since I was a boy. But his life, and the lives of his mother and sister, also victims of suicide, were marked by torment and tragedy."

***

Two People (1973)

In early February of 1972, Peter and his wife, Susan, decided to see if there was anything left of their ill-fated marriage. They flew to Morocco, where he was to begin shooting *Two People*.

Almost from the moment of their arrival, everything seemed to go wrong for them. "The old chemistry was gone," Peter confessed. "One day after rehearsing, I returned to our room to find my wife had gone. That was my birthday present for me when I turned 32. Lindsay Wagner gave me a lot of moral support—no sex, just tender, loving care."

The screenplay for *Two People* was written by Richard De Roy, the story of a brief involvement between a fashion model (Wagner) and a Vietnam War deserter (Peter Fonda).

"Bob (the film's director, Robert Wise) shot the film in sequence," Peter said, "the best way to go."

"After twelve days of rehearsal, the shooting began, lasting five weeks on the Marrakesh Express," Peter said, a reference to heavy hashish.

In the plot, fashion model Deirdre McCluskey (Lindsay Wagner) had finished a photo session in North Africa

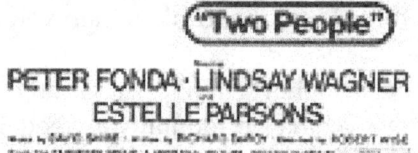

Peter Fonda, horizontal with **Lindsay Wagner** (her first leading role in a feature film) in *Two People*

for *Vogue*. The photographer, Ron Kesselman (actor Geoffrey Horne), had been her lover, but her passion for him had flickered out. Along for the shoot is Barbara Newman (Estelle Parsons), an editor at *Vogue*.

Deirdre becomes attracted to a fellow passenger, Evan Bonner (Peter Fonda).

The couple gravitate to each other, and she learns he is a deserter from the U.S. Army then fighting in Vietnam.

The plot reveals that for a while, he had fled to Moscow, and later to Sweden and (now) he's in Morocco. But by now, he has decided to return to America to face a court martial and a prison term.

After a day spent together in Paris, they fly to New York, where Evan, later on the day of their arrival, surrenders to the military authorities.

Arguably, Robert Wise was the best director with whom Peter ever worked. He'd won Academy Awards for Best Director and Best Picture for the musical films *West Side Story* (1961) and *The Sound of Music* (1965).

Actually, his first Oscar nomination had occurred in 1941 for his film editing of Orson Welles' *Citizen Kane*, a movie which is still hailed in some quarters as the best film ever made.

Wise also produced and directed *The Sand Pebbles* (1966) starring Steve McQueen. For it, Wise won an Oscar nomination for Best Picture that year.

In addition to all that, Wise was the President (from 1971 to 1975) of the Directors Guild of America, and President of the Academy of Motion Picture Arts and Sciences from 1985 to 1988.

"I didn't see them all," Peter said, "but I saw many of Robert's movies. The guy was fantastic—a master in many genres such as *film noir*, horror flicks, westerns, sci-fi, war stories, high drama, and, of course, musicals."

Lindsay Wagner, in the female lead of Deirdre McCluskey, had had a multi-faceted career as a star of film and television. She was also a model, author, singer, and acting coach.

Most of America knew her for her leading role in the sci-fi TV series, *The Bionic Woman*, that ran for two years beginning in 1976.

Two People was her first feature film role and her first lead.

In the third lead, the role of Barbara Newman, Estelle Parsons was one of the most talented actresses Peter would ever work with. Originally, she studied law before deciding to become a singer and later, an actress. Before that, as a teenager, her first boyfriend had been Jack Lemmon.

In her portrayal of Blanche Barrow in *Bonnie and Clyde* (1967), starring with Warren Beatty, she had won a Best Supporting Actress Oscar.

The following year, she was nominated for the same Oscar again for her role in *Rachel, Rachel* starring Joanne Woodward.

The film crew flew to Paris for the final shooting. As he wrote in his memoirs, Peter reported that once, when Jane called him, they talked about his failing marriage to Susan. He went on to state, whether it was true or not, that "Jane told me that if she were Susan, she would have stabbed me in the back with a large knife."

At the end of filming, Peter wanted to rent a yacht at a French port and sail back to California with a small crew. With him was a young (unnamed) woman whom he'd recently met. She agreed to go with him to America. "After my breakup with Susan, she offered me love and comfort—well, maybe not love, exactly."

After a few weeks at sea, their yacht sailed into California's port of Marina del Rey.

There, Federal agents, as if they'd been alerted in advance, came aboard for a thorough search.

"The bastards even looked inside our underwear to see what we were concealing. When they went to strip search our captain, 'Poncho Pollack,' he invited them 'to suck my dick.'"

In reference to *Two People*, *TV Guide* would claim, "Peter Fonda and Lindsay Wagner (in her film debut) just aren't able to pull it off."

Roger Ebert of the *Chicago Sun-Times* wrote: "The script for *Two People* must have sounded like such a good story idea, all those months or years ago when they were writing the film. What we have here, potentially, is a sort of bittersweet, radicalized *Love Story*, and that must have been what sold the director, Robert Wise, on the project. The movie sounds superficially as if it might have a comment to make on the effect of the war on its warriors. Well, that may be true, but true of a movie they did not make. What we're left with is an awkward journey into brutality."

Roger Greenspun of *The New York Times* claimed, "*Two People* is a very silly movie. I am tempted to hang the movie with quotations from its dialogue—which would be unfair. It is really equally bad in all departments. The film is remarkably of a piece—not with the consistency of a movie director like Robert Wise, but rather the consistency of something cooked up from the same package of synthetic soup."

Even its backers seemed surprised when it made money at the box office.

***

Dirty Mary, Crazy Larry (1974)

This car chase film was based on a novel by Richard Unekis which was aptly entitled *The Chase*. But both its director, John Hough, and Peter himself knew they could not use that title since it had been employed in a Jane Fonda movie in 1966. [*In it, she had famously co-starred with Marlon Brando and Robert Redford.*]

The title of the newer movie was therefore changed to *Dirty Mary, Crazy Larry*. "That title always embarrassed me," Peter later claimed.

The writing team of Leigh Chapman and Antonio Santean was hired by producer Norman T. Herman through the Academy Pictures Corporation. Shooting was set for distribution through 20th Century Fox on May 17, 1974. Hough was given a budget of $1.14 million—"and not a cent more"—for what he began marketing as "a brilliant and breathless film of pursuit."

A Londoner, Hough had been brought in to direct this very American film. In 1968, he had helmed *The Avengers*, a hit TV series. "The series was very disciplined," he told Peter. "It was like Michelangelo painting the Sistine Chapel on a nine-to-five work schedule."

Before shooting began, he invited Peter to sit through a screening of one of his efforts as a director, a film called *Twins of Evil* (1971). Peter defined it as "vampire erotica."

Although certainly not a blockbuster, *Dirty Mary, Crazy Larry* would become the biggest financial success for Hough. When Peter encountered him at a party three years later, he confessed, "I'm in a slump. No offers for film work. Each day I keep hoping something will turn up."

The filming of *Dirty Mary, Crazy Larry* took place in the late autumn of 1973 in and around Stockton, California, and included nearby fields of walnut groves.

In the runaway car, fleeing from police, Peter was cast as its driver, Larry Rayder. His passengers are Susan George, cast as Mary Coombs, and Adam Roarke in the role of Deke Sommers.

As NASCAR hopefuls, Larry and his mechanic, Deke, steal $150,000 in a supermarket heist as a means of financing their entry into big-time auto racing. They made off with it by holding the wife and daughter of the supermarket's manager as hostages.

Mary (Susan George) coerces Larry into taking her, in a souped-up 1966 Chevrolet Impala, for the ride of her life.

As Peter recalled, "Susan, Adam, and myself acted like a sort of Three Stooges, and had a hell of a good time making this movie."

In her capacity as a blonde-haired tramp, George is such an All-American girl that it seems odd that she'd been born in England.

Before working with Peter, she had appeared with Dustin Hoffman in *Straw Dogs* (1971). Her most notorious role was in the controversial film *Mandingo* (1975), in which she played the oversexed daughter of James Mason as a bigoted slave owner.

Before her marriage, George was known to have had a long affair with the singer, Jack Jones. In time, she would end up on a ranch raising Arabian horses.

Roarke was born in Brooklyn to a showgirl mother and a vaudeville comedian father. He'd already appeared in a number of biker films for American International Pictures, as had Jack Nicholson, Peter Fonda, and Bruce Dern.

Roarke's breakout role would come in 1980, when he portrayed Raymond Bailey in *The Stunt Man* with Peter O'Toole. He and the actor became drinking buddies, but Roarke (along with virtually everybody else) couldn't match the massive alcohol consumption of O'Toole. Once, during the peak of his friendship with O'Toole, after a drinking binge with him, Roarke had to be hospitalized for "delirium tremors."

Peter O'Toole as Lawrence of Arabia
"I can outdrink any bloke in the pub."

Adam Roarke, the binge-drinking motorcycle rider of B flickers.

Vic Marrow, as Police Captain Everett Franklin, obsessively pursues the trio, but his outmoded patrol cars are no match for the fleeing bandits, especially after they ditch the wrecked Impala for a 1969 Dodge Charger R/T.

Some of the scenes take place in a walnut grove where the nut-hearing trees provide cover from aerial tracking.

During the climatic chase, a Bell Jet/Ranger helicopter was flown by veteran film pilot James W. Gavin. The script called for a dangerous, high-speed trajectory between rows of trees and under powerlines.

Vic Morrow, from the Bronx, first rose to prominence as one of the leads in the ABC drama series *Combat!* (1962-1967), which earned him an Emmy nomination. Over the years, he appeared in such films as *Blackboard Jungle* (1965) with Glenn Ford, and *King Creole* (1958) with Elvis Presley.

Morrow died on July 23, 1982 during the filming of *Twilight Zone: The Movie.* He and two child actors were killed in the crash of a stunt helicopter.

Another son of England, Roddy McDowall, was cast as George Stanton. The former child actor, known for his sad eyes and sensitivity, was taking whatever roles were offered. In *Dirty Mary, Crazy Larry,* he played the supermarket manager. He referred to the movie as a "white trash car chase."

Roddy McDowall refused to see himself in the final cut of *Dirty Mary, Crazy Larry.*

"I was too ashamed."

"There would be no sequel," Hough said. "Since all the three leads explode in that fiery crash with an oncoming train, I wanted to show that speed kills."

Upon its release, the movie grossed some $15 million, which, in the words of Peter, was a "shit pile of dough. That was more money than any Dennis Hopper film except *Easy Rider*, our biggest moneymaker. I was surprised to hear that many young men across America went to see *Dirty Mary, Crazy Larry* five or six times. Our movie led to a cycle of action films in the years to come."

The ending is a shocker, horribly dramatic as the three leading stars, with Peter at the wheel, crash their car into an oncoming train, and it explodes in flames as THE END flashes on the screen. Critic John Miller wrote, "To me, the Fonda movie seemed inspired by one of those Burt Reynolds movies so popular in the 1970s."

Edgar Wright stated, "I felt sorry for Adam Roarke, who plays Deke Sommers, the third lead. I thought he would be killed at some point, so he's right there until the bloody end."

The movie should have been retitled *Dirty Mary, Crazy Larry, and Dangerous Deke.*"

Channing Roberts wrote: "In his latest movie, Peter Fonda is somewhat stoic as he picks up this little tramp played by Susan George. Apparently, she had a one-night stand with him, and joins him and his gangster friend, played by Adam Roarke. They flee the cops. Death is around the corner. Even when driving at a killer speed, Fonda seems to show no emotion in that stone face of his. Maybe he inherited that look from Henry Fonda himself."

***

Open Season (1974)

"What in hell am I doing in this piece of shit?"
—William Holden

Peter Collinson, the English director, was an odd choice to helm *Open Season,* a film about three homicidal veterans returning from the horrors of the Vietnam war.

Born in Lincolnshire, England, in 1936, he was only two years old when his parents divorced, sending him to live with his grandparents. Between the ages of 8 and 14, he was enrolled in the Actor's Orphanage in the county of Surrey, whose president was none other than Noël Coward.

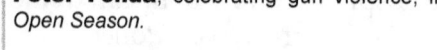

Peter Fonda, celebrating gun violence, in *Open Season.*

As the boy became a teenager, Coward took a keen interest in him and, in time, would help him find jobs in the entertainment business.

The playwright was rewarded by the then-teenaged Collinson, who allowed him to perform fellatio on him on several occasions.

Ironically, Collinson would end up directing Coward and Michael Caine in the film *The Italian* (1969).

Collinson later went to Turkey to helm Tony Curtis and Charles Bronson in *You Can't Win 'Em All* (1970). At one point, the tension between Curtis and Collins became so intense that they broke into a fistfight.

Back in England, he directed a thriller, *Fright* (1971) with Susan George, who would go on to co-star with Peter Fonda in *Dirty Mary, Crazy Larry.* She may have been Collinson's link to Peter, who lured him into directing *Open Season.*

Collinson was a war veteran himself, having been drafted into the Queen's Royal Regiment in West Surrey and sent to service in Malaya for two years.

The script for Peter's latest movie was loosely based on the novel, *The All Americans,* by David Osborn. Osborn joined Liz Charles-Williams in drafting a screenplay for a 104-minute film for Arpa Productions with a distribution deal through Columbia.

The plot follows a trio of Vietnam veterans who return from the battleground still stimulated by violence and the subjugation and debasement of people. The actors who portrayed the ex-soldiers were led by Peter as Ken; John Philip Law as Greg, and Richard Lynch as Art.

Every year, this trio vacations together in the

William Holden, desperately trying to salvage, without success, *Open Season.*

324

wilderness, where they engage in a spree of brutality, violence, and ultimately, murder. They kidnap a middle-aged man and his young mistress played by Cornelia Sharpe as Nancy Stillman.

A native of Selma, Alabama, she had appeared in *Serpico* (1973) and *The Reincarnation of Peter Proud* (1975). The veterans force the man into servitude, and the woman into a sex slave.

Ultimately, at the end of their trip, they will release their victims, give them a head start, and then hunt them down as they flee. When they find them, they will be shot. Finally, the killers themselves are eliminated by an unknown stalker.

The stalker turns out to be the father of a young girl who was raped by the group prior to their military service.

"I was surprised that John (Law) took the role," Peter said. "He was that beautiful angel who starred with my sister Jane in *Barbarella* (1968). I liked playing an evil guy for a change. But John didn't look all that evil. If anything, he was so beautiful that the killer veterans might kidnap him, instead of a girl, and take him into the wilderness for endless sexual assaults."

As the third villain, Brooklyn-born Richard Lynch was the ideal actor for the role, as he was best known for portraying villains in feature films and on television. He'd moved from such films as *Scarecrow* and *Halloween* into greater exposure in *Star Trek: The Next Generation*.

Lynch's disfigurement made him a popular nemesis in some 160 movies. His obvious scars stemmed from an incident in 1967 in Manhattan's Central Park. Heavily drugged, he set himself on fire, burning more than 70% of the surface of his body. After a year in recovery, he gave up drugs and joined the Actors Studio.

No fun and no surprises: Gun-crazy with **Richard Lynch** in *Open Season*

By 1970, he appeared in his first play, with a script by actress Shelley Winters: *One Night Stands of a Noisy Passenger* starred Robert De Niro, Sally Kirkland, and Diane Ladd.

Peter admired Lynch's skill as an actor, and one night in New York's Greenwich Village, went with him to a club. He found out that Lynch was also a musician and could play the piano, flute, guitar, and saxophone. Peter referred to him as a "one-man band."

In 1977, Peter showed up to see Lynch perform with one of his best friends, Al Pacino, in the Broadway play entitled *The Basic Training of Pavlo Hummel.* In it, as in *Open Season,* he played a Vietnam veteran. Instead of being an evil kidnapper, he had a sympathetic role based on a character who was confined to a wheelchair. For his efforts, he was nominated for a Tony Award.

Lynch's death on June 19, 2012, was somewhat mysterious. Neighbors in Yucca Valley, California, noticed that his front door had remained wide open and ajar for at least a full night and day. His friend and neighbor, actress Carol Vogel, decided to investigate and entered the house to find his dead body lying on the kitchen floor. The cause of his death was listed as a heart attack, but that didn't stop speculation that he might either have been murdered, or that he had committed suicide.

In his memoirs, Peter gave the reader no insight whatsoever into *Open Season*. He wrote only that he worked with Law, Lynch, and Bill Holden, and that he had a "grand time shooting the film."

Open Season opened on November 1, 1974 to poor box office and scathing reviews.

Frances Herridge, in the *New York Post,* wrote, "It's hard to believe Peter Fonda and John Philip Law as sadists. It's even harder to accept the contrived ending. The whole film reeks of cheap melodrama."

Nora Sayre of *The New York Times* weighed in, too: "William Holden appears briefly in an early scene. You then spend the rest of the movie waiting for him to come back. Perhaps he was just visiting the set or taking a short cut on his way to an appointment on the lot. A hundred minutes pass before you see his face again. Although there are a few shots of his boots, the film is innocent of all suspense, but it's not the very worst movie I've seen this year."

Variety called *Open Season* "an offensive, gamy potboiler about three amoral young men who each year kidnap innocent people to act as their servants on their hunting holiday, then stalk the victims to kill them. Peter Collinson's direction is routine. The R-rated Columbia release is mediocre exploitation fodder."

Author Lawrence J. Quirk wrote, "*Open Season* is a sordid, cheapjack amalgam of violence. Cornelia Sharpe is used for sexual hijinks, Holden plays a *deus ex machina* plot elucidator."

***

Race with the Devil (1975)

Once again, Peter teamed with his friend, character actor Warren Oates, to make a film about two couples who go on a road trip in an RV, heading for Aspen, Colorado, for a ski vacation.

A RACE WITH WHO?
HAD AMERICA BY NOW BECOME BORED WITH PETER FONDA?

Oversaturated moviegoers stayed away, in part because of the lurid taglines that **Peter Fonda** and **Warren Oates** dragged out of mothballs to promote it:

They included: BURNING THEIR BRIDGES AND A LOT OF RUBBER ON THE DEADLIEST STRETCH OF ROAD IN THE COUNTRY, and GOD HELP YOU WHEN THE DEVIL WANTS YOU.

But along the way, in central Texas, they encounter a coven of Satanists holding a nighttime ritual of human sacrifice. It's happening only a short distance from their campsite, on the other side of a river.

From that point on, they barely escape with their lives. They appeal to the local sheriff, played by R.G. Armstrong. He is of little help, telling them that what they saw was a bunch of hippies sacrificing a dog.

From there, it's a fight for their lives. Satanists kill their pet dog, put rattlesnakes into their RV, pursue them in high-speed car chases, and—clad in a variety of creepy disguises—confuse them into not knowing who, if anybody, to trust.

At the end, cult members (including Sheriff Taylor) wearing black robes with hoods, light a ring of fire around their RV, trapping the couples inside as their satanic chanting begins.

Jack Starrett was brought in to direct. The two lead roles for women went to Loretta Swit as Alice, and to Lara Parker as Kelly.

Race with the Devil, written by Les Frost and Wes Bishop, was a hybrid of the horror, action, and car chase genres. It was shot at various locations in Texas, including San Antonio. Director Starrett announced to the press that he hired actual Satanists to portray the cult figures. The following year, he would direct a similar B-grade action movie, *A Small Town in Texas.*

A Texan, Starrett was both an actor and a film director—in fact, he assigned himself the small role of a gas station attendant. He is best known for his performance as "Gabby," a parody of the Western character actor Gabby Hayes, who appeared in the 1974 film, *Blazing Saddles* produced by Mel Brooks. Mostly, Starrett was known for biker films such as *Hell's Angels on Wheels* (1967).

Loretta Swit, best know for her enduring comic presence in *M*A*S*H*.

Her involvement in Peter Fonda's low-rent *Race* did not particularly help her career.

Loretta Swit became famous portraying Major Margaret "Hot Lips" Houlihan in the long-running (1972-1983) TV series M*A*S*H, for which she won two Emmy Awards. In 1972, Swit inherited the star-making role of Hot Lips from Sally Kellerman, who had portrayed the character in *M*A*S*H*, the feature film.

In the series, Swit got involved with her married lover, Major Frank Burns, portrayed by Larry Linville.

Swit was one of only four cast members who remained employed throughout each of the eleven seasons of the show. The others were Alan Alda, Jamie Farr, and William Christopher.

Lara Parker of Knoxville, Tennessee, was a stage, film, and television actress best known for her performance as Angelique in the ABC-TV serial, *Dark Shadows* (1966-1971).

Among her feature films included roles opposite Robert De Niro in Brian De Palma's film, *Hi, Mom* (1970).

She was even better-known for the Oscar-winning drama, *Save the Tiger* (1973) with Jack Lemmon. In that movie, she played a sympathetic prostitute who is devastated when her client suffers a near-fatal heart attack.

Race with the Devil, with a running length of 88 minutes, was released by 20th Century Fox on June 27, 1975. It received mixed reviews. Despite that, it took in $12 million at the box office, having been made for a budget of only $1.7 million.

***

92 in the Shade (1975)

During one of his promotion and publicity tours for *Idaho Transfer*, Peter became acquainted with the novel in whose film adaptation he would star within a few months.

His last stop on the tour had been for a promotional visit to Chapel Hill, North Carolina. During his presentation there, he noted a young and male professor of English "giving me the eye. I thought he was gay and would come on to me after the audience filed out."

At the end, he did approach Peter, but not for sex. He asked him to read *92 in the Shade*, a then-recent novel by Thomas McGuane. The professor went on to tell Peter that the protagonist of the novel, Tom Skelton, "has your name written on it as a movie role."

Intrigued, Peter took the book with him aboard a flight to Los Angeles. By the time the plane landed in California, he agreed with that professor. "The novel was terrific, and I couldn't wait to get home to start reading it again. It would make a perfect movie."

The next day, he began to call around to learn more. He found out that its movie rights had already been acquired by producer Elliott Kastner.

He knew Kastner and admitted, "I wasn't crazy about him. After he gets a project off the ground, he usually doesn't give a rat's ass what happens to it."

That same year, Kastner also produced a movie whose screenplay was written by the same author, Thomas McGuane, *Rancho Deluxe*, directed by Frank Perry and starring Jeff Bridges and Sam Waterston as modern-day cattle rustlers. Peter soon learned that two of the stars of that movie, Henry Dean Stanton and Elizabeth Ashley, had been cast in *92 in the Shade*.

A Londoner, born to Jewish parents, Kastner was known for such works as *Where Eagles Dare* (1968), *The Long Goodbye* (1973), and *The Mis-*

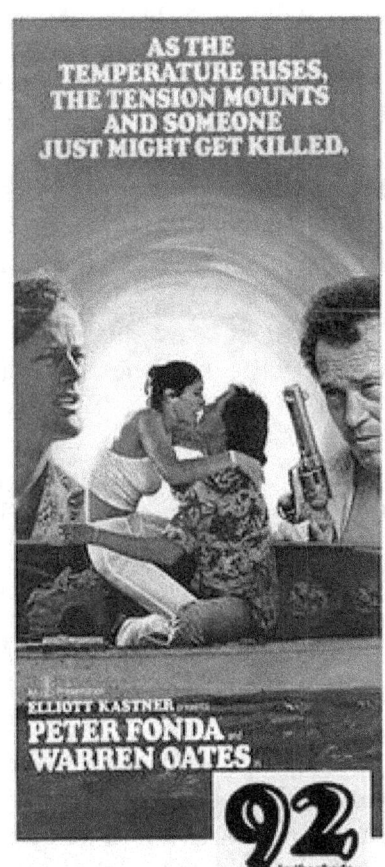

This occasionally funny movie was based on a novel by Thomas McGuane, one which was nominated for a National Book Award.

Filled with zany characters, it was a sex-laden saga of two rival fishing boat captains in the Florida Keys.

souri Breaks (1976).

Lew Wasserman, the CEO at Universal, had made Kastner Vice President in charge of Production. But he soon branched out to become an independent producer, hiring such stars as Elizabeth Taylor, Richard Burton, Paul Newman, Warren Beatty, Peter Sellers, and Marlon Brando.

Peter Fonda may not have been one of Kastner's admirers, but Mario Puzo called him "the greatest genius in the movie business."

Many others, however, agreed with Peter. Alan Parker, who would make *Angel Heart* (1987) with Kastner, called him an "irascible gadfly."

For *92 in the Shade*, Kastner hired Georges Pappas to produce it. He had just completed *Farewell, My Lovely* (1975).

When Peter heard that McGuane was also going to direct *92 in the Shade*, he obtained the novelist's unlisted phone number in Montana. McGuane was finishing the final pages of its script.

He made repeated calls to McGuane's home, but never got to speak to him. He was always told that he was living in the building's guesthouse, which had no phone. Actually, as Peter learned later, McGuane was lodged in a motel, having been alienated from his wife and with a divorce looming.

"I fell in love with that sweet voice on the phone," Peter said. "It was melodious and seductive. I didn't know what she looked like. For all I knew, she might weigh 300 pounds. But listening to that voice, I wanted to fuck her, sight unseen."

Actually, although he could hardly imagine it at the time, he was talking with the young woman with whom he would spend his next 36 years.

The voice that Peter heard was that of Portia Rebecca Crockett, whom McGuane had married in 1962 but would divorce in 1975. She was the great-great-great granddaughter of Davey Crockett.

[Famous during his lifetime for larger-than-life exploits popularized in the 20th Century by stage plays, TV series, and films, Davey Crockett ("King of the Wild Frontier;" 1786–1836) was an American frontiersman, folk hero, and politician.]

When, at last, Peter and McGuane got together, the novelist agreed that Peter would, indeed, be appropriately cast as the captain (Tom Skelton) of the charter boat. Peter then more or less got him to agree to assign him the role. But he went a step further and also asked him to cast his friend, Warren Oates, as the captain of the rival boat, too.

McGuane was already vaguely familiar with Oates, and he said he thought that that actor might be ideal. Finally, he agreed to give the role to Oates, but only after Peter lobbied hard to convince him. "The reason Warren held back was because both of us would practically have to work for nothing," Peter admitted.

92 in the Shade would mark the third time Peter and Oates had co-starred together. Before that, each had appeared in both *The Hired Hand* and *Race with the Devil*.

To prepare for his upcoming role, Peter let his hair grow long and he stopped shaving his beard. "When enough hair appeared on my head, I dyed it with henna, using more than Lucille Ball."

He also began to read other novels by McGuane. One critic cited the author's "comic appreciation for the irrational core of many human endeavors, presenting multiple takes on the counter-culture of the 1960s and 1970s."

The New York Times called McGuane "a talent of Faulknerian potential," and the novelist Saul Bellow labeled him "a language star."

After the completion of the film adaptation of *92 in the Shade*, McGuane would write the screenplay for *The Missouri Breaks* (1976), which would be directed by Arthur Penn and star both Marlon Brando and Jack Nicholson.

One night, Peter and McGuane spent a long evening together, ending it around 4AM. Peter concluded that the writer "was a font of creativity. They discussed McGuane's vision for an autobiographical novel, *Panama*, which

Portia Rebecca Crockett was descended from the legendary Davey Crockett.

In 1962, she was plunged into a marriage with the novelist Thomas McGuane.

In 1975, during the filming of his novel, *92 in the Shade*, she was charting her divorce.

would be published in 1978.

McGuane had based the character of Catherine in that book on Laura Buffett—the woman he would marry in 1977 who was, coincidentally, the sister of musician Jimmy Buffett—following his divorces from Portia Crockett and actress, Margot Kidder.

[*Panama, McGuane's novel, published in 1978, was marketed as "the story of a washed-up rock star turned casualty of illicit substances and kamikaze passion," received rave reviews from* The New York Times *and* The Village Voice, *but for the most part, it was massively attached by critics, despite McGuane's widely publicized belief that "it was my best work."*]

After Peter arrived for work in Key West for location shooting, McGuane ordered him to "get rid of that red beard." Nor did he like Peter's henna-colored hair, which, according to McGuane, "he could wear long, but in its natural color."

Warren Oates, who by now was one of Peter's best friends, was the first to greet him in Key West for a night of bar-hopping along Duval Street. On film, they were cast as enemies, operating rival fishing charters.

Oates played Nicholas Dance alongside his partner, Faron Carter (Harry Dean Stanton).

When Oates steals two of Tom's rich clients, he retaliates by blowing up Dance's boat. They remain bitter toward each other until the end, when Dance fatally shoots Tom as THE END flashes across the screen.

During filming, Peter also had a reunion with Elizabeth Ashley, who had returned to the state of her birth to portray Jeannie Carter, married to Faron Carter, played by Stanton.

She had married one of Peter's best friends, George Peppard, in 1966, divorcing him in 1972.

The couple had met on the set of *The Carpetbaggers* (1964), based on the novel by Harold Robbins, which had been inspired by Howard Hughes. At the time, she had described Peppard as "some kind of Nordic god—six feet tall with beautiful blonde hair and blue eyes and a body out of every high school teenager's lust fantasy."

But she had changed her mind over the years, and the marriage went sour.

Although she considered herself a major-league, A-list actress [on Broadway in 1962, she'd won a Tony for her performance in *Take Her, She's Mine*] Ashley had only a small role in this film.

She had also starred in the Broadway production of Neil Simon's *Barefoot in the Park*. Key roles in its film adaptation went to Jane Fonda and Robert Redford.

To Peter's surprise, he soon learned from Oates that Ashley was having an affair with the married McGuane.

Oates also told Peter that McGuane was having an affair with the third star of *92 in the Shade*, Margot Kidder, who had been cast as Miranda. According to what Oates told Peter, "Somehow, McGuane is managing to balance the two ac-

The unhappily married **George Peppard** with **Elizabeth Ashley,** as they appeared together in *The Third Day* (1965).

As Peter Fonda, his close friend, said, "George was just too good-looking and too well hung to give himself to just one woman. Where he was concerned, the line formed on the right. Gay guys went for him in droves."

Margot Kidder as Lois Lane flies high with **Christopher Reeve** as *Superman*. Each of them was headed, in their personal lives, for tragedy.

Reeve became an overnight tabloid sensation with his performance as a super hero, but after a string of spinoffs, he was ready to move on to other roles.

tresses both in and out of his bedroom, and his wife, Portia Crockett, is also here. And guess what? I'm carrying on with her behind McGuane's back."

A native of the Northwest Territories of Canada, Kidder would have a career spanning six decades. Her greatest fame came with her portrayal of Lois Lane in the first of four Superman movies. Her performance as Kathy Lutz in the blockbuster film, *The Amityville Horror* (1979) also gave her great exposure.

Big trouble lay ahead of her in the 1990s, when she suffered serious injuries in a car accident that left her temporarily paralyzed. She later had embarrassingly publicized manic episodes and nervous breakdowns stemming from her bipolar disorder.

Harry Dean Stanton played Faron Carter, the charter boat partner of Oates and the husband of the Ashley character. His career would span six decades. As he told Peter, "I was never pretty enough to be a leading man, so I ended up in supporting roles." He starred in such highly visible films as *Cool Hand Luke* (1967) with Paul Newman; *Kelly's Heroes* (1970), and *The Godfather: Part II* (1974).

Born in Kentucky, the son of a tobacco farmer, he grew up trying to decide if he wanted to be a singer or an actor.

In Hollywood, he made friends with director Sam Peckinpah and Francis Ford Coppola. McGuane and Jack Nicholson became so close that Nicholson designated him as his Best Man on the occasion of his marriage to Sandra Knight. *[This was Nicholson's only marriage.]*

Nicholson also got Stanton cast in *The Missouri Breaks* (1976) with Marlon Brando.

Veteran actor Burgess Meredith had long been a friend of both Henry Fonda and James Stewart. After Henry married

Burgess Meredith and **Paulette Goddard** are depicted here at one of the happier moments of thier doomed marriage. She had separated from Charlie Chaplin. The celebrated novelist, Erich Maria Remarque, lay in her future.

Of himself, Meredith said, "God knows I was not a dashing swain, but in a kind of mongrel way, I chased the foxes, not only Paulette, but Tallulah Bankhead, Ingrid Bergman, Hedy Lamarr, Ginger Rogers, and Norma Shearer.

Two views of **Sylvia Miles**: *Left photo*, as a con-artist prostitute with another prostitute, played by **Jon Voight** in *Midnight Cowboy*.

In the *right photo*, she's seen on Duval Street in Key West during the filming of *92 in the Shade*.

his second wife, Frances Seymour, in 1936, he moved out of Stewart's home. *[They had been roommates since their early days as unknown actors in New York in the 1930s.]*

To replace Henry, Stewart moved in Burgess Meredith. The three men had enjoyed long mutual friendships, and Peter enjoyed hearing tales of his father's early career.

Meredith had been famously married to actress Paulette Goddard after Charlie Chaplin dumped her. *[It was never really clear if she had been legally married to "The Little Tramp."]*

A "virtuosic actor," Meredith was one of the most accomplished actors in the history of Hollywood. He earned fame for performances in *Of Mice and Men* (1939) and as Ernie Pyle in *The Story of G.I. Joe* (1945). Most Americans, however, saw him as "The Penguin" in the 1960s *Batman* TV series, or as boxing trainer Mickey Goldmill in the "Rocky" film series with Sylvester Stallone.

In *92 in the Shade*, he played a bigoted redneck lawyer, Mr. Goldsboro. He had to deliver such lines as "I can't eat that nigger food."

Sylvia Miles is brilliant as Bella, who is having an affair with him. As he is seated in a chair, she sits on his lap as he fondles her crotch, telling her, "I call it pussy."

Miles recalled all the sexual couplings that flourished on the set of *92 in the Shade*, referring to the environment as "a sexual swamp meet."

"McGuane didn't seduce me because he was too busy plugging Kidder and Ashley. Oates was sleeping with McGuane's wife, Portia. Peter, for a while, had some dame stashed away in a motel, but he never introduced her to us. McGuane would later marry Kidder, but it lasted for only seven months before they headed for the divorce courts."

Miles was disappointed at how small her role was in *92 in the Shade*. She had previously appeared with Peter in *The Last Movie*. She'd also been twice nominated for a Best Supporting Actress Oscar—first for *Midnight Cowboy* (1969) and then for *Farewell, My Love* (1975).

For Andy Warhol, she'd also appeared in the controversial film, *Heat* (1972).

In honor of her visit to Key West, a local movie theater on Duval Street showed *Heat*, and Miles invited Peter to take her to see it. It was widely popular with gays.

Heat was written and directed by Paul Morrissey and produced by Andy Warhol. He envisioned it as a parody of Gloria Swanson's *Sunset Blvd.* (1950). Miles was cast as a fading star with sexy Joe Dallesandro cast as a hustler. He was never afraid of being photographed frontally nude.

For an ad in the *New York Daily News*, the art department had to put a T-shirt on Dellasandro and a bra to cover Miles' chest.

Otto Preminger had gone to see *Heat*, referring to it later as "depressingly entertaining." Another critic, in reference to his brand of "freestyle with lots of nudity" films, advised Warhol to "make them, make them, just don't show them to anybody."

***

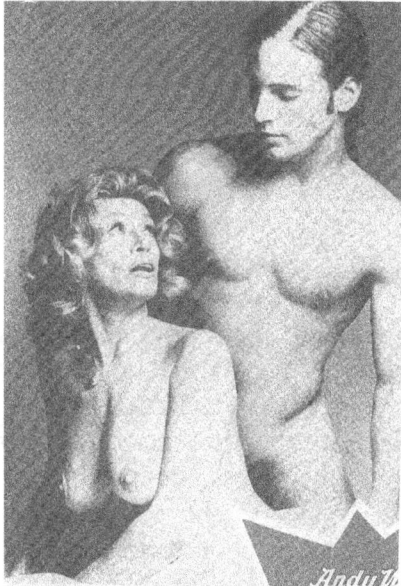

Sylvia Miles with **Joe Dallesandro** were cast together in Andy Warhol's *Heat*, a pornographic spoof of Gloria Swanson's *Sunset Blvd.* (1950).

"Joe got a hard-on pressed up this close to me," she later said to the co-author of this book, Darwin Porter.

Before filming began, she made it clear to Warhol that "I will not do a scene sucking off Joe. I'll do him in private, but not on camera." Warhol settled for having Miles, on camera, suck Joe's fingers.

Joe later relayed how he felt making the picture, "I was meat being marketed."

During the filming in Key West of *92 in the Shade*, **Peter Fonda** met **Portia Rebecca Crockett**.

He later said, "Thomas McGuane's loss was my gain...and what a prize trophy."

When Peter saw the first rushes of *92 in the Shade,* he was disappointed. "I had hoped that it would turn out better. I like some of the scenes but thought that overall, McGuane fucked up the picture. His editing was awful." He later told Oates, "The fart cut some of my best scenes but you came out terrific."

Both Peter and Oates accurately predicted that *92 in the Shade* would come under fire from critics and fail at the box office.

***

Before Peter flew back to California at the completion of *92 in the Shade,* he had visited the Bird Cage Bar in Key West, where Warren Oates introduced him to Portia Rebecca Crockett (otherwise known as Mrs. Thomas McGuane) to Peter.

It seemed that she and Oates were having a brief fling during the period when her husband took turns inviting Elizabeth Ashley or Margot Kidder to his boudoir.

"Becky, as she was called, was sensual, a vivacious blonde who evoked Barbara Stanwyck in those movies she made in the 1930s," Peter said. "I think I fell in love with her that very night. Warren (Oates) wasn't really in love with her, so it was easy to lure Becky—I had already stopped calling her Portia—away from him."

"At one point, Elizabeth Ashley came into the bar and walked over to greet us. "I was shocked at how Portia handled it."

"I think it's wonderful that you and Tom are having an affair," Portia said. "Normally, he picks up and screws bubbles. I'm not jealous, as I'm occupied myself. I guess he told you that we're getting a divorce?"

"Thank you for being so generous with your husband," Ashley remarked before moving on.

"My time with Portia was brief," Peter said. "But from the night I met her, I could think of no one else. I wanted her, needed her, and I was determined to have her. Warren didn't try to hold on to her. I think that very night he shacked up with Sylvia Miles, who was always on the lookout for the next stud. She rarely got a name star, although she'd once screwed Frank Sinatra and Robert Mitchum."

Oates later said, "I think Becky and Peter are perfect for each other. Nothing seems to faze her. I've never told anyone this, before, but Peter once confessed to me that as a teenager, he'd dreamed of seducing his older sister Jane. When he started screwing Becky, he told me it was like plugging Jane."

"That sounds like incest to me," Oates cautioned.

"Call it what you like," Peter responded. "Portia is now my gal."

She already had a son, Thomas, who later bonded with Peter, perhaps viewing him as his new stepfather. But after some walks along the beach, the boy asked him, "Do you think you'll love me more than you do your own son, Justin?"

After my divorce, I never planned to marry again," Peter said. "But along comes Portia.":

Before leaving Key West, Peter attended a cast party and Portia was there, too. "At the end of the party, I walked over and gave her a passionate kiss in front of everybody. I was staking out my territory."

He had to fly to San Antonio to fulfill a commitment. At this point, she had started writing him love letters, which led to long, late-night phone calls.

When she was free, he invited her to San Antonio. "Before her arrival, I founded up every yellow rose in Texas to decorate my suite. 'The Yellow Rose of Texas was on the way to my bed."

CHAPTER SIXTEEN

PETER DROPS OUT & FADES AWAY

"Nothing is so dangerous as being too modern. One is apt to grow old-fashioned quite suddenly."
—Oscar Wilde

O.J. SIMPSON CO-STARS WITH PETER IN
KILLER FORCE

The disgraced, "wife-murdering and slasher" football hero was Peter's friend and co-star in one of his most violent movies. Before filming began in South Africa, he almost got arrested for using the "Whites Only" men's room.

NAVIGATING THE SOUTH PACIFIC

In his own ketch, Peter, with his future wife, Portia, and her son, Thomas, sail together as an isolated trio through French Polynesia in a bid to get away from California and the Entertainment Industry

FIGHTING MAD

Peter stars as a vigilante riding a motorcycle with a toddler and carrying a crossbow to ward off any enemy

FUTURE WORLD

In this movie, based on a bestseller by Michael Crichton. Robots are available for sex.

OUTLAW BLUES
with Susan Saint James

Songwriter Peter is on the run from a crime he did not commit. His co-star played Rock Hudson's "wife," at least in a TV serial. Between takes, he gets high on mushrooms growing out of cow turds.

WANDA NEVADA

Peter rides off with 13-year-old jailbait, model Brooke Shields. For the first time, he directs Henry Fonda, casting his father as a grizzled old desert rat.

Disappointed with changing times and the evolution of Hollywood, and with dreams of exploring Tahiti and the South Seas, Peter purchased a yacht he named *Tatoosh* with the intention of sailing on it with Portia for three months in the South Pacific.

But first, he had to fly to South Africa to film *The Diamond Mercenaries*, later retitled *Killer Force*.

***

Killer Force (aka *The Diamond Mercenaries*; 1976)

He would be working with a new director, Val Guest, a Londoner, who had already cast the picture and scouted the location terrain for shooting in both South Africa and the deserts of Namibia.

Peter knew nothing about Guest, and tried to learn as much about him as he could. Born in 1911, the son of a jute broker, he had spent his childhood in India, so he was used to exotic settings. He returned to England and, at one point, had been told that his mother had died. That was not true. The accurate story was that she had divorced her husband and abandoned her child.

When he grew up, Guest became a newspaper columnist, later branching out to write screenplays for long-forgotten light comedies such as *Hi Gang!* (1941), starring Ben Lyon and Bebe Daniels. By 1940, he had become a film director. Most of the players he cast were strictly B picture actors, although on occasion, he would helm a player with greater name recognition—David Niven, Douglas Fairbanks Jr., Margaret Lockwood, or Dirk Bogarde.

In *Killer Force*, Peter would have second billing to Telly Savalas. Supporting players would include Hugh O'Brian, Christopher Lee, Maud Adams, and O.J. Simpson.

Savalas was both an actor and a singer, with a career that would span four decades. He was noted for his bald head, bitter humor, and a deep, resonant voice. He'd become best known for his portrayal of Lt. Theo Kojak in the TV crime series, *Kojak* (1973-1978) and for the James Bond archvillain Ernest Stavro Blofeld in *On Her Majesty's Secret Service* (1969). Another notable feature film was *The Birdman of Alcatraz* (1962) starring Burt Lancaster. For his performance in that movie, Savalas was nominated for a Best Supporting Actor Osar.

He later claimed, "I will become known for one thing, and that was introducing Americans to Diet Coke in a series of television commercials."

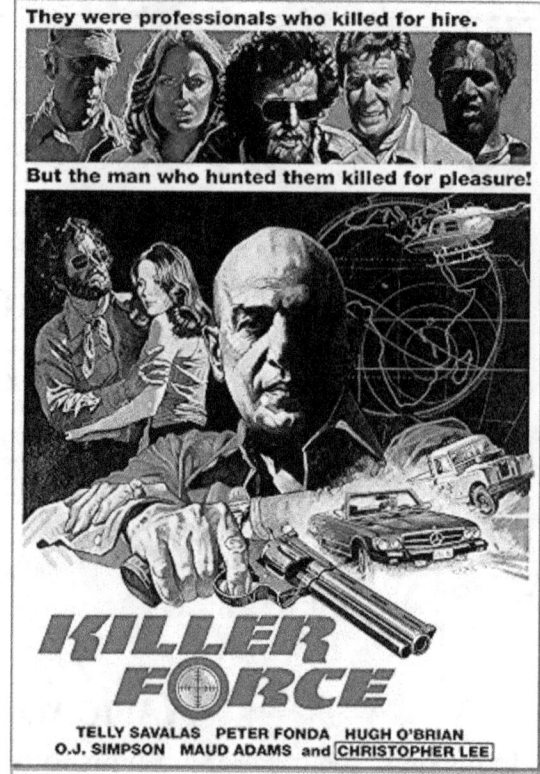

Some viewers interpreted **Telly Savalas a**s the film's most interesting male character. In the poster above, he's featured prominently as "the scariest force" within *Killer Force*.

Armed, dangerous, and looking tired of roles whose themes he had, by now, repeated frequently, here's **Peter** ("more macho") **Fonda** in *Killer Force*:

Tall, handsome, and studly, Hugh O'Brian was best known for his starring role in the ABC-TV Western series, *The Life and Legend of Wyatt Earp* (1955-1961). One of his most notable films had been the adaptation of Agatha Christie's *Ten Little Indians* (1965). He also played the last character John Wayne ever killed on screen in The Duke's farewell movie, *The Shootist* (1976).

Another Londoner, Christopher Lee, had a career that would span seven decades, often cast as a villain. In nine feature films, he played Count Dracula, and he also starred, with chilling effects, in *The Curse of Frankenstein* (1957).

He was in the James Bond film, *The Man with the Golden Gun* (1974). He would also be seen in *Star Wars* movies and as fear-inducing sorcerers within *The Lord of the Rings* and *The Hobbit* series.

Peter's leading lady in *Killer Force* was the Swedish actress, Maud Adams. Born the daughter of two government tax bureaucrats in the isolated far north of Sweden, and fluent in five languages, she abandoned her plans to become an interpreter and chose to become a model and later, an actress.

Left photo: **O.J. Simpson,** theatrically playing to the cameras and trying on a pair of gloves at his criminal trial

Righrt photo: **O.J. Simpson's** mugshot from June 17, 1994.

Guerrilla fighting and on the defensive in the Desert of Namibia: **Hugh O'Brian** in *Killer Force*

Here's **Maud Adams**, looking more like a weather-beaten frontierswoman than the glamorous international film star many of her fans had expected, in *Killer Force.*

She shot to fame as the doomed mistress of the villain, Christopher Lee in *The Man with the Golden Gun*. Producer Albert Broccoli liked her so much he brought her back to star in *Octopussy* (1983) as the title character, an exotic and mysterious smuggler, opposite Roger Moore.

["Maud Adams," born in 1945, is sometimes confused with "Maude Adams" (1872-1953), an actress from another era. The "earlier" Maude, spelled with an "e," achieved her greatest success on Broadway in 1905 when she starred as Peter Pan. *She became one of the highest paid actresses of her day, earning one million dollars a year, a fantastic sum at the turn of the 20th Century.]*

Rounding out the cast was O. J. Simpson, nicknamed "Juice," and later, "Slasher." Born in San Francisco in the summer of 1947, he stood 6' 1" and weighed 212 pounds. During the course of his career, he was famous as a football running back, a broadcaster, actor, and advertising spokesman for Hertz.

At the University of Southern California, he played football for the U.S. Trojans and won the Heisman Trophy in 1968. He played professionally as a running back in the NFL (National Football League) for eleven seasons, primarily for the Buffalo Bills (1967-1977).

After retiring from football, he began new careers in broadcasting and as an actor. He was seen in the television series *Roots* (1977) and in such feature film dramas as *The Klansman* (1974), *The Towering Inferno* (also 1974), and *The Cassandra Crossing* (1976). He later claimed that he learned how to act by watching the film performances of Lee Marvin and Richard Burton.

[In 1994, Simpson was arrested after police pursued him in the most famous car chase in American history. He was charged with the murder, by stabbing, of his ex-wife, Nicole Brown Simpson, and her friend, Ron Goldman.

After a lengthy trial that was broadcast on televisions across the nation, a jury acquitted him.

The families of the victims later filed a civil suit against him. He lost that case and was ordered to pay $33.5 million for their wrongful deaths. He fled from California to Miami to avoid paying the liability judgment, which was never settled.

In 2007, he was arrested in Las Vegas and charged with the felonies of armed robbery and kidnapping. The following year, he was convicted and sentenced to 33 years in prison, with a minimum of nine years before any possibility of parole. On December 14, 2021, he was granted early release from the Nevada Division of Parole and Probation.

Today, wherever he goes, he is mobbed by autograph seekers.]

***

The year of the release of *Killer Force*, Peter would marry Portia Crockett, the union lasting until he divorced her in 2011.

He had been in South Africa for two weeks before Portia flew to join him. She arrived at the airport in Johannesburg aboard the same plane as fellow passenger O. J. Simpson. She knew who he was, but he didn't know who she was.

In South Africa, long before Simpson's acquittal for the murder of Nicole Brown Simpson, Peter remembered O.J. as looking "like a fashion plate wearing Pierre Cardin clothing."

He rushed to take Portia in his arms before introducing her to O. J. He had a new nickname for her, calling her "Bundle of Joy," because of her small stature and her use of only Joy perfume.

Waiting to retrieve their luggage, O.J. told Peter, "I have to take a piss." So did Peter. They walked together until they found a sign that announced WHITES ONLY.

Reluctant to enter, O. J. held back, but Peter urged him on. At the urinal, O. J. couldn't bring relief to his bladder because of the hostile stares from most of the white men in the room.

Finally, Peter escorted and guided the football star upstairs to another toilet, this one marked with signs that said NONWHITE PEOPLE.

"I stood by O. J. as both of us poured out a stream," Peter recalled. "At first, I was hesitant to stand beside him, fearing that he might pull out a Mandingo-sized dong to put me to shame. I need not have feared. We looked about equal."

As they were leaving the "NONWHITE PEOPLE'S" men's toilet, Peter noticed five policemen in pursuit of them. Obviously, someone had reported the illegal entry of O. J. to a point too close to the segregated urinal. From there, he and Peter fled to join the accumulated ranks of other cast and crew members near the airport's exit. As such, the police apparently decided not to make an arrest.

After making love to Portia, Peter studied the script written by director Guest in collaboration with two other writers he'd hired.

Killer Force, even when it was still entitled *The Diamond Mercenaries*, was marketed with taglines that included "They were professionals who killed for a living. But the man who hunted them killed for pleasure."

Peter interpreted its plot as "murky": Working for a diamond mining complex in the desert, Harry Webb (Telly Savalas) as head of security suspects that a diamond theft is imminent.

His zealous, oft-expressed fears have antagonized Claire Chambers (Maud Adams) a cover girl and the daughter of the mine's administrator. She is visiting the mine for a reunion with her boyfriend, Mike Bradley (Peter Fonda).

Mr. Nelson (Victor Melleney), the administrator of the mine, gives Bradley an odd assignment. He is ordered to steal a diamond, thereby attracting the attention of Lewis (Hugh O'Brian), who invites him to join his gang of robbers.

There's a catch: One of the members of the gang plotting the "real" robbery is known as "Father Christmas" (i.e., Peter himself), who, ironically, had been intent on robbery even before he was approached by the mine administrator with what he thought was a ruse.

At the end of the film, Bradley (Fonda), pursued by Lewis (Hugh O'Brian) flees into the desert with the only other survivors the plot.

For the desert scenes, the cast and crew flew to Windhoek, the capital and largest city of Namibia. At that time, it was still under the control of South Africa. On its north, it shared borders with Angola and Zambia.

Namibia, an arid and stiflingly hot region known for its diamond mines and its former status as a colony of Imperial Germany, would gain independence in 1990. In part because of its sprawling and suffocatingly hot desert, ("The Namib") it's one of the least-populated countries in the world.

Some of the film's scenes were shot at Swakopmuno in the country's (relatively cool, but still very hot) inlands. Established by German colonists in 1892, It retains some remaining examples of German colonial architecture. A travel article in *The New York Times* called it "more German than Germany."

The final scenes of the movie were shot in Johannesburg, but before that, Peter put Portia on a plane back to the United States. It was understood that before going on her cruise with Peter to the South Pacific, she wanted to spend some time with her son, Thomas. She had bought a ranch near the one owned by Thomas McGuane, in part because her son would be near his father.

At the end of the shoot, Peter attended a party for film's cast and crew, where he relayed the details of his exotic (upcoming) cruise.

His colleagues had told him how much they admired Portia's beauty. However, each of them found her nickname for Peter a bit puzzling. She either called him "Peach Pit" or "Tuna Trousers."

***

By now, Peter was in Hawaii preparing for his South Pacific adventure with Portia. She was in Montana at the time, having a reunion with her son, Thomas.

Peter had bought an 81-foot ketch from an executive at Boeing. He dubbed it *Taltoosk,* a word that translates as "breast" in a native American dialect.

He had already made frequent excursions in the ketch from the California coast to Catalina and from there, also several trans-Pacific transits to Hawaii.

Now, he was preparing and stocking it with provisions for his most ambitious trek yet for himself, Portia, and her son, Thomas. His son, Justin, was too young for such a trip.

Peter was at the airport to welcome Portia to Honolulu. From there, on the fourth of July, 1975, they set sail for Lahaina, the largest island in West Maui. During tourist season, its population swelled to 40,000. It was also the site of some of the state's most expensive homes, with many houses and condos beginning at $5 million.

On the fifth of July, they celebrated at an "aloha party." Festivities were interrupted when in the distance, they saw the sky lit up from the eruption of Mauna Loa.

The very next day, they set sail for the Marquesas Islands, a cluster of volcanic islands in French Polynesia. Indigenous voyagers had colonized them as early as the 10th Century. Peter and his tribe arrived at Taiohae, a settlement on the small island of Nuku Hiva.

Fewer than 10,000 people inhabited the entire archipelago. As he later wrote, "I was living life as in a dream, spending every night in the arms of my "Bundle of Joy."

They would spend three weeks just cruising the Marquesas, stopping at Fatu Hutu, Tahuata, and Ua Pou. On one of the islands, the locals staged a big luau for them, roasting a goat in a pit.

At one point, they visited the grave of Paul Gauguin, the brilliant French Post-Impressionistic painter who had died of complications from syphilis beside Atuona Bay on the southern side of Hiva Oa island at the age of 54.

The ketch then sailed for the Tuamotus archipelago, with its dangerous atolls, raised about ten feet above the sea. Over the centuries, many mariners had run afoul in the rough waters.

They anchored at the little port of Rangiroa, the most populated settlement in the archipelago, where they purchased provisions. A week was spent there, as they went snorkeling and scuba diving.

Tahiti, the retreat of Marlon Brando, was next on their itinerary. The archipelago seemed lonely and isolated in a remote part of the Pacific, with nearest major landmass being Australia.

They anchored at Papeete, the capital city of French Polynesia. To Peter's astonishment, the restaurant they visited for lunch was decorated with posters from his films, *Easy Rider, The Hired Hand,* and *The Wild Angels.*

It was in Tahiti that the *HMS Bounty* arrived in October of 1788 under the command of Captain William Bligh. Three weeks after leaving Tahiti, in April of 1789, the crew mutinied on the initiative of Fletcher Christian. He was portrayed in two big-budget, critically acclaimed movies, first by Clark Gable and then by Marlon Brando. It was from Papeete that Portia and Peter headed west again aboard a flight to Honolulu, leaving the crew to sail the ketch back to Hawaii.

Whereas Portia wanted to return to her ranch in Montana. Peter was anxious for a reunion with his children, Justin and Bridget. He flew into Honolulu where his kids were waiting with Larry Hagman.

He took them to the vacation hacienda owned by his mother, Mary Martin.

By Labor Day, Peter and his children were back in Montana, reunited with Portia.

It was time to go back to work for him, and he had two more films to release in 1976: *Fighting Mad* and *Futureworld.*

***

Fighting Mad (1976)

Peter flew to Arkansas to shoot his next movie and once again found himself working for Roger Corman. That widely acclaimed producer had analyzed three low-budget, potentially blockbuster hits—each of them action films: *Billy Jack* (1973), *Walking Tall* (1973), and *Dirty Mary, Crazy Larry* (1974). They each had something in common: A hero with an offbeat sidekick, an unusual mode of transport, and an intriguing weapon.

In Corman's new vigilante thriller, Peter's character of Tom Hunter travels on an old motorcycle with his toddler son and uses a crossbow. He also employs guerrilla tactics against corrupt developers attempting to evict his family and his neighbors so that they can strip-mine their land.

Corman hired Jonathan Demme to write the script and to direct it. The film's budget was established at $800,000.

Demme had made his directorial debut with a profitable B movie, *Caged Heat* (1974), a tale of women in prison. He later became known for his "casually humanist" movies such as *Melvin and Howard* (1980).

His greatest triumph lay in his future when he won a Best Director Oscar for *The Silence of the Lambs* (1991) starring Jodie Foster.

Peter would agree with Foster's assessment of Demme: "He was so dynamic you'd have to design a hurricane to contain him. He was pure energy, an unstoppable cheerleader for anyone creative, a champion of the soul."

He's aiming a gun again?

At this point in his fading career, **Peter Fonda** had evolved into something of a poster boy for the "*shoot 'em up and kill 'em, 'cause I'm mad as hell*" school of B-list movie-making.

Lynn Lowry was hired as the female lead for the role of Lorene Maddox. She had attended the University of Georgia, and for a time, she worked as a bunny at the Playboy Club in Atlanta. She later became known for appearances in horror movies such as *I Drink Your Blood* (1971). Finally, she tired of "all that Hollywood bullshit" and went to sing with a band.

The project's most employable actor was John Douchette who, with his stocky build and deep, rich voice, was featured, during the course of his career, in some 280 films or television productions. His roles ranged from plays by Shakespeare to Western or crime *noirs.*

He played an architect in Gary Cooper's *The Fountainhead* (1949) and worked with Coop again in *High Noon* (1952). He appeared even more frequently with John Wayne in movies such as *The Sea Chase*, *The Sons of Katie Elder*, and *True Grit*.

Phil Carey, in the role of Pierce Crabtree, sometimes worked with far bigger names than he encountered in *Fighting Mad*. His pictures included roles in *This Woman is Dangerous* (1952) with Joan Crawford; *Calamity Jane* (1953) with Doris Day; and *Mister Roberts* (1955) with Henry Fonda.

Peter would hardly remember shooting the film in Arkansas except for one major event in his life: On Armistice Day, November 11, 1975, he married Portia Rebecca Crockett McGuane. Presiding at the ceremony was Washington County (Arkansas) Judge Val B. Lester.

Peter and Portia's honeymoon was spent at the local Ramada Inn.

He would not divorce her until 2011, when he was 71.

That same year, he would marry his final wife, Margaret DeVogelaere, a union that lasted until his death at the age of 79 in 2019.

***

Futureworld (1976)

It all began with *Westworld,* that 1973 science fiction movie. That film was written and directed by Michael Critchon. It follows visitors attending an amusement park that turns out to contain lifelike androids who unexpectedly begin to malfunction. *Westworld* starred Yul Brynner and was released by Metro-Goldwyn-Mayer.

The books of Crichton sold more than 200 million copies worldwide. More than a dozen of them were adapted into films. In time, he wrote 20 novels such as *The Andromeda Strain* (1969) and *Jurassic Park* (1990).

Futureworld was a sequel to the 1973 film *Westworld*. MGM did not want to get involved in the sequel, so it was made by American International instead. Crichton also did not want to work on it.

It was shot in the Greater Houston area at sites that included the Johnson Space Center. *Futureworld* became the first modern American film to be given a theatrical release in China.

Richard T. Heffron helmed a cast led by Peter Fonda, co-starring Blythe Danner as the female lead, supported by Arthur Hill. Yul Brynner, the original star of *Westworld*, appeared in a dream sequence.

Heffron was a very minor director who mainly worked in television series such as *The Rockford Files*. He helmed six episodes of the miniseries *North and South*.

During World War II, a Canadian actor, Arthur Hill, joined the Royal Canadian Air Force. In time, he gravitated to Broadway, where he won a Tony for Best Dramatic Actor in Edward Albee's *Who's Afraid of Virginia Woolf?* Later, he played Jane Fonda's husband in the movie *In the Cool of the Day* (1963).

Blythe Danner is known today as the mother of actress Gwyneth Paltrow, but in her heyday, she was also an award-winning actress, the recipient of both Emmy and Tony Awards. Woody Allen cast her in three of his films, including *Husband and Wives* (1992). Danner also played the mother of Paltrow in *Sylvia* (2003), based on the life of writer Sylvia Plath.

Futureworld begins where the *Westworld* film left off. Newspaper reporters Chuck Browning (Fonda) and TV newscaster Tracy Ballard (Danner) are invited to tour the park after $1.5 billion has been spent on safety improvements.

[Futureworld, *it's revealed, is one of four theme parks, including* Spaworld, *"where age and pain have been eliminated." The reporters focus their coverage on* Futureworld, *which simulates an orbiting space station. Robots are available for sex as well as such amusements as boxing.]*

They are shown through the complex by Dr. Duffy (Arthur Hill). On the premises, the night after their arrival, they are drugged. As they sleep, Duffy orders medical tests on them with the intention of using them to generate clones.

The following day, Ballard is testing a dream-recording device that leads to her making love to Yul Brynner, cast as "The Gunslinger."

The movie heats up with unexpected consequences. Browning and Ballard discover that they have been cloned, and their clones have been programmed to murder them.

Futureworld got mixed reviews, generating $4.2 million at the box office, having been made on a budget of $2.5 million.

The New York Times critic, Richard Elder, attacked it, describing it as "as much fun as running barefoot on Astroturf. It is all the most ordinary kind of hardware science fiction, full of computers and empty of thought. Starring in the movie must be the actor's equivalent of going on welfare."

Gene Siskel didn't like the film either but wrote that it has "some of the best gadgets since the early James Bond films."

Variety found that "*Futureworld* shapes up as a strong sequel to MGM's *Westworld* of three years ago."

Keven Thomas of the *Los Angeles Times* found that "the film is an extreme rarity, a sequel that's a decided improvement over the original."

The Monthly Film Bulletin wrote that the sequel "seems content to do little more than lead the players through the standard diversions of a caper movie."

***

Outlaw Blues (1977)

Richard T. Heffron, the director who had helmed Peter in *Futureworld*, was tapped once again to direct him in *Outlaw Blues*, a movie that teamed him with Susan Saint James.

Written by Bill L. Norton, the drama is about an ex-convict and songwriter trying to break into the music business in Austin, Texas.

The soundtrack of the film includes a title song written by John Oates and a trio of songs by Hoyt Axton. Some of the songs *[surprise, surprise]* were sung by Peter himself.

At the beginning of the film, Bobby Ogden (Fonda) makes a mistake by showing some of his tunes to Garland Dupree, a Nashville star in a role played by James Callahan. Dupree pilfers a copy of "Outlaw Blues" and records it as his own with no credit to the *bona-fide* author, Bobby (Peter).

In a confrontation, Dupree pulls a gun on Bobby. In the ensuing struggle, he accidentally shoots himself. Later, in the hospital, Dupree claims that Bobby shot him. It forces Bobby to go on the run for a crime he didn't commit. He flees with Tina Waters (Saint James), who had recently been fired by Dupree as his back-up singer.

Saint James, six years younger than Peter, became a virtual household name for her role in television from the 1960s to the 1980s. Her fist big break came with her starring role as Rock Hudson's younger, very supportive wife, Sally McMillan, in the popular, light-hearted crime series, *McMillan & Wife* (1971-1976), for which she received four Emmy nominations.

She later dropped out of the series because of a contract dispute over money.

After working in a number of films, including with Peter in *Outlaw Blues*, she returned to television, starring in the comedy

Back to Basics

Outlaw Blues: Love, Pain, Euphoria, and Country/Western Music

series, *Kate & Allie* opposite Jane Curtin from 1984-1989. She received three Emmy Award nominations for this role.

Most of the scenes for *Outlaw Blues* were shot in Huntsville and Austin, both in the state of Texas.

[Huntsville Prison is the site of the largest state prison in the country. "To go to that jail meant you have really fucked up in a big way," Peter said.]

"To get high, the crew and I found mushrooms—yes, that kind—growing out of cow piles," Peter said. "I had to pop one in my mouth first to convince the guys that they were not poisonous. Incidentally, don't tell anyone, but I hated that god damn song, 'Outlaw Blues.'"

Warner Brothers released the film on August 15, 1977, where it did moderate business, receiving mixed reviews.

Film critic A. H Weiler in *The New York Times* claimed that the movie "was pleasantly palatable if not especially nutritious. It is amiable, lilting, if lightweight diversion. The cast makes the most of a musical genre that has millions of devoted fans."

***

High-Ballin' (1978)

Peter Fonda's next film, *High-Ballin'*, was marketed as "a modern-day Western with good ol' boys and trucks instead of horses."

It was also summarized as *"pow, crash, screw, fight, collide, punch, slam, crash, and screw."*

"I flew to Toronto for the shoot, suffering "from the world's worst case of the flu," Peter claimed. "The weather there didn't help either."

Scenes for the movie were shot on the waterfront in Toronto as well as in and around the town of Milton, Ontario. Its special effects included "a flaming cannon roll," which had not previously been attempted in a motion picture.

Peter Carter, a British-Canadian film and television director, was called in to handle cast and crew in this rollicking drama of "rough, tough, and ready-for-a-brawl" truckers "who make a 900-mile run in a blizzard look like a trek to church."

Carter's career had begun in England when he worked at the J. Arthur Rank Studios. He moved to Canada in 1963, where he helmed a number of low-budget flickers with names like *Highpoint* and *Rituals.*

For distribution of the 97-minute movie, a deal was made with America International Pictures, familiar turf to Peter Fonda.

"Iron Duke" Boykin (cast with Jerry Reed) is a proudly independent trucker who stands up to the local truck boss, the corrupt "King Carroll" (Chris Wiggins).

The mobster tries to force independent truckers out of business, using intimidating tactics by gang leader Harvey (David Ferry). Enter Peter in the role of trucker "Rane," who ends up helping his friend, the Iron Duke.

Later, Duke is shot, and Rane and other independent truckers confront King and Harvey for a showdown.

High Ballin': Repetive and grating.

Peter Fonda with more of the same.

The film's producer, Jon Slan, was given a budget that totaled $2 million. He had ten weeks (it stretched from October and December of 1977) to bring the film in on time and on budget.

Peter could not seem to get over the flu—that is, until he flew to Key West to recover after the shoot. But during filming, he struggled bravely through, despite the cold weather.

During filming, the movie's title was changed from *P.F. Flyer* to *High-Ballin'*. When shown in Canada, it was sometimes billed as *Death Toll*.

The Globe and Mail wrote, "As much money seems to have been spent on stuntmen as actors. Cars screech, do 'wheelies,' file off a large hauler, turn somersaults, burst into flames, and generally do everything but tapdance on their reckless way to oblivion."

The *Toronto Star* labeled the film a popcorn movie, intended to be half-watched while your mind is coping with other matters."

Motion Picture Products called it "an exploitation film, existing not to provide any kind of realistic picture of the trucking industry, but to exploit it for a standard action movie with a lot of violence."

The *Independent Film Journal* noted that "Although *High Ballin'* is no great shades in terms of original story telling, director Peter Carter provides a good deal more polish and flash than one might expect of the raucous road genre."

***

Wanda Nevada (1979)

Peter Fonda was both the star and director of a Western that featured child model Brooke Shields cast in the title role.

Henry Fonda (Peter's father) was out of work at the time. He phoned Peter and asked if he had a part for him. The role most suitable was that of a grizzled old desert rat, an untitled character I.D.'d as "the Prospector." The role, theoretically at least, could be shot in one day.

"I'm your man," Henry said.

Pre-production was halted for a while when Peter came down with chicken pox. "Severe sores covered my body," he claimed. "Even my dick."

The script by Dennis Hackin takes place in 1950s Arizona, and is centered on a drifter and gambler (Peter) who cast himself as Beaudray Demerille.

In a card game, he wins the film's title character, Wanda Nevada. She is Brooke Shields cast as a 13-year-old orphan who dreams of singing onstage at the Grand Ole Opry. The adventures have only begun.

With a gang of cutthroat villains hot on his trail, Demerille hauls this sexy adolescent around the countryside as he searches for gold in the Grand Canyon.

As a Manhattan-born child model, Shields was born in 1965. At the age of 12, she was awarded the leading role in the Louis Malle movie, *Pretty Baby* (1978), where she played a prostitute. The film was so controversial that thousands of people demanded it not be exhibited.

Eileen Ford, founder of the Ford modeling Agency, claimed that Shields "looks like an adult and thinks like one."

In 1980, when she was 14, Shields became the youngest fashion model ever to appear on the cover of *Vogue*. The same year, she became famous when she appeared in sexually suggestive television ads for Calvin Klein jeans. Her tagline became a widely familiar refrain: "You want to know what comes between me and my Calvins? Nothing!"

These ads *[which were followed by equivalent ads with other models]* helped catapult Klein's products into the stratosphere of "super-designer chic."

Henry Fonda (*père*) arrived on the set a day early to experience (and accustom himself) to the 120-degree desert heat. For his work in the film, his son paid him $1,500.

The role called for Henry to chew tobacco and do a lot of spitting. Peter offered to let him use licorice, but he refused, claiming that Bill Cosby had given him some Red Man chewing tobacco, and that he was going to spit it out in attempts to appear as authentic as possible.

Two views of **Peter Fonda** with a very young **Brooke Shields** in *Wanda Nevada*.

However, by noon, the nicotine and the heat caused him to pass out in his dressing room. Fortunately, the footage recorded earlier that day was evaluated as sufficient for the final cut. As such, Henry flew back to Los Angeles and Shirlee the following day.

The critic for the *Motion Picture Guide* called *Wanda Nevada* "pretty bad, with a brief cameo by Peter Fonda's dad cast as a grizzled desert rat. He was the movie's only point of interest."

Rich Groen of *The Globe and Mail* declared the movie as "the least able fable imaginable. It contains every piece of *clichéd* Western dialogue ever uttered."

Todd McCarthy labeled the picture as "a serio-comic romance which is unconvincing on virtually every level. Peter Fonda's third directorial outing is all but sunk by Brooke Shields' critically deficient performance."

HENRY FONDA? Who knew?

That's **Henry Fonda**, *pére*, convincingly cast as a grizzled and alienated old prospector, lurking behind an enigmatic facade in *Wanda Nevada*. Father and son, on the same movie set together, stumbled through their scenes, dysfunctionally. Henry told anyone who would listen that he was only doing it for the money. Critics reviewed him as "the film's only point of interest."

***

The Hostage Tower (1980)

Peter Fonda launched the new decade of the 1980s by appearing with a star-studded cast in a relatively minor spy thriller, a made-for-TV film. His co-star was Douglas Fairbanks Jr., supported by Maud Adams, Billy Dee Williams, Keir Dullea, Britt Ekland, and Rachel Roberts.

The movie was directed by Claudio Guzman and based on a story by Alistair MacLean.

Born in Glasgow, MacLean became one of the best-selling authors of all time, selling some 150 different books, many of them thrillers and adventure stories.

Some of his "adapted by Hollywood" works reached the screen as movies that included *The Guns of Navarone* (1957) and *Ice Station Zebra* (1963). Readers devoured his "hot macho action," often wartime, commando sagas in exotic settings ranging from the Alaska oil fields to Greek islands.

The director, Claudio Guzmán, was from Chile. He set out to study architecture but switched to film and set design. In Hollywood, he met Desi Arnaz, who hired him to work for Desilu Productions as an art director.

Guzmán had married his second wife, actress Anna Maria Alberghetti, in 1964, divorcing her a decade later. Around the time of their divorce, they sold their home in Benedict Canyon to the then-lovers, Liza Minnelli and Desi Arnaz Jr.

Filming of *The Hostage Tower,* budgeted at $5 million, was shot in Paris beginning in October of 1979. Three weeks of it transpired at the Eiffel Tower. Originally, decision-makers at CBS-TV wanted to switch the venue to the Statue of Liberty in New York Harbor, but MacLean refused.

Fairbanks Jr., defined by some in the marketing department as "a vintage actor," had been away from the screen for a long absence before he returned to co-star with Peter Fonda.

Both of them were the sons of famous fathers. During the marriage (1920-1936) of Fairbanks' father to silent screen star Mary Pickford, they were, according to the Gallup Poll, "the most famous couple on earth."

Fairbanks Jr. was famously married (1929-1933) to Joan Crawford when she wasn't in the arms of Clark Gable. His most notable films were *The Prisoner of Zenda* (1937), *Gunga Din* (1939), and *The Corsican Brothers* (1941). He told Peter, "When I'm not making movies, I manufacture ball point pens."

Keir Dullea was best known for his performance in *2001: A Space Odyssey* (1968). He had also appeared in such notable movies as *David and Lisa* (1982). He was cast as the son of Lana Turner in the 1966 remake of *Madame X,* but he had more success with the Canadian film, *The Fox* (1967) with Sandy Dennis and Anne Heywood.

Dullea had co-starred with Laurence Olivier and Noël Coward in *Bunny Lake Is Missing* (1965). It was at this

Two views of **Douglas Fairbanks, Jr.:** *Left photo*, as he appeared, after a long absence from filmmaking, in *The Hostage Tower,* and *right photo*, with then-flapper **Joan Crawford** on their wedding day in 1929.

time that Coward made the famous quote, later repeated and amplified to embarrassing effect by Gore Vidal, "Keir Dullea, gone tomorrow."

An African American, Billy Dee Williams, who grew up in Harlem, made his Broadway debut at the age of seven. Over the course of six decades, he would appear in some seventy movies, including *The Lady Sings the Blues* (1972).

Right after working with Peter, Williams would star in his most widely known roles in the *Star Wars* franchise—first in *The Empire Strikes Back* (1980), and later in *The Return of the Jedi* (1983).

Both Maud Adams and Britt Ekland were seen together as Bond girls in *The Man with the Golden Gun.*

Adams had been Peter's leading lady in *Killer Force* (1974).

Stockholm-born Ekland was a model, singer, and actress. Her heyday on the screen was in the 1960s and 70s when she was widely publicized as a sex symbol in films such as *The Night They Raided Minsky's* (1968) and *Machine Gun McCain* (1969).

Her 1964 marriage to Peter Sellers was publicized around the world, although they divorced after only two years. She also attracted a lot of press attention from her affair with Rod Stewart. Ekland inspired his hit song, "Tonight's the Night (Gonna Be Alright)," which evolved into 1977's overall hit song.

The Welsh-born actress Rachel Roberts appeared emotionally disturbed throughout the movie. She is best remembered for *Saturday Night and Sunday Morning* (1960) and for *The Sporting Life* (1963), which brought her an Oscar nod for Best Supporting Actress.

Keir Dullea in 1962: His greatest role was in *2002: A Space Odyssey*.

Billy Dee Williams: A hero in Outer Space.

In 1962, she married Rex Harrison, but he divorced her in 1971. Later that year, he wed British socialite Elizabeth Rees-Williams, who had been Roberts' best friend.

She began to drink heavily. At a party thrown by actor Richard Harris, she attacked Robert Mitchum on all fours, playfully unzipping him and chomping on his penis until she was pulled off him by Harris.

She never got over her loss of Rex Harrison. In the year she worked with Peter, she was trying to get him back, but he had already moved on to his sixth and final wife, Mercia Tinker.

Rachel Roberts: Her greatest love was Rex Harrison.

On November 16, 1980, Roberts was found dead at her home in Los Angeles. She was only 53 years old. Lying amidst shards of broken glass, she had swallowed lye after drinking heavily all day.

The plot of *The Hostage Tower* was devised by Robert Carrington. It depicted criminal mastermind, "Mr. Smith" (Keir Dullea) being thwarted by Malcolm Philpott (Fairbanks Jr.), the head of an international peace organization.

Smith has gathered a team to capture the Eiffel Tower, using weapons expert Mike Graham (Fonda) who had worked for the CIA. Together, their gang captures both the Eiffel Tower and the mother of the President of the United States, played by Celia Johnson.

Philpott then enlists the help of spies to take down Mr. Smith, who is demanding a ransom of $30 million and threatening to blow up the Eiffel Tower.

The film attracted a wide audience for its telecast on May 13, 1980.

The critic for the *Los Angeles Times* defined *The Hostage Tower* as "a preposterous but rather charming piece of escapism."

Others described it as "absurd, inane trash, but charming trash."

Peter had a final comment. expressed in his own unique way, about revisiting Paris to shoot it. He wrote, "Paris hadn't changed much since Warren Oates and I rolled through in '71. Fart fart."

***

Split Image (1982)

Peter was demoted to third billing in his next picture, *Split Image*. In some releases, its title was changed to *Capture*. Directed by Ted Kotchoff, it starred Michael O'Keefe and Karen Allen. Supporting players included James Woods and Elizabeth Ashley.

[*Kotcheff had directed Jane Fonda and George Segal in* Fun with Dick and Jane *in 1977.*]

Fifteen years younger than Peter, O'Keefe, who hailed from Mount Vernon, New York, took the role of Danny Stetson, a clean-cut, All-American college student and gymnast with dreams of Olympic gold. He is lured into "Homeland," a youth-oriented religious commune, by a compellingly beautiful girl, Rebecca (Karen Allen).

At their cult-like gatherings, he is "programmed" by the charismatic leader, Neil Kirklander (Fonda) to believe that his new life has the true meaning that his previous one had lacked.

Anguished by their son's disappearance, Diana and Kevin Stetson (Elizabeth Ashley and Brian Dennehy), hire a modern-day bounty hunter, Charles Pratt (James Woods) to abduct Danny from the cult he joined, and to exorcise his brainwashed mind, despite dire warnings that the psychological "purge" could be traumatizing.

The oldest of seven children in an Irish American family, O'Keefe had attended the American Academy of Dramatic Arts and New York University. In films, he received a Best Supporting Actor nomination for his performance as Ben, the oldest son of a Marine aviator in *The Great Santini* (1979), starring Robert Duval. In his later career, he worked with such stars as Tommy Lee Jones, George Clooney, and Jack Nicholson (twice).

O'Keefe's highest-profile role was as Fred, the husband of Jackie Harris (Laurie Metcalf) in the hit ABC series, *Roseanne*, from 1993 to 1995.

From 1991 to 1999, he was famously married to the rock singer, Bonnie Raitt.

Karen Allen made her film debut in *National Lampoon's Animal House* (1978) before working with Peter and O'Keefe.

Michael O'Keefe being kidnapped in *Split Image* (1982)

She became known for her portrayal of Marion Ravenwood opposite Harrison Ford in *Raiders of the Lost Ark* (1981). Directed by Steven Spielberg, she was the love interest of Indiana Jones.

She was also a stage actress. In 1987, Paul Newman, as director, cast her as Laura in a remake of Tennessee Williams' *The Glass Menagerie* alongside his wife, Joanne Woodward.

James Wood was a very talented actor and producer, equally adept on the stage as in film and TV.

In 1978, he made his TV breakthrough role as the husband of Meryl Streep in the critically acclaimed four-part mini-series, *Holocaust*.

He later worked with some of the top directors in Hollywood: Sergio Leone, Oliver Stone, Martin Scorsese, and Clint Eastwood.

Twice, Woods was nominated for an Oscar—first for Best Actor in Oliver Stones' *Salvador* (1986) and again for Best Supporting Actor in Bob Reiner's *Ghosts of the Mississippi* (1996).

Split Image was a bitter disappointment at the box office and came under heavy fire from critics. Its production company, Polygram, had spent $8 million on production but took in only $250,000 at the box office. Its obvious and very embarrassing failure made it tough going for Peter in his ongoing search for roles later in the 1980s.

***

Peter Fonda would continue to star in movies in the 1980s and '90s, and even into the 21st Century, working until months before his death in August of 2019.

Sometimes, he worked with producers as diverse as those in Germany or Japan. His co-stars ranged from Oliver Reed to Tatum O'Neal, from Liv Ullman to his own daughter, Bridget Fonda, in *Bodies, Rest & Motion* (1993).

Many of his films lost money; others made a small profit. His luck changed when he starred in *Ulee's Gold* in 1997. He played a taciturn North Florida bookkeeper and Vietnam vet who tries so save his son and granddaughter from a life of drug abuse. For his efforts, he was nominated for a Best Actor Oscar.

After yet another absence, he returned to the screen as the bounty hunter Byron McElroy in *3:10 to Yuma* (2007), a remake of the Glenn Ford/Van Heflin classic from 1957. His co-stars were Russell Crowe and Christian Bale.

Peter Fonda's final portrayal was in the Vietnam war movie, *The Last Full Measure* (2019). Its director, Todd Robinson, arranged for him to see a screening of the film in its entirety right before the actor's death. "Peter cried through most of the screening. We both knew it was his farewell to the screen that had absorbed his life."

PETER FONDA
(1939-2019)

EPILOGUE

TWILIGHT TIME ON
GOLDEN POND

"Norman it's the loons. Listen...they're welcoming us back."
—Katharine Hepburn to Henry Fonda in *On Golden Pond*

"You know, I'm not religious, but I thank God every day for letting me live long enough to complete this picture."
—Henry Fonda to his daughter, Jane

***On Golden Pond* (1981) capped Henry Fonda's fabled film career,** winning him—at long last—his first and only Best Actor Oscar. In it, he played Norman Thayer Jr., an 80-something curmudgeon with a strained relationship with his daughter, Chelsea (Jane Fonda).

He and his loving wife, Ethel (Katharine Hepburn), arrive at their lakeside cottage on Golden Pond, the far reaches of Northern New England, to spend their last summer here. The loons on the lake seem to be welcoming them back.

In one of her greatest roles, Hepburn, also an Oscar winner, plays Ethel, his loyal wife of half a century. The screenplay was by Ernest Thompson based on his play on Broadway.

There were difficulties in getting the film launched. The first Broadway production of *On Golden Pond* opened in February of 1979 in Manhattan at the New Apollo Theatre. It ran for 126 performances. The cast starred Tom Aldredge and Frances Sternhagen in the lead roles. After a summer break, it came back, reopening at the Century Theater, a small playhouse in the basement of the Paramount Hotel, where it ran for an additional 256 performances.

In 1981, Thompson himself adapted his play for the big screen. For his effort, he won an Oscar for Best Adapted Screenplay. Although his drama was about aging, he was only 28 when he wrote it.

His second most popular play, *The West Side Waltz,* opened on Broadway in November of 1981, starring Katharine Hepburn.

In 1995, he would write a television version of *On Golden Pond,* starring Shirley MacLaine and Liza Minnelli as mother and daughter.

In 2001, Thompson would direct his own live tel-

Ecology experts assert that only about 400 loons remain alive and thriving today in New Hampshire. In *On Golden Pond*, they were configured as symbols of the family dynamic of **Henry Fonda,** his oft-estranged daughter, **Jane Fonda**, and their onscreen matriarch, as portrayed by the tough and relentlessly formidable **Katharine Hepburn,**

Throughout the context of the film, loons were presented as symbols of marital collaboration. They're known to forge and remain in long-time "family units" (in their case, an average of seven years) and to collaborate in the rearing and training of their offspring.

Thus, a dramatic context was crafted and created, the end result being a poignant and evocative family saga that pulled at the heartstrings of **Jane** Fonda, her biological father, **Henry,** and the *grande dame* of Vintage Hollywood, **Katharine Hepburn**, a force of nature who understood, at her age, better than anyone alive how to portray nostalgia, poignancy, and complicated rites of passage onscreen.

KATHARINE HEPBURN
1907-2003

Until they were "united and paired" under stressful circumstances by Hollywood deal-makers who included Jane Fonda, vintage screen diva **Katharine Hepburn** had never met **Henry Fonda**, despite the decades each had spent as players within the inner workings of the entertainment industry.

Belligerent and "impossibly prickly," the Connecticut Yankee (Hepburn), in tandem with the father-daughter team making news at the time, evoked the poignant dilemmas of aging gracefully and soldiering on in ways "the Greatest Generation" admired and understood.

Years after the completion and Oscar-approved success of *On Golden Pond*, movie fans still remember the sheer "emotional intelligence," delivered as intergenerational *tours de force* by the acting skills of all parties involved.

evision version of *On Golden Pond,* starring Julie Andres and Christopher Plummer.

The English actress, turned producer, Greer Garson, who had thrilled MGM audiences with her wartime movies, was deeply involved in history's first attempts to bring the play to the attention of the theater-going public. Although she succeeded at mounting a production at theaters that included the Kennedy Center in Washington, D.C., a Broadway production eluded her. At the Kennedy Center in Washington, where Garson's version was, indeed, presented in September of 2004, Hepburn was seen attending the play three times, perhaps as a "rehearsal" for a role she hoped would eventually become hers.

Whereas Henry had once performed in a very brief cameo directed by his son, Peter, for Peter's movie, *Wanda Nevada* (1979), he had never appeared in a film with Jane before. *[Jane and Henry had once been publicized as his co-stars in a film entitled The Journey of Simon McKeever, but the deal had fallen through.]*

Then Jane acquired the rights to *On Golden Pond*. She claimed, "I wanted it to be a tribute to my dying father. I feared it would be his last hurrah. I had another reason: I hoped it would bring us together in his final weeks."

Her friend, Brooke Hayward, was quoted as saying, "Henry still treats Jane like a gruff Army sergeant dealing with a new recruit."

In his defense, Henry responded, "I may not have been the world's greatest father, but I sure raised two talented kids."

The on-screen strained relationship of Henry with Jane paralleled their private lives.

For her producer, Jane turned once again to Bruce Gilbert, who combined the financial backing of both ITC Films and IPC Films. He had produced *The China Syndrome* (1979) and *9 to 5* (1980) with her.

On Golden Pond was the tender, rather heart-rending story of a married couple who had lived and loved each other for fifty years. With a bittersweet understanding that things are about to radically change, they have returned to their summer vacation retreat on a Golden Pond in Maine.

In the play, the family patriarch, Norman Thayer, is suffering from heart disease, as indeed, was Henry in real life. During the previous few years, Henry had been rushed to the hospital eight times. There, surgeons had removed a benign tumor the size of a grapefruit from Henry's diaphragm. His doctors had also discovered that he had prostate cancer, which had metastasized.

Five years before his casting in *On Golden Pond*, Henry had had a pacemaker installed. Because of his ailing health, no insurance company would issue a policy to ensure his collaboration in *On Golden Pond*.

Hepburn herself, at the age of 73, was also viewed by insurance actuaries as a risk. During the previous three years, her head-shaking palsy had worsened.

On Golden Pond came very close to never making it before the cameras. Possible financial backers derided the idea. One of them asked, "Who wants to sit through a movie starring two old codgers? Maybe a few people in their 80s might hobble to the box office with the aid of a cane."

Yet the project forged on.

In the pilot, Chelsea (Jane) is an attractive woman in her early 40s. She arrives at the Thayer family's summer retreat with the new man in her life, a dentist, Dr. Bill Ray.

Along with them is his son from a previous marriage, Billy Ray Jr. The couple are going to Europe for a month and want the little boy to stay with Norman and Ethel. Doug McKeon was cast as the youth, with Dr. Ray played by Dabney Coleman.

In a remarkable shift, Coleman, a native of Austin, Texas, had played the boss of Jane, Dolly Parton, and Lily Tomlin in *9 to 5* (1980).

Coleman had followed his involvement in *9 to 5* with a performance as the arrogant, sexist, soap opera director in *Tootsie* (1982) starring Dustin Hoffman in drag.

In *On Golden Pond*, **Jane Fonda** played a fully mature daughter who dreads late-in-life arguments with her remote on-screen father.

She admitted frequently to moments of emotional anguish associated with accurately portraying, on-screen, the "remembered but unresolved issues of her Hollywood childhood."

Thousands of "Jane" fans admired how gracefully she played it.

Jane flew to Manhattan to meet with Hepburn at her townhouse on East 49th Street. She arrived right on time to show how punctual she could be.

Hepburn herself opened the door. Her first words to Jane were, "I don't like you." She stabbed the air with her index finger only inches from Jane's face.

Finally, after pressing on, Jane found out what her problem was. It was about billing for the movie they were about to make.

Hepburn softened her attitude when she realized she was "no arrogant, upstart whippersnapper." Once Hepburn was assured that she would get top billing over Henry, and with Jane in the third slot in the supporting role, she became more relaxed and friendly.

Despite the fact that both Hepburn and Fonda had each arrived in Hollywood at the advent of the talkies, they had never worked together. In fact, they had never even met before.

On a sound stage in Hollywood, on the first day of filming, Hepburn walked right up to Henry and said, "It's about time. I guess we'll get better acquainted."

He responded with, "We'll be shipped off to New England to spend the summer together."

Right before shooting began, Hepburn feared she might have to drop out because she had injured her shoulder playing tennis.

Jane told her, "Then we'll just have to wait before shooting begins. You're vital to the project. In fact, we only got the money to finance our movie because of your name. Without Hepburn, no movie."

"Hearing that will speed my recovery," Hepburn assured her.

A crew searched New England before deciding to film on Squam Lake near Holdernes,, in central New Hampshire.

Hepburn eventually presented Henry with Spencer Tracy's "lucky hat," which he had worn in several films. Henry was honored with the gift and wore it in the picture.

During a fishing trip on the lake, Norman and Billy survive a boating accident in which Norman suffers a head injury. The accident makes their bond stronger. Before Chelsea returns, Norman and Billy are "good buddies."

During the course of the summer, Jane practiced for weeks, perfecting a back flip as part of an upcoming scene on the lake. Privately, she was determined to do it, despite the easy availability of a stunt extra who could have performed it beautifully.

In addition to his skills as a producer and actor, Mark Rydell, a New Yorker, was a much honored director. He had previously been Oscar-nominated for *The Fox* (1967); *The Rievers* (1969); *Cinderella Liberty* (1967), *The Rose* (1979); and *For the Boys* (1991). He would be nominated as Best Director for *On Golden Pond* too, but lost.

Rydell had worked with some of the top pros in the entertainment industry: Steve McQueen, John Wayne, Bette Midler, James Caan, Marsha Mason, Mel Gibson, Sissy Spacek, and James Franco.

Even so, he feared that directing the aging but notoriously strong-willed film veterans, Henry Fonda and Katharine Hepburn, "will be the challenge of my life."

Near the end of the film, Norman and Ethel bid a farewell to the loons and the lake, perhaps knowing that they will never return. Summer is coming to an end, as is Norman's life. The plot reveals that that summer alone, his character had suffered a mild heart attack, equivalent to those which Henry himself had suffered several times in real life.

At the end of the shoot, Henry told Jane, "You know, I'm not religious, but I thank God every day for letting me live long enough to complete this picture."

Critics tend to never agree on anything, including *Time Out London,* whose writers said, "Two of Hollywood's best-loved veterans deserve a far better swan song than this sticky confection."

Mad magazine satirized it as "*On Olden Pond."*

In the *Chicago Reader*, David Kehr wrote that *On Golden Pond* is "the cinematic equivalent of shrink-wrapping, in which all of the ideas, feelings, characters, and images are neatly separated and hermetically sealed to prevent spoilage, abrasion, or any contact with the natural world. Mark Rydell's bright, banal, visual style further sterilizes the issues. The film exudes complacency and self-congratulation: it is a very cowardly, craven piece of ersatz art."

These negative reviews, however, were mostly drowned out with high praise.

Vincent Canby in *The New York Times* stated, "Henry Fonda gives one of the great performances of his long, truly distinguished career. Here is film acting of the highest order. He is the best thing that has happened to Katharine Hepburn since Spencer Tracy and Humphrey Bogart. *On Golden Pond* is a mixed blessing, but it offers one performance of rare quality (Henry Fonda) and two others that are very good. That's not half bad."

Channel 4 summed up its review with: "Henry Fonda and Katharine Hepburn both shine in an impressively executed Hollywood drama. It has its mawkish moments, but there's a certain pleasure in that, and writer Thompson's analysis of old age is sensitive, thought-provoking, and credible."

Philip Strick in the *Monthly Film Bulletin* wrote: "Katharine Hepburn and Henry Fonda make a uniquely appealing couple. Their farewell concert may not be quite as elegant as one could have wished, but it does record, with a genuine pang, that in all probability we shall not see their likes again."

David Sterritt in the *Christian Science Monitor* said, "Henry Fonda delivers his irascible lines with a tender toughness that's a wonder to behold. He's so strong—not redeeming, but somehow avoiding the gushier aspects of the script.

TV Guide labeled it "a beautifully photographed movie filled with poignancy and (of course) superb acting. There could have been no finer curtain for Henry Fonda than this."

Variety found that "Fonda (*père*) and Hepburn are miraculous together, conveying heart-rendering intimations of mortality which are doubly powerful due to the stars' vulnerable status and, let's face it, general knowledge of Fonda's recent ailments."

Roger Ebert of the *Chicago Sun-Times* called *On Golden Pond* "a cinematic treasure. I felt I was watching something rare and valuable."

"Norman Thayer may be Henry Fonda's finest screen performance." So wrote Sheila Benson of the *Los Angeles Times*. "*On Golden Pond* is a distillation of everything Henry Fonda has mastered."

Rotten Tomatoes gave the film one of its highest ratings, saying, "Catch Katharine Hepburn and Henry Fonda, a wondrous duo in *On Golden Pond*, a wistful drama that movingly expresses the twilight years of a loving marriage."

In terms of box office, *On Golden Pond* was one of the most profitable movies Henry ever made, taking in $120 million at the box office. It became the second-highest grossing film of 1981, bowing only to *The Raiders of the Lost Ark* which took in a whopping $210 million.

***

In anticipation of the Oscar ceremony that year, Henry told his wife Shirlee, "As you know, I've never won an Oscar before. I don't expect to this time around, but in case I win, I want you to go before the world and accept the prize for me."

She turned him down, claiming, "I want to be by your side, watching it on television."

Then he called Jane and asked her if she'd accept the prize if it were offered. She was most willing to do so. Before a nation-wide audience watching from their homes, she held up the statuette awarded to Henry few moments before and said, "Oh, Dad, I'm so happy for you."

She then addressed the audience: "My father really didn't believe this was going to happen. His wife, Shirlee, whom he had wanted to accept, preferred to be with him at home. The role of acceptance then went to me, for which I am grateful. I'm sure my dad is highly grateful too."

Forever etched in Jane's mind was the happy look on her father's face as she presented him later with his Oscar. "For him, the clock was ticking. We both knew what time it was."

Jane had been nominated for a Best Supporting Actress Oscar but lost to Maureen Stapleton for her performance as the radical Emma Goldman in the movie *Reds*.

For Henry, this was his second Oscar nomination. In 1940, he'd been nominated for his role of Tom Joad in *The Grapes of Wrath*, but had lost to his best friend, James Stewart, for *The Philadelphia Story*, co-starring Cary Grant and Katharine Hepburn.

This time, Henry faced some stiff competition: Paul Newman, Warren Beatty, Burt Lancaster, and Dudley Moore.

On the morning that followed the Oscar ceremony, Jane phoned Hepburn to congratulate her: "You'll never catch up with me now," the aging actress said.

Jane knew what she was referencing: The previous night's Oscar was her fourth. Jane had only two.

***

At least on three afternoons a week, another old and graying man, in feeble condition and unsteady on his feet, arrived at the Fonda home to see his longtime best friend. It was James Stewart. Both actors were nearly deaf, so they shouted at each other.

On Stewart's last visit to Henry, he said, "Hank, you and I have become historical figures in the saga of the movies. How does it feel to be historical?"

"About the same way Marie Antoinette felt on her way to the guillotine."

Barbara Stanwick, Henry's former co-star, was a frequent visitor to Henry's bedside. "Oh, Hank," she told him. "If I'd only married you, a straight man—not Robert Taylor, a gay man."

***

Five months after the release of *On Golden Pond*, on August 12, 1982, Henry Fonda died. His wife, Shirlee, along with his son, Peter, were at his side. As soon as she heard the news, Jane rushed there, but arrived too late for a farewell.

"There was a bright star twinkling in the sky tonight, one I'd never seen before," Stewart told a reporter. "It was twinkling down at me. It sent a signal that I'd soon be joining Hank. We'll be two shining stars forever glowing."

In his last will and testament, Henry left his estate to his wife, Shirlee "and to my daughter Amy, because they are dependent on me for support. I have made no provision in my will for Jane or Peter, or for their families, solely because in my opinion, they are financially independent. My decision is not in any sense a measure of my deep affection for them."

The reference to Amy was aimed at the daughter he adopted during the course of his marriage to his third wife, Susan Blanchard, Amy Fonda Fishman.

In the years after his death, Henry Fonda has been held in even higher regard than he was during the course of his lifetime. Now recognized as one of the Hollywood greats of the classic golden age, he was named number six on the list of the greatest movie actors of all time by the American Film Institute.

THE END

HENRY FONDA

1905-1982

DARWIN PORTER

As a precocious nine-year-old, **Darwin Porter** *began meeting entertainers through his mother, Hazel, a charismatic Southern girl whose husband had died in World War II. Migrating from the Depression-ravaged valleys of western North Carolina to Miami Beach during its most ebullient heyday, Hazel became a personal assistant to the vaudeville comedienne* **Sophie Tucker***, the kind-hearted "Last of the Red Hot Mamas."*

Loosely supervised by his mother, Darwin was regularly dazzled by the likes of **Judy Garland, Dinah Shore, Frank Sinatra, Ronald Reagan** *(at the time near the end of his Hollywood gig), and* **Marilyn Monroe***. Each of them made it a point, whenever they were in Miami (either on or off the record), to visit and pay their respects to "Miss Sophie."*

At the University of Miami, Darwin edited the school newspaper, raising its revenues, through advertising and public events, to unheard-of new levels. He met and interviewed **Eleanor Roosevelt** *and later invited her, as part of a sponsored event he crafted, to spend a day ("Eleanor Roosevelt Day") at the university, and to his delight, she accepted. Years later, in Manhattan, during her work as a human rights activist, he escorted her, at her request, to many public functions.*

On another occasion, he invited **Lucille Ball and Desi Arnaz***, then at the pinnacle of their fame and popularity, to the University. On campus, after the photographers and fans departed, Lucille launched a bitter attack on her husband, accusing him of having had sex the previous night with two showgirls. Because of that and other upsets that unfolded that day, Darwin learned early in his life that Lucille Ball and Desi Arnaz were definitely not Ricky and Lucy Ricardo.*

After his graduation, Darwin, in a graceful transition from his work as editor of the University's newspaper and his sponsorship by **Wilson Hicks** *(Photo Editor and then Executive Editor of* Life *magazine) became a Bureau Chief of The Miami Herald (the youngest in that publication's history) assigned to its branch in Key West. At the time the island outpost was an avant-garde literary mecca and—thanks to the Cuban missile crisis—a flash point of the Cold War.*

Key West had been the site of **Harry S Truman***'s "Winter White House" and Truman returned a few months before his death for a final visit. He invited young Darwin for "early morning walks" where he used the young emissary of* The Miami Herald *to "set the record straight."*

Through Truman, Darwin was introduced and later joined the staff of **Senator George Smathers** *of Florida. Smathers' best friend was a young senator,* **John F. Kennedy.** *Through "Gorgeous George," as Smathers was known in the Senate, Darwin got to meet Jack and Jacqueline in Palm Beach. He later wrote two books about them—*The Kennedys, All the Gossip Unfit to Print, *and one of his all-time bestsellers,* Jacqueline Kennedy Onassis—A Life Beyond Her Wildest Dreams. *(A commemorative new edition was released in 2022 as* JKO: Her Tumultuous Life & Her Love Affairs).

Buttressed by his status as The Miami Herald's *Key West Bureau Chief, Darwin met, interviewed, and often befriended* **Tennessee Williams. Ernest Hemingway, Tallulah Bankhead, Gore Vidal, Truman Capote, Carson McCullers,** *and a gaggle of other internationally famous writers and entertainers:* **Cary Grant, Rock Hudson, Marlon Brando, Montgomery Clift, Susan Hayward, Warren Beatty, Christopher Isherwood, Anne Bancroft, Angela Lansbury,** *and* **William Inge.**

Eventually transferred to Manhattan, Darwin worked for a decade in television advertising with the producer and arts-industry socialite **Stanley Mills Haggart***. In addition to some speculative ventures associated with Marilyn Monroe, they also jointly produced TV commercials that included testimonials from* **Joan Crawford** *(then feverishly promoting Pepsi-Cola);* **Ronald Reagan** *(General Electric); and* **Debbie Reynolds** *(Singer sewing machines). Other personalities they promoted, each delivering televised sales pitches, included* **Louis Armstrong, Lena Horne, Rosalind Russell, William Holden,** *and* **Arlene Dahl,** *each of them hawking a commercial product.*

Beginning in the early 1960s, Darwin joined forces with the then-fledgling **Arthur Frommer** *organization, playing a key role in researching and writing more than 50 titles and defining the style and values that later emerged as the world's leading travel guidebooks,* **The Frommer Guides.** *Darwin's particular journalistic expertise on Europe, New Eng-*

YESTERDAY, WHEN HE WAS YOUNG

DARWIN PORTER
A social historian fascinated by biographies and the ironies of the American Experience.

land, California, and the Caribbean eventually propelled him into authorship of (depending on the era and whatever crises were brewing at the time), between 70 and 80% of their titles. Even during the research of his travel guides, he continued to interview show-biz celebrities, discussing their triumphs, feuds, and frustrations. At this point in their lives, many were retired and reclusive. Darwin either pursued them (sometimes though local tourist offices) or encountered them randomly as part of his extensive travels. **Ava Gardner, Lana Turner, Hedy Lamarr, Ingrid Bergman, Ethel Merman, Andy Warhol, Elizabeth Taylor, Marlene Dietrich, Bette Davis**, **Judy Garland,** and **Paul Newman** were particularly insightful.

Porter's biographies—at this writing, they number sixty-three—have won thirty first prize or "runner-up to first prize" awards at literary festivals in cities or regions which include New England, New York, Los Angeles, Hollywood, San Francisco, Florida, California, and Paris.

Darwin, also a magazine columnist, can be heard at regular intervals as a radio and podcast commentator, reviewing the ironies of celebrities, tabloid culture, politics, and scandal.

A resident of New York City, where he spent years within the social orbit of the Queen of Off-Broadway (the eccentric and very temperamental philanthropist, **Lucille Lortel**), Darwin is currently at work on a series of books with eyebrow-raising revelations about the dazzling personalities who kept the lights sparkling both On and Off Broadway in the 70s and 80s.

DANFORTH PRINCE

A graduate of Hamilton College and a native of Easton and Bethlehem, Pennsylvania, he's president and founder (in 1983) of the Porter and Prince Corporation, the entity that produced the original texts and updates for dozens of key titles of **THE FROMMER GUIDES**—travel "bibles" for millions of readers during the travel industry's go-go years in the 80s, 90s, and early millennium.

He also founded, in 1996, the Georgia Literary Association, precursor to what morphed, in 2004, into **Blood Moon Productions**, the corporate force behind dozens of political and Hollywood biographies. Its vaguely apocalyptic name was inspired by one of Darwin Porter's popular early novels, **Blood Moon**, a thriller about the false gods of power, wealth, and physical beauty. In 2011, Prince was named "Publisher of the Year" by a consortium of literary critics and marketers spearheaded by the J.M. Northern Media Group.

Prince has electronically documented his stewardship of Blood Moon in at least 50 videotaped documentaries, book trailers, public speeches, and TV or radio interviews. Most of these are available on **YouTube.com** and **Facebook** (keyword: "Danforth Prince"); on **Twitter** (#BloodyandLunar); or by clicking on **BloodMoonProductions.com**.

Hearkening back to his days as a travel writer, Prince is also an innkeeper, maintaining and managing a historic bed & breakfast, **Magnolia House (www.MagnoliaHouseSaintGeorge.com)**. Affiliated with AirBnb, and increasingly sought out by filmmakers as an evocative locale for moviemaking, it lies in St. George, at the northern tip of Staten Island, the "sometimes forgotten Outer Borough" of New York City. A landmarked building with a formidable historic and literary pedigree, it lies in a neighborhood closely linked to Henry James, Theodore Dreiser, the Vanderbilts, and key moments in America's colonial history.

Set in a terraced garden with views over New York Harbor and nearby Manhattan, it's been visited by show-biz stars who have included **Tennessee Williams, Gloria Swanson, Joan Blondell, Edward Albee, Jolie Gabor** (mother of Zsa Zsa, Eva, and Magda), soap opera queen **Ruth Warrick**, the Viennese chanteuse **Greta Keller**, and many of the luminaries of Broadway. It lies within a twelve-minute walk from the ferries regularly chugging their way across the harbor to Wall Street and Lower Manhattan.

Publicized as "a reasonably priced celebrity-centric bed & breakfast with links to the book trades," and the beneficiary of rave ("superhost") reviews (including "New York's most fascinating B&B") from hundreds of previous guests, **Magnolia House** is loaded with furniture and memorabilia collected from around the world during his decades as a travel journalist for the Frommer Guides. **Since the onset of the Covid Crisis, social distancing and regular decontamination regimens have been rigorously enforced.** For photographs, testimonials from previous guests, more information, and reservations, click on

www.AirBnb/H/Magnolia-House

In reference to historic Magnolia House's status as a "super-hosted" AirBnb, your handler, concierge, and problem-solver is **Danforth Prince**, who says, "It's more interesting than a cookie-cutter bandbox, and the resident ghosts and spirits will usually be glad to know you're here. Come with your friends and/or family (children and well-behaved dogs are welcome) for the night, and use it as your base for exploring nearby Manhattan."

Even with social distancing, Covid cautiousness, and a lot more 'scrub-a-dub-dubbing,' it's about healing, recuperation, razzmatazz, show-biz, Classic Hollywood, sightseeing, and conversation—if it interests you—in the greatest city in the world.

photo courtesy Frank Lugo

Magnolia House is a proud, architecturally protected landmark within the St. George, Staten Island Historical District.

It's depicted here in a photo snapped by New York City's Department of Finance as part of its 1940 Tax Census.

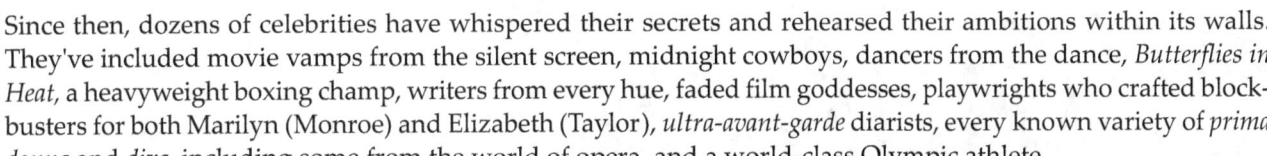

Some visitors liken Magnolia House to a *grande dame* with a centuries-old knack for nourishing high-functioning eccentrics. Many have lived or been entertained here since New York's State Senator Howard Bayne, a transplanted Southerner, moved in with his wife, the daughter of the Surgeon General of the Confederate States of America, in the aftermath of that bloodiest of wars on North American soil, the War Between the American States.

Since then, dozens of celebrities have whispered their secrets and rehearsed their ambitions within its walls. They've included movie vamps from the silent screen, midnight cowboys, dancers from the dance, *Butterflies in Heat*, a heavyweight boxing champ, writers from every hue, faded film goddesses, playwrights who crafted blockbusters for both Marilyn (Monroe) and Elizabeth (Taylor), *ultra-avant-garde* diarists, every known variety of *prima donna* and *diva*, including some from the world of opera, and a world-class Olympic athlete.

They've also included authors Darwin Porter and Danforth Prince, who spent decades here renovating it and producing, within its walls, a stream of FROMMER TRAVEL GUIDES and award-winning celebrity biographies.

HOW DO YOU DESCRIBE A BOOKISH, MAGNOLIA-SCENTED MONUMENT?

As depicted below, **Volumes One and Two** of Blood Moon's **Magnolia House Series** were conceived as affectionate testimonials to a great American monument, **MAGNOLIA HOUSE,** a nurturing and very tolerant historic home in NYC with a raft of stories to tell—some of them about how it adapted to America's radically changing tastes, times, circumstances, and values.

VOLUME ONE (ISBN 978-1-936003-65-5) focuses on its construction by a prominent lawyer during the booming (Northern) economy before the Civil War; its Gilded-Age purchase by the widow of the Surgeon General of the Confederate States of America; and later, its role as a branch office for dozens of travel titles during the heyday of THE FROMMER GUIDES, with detailed insights into the celebrity secrets their reporters (privately, until now) unveiled.

VOLUME TWO (ISBN 978-1-936003-73-0) is an *haute* celebrity romp through the half-century of Broadway, Hollywood, and publishing scandals swirling around Magnolia House's visitors and their frenemies…a "Reporters' Notebook" with everything that arts industry publicists didn't want fans and critics to know about at the time.

Each of these books is a celebration of the fast-disappearing
PRE-COVID AMERICAN CENTURY,
And both are available now through internet purveyors worldwide.

BLOOD MOON PRODUCTIONS at MAGNOLIA HOUSE:
Award-Winning Entertainment about
America's Legends, Icons, & Celebrities

LUCILLE BALL & DESI ARNAZ

BECAME THE MOST CELEBRATED DUO IN THE HISTORY OF TELEVISION

Half of America gathered every Monday night around the little black box in their living rooms to watch the antics of Lucy and Ricky Ricardo, a Cuban bandleader with his wacky, high-spirited wife.

The early struggles of Lucy and Desi were epic. As a girl, she at times was literally chained in her backyard in Jamestown, New York. As a teenager, she broke away and earned a reputation as "The Jamestown hussy," riding around with Johnny DeVita, a local hoodlum.

Born to wealth and privilege in Cuba, Desi, at the age of twelve, was escorted to the local bordello by his father to lose his virginity.

His family lost everything in the Cuban Revolution and fled to America. In Miami, Desi got a job cleaning out canary cages. He was eventually hired by bandleader Xavier Cugat because, "I beat hell out of those Afro-Cuban drums."

Meanwhile, in Manhattan, Lucy was struggling to break into show business, hustling "sugar daddies" and stage-door Johnnies who gave her money and gifts. Once, when desperate, she became a nude model. "A gal's gotta eat."

In the 1930s, she made it to Hollywood and worked making films for RKO. The executives used her as a gussied-up hooker to "entertain" out-of-town film exhibitors.

[Ultimately, she got her revenge. In one of the most ironic "fiscal revolutions" in show-biz history, she bought the studio.]

Drifting to Hollywood, Desi spotted Lucy on a sound stage "dressed like a two-dollar whore who had been badly beaten by her pimp." Their tempestuous marriage, characterized by long separations, staggered along for two decades.

By the early 1950s, the careers of both Desi and Lucy had headed south. There was a lot of resistance among TV executives who objected to his Cuban accent. But *I Love Lucy* was launched nevertheless and shot up in the ratings like a rocket, morphing into the most successful sitcom in TV history.

"With gold arriving in wheelbarrows" (Desi's words), they bought the four-block RKO Studios. Desilu Productions was launched, becoming the largest motion picture and television studio in the world.

In 1960, after their divorce, Lucy appraised her husband: "He is a Jekyll and Hyde type. He drinks, gambles, and chases the broads from thirteen to thirty, even Carrie Fisher. He's awash in broads, lots of booze, and that gay actor, Cesar Romero, is his devoted slave. Desi is destructive, but always building something. If it's big, he has to break it down."

"Love?" she asked. "I was always falling in love with the wrong man. Even Desi."

Desi, too, summed up his many years of marriage: "We were anything but Lucy and Ricky Ricardo on the tube. Those guys had nothing to do with us. Lucy and I dreamed of success, fame, and fortune. Guess what? ***It all led to hell.***"

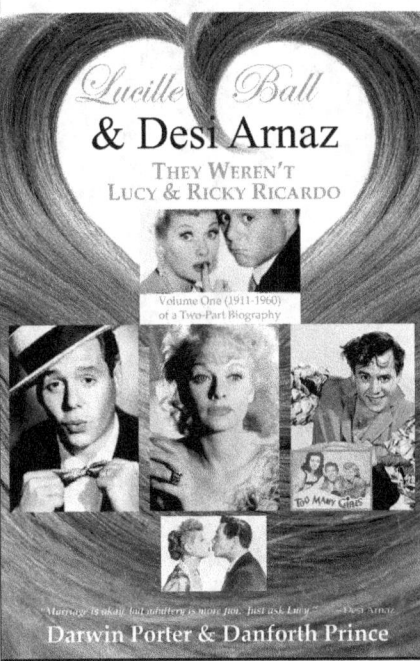

LUCILLE BALL & DESI ARNAZ

THEY WEREN'T LUCY AND RICKY RICARDO

VOLUME ONE (1911-1960)
OF A TWO-PART BIOGRAPHY

Darwin Porter and Danforth Prince
ISBN 978-1-936003-71-6
Softcover, 530 pages, with photos,
available everywhere now

THE SAD & TRAGIC ENDING OF LUCILLE BALL

VOLUME TWO (1961-1989)
OF A TWO-PART BIOGRAPHY

Darwin Porter and Danforth Prince
ISBN 978-1-936003-80-8
Softcover, 550 pages, with photos, available
everywhere now

Judy Garland & Liza Minnelli

Too Many Damn Rainbows

Judy and Liza were the greatest, most colorful, and most tragic mother-daughter saga in show biz history. They live, laugh, and weep again in the tear-soaked pages of this remarkable biography. Darwin Porter and Danforth Prince have compiled a compelling "post-modern" spin.

According to Liza, "My mother—hailed as the world's greatest entertainer—lived eighty lives during her short time with us."

Their memorable stories unfold through eyewitness accounts of the typhoons that engulfed them. They swing across glittery landscapes of euphoria and glory, detailing the betrayals and treachery which the duo encountered almost daily. There were depressions "as deep as the Mariana Trench," suicide attempts, and obsessive identifications on deep psychological levels with roles that include Judy's Vicky Lester in *A Star is Born* (1954) and Liza's Sally Bowles in *Cabaret* (1972).

Lesser known are the jealous actress-to-actress rivalries. Fueled by klieg lights and rivers of negative publicity, they sprouted like malevolent mushrooms on steroids.

As Judy faded into the 1960s, Liza roaringly emerged as a star in her own right. "I did it my way," Liza said. She survived the whirlwinds of her mother's drug addiction with a yen for choosing all the wrong men in patterns that weirdly evoked those of Judy herself.

For millions of fans, Judy will forever remain the cheerful adolescent (Dorothy) skipping along a yellow brick road toward the other side of the rainbow. Liza followed her down that hallucinogenic path, searching for the childhood, the security, and the love that eluded her.

Judy Garland, an icon whose memory is permanently etched into the American psyche, continues to thrive as a cult goddess. Revered by thousands of die-hard fans, she's the most poignant example of both the manic and depressive (some say "schizophrenic") sides of the Hollywood myth.

Deep in her 70s, Liza is still with us, too, nursing memories of her former acclaim and her first visit as a little girl to her parents at MGM, the "Dream Factory," during the Golden Age of Hollywood.

Judy Garland & Liza Minnelli: Too Many Damn Rainbows
Darwin Porter & Danforth Prince
Softcover, 6" x 9", with hundreds of photos.   ISBN 9781936003693
Available Everywhere Now

The Seductive Sapphic Exploits of
MERCEDES DE ACOSTA
Hollywood's Greatest Lover

IF YOU ASSUMED THAT THE GREATEST LOVERS ARE MEN, some of the most famous "cult goddesses" of the early- and mid-20th-Century might emphatically disagree.

At Magnolia House, in the final years of her life, the celebrated, notorious, and once-fabled Spanish beauty, **MERCEDES DE ACOSTA** (1892-1968) was a frequent visitor. To Darwin Porter, she confessed and recited fabulously indiscreet stories about her romantic same-sex exploits among the theatrical and cinematic elite of New York, London, Paris, and Hollywood.

It reveals "Sapphic Standards" from the heyday of Silent Film and the early Talkies that no other book—even her own (Here Lies the Heart, *published in 1960)— ever dared to make public.*

Mercedes de Acosta's love affairs were with women, each a figurehead in art, the theater, and the filmmaking and literary scenes. They included Greta Garbo, Marlene Dietrich, Nazimova, Gertrude Stein, Alice B. Toklas, Eva Le Gallienne, Tallulah Bankhead, Jeanne Eagels, Katharine Cornell, Eleanora Duse, Isadora Duncan, and both of Valentino's wives. This is probably the best portrait of *avant-garde* Broadway and early 20th-century filmmaking ever published.

Read all about it in the most recent installment of Blood Moon's MAGNOLIA HOUSE SERIES

The Seductive Sapphic Exploits of
MERCEDES DE ACOSTA
Hollywood's Greatest Lover

Darwin Porter and Danforth Prince ISBN 978-1-936003-75-4.
A pithy, photo-packed softcover with 474 pages and many dozens of photos
available now from Ingram's Lightning Source and Amazon.com

LOVE TRIANGLE
Ronald Reagan, Jane Wyman, & Nancy Davis

HOW MUCH DO YOU REALLY KNOW ABOUT THE REAGANS?

THIS BOOK TELLS EVERYTHING ABOUT THE SHOW-BIZ SCANDALS THEY DESPERATELY WANTED TO FORGET.

UNIQUE IN THE HISTORY OF PUBLISHING, THIS SCANDALOUS TRIPLE BIOGRAPHY focuses on the Hollywood indiscretions of former U.S. president Ronald Reagan and his two wives. A proud and Presidential addition to Blood Moon's Babylon series, it digs deep into what these three young and attractive movie stars were doing decades before two of them took over the Free World.

As reviewed by Diane Donovan, Senior Reviewer at the California Bookwatch section of the Midwest Book Review: "Love Triangle: Ronald Reagan, Jane Wyman & Nancy Davis may find its way onto many a Republican Reagan fan's reading shelf; but those who expect another Reagan celebration will be surprised: this is lurid Hollywood exposé writing at its best, and outlines the truths surrounding one of the most provocative industry scandals in the world.

"There are already so many biographies of the Reagans on the market that one might expect similar mile-markers from this: be prepared for shock and awe; because Love Triangle doesn't take your ordinary approach to biography and describes a love triangle that eventually bumped a major Hollywood movie star from the possibility of being First Lady and replaced her with a lesser-known Grade B actress (Nancy Davis).

"From politics and betrayal to romance, infidelity, and sordid affairs, Love Triangle is a steamy, eye-opening story that blows the lid off of the Reagan illusion to raise eyebrows on both sides of the big screen.

"Black and white photos liberally pepper an account of the careers of all three and the lasting shock of their stormy relationships in a delightful pursuit especially recommended for any who relish Hollywood gossip."

In 2015, LOVE TRIANGLE, Blood Moon Productions' overview of the early dramas associated with Ronald Reagan's scandal-soaked career in Hollywood, was designated by the Awards Committee of the HOLLYWOOD BOOK FESTIVAL as Runner-Up to Best Biography of the Year.

LOVE TRIANGLE: Ronald Reagan, Jane Wyman, & Nancy Davis
Darwin Porter & Danforth Prince
Softcover, 6" x 9", with hundreds of photos.   ISBN 978-1-936003-41-9

THIS BOOK ILLUSTRATES WHY *GENTLEMEN PREFER BLONDES*, AND WHY MARILYN MONROE WAS TOO DANGEROUS TO BE ALLOWED TO GO ON LIVING.

Less than an hour after the discovery of Marilyn Monroe's corpse in Brentwood, a flood of theories, tainted evidence, and conflicting testimonies began pouring out into the public landscape.

Filled with rage, hysteria, and depression, "and fed up with Jack's lies, Bobby's lies," Marilyn sought revenge and mass vindication. Her revelations at an imminent press conference could have toppled political dynasties and destroyed criminal empires. Marilyn had to be stopped…

Into this steamy cauldron of deceit, Marilyn herself emerges as a most unreliable witness during the weeks leading up to her murder. Her own deceptions, vanities, and self-delusion poured toxic accelerants on an already raging fire.

"This is the best book about Marilyn Monroe ever published."
—**David Hartnell**, Recipient, in 2011, of New Zealand's Order of Merit (MNZM) for services to the entertainment industry, as defined by Her Majesty, Queen Elizabeth II.

Winner of literary awards from the New York, Hollywood, and San Francisco Book Festivals

"Darwin Porter is fearless, honest and a great read. He minces no words. If the truth makes you wince and honesty offends your sensibility, stay away. It's been said that he deals in muck because he can't libel the dead. Well, it's about time someone started telling the truth about the dead and being honest about just what happened to get us in the mess in which we're in. If libel is lying, then Porter is so completely innocent as to deserve an award. In all of his works he speaks only to the truth, and although he is a hard teacher and task master, he's one we ignore at our peril. To quote Gore Vidal, power is not a toy we give to someone for being good. If we all don't begin to investigate where power and money really are in the here and now, we deserve what we get. Yes, Porter names names. The reader will come away from the book knowing just who killed Monroe. Porter rather brilliantly points to a number of motives, but leaves it to the reader to surmise exactly what happened at the rainbow's end, just why Marilyn was killed. And, of course, why we should be careful of getting exactly what we want. It's a very long tumble from the top."

—ALAN PETRUCELLI, Examiner.com, May 13, 2012

MARILYN: DON'T EVEN DREAM ABOUT TOMORROW

SEX, LIES, MURDER, AND THE GREAT COVER-UP, BY DARWIN PORTER
ISBN 978-1-936003-79-2   A Revised Edition of Darwin Porter's Investigative Classic from 2012
MARILYN AT RAINBOW'S END

CARRIE FISHER & DEBBIE REYNOLDS
PRINCESS LEIA & UNSINKABLE TAMMY IN HELL

It's history's first comprehensive, unauthorized overview of one of the greatest mother-daughter acts in showbiz history, Debbie Reynolds ("hard as nails and with more balls than any five guys I've ever known") and her talented, often traumatized daughter, Carrie Fisher ("one of the smartest, hippest chicks in Hollywood"). Evolving for decades under the unrelenting glare of public scrutiny, each became a world-class symbol of the social and cinematic tastes that prevailed during their heydays as celebrity icons in Hollywood.

It's a scandalous saga of the ferociously loyal relationship of the "boop-boop-a-doop" girl with her intergalactic STAR WARS daughter, and their iron-willed, "true grit" battles to out-race changing tastes in Hollywood.

Loaded with revelations about "who was doing what to whom" during the final gasps of Golden Age Hollywood, it's an All-American story about the price of glamour, career-related pain, family anguish, romantic betrayals, lingering guilt, and the volcanic shifts that affected a scrappy, mother-daughter team—and everyone else who ever loved the movies.

"Feeling misunderstood by the younger (female) members of your gene pool? This is the Hollywood exposé every grandmother should give to her granddaughter, a roadmap like Debbie Reynolds might have offered to Billie Lourd."
—Marnie O'Toole

"Hold onto your hats, the "bad boys" of Blood Moon Productions are back. This time, they have an exhaustively researched and highly readable account of the greatest mother-daughter act in the history of show business: Debbie Reynolds and Carrie (Princess Leia) Fisher. If celebrity gossip and inside dirt is your secret desire, check it out. This is a fabulous book that we heartily recommend. It will not disappoint. We rate it worthy of four stars."
—MAJ Glenn MacDonald, U.S. Army Reserve (Retired), © MilitaryCorruption.com

"How is a 1950s-era movie star, (TAMMY) supposed to cope with her postmodern, substance-abusing daughter (PRINCESS LEIA), the rebellious, high-octane byproduct of Rock 'n Roll, Free Love, and postwar Hollywood's most scandal-soaked marriage? Read about it here, in Blood Moon's unauthorized double exposé about how Hollywood's toughest (and savviest) mother-daughter team maneuvered their way through shifting definitions of fame, reconciliation, and fortune."
—Donna McSorley

Winner of the coveted "Best Biography" Award from the 2018
New York Book Festival

CARRIE FISHER & DEBBIE REYNOLDS,
UNSINKABLE TAMMY & PRINCESS LEIA IN HELL
Darwin Porter & Danforth Prince

630 pages Softcover with photos. Now online and in bookstores everywhere
ISBN 978-1-936003-57-0

This is What Happens When A Demented Billionaire Hits Hollywood

HOWARD HUGHES

HELL'S ANGEL

DARWIN PORTER

From his reckless pursuit of love as a rich teenager to his final days as a demented fossil, Howard Hughes tasted the best and worst of the century he occupied. Along the way, he changed the worlds of aviation and entertainment forever.

This biography reveals inside details about his destructive and usually scandalous associations with other Hollywood players.

"The Aviator flew both ways. Porter's biography presents new allegations about Hughes' shady dealings with some of the biggest names of the 20th century"
—*New York Daily News*

"Darwin Porter's access to film industry insiders and other Hughes confidants supplied him with the resources he needed to create a portrait of Hughes that both corroborates what other Hughes biographies have divulged, and go them one better."
—*Foreword Magazine*

"Thanks to this bio of Howard Hughes, we'll never be able to look at the old pinups in quite the same way again."
—*The Times* (London)

Winner of a respected literary award from the Los Angeles Book Festival, this book gives an insider's perspective about what money can buy
—and what it can't.

814 pages, with photos. **Available everywhere now.**
ISBN 978-1-936003-13-6

LANA TURNER

THE SWEATER GIRL, CELLULOID VENUS, SEX NYMPH TO THE G.I.s WHO WON WORLD WAR II, AND HOLLYWOOD'S OTHER MOST NOTORIOUS BLONDE

BEAUTIFUL AND BAD, HER FULL STORY HAS NEVER BEEN TOLD. UNTIL NOW!

Lana Turner was the most scandalous, most copied, and most gossiped-about actress in Hollywood. When her abusive Mafia lover was murdered in her house, every newspaper in the Free World described the murky dramas with something approaching hysteria.

Blood Moon's salacious but empathetic new biography exposes the public and private dramas of the girl who changed the American definition of what it REALLY means to be a blonde.

Here's how CALIFORNIA BOOKWATCH and THE MIDWEST BOOK REVIEW described the mega-celebrity as revealed in this book:

"Lana Turner: Hearts and Diamonds Take All belongs on the shelves of any collection strong in movie star biographies in general and Hollywood evolution in particular, and represents no lightweight production, appearing on the 20th anniversary of Lana Turner's death to provide a weighty survey packed with new information about her life.

"One would think that just about everything to be known about The Sweater Girl would have already appeared in print, but it should be noted that Lana Turner: Hearts and Diamonds Take All offers many new revelations not just about Turner, but about the movie industry in the aftermath of World War II.

"From Lana's introduction of a new brand of covert sexuality in women's movies to her scandalous romances among the stars, her extreme promiscuity, her search for love, and her notorious flings - even her involvement in murder - are all probed in a revealing account of glamour and movie industry relationships that bring Turner and her times to life.

"Some of the greatest scandals in Hollywood history are intricately detailed on these pages, making this much more than another survey of her life and times, and a 'must have' pick for any collection strong in Hollywood history in general, gossip and scandals and the real stories behind them, and Lana Turner's tumultuous career, in particular."

Lana Turner, Hearts & Diamonds Take All
Winner of the coveted "Best Biography" Award from the San Francisco Book Festival

By Darwin Porter and Danforth Prince
Softcover, 622 pages, with photos. ISBN 978-1-936003-53-2
Available everywhere, online and in bookstores.

SCARLETT O'HARA,

DESPERATELY IN LOVE WITH HEATHCLIFF,

TOGETHER ON THE ROAD TO HELL

Here, for the first time, is a biography that raises the curtain on the secret lives of **Lord Laurence Olivier**, often cited as the finest actor in the history of England, and **Vivien Leigh**, who immortalized herself with her Oscar-winning portrayals of Scarlett O'Hara in *Gone With the Wind*, and as Blanche DuBois in Tennessee Williams' *A Streetcar Named Desire.*

Dashing and "impossibly handsome," Laurence Olivier was pursued by the most dazzling luminaries, male and female, of the movie and theater worlds.

Lord Olivier's beautiful and brilliant but emotionally disturbed wife (Viv to her lovers) led a tumultuous off-the-record life whose paramours ranged from the A-list celebrities to men she selected randomly off the street. But none of the brilliant roles depicted by Lord and Lady Olivier, on stage or on screen, ever matched the power and drama of personal dramas which wavered between Wagnerian opera and Greek tragedy. Damn You, Scarlett O'Hara is the definitive and most revelatory portrait ever published of the most talented and tormented actor and actress of the 20th century.

Darwin Porter is the principal author of this seminal work.

"The folks over at TMZ would have had a field day tracking Laurence Olivier and Vivien Leigh with flip cameras in hand. Damn You, Scarlett O'Hara can be a dazzling read, the prose unmannered and instantly digestible. The authors' ability to pile scandal atop scandal, seduction after seduction, can be impossible to resist."

—THE WASHINGTON TIMES

DAMN YOU, SCARLETT O'HARA
THE PRIVATE LIFES OF LAURENCE OLIVIER AND VIVIEN LEIGH

Darwin Porter and Roy Moseley

Winner of four distinguished literary awards, this is the best biography of Vivien Leigh and Laurence Olivier ever published, with hundreds of insights into the London Theatre, the role of the Oliviers in the politics of World War II, and the passion, fury, and frustration of their lives together as actors in the West End, on Broadway, and in Hollywood.

ISBN 978-1-936003-15-0   Hardcover, 708 pages, with about a hundred photos.

DONALD TRUMP
WAS THE MAN WHO WOULD BE KING

This is the most famous book about our incendiary ex-President you've probably never heard of.

Winner of three respected literary awards, and released three months before the Presidential elections of 2016, it's an entertainingly packaged, artfully salacious bombshell, a scathingly historic overview of America during its 2016 election cycle, a portrait unlike anything ever published on CANDIDATE DONALD and the climate in which he thrived and massacred his political rivals.

Its volcanic, much-suppressed release during the heat and venom of the 2016 Presidential campaign has already been heralded by the Midwestern Book Review, California Book Watch, the Seattle Gay News, the staunchly right-wing WILS-AM radio, and also by the editors at the most popular Seniors' magazine in Florida, BOOMER TIMES, which designated it as one of their BOOKS OF THE MONTH.

TRUMPOCALYPSE: *"Donald Trump: The Man Who Would Be King* is recommended reading for all sides, no matter what political stance is being adopted: Republican, Democrat, or other.

"One of its driving forces is its ability to synthesize an unbelievable amount of information into a format and presentation which blends lively irony with outrageous observations, entertaining even as it presents eye-opening information in a format accessible to all.

"Politics dovetail with American obsessions and fascinations with trends, figureheads, drama, and sizzling news stories, but blend well with the observations of sociologists, psychologists, politicians, and others in a wide range of fields who lend their expertise and insights to create a much broader review of the Trump phenomena than a more casual book could provide.

"The result is a 'must read' for any American interested in issues of race, freedom, equality, and justice—and for any non-American who wonders just what is going on behind the scenes in this country's latest election debacle."

Diane Donovan, Senior Editor, California Bookwatch

DONALD TRUMP, THE MAN WHO WOULD BE KING
WINNER OF "BEST BIOGRAPHY" AWARDS FROM BOOK FESTIVALS IN NEW YORK, CALIFORNIA, AND FLORIDA
by Darwin Porter and Danforth Prince
Softcover, with 822 pages and hundreds of photos. ISBN 978-1-936003-51-8.

Available now from Ingram, Amazon.com and other purveyors, worldwide.

LINDA LOVELACE

INSIDE LINDA LOVELACE'S DEEP THROAT
Degradation, Porno Chic, and the Rise of Feminism

The most comprehensive biography ever written of an adult entertainment star, her tormented relationship with Hollywood's underbelly, and how she changed forever the world's perceptions about censorship, sexual behavior patterns, and pornography.

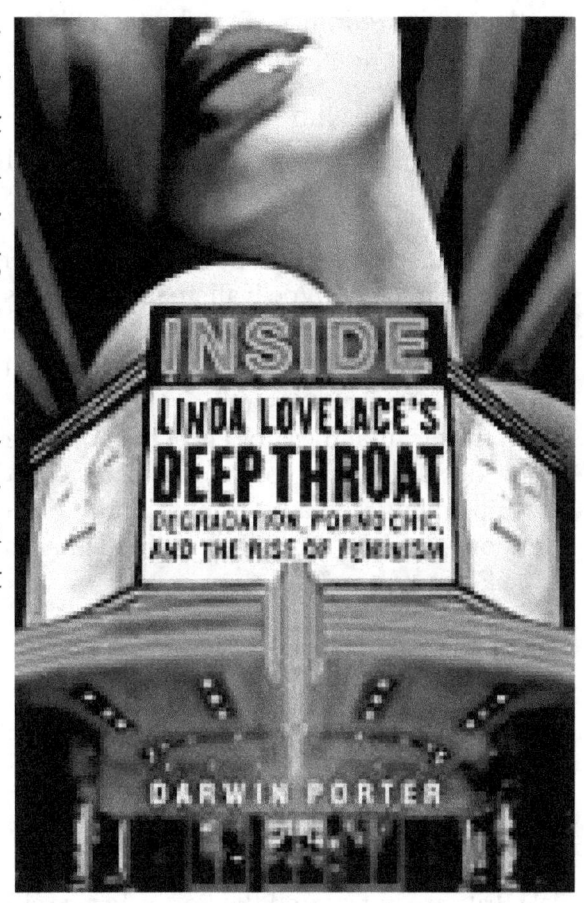

Darwin Porter, author of more than thirty critically acclaimed celebrity exposés of behind-the-scenes intrigue in the entertainment industry, was deeply involved in the Linda Lovelace saga as it unfolded in the 70s, interviewing many of the players, and raising money for the legal defense of the film's co-star, Harry Reems.

In this book, emphasizing her role as an unlikely celebrity interacting with other celebrities, he brings inside information and a never-before-published revelation to almost every page.

"This book drew me in..How could it not?"
Coco Papy, Bookslut.

The Beach Book Festival's Grand Prize Winner for Best Summer Reading of 2013"

Runner-Up to "Best Biography of 2013" The Los Angeles Book Festival

---

Another hot and insightful commentary about major and sometimes violently controversial conflicts of the American Century, from Blood Moon Productions.

Inside Linda Lovelace's Deep Throat, by Darwin Porter
Softcover, 640 pages, 6"x9" with photos.
ISBN 978-1-936003-33-4

PINK TRIANGLE

The Feuds and Private Lives of
TENNESSEE WILLIAMS, GORE VIDAL, TRUMAN CAPOTE,
& Famous Members of their Entourages

Darwin Porter & Danforth Prince

This book, the only one of its kind, reveals the backlot intrigues associated with the literary and script-writing *enfants terribles* of America's entertainment community during the mid-20th century.

It exposes their bitchfests, their slugfests, and their relationships with the glitterati—Marilyn Monroe, Brando, the Oliviers, the Paleys, U.S. Presidents, a gaggle of other movie stars, millionaires, and international débauchés.

This is for anyone who's interested in the formerly concealed scandals of Hollywood and Broadway, and the values and pretentions of both the literary community and the entertainment industry.

"A banquet... If PINK TRIANGLE had not been written for us, we would have had to research and type it all up for ourselves...Pink Triangle is nearly seven hundred pages of the most entertaining histrionics ever sliced, spiced, heated, and serviced up to the reading public. Everything that Blood Moon has done before pales in comparison.
Given the fact that the subjects of the book themselves were nearly delusional on the subject of themselves (to say nothing of each other) it is hard to find fault. Add to this the intertwined jungle that was the relationship among Williams, Capote, and Vidal, of the times they vied for things they loved most—especially attention—and the times they enthralled each other and the world, [Pink Triangle is] the perfect antidote to the Polar Vortex."

—Vinton McCabe in the NY JOURNAL OF BOOKS

"Full disclosure: I have been a friend and follower of Blood Moon Productions' tomes for years, and always marveled at the amount of information in their books—it's staggering. The index alone to Pink Triangle runs to 21 pages—and the scale of names in it runs like a Who's Who of American social, cultural and political life through much of the 20th century."

—Perry Brass in THE HUFFINGTON POST

"We Brits are not spared the Porter/Prince silken lash either. PINK TRIANGLE's research is, quite frankly, breathtaking. PINK TRIANGLE will fascinate you for many weeks to come. Once you have made the initial titillating dip, the day will seem dull without it."

—Jeffery Tayor in THE SUNDAY EXPRESS (UK)

PINK TRIANGLE—The Feuds and Private Lives of Tennessee Williams, Gore Vidal, Truman Capote, and Famous Members of their Entourages

Darwin Porter & Danforth Prince
Softcover, 700 pages, with photos   ISBN 978-1-936003-37-2   Also Available for E-Readers

THOSE GLAMOROUS GABORS
Bombshells from Budapest

Zsa Zsa, Eva, and Magda Gabor transferred their glittery dreams and gold-digging ambitions from the twilight of the Austro-Hungarian Empire to Hollywood. There, more effectively than any army, these Bombshells from Budapest broke hearts, amassed fortunes, lovers, and A-list husbands, and amused millions of voyeurs through the medium of television, movies, and the social registers. In this astonishing "triple-play" biography, designated "Best Biography of the Year" by the Hollywood Book Festival, Blood Moon lifts the "mink-and-diamond" curtain on this amazing trio of blood-related sisters, whose complicated intrigues have never been fully explored before.

***

"You will never be Ga-bored...this book gives new meaning to the term compelling. Be warned, Those Glamorous Gabors is both an epic and a pip. Not since Gone With the Wind have so many characters on the printed page been forced to run for their lives for one reason or another. And Scarlett making a dress out of the curtains is nothing compared to what a Gabor will do when she needs to scrap together an outfit for a movie premiere or late-night outing.

"For those not up to speed, Jolie Tilleman came from a family of jewelers and therefore came by her love for the shiny stones honestly, perhaps genetically. She married Vilmos Gabor somewhere around World War 1 (exact dates, especially birth dates, are always somewhat vague in order to establish plausible deniability later on) and they were soon blessed with three daughters: Magda, the oldest, whose hair, sadly, was naturally brown, although it would turn quite red in America; Zsa Zsa (born 'Sari') a natural blond who at a very young age exhibited the desire for fame with none of the talents usually associated with achievement, excepting beauty and a natural wit; and Eva, the youngest and blondest of the girls, who after seeing Grace Moore perform at the National Theater, decided that she wanted to be an actress and that she would one day move to Hollywood to become a star.

"Given that the Gabor family at that time lived in Budapest, Hungary, at the period of time between the World Wars, that Hollywood dream seemed a distant one indeed. The story—the riches to rags to riches to rags to riches again myth of survival against all odds as the four women, because of their Jewish heritage, flee Europe with only the minks on their backs and what jewels they could smuggle along with them in their decolletage, only to have to battle afresh for their places in the vicious Hollywood pecking order—gives new meaning to the term 'compelling.' The reader, as if he were witnessing a particularly gore-drenched traffic accident, is incapable of looking away."

—*New York Review of Books*

THOSE GLAMOROUS GABORS
Bombshells from Budapest,
by Darwin Porter & Danforth Prince
Softcover, 730 pages, with hundreds of photos
ISBN 978-1-936003-35-8

ROCK HUDSON

> In the dying days of Hollywood's Golden Age, Rock Hudson was the most celebrated phallic symbol and lust object in America.
>
> This book describes his rise and fall, and the Industry that created him.

Rock Hudson charmed every casting director in Hollywood (and movie-goers throughout America) as the megastar they most wanted to share PILLOW TALK with. This book describes his rise and fall, and how he handled himself as a closeted but promiscuous bisexual during an age when EVERYBODY tried to throw him onto a casting couch.

Based on dozens of face-to-face interviews with the actor's friends, co-conspirators, and enemies, and researched over a period of a half century, this biography reveals the shame, agonies, and irony of Rock Hudson's complete, never-before-told story.

In 2017, the year of its release, it was designated as winner ("BEST BIOGRAPHY") at two of the Golden State's most prestigious literary competitions, the Northern California and the Southern California Book Festivals.

It was also favorably reviewed by the *Midwestern Book Review, California Book Watch, KNEWS RADIO, the New York Journal of Books,* and the editors at the most popular Seniors' magazine in Florida, *BOOMER TIMES.*

ROCK HUDSON EROTIC FIRE
By Darwin Porter & Danforth Prince
Softcover, 624 pages, with dozens of photos, 6" x 9"
ISBN 978-1-936003-55-6

Available everywhere now

BILL & HILLARY
So This Is That Thing Called Love

CONFUSED ABOUT HOW TO INTERPRET THEIR RAUCOUS PASTS?
THIS UNCENSORED TALE ABOUT A LOVE AFFAIR THAT CHANGED THE COURSE OF POLITICS AND THE PLANET IS OF COMPELLING INTEREST TO ANYONE INVOLVED IN THE SLUGFESTS AND INCENDIARY WARS OF THE CLINTONS.

"This is both a biographical coverage of the Clintons and a political exposé; a detailed, weighty exploration that traces the couple's social and political evolution, from how each entered the political arena to their White House years under Bill Clinton's presidency.

"Containing gossip, scandal, and biographical sketches, it delves deeply into the news and politics of its times, presenting enough historical background to fully explore the underlying controversies affecting the Clinton family and their choices.

"Sidebars of information and black and white photos liberally peppered throughout the account offer visual reinforcement to the exploration, lending it the feel and tone of both a gossip column and political piece - something that probes not just Clinton interactions but the D.C. political milieu as a whole.

"The result may appear weighty, sporting over five hundred pages, but is an absorbing, top recommendation for readers of both biographical and political pieces who will thoroughly enjoy this spirited, lively, and thought-provoking analysis."

—THE MIDWEST BOOK REVIEW

***

Shortly after its release in December of 2015, this book received a literary award (Runner-up to Best Biography of the Year) from the New England Book Festival. As stated by a spokesperson for the Awards, "The New England Book Festival is an annual competition honoring excellence in books, with particular focus on projects that deserve closer attention from the academic community. Congratulations to Blood Moon and its authors, especially Darwin Porter, for his highly entertaining analysis of Clinton's double-barreled presidential regime, and the sometimes hysterical overreaction of their enemies."

BILL & HILLARY—SO THIS IS THAT THING CALLED LOVE
Softcover, with photos. ISBN 978-1-936003-47-1

BURT REYNOLDS
PUT THE PEDAL TO THE METAL
How a Nude Centerfold Sex Symbol Seduced Hollywood

In the 1970s and '80s, Burt Reynolds represented a new breed of movie star.

Charming and relentlessly macho, he was a good old Southern boy who made hearts throb and audiences laugh. He was Burt Reynolds, a football hero and a guy you might have shared some jokes with in a redneck bar. After an impressive but tormented career, rivers of negative publicity, a self-admitted history of bad choices, and a spectacular fall from Hollywood grace, he died in Jupiter, Florida, at the age of 82 in September of 2018.

For five years, both in terms of earnings and popularity, he was the number one box office star in the world. *Smokey and the Bandit* (1977) became the biggest-grossing car-chase film of all time. As he put it, perhaps as a means of bolstering his image, "I like nothing better than making love to some of the most beautiful women in the world." Perhaps he was referring to his romantic and sexual involvements with dozens of celebrities from New Hollywood. More unusual dalliances occurred with Marilyn Monroe, whom he once picked up on his way to the Actors Studio in New York City. Love with another VIP came in the form of that "Sweetheart of the G.I.s," Dinah Shore, sparking chatter. "I appreciate older women," he once said in a moment of self-revelation. According to Sally Field, "Burt still lives in my heart." But then she expressed relief that, because of his recent death, he never read what she'd said about him in her memoir.

Men liked him too: He played poker with Frank Sinatra; shared boozy nights with John Wayne; intercepted a "pass" from closeted Spencer Tracy; talked "penis size" with Mark Wahlberg; went "wench-hunting" with Johnny Carson; and threatened to kill Marlon Brando, to whom his appearance was often compared. He also hung out with Bette Davis. ("I always had a thing for her.")

His least happy (some said "most poisonous") marriage—to Loni Anderson—was rife with dramas played out more in the tabloids than in the boudoir. According to Reynolds, "She's vain, she's a rotten mother, she sleeps around, and she spent all my money."

This biography—the first comprehensive overview of the "redneck icon" ever published—reveals the joys and sorrows of a movie star who thrived in, but who was then almost buried by the pressures and insecurities of the New Hollywood. A tribute to "truck stop" America, it's about the accelerated life of a courageous spirit who "Put His Pedal to the Metal" with humor, high jinx, and pizzazz. He predicted his own death: "Soon, I'll be racing a hotrod in Valhalla in my cowboy hat and a pair of aviators." On his tombstone, he wanted it writ: "He was not the best actor in the world, but he was the best Burt Reynolds in the world."

BURT REYNOLDS
PUT THE PEDAL TO THE METAL

Darwin Porter & Danforth Prince; ISBN 978-1-936003-63-1; 450 pages with photos.
Available Everywhere Now

PETER O'TOOLE

Hellraiser, Sexual Outlaw, Irish Rebel

When it was published, early in 2015, this book was widely publicized in the *Daily Mail*, the *New York Daily News*, the *New York Post*, the *Midwest Book Review, The Express (London), The Globe*, the *National Enquirer*, and in equivalent publications worldwide

One of the world's most admired (and brilliant) actors, Peter O'Toole wined and wenched his way through a labyrinth of sexual and interpersonal betrayals, sometimes with disastrous results. Away from the stage and screen, where such films as *Becket* and *Lawrence of Arabia*, made film history, his life was filled with drunken, debauched nights and edgy sexual experimentations, most of which were never openly examined in the press. A hellraiser, he shared wild times with his "best blokes" Richard Burton and Richard Harris. Peter Finch, also his close friend, once invited him to join him in sharing the pleasures of his mistress, Vivien Leigh.

"My father, a bookie, moved us to the Mick community of Leeds," O'Toole once told a reporter. "We were very poor, but I was born an Irishman, which accounts for my gift of gab, my unruly behavior, my passionate devotion to women and the bottle, and my loathing of any authority figure."

Author Robert Sellers described O'Toole's boyhood neighborhood. "Three of his playmates went on to be hanged for murder; one strangled a girl in a lovers' quarrel; one killed a man during a robbery; another cut up a warden in South Africa with a pair of shears. It was a heavy bunch."

Peter O'Toole's hell-raising life story has never been told, until now. Hot and uncensored, from a writing team which, even prior to O'Toole's death in 2013, had been collecting under-the-radar info about him for years, this book has everything you ever wanted to know about how THE LION navigated his way through the boudoirs of the Entertainment Industry IN WINTER, Spring, Summer, and a dissipated Autumn as well.

Blood Moon has ripped away the imperial robe, scepter, and crown usually associated with this quixotic problem child of the British Midlands. Provocatively uncensored, this illusion-shattering overview of Peter O'Toole's hell-raising (or at least very naughty) and demented life is unique in the history of publishing.

PETER O'TOOLE
Hellraiser, Sexual Outlaw, Irish Rebel
Darwin Porter & Danforth Prince
Softcover, with photos. ISBN 978-1-936003-45-7
Available Now

PAUL NEWMAN

The Man Behind the Baby Blues
His Secret Life Exposed

Drawn from firsthand interviews with insiders who knew Paul Newman intimately, and compiled over a period of nearly a half-century, this is the world's most honest and most revelatory biography about Hollywood's pre-eminent male sex symbol.

This is a respectful but candid cornucopia of once-concealed information about the sexual and emotional adventures of an affable, impossibly good-looking workaday actor, a former sailor from Shaker Heights, Ohio, who parlayed his ambisexual charm and extraordinary good looks into one of the most successful careers in Hollywood.

Whereas the situations it exposes were widely known within Hollywood's inner circles, they've never before been revealed to the general public.

But now, the full story has been published—the giddy heights and agonizing crashes of a great American star, with revelations and insights never before published in any other biography.

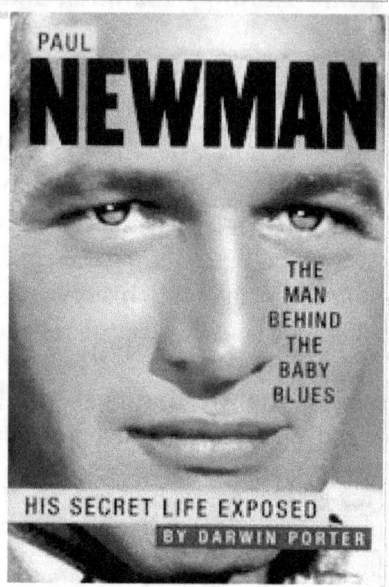

***

"Paul Newman had just as many on-location affairs as the rest of us, and he was just as bisexual as I was. But whereas I was always getting caught with my pants down, he managed to do it in the dark with not a paparazzo in sight. He might have bedded Marilyn Monroe or Elizabeth Taylor the night before, but he always managed to show up for breakfast with Joanne Woodward, with those baby blues, looking as innocent as a Botticelli angel. He never fooled me. It takes an alleycat to know another one. Did I ever tell you what really happened between Newman and me? If that doesn't grab you, what about what went on between James Dean and Newman? Let me tell you about this co-called model husband if you want to look behind those famous peepers."

—Marlon Brando

PAUL NEWMAN, THE MAN BEHIND THE BABY BLUES,
His Secret Life Exposed, by Darwin Porter
Recipient of an Honorable Mention from the New England Book Festival
Hardcover, 520 pages, with dozens of photos.
ISBN 978-0-9786465-1-6   Available everywhere now.

JAMES DEAN
Tomorrow Never Comes

Honoring the 60th Anniversary of His Violent and Early Death

America's most enduring and legendary symbol of young, enraged rebellion, James Dean continues into the 21st Century to capture the imagination of the world.

After one of his many flirtations with Death, which caught up with him when he was a celebrity-soaked 24-year-old, he said, "If a man can live after he dies, then maybe he's a great man." Today, bars from Nigeria to Patagonia are named in honor of this international, spectacularly self-destructive movie star icon.

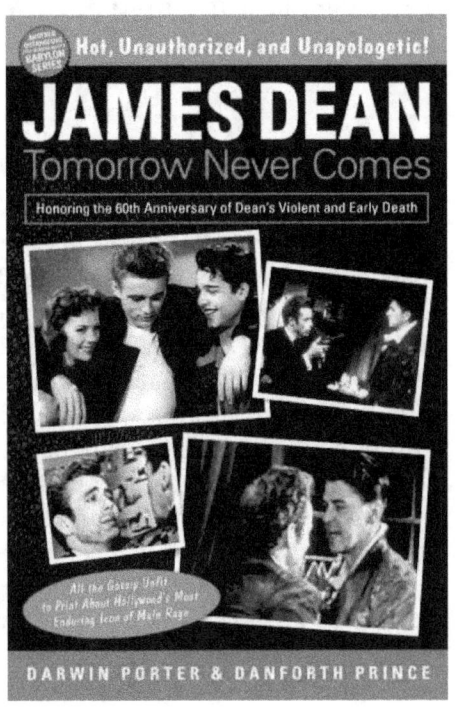

Migrating from the dusty backroads of Indiana to center stage in the most formidable boudoirs of Hollywood, his saga is electrifying.

A strikingly handsome heart-throb, Dean is a study in contrasts: Tough but tender, brutal but remarkably sensitive; he was a reckless hellraiser badass who could revert to a little boy in bed.

A rampant bisexual, he claimed that he didn't want to go through life "with one hand tied behind my back." He demonstrated that during bedroom trysts with Marilyn Monroe, Rock Hudson, Elizabeth Taylor, Paul Newman, Natalie Wood, Shelley Winters, Marlon Brando, Steve McQueen, Ursula Andress, Montgomery Clift, Pier Angeli, Tennessee Williams, Susan Strasberg, Tallulah Bankhead, and FBI director J. Edgar Hoover.

Woolworth heiress Barbara Hutton, one of the richest and most dissipated women of her era, wanted to make him her toy boy.

Tomorrow Never Comes is the most penetrating look at James Dean to have emerged from the wreckage of his Porsche Spyder in 1955.

Before setting out on his last ride, he said, "I feel life too intensely to bear living it." *Tomorrow Never Comes* presents a damaged but beautiful soul.

JAMES DEAN—TOMORROW NEVER COMES
Darwin Porter & Danforth Prince
Softcover, with photos. ISBN 978-1-936003-49-5

BLOOD MOON'S RESPECTFUL FAREWELL TO A GREAT AMERICAN MOVIE STAR

KIRK DOUGLAS
MORE IS NEVER ENOUGH

OOZING MASCULINITY, A YOUNG HORNDOG SETS OUT TO CONQUER HOLLYWOOD

Of the many male stars of Golden Age Hollywood, Kirk Douglas became the final survivor, the last icon of a fabled, optimistic era that the world will never see again. When he celebrated his birthday in 2016, a headline read: LEGENDARY HOLLYWOOD HORNDOG TURNS 100.

He was both a charismatic actor and a man of uncommon force and vigor. His restless and volcanic spirit is reflected both in his films and through his many sexual conquests.

Douglas was the son of Russian-Jewish immigrants, his father a collector and seller of rags. After service in the Navy during World War II, he hit Hollywood, oozing masculinity and charm. Conquering Tinseltown and bedding its leading ladies, he became the personification of the American dream, moving from obscurity and (literally) rags to riches and major-league fame.

The *Who's Who* cast of characters roaring through his life included not only a daunting list of Hollywood goddesses, but the town's most colossal male talents and egos, too. They included his kindred hellraiser and best buddy Burt Lancaster, John Wayne, Henry Fonda, Billy Wilder, Laurence Olivier, Rock Hudson, and a future U.S. President, Ronald Reagan, when winning the highest office in the land was virtually unthinkable.

Over the decades, he immortalized himself in film after film, delivering, like a Trojan, one memorable performance after another. He was at home in *film noir*, as a western gunslinger, as an adventurer (in both ancient and modern sagas), as a juggler, as Tennessee Williams' "gentleman caller," as a Greek super-hero from Homer's *Odyssey*, and as roguish sailor in the Jules Verne yarn, exploring the mysteries of the ocean's depths.

En route to his status as a myth and legend, his performances reflected both his personal pain and the brutalization of the characters he played, too. In *Champion* (1949), he was beaten to a fatal bloody pulp. As the sleazy, heartless reporter in *Ace in the Hole* (1951), he was stabbed with a knife in his gut. As Van Gogh in *Lust for Life* (1956), he writhed in emotional agony and unrequited love before slicing off his ear with a razor. His World War I movie, *Paths of Glory* (1957) grows more profound over the years. He lost an eye in *The Vikings* (1958), and, as the Thracian slave leading a revolt against Roman legions in *Spartacus* (1960), he was crucified.

All of this is brought out, with photos, in this remarkable testimonial to the last hero of Hollywood's cinematic and swashbuckling Golden Age, an inspiring testimonial to the values and core beliefs of an America that's Gone With the Wind, yet lovingly remembered as a time when it, in many ways, was truly great.

KIRK DOUGLAS: MORE IS NEVER ENOUGH

Darwin Porter & Danforth Prince; ISBN 978-1-936003-61-7; 550 pages with photos. Available everywhere now

Available Now From Blood Moon: The Comprehensive, Unauthorized Exposé that Every Survivor of the Sexual Revolution Will Want to Read

Hugh Hefner, the most iconic Playboy in human history, was a visionary, an empire-builder, and a pajama-clad pipe-smoker with a pre-coital grin.

In 1953, he published his first edition of *Playboy* with money borrowed from his puritanical, Nebraska-born mother. Marilyn Monroe appeared on the cover, with her nude calendar inside.

Rebelling against his strict upbringing, he lost his virginity at the age of 22.

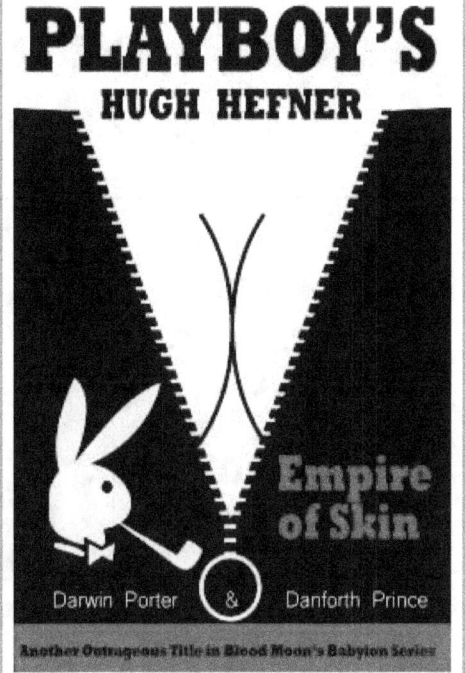

His magazine, punctuated with nudes and studded with articles by major literary figures, reached its zenith at eight million readers. As a "tasteful pornographer," Hef became a cultural warrior, fighting government censorship all the way to the U.S. Supreme Court. As the years and his notoriety progressed, he became an advocate of abortion, LGBT equality, and the legalization of pot. Eventually, he engaged in "pubic wars" with Bob Guccione, the flamboyant founder of Penthouse, which cut into Hef's sales.

Lauded by millions of avid readers, he was denounced as "the father of sex addiction," "a huckster," "a lecherous low-brow feeder of our vices," "a misogynist," and, near the end of his life, "a symbol of priapic senility."

During his heyday, some of the biggest male stars in Hollywood, including Warren Beatty, Sammy Davis, Jr., Mick Jagger, and Jack Nicholson, came to frolic behind Hef's guarded walls, stripping nude in the hot tub grotto before sampling the rotating beds upstairs. Even a future U.S. president came to call. "Donald Trump had an appreciation of Bunny tail," Hef said.

Hefner's last Viagra-fueled marriage was to a beautiful blonde, Crystal Harris, 60 years his junior. "There's nothing wrong in a man marrying a girl who could be his great-granddaughter," he was famously quoted as saying.

This ground-breaking biography, the latest in Blood Moon's string of outrageously unvarnished myth-busters, was the first published since Hefner's death at the age of 91 in 2017. It's a provocative saga, rich in tantalizing, often shocking detail. Not recommended for the sanctimonious or the faint of heart, and loaded with ironic, little-known details about the trendsetter's epic challenges and the solutions he devised.

PLAYBOY'S HUGH HEFNER EMPIRE OF SKIN

by Darwin Porter and Danforth Prince
978-1-936003-59-4

Blood Moon Productions proudly announces its compilation of lurid, vintage scandals from the Golden Age of Camelot.

It's in the form of a new edition of Darwin Porter's classic 2014 biography of the most watched, most enigmatic, and most controversial woman of the 20th Century,

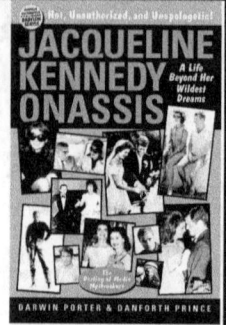

JACQUELINE KENNEDY ONASSIS
Her Tumultous Life & Her Love Affairs

JACKIE INVADES WASHINGTON BABYLON, EUROPE, and BEYOND

This is a new edition of the most compelling compilation of cash-soaked ambition, sexual indiscretion, and social embarrassment about a former first lady ever published,

Available now from **Ingram** and from **Amazon.com** worldwide, in honor of one of America's favorite Valentines

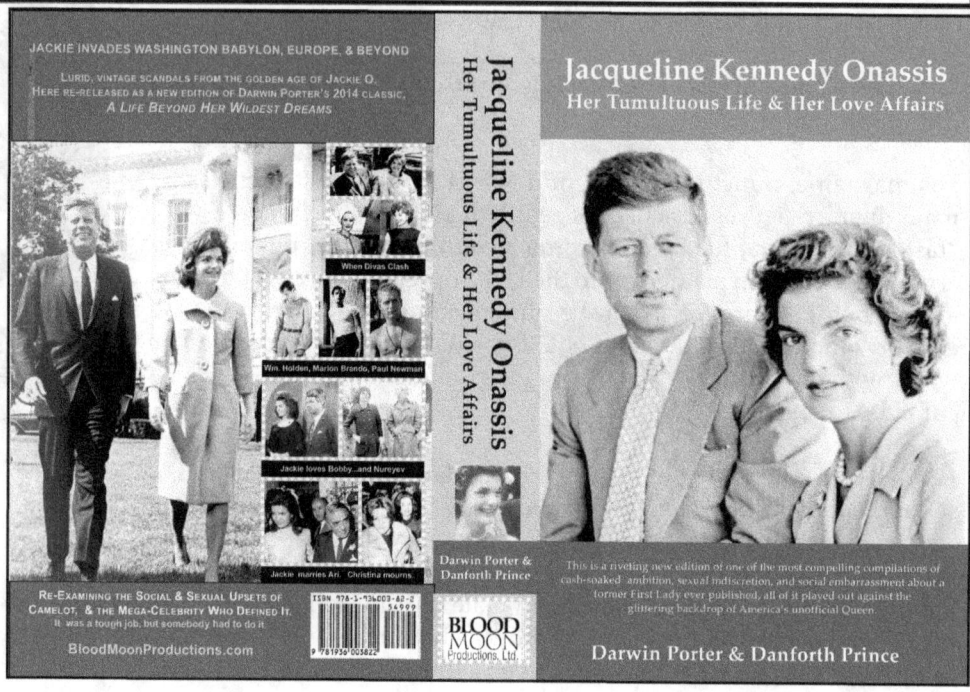

JAQUELINE KENNEDY ONASSIS
Her Tumultuous Life & Her Love Affairs
ISBN 978-1-936003-82-2   Originally published in 2014 as
A LIFE BEYOND HER WILDEST DREAMS by Darwin Porter & Danforth Prince
700 fascinating pages with hundreds of photos

Conceived in direct and sometimes defiant contrast to the avalanche of more breathlessly respectful testimonials to the life and legacy of "America's Queen," this book is the latest installment in Blood Moon's endlessly irreverent MAGNOLIA HOUSE series.

RE-EXAMINING THE SOCIAL AND SEXUAL UPSETS OF CAMELOT AND THE MEGA-CELEBRITY WHO DEFINED IT.

It was a tough job, but somebody had to do it.